VW Beetle & Karmann Ghia Automotive Repair Manual

by Ken Freund, Mike Stubblefield and John H Haynes

Member of the Guild of Motoring Writers

Models covered:

All VW Beetles and Karmann Ghias
1954 through 1979

(1W4 – 159)

ABCDE
FG

Haynes Publishing Group
Sparkford Nr Yeovil
Somerset BA22 7JJ England

Haynes North America, Inc.
861 Lawrence Drive
Newbury Park
California 91320 USA

Acknowledgements
We are grateful for the help and cooperation of Volkswagen of America, Inc., for assistance with technical information, certain illustrations and vehicle photos. The Champion Spark Plug Company supplied the illustrations of various spark plug conditions.

© **Haynes North America, Inc.   1991**

With permission from J.H. Haynes & Co. Ltd.

A book in the **Haynes Automotive Repair Manual Series**

Printed in the USA

ISBN 1 85010 729 7

Library of Congress Catalog Card Number 91-70148

Contents

1967 VW Beetle

1974 VW Super Beetle

About this manual

Its purpose

The purpose of this manual is to help you get the best value from your vehicle. It can do so in several ways. It can help you decide what work must be done, even if you choose to have it done by a dealer service department or a repair shop; it provides information and procedures for routine maintenance and servicing; and it offers diagnostic and repair procedures to follow when trouble occurs.

We hope you use the manual to tackle the work yourself. For many simpler jobs, doing it yourself may be quicker than arranging an appointment to get the vehicle into a shop and making the trips to leave it and pick it up. More importantly, a lot of money can be saved by avoiding the expense the shop must pass on to you to cover its labor and overhead costs. An added benefit is the sense of satisfaction and accomplishment that you feel after doing the job yourself.

Using the manual

The manual is divided into Chapters. Each Chapter is divided into numbered Sections, which are headed in bold type between horizontal lines. Each Section consists of consecutively numbered paragraphs.

At the beginning of each numbered Section you will be referred to any illustrations which apply to the procedures in that Section. The reference numbers used in illustration captions pinpoint the pertinent Section and the Step within that Section. That is, illustration 3.2 means the illustration refers to Section 3 and Step (or paragraph) 2 within that Section.

Procedures, once described in the text, are not normally repeated. When it's necessary to refer to another Chapter, the reference will be given as Chapter and Section number. Cross references given without use of the word "Chapter" apply to Sections and/or paragraphs in the same Chapter. For example, "see Section 8" means in the same Chapter.

References to the left or right side of the vehicle assume you are sitting in the driver's seat, facing forward.

Even though we have prepared this manual with extreme care, neither the publisher nor the author can accept responsibility for any errors in, or omissions from, the information given.

NOTE

A **Note** provides information necessary to properly complete a procedure or information which will make the procedure easier to understand.

CAUTION

A **Caution** provides a special procedure or special steps which must be taken while completing the procedure where the **Caution** is found. Not heeding a **Caution** can result in damage to the assembly being worked on.

WARNING

A **Warning** provides a special procedure or special steps which must be taken while completing the procedure where the **Warning** is found. Not heeding a **Warning** can result in personal injury.

Introduction to the Volkswagen Beetle and Karmann Ghia

The vehicles covered by this manual are very similar in design. Although the Karmann Ghia may appear to be a completely different vehicle, it shares the same basic platform and components.

The horizontally opposed, four-cylinder engine used in these models is equipped with either a carburetor or electronic fuel injection. All models utilize a breaker points-type ignition system.

The engine drives the rear wheels through a 4-speed manual or 3-speed semi-automatic transaxle via independent axles. Early models employ a swing axle-type rear suspension, in which the axles are stressed members of the suspension. Later models use driveaxles, which are used only for the transmission of power to the rear wheels.

Independent suspension, featuring torsion bars, trailing arms, and telescopic shock absorbers is used on the front wheels of most models.

Beginning with the 1971 Super Beetle, some models were equipped with a MacPherson strut-type front suspension (all 1975 and later models were equipped with this type of front suspension). Most models use a worm-and-roller type steering gear, with the steering gearbox mounted to the front axle beam. Later models were equipped with a rack-and-pinion style steering gear.

The rear suspension on all models is of a torsion bar design, although there are significant differences between models with swing axles and models with driveaxles (see Chapter 8 for more details). Telescopic shock absorbers are also used at the rear.

All models are equipped with drum brakes on all four wheels, with the exception of later model Karmann Ghias, which were equipped with disc brakes on the front wheels.

Vehicle identification numbers

Modifications are a continuing and unpublicized process in vehicle manufacturing. Since spare parts manuals and lists are compiled on a numerical basis, the individual vehicle numbers are essential to correctly identify the component required.

Chassis identification number

This very important identification number is found in three different places: on the frame tunnel under the rear seat, under the hood, and on the dashboard. It also appears on the Vehicle Certificate of Title and Registration. It contains information such as where and when the vehicle was manufactured, the model year and the body style.

Engine number

The engine identification number is stamped on the engine case, just below the generator pedestal **(see illustration)**. See Chapter 2 for a breakdown of engine identification numbers for the different model years.

The engine identification number is stamped on the engine case, just below the generator pedestal

Buying parts

Replacement parts are available from many sources, which generally fall into one of two categories – authorized dealer parts departments and independent retail auto parts stores. Our advice concerning these parts is as follows:

Retail auto parts stores: Good auto parts stores will stock frequently needed components which wear out relatively fast, such as clutch components, exhaust systems, brake parts, tune-up parts, etc. These stores often supply new or reconditioned parts on an exchange basis, which can save a considerable amount of money. Discount auto parts stores are often very good places to buy materials and parts needed for general vehicle maintenance such as oil, grease, filters, spark plugs, belts, touch-up paint, bulbs, etc. They also usually sell tools and general accessories, have con-venient hours, charge lower prices and can often be found not far from home.

Authorized dealer parts department: This is the best source for parts which are unique to the vehicle and not generally available else-where (such as major engine parts, transmission parts, trim pieces, etc.).

Warranty information: If the vehicle is still covered under warranty, be sure that any replacement parts purchased – regardless of the source – do not invalidate the warranty!

To be sure of obtaining the correct parts, have engine and chassis numbers available and, if possible, take the old parts along for positive identification.

Maintenance techniques, tools and working facilities

Maintenance techniques

There are a number of techniques involved in maintenance and repair that will be referred to throughout this manual. Application of these tech-niques will enable the home mechanic to be more efficient, better orga-nized and capable of performing the various tasks properly, which will ensure that the repair job is thorough and complete.

Fasteners

Fasteners are nuts, bolts, studs and screws used to hold two or more parts together. There are a few things to keep in mind when working with fasteners. Almost all of them use a locking device of some type, either a lockwasher, locknut, locking tab or thread adhesive. All threaded fasten-ers should be clean and straight, with undamaged threads and undam-aged corners on the hex head where the wrench fits. Develop the habit of replacing all damaged nuts and bolts with new ones. Special locknuts with nylon or fiber inserts can only be used once. If they are removed, they lose their locking ability and must be replaced with new ones.

Rusted nuts and bolts should be treated with a penetrating fluid to ease removal and prevent breakage. Some mechanics use turpentine in a spout-type oil can, which works quite well. After applying the rust pene-trant, let it work for a few minutes before trying to loosen the nut or bolt. Badly rusted fasteners may have to be chiseled or sawed off or removed with a special nut breaker, available at tool stores.

If a bolt or stud breaks off in an assembly, it can be drilled and removed with a special tool commonly available for this purpose. Most automotive machine shops can perform this task, as well as other repair procedures, such as the repair of threaded holes that have been stripped out.

Flat washers and lockwashers, when removed from an assembly, should always be replaced exactly as removed. Replace any damaged washers with new ones. Never use a lockwasher on any soft metal surface (such as aluminum), thin sheet metal or plastic.

Fastener sizes

For a number of reasons, automobile manufacturers are making wider and wider use of metric fasteners. Therefore, it is important to be able to tell the difference between standard (sometimes called U.S. or SAE) and metric hardware, since they cannot be interchanged.

All bolts, whether standard or metric, are sized according to diameter, thread pitch and length. For example, a standard 1/2 – 13 x 1 bolt is 1/2 inch in diameter, has 13 threads per inch and is 1 inch long. An M12 – 1.75 x 25 metric bolt is 12 mm in diameter, has a thread pitch of 1.75 mm (the distance between threads) and is 25 mm long. The two bolts are nearly identical, and easily confused, but they are not interchangeable.

In addition to the differences in diameter, thread pitch and length, metric and standard bolts can also be distinguished by examining the bolt heads. To begin with, the distance across the flats on a standard bolt head is measured in inches, while the same dimension on a metric bolt is sized in millimeters (the same is true for nuts). As a result, a standard wrench should not be used on a metric bolt and a metric wrench should not be used on a standard bolt. Also, most standard bolts have slashes radiating out from the center of the head to denote the grade or strength of the bolt, which is an indication of the amount of torque that can be applied to it. The greater the number of slashes, the greater the strength of the bolt. Grades 0 through 5 are commonly used on automobiles. Metric bolts have a property class (grade) number, rather than a slash, molded into their heads to indicate bolt strength. In this case, the higher the number, the stronger the bolt. Property class numbers 8.8, 9.8 and 10.9 are commonly used on automobiles.

Strength markings can also be used to distinguish standard hex nuts from metric hex nuts. Many standard nuts have dots stamped into one side, while metric nuts are marked with a number. The greater the number of dots, or the higher the number, the greater the strength of the nut.

Metric studs are also marked on their ends according to property class (grade). Larger studs are numbered (the same as metric bolts), while smaller studs carry a geometric code to denote grade.

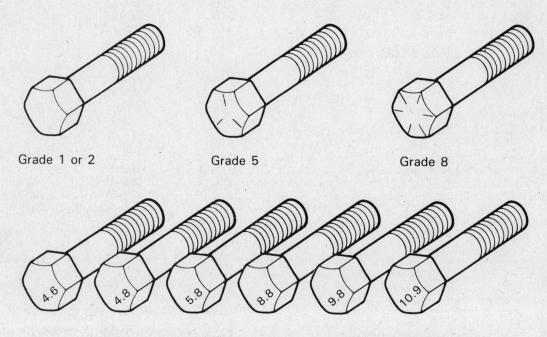

Grade 1 or 2   Grade 5   Grade 8

Bolt strength markings (top – standard/SAE/USS; bottom – metric)

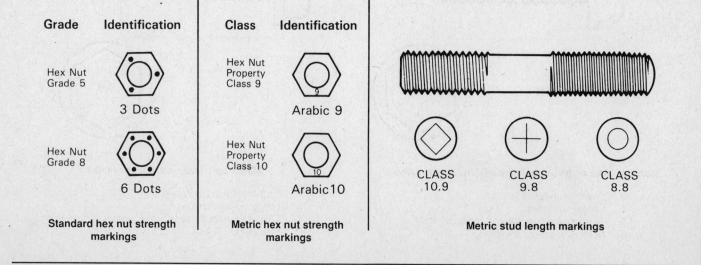

Grade	Identification
Hex Nut Grade 5	3 Dots
Hex Nut Grade 8	6 Dots

Standard hex nut strength markings

Class	Identification
Hex Nut Property Class 9	Arabic 9
Hex Nut Property Class 10	Arabic 10

Metric hex nut strength markings

CLASS 10.9   CLASS 9.8   CLASS 8.8

Metric stud length markings

It should be noted that many fasteners, especially Grades 0 through 2, have no distinguishing marks on them. When such is the case, the only way to determine whether it is standard or metric is to measure the thread pitch or compare it to a known fastener of the same size.

Standard fasteners are often referred to as SAE, as opposed to metric. However, it should be noted that SAE technically refers to a non-metric *fine thread* fastener only. Coarse thread non-metric fasteners are referred to as USS sizes.

Since fasteners of the same size (both standard and metric) may have different strength ratings, be sure to reinstall any bolts, studs or nuts removed from your vehicle in their original locations. Also, when replacing a fastener with a new one, make sure that the new one has a strength rating equal to or greater than the original.

Tightening sequences and procedures

Most threaded fasteners should be tightened to a specific torque value (torque is the twisting force applied to a threaded component such as a nut or bolt). Overtightening the fastener can weaken it and cause it to break, while undertightening can cause it to eventually come loose. Bolts, screws and studs, depending on the material they are made of and their thread diameters, have specific torque values, many of which are noted in the Specifications at the beginning of each Chapter. Be sure to follow the torque recommendations closely. For fasteners not assigned a specific torque, a general torque value chart is presented here as a guide. These torque values are for dry (unlubricated) fasteners threaded into steel or cast iron (not aluminum). As was previously mentioned, the size and grade of a fastener determine the amount of torque that can safely be

Metric thread sizes	Ft-lbs	Nm
M-6	6 to 9	9 to 12
M-8	14 to 21	19 to 28
M-10	28 to 40	38 to 54
M-12	50 to 71	68 to 96
M-14	80 to 140	109 to 154

Pipe thread sizes		
1/8	5 to 8	7 to 10
1/4	12 to 18	17 to 24
3/8	22 to 33	30 to 44
1/2	25 to 35	34 to 47

U.S. thread sizes		
1/4 – 20	6 to 9	9 to 12
5/16 – 18	12 to 18	17 to 24
5/16 – 24	14 to 20	19 to 27
3/8 – 16	22 to 32	30 to 43
3/8 – 24	27 to 38	37 to 51
7/16 – 14	40 to 55	55 to 74
7/16 – 20	40 to 60	55 to 81
1/2 – 13	55 to 80	75 to 108

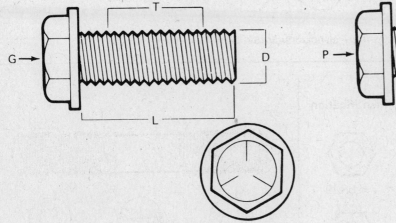

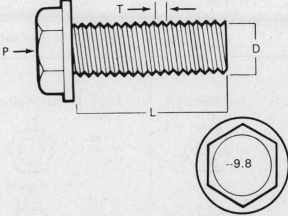

Standard (SAE and USS) bolt dimensions/grade marks

- G   Grade marks (bolt length)
- L   Length (in inches)
- T   Thread pitch (number of threads per inch)
- D   Nominal diameter (in inches)

Metric bolt dimensions/grade marks

- P   Property class (bolt strength)
- L   Length (in millimeters)
- T   Thread pitch (distance between threads in millimeters)
- D   Diameter

applied to it. The figures listed here are approximate for Grade 2 and Grade 3 fasteners. Higher grades can tolerate higher torque values.

Fasteners laid out in a pattern, such as cylinder head bolts, oil pan bolts, differential cover bolts, etc., must be loosened or tightened in sequence to avoid warping the component. This sequence will normally be shown in the appropriate Chapter. If a specific pattern is not given, the following procedures can be used to prevent warping.

Initially, the bolts or nuts should be assembled finger-tight only. Next, they should be tightened one full turn each, in a criss-cross or diagonal pattern. After each one has been tightened one full turn, return to the first one and tighten them all one-half turn, following the same pattern. Finally, tighten each of them one-quarter turn at a time until each fastener has been tightened to the proper torque. To loosen and remove the fasteners, the procedure would be reversed.

Component disassembly

Component disassembly should be done with care and purpose to help ensure that the parts go back together properly. Always keep track of the sequence in which parts are removed. Make note of special characteristics or marks on parts that can be installed more than one way, such as a grooved thrust washer on a shaft. It is a good idea to lay the disassembled parts out on a clean surface in the order that they were removed. It may also be helpful to make sketches or take instant photos of components before removal.

When removing fasteners from a component, keep track of their locations. Sometimes threading a bolt back in a part, or putting the washers and nut back on a stud, can prevent mix-ups later. If nuts and bolts cannot be returned to their original locations, they should be kept in a compartmented box or a series of small boxes. A cupcake or muffin tin is ideal for this purpose, since each cavity can hold the bolts and nuts from a particular area (i.e. oil pan bolts, valve cover bolts, engine mount bolts, etc.). A pan of this type is especially helpful when working on assemblies with very small parts, such as the carburetor, alternator, valve train or interior dash and trim pieces. The cavities can be marked with paint or tape to identify the contents.

Whenever wiring looms, harnesses or connectors are separated, it is a good idea to identify the two halves with numbered pieces of masking tape so they can be easily reconnected.

Gasket sealing surfaces

Throughout any vehicle, gaskets are used to seal the mating surfaces between two parts and keep lubricants, fluids, vacuum or pressure contained in an assembly.

Many times these gaskets are coated with a liquid or paste-type gasket sealing compound before assembly. Age, heat and pressure can sometimes cause the two parts to stick together so tightly that they are very difficult to separate. Often, the assembly can be loosened by striking it with a soft-face hammer near the mating surfaces. A regular hammer can be used if a block of wood is placed between the hammer and the part. Do not hammer on cast parts or parts that could be easily damaged. With any particularly stubborn part, always recheck to make sure that every fastener has been removed.

Avoid using a screwdriver or bar to pry apart an assembly, as they can easily mar the gasket sealing surfaces of the parts, which must remain smooth. If prying is absolutely necessary, use an old broom handle, but keep in mind that extra clean up will be necessary if the wood splinters.

After the parts are separated, the old gasket must be carefully scraped off and the gasket surfaces cleaned. Stubborn gasket material can be soaked with rust penetrant or treated with a special chemical to soften it so it can be easily scraped off. A scraper can be fashioned from a piece of copper tubing by flattening and sharpening one end. Copper is recommended because it is usually softer than the surfaces to be scraped, which reduces the chance of gouging the part. Some gaskets can be removed with a wire brush, but regardless of the method used, the mating surfaces must be left clean and smooth. If for some reason the gasket surface is gouged, then a gasket sealer thick enough to fill scratches will have to be used during reassembly of the components. For most applications, a non-drying (or semi-drying) gasket sealer should be used.

Hose removal tips

Warning: *If the vehicle is equipped with air conditioning, do not disconnect any of the A/C hoses without first having the system depressurized by a dealer service department or a service station.*

Hose removal precautions closely parallel gasket removal precautions. Avoid scratching or gouging the surface that the hose mates against or the connection may leak. This is especially true for radiator hoses. Because of various chemical reactions, the rubber in hoses can bond itself to the metal spigot that the hose fits over. To remove a hose, first loosen the hose clamps that secure it to the spigot. Then, with slip-joint pliers, grab the hose at the clamp and rotate it around the spigot. Work it back and forth until it is completely free, then pull it off. Silicone or other lubricants will ease removal if they can be applied between the hose and the outside of the spigot. Apply the same lubricant to the inside of the hose and the outside of the spigot to simplify installation.

As a last resort (and if the hose is to be replaced with a new one anyway), the rubber can be slit with a knife and the hose peeled from the spigot. If this must be done, be careful that the metal connection is not damaged.

If a hose clamp is broken or damaged, do not reuse it. Wire-type clamps usually weaken with age, so it is a good idea to replace them with screw-type clamps whenever a hose is removed.

Tools

A selection of good tools is a basic requirement for anyone who plans to maintain and repair his or her own vehicle. For the owner who has few tools, the initial investment might seem high, but when compared to the spiraling costs of professional auto maintenance and repair, it is a wise one.

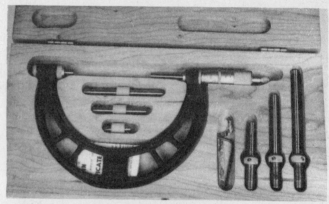

Micrometer set

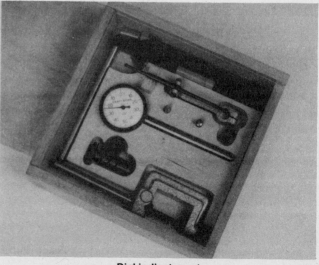

Dial indicator set

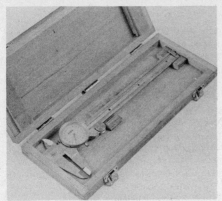
Dial caliper

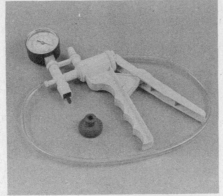
Hand-operated vacuum pump

Timing light

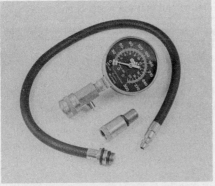
Compression gauge with spark plug hole adapter

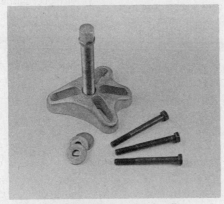
Damper/steering wheel puller

General purpose puller

Hydraulic lifter removal tool

Valve spring compressor

Valve spring compressor

Ridge reamer

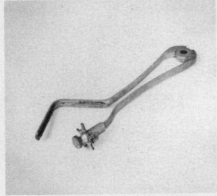
Piston ring groove cleaning tool

Ring removal/installation tool

Ring compressor

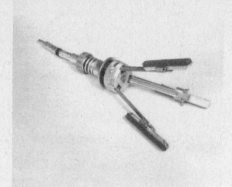

Cylinder hone

Brake hold-down spring tool

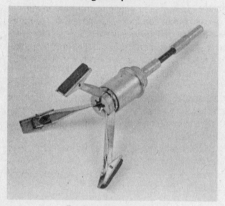

Brake cylinder hone

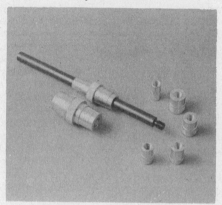

Clutch plate alignment tool

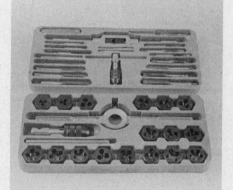

Tap and die set

To help the owner decide which tools are needed to perform the tasks detailed in this manual, the following tool lists are offered: *Maintenance and minor repair, Repair/overhaul* and *Special*.

The newcomer to practical mechanics should start off with the maintenance and minor repair tool kit, which is adequate for the simpler jobs performed on a vehicle. Then, as confidence and experience grow, the owner can tackle more difficult tasks, buying additional tools as they are needed. Eventually the basic kit will be expanded into the repair and overhaul tool set. Over a period of time, the experienced do-it-yourselfer will assemble a tool set complete enough for most repair and overhaul procedures and will add tools from the special category when it is felt that the expense is justified by the frequency of use.

Maintenance and minor repair tool kit

The tools in this list should be considered the minimum required for performance of routine maintenance, servicing and minor repair work. We recommend the purchase of combination wrenches (box-end and open-end combined in one wrench). While more expensive than open end wrenches, they offer the advantages of both types of wrench.

Combination wrench set (1/4-inch to 1 inch or 6 mm to 19 mm)
Adjustable wrench, 8 inch
Spark plug wrench with rubber insert
Spark plug gap adjusting tool
Feeler gauge set
Brake bleeder wrench
Standard screwdriver (5/16-inch x 6 inch)
Phillips screwdriver (No. 2 x 6 inch)
Combination pliers – 6 inch
Hacksaw and assortment of blades
Tire pressure gauge
Grease gun
Oil can
Fine emery cloth
Wire brush

Battery post and cable cleaning tool
Oil filter wrench
Funnel (medium size)
Safety goggles
Jackstands(2)
Drain pan

Note: *If basic tune-ups are going to be part of routine maintenance, it will be necessary to purchase a good quality stroboscopic timing light and combination tachometer/dwell meter. Although they are included in the list of special tools, it is mentioned here because they are absolutely necessary for tuning most vehicles properly.*

Repair and overhaul tool set

These tools are essential for anyone who plans to perform major repairs and are in addition to those in the maintenance and minor repair tool kit. Included is a comprehensive set of sockets which, though expensive, are invaluable because of their versatility, especially when various extensions and drives are available. We recommend the 1/2-inch drive over the 3/8-inch drive. Although the larger drive is bulky and more expensive, it has the capacity of accepting a very wide range of large sockets. Ideally, however, the mechanic should have a 3/8-inch drive set and a 1/2-inch drive set.

Socket set(s)
Reversible ratchet
Extension – 10 inch
Universal joint
Torque wrench (same size drive as sockets)
Ball peen hammer – 8 ounce
Soft-face hammer (plastic/rubber)
Standard screwdriver (1/4-inch x 6 inch)
Standard screwdriver (stubby – 5/16-inch)
Phillips screwdriver (No. 3 x 8 inch)
Phillips screwdriver (stubby – No. 2)

Pliers – vise grip
Pliers – lineman's
Pliers – needle nose
Pliers – snap-ring (internal and external)
Cold chisel – 1/2-inch
Scribe
Scraper (made from flattened copper tubing)
Centerpunch
Pin punches (1/16, 1/8, 3/16-inch)
Steel rule/straightedge – 12 inch
Allen wrench set (1/8 to 3/8-inch or 4 mm to 10 mm)
A selection of files
Wire brush (large)
Jackstands (second set)
Jack (scissor or hydraulic type)

Note: *Another tool which is often useful is an electric drill with a chuck capacity of 3/8-inch and a set of good quality drill bits.*

Special tools

The tools in this list include those which are not used regularly, are expensive to buy, or which need to be used in accordance with their manufacturer's instructions. Unless these tools will be used frequently, it is not very economical to purchase many of them. A consideration would be to split the cost and use between yourself and a friend or friends. In addition, most of these tools can be obtained from a tool rental shop on a temporary basis.

This list primarily contains only those tools and instruments widely available to the public, and not those special tools produced by the vehicle manufacturer for distribution to dealer service departments. Occasionally, references to the manufacturer's special tools are included in the text of this manual. Generally, an alternative method of doing the job without the special tool is offered. However, sometimes there is no alternative to their use. Where this is the case, and the tool cannot be purchased or borrowed, the work should be turned over to the dealer service department or an automotive repair shop.

Valve spring compressor
Piston ring groove cleaning tool
Piston ring compressor
Piston ring installation tool
Cylinder compression gauge
Cylinder ridge reamer
Cylinder surfacing hone
Cylinder bore gauge
Micrometers and/or dial calipers
Hydraulic lifter removal tool
Balljoint separator
Universal-type puller
Impact screwdriver
Dial indicator set
Stroboscopic timing light (inductive pick-up)
Hand operated vacuum/pressure pump
Tachometer/dwell meter
Universal electrical multimeter
Cable hoist
Brake spring removal and installation tools
Floor jack

Buying tools

For the do-it-yourselfer who is just starting to get involved in vehicle maintenance and repair, there are a number of options available when purchasing tools. If maintenance and minor repair is the extent of the work to be done, the purchase of individual tools is satisfactory. If, on the other hand, extensive work is planned, it would be a good idea to purchase a modest tool set from one of the large retail chain stores. A set can usually be bought at a substantial savings over the individual tool prices, and they often come with a tool box. As additional tools are needed, add–on sets, individual tools and a larger tool box can be purchased to expand the tool selection. Building a tool set gradually allows the cost of the tools to be spread over a longer period of time and gives the mechanic the freedom to choose only those tools that will actually be used.

Tool stores will often be the only source of some of the special tools that are needed, but regardless of where tools are bought, try to avoid cheap ones, especially when buying screwdrivers and sockets, because they won't last very long. The expense involved in replacing cheap tools will eventually be greater than the initial cost of quality tools.

Care and maintenance of tools

Good tools are expensive, so it makes sense to treat them with respect. Keep them clean and in usable condition and store them properly when not in use. Always wipe off any dirt, grease or metal chips before putting them away. Never leave tools lying around in the work area. Upon completion of a job, always check closely under the hood for tools that may have been left there so they won't get lost during a test drive.

Some tools, such as screwdrivers, pliers, wrenches and sockets, can be hung on a panel mounted on the garage or workshop wall, while others should be kept in a tool box or tray. Measuring instruments, gauges, meters, etc. must be carefully stored where they cannot be damaged by weather or impact from other tools.

When tools are used with care and stored properly, they will last a very long time. Even with the best of care, though, tools will wear out if used frequently. When a tool is damaged or worn out, replace it. Subsequent jobs will be safer and more enjoyable if you do.

Working facilities

Not to be overlooked when discussing tools is the workshop. If anything more than routine maintenance is to be carried out, some sort of suitable work area is essential.

It is understood, and appreciated, that many home mechanics do not have a good workshop or garage available, and end up removing an engine or doing major repairs outside. It is recommended, however, that the overhaul or repair be completed under the cover of a roof.

A clean, flat workbench or table of comfortable working height is an absolute necessity. The workbench should be equipped with a vise that has a jaw opening of at least four inches.

As mentioned previously, some clean, dry storage space is also required for tools, as well as the lubricants, fluids, cleaning solvents, etc. which soon become necessary.

Sometimes waste oil and fluids, drained from the engine or cooling system during normal maintenance or repairs, present a disposal problem. To avoid pouring them on the ground or into a sewage system, pour the used fluids into large containers, seal them with caps and take them to an authorized disposal site or recycling center. Plastic jugs, such as old antifreeze containers, are ideal for this purpose.

Always keep a supply of old newspapers and clean rags available. Old towels are excellent for mopping up spills. Many mechanics use rolls of paper towels for most work because they are readily available and disposable. To help keep the area under the vehicle clean, a large cardboard box can be cut open and flattened to protect the garage or shop floor.

Whenever working over a painted surface, such as when leaning over a fender to service something under the hood, always cover it with an old blanket or bedspread to protect the finish. Vinyl covered pads, made especially for this purpose, are available at auto parts stores.

Booster battery (jump) starting

Observe these precautions when using a booster battery to start a vehicle:

a) Before connecting the booster battery, make sure the ignition switch is in the Off position. The battery is under the rear seat.

b) Turn off the lights, heater and other electrical loads.

c) Your eyes should be shielded. Safety goggles are a good idea.

d) Make sure the booster battery is the same voltage as the dead one in the vehicle.

e) The two vehicles MUST NOT TOUCH each other!

f) Make sure the transaxle is in Neutral (manual) or Park (automatic).

g) If the booster battery is not a maintenance-free type, remove the vent caps and lay a cloth over the vent holes.

Connect the red jumper cable to the positive (+) terminals of each battery **(see illustration)**.

Connect one end of the black jumper cable to the negative (−) terminal of the booster battery. The other end of this cable should be connected to a good ground on the vehicle to be started, such as a bolt or bracket on the body.

Start the engine using the booster battery, then, with the engine running at idle speed, disconnect the jumper cables in the reverse order of connection.

The negative terminal (1) has a ground strap connected to it; the positive cable (2) has an insulated cable connected to it – note that this is a six-volt battery (it has three cell caps), so the booster battery must also be six volts (12-volt batteries have six cell caps)

Jacking and towing

Jacking

Warning: *The jack supplied with the vehicle should only be used for changing a tire or placing jackstands under the frame. Never work under the vehicle or start the engine while this jack is being used as the only means of support.*

The vehicle should be on level ground. Place the shift lever in Reverse. Set the parking brake use wood blocks to block the wheels still on the ground.

Remove the spare tire and jack from stowage. Remove the wheel cover and trim ring (if so equipped) with the tapered end of the lug bolt wrench by inserting and twisting the handle and then prying against the back of the wheel cover. Loosen, but do not remove, the lug bolts (one-half turn is sufficient).

Insert the arm of the jack into the square socket under the running board. Insert the lug bolt wrench into the upper link of the jack and pump it up and down to raise the vehicle (the front and rear wheels will be raised off the ground) **(see illustration)**. If the ground underneath the jack is soft, you may have to place a wood board under the foot of the jack. Never use rocks or bricks, because these materials could crumble under the weight of the vehicle.

Continue to operate the jack until the wheel is off the ground. Support the wheel, remove the lug bolts and pull the wheel off.

Raise the spare into position and install the lug bolts, tightening them snugly. Don't attempt to tighten them completely until the vehicle is lowered or it could slip off the jack. Insert the lug wrench into the lower link of the jack and pump it up and down to lower the vehicle. Remove the jack and tighten the lug bolts in a criss-cross pattern. Stow the tire, jack and wrench. Unblock the wheels.

If the front of the vehicle must be raised for service, jack up one side as described above, then place a jackstand under the front axle beam (torsion bar models) **(see illustration)** or under the frame head (models with strut front suspension) (see Chapter 10). Carefully lower the vehicle onto the jackstand, then repeat the procedure to the other side. If, however, the entire axle beam is to be removed, place the jackstands under the reinforced side rails of the floorpan, at the rear of the front wheel wells.

If the rear of the vehicle must be raised for service, raise one side of the vehicle as described above, then place a jackstand under the rear torsion housing (NOT the spring plate or the axle tube – see Chapter 10). Carefully lower the vehicle onto the jackstand, then repeat the procedure to the other side.

Towing

As a general rule, the vehicle should be towed with the rear wheels off the ground. If they can't be raised, place them on a dolly. The vehicle can be towed with all four wheels on the ground, but this method isn't recommended for long distances or high speeds. If the vehicle must be towed with all four wheels on the ground, make sure the shift lever is placed in Neutral and the ignition key is turned to the On position (disconnect the ground strap from the battery, too) so the steering lock will not become engaged.

Equipment specifically designed for towing should be used. Safety is a major consideration when towing and all applicable state and local laws must be obeyed. A safety chain system must be used at all times.

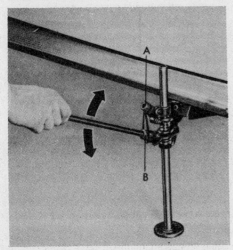

The vehicle jack engages with the socket near the rear of the running board – use the upper link of the jack (A) to raise the vehicle and the bottom link (B) to lower it

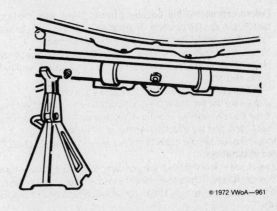

© 1972 VWoA—961

On models with torsion bar front suspension, place the jackstands under the front axle beam

Automotive chemicals and lubricants

A number of automotive chemicals and lubricants are available for use during vehicle maintenance and repair. They include a wide variety of products ranging from cleaning solvents and degreasers to lubricants and protective sprays for rubber, plastic and vinyl.

Cleaners

Carburetor cleaner and choke cleaner is a strong solvent for gum, varnish and carbon. Most carburetor cleaners leave a dry-type lubricant film which will not harden or gum up. Because of this film it is not recommended for use on electrical components.

Brake system cleaner is used to remove grease and brake fluid from the brake system, where clean surfaces are absolutely necessary. It leaves no residue and often eliminates brake squeal caused by contaminants.

Electrical cleaner removes oxidation, corrosion and carbon deposits from electrical contacts, restoring full current flow. It can also be used to clean spark plugs, carburetor jets, voltage regulators and other parts where an oil-free surface is desired.

Demoisturants remove water and moisture from electrical components such as alternators, voltage regulators, electrical connectors and fuse blocks. They are non-conductive, non-corrosive and non-flammable.

Degreasers are heavy-duty solvents used to remove grease from the outside of the engine and from chassis components. They can be sprayed or brushed on and, depending on the type, are rinsed off either with water or solvent.

Lubricants

Motor oil is the lubricant formulated for use in engines. It normally contains a wide variety of additives to prevent corrosion and reduce foaming and wear. Motor oil comes in various weights (viscosity ratings) from 5 to 80. The recommended weight of the oil depends on the season, temperature and the demands on the engine. Light oil is used in cold climates and under light load conditions. Heavy oil is used in hot climates and where high loads are encountered. Multi-viscosity oils are designed to have characteristics of both light and heavy oils and are available in a number of weights from 5W-20 to 20W-50.

Gear oil is designed to be used in differentials, manual transmissions and other areas where high-temperature lubrication is required.

Chassis and wheel bearing grease is a heavy grease used where increased loads and friction are encountered, such as for wheel bearings, balljoints, tie-rod ends and universal joints.

High-temperature wheel bearing grease is designed to withstand the extreme temperatures encountered by wheel bearings in disc brake equipped vehicles. It usually contains molybdenum disulfide (moly), which is a dry-type lubricant.

White grease is a heavy grease for metal-to-metal applications where water is a problem. White grease stays soft under both low and high temperatures (usually from –100 to +190-degrees F), and will not wash off or dilute in the presence of water.

Assembly lube is a special extreme pressure lubricant, usually containing moly, used to lubricate high-load parts (such as main and rod bearings and cam lobes) for initial start-up of a new engine. The assembly lube lubricates the parts without being squeezed out or washed away until the engine oiling system begins to function.

Silicone lubricants are used to protect rubber, plastic, vinyl and nylon parts.

Graphite lubricants are used where oils cannot be used due to contamination problems, such as in locks. The dry graphite will lubricate metal parts while remaining uncontaminated by dirt, water, oil or acids. It is electrically conductive and will not foul electrical contacts in locks such as the ignition switch.

Moly penetrants loosen and lubricate frozen, rusted and corroded fasteners and prevent future rusting or freezing.

Heat-sink grease is a special electrically non-conductive grease that is used for mounting electronic ignition modules where it is essential that heat is transferred away from the module.

Sealants

RTV sealant is one of the most widely used gasket compounds. Made from silicone, RTV is air curing, it seals, bonds, waterproofs, fills surface irregularities, remains flexible, doesn't shrink, is relatively easy to remove, and is used as a supplementary sealer with almost all low and medium temperature gaskets.

Anaerobic sealant is much like RTV in that it can be used either to seal gaskets or to form gaskets by itself. It remains flexible, is solvent resistant and fills surface imperfections. The difference between an anaerobic sealant and an RTV-type sealant is in the curing. RTV cures when exposed to air, while an anaerobic sealant cures only in the absence of air. This means that an anaerobic sealant cures only after the assembly of parts, sealing them together.

Thread and pipe sealant is used for sealing hydraulic and pneumatic fittings and vacuum lines. It is usually made from a Teflon compound, and comes in a spray, a paint-on liquid and as a wrap-around tape.

Chemicals

Anti-seize compound prevents seizing, galling, cold welding, rust and corrosion in fasteners. High-temperature anti-seize, usually made with copper and graphite lubricants, is used for exhaust system and exhaust manifold bolts.

Anaerobic locking compounds are used to keep fasteners from vibrating or working loose and cure only after installation, in the absence of air. Medium strength locking compound is used for small nuts, bolts and screws that may be removed later. High-strength locking compound is for large nuts, bolts and studs which aren't removed on a regular basis.

Oil additives range from viscosity index improvers to chemical treatments that claim to reduce internal engine friction. It should be noted that most oil manufacturers caution against using additives with their oils.

Gas additives perform several functions, depending on their chemical makeup. They usually contain solvents that help dissolve gum and varnish that build up on carburetor, fuel injection and intake parts. They also serve to break down carbon deposits that form on the inside surfaces of the combustion chambers. Some additives contain upper cylinder lubricants for valves and piston rings, and others contain chemicals to remove condensation from the gas tank.

Miscellaneous

Brake fluid is specially formulated hydraulic fluid that can withstand the heat and pressure encountered in brake systems. Care must be taken so this fluid does not come in contact with painted surfaces or plastics. An opened container should always be resealed to prevent contamination by water or dirt.

Weatherstrip adhesive is used to bond weatherstripping around doors, windows and trunk lids. It is sometimes used to attach trim pieces.

Undercoating is a petroleum-based, tar-like substance that is designed to protect metal surfaces on the underside of the vehicle from corrosion. It also acts as a sound-deadening agent by insulating the bottom of the vehicle.

Waxes and polishes are used to help protect painted and plated surfaces from the weather. Different types of paint may require the use of different types of wax and polish. Some polishes utilize a chemical or abrasive cleaner to help remove the top layer of oxidized (dull) paint on older vehicles. In recent years many non-wax polishes that contain a wide variety of chemicals such as polymers and silicones have been introduced. These non-wax polishes are usually easier to apply and last longer than conventional waxes and polishes.

Safety first!

Regardless of how enthusiastic you may be about getting on with the job at hand, take the time to ensure that your safety is not jeopardized. A moment's lack of attention can result in an accident, as can failure to observe certain simple safety precautions. The possibility of an accident will always exist, and the following points should not be considered a comprehensive list of all dangers. Rather, they are intended to make you aware of the risks and to encourage a safety conscious approach to all work you carry out on your vehicle.

Essential DOs and DON'Ts

DON'T rely on a jack when working under the vehicle. Always use approved jackstands to support the weight of the vehicle and place them under the recommended lift or support points.

DON'T attempt to loosen extremely tight fasteners (i.e. wheel lug nuts) while the vehicle is on a jack – it may fall.

DON'T start the engine without first making sure that the transmission is in Neutral (or Park where applicable) and the parking brake is set.

DON'T remove the radiator cap from a hot cooling system – let it cool or cover it with a cloth and release the pressure gradually.

DON'T attempt to drain the engine oil until you are sure it has cooled to the point that it will not burn you.

DON'T touch any part of the engine or exhaust system until it has cooled sufficiently to avoid burns.

DON'T siphon toxic liquids such as gasoline, antifreeze and brake fluid by mouth, or allow them to remain on your skin.

DON'T inhale brake lining dust – it is potentially hazardous (see *Asbestos* below)

DON'T allow spilled oil or grease to remain on the floor – wipe it up before someone slips on it.

DON'T use loose fitting wrenches or other tools which may slip and cause injury.

DON'T push on wrenches when loosening or tightening nuts or bolts. Always try to pull the wrench toward you. If the situation calls for pushing the wrench away, push with an open hand to avoid scraped knuckles if the wrench should slip.

DON'T attempt to lift a heavy component alone – get someone to help you.

DON'T rush or take unsafe shortcuts to finish a job.

DON'T allow children or animals in or around the vehicle while you are working on it.

DO wear eye protection when using power tools such as a drill, sander, bench grinder, etc. and when working under a vehicle.

DO keep loose clothing and long hair well out of the way of moving parts.

DO make sure that any hoist used has a safe working load rating adequate for the job.

DO get someone to check on you periodically when working alone on a vehicle.

DO carry out work in a logical sequence and make sure that everything is correctly assembled and tightened.

DO keep chemicals and fluids tightly capped and out of the reach of children and pets.

DO remember that your vehicle's safety affects that of yourself and others. If in doubt on any point, get professional advice.

Asbestos

Certain friction, insulating, sealing, and other products – such as brake linings, brake bands, clutch linings, torque converters, gaskets, etc. – contain asbestos. *Extreme care must be taken to avoid inhalation of dust from such products, since it is hazardous to health.* If in doubt, assume that they *do* contain asbestos.

Fire

Remember at all times that gasoline is highly flammable. Never smoke or have any kind of open flame around when working on a vehicle. But the risk does not end there. A spark caused by an electrical short circuit, by two metal surfaces contacting each other, or even by static electricity built up in your body under certain conditions, can ignite gasoline vapors, which in a confined space are highly explosive. Do not, under any circumstances, use gasoline for cleaning parts. Use an approved safety solvent.

Always disconnect the battery ground (–) cable *at the battery* before working on any part of the fuel system or electrical system. Never risk spilling fuel on a hot engine or exhaust component.

It is strongly recommended that a fire extinguisher suitable for use on fuel and electrical fires be kept handy in the garage or workshop at all times. Never try to extinguish a fuel or electrical fire with water.

Fumes

Certain fumes are highly toxic and can quickly cause unconsciousness and even death if inhaled to any extent. Gasoline vapor falls into this category, as do the vapors from some cleaning solvents. Any draining or pouring of such volatile fluids should be done in a well ventilated area.

When using cleaning fluids and solvents, read the instructions on the container carefully. Never use materials from unmarked containers.

Never run the engine in an enclosed space, such as a garage. Exhaust fumes contain carbon monoxide, which is extremely poisonous. If you need to run the engine, always do so in the open air, or at least have the rear of the vehicle outside the work area.

If you are fortunate enough to have the use of an inspection pit, never drain or pour gasoline and never run the engine while the vehicle is over the pit. The fumes, being heavier than air, will concentrate in the pit with possibly lethal results.

The battery

Never create a spark or allow a bare light bulb near a battery. They normally give off a certain amount of hydrogen gas, which is highly explosive.

Always disconnect the battery ground (–) cable *at the battery* before working on the fuel or electrical systems.

If possible, loosen the filler caps or cover when charging the battery from an external source (this does not apply to sealed or maintenance-free batteries). Do not charge at an excessive rate or the battery may burst.

Take care when adding water to a non maintenance-free battery and when carrying a battery. The electrolyte, even when diluted, is very corrosive and should not be allowed to contact clothing or skin.

Always wear eye protection when cleaning the battery to prevent the caustic deposits from entering your eyes.

Household current

When using an electric power tool, inspection light, etc., which operates on household current, always make sure that the tool is correctly connected to its plug and that, where necessary, it is properly grounded. Do not use such items in damp conditions and, again, do not create a spark or apply excessive heat in the vicinity of fuel or fuel vapor.

Secondary ignition system voltage

A severe electric shock can result from touching certain parts of the ignition system (such as the spark plug wires) when the engine is running or being cranked, particularly if components are damp or the insulation is defective. In the case of an electronic ignition system, the secondary system voltage is much higher and could prove fatal.

Conversion factors

Length (distance)

Inches (in)	X	25.4	= Millimetres (mm)	X	0.0394 = Inches (in)
Feet (ft)	X	0.305	= Metres (m)	X	3.281 = Feet (ft)
Miles	X	1.609	= Kilometres (km)	X	0.621 = Miles

Volume (capacity)

Cubic inches (cu in; in³)	X	16.387	= Cubic centimetres (cc; cm³)	X	0.061 = Cubic inches (cu in; in³)
Imperial pints (Imp pt)	X	0.568	= Litres (l)	X	1.76 = Imperial pints (Imp pt)
Imperial quarts (Imp qt)	X	1.137	= Litres (l)	X	0.88 = Imperial quarts (Imp qt)
Imperial quarts (Imp qt)	X	1.201	= US quarts (US qt)	X	0.833 = Imperial quarts (Imp qt)
US quarts (US qt)	X	0.946	= Litres (l)	X	1.057 = US quarts (US qt)
Imperial gallons (Imp gal)	X	4.546	= Litres (l)	X	0.22 = Imperial gallons (Imp gal)
Imperial gallons (Imp gal)	X	1.201	= US gallons (US gal)	X	0.833 = Imperial gallons (Imp gal)
US gallons (US gal)	X	3.785	= Litres (l)	X	0.264 = US gallons (US gal)

Mass (weight)

Ounces (oz)	X	28.35	= Grams (g)	X	0.035 = Ounces (oz)
Pounds (lb)	X	0.454	= Kilograms (kg)	X	2.205 = Pounds (lb)

Force

Ounces-force (ozf; oz)	X	0.278	= Newtons (N)	X	3.6 = Ounces-force (ozf; oz)
Pounds-force (lbf; lb)	X	4.448	= Newtons (N)	X	0.225 = Pounds-force (lbf; lb)
Newtons (N)	X	0.1	= Kilograms-force (kgf; kg)	X	9.81 = Newtons (N)

Pressure

Pounds-force per square inch (psi; lbf/in²; lb/in²)	X	0.070	= Kilograms-force per square centimetre (kgf/cm²; kg/cm²)	X	14.223 = Pounds-force per square inch (psi; lbf/in²; lb/in²)
Pounds-force per square inch (psi; lbf/in²; lb/in²)	X	0.068	= Atmospheres (atm)	X	14.696 = Pounds-force per square inch (psi; lbf/in²; lb/in²)
Pounds-force per square inch (psi; lbf/in²; lb/in²)	X	0.069	= Bars	X	14.5 = Pounds-force per square inch (psi; lbf/in²; lb/in²)
Pounds-force per square inch (psi; lbf/in²; lb/in²)	X	6.895	= Kilopascals (kPa)	X	0.145 = Pounds-force per square inch (psi; lbf/in²; lb/in²)
Kilopascals (kPa)	X	0.01	= Kilograms-force per square centimetre (kgf/cm²; kg/cm²)	X	98.1 = Kilopascals (kPa)

Torque (moment of force)

Pounds-force inches (lbf in; lb in)	X	1.152	= Kilograms-force centimetre (kgf cm; kg cm)	X	0.868 = Pounds-force inches (lbf in; lb in)
Pounds-force inches (lbf in; lb in)	X	0.113	= Newton metres (Nm)	X	8.85 = Pounds-force inches (lbf in; lb in)
Pounds-force inches (lbf in; lb in)	X	0.083	= Pounds-force feet (lbf ft; lb ft)	X	12 = Pounds-force inches (lbf in; lb in)
Pounds-force feet (lbf ft; lb ft)	X	0.138	= Kilograms-force metres (kgf m; kg m)	X	7.233 = Pounds-force feet (lbf ft; lb ft)
Pounds-force feet (lbf ft; lb ft)	X	1.356	= Newton metres (Nm)	X	0.738 = Pounds-force feet (lbf ft; lb ft)
Newton metres (Nm)	X	0.102	= Kilograms-force metres (kgf m; kg m)	X	9.804 = Newton metres (Nm)

Power

Horsepower (hp)	X	745.7	= Watts (W)	X	0.0013 = Horsepower (hp)

Velocity (speed)

Miles per hour (miles/hr; mph)	X	1.609	= Kilometres per hour (km/hr; kph)	X	0.621 = Miles per hour (miles/hr; mph)

Fuel consumption*

Miles per gallon, Imperial (mpg)	X	0.354	= Kilometres per litre (km/l)	X	2.825 = Miles per gallon, Imperial (mpg)
Miles per gallon, US (mpg)	X	0.425	= Kilometres per litre (km/l)	X	2.352 = Miles per gallon, US (mpg)

Temperature

Degrees Fahrenheit $= (°C \times 1.8) + 32$

Degrees Celsius (Degrees Centigrade; °C) $= (°F - 32) \times 0.56$

*It is common practice to convert from miles per gallon (mpg) to litres/100 kilometres (l/100km), where mpg (Imperial) x l/100 km = 282 and mpg (US) x l/100 km = 235

Troubleshooting

Contents

This section provides an easy reference guide to the more common problems which may occur during the operation of your vehicle. These problems and their possible causes are grouped under headings denoting various components or systems, such as Engine, Cooling system, etc. They also refer you to the chapter and/or section which deals with the problem.

Remember that successful troubleshooting is not a mysterious black art practiced only by professional mechanics. It is simply the result of the right knowledge combined with an intelligent, systematic approach to the problem. Always work by a process of elimination, starting with the simplest solution and working through to the most complex – and never overlook the obvious. Anyone can run the gas tank dry or leave the lights on overnight, so don't assume that you are exempt from such oversights.

Finally, always establish a clear idea of why a problem has occurred and take steps to ensure that it doesn't happen again. If the electrical system fails because of a poor connection, check the other connections in the system to make sure that they don't fail as well. If a particular fuse continues to blow, find out why – don't just replace one fuse after another. Remember, failure of a small component can often be indicative of potential failure or incorrect functioning of a more important component or system.

Engine and performance

1 Engine will not rotate when attempting to start

1 Battery terminal connections loose or corroded (Chapter 1).
2 Battery discharged or faulty (Chapter 1).
3 Automatic Stick Shift not in Neutral (Chapter 7B).
4 Broken, loose or disconnected wiring in the starting circuit (Chapters 5 and 12).
5 Starter motor pinion jammed in flywheel ring gear (Chapter 5).
6 Starter solenoid faulty (Chapter 5).
7 Starter motor faulty (Chapter 5).
8 Ignition switch faulty (Chapter 12).
9 Starter pinion or flywheel teeth worn or broken (Chapter 5).

2 Engine rotates but will not start

1 Fuel tank empty.
2 Battery discharged (engine rotates slowly) (Chapter 5).
3 Battery terminal connections loose or corroded (Chapter 1).
4 Leaking fuel injector(s), faulty cold start valve, fuel pump, pressure regulator, etc. (Chapter 4).
5 Fuel not reaching main ring, or other fuel injection problem (Chapter 4).
6 Fuel not reaching carburetor (Chapter 4).
7 Ignition components damp or damaged (Chapter 5).
8 Worn, faulty or incorrectly gapped spark plugs (Chapter 1).
9 Broken, loose or disconnected wiring in the starting circuit (Chapter 5).
10 Ignition points incorrectly gapped (Chapter 5).
11 Broken, loose or disconnected wires at the ignition coil or faulty coil (Chapter 5).

3 Engine hard to start when cold

1 Battery discharged or low (Chapter 1).
2 Choke defective or not adjusted properly (Chapter 4).
3 Malfunctioning fuel system (Chapter 4).
4 Faulty cold start injector (Chapter 4).
5 Injector(s) leaking (Chapter 4).
6 Faulty ignition system (Chapter 5).

4 Engine hard to start when hot

1 Air filter clogged (Chapter 1).
2 Fuel not reaching the fuel pump, carburetor or fuel injection system (Chapter 4).
3 Corroded battery connections, especially ground (Chapter 1).
4 Worn starter motor (Chapter 5).
5 Leaking injector(s).
6 Defective thermo-time switch (Chapter 4)
7 Choke defective or not adjusted properly (Chapter 4).

5 Starter motor noisy or excessively rough in engagement

1 Pinion or flywheel gear teeth worn or broken (Chapter 5).
2 Starter motor mounting bolts loose or missing (Chapter 5).

6 Engine starts but stops immediately

1 Loose or faulty electrical connections at coil or distributor (Chapter 5).
2 Defective coil (Chapter 5)
3 Insufficient fuel reaching the carburetor or fuel injector(s) (Chapters 1 and 4).
4 Vacuum leak at the gasket between the intake manifold/plenum and throttle body (Chapter 4).
5 Defective pilot jet cutoff valve (Chapter 4).

7 Oil puddle under engine

1 Oil strainer cover plate or drain bolt washer leaking (Chapter 1).
2 Oil pressure sending unit leaking (Chapter 2).
3 Valve cover leaking (Chapter 2).
4 Pushrod tubes leaking (Chapter 2).
5 Oil cooler or oil cooler seals leaking (Chapter 3).
6 Engine oil seals leaking (Chapter 2).

8 Engine lopes while idling or idles erratically

1 Vacuum leakage (Chapters 2 and 4).
2 Leaking EGR valve (Chapter 6).
3 Air filter clogged (Chapter 1).
4 Fuel pump not delivering sufficient fuel (Chapter 4).
5 Timing gears worn (Chapter 2).
6 Camshaft lobes worn (Chapter 2).
7 Throttle body ports clogged (Chapter 4).
8 Carburetor misadjusted or worn (Chapter 4).

9 Engine misses at idle speed

1 Spark plugs worn or not gapped properly (Chapter 1).
2 Faulty spark plug wires (Chapter 1).
3 Vacuum leaks (Chapter 1).
4 Incorrect ignition timing (Chapter 1).
5 Uneven or low compression (Chapter 2).
6 Incorrect air/fuel mixture (Chapter 4).

10 Engine misses throughout driving speed range

1 Fuel filter/carburetor/injectors clogged and/or impurities in the fuel system (Chapter 1).

2 Low fuel output at the injector(s) (Chapter 4).
3 Faulty or incorrectly gapped spark plugs (Chapter 1).
4 Incorrect ignition timing (Chapter 5).
5 Cracked distributor cap or rotor (Chapters 1 and 5).
6 Leaking spark plug wires (Chapters 1 or 5).
7 Faulty emission system components (Chapter 6).
8 Low or uneven cylinder compression pressures (Chapter 2).
9 Weak or faulty ignition system (Chapter 5).
10 Vacuum leak in fuel injection system, intake manifold, air regulator valve or vacuum hoses (Chapter 4).

11 Engine stumbles on acceleration

1 Spark plugs fouled (Chapter 1).
2 Carburetor/fuel injection system needs adjustment or repair (Chapter 4).
3 Fuel filter clogged (Chapters 1 and 4).
4 Incorrect ignition timing (Chapter 5).
5 Intake manifold vacuum leak (Chapters 2 and 4).

12 Engine surges while holding accelerator steady

1 Intake air leak (Chapter 4).
2 Fuel pump faulty (Chapter 4).
3 Loose fuel injector electrical connectors (Chapter 4).
4 Defective ECU (Chapter 6).
5 Damaged air flow sensor (Chapter 4).

13 Engine stalls

1 Idle speed incorrect (Chapter 1).
2 Fuel filter clogged and/or water and impurities in the fuel system (Chapters 1 and 4).
3 Distributor components damp or damaged (Chapter 5).
4 Faulty emissions system components (Chapter 6).
5 Faulty or incorrectly gapped spark plugs (Chapter 1).
6 Faulty spark plug wires (Chapter 1).
7 Vacuum leak in the intake manifold or vacuum hoses (Chapters 2 and 4).
8 Valve clearances incorrectly set (Chapter 1).
9 Defective pilot jet cutoff valve.

14 Engine lacks power

1 Incorrect ignition timing (Chapter 5).
2 Excessive play in distributor shaft (Chapter 5).
3 Worn rotor, distributor cap, points or wires (Chapters 1 and 5).
4 Faulty or incorrectly gapped spark plugs (Chapter 1).
5 Carburetor or fuel injection system out of adjustment or excessively worn (Chapter 4).
6 Faulty coil (Chapter 5).
7 Brakes binding (Chapter 9).
8 Automatic Stick Shift fluid level incorrect (Chapter 1).
9 Clutch slipping (Chapter 7B or 8).
10 Fuel filter clogged and/or impurities in the fuel system (Chapters 1 and 4).
11 Emission control system not functioning properly (Chapter 6).
12 Low or uneven cylinder compression pressures (Chapter 2).
13 Exhaust system plugged (Chapter 4).

15 Engine backfires

1 Emission control system not functioning properly (Chapter 6).
2 Ignition timing incorrect (Chapter 5).
3 Faulty secondary ignition system (cracked spark plug insulator, faulty plug wires, distributor cap and/or rotor) (Chapters 1 and 5).
4 Carburetor/fuel injection system in need of adjustment or worn excessively (Chapter 4).
5 Vacuum leak at fuel injector(s), intake manifold, air regulator valve or vacuum hoses (Chapters 2 and 4).
6 Valve clearances incorrectly set and/or valves sticking (Chapter 1).

16 Pinging or knocking engine sounds during acceleration or uphill

1 Incorrect grade of fuel.
2 Ignition timing incorrect (Chapter 5).
3 Carburetor/fuel injection system in need of adjustment (Chapter 4).
4 Improper or damaged spark plugs or wires (Chapter 1).
5 Worn or damaged ignition components (Chapter 5).
6 Faulty emission system (Chapter 6).
7 Vacuum leak (Chapters 2 and 4).

17 Engine runs with oil pressure light on

1 Low oil level (Chapter 1).
2 Idle rpm below specification (Chapter 1).
3 Short in wiring circuit (Chapter 12).
4 Faulty oil pressure sender (Chapter 2).
5 Worn engine bearings and/or oil pump (Chapter 2).

18 Engine diesels (continues to run) after switching off

1 Idle speed too high (Chapter 1).
2 Excessive engine operating temperature (Chapter 3).
3 Defective pilot jet cutoff valve (Chapter 4).

Engine electrical system

19 Battery will not hold a charge

1 Alternator/generator drivebelt defective or not adjusted properly (Chapter 1).
2 Battery electrolyte level low (Chapter 1).
3 Battery terminals loose or corroded (Chapter 1).
4 Alternator/generator not charging properly (Chapter 5).
5 Loose, broken or faulty wiring in the charging circuit (Chapter 5).
6 Short in vehicle wiring (Chapter 12).
7 Internally defective battery (Chapters 1 and 5).

20 Alternator/generator light fails to go out

1 Faulty alternator/generator or charging circuit (Chapter 5).
2 Alternator/generator drivebelt defective or out of adjustment (Chapter 1).
3 Alternator/generator voltage regulator inoperative (Chapter 5).

21   Alternator/generator light fails to come on when key is turned on

Warning light bulb or circuit defective (Chapter 12).

Fuel system

22   Excessive fuel consumption

1   Dirty or clogged air filter element (Chapter 1).
2   Incorrectly set ignition timing (Chapter 5).
3   Emissions system not functioning properly (Chapter 6).
4   Carburetor/fuel injection internal parts excessively worn or damaged (Chapter 4).
5   Low tire pressure or incorrect tire size (Chapter 1).

23   Fuel leakage and/or fuel odor

1   Leaking fuel feed or return line (Chapters 1 and 4).
2   Tank overfilled.
3   Evaporative canister filter clogged (Chapters 1 and 6).
4   Fuel injector internal parts excessively worn (Chapter 4).
5   Leaking fuel injector(s) (Chapter 4).
6   Carburetor worn (Chapter 4).

Cooling system

24   Overheating

1   Drivebelt slipping (Chapter 1).
2   Fan air intake behind shroud blocked or restricted (Chapter 3).
3   Thermostat faulty (Chapter 3).
4   Ignition timing incorrect (Chapter 5).
5   Air/fuel mixture incorrect (Chapter 4).

25   Overcooling

Faulty thermostat (Chapter 3).

Clutch

26   Pedal travels to floor – no pressure or very little resistance

1   Broken release bearing or fork (Chapter 8).
2   Collapsed diaphragm spring in clutch pressure plate (Chapter 8).

27   High pedal effort

1   Clutch cable worn (Chapter 8).
2   Clutch release shaft/housing worn (Chapter 8).

28   Unable to select gears

1   Faulty transaxle (Chapter 7).
2   Faulty clutch disc (Chapter 8).

3   Faulty pressure plate (Chapter 8).
4   Pressure plate-to-flywheel bolts loose (Chapter 8).
5   Coupling pin on shift rod loose or missing (Chapter 7A).

29   Clutch slips (engine speed increases with no increase in vehicle speed)

1   Clutch plate worn (Chapter 8).
2   Clutch plate is oil soaked by leaking rear main seal (Chapter 8) or transaxle input shaft seal (Chapter 7A).
3   Clutch plate not seated. It may take 30 or 40 normal starts for a new one to seat.
4   Warped pressure plate or flywheel (Chapter 8).
5   Weak clutch springs (Chapter 8).
6   Clutch plate overheated. Allow to cool.

30   Grabbing (chattering) as clutch is engaged

1   Oil on clutch plate lining, burned or glazed facings (Chapter 8).
2   Worn or loose engine or transaxle mounts (Chapters 2 and 7).
3   Worn splines on clutch plate hub (Chapter 8).
4   Warped pressure plate or flywheel (Chapter 8).
5   Burned or smeared resin on flywheel or pressure plate (Chapter 8).

31   Noise in clutch area

1   Release shaft improperly installed (Chapter 8).
2   Faulty bearing (Chapter 8).
3   Clutch plate damper spring failure (Chapter 8).

32   Clutch pedal stays on floor

1   Binding release cable (Chapter 8).
2   Broken release bearing or fork (Chapter 8).

Manual transaxle

33   Knocking noise at low speeds

Worn driveaxle constant velocity (CV) joint(s) (Chapter 8).

34   Noise most pronounced when turning

Differential gear noise (Chapter 7A).*

35   Clunk on acceleration or deceleration

1   Loose engine or transaxle mounts (Chapters 2 and 7A).
2   Worn differential pinion shaft in case.*
3   Worn or damaged driveaxle CV joints (Chapter 8).

36   Vibration

1   Rough wheel bearing (Chapters 1 and 10).
2   Damaged driveaxle (Chapter 8).

3   Out of round tires (Chapter 1).
4   Tire out of balance (Chapters 1 and 10).
5   Worn CV joint (Chapter 8).

37   Noisy in neutral with engine running

Damaged input gear bearing (Chapter 7A).*

38   Noisy in one particular gear

1   Damaged or worn constant mesh gears (Chapter 7A).*
2   Damaged or worn synchronizers (Chapter 7A).*
3   Bent reverse fork (Chapter 7A).*
4   Damaged fourth speed gear or output gear (Chapter 7A).*
5   Worn or damaged reverse idler gear or idler bushing (Chapter 7A).*

39   Noisy in all gears

1   Insufficient lubricant (Chapter 7A).
2   Damaged or worn bearings (Chapter 7A).*
3   Worn or damaged input gear shaft (Chapter 7A).*

40   Slips out of gear

1   Worn or improperly adjusted linkage (Chapter 7A).
2   Transaxle/engine mounts loose or worn (Chapter 7A).
3   Shift linkage does not work freely, binds (Chapter 7A).
4   Worn shift fork (Chapter 7A).*

41   Leaks lubricant

1   Final drive flange seals worn (Chapter 8).
2   Excessive amount of lubricant in transaxle (Chapters 1 and 7A).
3   Input gear shaft seal damaged (Chapter 7A).*
4   Torn axle boot (Chapter 8).
5   Leaking axle tube retainer gasket (Chapter 8).

42   Locked in gear

1   Lock pin or interlock pin missing (Chapter 7A).*
2   Coupling pin for shift rod loose or missing (Chapter 8).

* Although the corrective action necessary to remedy the symptoms described is beyond the scope of the home mechanic, the above information should be helpful in isolating the cause of the condition so the owner can communicate clearly with a professional mechanic.

Automatic Stick Shift

43   Fluid leakage

1   Automatic transmission fluid is a deep red color. Fluid leaks should not be confused with engine oil, which can easily be blown onto the transaxle by air flow.

2   To pinpoint a leak, first remove all built-up dirt and grime from the transaxle housing with degreasing agents and/or steam cleaning. Then drive the vehicle at low speeds so air flow will not blow the leak far from its source. Raise the vehicle and determine where the leak is coming from.

44   Transaxle fluid brown or has a burned smell

Transaxle fluid burned (Chapter 1).

45   Clutch slips at full throttle

1   Insufficient freeplay (Chapter 7B).
2   Clutch linings contaminated (Chapter 2 and Chapter 7B).
3   Clutch linings worn (Chapter 7B).

46   Excessive clutch slippage after gear selection

1   Leaking hose between carburetor and control valve (Chapter 7B).
2   Control valve filter blocked (Chapter 7B).
3   Adjusting screw on reduction valve in too far (Chapter 7B).

47   Clutch disengaging improperly

1   Vacuum hose or vacuum tank leaking (Chapter 7B).
2   Excessive freeplay (Chapter 7B).
3   Servo defective (Chapter 7B).

48   Clutch not disengaging

1   Solenoid circuit open (Chapter 7B).
2   Bad ground connection between selector lever and frame (Chapter 7B).
3   Hoses to servo kinked or collapsed (Chapter 7B).
4   Defective servo (Chapter 7B).

49   Engine stalls when gear is selected

1   Leaking hose between servo and control valve (Chapter 7B).
2   Defective servo (Chapter 7B).

50   Engine stalls and won't restart

1   Hose between control valve and carburetor or vacuum tank leaking (Chapter 7B).
2   Vacuum tank leaking (Chapter 7B).

51   Clutch doesn't engage after gear selection

1   Sticking selector lever switch (Chapter 7B).
2   Short in solenoid circuit (Chapter 7B).
3   Solenoid in control valve sticking (Chapter 7B).

52   Clutch grabs after gear selection

1   Clutch linings contaminated with oil (Chapter 7B).
2   Distorted carrier plate (Chapter 7B).

53   Vehicle jerks at idle when shift lever is released

1   Idle speed too high (Chapter 1).
2   Misadjusted control valve (Chapter 7B).

54   Torque converter noisy (high-pitched hissing)

1   Low ATF level (Chapter 1).
2   Low ATF pressure (Chapter 7B).
3   Leaking converter or converter seal (Chapter 7B).

55   Poor acceleration (engine output satisfactory)

Faulty one-way clutch in the torque converter (Chapter 7B).

56   Engine will start in gears other than Neutral

Neutral start switch malfunctioning (Chapter 7B).

Driveaxles

57   Shudder or vibration during acceleration

1   Excessive toe-in (Chapter 10).
2   Incorrect spring heights (Chapter 10).
3   Worn or damaged inboard or outboard CV joints (Chapter 8).
4   Sticking inboard CV joint assembly (Chapter 8).

58   Vibration at highway speeds

1   Out of balance front wheels and/or tires (Chapters 1 and 10).
2   Out of round front tires (Chapters 1 and 10).
3   Worn CV joint(s) (Chapter 8).

Brakes

Note: *Before assuming that a brake problem exists, make sure that:*
    a) The tires are in good condition and properly inflated (Chapter 1).
    b) The front end alignment is correct (Chapter 10).
    c) The vehicle is not loaded with weight in an unequal manner.

59   Vehicle pulls to one side during braking

1   Incorrect tire pressures (Chapter 1).
2   Front end out of line (have the front end aligned).
3   Front, or rear, tires not matched to one another.
4   Restricted brake lines or hoses (Chapter 9).
5   Malfunctioning drum brake or caliper assembly (Chapter 9).
6   Loose suspension parts (Chapter 10).
7   Loose backing plates or calipers (Chapter 9).
8   Excessive wear of brake shoe or pad material or disc/drum on one side.

60   Noise (high-pitched squeal when the brakes are applied)

Brake pads or shoes worn out. Replace pads/shoes with new ones immediately (Chapter 9). Be sure to check the disc/drums for damage as well.

61   Brake roughness or chatter (pedal pulsates)

1   Excessive disc lateral runout (Chapter 9).
2   Uneven pad wear (Chapter 9).
3   Defective disc (Chapter 9).
4   Drum out-of-round (Chapter 9).

62   Excessive brake pedal effort required to stop vehicle

1   Partial system failure (Chapter 9).
2   Excessively worn pads or shoes (Chapter 9).
3   Piston in caliper or wheel cylinder stuck or sluggish (Chapter 9).
4   Brake pads or shoes contaminated with oil or grease (Chapter 9).
5   New pads or shoes installed and not yet seated. It will take a while for the new material to seat against the rotor or drum.

63   Excessive brake pedal travel

1   Partial brake system failure (Chapter 9).
2   Insufficient fluid in master cylinder (Chapters 1 and 9).
3   Air trapped in system (Chapters 1 and 9).
4   Brakes in need of adjustment (Chapter 9).

64   Dragging brakes

1   Master cylinder pistons not returning correctly (Chapter 9).
2   Restricted brake lines or hoses (Chapters 1 and 9).
3   Incorrect parking brake adjustment (Chapter 9).

65   Grabbing or uneven braking action

1   Binding brake pedal mechanism (Chapter 9).
2   Grease or oil on brake lining (Chapter 9).

66   Brake pedal feels spongy when depressed

1   Air in hydraulic lines (Chapter 9).
2   Master cylinder mounting bolts loose (Chapter 9).
3   Master cylinder defective (Chapter 9).

67   Brake pedal travels to the floor with little resistance

1   Little or no fluid in the master cylinder reservoir caused by leaking caliper or wheel cylinder piston(s) (Chapter 9).
2   Loose, damaged or disconnected brake lines (Chapter 9).

68   Parking brake does not hold

Parking brake cable improperly adjusted (Chapter 9).

Suspension and steering systems

Note: *Before attempting to diagnose the suspension and steering systems, perform the following preliminary checks:*

   a) Tires for wrong pressure and uneven wear.
   b) Steering couplings from the column to the steering gear for loose connectors or wear.
   c) Front and rear suspension and the steering gear assembly for loose or damaged parts.
   d) Out-of-round or out-of-balance tires, bent rims and loose and/or rough wheel bearings.

69   Vehicle pulls to one side

1   Mismatched or uneven tires (Chapter 10).
2   Broken or sagging torsion bars (Chapter 10).
3   Wheel alignment (Chapter 10).
4   Front brake dragging (Chapter 9).

70   Abnormal or excessive tire wear

1   Incorrect wheel alignment (Chapter 10).
2   Sagging or broken torsion bars (Chapter 10).
3   Tire out of balance (Chapter 10).
4   Worn shock absorber or strut damper (Chapter 10).
5   Overloaded vehicle.
6   Tires not rotated regularly.

71   Wheel makes a thumping noise

1   Blister or bump on tire (Chapter 10).
2   Improper shock absorber or strut damper action (Chapter 10).

72   Shimmy, shake or vibration

1   Tire or wheel out-of-balance or out-of-round (Chapter 10).
2   Loose or worn wheel bearings (Chapters 1 and 10).
3   Worn tie-rod ends (Chapter 10).
4   Worn balljoints (Chapters 1 and 10).
5   Excessive wheel runout (Chapter 10).
6   Blister or bump on tire (Chapter 10).

73   Hard steering

1   Lack of lubrication at balljoints, tie-rod ends and steering gear assembly (Chapter 10).
2   Incorrect front wheel alignment (Chapter 10).
3   Low tire pressure(s) (Chapter 1).

74   Poor returnability of steering to center

1   Lack of lubrication at balljoints and tie-rod ends (Chapter 10).
2   Binding in balljoints (Chapter 10).
3   Binding in steering column (Chapter 10).
4   Lack of lubricant in steering gear (Chapter 10).
5   Incorrect front wheel alignment (Chapter 10).

75   Abnormal noise at the front end

1   Lack of lubrication at balljoints and tie-rod ends (Chapters 1 and 10).
2   Damaged shock absorber or strut (Chapter 10).
3   Worn control arm bushings or tie-rod ends (Chapter 10).
4   Loose stabilizer bar (Chapter 10).
5   Loose wheel lug bolts (Chapters 1 and 10).
6   Loose suspension bolts (Chapter 10).

76   Wander or poor steering stability

1   Mismatched or uneven tires (Chapter 10).
2   Lack of lubrication at balljoints and tie-rod ends (Chapters 1 and 10).
3   Worn shock absorbers or strut assemblies (Chapter 10).
4   Loose stabilizer bar (Chapter 10).
5   Broken or sagging torsion bars (Chapter 10).
6   Incorrect wheel alignment (Chapter 10).

77   Erratic steering when braking

1   Wheel bearings worn or out of adjustment (Chapter 10).
2   Broken or sagging torsion bars (Chapter 10).
3   Leaking wheel cylinder or caliper (Chapter 10).
4   Warped discs or drums (Chapter 10).

78   Excessive pitching and/or rolling around corners or during braking

1   Loose stabilizer bar (Chapter 10).
2   Worn shock absorbers or strut dampers (Chapter 10).
3   Broken or sagging torsion bars (Chapter 10).
4   Overloaded vehicle.

79   Suspension bottoms

1   Overloaded vehicle.
2   Worn shock absorbers or strut dampers (Chapter 10).
3   Incorrect, broken or sagging torsion bars (Chapter 10).

80   Cupped tires

1   Incorrect front wheel or rear wheel alignment (Chapter 10).
2   Worn strut dampers or shock absorbers (Chapter 10).
3   Wheel bearings worn (Chapter 10).
4   Excessive tire or wheel runout (Chapter 10).
5   Worn balljoints (Chapter 10).

81   Excessive tire wear on outside edge

1   Inflation pressures incorrect (Chapter 1).
2   Excessive speed in turns.
3   Front end alignment incorrect. Have professionally aligned.

82   Excessive tire wear on inside edge

1   Inflation pressures incorrect (Chapter 1).
2   Front end alignment incorrect. Have professionally aligned.

83   Tire tread worn in one place

1   Tires out of balance.
2   Damaged or buckled wheel. Inspect and replace if necessary.
3   Defective tire (Chapter 1).

84   Excessive play or looseness in steering system

1   Wheel bearing(s) worn or out of adjustment (Chapter 10).

2   Tie-rod end loose (Chapter 10).
3   Steering gear loose (Chapter 10).
4   Worn or loose steering intermediate shaft (Chapter 10).

85   Rattling or clicking noise in steering gear

1   Insufficient or improper lubricant in steering gear (Chapter 10).
2   Steering gear attachment loose (Chapter 10).
3   Internal steering gear problem (Chapter 10).

Chapter 1 Tune-up and routine maintenance

Contents

1

Specifications

Recommended lubricants and fluids

Engine oil type	API grade SG or SG/CE multigrade and fuel efficient oil
Engine oil viscosity	See accompanying chart
Automatic stick shift torque converter fluid type	Dexron II automatic transmission fluid
Automatic stick shift differential/gearbox lubricant type	API GL-5 SAE 75W90W or 80W90W Hypoid gear oil
Manual transaxle lubricant type	API GL-5 SAE 75W90W or 80W90W Hypoid gear oil
Brake fluid type	DOT 3 or DOT 4 brake fluid

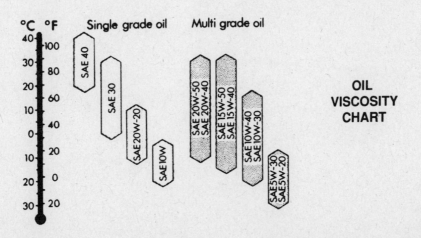

OIL VISCOSITY CHART

Tune-up specifications

Spark plug type	Refer to the spark plug manufacturer's catalog, owner's manual or emission control information label on the engine
Spark plug gap	0.024 to 0.028 in
Ignition point gap	0.016 in
Dwell angle	44 to 50-degrees

Ignition timing
  1954 through 1965 models .... 10-degrees BTDC
  1966 and 1967 models with engine numbers
    beginning with FO or HO .... 7.5-degrees BTDC
  1967 through 1970 models with engine numbers
    beginning with H5 and fuel injected models
    with automatic stick shift .... 0-degrees (TDC)
  August 1970 through spring 1973 carbureted
    models and fuel injected models with manual transaxles .... 5-degrees After Top Dead Center (ATDC)
  Spring 1973 and 1974 carbureted models .... 7.5-degrees BTDC
  1975 and later with manual transaxle .... 5-degrees ATDC
  1975 and later with automatic stick shift .... 0-degrees (TDC)
Spark plug connector resistance .... 5,000 to 10,000 ohms
Engine firing order 1-4-3-2
Idle speed
  Carbureted models
    With manual transaxle .... 800 to 900 rpm
    With Automatic Stick Shift .... 900 to 1000 rpm
  Fuel injected models
    With manual transaxle .... 800 to 950 rpm
    With Automatic Stick Shift .... 850 to 1000 rpm
Valve clearances (engine cold)
  1954 through 1960 (36 hp)
    Intake valve .... 0.004 in
    Exhaust valve .... 0.004 in
  1961 through 1965 (40 hp)
    Intake valve .... 0.008 in*
    Exhaust valve .... 0.012 in*
  All other models
    Intake valve .... 0.006 in
    Exhaust valve .... 0.006 in
* See Note in Section 30

Cylinder numbering diagram

Drivebelt deflection .... 1/2 in

Clutch pedal freeplay .... 1/2 to 3/4 in

Brakes

Disc brake pad lining thickness (minimum) .... 1/16 in
Drum brake shoe lining thickness (minimum)
  Riveted lining .... 1/16 in
  Bonded lining .... 3/64 in
Parking brake adjustment .... 4 clicks

Suspension and steering

Steering wheel freeplay limit .... 1.0 in
Tire pressures
  Bias ply
    Front .... 16 psi
    Rear .... 24 psi
  Radial
    Front 18
    Rear 27

Torque specifications

	Ft-lbs
Oil screen cover	5
Wheel lug bolts	
Five lug wheels	72
Four lug wheels	90

1 Volkswagen Maintenance schedule

The maintenance intervals in this manual are provided with the assumption that you, not the dealer, will be doing the work. These are the minimum maintenance intervals recommended for Volkswagens that are driven daily. If you wish to keep your vehicle in peak condition at all times, you may wish to perform some of these procedures even more often. Because frequent maintenance enhances the efficiency, performance and resale value of your car, we encourage you to do so. If you drive in dusty areas, idle or drive at low speeds for extended periods or drive for short distances (less than four miles) in below freezing temperatures, shorter intervals are also recommended.

Every 250 miles or weekly, whichever comes first

Check the engine oil level (Section 4)
Check the windshield washer fluid level (Section 4)
Check the brake fluid level (Section 4)
Check the tires and tire pressures (Section 5)

Every 3000 miles or 3 months, whichever comes first

All items listed above plus:
Check the automatic stick shift fluid level (Section 4)
Change the engine oil (Section 9)
Lubricate the chassis (Section 20)
Check and service the battery (Section 6)
Check and adjust if necessary the engine drivebelt(s) (Section 18)

Every 6000 miles or 6 months, whichever comes first

All items listed above plus:
Inspect the windshield wiper blades and replace if necessary (Section 8)
Check the clutch pedal for proper freeplay and adjust if necessary (Section 31)
Inspect all underhood hoses and replace if necessary (Section 7)
Rotate the tires (Section 14)
Check and if necessary adjust the valve clearance (Section 30)
Inspect the brake system (Section 15)*

Check the driveaxle boots and CV joints (Section 10)
Check the starter safety switch check – automatic stick shift only (Section 19)

Every 12,000 miles or 12 months, whichever comes first

All items listed above plus:
Service the air filter (Section 17)
Service the fuel filter (Section 21)
Inspect the fuel system (Section 16)
Check compression (see Chapter 2)
Replace the spark plugs (Section 25)
Replace the ignition points and condenser (Section 27)
Inspect and replace if necessary the spark plug wires, distributor cap and rotor (Section 26)
Check the engine idle speed and adjust if necessary (Section 29)
Check the ignition timing and adjust if necessary (Section 28)
Check the valve clearance and adjust if necessary (Section 30)
Check the transaxle lubricant level (Section 13)*
Inspect the suspension and steering components (Section 11)*
Inspect the emission control system (if equipped) (Section 24)
Inspect the exhaust system (Section 12)
Service the automatic stick shift (Section 22)
Rotate the tires (Section 14)

Every 30,000 miles or 24 months, whichever comes first

Check and repack the wheel bearings (Section 32)
Change the transaxle lubricant (Section 23)*
Replace the catalytic converter (Section 24)
Service the EGR system (Section 33)

* This item is affected by "severe" operating conditions as described below. If your vehicle is operated under "severe" conditions, perform all maintenance indicated with an asterisk (*) twice as often. Severe conditions are indicated if you mainly operate your vehicle under one or more of the following conditions:
   Operating in dusty areas
   Idling for extended periods and/or low speed operation
   Operating when outside temperatures remain below freezing and when most trips are less than four miles

2   Introduction

This chapter is designed to help the home mechanic maintain the Volkswagen Beetle/Karmann Ghia for peak performance, economy, safety and long life.

In the beginning of this Chapter is a master maintenance schedule. Refer to the accompanying illustrations of the engine compartment and the underside of the vehicle for the location of various components.

Servicing your Volkswagen in accordance with the mileage/time maintenance schedule and the following Sections will provide it with a planned maintenance program that should result in a long and reliable service life. This is a comprehensive plan, so maintaining some items but not others at the specified service intervals will not produce the same results.

As you service your Volkswagen, you will discover that many of the procedures can – and should – be grouped together because of the nature of the particular procedure you're performing or because of the close proximity of two otherwise unrelated components to one another.

For example, if the vehicle is raised for chassis lubrication, you should inspect the exhaust, suspension, steering and fuel systems while you're under the vehicle. When you're rotating the tires, it makes good sense to check the brakes and wheel bearings since the wheels are already removed.

Finally, let's suppose you have to borrow or rent a torque wrench. Even if you only need to tighten the spark plugs, you might as well check the torque of as many critical fasteners as time allows.

The first step of this maintenance program is to prepare yourself before the actual work begins. Read through all sections pertinent to the procedures you're planning to do, then make a list of and gather together all the parts and tools you will need to do the job. If it looks as if you might run into problems during a particular segment of some procedure, seek advice from your local parts counterperson or dealer service department.

3   Tune-up general information

The term tune-up is used in this manual to represent a combination of individual operations rather than one specific procedure.

If, from the time the vehicle is new, the routine maintenance schedule is followed closely and frequent checks are made of fluid levels and high wear items, as suggested throughout this manual, the engine will be kept in relatively good running condition and the need for additional work will be minimized.

More likely than not, however, there will be times when the engine is running poorly due to lack of regular maintenance. This is even more likely if a used vehicle, which has not received regular and frequent maintenance checks, is purchased. In such cases, an engine tune-up will be needed outside of the regular routine maintenance intervals.

The first step in any tune-up or engine diagnosis to help correct a poor running engine would be a cylinder compression check. A check of the engine compression (see Chapter 2) will give valuable information regarding the overall performance of many internal components and should be used as a basis for tune-up and repair procedures. If, for instance, a compression check indicates serious internal engine wear, a conventional tune-up will not help the running condition of the engine and would be a waste of time and money. Because of its importance, compression checking should be performed by someone with the proper compression testing gauge and the knowledge to use it properly.

The following series of operations are those most often needed to bring a poor running engine back into a proper state of tune.

Minor tune-up

Clean, inspect and test the battery
Check all engine related fluids
Check and adjust the drivebelt
Clean and regap the spark plugs
Inspect the distributor cap and rotor
Inspect the spark plug and coil wires
Check and adjust the ignition points
Check and adjust the ignition timing
Check and adjust the valve clearance
Check and adjust the idle speed
Check the air filter
Check all underhood hoses

Major tune-up

All items listed under minor tune-up, plus . . .
Replace the spark plugs
Service the fuel filter
Service the air filter
Check the EGR and emission systems (if equipped)
Check the ignition system
Check the charging system
Check the fuel system
Service or replace the air filter
Replace the distributor cap and rotor
Replace the spark plug wires
Replace the ignition points and condenser

4   Fluid level checks

1   Fluids are an essential part of the lubrication, cooling, brake and other systems. Because these fluids gradually become depleted and/or contaminated during normal operation of the vehicle, they must be periodically replenished. See Recommended lubricants, fluids and capacities at the beginning of this Chapter before adding fluid to any of the following components. **Note:** *The vehicle must be on level ground before fluid levels can be checked.*

Engine oil

Refer to illustrations 4.2, 4.4 and 4.6

2   The engine oil level is checked with a dipstick located adjacent to the generator/alternator **(see illustration)**. The dipstick extends through a metal tube from which it protrudes down into the engine oil sump.

3   The oil level should be checked before the vehicle has been driven, or about 15 minutes after the engine has been shut off. If the oil is checked immediately after driving the vehicle, some of the oil will remain in the upper engine components, producing an inaccurate reading on the dipstick.

4   Pull the dipstick from the tube and wipe all the oil from the end with a clean rag or paper towel. Insert the clean dipstick all the way back into its metal tube and pull it out again. Observe the oil at the end of the dipstick. The level should be between the high and low marks **(see illustration)**.

5   It takes one pint of oil to raise the level from the low mark to the high mark on the dipstick. Do not allow the level to drop below the low mark or oil starvation may cause engine damage. Conversely, overfilling the engine (adding oil above the full mark) may cause oil fouled spark plugs, oil leaks or oil seal failures.

6   Remove the filler cap to add oil **(see illustration)**. Use an oil can spout or funnel to prevent spills. After adding the oil, install the filler cap. Start the engine and look carefully for any small leaks around the oil screen cover or drain plug. Stop the engine and check the oil level again after it has had sufficient time to drain back into the sump.

7   Checking the oil level is an important preventive maintenance step. A continually dropping oil level indicates oil leakage through damaged seals, from loose connections, or past worn rings or valve guides. The condition of the oil should also be checked. Each time you check the oil level, slide your thumb and index finger up the dipstick before wiping off the oil. If you see small dirt or metal particles clinging to the dipstick, the oil should be changed (see Section 9).

Windshield washer fluid

Refer to illustration 4.8

8   Fluid for the windshield washer system is stored in a plastic reservoir which is located under the front hood adjacent to the spare tire **(see illustration)**. In milder climates, plain water can be used to top up the reservoir,

4.2   The engine oil dipstick is located below the generator/alternator

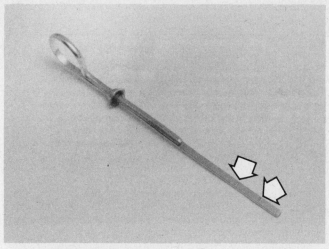

4.4   Maintain the oil level between the high and low marks

4.6   The oil filler cap is on the right (passenger's) side of the generator/alternator

4.8   Detach the hose and remove the washer fluid filler cap

but the reservoir should be kept no more than 3/4 full to allow for air pressure above the fluid. In colder climates, the use of a specially designed windshield washer fluid, available at your dealer or any auto parts store, will lower the freezing point of the fluid. Mix the solution with water in accordance with the manufacturer's directions on the container. Do not use regular antifreeze. It will damage the vehicle's paint. Be sure the spare tire has enough pressure in it and reconnect the hose between the tire and reservoir.

Battery electrolyte
Refer to illustration 4.9

9   The battery on Beetles is located under the rear seat cushion. On Karmann Ghias it is in the engine compartment. Remove the protective cover and check the electrolyte level of all the battery cells. It must be between the upper and lower levels **(see illustration)**. If the level is low, unscrew or lift off the filler/vent cap and add distilled water (except maintenance free batteries). Install and securely retighten the cap. **Caution:** *Overfilling the cells may cause electrolyte to spill over during periods of heavy charging, causing corrosion or damage. Failure to install the battery cover may result in a short circuit from the seat springs.*

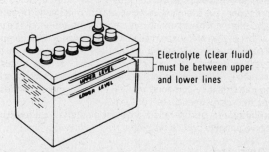

4.9   Keep the electrolyte level of all the cells in the battery between the Upper and Lower levels – use only distilled water to replenish a cell and never overfill it or electrolyte may squirt out of the battery during periods of heavy charging

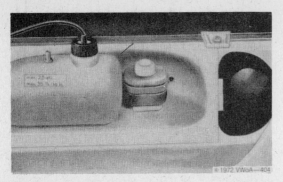

4.10a   On early models, the brake fluid reservoir is located behind the spare tire next to the windshield washer reservoir

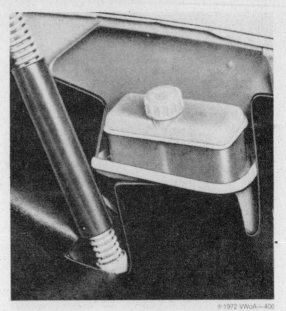

4.10b   On later models, the reservoir is adjacent to the hood spring

4.10c   On Karmann Ghias, the reservoir is behind the instrument panel cover

Brake fluid

Refer to illustrations 4.10a, 4.10b and 4.10c

10   The brake fluid reservoir is located under the front hood. On early models, it is near the spare tire, on later models the reservoir is near the driver's side hood spring. Karmann Ghias have the reservoir located behind the instrument panel cover **(see illustrations)**.

11   To check the brake fluid level on models with see-through reservoirs, simply look at the MAX and MIN marks on the reservoir. Early models require cap removal. The level should be within the specified distance from the maximum fill line for the reservoir.

12   If the level is low, wipe the top of the reservoir cover with a clean rag to prevent contamination of the brake system before lifting the cover.

13   Add only the specified brake fluid to the brake reservoir (refer to Recommended lubricants and fluids at the front of this chapter or to your owner's manual). Mixing different types of brake fluid can damage the system. Fill the brake master cylinder reservoir only to the max fill line – this brings the fluid to the correct level when you put the cover back on. **Warning:** *Use caution when filling the reservoir – brake fluid can harm your eyes and damage painted surfaces. Do not use brake fluid that has been opened for more than one year or has been left open. Brake fluid absorbs moisture from the air. Excess moisture can cause a dangerous loss of braking.*

14   While the reservoir cap is removed, inspect the master cylinder reservoir for contamination. If deposits or dirt particles are present, the system should be drained and refilled.

15   After filling the reservoir to the proper level, make sure the lid is properly seated to prevent fluid leakage and/or system pressure loss.

16   The brake fluid in the reservoir will drop slightly as the brake linings at each wheel wear down during normal operation. If the master cylinder requires frequent replenishing to keep it at the proper level, this is an indication of leakage in the brake system, which should be corrected immediately. Check all brake lines and connections, along with the wheel cylinders or calipers.

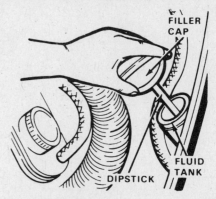

4.20   The automatic stick shift dipstick is located on the right (passenger's) side of the engine compartment

17   If, upon checking the master cylinder fluid level, you discover the reservoir is empty or nearly empty, the brake system should be refilled and carefully checked for leaks before the vehicle is returned to service (see Chapter 9).

Automatic stick shift fluid

Refer to illustration 4.20

18   The level of the automatic stick shift fluid should be carefully maintained. Low fluid level can lead to slipping or loss of drive, while overfilling can cause foaming, loss of fluid and damage.

19   Park the vehicle on level ground and set the parking brake.

20   With the engine OFF, remove the dipstick **(see illustration)**. The dipstick is located on the right (passenger's) side of the engine compartment near the firewall.

21   Wipe the fluid from the dipstick with a clean rag and reinsert it back into the filler tube until the cap seats.

22   Pull the dipstick out and note the fluid level and its condition. If the level is low, add the specified automatic transmission fluid through the dipstick tube with a funnel.

23   Add just enough of the recommended fluid to reach the proper level. Add the fluid a little at a time and keep checking the level until it is correct.

24   The condition of the fluid should also be checked along with the level. If the fluid at the end of the dipstick is black or a dark reddish brown color, or if it emits a burned smell, the fluid should be changed (see Section 22). If

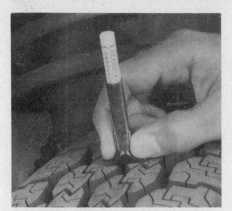

5.2   A tire tread depth indicator should be used to monitor tire wear – they are available at auto parts stores and service stations and cost very little

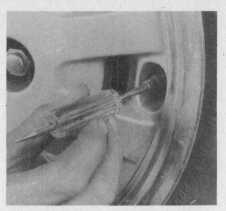

5.4a   If a tire loses air on a steady basis, check the valve core first to make sure it's snug (special inexpensive wrenches are commonly available at auto parts stores)

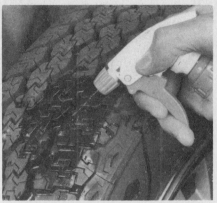

5.4b   If the valve core is tight, raise the corner of the vehicle with the low tire and spray a soapy water solution onto the tread as the tire is turned slowly – leaks will cause small bubbles to appear

you are in doubt about the condition of the fluid, purchase some new fluid and compare the two for color and smell.

Transaxle lubricant

25   Both the automatic stick shift and manual transaxle have a check/fill plug which must be removed to check the lubricant level. See Section 13 for information.

5   Tire and tire pressure checks

Refer to illustrations 5.2, 5.3, 5.4a, 5.4b and 5.8

1   Periodic inspection of the tires may spare you from the inconvenience of being stranded with a flat tire. It can also provide you with vital information regarding possible problems in the steering and suspension systems before major damage occurs.

2   Normal tread wear can be monitored with a simple, inexpensive device known as a tread depth indicator (**see illustration**). When the tread

depth reaches about 1/16 inch, replace the tire(s).

3   Note any abnormal tread wear (**see illustration**). Tread pattern irregularities such as cupping, flat spots and more wear on one side than the other are indications of front end alignment and/or balance problems. If any of these conditions are noted, take the vehicle to a tire shop or service station to correct the problem.

4   Look closely for cuts, punctures and embedded nails or tacks. Sometimes a tire will hold its air pressure for a short time or leak down very slowly even after a nail has embedded itself into the tread. If a slow leak persists, check the valve stem core to make sure it is tight (**see illustration**). Examine the tread for an object that may have embedded itself into the tire or for a "plug" that may have begun to leak (radial tire punctures are often repaired with a plug that is installed in a puncture). Sometimes rust will form between the tire and rim on tubeless tires, causing a leak. If a leak is suspected, it can be easily verified by spraying a solution of soapy water onto the suspect area (**see illustration**). The soapy solution will bubble if there is a leak. Unless the puncture is inordinately large, a tire shop or gas station can usually repair the punctured tire.

Condition	Probable cause	Corrective action	Condition	Probable cause	Corrective action
Shoulder wear	• Underinflation (both sides wear) • Incorrect wheel camber (one side wear) • Hard cornering • Lack of rotation	• Measure and adjust pressure. • Repair or replace axle and suspension parts. • Reduce speed. • Rotate tires.	Feathered edge Toe wear	• Incorrect toe	• Adjust toe-in.
Center wear	• Overinflation • Lack of rotation	• Measure and adjust pressure. • Rotate tires.	Uneven wear	• Incorrect camber or caster • Malfunctioning suspension • Unbalanced wheel • Out-of-round brake drum • Lack of rotation	• Repair or replace axle and suspension parts. • Repair or replace suspension parts. • Balance or replace. • Turn or replace. • Rotate tires.

5.3   This chart will help you determine the condition of your tires, the probable cause(s) of abnormal wear and the corrective action necessary

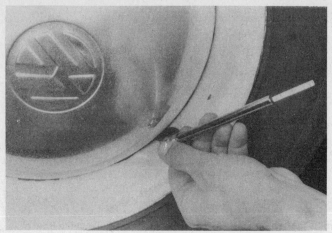

5.8   To extend the life of the tires, check the air pressure at least once a week with an accurate gauge (don't forget the spare!)

5   Carefully inspect the inner sidewall of each tire for evidence of brake fluid leakage. If you see any, inspect the brakes immediately.

6   Correct tire air pressure adds miles to the lifespan of the tires, improves mileage and enhances overall ride quality. Tire pressure cannot be accurately estimated by looking at a tire, particularly if it is a radial. A tire pressure gauge is therefore essential. Keep an accurate gauge in the glovebox. The pressure gauges fitted to the the the nozzles of air hoses at gas stations are often inaccurate.

7   Always check tire pressure when the tires are cold. "Cold," in this case, means the vehicle has not been driven over a mile in the three hours preceding a tire pressure check. A pressure rise of four to eight pounds is not uncommon once the tires are warm.

8   Unscrew the valve cap protruding from the wheel and push the gauge firmly onto the valve **(see illustration)**. Note the reading on the gauge and compare this figure to the recommended tire pressure shown on the tire placard on the left door (if equipped), the tire itself, or the pressure listed in this Chapter's Specifications. Be sure to reinstall the valve cap to keep dirt and moisture out of the valve stem mechanism. Check all four tires and, if necessary, add enough air to bring them up to the recommended pressure levels.

9   Don't forget to keep the spare tire inflated to the specified pressure (consult your owner's manual).

---

6   Battery check and maintenance

Refer to illustrations 6.1, 6.3, 6.6a, 6.6b, 6.7a and 6.7b

1   A routine preventive maintenance program for the battery in your vehicle is the only way to ensure quick and reliable starts. But before performing any battery maintenance, make sure that you have the proper equipment necessary to work safely around the battery **(see illustration)**.

2   There are also several precautions that should be taken whenever battery maintenance is performed. Before servicing the battery, always turn the engine and all accessories off. Remove the lower cushion from the rear seat and disconnect the cable from the negative terminal of the battery.

3   The battery produces hydrogen gas, which is both flammable and explosive. Never create a spark, smoke or light a match around the battery. If the vehicle you are working on has removable caps on top of the battery, open them and check the electrolyte level **(see illustration)**. Always charge the battery in a ventilated area.

4   Electrolyte contains poisonous and corrosive sulfuric acid. Do not allow it to get in your eyes, on your skin on on your clothes. Never ingest it. Wear protective safety glasses when working near the battery. Keep children away from the battery.

5   Note the external condition of the battery. If the positive terminal and cable clamp on your vehicle's battery is usually equipped with a rubber or

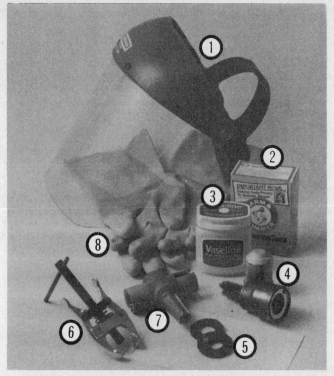

6.1   Tools and materials required for battery maintenance

1   *Face shield/safety goggles – When removing corrosion with a brush, the acidic particles can easily fly up into your eyes*

2   *Baking soda – A solution of baking soda and water can be used to neutralize corrosion*

3   *Petroleum jelly – A layer of this on the battery posts will help prevent corrosion*

4   *Battery post/cable cleaner – This wire brush cleaning tool will remove all traces of corrosion from the battery posts and cable clamps*

5   *Treated felt washers – Placing one of these on each post, directly under the cable clamps, will help prevent corrosion*

6   *Puller – Sometimes the cable clamps are very difficult to pull off the posts, even after the nut/bolt has been completely loosened. This tool pulls the clamp straight up and off the post without damage.*

7   *Battery post/cable cleaner – Here is another cleaning tool which is a slightly different version of number 4 above, but it does the same thing*

8   *Rubber gloves – Another safety item to consider when servicing the battery; remember that's acid inside the battery!*

plastic protector, make sure that it's not torn or damaged. It should completely cover the terminal. Look for any corroded or loose connections, cracks in the case or cover or loose hold-down clamps. Also check the entire length of each cable for cracks and frayed conductors.

6   If corrosion, which looks like white, fluffy deposits **(see illustration)** is evident, particularly around the terminals, the battery should be removed for cleaning. Loosen the cable clamp bolts with a wrench, being careful to remove the ground cable first, and slide them off the terminals **(see illustration)**. Then disconnect the hold-down clamp bolt and nut, remove the clamp and lift the battery from its compartment.

7   Clean the cable clamps thoroughly with a battery brush or a terminal cleaner and a solution of warm water and baking soda **(see illustration)**. Wash the terminals and the top of the battery case with the same solution but make sure that the solution doesn't get into the battery. When cleaning the cables, terminals and battery top, wear safety goggles and rubber gloves to prevent any solution from coming in contact with your eyes or

6.3 Remove the cell caps to check the electrolyte level in the battery – if the level is low, add distilled water only

6.6a Battery terminal corrosion usually appears as light, fluffy powder

6.6b Removing the cable from a battery post with a wrench – sometimes a special battery pliers is required for this procedure if corrosion has caused deterioration of the nut hex (always remove the ground cable first and hook it up last!)

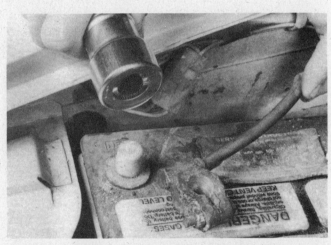

6.7a Regardless of the type of tool used on the battery posts, a clean, shiny surface should be the result

6.7b When cleaning the cable clamps, all corrosion must be removed (the inside of the clamp is tapered to match the taper on the post, so don't remove too much material)

hands. Wear old clothes too – even diluted, sulfuric acid splashed onto clothes will burn holes in them. If the terminals have been extensively corroded, clean them up with a terminal cleaner (see illustration). Thoroughly wash all cleaned areas with plain water.

8   Before reinstalling the battery into its compartment, inspect the battery tray. If it's dirty or covered with corrosion, remove it and clean it in the same solution of warm water and baking soda. Inspect the brackets which support the carrier to make sure that they are not covered with corrosion. If they are, wash them off. If corrosion is extensive, sand the brackets down to bare metal and spray them with a zinc-based primer (available in spray cans at auto paint and body supply stores).

9   Reinstall the battery carrier and the battery. Make sure that no parts or wires are laying on the carrier during installation of the battery.

10   Install a pair of specially treated felt washers around the terminals (available at auto parts stores). Install the cable clamps and tighten the bolts, being careful to install the negative cable last. Then coat the terminals and the cable clamps with petroleum jelly or grease to prevent further corrosion.

11   Install the hold-down clamp and bolts. Tighten the bolts only enough to hold the battery firmly in place. Overtightening these bolts can crack the battery case.

12   Further information on the battery, charging and jump starting can be found in Chapter 5 and at the front of this manual.

7   Underhood hose check and replacement

General

1   High temperatures in the engine compartment can cause the deterioration of the rubber and plastic hoses used for engine, accessory and emission systems operation. Periodic inspection should be made for cracks, loose clamps, material hardening and leaks.

2   Some, but not all, hoses are secured to the fittings with clamps. Where clamps are used, check to be sure they haven't lost their tension, allowing the hose to leak. If clamps aren't used, make sure the hose has not expanded and/or hardened where it slips over the fitting, allowing it to leak.

Vacuum hoses

3   Various systems require hoses with different wall thicknesses, collapse resistance and temperature resistance. When replacing hoses, be sure the new ones are equivalent.

4   Often the only effective way to check a hose is to remove it completely from the vehicle. If more than one hose is removed, be sure to label the hoses and fittings to ensure correct installation.

5   When checking vacuum hoses, be sure to include any fittings in the check. Inspect the fittings for cracks and the hose where it fits over the fitting for distortion, which could cause leakage.

6   A small piece of vacuum hose (1/4-inch inside diameter) can be used as a stethoscope to detect vacuum leaks. Hold one end of the hose to your ear and probe around vacuum hoses and fittings, listening for the "hissing" sound characteristic of a vacuum leak. **Warning:** *When probing with the vacuum hose stethoscope, be very careful not to come into contact with moving engine components such as the drivebelts and pulleys.*

Fuel hose

Warning: *Gasoline is extremely flammable, so take extra precautions when you work on any part of the fuel system. Don't smoke or allow open flames or bare light bulbs near the work area, and don't work in a garage where a natural gas-type appliance (such as a water heater or clothes dryer) with a pilot light is present. If you spill any fuel on your skin, rinse it off immediately with soap and water. When you perform any kind of work on the fuel system, wear safety glasses and have a Class B type fire extinguisher on hand. On vehicles equipped with fuel injection, the fuel system is under pressure, so if any fuel lines are to be disconnected, the pressure in the system must be relieved first (see Chapter 4 for more information).*

7   Check all rubber fuel lines for deterioration and chafing. Check especially for cracks in areas where the hose bends and just before fittings, such as where a hose attaches to the fuel filter.

8   High quality fuel line, often identified by the word Fluroelastomer printed on the hose, should be used for fuel line replacement. Never, under any circumstances, use unreinforced vacuum line, clear plastic tubing or water hose for fuel lines.

9   Spring-type clamps are commonly used on fuel lines. These clamps often lose their tension over a period of time, and can be "sprung" during removal. Replace all spring-type clamps with screw clamps whenever a hose is replaced.

Metal lines

10   Sections of metal line are often used for fuel line between the fuel pump and fuel injection unit. Check carefully to be sure the line has not been bent or crimped and that cracks have not started in the line.

11   If a section of metal fuel line must be replaced, only seamless steel tubing should be used, since copper and aluminum tubing don't have the strength necessary to withstand normal engine vibration.

12   Check the metal brake lines where they enter the master cylinder and brake proportioning unit (if used) for cracks in the lines or loose fittings. Any sign of brake fluid leakage calls for an immediate thorough inspection of the brake system.

8   Wiper blade check and replacement

Refer to illustration 8.6

1   Windshield wiper and blade assemblies should be inspected periodically for damage, loose components and cracked or worn blade elements.

2   Road film can build up on the wiper blades and affect their efficiency, so they should be washed regularly with a mild detergent solution.

3   The action of the wiping mechanism can loosen bolts, nuts and fasteners, so they should be checked and tightened, as necessary, at the same time the wiper blades are checked.

4   If the wiper blade elements are cracked, worn or warped, or no longer clean adequately, they should be replaced with new ones.

5   On early models, the wiper blades are held on the arms by a small setscrew. Lift the arm assembly away from the glass for clearance. Loosen the screw and slip the blade assembly off the arm. The rubber blade is permanently attached to the metal backing; replace the blade as an assembly. Installation is the reverse of removal.

6   On later models, a large variety of wiper blades are used. However, most of them utilize a "shepherd's hook" type wiper arm. Lift the arm assembly away from the glass for clearance and pinch the retaining spring to release the blade. Slide the blade inward until the blade is free of the hook, then slip it around the hook and off the arm **(see illustration)**.

7   Remove the rubber blade from the frame and discard it.

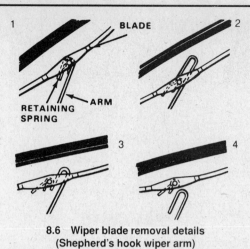

8.6   Wiper blade removal details (Shepherd's hook wiper arm)

8   To install a new rubber wiper element, follow the instructions included in the package. Be sure the elements are securely seated.

9   Reinstall the blades in the arms in the reverse order of installation. Make sure the spring retainers click into place securely.

9   Engine oil change

Refer to illustrations 9.7 and 9.14

1   Frequent oil changes are the best preventive maintenance the home mechanic can give the engine, because aging oil becomes diluted and contaminated, which leads to premature engine wear.

2   Make sure that you have all the necessary tools before you begin this procedure. You should have a drain pan, wrenches and plenty of rags or newspapers handy for mopping up any spills.

3   Access to the underside of the vehicle is greatly improved if the vehicle can be lifted on a hoist, driven onto ramps or supported by jackstands. **Warning:** *Do not work under a vehicle which is supported only by a jack.*

4   If this is your first oil change, get under the vehicle and familiarize yourself with the location of the oil screen cover and the oil drain plug, if equipped. The engine and exhaust components will be warm during the actual work, so try to anticipate any potential problems before the engine and accessories are hot.

5   Park the vehicle on a level spot. Start the engine and allow it to reach its normal operating temperature. Warm oil and sludge will flow out more easily. Turn off the engine when it's warmed up. Remove the oil filler cap.

6   Raise the vehicle and support it on jackstands. **Warning:** *To avoid personal injury, never get beneath the vehicle when it is supported by only by a jack. The jack provided with your vehicle is designed solely for raising the vehicle to remove and replace the wheels. Always use jackstands to support the vehicle when it becomes necessary to place your body underneath the vehicle.*

7   Being careful not to touch the hot exhaust components, place the drain pan under the bottom of the sump and remove the plug, if equipped **(see illustration)**. **Note:** *On 36-horsepower engines, the oil drain plug is slightly off-center. You may want to wear gloves while unscrewing the plug the final few turns if the engine is really hot. If the vehicle you are working on doesn't have a drain plug (later models), loosen the nuts around the perimeter of the oil screen cover.*

8   Allow the old oil to drain into the pan. Inspect the old oil for the presence of metal shavings and chips.

9   After all the oil has drained, wipe off the drain plug with a clean rag. Even minute metal particles clinging to the plug would immediately contaminate the new oil.

10   Clean the area around the drain plug opening, reinstall the plug and tighten it securely, but do not strip the threads.

11   Remove the nuts around the perimeter of the oil screen cover. Remove the cover and screen.

12   Clean and inspect the oil screen and cover.

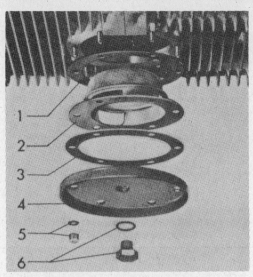

9.7 Typical drain plug/oil screen assembly

1	Gasket	4	Cover plate
2	Oil screen	5	Cap nut and washer
3	Gasket	6	Drain plug and washer

13 Make sure that none of the old gasket remains stuck to the mounting surfaces. It can be removed with a scraper if necessary. With a clean rag, wipe off the mounting surface on the block.

14 Using new gaskets and crush washers, install the oil screen and cover. Tighten the nuts in the sequence shown **(see illustration)** to the torque listed in this Chapter's Specifications.

15 Remove all tools, rags, etc. from under the vehicle, being careful not to spill the oil in the drain pan, then lower the vehicle.

16 Add new oil to the engine through the oil filler opening adjacent to the generator/alternator. Use a spout or funnel to prevent oil from spilling onto the top of the engine. Pour two and one-half quarts of fresh oil into the engine. Wait a few minutes to allow the oil to drain into the sump, then check the level on the oil dipstick (see Section 4 if necessary). If the oil level is at or near the top mark, install the filler cap hand tight, start the engine and allow the new oil to circulate.

17 Allow the engine to run for about a minute. While the engine is running, look under the vehicle and check for leaks at the oil pan drain plug and around the oil screen cover. If either is leaking, stop the engine and tighten the plug or cover slightly.

18 Wait a few minutes to allow the oil to trickle down into the sump, then recheck the level on the dipstick and, if necessary, add enough oil to bring the level to the top mark.

19 During the first few trips after an oil change, make it a point to check

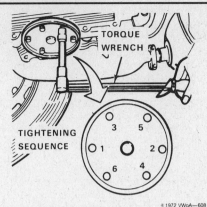

9.14 Tighten the nuts in the sequence shown

frequently for leaks and proper oil level.

20 The old oil drained from the engine cannot be reused in its present state and should be discarded. Oil reclamation centers, auto repair shops and gas stations will normally accept the oil, which can be refined and used again. After the oil has cooled, it can be drained into a suitable container (capped plastic jugs, topped bottles, milk cartons, etc.) for transport to one of these disposal sites.

10 Driveaxle boot and CV joint check

Driveaxle boot check
Refer to illustrations 10.3, 10.5 and 10.6

1 The driveaxle boots are very important because they prevent dirt, water and foreign material from entering and damaging the inner axle joints (early models) or Constant Velocity (CV) joints (1968 and later automatic stick shift and 1969 and later manual transaxles).

2 Raise the vehicle and support it securely on jackstands.

3 Inspect the boots for tears and cracks as well as loose clamps **(see illustration)**. If there is any evidence of cracks or leaking lubricant, they must be replaced as described in Chapter 8.

Constant Velocity (CV) joint check (later models)

4 The most common symptom of driveaxle or CV joint failure is knocking or clicking noises coming from the affected area while the vehicle is moving.

5 Grasp each axle and rotate it in both directions while holding the CV joint housings to check for excessive movement **(see illustration)**, indicating worn splines or loose CV joints.

6 Check the mounting bolts for looseness **(see illustration)**. Tighten the bolts to the torque listed in the Chapter 8 Specifications.

7 Replace any joints that are faulty (see Chapter 8).

10.3 Inspect the boots for cracks, tears and loose clamps

10.5 Rotate the axles back-and-forth to check for play

10.6 Tighten the mounting bolts

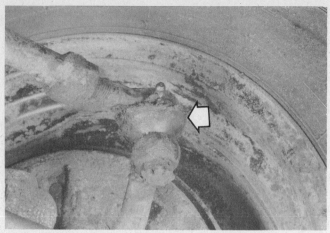

11.9   Check the balljoint boots for damage

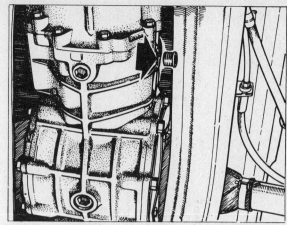

13.1   Remove the plug (arrow) on the left (driver's side)
of the transaxle (viewed from below)

11   Suspension and steering check

Refer to illustration 11.9

Note: *For detailed illustrations of the steering and suspension components, refer to Chapter 10.*

With the wheels on the ground

1   With the vehicle stopped and the front wheels pointed straight ahead, rock the steering wheel gently back-and-forth. If freeplay is excessive , a front wheel bearing, king and/or link pins, balljoint or steering system joint is worn or the steering gear is out of adjustment or worn. Refer to Chapter 10 for the appropriate repair procedure.

2   Other symptoms, such as excessive vehicle body movement over rough roads, swaying, leaning around corners and binding as the steering wheel is turned, may indicate faulty steering and/or suspension components.

3   Check the shock absorbers by pushing down and releasing the vehicle several times at each corner. If the vehicle does not come back to a level position within one or two bounces, the shocks/struts are worn and must be replaced. When bouncing the vehicle up and down, listen for squeaks and noises from the suspension components. Additional information on suspension components can be found in Chapter 10.

4   Measure the front and rear chassis clearance (the height of the vehicle above the ground) by measuring the distance from the ground to the bottom of the floor pan at the same point on each side. Also note whether the vehicle looks canted to one side or corner. If the clearance of the vehicle is unequal or if it is canted to one side or corner, try to level the vehicle by rocking it. If this doesn't work, look for out of adjustment torsion bars or worn or loose suspension parts (see Chapter 10).

Under the vehicle

5   Raise the vehicle with a floor jack and support it securely on jackstands. See Jacking and towing at the front of this book for the proper jacking points.

6   Check the tires for irregular wear patterns and proper inflation (see Section 5). If the wheel bearings are rough or noisy, see Chapter 10 for wheel bearing replacement procedures.

7   Inspect the universal joint(s) between the steering shaft and the steering gear. Check the steering gear housing for lubricant leakage or oozing. Make sure that the dust seals and boots are not damaged and that the boot clamps are not loose. Check the steering linkage for looseness or damage. Check the tie-rod ends for excessive play. Look for loose bolts, broken or disconnected parts and deteriorated rubber bushings on all suspension and steering components. While an assistant turns the steering wheel from side to side, check the steering components for free movement, chafing and binding. If the steering components do not seem to be reacting with the movement of the steering wheel, try to determine where the slack is located

8   Check the balljoints (1966 and later models) for wear. Raise the front of the vehicle and support it securely on jackstands. Make sure the front wheels are in a straight forward position and block the wheels with chocks. Remove the front wheels and tires. Place a floor jack under the lower torsion arms (except MacPherson struts), one side at a time. Grasp the brake and backing plate assembly at the top and bottom and rock the spindle up and down to ensure that it has no play. If any parts have noticeable play, replace them. Refer to Chapter 10 for the front balljoint replacement procedure.

9   Inspect the balljoint boots for damage and leaking grease **(see illustration)**. Replace the boots with new ones if they are damaged (see Chapter 10).

12   Exhaust system check

1   With the engine cold (at least three hours after the vehicle has been driven), check the complete exhaust system from its starting points at the engine to the end of the tailpipe(s). Raise the vehicle and support it securely on jackstands.

2   Check the pipes and connections for evidence of leaks, severe corrosion or damage. Make sure that all braces and clamps are in good condition and tight.

3   At the same time, inspect the underside of the body for holes, corrosion, open seams, etc. which may allow exhaust gases to enter the passenger compartment. Seal all body openings with silicone or body putty.

4   Rattles and other noises can often be traced to the exhaust system. Try to move the pipes, muffler and catalytic converter (if equipped). If the components can come in contact with body parts, realign the exhaust system.

5   Check the running condition of the engine by inspecting inside the end of the tailpipe. The exhaust deposits here are an indication of engine state-of-tune. If the pipe is black and sooty or coated with white deposits, the engine may be in need of service, including a thorough fuel system inspection and adjustment.

13   Transaxle lubricant level check

Refer to illustration 13.1

1   To check the fluid level, raise the vehicle and support it securely on jackstands. On the driver's side of the transaxle housing, you will see a plug **(see illustration)**. Remove it with a 17 mm hex wrench. Use your finger as a dipstick. If the lubricant level is correct, it should be up to the lower edge of the hole.

2   If the transaxle needs more lubricant (if the level is not up to the hole), use a lubricant pump to add more. Use the type listed in this Chapter's

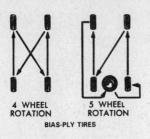

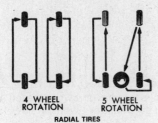

14.2   Tire rotation diagram

Specifications. Stop filling the transaxle when the lubricant begins to run out the hole.

3   Install the plug and tighten it securely. Drive the vehicle a short distance, then check for leaks.

14   Tire rotation

Refer to illustration 14.2

1   The tires should be rotated at the specified intervals and whenever uneven wear is noticed. Since the vehicle will be raised and the tires removed anyway, check the brakes (see Section 15) at this time.

2   Radial tires should be rotated in a specific pattern **(see illustration)**.

3   Refer to the information in *Jacking and towing* at the front of this manual for the proper procedures to follow when raising the vehicle and changing a tire. If the rear brakes are to be checked, do not apply the parking brake as stated. Make sure the tires are blocked to prevent the vehicle from rolling.

4   Preferably, the entire vehicle should be raised at the same time. This can be done on a hoist or by jacking up each corner and then lowering the vehicle onto jackstands placed under the jacking points. Always use four jackstands and make sure the vehicle is firmly supported.

5   After rotation, check and adjust the tire pressures as necessary and be sure to check the lug nut tightness.

6   For further information on the wheels and tires, refer to Chapter 10.

15   Brake check

Note: *The first step of this maintenance program is to prepare yourself before the actual work begins. Read through all sections pertinent to the procedures you're planning to do, then make a list of and gather together all the parts and tools you will need to do the job. If it looks as if you might run into problems during a particular segment of some procedure, seek advice from your local parts counterperson or dealer service department. For detailed photographs of the brake system, refer to Chapter 9.*

1   In addition to the specified intervals, the brakes should be inspected every time the wheels are removed or whenever a defect is suspected. Any of the following symptoms could indicate a potential brake system defect: The vehicle pulls to one side when the brake pedal is depressed; the brakes make squealing or dragging noises when applied; brake pedal travel is excessive; the pedal pulsates; brake fluid is leaking onto the inside of the tire or wheel.

2   Regular inspection of brake lining is necessary because there are no brake wear sensors on these vehicles.

3   Remove the wheel covers and loosen (but don't remove) the wheel lug bolts.

4   Raise the vehicle and place it securely on jackstands.

5   Remove the wheels (see *Jacking and towing* at the front of this book, or your owner's manual, if necessary).

Front disc brakes (models so equipped)

Refer to illustration 15.7

6   On models equipped with front disc brakes, there are two pads – an outer and an inner – in each caliper. The pads are visible through inspection holes in each caliper.

7   Check the pad thickness by looking at each end of the caliper and through the inspection hole in the caliper body **(see illustration)**. Replace the pads if the lining material is less than the minimum thickness listed in this Chapter's Specifications. When you're rotating the tires, it makes good sense to check the brakes and wheel bearings since the wheels are already removed.

Drum brakes (front and rear)

Refer to illustrations 15.8, 15.9, 15.12 and 15.14

8   To check the brake shoe lining thickness on vehicles with five lug wheels without removing the brake drums, remove the wheel covers and look through the inspection hole in the outside of the drum as the wheel is turned **(see illustration)**.

9   To check the brake shoe lining thickness on vehicles with four lug wheels without removing the brake drums, remove the rubber plugs from the backing plate and use a flashlight to inspect the linings **(see illustration)**. For a more thorough brake inspection, follow the procedure below.

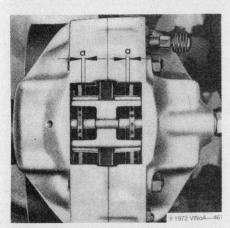

15.7   Check the brake lining thickness "a"

15.8   On models with five lug wheels, look through the inspection hole in the drum

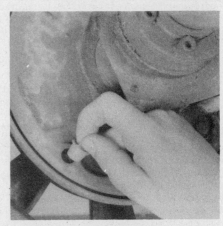

15.9   On models with four lug wheels, remove the inspection plugs to check the brake shoes

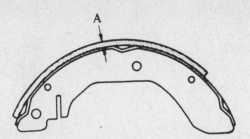

15.12 If the lining is bonded to the brake shoe, measure the lining thickness from the outer surface to the metal shoe, as shown here; if the lining is riveted to the shoe, measure from the lining outer surface to the rivet head

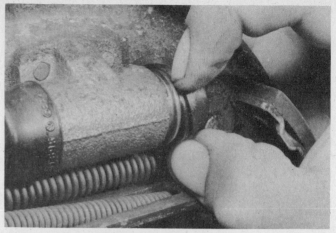

15.14 Peel the wheel cylinder boot back carefully and check for leaking fluid indicating that the cylinder must be replaced or rebuilt

10   Refer to Chapter 9 and remove the rear brake drums, and Section 32 of this Chapter to remove the front brake drums.

11   **Warning:** *Brake dust produced by lining wear and deposited on brake components may contain asbestos, which is hazardous to your health. DO NOT blow it out with compressed air and DO NOT inhale it! DO NOT use gasoline or solvents to remove the dust. Brake system cleaner should be used to flush the dust into a drain pan. After the brake components are wiped clean with a damp rag, dispose of the contaminated rag(s) and cleaner in a covered and labelled container. Use non-asbestos replacement linings whenever possible.*

12   Note the thickness of the lining material on the brake shoes **(see illustration)** and look for signs of contamination by brake fluid and grease. If the lining material is within 1/16-inch of the recessed rivets or metal shoes, replace the brake shoes with new ones. The shoes should also be replaced if they are cracked, glazed (shiny lining surfaces) or contaminated with brake fluid or grease. See Chapter 9 for the replacement procedure.

13   Check the shoe return and hold-down springs and the adjusting mechanism to make sure they're installed correctly and in good condition. Deteriorated or distorted springs, if not replaced, could allow the linings to drag and wear prematurely.

14   Check the wheel cylinders for leakage by carefully peeling back the rubber boots **(see illustration)**. If brake fluid is noted behind the boots, the wheel cylinders must be replaced (see Chapter 9).

15   Check the drums for cracks, score marks, deep scratches and hard spots, which will appear as small discolored areas. If imperfections cannot be removed with emery cloth, the drums must be resurfaced by an automotive machine shop (see Chapter 9 for more detailed information).

16   Refer to Chapter 9 and Section 32 of this Chapter and install the brake drums.

17   Install the wheels and snug the wheel lug bolts finger tight.

18   Remove the jackstands and lower the vehicle.

19   Tighten the wheel lug bolts to the torque listed in this Chapter's Specifications.

Parking brake

20   Slowly pull up on the parking brake and count the number of clicks you hear until the handle is up as far as it will go. The adjustment is correct if you hear the number of clicks listed in this Chapter's Specifications. If you hear more or fewer clicks, it's time to adjust the parking brake (refer to Chapter 9).

21   An alternative method of checking the parking brake is to park the vehicle on a steep hill with the parking brake set and the transmission in Neutral (make sure you're in the vehicle when performing this check). If the parking brake cannot prevent the vehicle from rolling, it is in need of adjustment (see Chapter 9).

16   Fuel system check

Warning: *Gasoline is extremely flammable, so take extra precautions when you work on any part of the fuel system. Don't smoke or allow open flames or bare light bulbs near the work area, and don't work in a garage where a natural gas-type appliance (such as a water heater or clothes dryer) with a pilot light is present. If you spill any fuel on your skin, rinse it off immediately with soap and water. When you perform any kind of work on the fuel system, wear safety glasses and have a Class B type fire extinguisher on hand.*

1   If you smell gasoline while driving or after the vehicle has been parked, inspect the fuel system immediately.

2   Remove the gas filler cap and inspect if for damage and corrosion. The gasket should have an unbroken sealing imprint. If the gasket is damaged or corroded, replace it.

3   Inspect the fuel feed and return lines for cracks. Make sure that the clamps which secure the fuel lines are tight, especially on fuel injected models. **Warning:** *It is necessary to relieve the fuel system pressure on fuel-injected models before servicing fuel system components. The correct procedures for fuel system pressure relief are outlined in Chapter 4.*

4   Since some components of the fuel system are underneath the vehicle, they can be inspected more easily with the vehicle raised on a hoist. If that's not possible, raise the vehicle and secure it on jackstands. Inspect the bottom of the gas tank for punctures, cracks and other damage.

5   The connection between the filler neck and the tank is particularly critical. Sometimes a rubber filler neck will leak because of loose clamps or deteriorated rubber. These are problems a home mechanic can usually rectify. **Warning:** *Do not, under any circumstances, try to repair a fuel tank (except rubber components). A welding torch or any open flame can easily cause fuel vapors inside the tank to explode.*

6   Carefully check all rubber hoses and metal lines connected to the fuel tank. Check for loose connections, deteriorated hoses, crimped lines and other damage. Be especially thorough when inspecting the lines on fuel injected models. Repair or replace damaged sections as necessary.

17   Air filter service

Oil bath air cleaners

Refer to illustration 17.5

1   Remove the air cleaner as described in Chapter 4.

2   Place the air cleaner assembly in an empty oil drain pan.

3   Unsnap the clips and lift the cover off.

4   Pour out all of the oil inside the housing. Thoroughly clean the housing and cover portion with solvent and allow it to dry.

5   Install the lower air cleaner housing on the engine. Refill the housing up to the fill marks **(see illustration)** with the same grade and viscosity of motor oil that is recommended in this Chapter's Specifications.

6   Reinstall the air cleaner cover.

17.5 Add oil up to the line marked "Olstand" (German for oil level)

17.8 The housing is held together with clips

SMALL CRACKS

GREASE

GLAZED

ALWAYS CHECK the underside of the belt.

18.2 Here are some of the more common problems associated with drivebelts (check the belts very carefully to prevent an untimely breakdown)

18.3 Push in on the belt and measure the deflection (a)

18.4 Use a screwdriver to keep the pulley from turning while you loosen the nut

18.5 Add or subtract shims as necessary

Air filter replacement

Refer to illustration 17.8

7   1973 and later models have a replaceable paper air filter located inside a housing in the engine compartment. To remove the air filter, release the spring clips that keep the two halves of the air cleaner housing together.

8   Lift the cover up and remove the air filter element **(see illustration)**.

9   Inspect the outer surface of the filter element. If it is dirty, replace it. If it is only slightly dusty, it can be reused by blowing it clean from the back to the front surface with compressed air. **Warning:** *Wear eye protection.* Because it is a pleated paper type filter, it cannot be washed or oiled. If it cannot be cleaned satisfactorily with compressed air, discard and replace it. **Caution:** *Never drive the vehicle with the air cleaner removed. Excessive engine wear could result and backfiring could even cause a fire under the hood.*

10   Installation is the reverse of removal.

---

18   Drivebelt check, adjustment and replacement

Refer to illustrations 18.2, 18.3, 18.4, 18.5, 18.6a and 18.6b

Check

1   The generator/alternator drivebelt, also referred to as a V-belt or simply "fan" belt, is located at the rear of the engine. The good condition and proper adjustment of the belt is critical to the operation of the engine. Because of their composition and the high stresses to which they are subjected, drivebelts stretch and deteriorate as they get older. They must therefore be periodically inspected.

2   With the engine off, open the rear hood and locate the drivebelt at the rear of the engine. Check the belt for separation of the adhesive rubber on both sides of the core, core separation from the belt side and/or a severed core **(see illustration)**. Also check for fraying and glazing, which gives the belt a shiny appearance. Both sides of the belt should be inspected, which means you will have to twist the belt to check the underside. Use your fingers to feel the belt where you can't see it. If any of the above conditions are evident, replace the belt.

3   To check belt tension, push in on the belt midway between the pulleys **(see illustration)** and measure the deflection with a ruler. Compare your measurement to that listed in this Chapter's Specifications. **Note:** *Recheck belt tension after about 100 miles whenever a new belt is installed.*

Adjustment

4   Hold a screwdriver in the cutout in the upper pulley to keep the crankshaft from turning **(see illustration)**. Remove the nut on the generator/alternator shaft. Slip off the washer, any spare shims and the outer pulley half.

5   Belt tension is adjusted by changing the number of shims between the pulley halves **(see illustration)**. Removing shims tightens the belt. **Note:** *Although the shims are thin, removing or adding even one makes a considerable difference in belt tension.*

18.6a   Hold the belt in place as you install the outer pulley

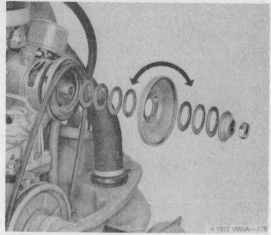

18.6b   Pulley components – exploded view

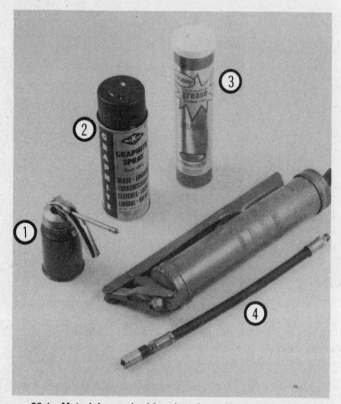

20.1   Materials required for chassis and body lubrication

1   **Engine oil** – *Light engine oil in a can like this can be used for door and hood hinges*
2   **Graphite spray** – *Used to lubricate lock cylinders*
3   **Grease** – *Grease, in a variety of types and weights, is available for use in a grease gun. Check the Specifications for your requirements.*
4   **Grease gun** – *A common grease gun, shown here with a detachable hose and nozzle, is needed for chassis lubrication. After use, clean it thoroughly!*

6   Install the belt, shims as needed, outer pulley, spare shims, washers and nut **(see illustrations)**. Hold the pulleys from turning as described above and tighten the nut securely.
7   Recheck the belt tension and repeat until the drivebelt tension is correct.

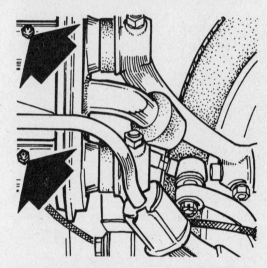

20.4   Grease the fittings (arrows) on both sides of the axle beam

Replacement

8   To replace a belt, follow the above procedures for drivebelt adjustment but slip the belt off the crankshaft pulley and remove it.
9   Take the old belt to the parts store in order to make a direct comparison for length, width and design.
10   After replacing the drivebelt, make sure that it fits properly in the pulleys.
11   Adjust the belt in accordance with the procedure outlined above.

---

19   Neutral start switch check (automatic stick shift models only)

Warning: *During the following checks there is a chance that the vehicle could lunge forward, possibly causing damage or injuries. Allow plenty of room around the vehicle, apply the parking brake firmly and hold down the foot brake pedal during the checks.*

1   Automatic stick shift models are equipped with neutral start switch which prevents the engine from starting unless the shift lever is in the Neutral position.
2   Try to start the engine in each gear. The engine should crank only in Neutral.
3   See Chapter 7B for the neutral start switch replacement procedure.

21.4a   Remove the cover bolt (early model shown)

21.4b   A screen is located under the cover (later model shown)

21.5   Clean or replace the screen

21.7   On fuel-injected models, the filter is located under the gas tank

20   Chassis lubrication

Refer to illustrations 20.1 and 20.4

1   Only a few simple items are required for chassis lubrication other than some clean rags and equipment needed to raise and support the vehicle safely (see illustration).
2   Raise the vehicle and support it securely on jackstands.
3   Force a little grease out of the gun nozzle to remove any dirt, then wipe it clean with a rag.
4   There are four grease fittings on the front axle beam (see illustration) that need to be greased (except Super Beetles with MacPherson strut front suspension). Additionally, some early models have grease fittings on the tie-rod ends.
5   Wipe the grease fitting with a clean cloth and push the nozzle firmly over it. Squeeze the lever on the grease gun to force grease into the fitting until it begins to escape from the ends of the axle beam or tie-rod end dust boots.
6   Wipe excess grease from the components and fittings.
7   Lower the vehicle to the ground for the remaining Steps.
8   Open the front and rear hoods and smear a little grease on the latch mechanisms. Have an assistant operate the front hood release knob from inside the vehicle as you lube the cable at the latch. Apply a light coat of grease to the seat tracks as well.
9   Lubricate all the hinges (doors and hoods) and the throttle linkage at the carburetor with a few drops of light engine oil to keep them in proper working order. Also, add a drop or two of oil to the wick in the center of the distributor shaft under the rotor.
10   Lubricate the key lock cylinders with spray-on graphite, which is avail

able at auto parts stores.
11   On 1965 and earlier models, remove the filler plug on top of the steering gear. The plug may be accessed by removing the inspection plate behind the spare tire on the left (driver's) side. Oil level should reach the bottom of the filler hole threads. Add the same lubricant used in the manual transaxle (see this Chapter's Specifications) if necessary.

21   Fuel filter service

Warning: Gasoline is extremely flammable, so take extra precautions when you work on any part of the fuel system. Don't smoke or allow open flames or bare light bulbs near the work area, and don't work in a garage where a natural gas-type appliance (such as a water heater or clothes dryer) with a pilot light is present. If you spill any fuel on your skin, rinse it off immediately with soap and water. When you perform any kind of work on the fuel system, wear safety glasses and have a Class B type fire extinguisher on hand.

Carbureted models

Refer to illustrations 21.4a, 21.4b and 21.5

1   Remove the air cleaner assembly if necessary for access (see Chapter 4).
2   Examine the fuel hoses adjacent to the fuel pump. Most models have a small plastic inline filter located in the hose between the pump and carburetor.
3   If the vehicle you're working on has an inline fuel filter, quickly detach the hoses and insert a new filter. Be sure the arrow on the filter points in the direction of fuel flow (from the fuel pump to the carburetor).
4   Most models have a filter screen in the fuel pump. Remove the screw or bolt and lift the cover off. Remove the screen (see illustrations).
5   Later models with four screws in the top of the fuel pump have a screen at the rear. Remove the banjo bolt and lift the screen out (see illustration).
6   Clean the screen with solvent and reinstall it, along with a new gasket.

Fuel-injected models

Refer to illustration 21.7

7   The fuel filter is located below the fuel tank (see illustration). Raise the front of the vehicle and support it securely on jackstands.
8   Before removing the fuel filter on fuel injected models, temporarily clamp the fuel line between the filter and fuel tank.
9   Place a drain pan under the fuel filter. Detach the filter from its bracket. Remove the hose clamps and detach the fuel lines from the filter. **Warning:** Wear eye protection.
10   Install the new filter with the arrow pointing in the direction of fuel flow (from the tank to the engine). Install the hose clamps and tighten them securely. Snap the filter into its bracket, if equipped.
11   Remove the jackstands and lower the vehicle.
12   Start the engine and check for fuel leaks.

22.5   Remove the filter (arrow) from the control valve

23.2   Remove the drain plugs

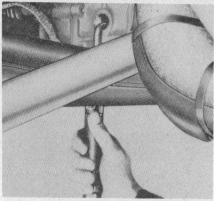

23.4   Add lubricant into the opening on the side

22   Automatic stick shift service

Refer to illustration 22.5

Fluids

1   The automatic stick shift transaxle uses two different fluids. The gearbox/differential portion of the transaxle assembly uses gear lubricant (see Section 13) and the torque converter uses automatic transmission fluid.
2   Check and add fluid to the torque converter as necessary (see Section 4). The factory does not recommend periodic fluid changes.

Clutch freeplay

3   Normal wear reduces clutch freeplay, eventually leading to complete failure if maintenance is ignored. See Chapter 7B for the check and adjustment procedure.

Clutch engagement speed

4   If the clutch engages too slowly (slips) or too abruptly (harsh), the control valve may need adjustment. See Chapter 7B for the procedure.

Control valve filter

5   Replace the control valve filter **(see illustration)** whenever the transaxle is serviced by unscrewing the old one and installing a new one in its place.

Shifter contacts

6   The shift lever contains electrical contacts that control the clutch. As they wear, operation deteriorates. See Chapter 7B for cleaning and adjustment procedures.

23   Transaxle lubricant change

Refer to illustration 23.2 and 23.4

1   Raise the vehicle and support it securely on jackstands.
2   Place a drain pan under the transaxle. Using a 17 mm Allen wrench or hex drive, remove the drain plugs **(see illustration)** and allow the lubricant to drain completely. **Note:** *Some automatic stick shift models do not have drain plugs. Use a suction gun to remove the lubricant through the filler plug opening.*
3   Reinstall the drain plug and tighten it securely. Using the same tool, remove the filler plug, which is located on the left (driver's) side of the transaxle ahead of the driveaxle.
4   Add new lubricant until it begins to run out of the filler hole **(see illustration)**. See *Recommended Lubricants and Fluids* in this Chapter's Specifications for the specified lubricant type.
5   Reinstall the plug and tighten securely. Remove the jackstands and lower the vehicle.

24   Emissions control system check

Evaporative emissions control system

1   The function of the Fuel Evaporative Emission Control (EVAP) System is to store fuel vapors from the fuel tank in a charcoal canister until they can be routed to the intake manifold where they mix with incoming air before being burned in the cylinder combustion chambers.
2   The most common symptom of a faulty evaporative emissions system is a strong fuel odor in the engine compartment. If a fuel odor is detected, inspect the charcoal canister (located inside the right rear fender on Beetles and in the engine compartment on Karmann Ghias), and the EVAP system hoses.
3   If the canister is due for replacement (it should be replaced at 40,000 mile intervals) or is clogged or leaking charcoal, replace it.
4   See Chapter 6 for replacement instructions.

Positive Crankcase Ventilation (PCV) system

5   The Positive Crankcase Ventilation (PCV) system merely consists of a breather hose from the crankcase to the air cleaner, with no PCV valve. The only maintenance required is to inspect the hose and replace if necessary.

Catalytic converter

6   The catalytic converter, introduced on the 1975 models, cleanses the exhaust by sustaining chemical reactions. Eventually the materials in the catalyst lose their effectiveness and need to be replaced. The factory recommends replacement every 30,000 miles, see Chapter 6 for further information. Due to the high cost of replacement, many owners have them tested to determine their effectiveness. Take the vehicle to a dealer service department or other service station to have the exhaust emissions checked.

Exhaust Gas Recirculation (EGR) system

7   See Section 33 and Chapter 6 for information on this system.

25   Spark plug check and replacement

Refer to illustrations 25.1, 25.4a, 25.4b and 25.10

1   Spark plug replacement requires a spark plug socket which fits onto a ratchet wrench. This socket should be lined with a rubber grommet to protect the porcelain insulator of the spark plug and to hold the plug while you insert it into the spark plug hole. You will also need a wire-type feeler gauge to check and adjust the spark plug gap **(see illustration)**.
2   If you're replacing the plugs, purchase the new plugs, adjust them to the proper gap and then replace each plug one at a time. **Note:** *When buying new spark plugs, it's essential that you obtain the correct plugs for your specific vehicle. Consult the catalogs provided by spark plug manufacturers (most auto parts stores have these catalogs) or look in the owner's*

CARBON DEPOSITS

Symptoms: Dry sooty deposits indicate a rich mixture or weak ignition. Causes misfiring, hard starting and hesitation.

Recommendation: Check for a clogged air cleaner, high float level, sticky choke and worn ignition points. Use a spark plug with a longer core nose for greater anti-fouling protection.

OIL DEPOSITS

Symptoms: Oily coating caused by poor oil control. Oil is leaking past worn valve guides or piston rings into the combustion chamber. Causes hard starting, misfiring and hesition.

Recommendation: Correct the mechanical condition with necessary repairs and install new plugs.

TOO HOT

Symptoms: Blistered, white insulator, eroded electrode and absence of deposits. Results in shortened plug life.

Recommendation: Check for the correct plug heat range, over-advanced ignition timing, lean fuel mixture, intake manifold vacuum leaks and sticking valves. Check the coolant level and make sure the radiator is not clogged.

PREIGNITION

Symptoms: Melted electrodes. Insulators are white, but may be dirty due to misfiring or flying debris in the combustion chamber. Can lead to engine damage.

Recommendation: Check for the correct plug heat range, over-advanced ignition timing, lean fuel mixture, clogged cooling system and lack of lubrication.

HIGH SPEED GLAZING

Symptoms: Insulator has yellowish, glazed appearance. Indicates that combustion chamber temperatures have risen suddenly during hard acceleration. Normal deposits melt to form a conductive coating. Causes misfiring at high speeds.

Recommendation: Install new plugs. Consider using a colder plug if driving habits warrant.

GAP BRIDGING

Symptoms: Combustion deposits lodge between the electrodes. Heavy deposits accumulate and bridge the electrode gap. The plug ceases to fire, resulting in a dead cylinder.

Recommendation: Locate the faulty plug and remove the deposits from between the electrodes.

NORMAL

Symptoms: Brown to grayish-tan color and slight electrode wear. Correct heat range for engine and operating conditions.

Recommendation: When new spark plugs are installed, replace with plugs of the same heat range.

ASH DEPOSITS

Symptoms: Light brown deposits encrusted on the side or center electrodes or both. Derived from oil and/or fuel additives. Excessive amounts may mask the spark, causing misfiring and hesitation during acceleration.

Recommendation: If excessive deposits accumulate over a short time or low mileage, install new valve guide seals to prevent seepage of oil into the combustion chambers. Also try changing gasoline brands.

WORN

Symptoms: Rounded electrodes with a small amount of deposits on the firing end. Normal color. Causes hard starting in damp or cold weather and poor fuel economy.

Recommendation: Replace with new plugs of the same heat range.

1

DETONATION

Symptoms: Insulators may be cracked or chipped. Improper gap setting techniques can also result in a fractured insulator tip. Can lead to piston damage.

Recommendation: Make sure the fuel anti-knock values meet engine requirements. Use care when setting the gaps on new plugs. Avoid lugging the engine.

SPLASHED DEPOSITS

Symptoms: After long periods of misfiring, deposits can loosen when normal combustion temperature is restored by an overdue tune-up. At high speeds, deposits flake off the piston and are thrown against the hot insulator, causing misfiring.

Recommendation: Replace the plugs with new ones or clean and reinstall the originals.

MECHANICAL DAMAGE

Symptoms: May be caused by a foreign object in the combustion chamber or the piston striking an incorrect reach (too long) plug. Causes a dead cylinder and could result in piston damage.

Recommendation: Remove the foreign object from the engine and/or install the correct reach plug.

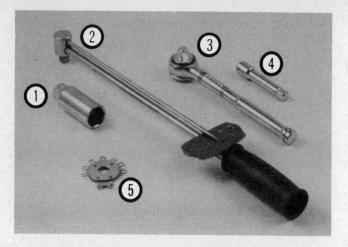

25.1   Tools required for changing spark plugs

1   **Spark plug socket** – This will have special padding inside to protect the spark plug's porcelain insulator
2   **Torque wrench** – Although not mandatory, using this tool is the best way to ensure the plugs are tightened properly
3   **Ratchet** – Standard hand tool to fit the spark plug socket
4   **Extension** – Depending on model and accessories, you may need special extensions and universal joints to reach one or more of the plugs
5   **Spark plug gap gauge** – This gauge for checking the gap comes in a variety of styles. Make sure the gap for your engine is included.

25.4a   Spark plug manufacturers recommend using a wire type gauge when checking the gap – if the wire does not slide between the electrodes with a slight drag, adjustment is required

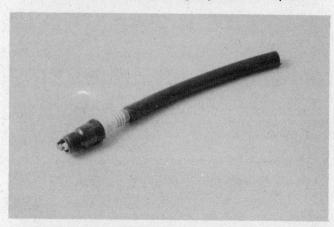

25.10   A length of 3/16-inch ID rubber hose will save time and prevent damaged threads when installing the spark plugs

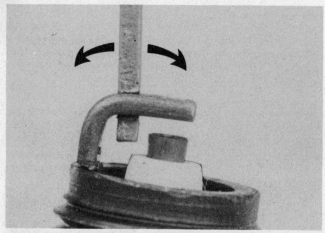

25.4b   To change the gap, bend the *side* electrode only, as indicated by the arrows, and be very careful not to crack or chip the porcelain insulator surrounding the center electrode

manual. On later models, spark plug information may be found on the Vehicle Emissions Control Information (VECI) label located on the engine shroud. If these sources specify different plugs, purchase the spark plug type specified on the VECI label because that information is provided specifically for your engine.
3   Inspect each of the new plugs for defects. If there are any signs of cracks in the porcelain insulator of a plug, don't use it.
4   Check the electrode gaps of the new plugs. Check the gap by inserting the wire gauge of the proper thickness between the electrodes at the tip of the plug **(see illustration)**. The gap between the electrodes should be identical to that specified by the spark plug manufacturer or on the VECI label. If the gap is incorrect, use the notched adjuster on the feeler gauge body to bend the curved side electrode slightly **(see illustration)**.
5   If the side electrode is not exactly over the center electrode, use the notched adjuster to align them. **Caution:** If the gap of a new plug must be adjusted, bend only the base of the ground electrode; do not touch the tip.

Removal

6   To prevent the possibility of mixing up spark plug wires, work on one spark plug at a time. Remove the wire and boot from one spark plug. Grasp the connector – not the cable, give it a half twisting motion and pull straight up.
7   If compressed air is available, blow any dirt or foreign material away from the spark plug area (wear eye protection) before proceeding (a common bicycle pump will also work).
8   Remove the spark plug.
9   Whether you are replacing the plugs at this time or intend to reuse the old plugs, compare each old spark plug with those shown in the accompanying photos to determine the overall running condition of the engine.

Installation

10   It's often difficult to insert spark plugs into their holes without cross-threading them. To avoid this possibility, fit a short piece of 3/16-inch ID rubber hose over the end of the spark plug **(see illustration)**. The flexible hose acts as a universal joint to help align the plug with the plug hole. Should the plug begin to cross-thread, the hose will slip on the spark plug, preventing thread damage. Apply a light coating of anti-seize compound to the threads. Once the plug threads are started correctly, tighten the plug securely. **Note:** If the threads in the head are damaged, they may be repaired with thread insert kits available at auto parts stores.

26.11a   Pop the two retaining clips (arrows) off and lift the cap

11   Attach the plug wire to the new spark plug, again using a twisting motion on the connector until it is firmly seated on the end of the spark plug. Be sure the air seal is intact.

12   Follow the above procedure for the remaining spark plugs, replacing them one at a time to prevent mixing up the spark plug wires.

26   Spark plug wire, distributor cap and rotor check and replacement

Refer to illustrations 26.11a, 26.11b, 26.12a, 26.12b and 26.12c

1   The spark plug wires should be checked whenever new spark plugs are installed.

2   Begin this procedure by making a visual check of the spark plug wires while the engine is running. In a darkened garage (make sure there is ventilation) start the engine and observe each plug wire. Be careful not to come into contact with any moving engine parts. If there is a break in the wire, you will see arcing or a small spark at the damaged area. If arcing is noticed, make a note to obtain new wires, then allow the engine to cool and check the distributor cap and rotor.

3   The spark plug wires should be inspected one at a time to prevent mixing up the order, which is essential for proper engine operation. Each original plug wire should be numbered to help identify its location. If the number is illegible, a piece of tape can be marked with the correct number and wrapped around the plug wire.

4   Disconnect the plug wire from the spark plug. A removal tool can be used for this purpose or you can grasp the connector, twist it half a turn and pull the connector free. Do not pull on the wire itself.

5   Check inside the connector for corrosion, which may look like a white crusty powder.

6   Push the wire and terminal back onto the end of the spark plug. It should fit tightly onto the end of the plug.

7   Using a clean rag, wipe the entire length of the wire to remove built-up dirt and grease. Once the wire is clean, check for burns, cracks and other damage. Check the air seals that fit around the connectors for cracks and damage, replace as necessary.

8   Disconnect the wire from the distributor. Again, pull only on the connector. Check for corrosion and a tight fit. Reinstall the wire in the distributor.

9   Inspect the remaining spark plug wires, making sure that each one is securely fastened at the distributor and spark plug when the check is complete.

10   If new spark plug wires are required, purchase a set for your specific model. Pre-cut wire sets with the connectors already installed are available. Remove and replace the wires one at a time to avoid mix-ups in the firing order.

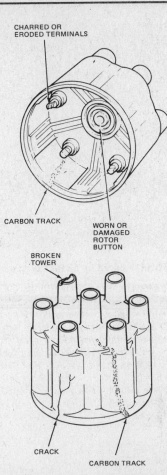

26.11b   Shown here are some of the common defects to look for when inspecting the distributor cap (if in doubt about its condition, install a new one)

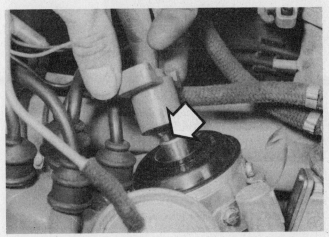

26.12a   Pull the rotor straight up – note the notch in the distributor shaft (arrow) must align with the tab in the rotor

11   Detach the distributor cap by unclipping the two cap retaining clips. Look inside it for cracks, carbon tracks and worn, burned or loose contacts **(see illustration)**. Be sure the center post and spring are intact.

12   Pull the rotor off the distributor shaft and examine it for cracks and carbon tracks. Some models also have a dust cover which is held in place by the distributor cap **(see illustrations)**. Replace the cap and rotor if any damage or defects are noted.

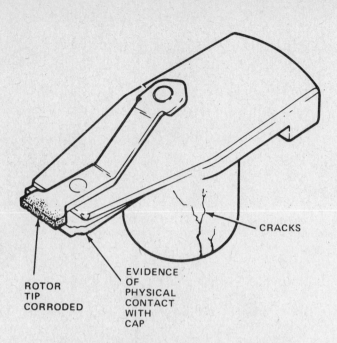

26.12b   The ignition rotor should be checked for wear and corrosion as indicated here (if in doubt about its condition, buy a new one)

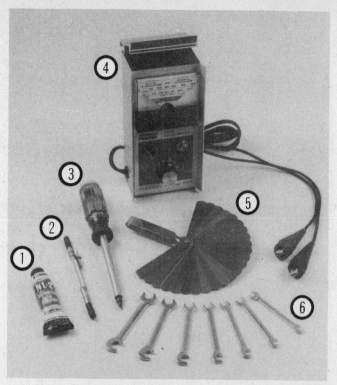

27.3   Tools and materials needed for contact point replacement and dwell angle adjustment

1   **Distributor cam lube** – *Sometimes this special lubricant comes with the new points; however, it's a good idea to buy a tube and have it on hand*
2   **Screw starter** – *This tool has special claws which hold the screw securely as it's started, which helps prevent accidental dropping of the screw*
3   **Magnetic screwdriver** – *Serves the same purpose as 2 above. If you don't have one of these special screwdrivers, you risk dropping the point mounting screws down into the distributor body.*
4   **Dwell meter** – *A dwell meter is the only accurate way to determine the point setting (gap). Connect the meter according to the instructions supplied with it.*
5   **Blade-type feeler gauges** – *These are required to set the initial point gap (space between the points when they are open)*
6   **Ignition wrenches** – *These special wrenches are made to work within the tight confines of the distributor. Specifically, they are needed to loosen the nut/bolt which secures the leads to the points.*

26.12c   Lift the dust cover off – note the locating tab (arrow) must fit in the housing notch

13   When installing a new cap, remove the wires from the old cap one at a time and attach them to the new cap in the exact same location – do not simultaneously remove all the wires from the old cap or firing order mix-ups may occur.

27   Ignition points and condenser check and replacement

Refer to illustrations 27.3, 27.5a, 27.5b, 27.5c, 27.6, 27.9a, 27.9b, 27.10 and 27.11

Check

1   Position the engine at Top Dead Center (see Chapter 2).
2   Remove the distributor cap and rotor (and dust cover, if equipped) – see Section 26.
3   Visually inspect the contact points for signs of burning and arcing. The contact surfaces should be clean and smooth. If a crater has formed on one side and a buildup of metal on the other, replace the points. Some special tools will be necessary for this procedure (**see illustration**).

Replacement

4   Several types of points and condensers were used over the years. Early models have two-piece point sets and later models have one-piece sets. Additionally, some models have the condenser mounted on the outside of the distributor and others have the condenser mounted inside. Use

27.5a Disconnect the wire from the points at the terminal

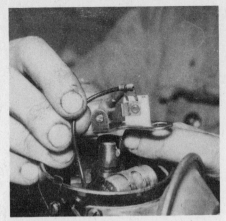

27.5b On some early models, the wire connector is attached with a screw

27.5c Remove the hold-down screw (arrow)

the distributor number (found on the housing) to purchase new ignition parts. Compare the new and old points and condenser to ensure you have the correct type. Note the way the old ones are mounted prior to removal.

5   Detach the wire from the points (see illustrations) and remove the hold-down screw (see illustration) and clip, if equipped. Lift the points out.

6   Loosen the condenser mounting screw and remove the condenser (see illustration). Note: On some models, it may be necessary to remove the distributor to access the mounting screw (see Chapter 5).

7   Inspect the distributor for wear and damage. Also check for shaft bushing looseness.

8   Apply a light coating of distributor grease to the lobes of the cam where it contacts the ignition points. Squirt a drop of oil on the center of the shaft.

9   Install the condenser and points (see illustrations) and lightly tighten the points hold-down screw.

27.6 If the points are mounted externally like this, remove the screw (arrow) and pull the connector block out of the housing

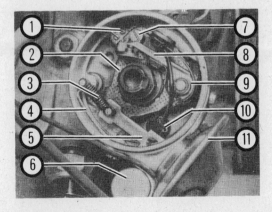

27.9a Ignition components – Bosch distributor

1	Pins and adjusting slot	7	Hold-down screw
2	Advance plate	8	Moving contact arm
3	Return spring	9	Breaker arm spring
4	Ground connection	10	Primary wire
5	Pullrod	11	Vacuum unit
6	Condenser		

27.9b Ignition components – VW distributor

1	Primary wire connection	8	Pullrod
2	Securing screw	9	Fixed point
3	Spring	10	Adjusting slot
4	Hex head screw	11	Threaded rod
5	Stop bracket	12	Spring
6	Fiber block	13	Leaf spring for breaker plate
7	Breaker arm spring	14	Breaker plate

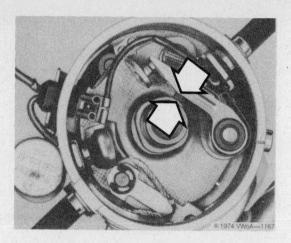

27.10   Be sure the rubbing block is positioned on the high point of the lobe (arrows)

27.11   Adjust the points with a screwdriver as shown here

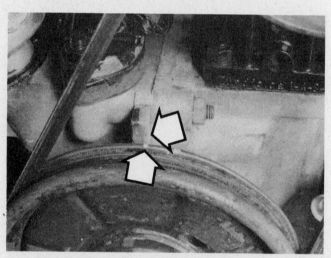

28.1   The timing mark must align with the seam in the crankcase (arrows)

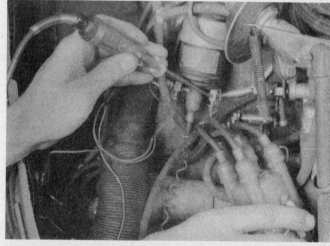

28.3   Connect a test light and turn the distributor until you find the point where the light just comes on and off

10   The rubbing block on the ignition points must be positioned on the high point of a distributor cam lobe (**see illustration**). This is where the points are open widest.

11   Using a small screwdriver, adjust the moveable point until the gap listed in this Chapter's Specifications is obtained. Measure the gap with a clean feeler gauge (**see illustration**).

12   Tighten the screw to hold the points securely after adjustment and re-check the gap.

13   Ignition point gap may be double-checked with a dwell meter (**see illustration**). Follow the instructions provided with the meter and adjust the points until the dwell angle is within the range listed in this Chapter's Specifications.

14   After point gap adjustment (or dwell adjustment), set the ignition timing (see Section 28).

28   Ignition timing check and adjustment

Note: *Ignition timing should be checked and adjusted AFTER ignition point gap is adjusted (see Section 27) and the engine is warmed up to operating temperature.*

Static-timing method (all models through 1967)
Refer to illustrations 28.1 and 28.3

1   Position the engine at Top Dead Center (see Chapter 2). With the ignition OFF, turn the crankshaft pulley clockwise with a wrench until the proper notch in the pulley is exactly aligned with the the seam in the crankcase (**see illustration**).

2   Loosen the bolt and nut near the base of the distributor just enough so the distributor can be turned by hand.

3   Connect a test light ground wire to a clean ground on the engine. **Note:** *Use a bulb that is compatible with the electrical system (6 or 12 volt).* Turn the ignition ON, but don't activate the starter. Hold the probe of the test light to the no. 1 connection, or negative (-) side, on the ignition coil where the thin wire (usually green) comes from the distributor (**see illustration**).

Timing light method (all 1968 and later models, optional on earlier models)
Refer to illustration 28.5

Warning: *This procedure requires the engine to be running. Keep hands and wires clear of the drivebelt and other moving parts. Do not wear loose clothing or allow long hair or neckties, etc., to become entangled.*

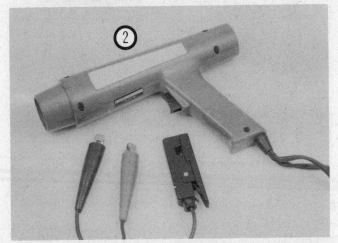

28.5   Tools needed to check and adjust the ignition timing

1   *Vacuum plugs* – *Vacuum hoses will, in most cases, have to be disconnected and plugged. Molded plugs in various shapes and sizes are available for this.*
2   *Inductive pick-up timing light* – *Flashes a bright concentrated beam of light when the number one spark plug fires. Connect the leads according to the instructions supplied with the light.*

29.6   Turn the throttle valve screw until it just stops touching the fast idle cam

29.7   The volume control screw is located near the base of the carburetor

4   Turn the distributor slightly in the direction of rotor rotation (see this Chapter's Specifications). The test light should be off. Now, turn the distributor slowly against the direction of rotor rotation until the test light comes on. Find the exact spot where the light comes on and tighten the distributor lockbolt. Reinstall the distributor cap.
Note: *The following ignition timing procedure applies to most all vehicles from model year 1968 and later. However, if the procedure specified on the VECI label attached to the engine differs from this one, follow the one on the label.*
5   Connect a timing light **(see illustration)** to the spark plug wire of the number one cylinder, in accordance with the manufacturer's instructions. Keep the wires away from the drivebelt. **Note:** *Battery voltage for the timing light is available at the positive terminal (#15) of the ignition coil when the ignition is On.*
6   Loosen the bolt and nut near the base of the distributor just enough so the distributor can be turned by hand.
7   Locate the timing marks on the crankshaft pulley and the seam in the crankcase **(see illustration 28.1)**. On engines manufactured before August 1967 there are two marks on the crankshaft pulley. The left mark is 7.5-degrees Before Top Dead Center (BTDC) and the right mark is 10-degrees BTDC. Later models have more marks. On engines with three marks, the left mark is 0-degrees (TDC), the middle mark is 7.5-degrees BTDC and the right mark is 10-degrees BTDC. **Note:** *On all 1970 models and on Spring 1973 through 1974 models (starting chassis numbers 11326474897 manual transaxle and 1132690032 automatic transaxle) with one vacuum hose to the distributor, adjust the timing with the hose disconnected and plugged. If the distributor has two hoses, leave them both connected. On 1975 and later models, disconnect and plug the charcoal canister hose at the air cleaner.*
8   Start the engine and allow it to idle. The idle speed must be within the range listed in this Chapter's Specifications (see Section 29). Check the timing with the timing light and, if necessary, turn the distributor until the

desired timing mark (see this Chapter's Specifications) is aligned with the seam in the crankcase.
9   Shut the engine OFF and tighten the distributor lockbolt securely.
10   Start the engine and recheck the timing.
11   Shut off the engine and remove the timing light.

---

29   Idle speed check and adjustment

---

1   Engine idle speed should only be adjusted after the ignition points and timing have been checked and/or adjusted. This speed is critical to the performance and exhaust emissions of the engine.
2   Set the parking brake firmly and block the wheels to prevent the vehicle from rolling. Put the transaxle in Neutral.
3   Connect a hand held tachometer to the no. 1 in accordance with the manufacturer's instructions.
4   Start the engine and run it for at least five minutes to warm it up.
5   Allow the engine to idle. Note the indicated idle rpm on the tachometer and compare it to the idle speed listed in this Chapter's Specifications. If the idle speed is too low or too high, adjust it as described below.

1969 and earlier models
Refer to illustrations 29.6 and 29.7
6   Adjust the screw on the throttle arm **(see illustration)** until it just stops touching the fast idle cam.
7   Turn the volume control screw **(see illustration)** in until engine speed begins to drop. Now, turn the screw out until the highest idle speed is achieved. Finally, readjust the screw on the throttle arm until you obtain the idle speed listed in this Chapter's Specifications.

29.8   1970 and later carburetor adjustments

1   Throttle valve adjustment
2   Volume control screw
3   Bypass screw

30.5   Check the studs to see if they protrude

1970 models (30 PICT-3 carburetors)

Refer to illustration 29.8

8   Adjust the idle speed by turning the bypass screw **(see illustration)** until you obtain the idle speed listed in this Chapter's Specifications. Do not turn the throttle valve adjustment.

1971 through 1974 models (34 PICT-3 carburetors)

9   Turn the throttle valve adjustment screw **(see illustration 29.8)** until it just touches the fast idle cam. Then turn it in 1/4 turn.

10   Slowly turn in the volume control screw until it bottoms lightly. Then back it out 2 and 1/2 to 3 turns.

11   Adjust the bypass screw until you obtain the idle speed listed in this Chapter's Specifications.

12   Turn the volume control screw to obtain the highest idle speed, then turn the volume control screw clockwise slowly until the rpm drops by about 25.

29.14   Location of the idle speed screw (arrow) on fuel-injected models

13   Using the bypass screw, reset the idle to obtain the idle speed listed in this Chapter's Specifications.

Fuel-injected models

Refer to illustration 29.14

14   Turn the idle speed screw **(see illustration)** to obtain the idle speed listed in this Chapter's Specifications.

All models

15   Manually snap the throttle open and allow the engine to return to an idle. Recheck the idle speed. Turn off the engine and disconnect the tachometer.

---

30   Valve clearance check and adjustment

Refer to illustrations 30.5 and 30.6

1   Allow the engine to cool completely (preferably, allow it to sit overnight).

2   With the engine Off and the transaxle in neutral, position the number one cylinder at Top Dead Center on the compression stroke (see Chapter 2).

3   Remove the valve covers (see Chapter 2).

4   Working under the vehicle, begin with the number one cylinder (see the diagram in this Chapter's Specifications). Both valves should be closed completely. If not, recheck the Top Dead Center Procedure.

5   Try to slide a feeler gauge of the thickness listed in this Chapter's Specifications (see note below) between the tip of the adjusting screw and the tip of the valve stem. If the gauge slips through with only a slight drag, the clearance is correct. **Note:** *On 1961 through 1965 models, most engines have long rocker arm shaft mounting studs. Additionally, some engines through 1971 had long studs. You can determine this by checking the other side of the cylinder head* **(see illustration)***. If the studs protrude, they are the long variety. Be sure to check all of them. The factory revised the original specifications due to problems with valves burning. Therefore, we recommend adjusting long stud models at 0.008 inch on both intake and exhaust and short stud models at 0.006 inch on both intake and exhaust.*

6   If the feeler gauge won't fit or is too loose, loosen the locknut and turn the adjustment screw out or in as necessary until a slight drag is felt on the feeler gauge as it is slid between the valve and screw tip **(see illustration)**. Tighten the locknut and recheck the clearance.

7   Repeat this procedure for the other valve in the cylinder.

8   Mark the crankshaft pulley 180-degrees opposite the TDC mark. Using a wrench on the crankshaft pulley bolt, turn the crankshaft 180-degrees (1/2 turn) clockwise. This will put the next cylinder in the firing order

30.6 Turn the screw to adjust the clearance and then tighten the locknut

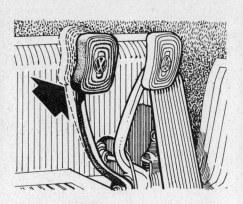

31.1 Check the clutch pedal freeplay

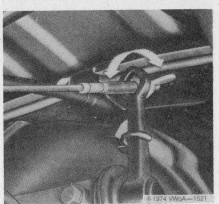

31.3 Later models use a wingnut for clutch adjustment

32.6 Pry the dust cap off

32.8 Loosen the lock bolt (arrow) and back the nut off

32.11 Pry the seal out of the hub

at TDC. Repeat Steps 4, 5 and 6 above. Do this for each cylinder in turn, following the firing order 1-4-3-2.

9   Reinstall the valve covers.

31   Clutch pedal freeplay check and adjustment

Refer to illustrations 31.1 and 31.3

1   Press down lightly on the clutch pedal and, with a ruler, measure the distance that it moves freely before the clutch resistance is felt **(see illustration)**. The freeplay should be within the limits listed in this Chapter's Specifications. If it isn't, it must be adjusted.

2   Raise the vehicle and support it securely on jackstands.

3   The clutch cable adjuster is located under the vehicle on the driver's side of the transaxle adjacent to the upper engine mounting. Loosen the locknut (if equipped) and turn the adjustment nut **(see illustration)** until freeplay is correct. It may be necessary to hold the cable with a locking plier to prevent it from twisting.

4   After adjusting the pedal freeplay, tighten the locknut (if equipped).

5   Recheck the pedal height.

32   Wheel bearing check, repack and adjustment

Front wheel bearings

Refer to illustrations 32.6, 32.8, 32.11 and 32.15

1   The front wheel bearings should be serviced every 30,000 miles and/or when the brake linings are changed. Additionally, the bearings should be checked whenever the front of the vehicle is raised for any reason.

2   Raise the vehicle and support it securely on jackstands. Spin each wheel and check for noise, rolling resistance and freeplay. The wheels should turn freely without binding.

3   Grasp the top of each tire with one hand and the bottom with the other. Move the wheel in-and-out on the spindle. If there's any noticeable movement, the bearings should be checked and then repacked with grease or replaced if necessary.

4   Remove the wheel.

5   On vehicles with disc brakes, fabricate a wood block which can be slid between the brake pads to keep them separated. Remove the brake caliper (see Chapter 9) and hang it out of the way on a piece of wire.

6   On the driver's side, remove the clip from the end of the speedometer cable. On both sides, pry the dust cap off the hub **(see illustration)**.

7   On early models with double nuts, bend the lock tab and unscrew the lock nut. On later models, loosen the spindle nut lockbolt with an Allen wrench.

8   Remove the spindle nut and washer from the end of the spindle **(see illustration)**. Note: *The left side spindle has left hand threads.*

9   Pull the hub assembly out slightly, then push it back into its original position. This should force the outer bearing off the spindle enough so it can be removed.

10   Pull the hub assembly off the spindle.

11   Use a screwdriver to pry the seal out of the rear of the hub **(see illustration)**. As this is done, note how the seal is installed.

12   Remove the inner wheel bearing from the hub.

13   Use solvent to remove all traces of the old grease from the bearings, hub and spindle. A small brush may prove helpful; however, make sure no bristles from the brush embed themselves inside the bearing rollers. Allow the parts to air dry.

14   Carefully inspect the bearings for cracks, heat discoloration, worn rollers, etc. Check the bearing races inside the hub for wear and damage.

32.15   Work the grease completely into the rollers

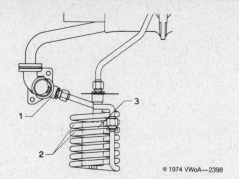

© 1974 VWoA—2398

33.3   1972 California EGR filtering system

| 1 | Exhaust flange of | 2 | Cooling coil |
| | Number 4 cylinder | 3 | Cyclone-type filter |

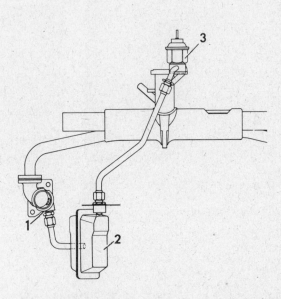

33.4   Some 1973 and all 1974 models have an element-type filter

1	Exhaust flange of Number 4	3	Exhaust gas recirculation
	cylinder		valve
2	Element-type filter		

If the bearing races are defective, the hubs should be taken to a machine shop with the facilities to remove the old races and press new ones in. Note that the bearings and races come as matched sets and old bearings should never be installed on new races.

15   Use high-temperature front wheel bearing grease to pack the bearings. Work the grease completely into the rollers, forcing it between the rollers, cone and cage from the back side **(see illustration)**.

16   Apply a thin coat of grease to the spindle at the outer bearing seat, inner bearing seat, shoulder and seal seat.

17   Put a small quantity of grease inboard of each bearing race inside the hub. Using your finger, form a dam at these points to provide extra grease availability and to keep thinned grease from flowing out of the bearing.

18   Place the grease-packed inner bearing into the rear of the hub and put a little more grease outboard of the bearing.

19   Place a new seal over the inner bearing and tap the seal evenly into place with a hammer and block of wood until it's flush with the hub.

20   Carefully place the hub assembly onto the spindle and push the grease-packed outer bearing into position.

21   Install the washer and spindle nut. Tighten the nut only until all freeplay is gone.

22   Spin the hub in a forward direction to seat the bearings and remove any grease or burrs which could cause excessive bearing play later.

23   Check to see that the tightness of the spindle nut is still the same.

24   Tighten the nut by hand until all looseness and freeplay is gone. Now tighten the nut with a wrench approximately an additional 1/4 turn to create a very slight preload, then back it off about 1/8 turn. The acceptable amount of endplay is 0.001 to 0.003 inch.

25   On early models, install the locking tab and outer nut. Tighten the outer nut against the inner nut and bend the lock tab. It will probably be necessary to hold the inner nut with a wrench to prevent it from turning. On later models, tighten the spindle nut lock bolt with an Allen wrench.

26   Install the dust cap, tapping it into place with a hammer.

27   On the driver's side, reach behind the spindle and push the speedometer cable through the dust cap. Reinstall the clip to hold it in place.

28   On disc brake models, place the brake caliper near the rotor and carefully remove the wood spacer. Install the caliper (see Chapter 9).

29   On all models, install the wheel on the hub and tighten the lug bolts.

30   Grasp the top and bottom of the tire and check the bearings in the manner described earlier in this Section.

31   Lower the vehicle.

Rear wheel bearings

32   **Note:** *This procedure only applies to 1972 and earlier models with CV joint type rear axles. Every 30,000 miles, the rear wheel bearings should be removed, cleaned and repacked with new multi-purpose grease. Because special tools and procedures are required to service the rear wheel bearings, we recommend taking the vehicle to a dealer service department or other repair shop. If you wish to try it yourself, see Chapter 10.*

33   Exhaust Gas Recirculation (EGR) system service

Refer to illustrations 33.3 and 33.4

1   EGR systems are original equipment on the following U.S.A. models: 1972 California models, all 1973 models with automatic stick shift and all 1974 and later models.

2   On 1975 and later models, the EGR service reminder light is designed to activate every 15,000 miles. Some later models don't have EGR filters, but the EGR valve should be removed and the carbon cleaned out (see Chapter 6 for EGR valve removal). To reset the service reminder light, press the reset button on the back of the light assembly.

3   Replace the EGR filter every 30,000 miles. On 1972 California models, unbolt the filter **(see illustration)** and flush it out with solvent. These filters may be replaced with the later disposable type, if desired.

4   Later models have a disposable element-type filter **(see illustration)**. Unbolt the filter from the exhaust flange on the muffler and from the intake manifold. Install the new filter and gaskets and tighten the bolts securely.

Chapter 2   Engine

Contents

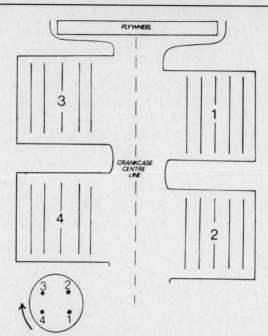

Cylinder numbering diagram

General

Firing order	1-4-3-2
Oil pressure (minimum at normal operating temperature)	28 psi at 2,500 rpm
Compression pressure	
Minimum pressure	100 psi
Maximum variation between cylinders	21 psi
Cylinder bore	
1200 cc	3.03 in (77 mm)
1300 cc	3.03 in (77 mm)
1500 cc	3.27 in (83 mm)
1600 cc	3.36 in (85.5 mm)
Stroke	
1200 cc	2.52 in (64 mm)
1300, 1500 and 1600 cc	2.72 in (69 mm)

Camshaft and bearings

Camshaft journal diameters (all)	0.9837 to 09842 in (24.99 to 25.0 mm)
Camshaft bearing clearance	
New	0.0008 to 0.0019 in (0.02 to 0.05 mm)
Wear limit	0.0047 in (0.12 mm)
Endplay	
New	0.0016 to 0.0051 in (0.4 to 0.13 mm)
Wear limit	0.0063 in (0.16 mm)
Gear backlash	0.0000 to 0.0019 in (0.0 to 0.05 mm)

Connecting rods and bearings

Connecting rod journal diameter	
1200 cc	2.1640 to 2.1648 in (54.97 to 54.99 mm)
1300, 1500 and 1600 cc	2.1644 to 2.1653 in (54.98 to 55.00 mm)
Connecting rod bearing clearance	
New	0.0008 to 0.0031 in (0.02 to 0.08 mm)
Wear limit	0.006 in (0.15 mm)
Connecting rod endplay (all)	
New	0.004 to 0.016 in (0.1 to 0.4 mm)
Wear limit	0.028 in (0.7 mm)
Wrist pin clearance (all)	
New	0.0004 to 0.0008 in (0.01 to 0.02 mm)
Wear limit	0.0016 in (0.04 mm)

Wrist pin diameter
  1200 cc . . . .   0.7871 to 0.7874 in (19.996 to 20.000 mm)
  1300, 1500 and 1600 cc . . . .   0.8658 to 0.8661 in (21.996 to 22.000 mm)
Connecting rod weight color code
  1200 cc . . . .   Brown or white . .   487 to 495 grams
  1200 cc . . . .   Grey or black   . . .   507 to 515 grams
  1300, 1500 and 1600 cc . . . .   Brown or white . . .   580 to 588 grams
  1300, 1500 and 1600 cc . . . .   Grey or black   . . .   592 to 600 grams
Connecting rod journal out-of-round limit . . . .   0.0011 in (0.03 mm)

Crankshaft and main bearings

Main bearing journal diameters
  Nos. 1, 2 and 3 . . . .   2.1640 to 2.1648 in (54.97 to 54.99 mm)
  No. 4 . . . .   1.5739 to 1.5748 in (39.98 to 40.00 mm)
Journal clearance
  Nos. 1 and 3
    New . . . .   0.0016 to 0.0047 in (0.04 to 0.10 mm)
    Wear limit . . . .   0.007 in (0.18 mm)
  No. 2
    New . . . .   0.0011 to 0.0035 in (0.03 to 0.09 mm)
    Wear limit . . . .   0.0066 in (0.17 mm)
  No. 4
    New . . . .   0.0019 to 0.0040 in (0.05 to 0.10 mm)
    Wear limit . . . .   0.0074 in (0.19 mm)
Crankshaft endplay
  New . . . .   0.0027 to 0.0051 in (0.07 to 0.13 mm)
  Wear limit . . . .   0.006 in (0.15 mm)
Main journal out-of-round (maximum) . . . .   0.0011 in (0.03 mm)

Oil pump

Gear/shaft endplay limit (no gasket) . . . .   0.004 in (0.1 mm)
Gear backlash . . . .   0.0012 to 0.0031 in (0.03 to 0.08 mm)

Pistons, cylinders and rings

Piston ring groove side clearance
  Top compression
    New . . . .   0.0027 to 0.0035 in (0.007 to 0.09 mm)
    Wear limit . . . .   0.0047 in (0.12 mm)
  Second compression
    New . . . .   0.0019 to 0.0027 in (0.05 to 0.07 mm)
    Wear limit . . . .   0.0039 in (0.10 mm)
  Oil control
    New . . . .   0.012 to 0.0019 in (0.03 to 0.05 mm)
    Wear limit . . . .   0.0039 in (0.10 mm)
Piston oversizes available . . . .   0.020 and 0.040 in (0.5 mm and 1.0 mm)
Piston ring end gaps
  Compression
    New . . . .   0.012 to 0.018 in (0.30 to 0.45 mm)
    Wear limit . . . .   0.35 in (0.90 mm)
  Oil control
    New . . . .   0.010 to 0.016 in (0.25 to 0.40 mm)
    Wear limit . . . .   0.037 in (0.95 mm)
Cylinder-to-piston clearance (all)
  New . . . .   0.0015 to 0.0019 in (0.04 to 0.05 mm)
  Wear limit . . . .   0.008 in (0.20 mm)
Cylinder out-of-round limit . . . .   0.0004 in (0.01 mm)

Valves/springs

Intake valve stem diameter
  New . . . .   0.3125 to 0.3129 in (7.94 to 7.95 mm)
  Wear limit . . . .   0.3109 in (7.90 mm)
Intake valve guide inside diameter . . . .   0.3149 to 0.3156 in (8.00 to 8.02 mm)
Exhaust valve stem diameter
  New . . . .   0.3114 to 0.3118 in (7.91 to 7.92 mm)
  Wear limit . . . .   0.3109 in (7.90 mm)
Exhaust valve guide inside diameter . . . .   0.3149 to 0.3156 in (8.00 to 8.02 mm)
Valve spring length (loaded)
  1200 cc . . . .   1.305 in @ 90 to 103 lbs
  1300, 1500 and 1600 cc . . . .   1.220 in @ 117 to 135 lbs
Valve margin (minimum) . . . .   1/32 in

2

Torque specifications

Ft-lbs (unless otherwise indicated)

Crankshaft pulley nut	33
Oil pump nuts	14
Cylinder head nuts (see text for tightening sequence)	
First step	84 in-lbs
Second step	
1969 and earlier models	23
1970 and later models	
M10 nuts	23
M8 nuts	18
Flywheel/driveplate gland nut	
1200, 1300 and 1500 cc	217
1600 cc	253
Crankcase nuts and bolts	
M8	14
M10 or M12	25
Connecting rod cap nuts	24
Rocker arm shaft nuts	18
Torque converter-to-driveplate bolts	18
Oil strainer cover plate nuts	See Chapter 1
Oil cooler nuts	See Chapter 3

1   General information

This Chapter covers in-vehicle engine repair, engine removal and installation and engine overhaul procedures. We have placed the in-vehicle procedures in the front of this Chapter, in Sections 2 through 9. Most repairs require engine removal; these procedures are covered in the remaining Sections.

The models covered by this manual are fitted with 1200, 1300, 1500 and 1600 cc engines. These four cylinder engines are of an air-cooled horizontally opposed design. The crankshaft runs in aluminum alloy shell bearings located between the two halves of a magnesium alloy crankcase. The camshaft runs centrally below the crankshaft and is gear driven from the rear end of the crankshaft. The camshaft is also located between the crankcase halves and, on 1966 and later models, runs in removable split shell bearings.

The distributor is driven by a removable shaft from a gear mounted on the rear end of the crankshaft. The same shaft incorporates a cam which operates the fuel pump operating plunger rod on carbureted models.

The gear type oil pump is mounted in the rear of the crankcase, held between the two halves and driven by a horizontal shaft. A tang on the inner end of the shaft engages in a slot in the end of the camshaft.

The four finned cylinder barrels are separately mounted and each pair has a common cylinder head containing the valves and rocker gear. The pushrods are actuated by valve lifters at the camshaft end and pass through sealed pushrod tubes clamped between the head and crankcase. Each valve cover is held to the head by spring hoops located in the cylinder head.

The flywheel/driveplate is located on the front of the crankshaft by four dowel pegs and secured by a single central bolt which also incorporates needle roller bearings for the manual transaxle input shaft. The front crankcase oil seal contacts the center hub of the flywheel. The rear end of the crankshaft has an oil slinger plate and a helical groove machined in the crankshaft pulley hub to contain the oil. An oil filter screen is mounted in the bottom center of the crankcase and the oil suction pipe for the pump comes from the center of it. There is no other form of oil filter incorporated.

The generator (or alternator on 1973 and later models) is mounted on a pedestal above the engine and driven by a "V"-belt from the crankshaft pulley. The cooling fan is mounted on the forward end of the generator/alternator shaft. This runs inside of a sheet steel housing which ducts air down to the cylinder barrels.

Engine identification

For many procedures it is essential to know what model engine you are working on. Many vehicles have had the original engine replaced with one from a different model year. The engine serial numbers begin with the identification codes (numbers/letters) shown in the chart below. These are located at the base of the generator/alternator pedestal:

Production date	Displacement	Engine code	Horsepower
Dec. 1953 through July 1960	1200 cc	1, 2, 3	36
August 1960 through July 1965	1200 cc	5, 6, 7, 8, 9	40
August 1965 through July 1966	1300 cc	FO	50
August 1966 through July 1967	1500 cc	HO	53
August 1967 through July 1969	1500 cc	H5	53
August 1969 through July 1970	1600 cc	B	57
August 1970 through Sept 1971	1600 cc*	AE	60
From August 1971 (Calif. only)	1600 cc *	AH	60
From Oct. 1972	1600 cc *	AK	46
From Dec 1974 (fuel-injected)	1600 cc*	AF, AJ, AS	48

Dual port version

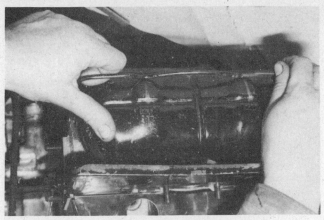

2.3   Pry off the wire clamp

2.6   Install a new gasket in the valve cover prior to installation

2

3.2   Remove the rocker shaft nuts (arrows)

3.3   Slip the rocker shaft assembly off the studs

3.4   Remove the stud seals on 1966 through 1976 models

2   Valve covers – removal and installation

Refer to illustrations 2.3 and 2.6

1   Block the front wheels to prevent the vehicle from rolling forward. Raise the rear of the vehicle and support it securely on jackstands.
2   Place a drain pan on the floor below the valve cover area.
3   Pry the wire clamp down off the valve cover **(see illustration)**.
4   Remove the valve cover. If the cover is stuck, carefully pry it off or tap it with a soft-face hammer. Do not bend or distort the cover.
5   Remove all traces of old gasket material. Clean the cover in solvent and allow it to dry.
6   Position a new gasket in the cover **(see illustration)** and install it on the cylinder head.
7   Snap the wire clamp in place over the cover.
8   Start the engine and check for oil leaks.

3   Rocker arms and pushrods – removal and installation

Refer to illustrations 3.2, 3.3, 3.4, 3.5a, 3.5b, 3.6a, 3.6b and 3.10

Removal

1   Remove the valve covers (see Section 2).
2   Remove the rocker shaft mounting nuts **(see illustration)**. These are special copper plated nuts; keep them separate from any others.

3.5a   Remove the pushrods . . .

3   Pull the rocker shaft assembly off the studs **(see illustration)**.
4   On 1966 through 1976 models, remove the stud seals **(see illustration)**.
5   Remove the pushrods and store them in an organized manner so they may be reinstalled in the same place **(see illustrations)**. **Note:** *On 36 horsepower models, the pushrods and lifters are combined. To remove*

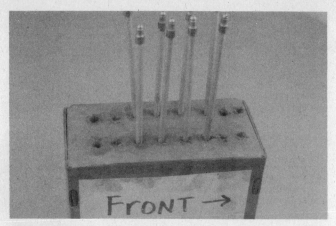

3.5b   . . . and store them in a box so they may be reinstalled in the same place

them, the engine must be removed and the cases must be separated.

6   If you intend to disassemble the rocker arms and shafts, mark the rockers so they may be reassembled in the same position. Remove the end clips and slide the parts from the shaft **(see illustrations)**.

7   Wash all parts in solvent and inspect them for wear and damage. Check the pushrod seats and adjustment screw tips and be sure the shafts are not deeply grooved. Roll the pushrods on a flat surface to check for straightness. Replace as necessary.

Installation

8   Lubricate all parts with assembly lube or clean engine oil. Reassemble the rockers, if necessary, and install the pushrods.

9   On 1966 through 1976 models, install new stud seals. There are two types of seals available. Use the type that was installed originally. Use the doughnut shaped seals unless there is a recessed groove around the stud.

10   Position the rocker assembly over the studs. On 1966 and later models, install the rockers with the chamfered supports facing out **(see illustration)**.

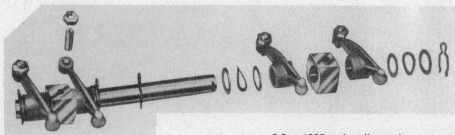

3.6a   1965 and earlier rocker arm assembly – exploded view

3.6b   1966 and later rocker arm assembly – exploded view

3.10   Install the rocker assembly with the chamfered edges facing out (arrow) and the slots facing up

4.2   Remove the shrouds around the preheater pipes

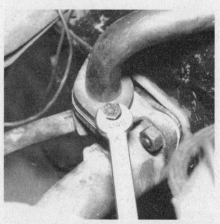

4.3   Unbolt the preheater tubes from the exhaust manifold and the intake manifold from the cylinder heads

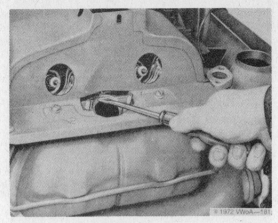

4.5a   Pry the old seals out of the cylinder heads

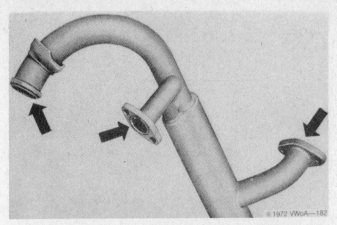

4.5b   Inspect all of the flanges (arrows) for damage and corrosion

4.6   Install new gaskets and seals

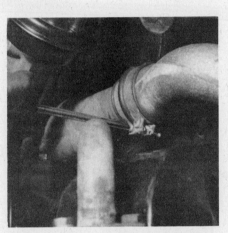

4.8   Loosen the clamps on the boots

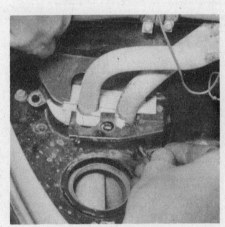

4.9a   Remove the shrouds . . .

11   Be sure all the pushrods seat into the rocker arms. Install the washers and special nuts and tighten them to the torque listed in this Chapter's Specifications.
12   Adjust the valve clearances (see Chapter 1).
13   Install the valve covers (see Section 2).

4   Intake manifold – removal and installation

Single port engines (1970 and earlier models)

Refer to illustrations 4.2, 4.3, 4.5a, 4.5b and 4.6

1   Label and remove the spark plug wires, then remove the carburetor (see Chapters 1 and 4).
2   Remove the cooling shrouds from around the intake manifold pre-heater tubes **(see illustration)**.
3   Unbolt the preheater tubes **(see illustration)**. Now, unbolt the intake manifold from the cylinder heads.
4   Detach the generator and lift the cooling fan housing enough to slip the manifold under it (see Chapters 3 and 5).
5   Remove the old gaskets and seals **(see illustration)**. Clean and inspect the manifold, paying extra attention to the flanges and preheat tubes **(see illustration)**. Remove any carbon buildup from the passages.
6   Using new seals and gaskets **(see illustration)**, install the manifold and tighten the fasteners securely.
7   Reinstall the remaining parts in the reverse order of removal.

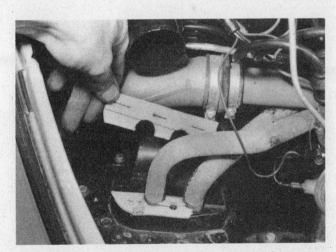

4.9b   . . . and insulators from the preheater tubes

Dual port engines (1971 and later models)

Refer to illustrations 4.8, 4.9a, 4.9b, 4.10, 4.13 and 4.15

8   Loosen the clamps on the boots **(see illustration)** and separate them from the end pieces.
9   Remove the shrouds from around the preheater tubes **(see illustrations)**.

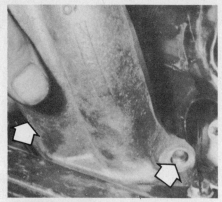

4.10   Remove the nuts from the mounting studs (arrows) and lift the end piece from the cylinder head

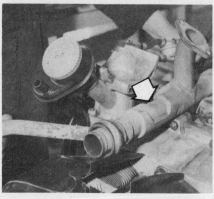

4.13   Remove the nut (arrow) and lift the manifold center section from the engine

4.15   Fit new gaskets over the studs and dowel

5.3   Remove the air shroud screws (arrows) – typical model shown

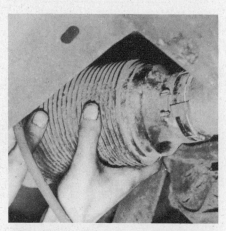

5.4   Loosen the clamps and compress the air ducts, then slip them off the end of the heat exchanger

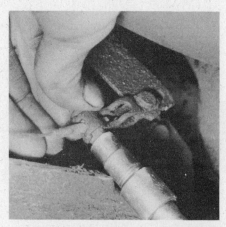

5.5   Loosen the clamps and detach the heater control cables from the front end of each heat exchanger

5.7   Remove the nuts (arrows) from the cylinder head studs

5.10   Slip a new gasket over the studs

5.11   Position the heat exchanger on the engine (early model shown)

10   Remove the mounting nuts and lift off the end pieces (see illustration).

11   Remove the carburetor or throttle valve assembly (see Chapter 4).

12   Detach the generator/alternator and lift the cooling fan housing enough to slip the manifold under it (see Chapters 3 and 5).

13   Remove the nut (see illustration) and lift the intake manifold center section off the engine.

14   Remove the old gaskets and seals. Clean and inspect the manifold, paying extra attention to the flanges and preheat tubes. Remove any carbon buildup from the passages.

15   Using new seals and gaskets (see illustration), install the manifold and tighten the fasteners securely.

16   Reinstall the remaining parts in the reverse order of removal.

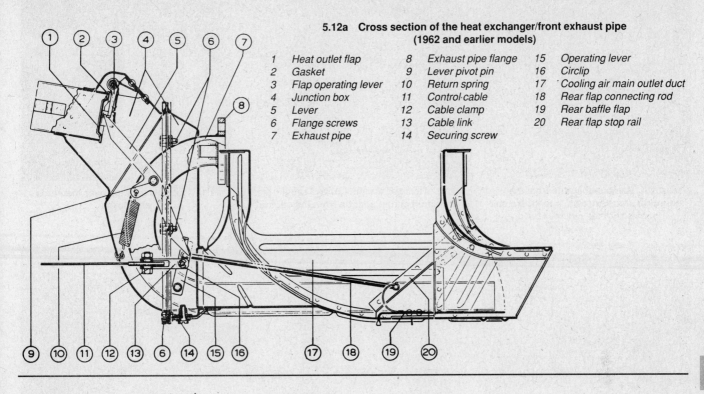

5.12a   Cross section of the heat exchanger/front exhaust pipe (1962 and earlier models)

1	Heat outlet flap	8	Exhaust pipe flange	15	Operating lever
2	Gasket	9	Lever pivot pin	16	Circlip
3	Flap operating lever	10	Return spring	17	Cooling air main outlet duct
4	Junction box	11	Control cable	18	Rear flap connecting rod
5	Lever	12	Cable clamp	19	Rear baffle flap
6	Flange screws	13	Cable link	20	Rear flap stop rail
7	Exhaust pipe	14	Securing screw		

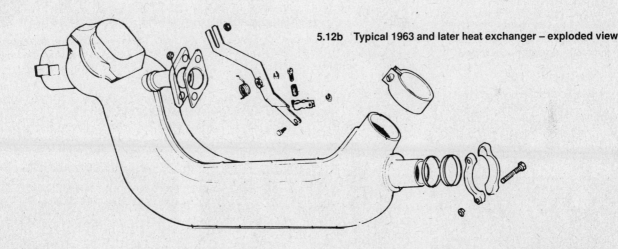

5.12b   Typical 1963 and later heat exchanger – exploded view

5   Exhaust manifold/heat exchanger – removal and installation

Refer to illustrations 5.3, 5.4, 5.5, 5.7, 5.10, 5.11, 5.12a and 5.12b

Removal

1   Block the front wheels so the vehicle can't roll forward.
2   Raise the rear of the vehicle and support it securely on jackstands.
3   Working under the vehicle, remove the air shrouds from the heat exchanger **(see illustration)**.
4   Remove the hot air ducts from each side **(see illustration)**.
5   Disconnect the heater control cables **(see illustration)**.
6   Remove the muffler (see Chapter 4).

7   Apply penetrating oil to the threads of the cylinder head-to-heat exchanger studs and remove the nuts **(see illustration)**.
8   Pull the heat exchanger toward the front of the vehicle until it is clear of the studs and lower it to the floor.
9   Remove the old gaskets from the mounting flanges.

Installation

10   Install a new gasket **(see illustration)** on each of the mounting flanges.
11   Position the heat exchanger on the engine **(see illustration)**. Install the mounting nuts and tighten them securely.
12   Reinstall the remaining components **(see illustrations)** in the reverse order of removal.

6.5   Insert a prybar through the pulley to keep the crankshaft from turning when loosening/tightening the crankshaft bolt

6.6   Remove the pulley with a special puller

6.7   Remove the two screws (arrows) and lift off the shroud

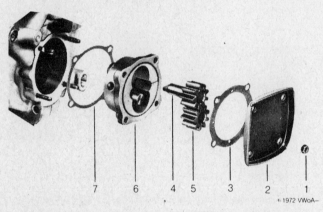

6.9a   Oil pump – exploded view (manual transaxle models)

1	Sealing nut (4)
2	Oil pump cover
3	Oil pump cover gasket
4	Driveshaft

5	Oil pump gear
6	Oil pump housing
7	Oil pump housing gasket

6   Oil pump – removal, inspection and installation

Note: *Several different types of oil pumps were used in these models over the years. Automatic Stick Shift models use a special two-part pump, and a larger capacity oil pump was introduced on all models in May 1971. Be sure to check with a dealer parts department or other auto parts store to determine interchangeability of any replacement pump.*

Removal

Refer to illustrations 6.5, 6.6, 6.7, 6.9a, 6.9b and 6.11

1   Disconnect the ground strap from the negative terminal of the battery.
2   Set the parking brake and place the transaxle in fourth gear to keep the crankshaft from turning (manual transaxle models only).
3   Remove the crankshaft pulley cover (if equipped) and the rear cover plate (over the muffler).
4   Remove the drivebelt (see Chapter 1).
5   Remove the crankshaft pulley bolt and washer **(see illustration)**.
6   Using a special puller, remove the crankshaft pulley **(see illustration)**. **Caution:** *Do not try to remove the pulley with an external jaw-type puller or by prying it off; the pulley and/or crankcase will be damaged.*
7   Remove the shroud **(see illustration)**.

6.9b   Oil pump – exploded view (Automatic Stick Shift models)

1	Housing gasket
2	Oil pump housing
3	Intermediate plate gasket (2)
4	Oil pump upper shaft with gear

5	Oil pump lower shaft with gear
6	Woodruff key
7	Oil seal (2)
8	Intermediate plate
9	ATF pump lower gear

10	ATF pump upper gear
11	Cover with ATF hose fitting
12	Sealing nut
13	ATF pressure relief piston
14	Relief spring
15	Plug

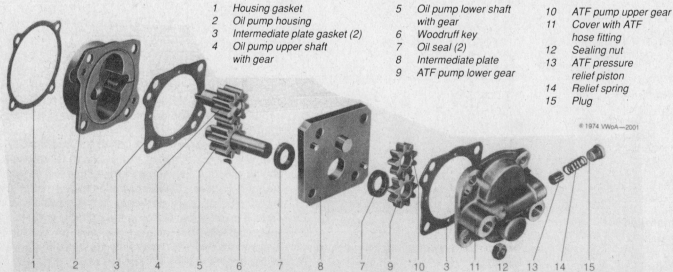

6.11 Use a special puller to remove the oil pump body

6.13 Measure the oil pump gear backlash

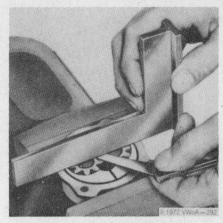

6.14 Measure gear endplay

6.16 Position a new gasket over the pump without using sealant

6.17 Slip the pump over the studs

6.18a Install the upper gear first, turn it until the tang meshes with the slot in the camshaft . . .

2

8   On Automatic Stick Shift models, detach the pressure line and return line from the pump.

9   On all models, remove the four sealing nuts **(see illustrations)** and remove the oil pump cover.

10   Remove the gears, gasket(s), plate and seals (as applicable) from the oil pump.

11   Mark the position of the pump housing-to-crankcase with a scribe. Using a special puller **(see illustration)**, remove the oil pump body from the crankcase. **Caution:** *Do not try to remove the oil pump by prying it out; the pump and/or crankcase will be damaged.* **Note:** *If the engine is being completely disassembled, the pump can be removed without the special puller after the crankcase halves are separated.*

Inspection

Refer to illustrations 6.13 and 6.14

12   Remove all traces of old gasket material. Clean all of the parts thoroughly with solvent and inspect them for wear and damage.

13   Measure the gear backlash **(see illustration)** and compare the clearance to the one listed in this Chapter's Specifications.

14   Check gear endplay **(see illustration)** and compare the clearance to that listed in this Chapter's Specifications.

15   Check the idler gear shaft(s) for play and replace the pump if any looseness is found.

Installation

Refer to illustrations 6.16, 6.17, 6.18a and 6.18b

16   Place a new gasket over the pump without using sealant **(see illustration)**.

6.18b   . . . then install the lower gear

17   Slide the pump into position over the studs **(see illustration)**.

18   Lubricate the gears with engine oil and install them into the pump **(see illustrations)**. Pack the spaces between the gears with petroleum jelly; this will help the pump prime quickly.

19   Complete the installation in the reverse order of removal. Use a new gasket and new sealing nuts on the pump cover. Be sure to tighten the oil pump cover nuts and the crankshaft pulley bolt to the torque listed in this Chapter's Specifications.

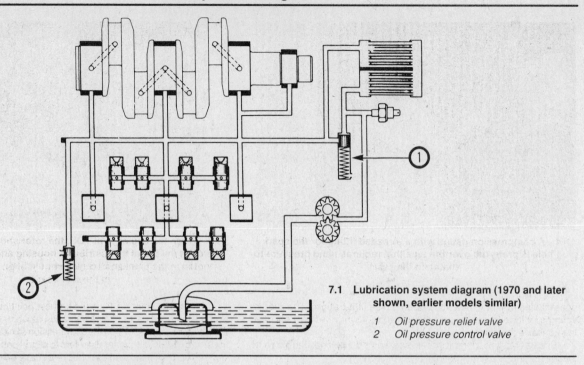

7.1   Lubrication system diagram (1970 and later shown, earlier models similar)

1   *Oil pressure relief valve*
2   *Oil pressure control valve*

7.4   Exploded view of the valves (1970 and later models)

1   *Oil pressure relief valve*   2   *Oil pressure control valve*

7   Oil pressure relief and control valves – removal and installation

Refer to illustrations 7.1, 7.4 and 7.6

Note: *On 1969 and earlier models, there is one oil pressure relief valve located near the oil pump. Beginning with 1970 models, the engines were equipped with an additional valve, known as the oil pressure control valve, located near the flywheel end of the engine. The oil pressure relief valve releases excessive oil pressure before it goes into the oil cooler when the oil is cold and thick. The oil pressure control valve serves to maintain oil pressure at the crankshaft bearings when the oil is hot and thin.*

Removal

1   The oil pressure relief and control valves are spring loaded pistons located in the left (driver's) side of the crankcase at front and rear by large screw plugs **(see illustration)**. They may be removed from underneath when the engine is in the vehicle.
2   Block the front wheels to prevent the vehicle from rolling. Raise the rear of the vehicle and support it securely on jackstands.
3   It is not necessary to drain the engine oil but be prepared to catch some oil when either of the valves is removed.

7.6   Oil pressure relief valve – exploded view

1   *Plunger*   3   *Gasket*
2   *Spring*   4   *Plug*

4   Remove the plug **(see illustration)** with a large screwdriver. The spring and plunger should drop out. If a plunger sticks in its bore in the crankcase, use a 10 mm (3/8 inch) tap to pull the plunger out. **Note:** *On 1970 and later models, remove both valves. The plungers and springs are not interchangeable, so don't mix them up. Beginning with 1967 model Chassis number 117054916, engine number HO 225117, the oil pressure relief valve plunger has an annular groove.*

Installation

5   The plunger(s) should be a sliding fit in the crankcase bore. Minor signs of scuffing may be cleaned up. If there is severe scoring of the piston or bore, the damaged parts must be replaced.
6   Lightly oil the plunger(s) and insert into the bore(s). On 1970 and later models, the larger of the two springs is for the oil pressure relief valve and

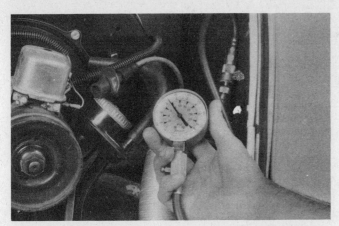

8.4   A compression gauge with a threaded fitting for the spark plug hole is preferred over the type that requires hand pressure to maintain the seal

9.7   When the engine is at TDC, the rotor should align with the notch in the top of the distributor housing and the "O" degree notch in the crankshaft pulley should align with the seam in the crankcase

goes into the rear bore near the oil pump **(see illustration)**. The shorter spring is for the oil pressure control valve and goes into the front bore near the transaxle mounting.

7   Ensure that the springs fit in their recesses in the plunger and plug and that a new seal is used. Tighten the plugs securely.

8   Compression check

Refer to illustration 8.4

1   A compression check will tell you what mechanical condition the pistons, rings and valves in your engine are in. Specifically, it can tell you if the compression is down due to leakage caused by worn piston rings or defective valves and seats. **Note:** *The engine must be at normal operating temperature for this check and the battery must be fully charged.*

2   Label and then remove the spark plug wires from the spark plugs. Begin by cleaning the area around the spark plugs before you remove them (compressed air works best for this). **Warning:** *Wear eye protection.* This will prevent dirt from getting into the cylinders as the compression check is being done. Remove all of the spark plugs from the engine.

3   Block the throttle wide open and temporarily disconnect the wire from the BAT (or no. 15) terminal on the ignition coil.

4   With the compression gauge in the number one spark plug hole, crank the engine over at least four compression strokes and watch the gauge **(see illustration)**. The compression should build up quickly in a healthy engine. Low compression on the first stroke, followed by gradually increasing pressure on successive strokes, indicates worn piston rings, pistons or cylinders. A low compression reading on the first stroke, which does not build up during successive strokes, indicates leaking valves or a cracked head. Record the highest gauge reading obtained.

5   Repeat the procedure for the remaining cylinders and compare the results to the pressures listed in this Chapter's Specifications.

6   Mechanics frequently squirt oil into the cylinders and perform a second "wet" compression test on conventional engines. However, this type of test is not reliable on horizontally opposed engines. If compression is way down or varies greatly between cylinders, have a leak-down test performed by an automotive repair shop before you remove the engine and begin an overhaul. This test will pinpoint exactly where the leakage is occurring and how severe it is.

9   Top Dead Center (TDC) for number one cylinder – locating

Refer to illustration 9.7

Note: *Refer to Chapter 5 for information on distributor removal and installation.*

1   Top Dead Center (TDC) is the farthest point out in the cylinder that each piston reaches as it travels in-and-out when the crankshaft turns. Each piston reaches TDC on the compression stroke and again on the exhaust stroke, but TDC generally refers to piston position on the compression stroke. The timing marks on the crankshaft pulley installed on the rear of the crankshaft are referenced to the number one piston at TDC on the compression stroke.

2   Positioning the pistons at TDC is an essential part of many procedures such as valve adjustment and distributor removal.

3   In order to bring any piston to TDC, the crankshaft must be turned using one of the methods outlined below. When looking at the engine, normal crankshaft rotation is clockwise. **Warning:** *Before beginning this procedure, be sure to place the transmission in Neutral and disable the ignition system by disconnecting the wire from terminal 15 on the ignition coil.*

   a)   The preferred method is to turn the crankshaft with a wrench on the crankshaft pulley bolt.

   b)   If you don't have a wrench that fits the crankshaft pulley bolt, turn the generator/alternator pulley nut. The drivebelt will turn the crankshaft.

4   Remove the distributor cap as described in Chapter 1.

5   There is a small notch on the distributor body directly below the number one spark plug wire terminal in the distributor cap.

6   Turn the crankshaft (see Step 3 above) until the line on the crankshaft pulley is aligned with the split in the crankcase.

7   The rotor should now be pointing directly at the mark on the distributor housing **(see illustration)**. If it's 180-degrees off, the piston is at TDC on the exhaust stroke.

8   If the rotor is 180-degrees off, turn the crankshaft one complete turn (360-degrees) clockwise. The rotor should now be pointing at the mark. When the rotor is pointing at the number one spark plug wire terminal in the distributor cap (which is indicated by the mark on the distributor body) and the timing marks are aligned, the number one piston is at TDC on the compression stroke.

9   After the number one piston has been positioned at TDC on the compression stroke, TDC for any of the remaining cylinders can be located by turning the crankshaft 180-degrees at a time and following the firing order (1-4-3-2).

10   Engine overhaul – general information

Refer to illustrations 10.4a and 10.4b

   It is not always easy to determine when, or if, an engine should be completely overhauled, as a number of factors must be considered.

   High mileage is not necessarily an indication that an overhaul is needed, while low mileage does not preclude the need for an overhaul. Frequency of servicing is probably the most important consideration. An engine that has had regular and frequent oil changes, as well as other re-

2

10.4a   Remove the oil pressure
sending unit . . .

10.4b   . . . and install a gauge in
its place

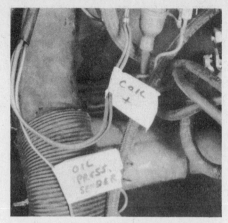

12.9   Clearly label the wires before
disconnecting them

quired maintenance, will most likely give many thousands of miles of reliable service. Conversely, a neglected engine may require an overhaul very early in its life.

Excessive oil consumption and blue exhaust smoke are indications that piston rings and/or valve guides are in need of attention. Make sure that oil leaks are not responsible before deciding that the rings and/or guides are bad. Have a compression or leakdown test performed by an experienced tune-up mechanic to determine the extent of the work required.

If the engine is making obvious knocking or rumbling noises, the connecting rod and/or main bearings are probably at fault. Check the oil pressure with a gauge temporarily installed in place of the oil pressure sending unit **(see illustrations)** and compare it to the Specifications in this Chapter. If the pressure is extremely low, the bearings and/or oil pump are probably worn out.

Loss of power, rough running, excessive valve train noise and high fuel consumption rates may also point to the need for an overhaul, especially if they are all present at the same time. If a complete tune-up does not remedy the situation, major mechanical work is the only solution.

An engine overhaul involves restoring the internal parts to the specifications of a new engine. During a complete overhaul, the pistons, cylinders and piston rings are replaced. Sometimes, wear is minimal and the cylinder walls are reconditioned (rebored and/or honed). If a rebore is done, new pistons are required. Usually it is less expensive to buy new aftermarket pistons, rings and cylinders as a set than it is to have the old ones rebored and purchase pistons and rings separately.

The main bearings, connecting rod bearings and camshaft bearings are replaced with new ones and, if necessary, the crankshaft may be reground to restore the journals. Usually, the valves are serviced as well, since they are normally in less-than-perfect condition at this point. While the engine is being overhauled, other components, such as the fuel pump (carbureted models), distributor, starter and generator/alternator, can be rebuilt as well. The end result should be a like-new engine that will give many trouble free miles. **Note:** *Critical cooling system components such as the ducts, the drivebelt and the thermostat MUST be replaced with new parts when an engine is overhauled. The oil cooler should be checked carefully to ensure that it isn't clogged or leaking. If in doubt, replace it with a new one. Also, we do not recommend overhauling the oil pump – always install a new one when an engine is rebuilt.*

Before beginning the engine overhaul, read through the entire procedure to familiarize yourself with the scope and requirements of the job. Overhauling an engine is not especially difficult, but it is time consuming. Plan on the vehicle being tied up for a minimum of two weeks, especially if parts must be taken to an automotive machine shop for repair or reconditioning. Check on availability of parts and make sure that any necessary special tools and equipment are obtained in advance. Most work can be done with typical hand tools, although a number of precision measuring tools are required. Often an automotive machine shop will handle the inspection of parts and offer advice concerning reconditioning and replacement. **Note:** *Always wait until the engine has been completely*

disassembled and all components, especially the engine crankcases, have been inspected before deciding what service and repair operations must be performed by an automotive machine shop. Since the crankcase's condition will be the major factor to consider when determining whether to overhaul the original engine or buy a rebuilt one, never purchase parts or have machine work done on other components until the engine cases have been thoroughly inspected. As a general rule, time is the primary cost of an overhaul, so it does not pay to install worn or substandard parts.

As a final note, to ensure maximum life and minimum trouble from a rebuilt engine, everything must be assembled with care in a spotlessly clean environment.

11   Engine removal – methods and precautions

If you've decided that an engine must be removed for overhaul or major repair work, several preliminary steps should be taken.

Locating a suitable place to work is extremely important. Adequate work space, along with storage space for the vehicle, will be needed. If a shop or garage isn't available, at the very least a flat, level, clean work surface made of concrete or asphalt is required.

Clean the engine compartment and engine before beginning the removal procedure. A floor jack and jackstands or a vehicle hoist will be necessary. Make sure the equipment is rated in excess of the vehicle weight. Safety is of primary importance, considering the potential hazards involved in lifting the engine out of the vehicle.

If the engine is being removed by a novice, a helper should be available. Advice and aid from someone more experienced would also be helpful. There are instances when one person cannot simultaneously perform all of the operations required when lifting the engine out of the vehicle.

Plan the operation ahead of time. Arrange for or obtain all of the tools and equipment you'll need prior to beginning the job. Some of the equipment necessary to perform engine removal and installation safely and with relative ease are a complete set of wrenches, screwdrivers and sockets as described in the front of this manual, wood blocks and plenty of rags and cleaning solvent for mopping up spilled oil, coolant and gasoline. If any equipment must be rented, make sure that you arrange for it in advance and perform all of the operations possible without it beforehand. This will save you money and time.

Plan for the vehicle to be out of use for quite a while. A machine shop will be required to perform some of the work which the do-it-yourselfer can't accomplish without special equipment. These shops often have a busy schedule, so it would be a good idea to consult them before removing the engine in order to accurately estimate the amount of time required to rebuild or repair components that may need work.

Always be extremely careful when removing and installing the engine. Serious injury can result from careless actions. Plan ahead, take your time and a job of this nature, although major, can be accomplished successfully.

12.11a   Remove the crankshaft pulley cover, if equipped . . .

12.11b   . . . then remove the preheater pipe covers on both sides (carbureted models) . . .

12.11c   . . . and detach the rear cover

12.15   On carbureted models, disconnect the fuel line above the heat exchanger on the driver's side

12.16   Remove the ducts which connect the heat exchangers to the ducts in the body

2

12   Engine – removal

Refer to illustrations 12.9, 12.11a, 12.11b, 12.11c, 12.15, 12.16, 12.17, 12.18a, 12.18b, 12.19, 12.20, 12.21, 12.22, 12.23a, 12.23b and 12.25

Warning: *Gasoline is extremely flammable, so take extra precautions when you work on any part of the fuel system. Don't smoke or allow open flames or bare light bulbs near the work area, and don't work in a garage when natural gas-type appliances (such as a water heater or clothes dryer) with a pilot light is present. When you perform any kind of work on the fuel system, wear safety glasses and have a fire extinguisher handy.*

1   Removal of the engine is fairly simple, provided the correct tools and equipment are assembled beforehand. If the engine is very dirty, clean it first.

2   The car is lifted up at the rear for engine removal. The engine is held to the transaxle by two studs and two bolts. It has to be pulled back from these and lowered out of the car. Support the engine with a floor jack as soon as it is detached from the transaxle.

3   You may remove the engine single-handedly if all the necessary equipment is available, but the trickiest part is lowering the engine to the floor level. Even a fall of a few inches could crack the aluminium crankcase. Note that the engine is reversed compared with a conventional layout, so that the flywheel/driveplate is at the front. All references to front and rear of the engine will be in relation to its position in the vehicle.

4   Park the vehicle on a level hard surface with the transaxle in neutral and block the front tires to prevent the vehicle from rolling.

5   Disconnect the ground strap from the negative terminal of the battery.

6   Drain the engine oil (see Chapter 1).

7   Prop open the rear hood or remove it (see Chapter 11).

8   Remove the air cleaner assembly, and on 1968 and 1969 models, remove the throttle positioner (see Chapter 4).

9   Carefully label and disconnect all vacuum lines, emissions hoses and wiring. Masking tape and felt tip pens work well for marking items **(see illustration)**. The main engine wiring harness may then be taken from the clips and tucked to one side of the engine compartment. If necessary, take instant photos or sketch the locations to ensure correct reinstallation.

10   Detach the accelerator cable (see Chapter 4).

11   Detach the air ducts from the fan housing (1963 and later models) and remove the rear cover plate **(see illustrations)**.

12   Loosen the clamping screw which holds the distributor in position and turn the distributor so the vacuum diaphragm faces the engine.

13   Raise the rear of the vehicle and support it securely on jackstands. Position the jackstands under the torsion arms, just forward of the rear wheels.

14   Working under the vehicle, disconnect the heater control cables from the heater flaps or heat exchangers (see Chapter 3, if necessary).

15   Disconnect the fuel line(s) between the engine and chassis and plug the ends. The fuel line runs along the left (drivers) side of the transaxle. On fuel-injected models, relieve fuel pressure first (see Chapter 4). On carbureted models, this should be pulled off at the end of the hose nearest the engine so that the hose can be plugged **(see illustration)**.

16   Pull off the flexible ducts which connect the heat exchangers to the body on each side of the engine **(see illustration)**.

Automatic Stick Shift models only

17   Detach the hydraulic pressure and suction lines near the engine **(see**

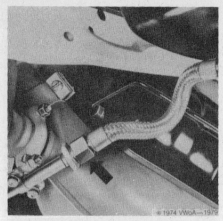

12.17   Disconnect the fitting (arrow) and plug the end with an M16x1.5 union that has been soldered closed

12.18a   On carbureted models, the torque converter bolts are accessed through this opening (arrow)

12.18b   On fuel-injected models, the torque converter bolts are accessed by removing a plug and working through this opening (arrow)

12.19   Remove the two lower mounting nuts or bolts

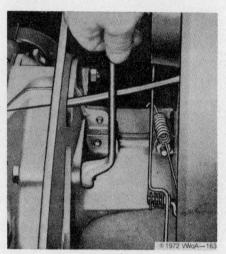

12.20   Reach between the fan housing and the firewall to access the upper nuts/bolts

12.21   Position the jack under the center of the engine

12.22   Pull back on the engine to disengage it from the transaxle

illustration). Have a drain pan positioned to catch fluid. Plug the ends to prevent fluid loss.

18   Remove the four torque converter-to-driveplate bolts with a 12 point socket. The bolts may be accessed through openings in the bellhousing **(see illustrations)**. Turn the crankshaft pulley bolt with a wrench to bring each bolt into the opening.

All models

19   Remove the two lower engine mounting nuts (manual transaxle) or bolts on Automatic Stick Shift models **(see illustration)**. The fasteners are positioned about four inches from each side of the engine center line and about two inches up from the bottom of the flange where the engine joins the transaxle.

20   On 1970 and earlier models, remove both upper engine mounting nuts from above by reaching between the fan housing and firewall **(see illustration)**. On later models, the bolt head has a flat on it which should lock into the transaxle. This enables the nut to be taken off without any difficulty, provided the bolt is not pushed out. **Note:** *It may help to use a locking plier to hold the bolts in place.* On 1971 and later models, remove the left (driver's) side top mounting bolt from underneath. This is best done with a socket and extension with a universal joint.

21   Support the engine with a floor jack as the last mounting bolt is removed. Position the jack head under the center of the crankcase with a large block of wood on top of the jack to extend its reach **(see illustration)**.

22   Pull the engine back about three inches to disengage it from the transaxle **(see illustration)**. It may need a bit of wiggling to get it free. When this is done slip the accelerator cable out of the tube in the fan housing and tape it up on the firewall.

23   Lower the engine carefully. **Caution:** *On manual transaxle models, be sure the input shaft of the transaxle is clear of the clutch* **(see illustration)**, *until it rests on blocks* **(see illustration)**.

12.23a On manual transaxle models, look between the engine and transaxle to be sure the clutch is not caught on the input shaft (arrow)

12.23b Let the engine down on blocks positioned under both heat exchangers

12.25 Secure the torque converter with a strap or wire

24   Remove the jack, then lift one side of the engine while an assistant removes the blocks under each side of the engine. Take out one at a time on each side so the engine doesn't tip over. When the engine is on the floor, it should be low enough to slide out from under the vehicle.
25   On Automatic Stick Shift models, secure the torque converter in place with a strap or wire **(see illustration)**.

13   Engine rebuilding alternatives

The do-it-yourselfer is faced with a number of options when performing an engine overhaul. The decision to replace the engine cases, piston/cylinder assemblies, cylinder heads and crankshaft depends on a number of factors, with the number one consideration being the condition of the engine cases. Other considerations are cost, access to machine shop facilities, parts availability, time required to complete the project and the extent of prior mechanical experience on the part of the do-it-yourselfer.
Some of the rebuilding alternatives include:
Individual parts – If the inspection procedures reveal that the engine cases and most engine components are in reusable condition, purchasing individual parts may be the most economical alternative.
The engine cases, cylinder heads, crankshaft and piston/connecting rod assemblies should all be inspected carefully. Even if the cylinder bores show little wear, they should be surface honed.
Short block – A short block consists of the engine cases with a camshaft and lifters, crankshaft and connecting rods already installed. All new bearings are incorporated and all clearances will be correct. The existing

valve train components, piston/cylinder assemblies and cylinder heads and external parts can be bolted to the short block with little or no machine shop work necessary.
Long block – A long block consists of a short block plus piston/cylinder assemblies, cylinder heads, valve covers, pushrods and valve train components. All components are installed with new bearings, seals and gaskets incorporated throughout. The installation of manifolds and external parts is all that's necessary.
Give careful thought to which alternative is best for you and discuss the situation with local automotive machine shops, auto parts dealers and experienced rebuilders before ordering or purchasing replacement parts.

14   Engine overhaul – disassembly sequence

Refer to illustrations 14.3a, 14.3b, 14.3c, 14.3d and 14.3e
1   It's much easier to disassemble and work on the engine if it's mounted on a portable engine stand. A stand can often be rented quite cheaply from an equipment rental yard. Before the engine is mounted on a stand, the flywheel/driveplate should be removed from the engine.
2   If a stand isn't available, it's possible to disassemble the engine with it blocked up on the floor or a sturdy workbench. Be extra careful not to tip or drop the engine when working without a stand.
3   If you're going to obtain a rebuilt engine, all external components **(see illustrations)** must come off first, to be transferred to the replacement engine, just as they will if you're doing a complete engine overhaul yourself. These include:

Air cleaner assembly
Clutch and flywheel or driveplate
Thermostat (1963 and later)
Generator/alternator and fan housing
Cooling shrouds
Oil cooler
Distributor and drive, spark plug wires and spark plugs
Fuel pump (carbureted models only)
Fuel injection components or carburetor
Intake manifold
Emissions control components (if equipped)
Exhaust manifolds/heat exchangers and muffler
Crankshaft pulley

Note: *When removing the external components from the engine, pay close attention to details that may be helpful or important during installation. Note the installed position of gaskets, seals, spacers, pins, brackets, washers, bolts and other small items.*

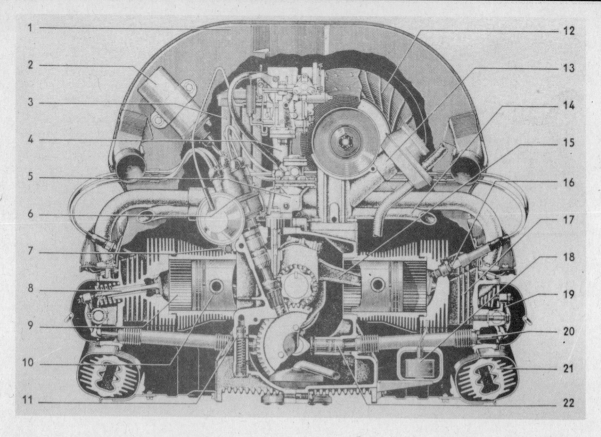

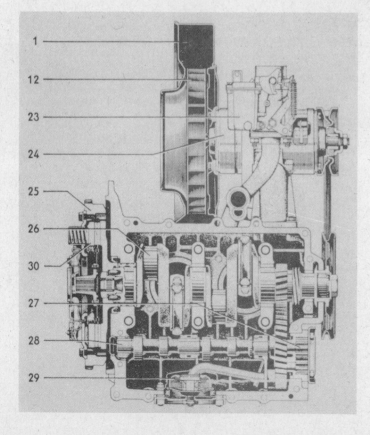

14.3a   Engine – cross-sections

1   Fan housing
2   Coil
3   Oil cooler
4   Intake manifold
5   Fuel pump
6   Distributor
7   Oil pressure switch
8   Valve
9   Cylinder
10   Piston
11   Oil pressure relief valve
12   Fan
13   Oil filter
14   Intake manifold preheater pipe
15   Connecting rod
16   Spark plug
17   Cylinder head
18   Thermostat
19   Rocker arm
20   Pushrod
21   Heat exchange
22   Valve lifter
23   Carburetor
24   Generator
25   Flywheel
26   Crankshaft
27   Oil pump
28   Camshaft
29   Oil strainer
30   Clutch

Note: This drawing does not show all the later modifications such as the three-section intake manifold and the one piece fuel pump, but the basic layout is the same.

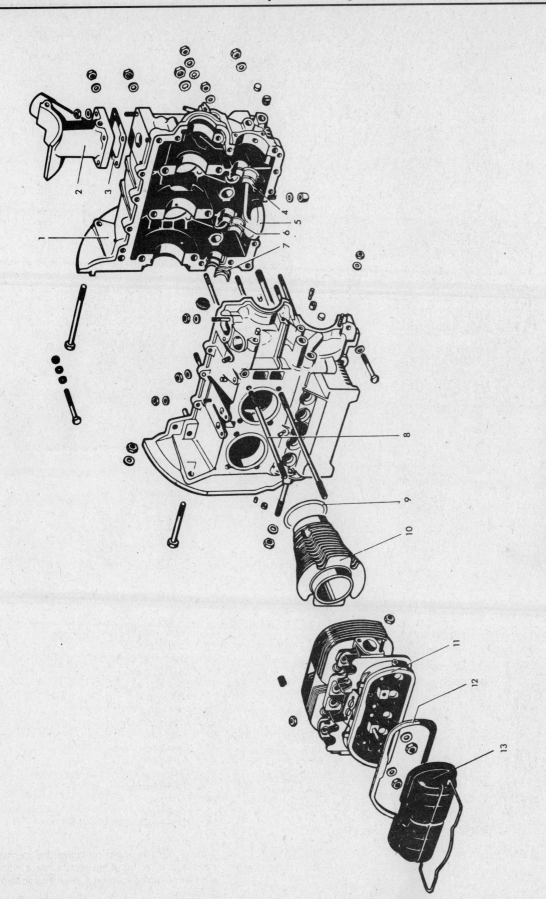

14.3b Engine components — exploded view

1 Crankcase – right half
2 Generator alternator pedestal
3 Gasket
4 Camshaft bearing – rear
5 Oil pickup tube

6 Camshaft bearing – center
7 Camshaft bearing – front
8 Cylinder head stud
9 Cylinder base gasket

10 Cylinder barrel
11 Cylinder head
12 Valve cover gasket
13 Valve cover

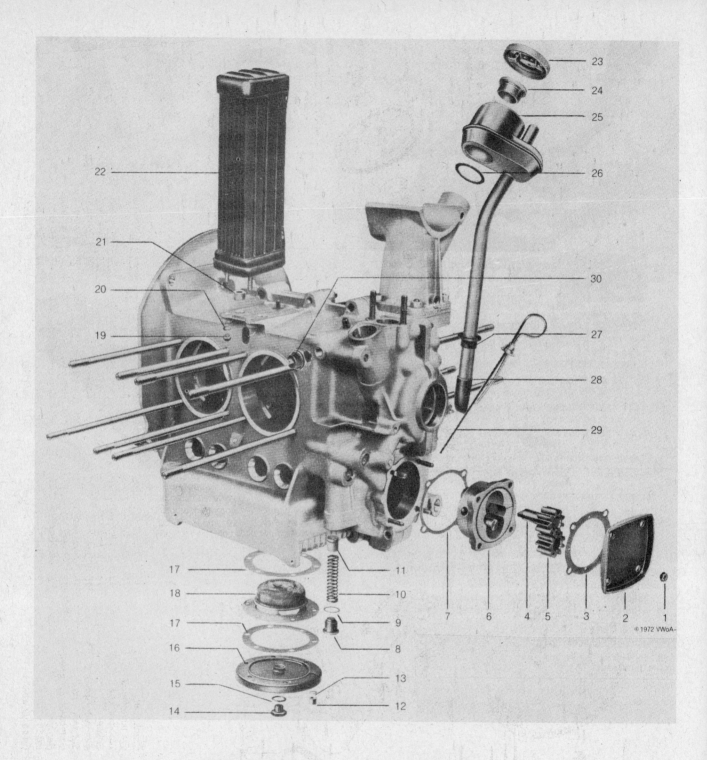

14.3c Typical crankcase components – exploded view

1	sealing nut (4)	9	Seal
2	Oil pump cover	10	Spring
3	Oil pump cover gasket	11	Plunger for oil pressure
4	Drive shaft		relief valve
5	Oil pump gear	12	Nut (6)
6	Oil pump housing	13	Seal (6)
7	Oil pump housing gasket	14	Oil drain plug
8	Plug	15	Seal

16	Oil strainer cover	24	Gland nut for breather
17	Gasket (2)	25	Oil filler and
18	Oil strainer		breather assembly
19	Nut (3)	26	Seal
20	Lock washer (3)	27	Grommet
21	Oil cooler seal (2)	28	Breather rubber valve
22	Oil cooler	29	Dipstick
23	Oil filler neck cap	30	Oil pressure switch

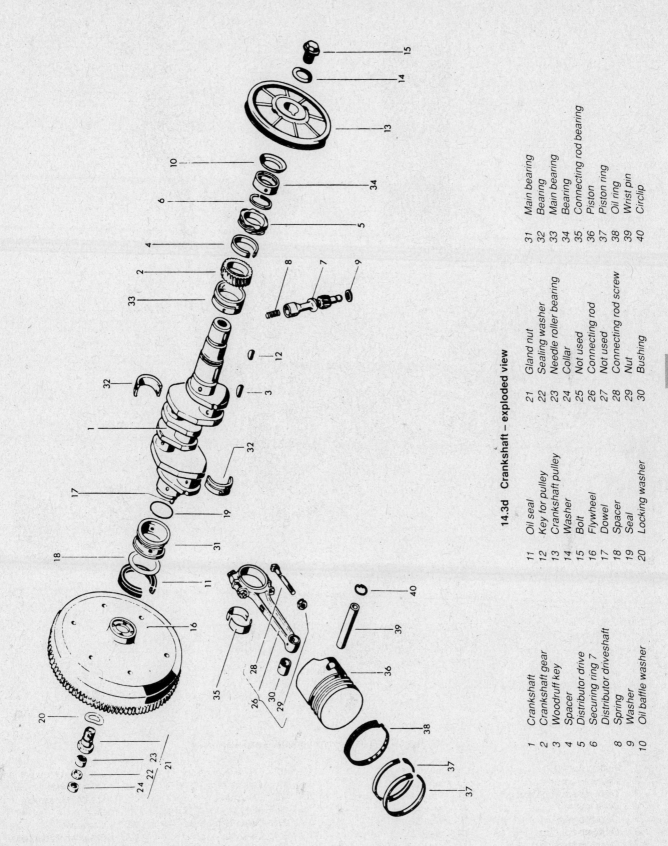

14.3d Crankshaft – exploded view

1 Crankshaft	21 Gland nut
2 Crankshaft gear	22 Sealing washer
3 Woodruff key	23 Needle roller bearing
4 Spacer	24 Collar
5 Distributor drive	25 Not used
6 Securing ring 7	26 Connecting rod
Distributor driveshaft	27 Not used
8 Spring	28 Connecting rod screw
9 Washer	29 Nut
10 Oil baffle washer.	30 Bushing
11 Oil seal	31 Main bearing
12 Key for pulley	32 Bearing
13 Crankshaft pulley	33 Main bearing
14 Washer	34 Bearing
15 Bolt	35 Connecting rod bearing
16 Flywheel	36 Piston
17 Dowel	37 Piston ring
18 Spacer	38 Oil ring
19 Seal	39 Wrist pin
20 Locking washer	40 Circlip

2

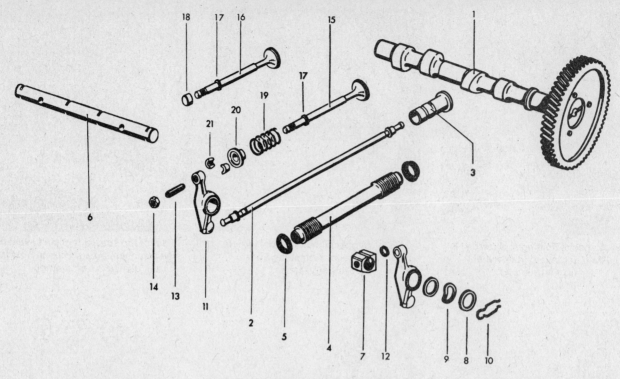

14.3e   Camshaft and valves – exploded view

1 Camshaft and gear	8 Thrust washer	15 Intake valve
2 Pushrod	9 Wave washer	16 Exhaust valve
3 Tappet (lifter)	10 Securing clip	17 Oil wiper
4 Pushrod tube	11 Rocker arm	18 Valve cap
5 Pushrod tube seal	12 Sealing ring	19 Valve spring
6 Rocker shaft	13 Valve adjusting screw	20 Valve spring seat
7 Shaft support bracket	14 Locknut	21 Valve keeper halves

4   If you're obtaining a short block, which consists of the engine cases, camshaft, lifters, crankshaft and connecting rods all assembled, then the cylinder heads, pistons and cylinders will have to be removed as well. See Engine rebuilding alternatives for additional information regarding the different possibilities to be considered.

5   If you're planning a complete overhaul, the engine must be disassembled and the internal components removed in the basic following order:

Valve covers
Rocker arms and pushrods
Intake and exhaust manifolds/heat exchangers
Cooling shrouds
Cylinder heads
Cylinders and pistons
Separate the crankcase halves
Oil pump
Camshaft and valve lifters
Crankshaft and connecting rod assemblies

6   Before beginning the disassembly and overhaul procedures, make sure the following items are available. Also, refer to Engine overhaul – reassembly sequence for a list of tools and materials needed for engine reassembly.

Common hand tools
Small cardboard boxes and plastic bags for storing parts
Gasket scraper
Crankshaft pulley removal tool
Micrometers
Telescoping gauges
Dial indicator set
Valve spring compressor
Cylinder surfacing hone and electric drill motor (optional)
Piston ring groove cleaning tool (optional)
Tap and die set
Wire brushes
Oil gallery brushes
Cleaning solvent

15   Flywheel/driveplate – removal

Refer to illustrations 15.3a, 15.3b, 15.3c and 15.10

1   After the engine is removed, unbolt the pressure plate and clutch disc as described in Chapter 8 (manual transaxle only). Be sure to mark the relative position of the pressure plate and flywheel to preserve the original balance.

2   The flywheel/driveplate is held by a single center bolt, which is also known as a gland nut. On manual transaxle models, the gland nut incorporates the pilot bearing, and should be replaced whenever the clutch is replaced.

3   The gland nut is very tight and special tools are available to prevent the crankshaft from turning while you loosen or tighten the gland nut **(see illustrations)**. If the special tools are unavailable, obtain a piece of angle iron to lock the flywheel. Install two of the clutch pressure plate bolts and put the angle iron across them **(see illustration). Caution:** *This may bend the bolts, so don't reuse them.*

4   Using a 36 mm (1 7/16 inch) socket with a breaker bar, remove the gland nut and washer. Make a paint mark on a crankshaft dowel and the

15.3a A special holding tool (arrow) is available to prevent the flywheel from turning

15.3b A special holding tool is also available for Automatic Stick Shift driveplates

15.3c If the special tool isn't available, use a section of angle iron to hold the flywheel from turning

2

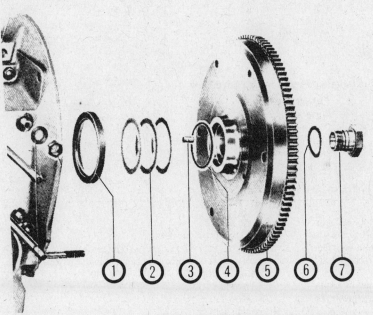

15.10 Flywheel/driveplate components – exploded view

1	Crankshaft oil seal	5	Flywheel	8	Drive plate
2	Shim (3)	6	Spring-type lock washer	9	Spring-type lock washer
3	Steel dowel pin (4)	7	Gland nut with bearing	10	Gland nut without bearing
4	O-ring				

flywheel hub next to the dowel so the flywheel can be reinstalled in the same position. The matching mark on the crankshaft can't be made until the flywheel/driveplate is off. Remember to make a corresponding mark on the crankshaft after the flywheel/driveplate is removed.

5   Rock the flywheel/driveplate on the four dowels which fit into holes in the end of the crankshaft to loosen it, then pull it straight off.

6   When the flywheel/driveplate is off, remove the metal or paper gasket (if equipped) fitted over the four dowel pegs in the flange, noting the type used. Make the alignment mark on the crankshaft next to the painted dowel as described above.

7   The dowels are a precision fit into both the crankshaft and flywheel/driveplate. If any of these are loose fitting there is considerable risk of the flywheel/driveplate working loose, despite the tightness of the gland nut. If

the flywheel/driveplate has worked loose and caused the holes to become elongated, a new flywheel/driveplate and crankshaft will be needed.

8   Examine the starter ring gear teeth; if the teeth are significantly damaged, replace the flywheel/driveplate.

9   Inspect the flywheel/driveplate boss where the oil seal contacts. If a groove is worn, replace the flywheel/driveplate.

10   On 1966 and later models (engine number FO 741385 and later), replace the rubber O-ring seal **(see illustration)** in the flywheel/driveplate.

11   Using a thin screwdriver, carefully pry out the oil seal. Be sure to save the shims.

12   Check crankshaft endplay before final flywheel/driveplate installation (see Section 36).

13   See Sections 37 and 38 for seal and flywheel/driveplate installation.

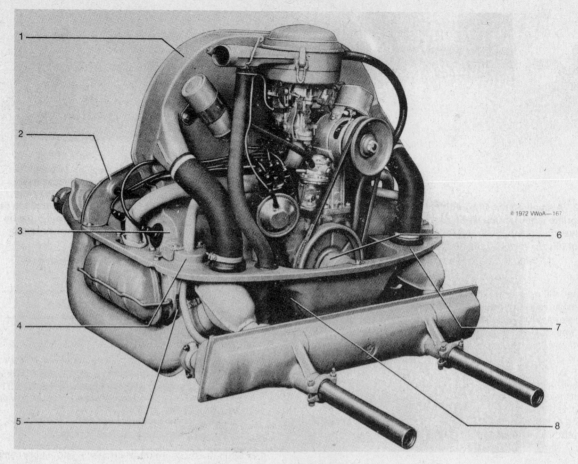

16.2   Cooling shroud details

1	Fan housing	3	Cylinder cover plate	5	Air deflector plate	7	Rear engine cover plate
2	Front engine cover plate	4	Pre-heater pipe sealing plate	6	Crankshaft pulley cover	8	Crankshaft pulley lower plate

---

16   External engine components – removal

Refer to illustration 16.2

1   Remove the alternator/generator and fan housing (see Chapter 5).
2   Remove the front engine cover plate **(see illustration)**.
3   Remove the crankshaft pulley cover.
4   Remove the preheater pipe sealing plate (if equipped).
5   Remove the intake manifold (see Section 4).
6   Remove the muffler and catalytic converter, if equipped (see Chapter 4).
7   Remove the exhaust manifolds/heat exchangers (see Section 5).
8   Remove the rear air deflector plate and the lower portion of the warm air duct.
9   Detach the cylinder cover plates.
10   Remove the crankshaft pulley and the cover plate behind the pulley (see Section 6).
11   Remove the oil cooler (see Chapter 3).
12   Remove the distributor and driveshaft (see Chapter 5).
13   Remove the oil pressure relief and control valves, as equipped (see Section 7).
14   On carbureted models, remove the fuel pump (see Chapter 4).
15   Remove the alternator/generator stand (except 36 horsepower models).

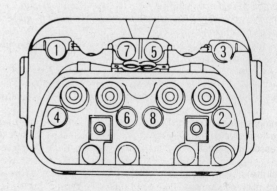

17.2   Loosen the cylinder head nuts in this sequence

17   Cylinder heads – removal

Refer to illustration 17.2

1   Remove the valve covers, rocker arms and pushrods and inspect the components as described in Sections 2 and 3.

18.2 A small plastic bag, with an appropriate label, can be used to store the valve train components so they can be kept together and reinstalled in the original location

18.3 Use a valve spring compressor to compress the spring, then remove the keepers from the valve stem

18.4 If the valve binds in the guide, deburr the area around the tip with a fine file or whetstone

2   Loosen the cylinder head nuts 1/4 to 1/2 turn each only, in the sequence shown **(see illustration)**. Continue releasing each nut a little at a time until they are all loose. When all are removed, the head may be pulled off a little way. **Note:** *Keep the special cylinder head washers together with a piece of wire for reassembly.*
3   Remove the pushrod tubes from between the head and crankcase and make sure the cylinders are disengaged from the head before pulling the head off. When the head is detached, the four pushrod tubes will be freed with the cylinders. On 1965 and earlier models, remove the copper head-to-cylinder seals. If you are only removing the heads, they will stay in position if the crankshaft is not turned. If the crankshaft must be turned, the cylinders should be temporarily tied to the crankcase with wire.

18   Cylinder head – disassembly

Refer to illustrations 18.2, 18.3 and 18.4
Note: *New and rebuilt cylinder heads are commonly available for most engines at dealerships and auto parts stores. Due to the fact that some specialized tools are necessary for the disassembly and inspection procedures, and replacement parts may not be readily available, it may be more practical and economical for the home mechanic to purchase replacement heads rather than taking the time to disassemble, inspect and recondition the originals.*
1   Cylinder head disassembly involves removal of the intake and exhaust valves and related components.
2   Before the valves are removed, arrange to label and store them, along with their related components, so they can be kept separate and reinstalled in the same valve guides they are removed from **(see illustration)**.
3   Compress the springs on the first valve with a spring compressor and remove the keepers **(see illustration)**. Carefully release the valve spring compressor and remove the retainer, the spring and the spring seat (if used).
4   Pull the valve out of the head. If the valve binds in the guide (won't pull through), push it back into the head and deburr the area around the keeper groove with a fine file or whetstone **(see illustration)**.
5   Repeat the procedure for the remaining valves. Remember to keep all the parts for each valve together so they can be reinstalled in the same locations.
6   Once the valves and related components have been removed and stored in an organized manner, the head should be thoroughly cleaned and inspected. If a complete engine overhaul is being done, finish the engine disassembly procedures before beginning the cylinder head cleaning and inspection process.

19   Cylinder head – cleaning and inspection

Refer to illustrations 19.11, 19.12, 19.13 and 19.15
1   Thorough cleaning of the cylinder head(s) and related valve train components, followed by a detailed inspection, will enable you to decide how much valve service work must be done during the engine overhaul. **Note:** *If the engine was severely overheated, the cylinder heads are probably warped (see Step 12).*

Cleaning
2   Scrape all traces of old gasket material and sealing compound off the head-to-intake manifold and exhaust manifold sealing surfaces. Be very careful not to gouge the cylinder head. Special gasket removal solvents that soften gaskets and make removal much easier are available at auto parts stores.
3   Run a stiff wire brush through the various holes to remove deposits that may have formed in them.
4   Run an appropriate size tap into each of the threaded holes to remove corrosion and thread sealant that may be present. If compressed air is available, use it to clear the holes of debris produced by this operation. **Warning:** *Wear eye protection when using compressed air!*
5   Clean the cylinder head with solvent and dry it thoroughly. Compressed air will speed the drying process and ensure that all holes and recessed areas are clean. **Warning:** *Wear eye protection when using compressed air!* **Note:** *Decarbonizing chemicals are available and may prove very useful when cleaning cylinder heads and valve train components. They are very caustic and should be used with caution. Be sure to follow the instructions on the container.*
6   Clean the rocker arms, shafts, adjustment screws, nuts and pushrods with solvent and dry them thoroughly (don't mix them up during the cleaning process). Compressed air will speed the drying process and can be used to clean out the oil passages.
7   Clean all the valve springs, spring seats, keepers and retainers with solvent and dry them thoroughly. Do the components from one valve at a time to avoid mixing up the parts.
8   Scrape off any heavy deposits that may have formed on the valves, then use a motorized wire brush to remove deposits from the valve heads and stems. Again, make sure the valves don't get mixed up.

Inspection
Note: *Be sure to perform all of the following inspection procedures before concluding that machine shop work is required. Make a list of the items that need attention.*

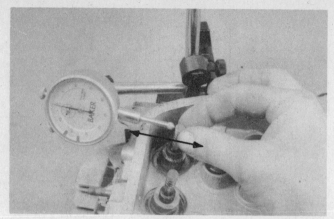

19.11 A dial indicator can be used to determine the valve stem-to-guide clearance – move the valve stem as indicated by the arrows

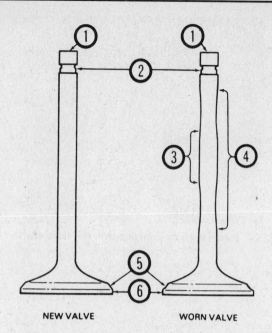

19.12 Check for valve wear at the points shown here

1 *Valve tip*	4 *Stem (most worn area)*
2 *Keeper groove*	5 *Valve face*
3 *Stem (least worn area)*	6 *Margin*

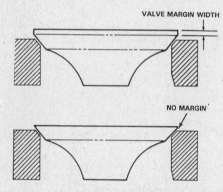

19.13 The margin width on each valve must be as specified (if no margin exists, the valve cannot be reused)

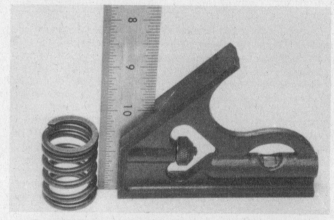

19.15 Check each valve spring for squareness

Cylinder head

9 Inspect the heads very carefully for cracks, evidence of coolant leakage and other damage. If cracks are found, check with an automotive machine shop concerning repair. If repair isn't possible, a replacement cylinder head should be obtained.

10 Examine the valve seats in each of the combustion chambers. If they're pitted, cracked or burned, the head will require valve service that's beyond the scope of the home mechanic.

11 Check the valve stem-to-guide clearance by measuring the lateral movement of the valve stem with a dial indicator attached securely to the head **(see illustration)**. The valve must be in the guide and approximately 1/16-inch off the seat. The total valve stem movement indicated by the gauge needle must be divided by two to obtain the actual clearance. After this is done, if there's still some doubt regarding the condition of the valve guides they should be checked by an automotive machine shop (the cost should be minimal).

Valves

12 Carefully inspect each valve face for uneven wear, deformation, cracks, pits and burned areas **(see illustration)**. Check the valve stem for scuffing and galling and the neck for cracks. Rotate the valve and check for any obvious indication that it's bent. Look for pits and excessive wear on the end of the stem. The presence of any of these conditions indicates the need for valve service by an automotive machine shop.

13 Measure the margin width on each valve **(see illustration)**. Any valve with a margin narrower than listed in this Chapter's Specifications will have to be replaced with a new one.

Valve components

14 Check each valve spring for wear (on the ends) and pits. The tension of all springs should be checked with a special fixture before deciding that they're suitable for use in a rebuilt engine (take the springs to an automotive machine shop for this check).

15 Stand each spring on a flat surface and check it for squareness **(see illustration)**. If any of the springs are distorted or sagged, replace all of them with new parts.

16 Check the spring retainers and keepers for obvious wear and cracks. Any questionable parts should be replaced with new ones, as extensive damage will occur if they fail during engine operation.

Rocker arm components

17 Check the rocker arm faces (the areas that contact the pushrod ends and valve stems) for pits, wear, galling, score marks and rough spots. Check the rocker arm pivot contact areas as well. Look for cracks in each rocker arm, adjuster screw and nut.

18 Inspect the pushrod ends for scuffing and excessive wear. Roll each pushrod on a flat surface, like a piece of plate glass, to determine if it's bent.

21.4a Install the stem seal ring over the valve stem

19 Check the rocker arm studs or bolt holes in the cylinder heads for damaged threads and/or secure installation.
20 Any damaged or excessively worn parts must be replaced with new ones.
21 If the inspection process indicates that the valve components are in generally poor condition and worn beyond the limits specified, which is usually the case in an engine that's being overhauled, reassemble the valves in the cylinder head and refer to Section 20 for valve servicing recommendations.

20 Valves – servicing

1 Because of the complex nature of the job and the special tools and equipment needed, servicing of the valves, the valve seats and the valve guides, commonly known as a valve job, should be done by a professional.
2 The home mechanic can remove and disassemble the head, do the initial cleaning and inspection, then reassemble and deliver it to a dealer service department or an automotive machine shop for the actual service work. Doing the inspection will enable you to see what condition the head and valvetrain components are in and will ensure that you know what work and new parts are required when dealing with an automotive machine shop.
3 The dealer service department, or automotive machine shop, will remove the valves and springs, recondition or replace the valves and valve seats, recondition the valve guides, check and replace the valve springs, spring retainers and keepers (as necessary), replace the valve seals with new ones, reassemble the valve components and make sure the installed spring height is correct. The cylinder head gasket surface will also be resurfaced if it's warped.
4 After the valve job has been performed by a professional, the head will be in like-new condition. When the head is returned, be sure to clean it again before installation on the engine to remove any metal particles and abrasive grit that may still be present from the valve service or head resurfacing operations. Use compressed air, if available, to blow out all the oil holes and passages.

21 Cylinder head – reassembly

Refer to illustrations 21.4a, 21.4b and 21.5
1 Regardless of whether or not the head was sent to an automotive repair shop for valve servicing, make sure it's clean before beginning reassembly.
2 If the head was sent out for valve servicing, the valves and related components will already be in place.
3 Beginning at one end of the head, lubricate and install the first valve. Apply moly-base grease or clean engine oil to the valve stem.

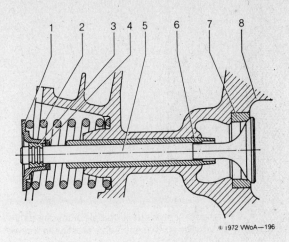

© 1972 VWoA—196

21.4b Valve assembly cross-section

1	*Spring retainer*	5	*Valve*
2	*Valve spring*	6	*Valve guide*
3	*Valve keeper*	7	*Valve seat insert*
4	*Stem seal ring*	8	*Cylinder head*

21.5 Apply a small dab of grease to each keeper as shown here before installation – it'll hold them in place on the valve stem as the spring is released

4 Drop the spring seat or shim(s), if equipped, over the valve guide and set the valve spring and retainer in place. On 1966 and later models, install the stem seal rings **(see illustrations)**.
5 Compress the springs with a valve spring compressor and carefully install the keepers in the upper groove, then slowly release the compressor and make sure the keepers seat properly. Apply a small dab of grease to each keeper to hold it in place if necessary **(see illustration)**.
6 Repeat the procedure for the remaining valves. Be sure to return the components to their original locations – don't mix them up!
Note: *1965 and earlier models don't use a stem seal ring*

22 Cylinders, pistons and rings – removal and inspection

Refer to illustrations 22.1a, 22.1b, 22.2a, 22.2b, 22.2c, 22.3, 22.6a, 22.6b, 22.10, 22.11, 22.12a, 22.12b and 22.12c
1 The cylinders may be removed after the cylinder heads are off, simply by sliding them over the pistons **(see illustration)**. Be sure that each one is marked so you know which number cylinder it came from and which way faces toward the flywheel. A good way is to temporarily paint the number and an arrow pointing toward the flywheel end on the crown before remov-

22.1a The cylinders are pulled off over the pistons and slipped over the studs – be sure the pistons are marked as shown

22.1b Mark the pistons and cylinders with a number to indicate which cylinder position they came from and an arrow toward the flywheel

22.2a Remove the circlip from one side of the piston . . .

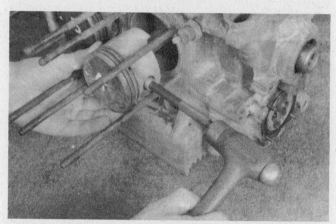

22.2b . . . and push the wrist pin out from the other side

al **(see illustration)**. After the pistons are removed, scratch the numbers in the tops before cleaning them. **Caution:** *If the crankshaft is turned after removing the cylinder, the piston skirts can be damaged by hitting the crankcase.*

2   To remove the pistons, remove the circlip from one side of the piston boss and push out the wrist pin **(see illustrations)**. Do not use great force to drive out the wrist pin if it's stuck – you may bend a connecting rod. If it binds, warm the piston with an electric hair dryer. It is only necessary to push out the pin far enough to enable the piston to be released from the connecting rod. After the piston is removed, carefully clean the top of the crown and look for identifying marks which indicate the diameter and the flywheel end **(see illustration)**.

3   The piston rings may be removed from the pistons by carefully spreading the ends of each ring and then slipping if over the top of the piston **(see illustration)**. New piston rings should be installed whenever the engine is disassembled.

4   Before the inspection process can be carried out, the pistons and cylinders must be cleaned.

5   Scrape all traces of carbon from the top of the piston. A hand held wire brush or a piece of fine emery cloth can be used once the majority of the deposits have been scraped away. **Caution:** *Do not use a wire brush mounted in a drill to remove deposits from the pistons. The piston material is soft and may be eroded away by the wire brush.*

6   Use a piston ring groove cleaning tool to remove carbon deposits from the ring grooves. If a tool isn't available, a piece broken off the old ring will do the job **(see illustrations)**. Be very careful to remove only the carbon deposits – don't remove any metal and do not nick or scratch the sides of the ring grooves.

7   Once the deposits have been removed, clean the pistons and rods with solvent and dry them with compressed air, if available. Make sure the

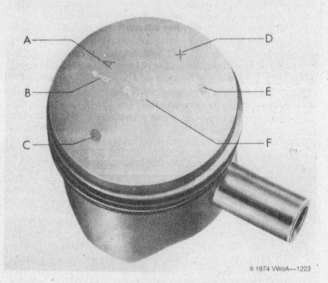

© 1974 VWoA—1223

22.2c Piston crown markings

A   Index letter of piston part number
B   Arrow that must point toward flywheel
C   Paint spot indicating matching cylinder size (blue, pink, green)
D   Weight grading (+ or -)
E   Paint spot indicating weight grading (brown for – weight, gray for + weight
F   Piston size in mm

22.3   Expand the rings with a special tool and slip them over the piston

bosses and at the ring lands.

9   Look for scoring and scuffing on the thrust faces of the skirt, holes in the piston crown and burned areas at the edge of the crown. If the skirt is scored or scuffed, the engine may have been suffering from overheating and/or abnormal combustion, which caused excessively high operating temperatures. The cooling and lubrication systems should be checked thoroughly. A hole in the piston crown is an indication that abnormal combustion (preignition) was occurring. Burned areas at the edge of the piston crown are usually evidence of spark knock (detonation). If any of the above problems exist, the causes must be corrected or the damage will occur again. The causes may include intake air leaks, incorrect fuel/air mixture, incorrect ignition timing and EGR system malfunctions.

10   Measure the piston ring side clearance by laying a new piston ring in each ring groove and slipping a feeler gauge in beside it **(see illustration)**. Check the clearance at three or four locations around each groove. Be sure to use the correct ring for each groove – they are different. If the side clearance is greater than the figure listed in this Chapter's Specifications, new pistons will have to be used.

11   Check the piston-to-bore clearance by measuring the bore and the piston diameter. Make sure the pistons and bores are correctly matched. Measure the piston across the skirt, at a 90-degree angle to and in line with the piston pin **(see illustration)**. Do this for each piston and record the results.

12   Measure the cylinder bores with an inside micrometer or bore gauge across the bore of the cylinder at right angles to the axis of the wrist pin **(see illustrations)**. Use the largest measurement obtained. Subtract the piston diameter from the bore diameter to obtain the clearance. If it's great-

oil return holes in the back sides of the ring grooves are clear. **Warning:** *Wear eye protection.*

8   Carefully inspect each piston for cracks around the skirt, at the pin

22.6a   The piston ring grooves can be cleaned with a special tool, as shown here, . . .

22.6b   . . . or a section of a broken ring

22.10   Measure the side clearance of each piston ring

22.11   Measure the piston diameter near the bottom of the skirt

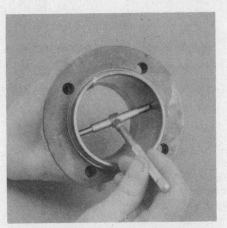

22.12a   Use a bore gauge to check cylinder wear

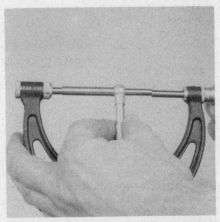

22.12b   The gauge is then measured with a micrometer to determine the bore size

2

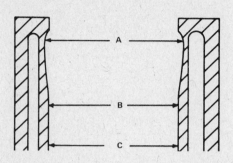

22.12c   Measure the diameter of each cylinder just under the wear ridge (A), at the center (B) and at the bottom (C)

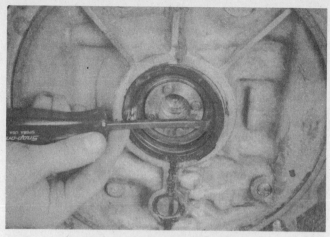

23.2   Carefully pry out the oil seal

23.3a   Remove the three crankshaft endplay shims

23.3b   Some models have paper or metal shims on the end of the crankshaft

er than that listed in this Chapter's Specifications, the cylinders will have to be rebored or replaced and new pistons and rings installed.

13   If the pistons and cylinder walls aren't damaged or worn excessively, and if the cylinders don't need to be rebored, new pistons won't be necessary. New piston rings, however, should always be used when an engine is rebuilt.

14   Factory replacement pistons are available in two different weight groups, identified by a "+" or "-" marked on the crown of the piston. This denotes a lighter (-) or heavier (+) weight by up to 10 grams. Pistons should be matched to retain balance. For best results, have an automotive machine shop balance the moving parts in the engine. **Note:** *1972 and later model pistons have a concave top and are not interchangeable with earlier models.*

15   Factory replacement wrist pins are available in two different diameters. The wrist pins may be identified by black or white painted color codes. The pistons are marked "W" for white and "S" for black. Be sure the codes match. Do not try to install larger pins to compensate for worn bushings.

23   Crankshaft – removal

Refer to illustrations 23.2, 23.3a, 23.3b, 23.5, 23.7, 23.9, 23.11a, 23.11b, 23.12a, 23.12b and 23.13

1   With the pistons, cylinders and flywheel/driveplate removed, prop the crankcase on its left side. The connecting rods may be left in place for now as these will be easier to remove after the crankcase is split.

2   Carefully pry the oil seal out of the crankcase with a screwdriver **(see illustration)**.

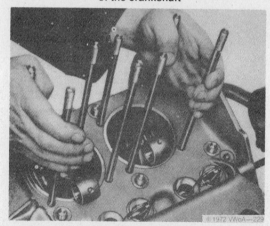

23.5   Lift the crankcase half by the studs

3   After the oil seal is removed, remove the three shims which fit between the flywheel hub and the flange on the front main bearing. These set the amount of crankshaft endplay – make sure they are not lost or damaged. Also check for a metal or paper shim on the end of the crankshaft **(see illustration)**. Note the type of material used, then remove it. Be sure to use a new shim of the same type on reassembly.

4   The two crankcase halves are held together by large and small studs with nuts and two bolts with nuts. Remove all the smaller nuts followed by

23.7 Lift the camshaft out of the crankcase half

23.9 Carefully lift the crankshaft out

23.11a Carefully remove the
Woodruff key

23.11b Remove the circlip

23.12a Mark the cylinder number on the
rods with a sharp punch – two dots for
number two cylinder, etc.

the large nuts. The crankshaft and camshaft are held between the crank-case halves and you do not want either to fall out. Keep the crankcase tilted to the left so they will both rest in that half.

5   Separate the two halves by tapping lightly at the projecting lugs on the left half with a soft-face mallet. This progressive gentle tapping at the four corners will gradually increase the gap between the two until the right-hand half will be free enough to lift off over the studs **(see illustration)**. When the right-hand half has moved out a little way, the valve lifters may begin to fall out. Try to get hold of these and arrange them in a numbered carton so that they may be put back in the same bore. Special spring clips are available to hold the lifters in place – use these if possible.

6   Put the crankcase half in a safe place.

7   Lift out the camshaft from the other half of the crankcase **(see illus-tration)**. The bearings may be left in position. If they fall out, note where they came from. One half of one bearing is flanged to take the camshaft end thrust. **Note:** *On 1965 and earlier models, the bearings are integral with the crankcase.*

8   The valve lifters from the left half of the crankcase may now be taken out. Keep them in order so they may be replaced in the same bores.

9   The crankshaft can now be lifted out **(see illustration)**. The halves of the number 2 bearing should be removed from their locations in each half of the crankcase. Note that each bearing is located by a dowel. These normally remain in the crankcase but if any have come out with the bearings, retrieve them now before they get lost.

10   Three of the four main bearings may be removed as soon as the crankshaft is taken from the crankcase. Number 1 is a circular flanged bearing which is slipped off the flywheel end. Number 2 is the split bearing and number 4 is a narrow circular bearing which can be drawn off the crankshaft pulley end. Number 3 however, is held by the helical gear which drives the camshaft. In front of this gear is a spacer and the distributor dri-

23.12b The rods have numbers such as this on them – be sure
they are kept together

veshaft worm gear, an oil slinger disc and Woodruff key.

11   To remove the number 3 main bearing, tap the Woodruff key out of the shaft **(see illustration)** and keep it safe. Take off the oil slinger disc and remove the circlip **(see illustration)**.

12   Mark the rods with a sharp punch **(see illustration)** to indicate the cyl-inder it goes to. Note that each rod also has a number **(see illustration)**. Keep them together with the numbers on the cap and rod adjacent.

13   The two gears are a tight, keyed fit onto the shaft and the only way to get them off is by using a puller which grips completely behind the helical

23.13　Use a puller to remove the gears

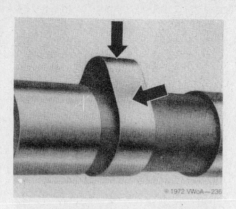

24.2　Look for wear on the lobes at these points (arrows)

24.4　Check the diameter of each camshaft bearing journal to pinpoint excessive wear and out-of-round conditions

25.1　Use a wire or stiff plastic bristle brush to clean the oil passages in the crankshaft

25.3　Rubbing a penny lengthwise on each journal will reveal its condition – if copper rubs off and is embedded in the crankshaft, the journals should be reground

25.4　The oil holes should be chamfered so sharp edges don't gouge or scratch the new bearings

gear **(see illustration)** so that both the gears and the spacer can be drawn off together. If you have difficulty in fitting the puller in the small gap between the bearing and gear, do not try to pull off the gear by gripping only against the gear teeth. You may either chip them or break them off. If necessary, take the crankshaft to a dealer service department, an automotive machine shop or other repair shop.

14　When you start applying pressure, if considerable force is needed, clamp the legs of the puller to prevent them spreading and possibly flying off. Some pullers have a clamp incorporated for such a purpose. **Caution:** *Do not try to hammer the gears off.*

15　With the two gears removed, the bearing can be slipped off the shaft.

16　Refer to Section 25 for crankshaft inspection procedures.

24　Camshaft and valve lifters – inspection

Refer to illustrations 24.2 and 24.4

1　After the crankcase is separated, the valve lifters should be checked in their bores in the crankcase and no noticeable side-play should be apparent. The faces of the valve lifters which contact the camshaft lobes should also have a smooth, shiny surface. If they show signs of pitting or wear they should be replaced.

2　Examine the lobes of the camshaft for any indications of flat spots, pitting or wear **(see illustration)**.

3　Inspect the camshaft bearing journals and the bearing surfaces in the crankcase the same way as those of the crankshaft. **Note:** *The camshaft bearings on 1966 and later models are replaceable.*

4　Measure the diameter of the camshaft bearing journals with a micrometer **(see illustration)** and record the results. Subtract this measurement from the bearing inside diameter listed in this Chapter's Specifications to determine the bearing clearance. Do this for each bearing.

5　The gear which is riveted to the end of the camshaft must be tight and the teeth should be examined for any signs of breakage or excessive wear. Replace as necessary. **Note:** *The camshaft driven gear is available in several pitch diameters to allow backlash adjustment. Always replace the drive gear whenever the driven gear is replaced.*

6　Always replace the camshaft and lifters as a set. **Note:** *Earlier model camshafts have gears retained by three rivets, later model camshafts have four rivets. These are not interchangeable.*

25　Crankshaft – inspection

Refer to illustrations 25.1, 25.3, 25.4 and 25.6

1　Clean the crankshaft with solvent and dry it with compressed air, if available. **Warning:** *Wear eye protection.* Be sure to clean the oil holes with a stiff brush **(see illustration)** and flush them with solvent.

2　Check the main and connecting rod bearing journals for uneven wear, scoring, pits and cracks.

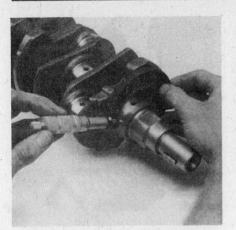

25.6 Measure the diameter of each crankshaft journal at several points to detect taper and out-of-round conditions

26.6 Measure the inside diameter of each bearing

27.3 Hold the piston and connecting rod and try to detect play

3   Rub a penny across each journal several times **(see illustration)**. If a journal picks up copper from the penny, it's too rough and must be reground.

4   Remove all burrs from the crankshaft oil holes with a stone, file or scraper **(see illustration)**.

5   Check the rest of the crankshaft for cracks and other damage. It should be magnafluxed to reveal hidden cracks – an automotive machine shop will handle the procedure.

6   Using a micrometer, measure the diameter of the main and connecting rod journals and compare the results to this Chapter's Specifications **(see illustration)**. By measuring the diameter at a number of points around each journal's circumference, you'll be able to determine whether or not the journal is out-of-round. Take the measurement at each end of the journal, near the crank throws, to determine if the journal is tapered.

7   If the crankshaft journals are damaged, tapered, out-of-round or worn beyond the limits given in the Specifications, have the crankshaft reground by an automotive machine shop. Be sure to use the correct size bearing inserts if the crankshaft is reconditioned or the crankcase is align bored. Such bearings will normally be supplied with a reground crankshaft. If the crankshaft does not need to be reground, make sure the bearings obtained are exactly the same dimensions as those removed. This can be verified by checking the markings on the back of the bearings to determine if they are standard or undersize. **Note:** *The crankcase may have been align bored to correct for warpage and/or the crankshaft may have been reground already. In either case, special oversize bearings are required.*

8   Refer to Section 29 and examine the main and rod bearing inserts.

26 Crankcase – cleaning and inspection

Refer to illustration 26.6

1   Inspect the crankcase for cracks or any other form of damage. The two mating edges must be free from dents, scratches and burrs which could affect their precise alignment when both are clamped together.

2   Check the crankshaft bearing locations for any signs of damage or distortion. In the engine has been run with worn out main bearings, it is possible that the bearings will be 'hammered' into the crankcase by the vibration of the crankshaft. If this occurs, new bearings will not be a tight fit in their crankcase locations. In such instances the crankcase must be align bored or replaced.

3   Make sure that the camshaft bearing surfaces are in good condition. On 1965 and earlier models, if the bearing surfaces are rough, replace the crankcase.

4   The studs in the crankcase must be tight in their holes. Any sign of looseness due to worn threads in the crankcase is repairable. Have an automotive machine shop install threaded inserts in the crankcase.

5   Determine what size bearings are probably needed from the measurements done in Section 25. Then verify this by temporarily installing the crankshaft bearings in the crankcase halves without the crankshaft. Refer to Section 32 for information on crankcase assembly. Do not use sealant.

6   Working through the openings in the crankcase, measure the inside diameters of the bearings **(see illustration)** and record the results. Subtract the crankshaft journal outside diameter from the bearing inside diameter to determine the main bearing clearance. Compare this figure to that listed in this Chapter's Specifications to decide if the bearing clearances are within factory tolerances.

7   If the clearances are within the "new" range, continue engine assembly. If the clearances are too small or too loose, try a different set of bearings or consult an automotive machine shop for corrective action.

27 Connecting rods – inspection

Refer to illustrations 27.3 and 27.5

1   Before the inspection process can be carried out, clean the connecting rods with solvent and dry them with compressed air, if available. **Warning:** *Wear eye protection.*

2   Check the connecting rods, bolts and nuts for cracks and other damage. On 1965 and earlier models, discard the old bolts. On 1966 and later models (engine number FO451421 – on), do not remove the bolts from the rods for inspection; if these bolts are defective, replace the rod. Temporarily remove the rod caps, lift out the old bearing inserts, wipe the rod and cap bearing surfaces clean and inspect them for nicks, gouges and scratches. After checking the rods, temporarily reinstall the old bearings, slip the caps into place and tighten the nuts finger tight. **Caution:** *On 1971 and earlier models, the connecting rod nuts could be staked in place with a hammer and chisel. If the nuts were staked in place, do not reuse them.* **Note:** *If the engine is being rebuilt because of a connecting rod knock, be sure to install new rods.*

3   Temporarily install the pistons and wrist pins onto their respective connecting rods without the circlips. Check the piston-to-rod clearance by twisting the piston and rod in opposite directions **(see illustration)**. Any noticeable play indicates excessive wear, which must be corrected. The pistons and connecting rods should be taken to an automotive machine shop to have them resized and new bushings installed. Have the connecting rods checked for bend and twist at the same time.

4   Factory replacement connecting rods are available in two different weight groups, identified by painted color code markings. Black or gray indicates heavier and white or brown indicates lighter weight by up to 10 grams. Connecting rods should be matched within ten grams to retain balance. For best results, have an automotive machine shop magnaflux and balance the moving parts of the engine.

2

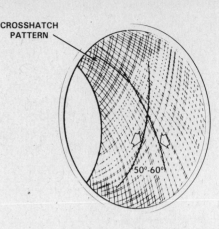

CROSSHATCH PATTERN

50°-60°

27.5   Measure connecting rod endplay with a feeler gauge

28.2a   If this is the first time you've ever honed cylinders, you'll get better results with a "bottle brush" hone than you will with a traditional spring-loaded hone

28.2b   The cylinder hone should leave a smooth, crosshatch pattern with the lines intersecting at approximately a 60-degree angle

5   Measure connecting rod endplay **(see illustration)** and compare the results to the dimensions listed in this Chapter's Specifications.

28   Cylinder honing

Refer to illustrations 28.2a and 28.2b

1   If the original cylinders are being reinstalled on the engine, the cylinder bores must be honed so the new piston rings will seat correctly and provide the best possible combustion chamber seal. **Note:** *If you don't have the tools or don't want to tackle the honing operation, most automotive machine shops will do it for a reasonable fee.*

2   Two types of cylinder hones are commonly available – the flex hone or "bottle brush" type and the more traditional surfacing hone with spring-loaded stones. Both will do the job, but for the less experienced mechanic the "bottle brush" hone will probably be easier to use. You'll also need some kerosene or honing oil, rags and an electric drill motor. Proceed as follows:

   a) Mount the hone in the drill motor, compress the stones and slip it into the first cylinder. Be sure to wear safety goggles or a face shield!

   b) Lubricate the cylinder with plenty of honing oil, turn on the drill and move the hone up-and-down in the cylinder at a pace that will produce a fine crosshatch pattern on the cylinder walls. Ideally, the crosshatch lines should intersect at approximately a 60-degree angle **(see illustrations)**. Be sure to use plenty of lubricant and don't take off any more material than is absolutely necessary to produce the desired finish. **Note:** *Piston ring manufacturers may specify a smaller crosshatch angle than the traditional 60-degrees – read and follow any instructions included with the new rings.*

   c) Don't withdraw the hone from the cylinder while it's running. Instead, shut off the drill and continue moving the hone up-and-down in the cylinder until it comes to a complete stop, then compress the stones and withdraw the hone. If you're using a "bottle brush" type hone, stop the drill motor, then turn the chuck in the normal direction of rotation while withdrawing the hone from the cylinder.

   d) Wipe the oil out of the cylinder and repeat the procedure for the remaining cylinders.

3   The cylinders must be washed again very thoroughly with warm, soapy water to remove all traces of the abrasive grit produced during the honing operation. **Note:** *The bores can be considered clean when a lint-free white cloth dampened with clean engine oil used to wipe them out doesn't pick up any more honing residue, which will show up as gray areas on the cloth.*

CRATERS OR POCKETS

BRIGHT (POLISHED) SECTIONS

FATIGUE FAILURE

IMPROPER SEATING

SCRATCHES

DIRT IMBEDDED INTO BEARING MATERIAL

OVERLAY WIPED OUT

SCRATCHED BY DIRT

LACK OF OIL

OVERLAY GONE FROM ENTIRE SURFACE

RADIUS RIDE

TAPERED JOURNAL

RADIUS RIDE

29.1   Typical bearing failures

4   After rinsing, dry the cylinders and apply a coat of light rust preventive oil to all machined surfaces. Wrap the cylinders in plastic to keep them clean and set them aside until reassembly.

29   Engine bearings – inspection

Refer to illustration 29.1

1   Even though the main and connecting rod bearings (and camshaft bearings on 1966 and later models) should be replaced with new ones during the engine overhaul, the old bearings should be retained for close examination, as they may reveal valuable information about the condition of the engine **(see illustration)**.

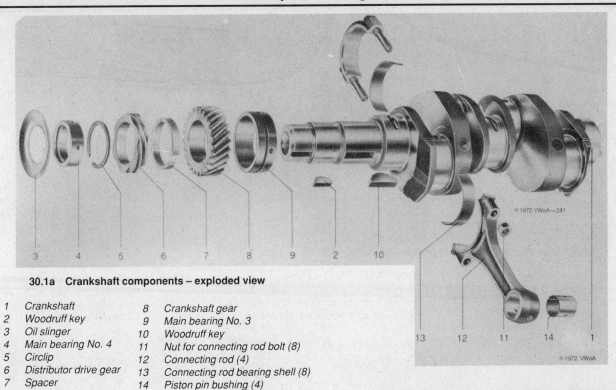

30.1a   Crankshaft components – exploded view

1   Crankshaft
2   Woodruff key
3   Oil slinger
4   Main bearing No. 4
5   Circlip
6   Distributor drive gear
7   Spacer
8   Crankshaft gear
9   Main bearing No. 3
10   Woodruff key
11   Nut for connecting rod bolt (8)
12   Connecting rod (4)
13   Connecting rod bearing shell (8)
14   Piston pin bushing (4)

2   Bearing failure occurs because of lack of lubrication, the presence of dirt or other foreign particles, overloading the engine and corrosion. Regardless of the cause of bearing failure, it must be corrected before the engine is reassembled to prevent it from happening again.

3   When examining the bearings, remove them from the crankcase, the crankshaft, the connecting rods and the rod caps and lay them out on a clean surface in the same general position as their location in the engine. This will enable you to match any bearing problems with the corresponding crankshaft or camshaft journal.

4   Dirt and other foreign particles get into the engine in a variety of ways. It may be left in the engine during assembly, or it may pass through filters or the PCV system. It may get into the oil, and from there into the bearings. Metal chips from machining operations and normal engine wear are often present. Abrasives are sometimes left in engine components after reconditioning, especially when parts are not thoroughly cleaned using the proper cleaning methods. Whatever the source, these foreign objects often end up embedded in the soft bearing material and are easily recognized. Large particles will not embed in the bearing and will score or gouge the bearing and journal. The best prevention for this cause of bearing failure is to clean all parts thoroughly and keep everything spotlessly clean during engine assembly. Frequent and regular engine oil changes and filter servicing are also recommended.

5   Lack of lubrication (or lubrication breakdown) has a number of interrelated causes. Excessive heat (which thins the oil), overloading (which squeezes the oil from the bearing face) and oil leakage or throw off (from excessive bearing clearances, worn oil pump or high engine speeds) all contribute to lubrication breakdown.
Blocked oil passages, which usually are the result of misaligned oil holes in a bearing shell, will also oil starve a bearing and destroy it. When lack of lubrication is the cause of bearing failure, the bearing material is wiped or extruded from the steel backing of the bearing. Temperatures may increase to the point where the metal backing turns blue from overheating.

6   Driving habits can have a definite effect on bearing life. Full throttle, low speed operation (lugging the engine) puts very high loads on bearings, which tends to squeeze out the oil film. These loads cause the bearings to flex, which produces fine cracks in the bearing face (fatigue failure). Eventually the bearing material will loosen in pieces and tear away from the steel backing. Short trip driving leads to corrosion of bearings because in-

30.1b   Lubricate the journal and slip the bearing into place with the offset hole (arrow) toward the flywheel end

sufficient engine heat is produced to drive off the condensed water and corrosive gases. These products collect in the engine oil, forming acid and sludge. As the oil is carried to the engine bearings, the acid attacks and corrodes the bearing material.

7   Incorrect bearing installation during engine assembly will lead to bearing failure as well. Tight fitting bearings leave insufficient bearing oil clearance and will result in oil starvation. Dirt or foreign particles trapped behind a bearing insert result in high spots on the bearing which lead to failure.

30   Crankshaft – reassembly

Refer to illustrations 30.1a, 30.1b, 30.2, 30.3, 30.4, 30.5, 30.6, 30.7, 30.8 and 30.9

1   With the crankshaft thoroughly clean and the oil passages blown out, lubricate number 3 journal with clean engine oil or assembly lube. Number 3 main bearing is one of the two large one-piece circular bearings and does not have a flange on it **(see illustration)**. Install this bearing with the

30.2   Install the camshaft drive gear with the chamfer facing the flywheel end

30.3   Slip the spacer in place

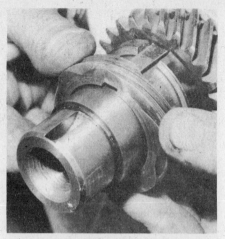

30.4   Carefully guide the distributor drive gear onto the crankshaft

30.5   Install the circlip in the groove next to the distributor drive gear

30.6   Install the number four bearing with the offset hole toward the flywheel end

30.7   Place the oil slinger on the crankshaft with the concave face out

30.8   Gently tap the Woodruff key into the keyway

30.9   Lubricate and install the flanged thrust main bearing on the flywheel end of the crankshaft with the offset hole toward the flywheel

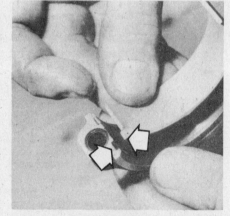

31.2   The bearing tang must engage the notch (arrows)

small offset dowel hole toward the flywheel end of the crankshaft **(see illustration).**

2   Next, install the camshaft drive gear. Before putting it on, examine the surfaces of the crankshaft and key and the bore of the gear. If there are signs of slight scoring from gear removal, clean it up with a very fine file. This will avoid a tendency to bind on installation. The gear keyway should be aligned with the key in the shaft and the chamfered edge of the gear bore must face the flywheel end **(see illustration).** Heat the gear to 176-degrees F. The gear may be difficult to start on the shaft, so keep it square and make sure that the keyway is precisely lined up. Press it on with firm, evenly spaced strikes, using a mallet against a pipe slipped over the shaft. Keep it square, particularly at the start, and, drive it on until fully seated. The crankshaft should be clamped between padded vise jaws for this operation. **Warning:** *Wear thick gloves to protect your hands from the hot gear.*

3   Next, install the spacer ring **(see illustration).**

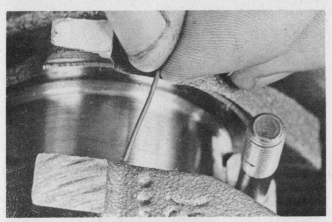

31.3   Lay the Plastigage strips on each rod bearing journal, parallel to the crankshaft centerline

31.4   Install the connecting rods onto the crankshaft

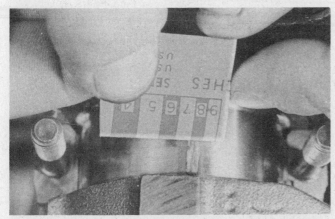

31.5   Measuring the width of the crushed Plastigage to determine the rod bearing oil clearance (be sure to use the correct scale – standard and metric ones are included)

31.7   Assemble the connecting rods on the crankshaft with the forging marks (arrows) up

4   Install the distributor drive gear. It can be installed either way, and the gear should be carefully moved up to the spacer without damaging the teeth **(see illustration)**. Heat the gear to 176-degrees F. Press it on with firm, evenly spaced strikes, using a mallet against a pipe slipped over the shaft. **Warning:** *Wear thick gloves to protect your hands from the hot gear.*
5   Fit the retaining circlip and make sure it fits snugly in its groove **(see illustration)**. If it will not go in the groove, then one of the gears has not been fully seated onto the crankshaft.
6   Lubricate and install the number four main bearing over the end journal, once again making sure that the offset dowel hole is towards the flywheel end of the crankshaft **(see illustration)**. Do not confuse the dowel hole with the circular groove machined in the outside of this bearing.
7   Next, install the oil slinger with the concave face out **(see illustration)**.
8   Gently tap the Woodruff key into the keyway **(see illustration)**.
9   Lubricate the flanged thrust bearing with clean engine oil or assembly lube and install with the offset hole toward the flywheel **(see illustration)**.

31   Connecting rods – installation

Refer to illustrations 31.2, 31.3, 31.4, 31.5, 31.7 and 31.9
1   Position the crankshaft on a clean workbench with the flywheel end away from you.
2   Wipe the bearing surfaces of the connecting rods perfectly clean and install the bearings with the tangs engaging in the corresponding notches in the rods. Install the other halves of the bearings to the cap in the same fashion **(see illustration)**.

3   The connecting rod bearing oil clearance must be checked before the rod is permanently bolted into place. Cut a piece of the appropriate size Plastigage slightly shorter than the width of the connecting rod bearing and lay it in place, parallel to the with the journal axis **(see illustration)**.
4   Temporarily install the connecting rods onto their respective journals on the crankshaft **(see illustration)** without lubrication. Place the rod cap with the numbers on the cap and rod next to each other. Install the nuts/ bolts and tighten them to the torque listed in this Chapter's Specifications, working up to it in three steps. Use a thin wall socket to avoid erroneous torque readings that can result if the socket becomes wedged between the rod cap and nut. Do each rod, beginning at one end of the crankshaft and working toward the other end. **Caution:** *Do not rotate the crankshaft or rod at any time during this operation.*
5   Remove the rod cap, being very careful not to disturb the Plastigage. Compare the width of the crushed Plastigage to the scale printed on the Plastigage envelope to obtain the oil clearance **(see illustration)**. Compare it to the clearance listed in this Chapter's Specifications to make sure the clearance is correct. If the clearance is not as specified, the bearing inserts may be the wrong size (which means other ones will be required).
6   Carefully scrape all traces of the Plastigage material off the rod journals and the bearing face. Be very careful not to scratch the bearing – use your fingernail or the edge of a credit card.
7   Apply oil or assembly lube to the crankshaft journals and slip the connecting rods back into place on the crankshaft. Arrange the connecting rods on the crankshaft with numbers 1 and 2 on the right, number 1 nearest the flywheel end, and number 3 and 4 on the left with number 3 nearest

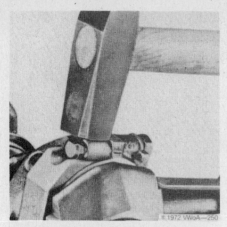

31.9   Lightly tap the shoulders of each rod with a soft-face hammer to seat the bearings

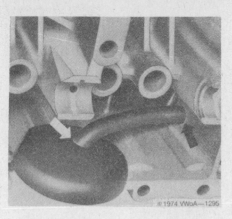

32.1   Check the oil pump suction tube for security at these points (arrows)

32.5a   Align the hole in the bearing with the dowel

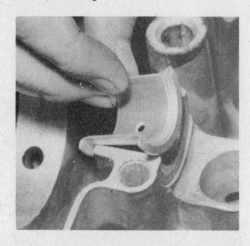

32.5b   The camshaft thrust bearing (with flanges) fits in the crankcase at the end opposite from the flywheel

32.6   Hold the crankshaft like this and slip the number three and four connecting rods through the crankcase openings

the flywheel end. The numbers on each connecting rod and cap must face down for each cylinder. There is a forging mark on each rod on the opposite side which faces up **(see illustration)**. The first throw on the crankshaft from the flywheel end is number 3. Match the two numbers on the shoulders of the connecting rods and caps. Install the cap and nuts finger tight.

8   Tighten the connecting rod nuts/bolts to the torque listed in this Chapter's Specifications. Again, work up to the torque in three steps.

9   When the cap bolts are fully tightened, lightly tap the shoulders of each rod with a mallet to relieve any tension between the mating surfaces of the cap and the rod **(see illustration)**. Also, peen the ridge of each nut into the notch in the connecting rod, using a hammer and a small punch. The connecting rods should be able to rotate around the journals under their own weight. There should be no tight or loose spots.

10   The crankshaft and connecting rod assembly is now ready for installation in the crankcase.

32   Crankcase – reassembly

Refer to illustrations 32.1, 32.5a, 32.5b, 32.6, 32.7a, 32.7b, 32.7c, 32.10, 32.11, 32.16 and 32.17

1   Both crankcase halves must be perfectly clean, inside and out. All traces of sealant must be removed from the mating faces, the base of the studs, and the chamfers in the stud hole mating faces. The oil pump suc-

tion tube **(see illustration)** must be tightly installed; if it's loose it must be peened in position as necessary.

2   Place the left half of the crankcase on the bench with the flywheel side away from you and leaning over so that it rests on the cylinder head studs (or tilt the head of the engine stand so the cylinder head studs of the left half of the crankcase are pointing down).

3   Apply assembly lube to the four valve lifters for the left half of the crankcase and place them in their bores. The grease will hold them in place during assembly. If new valve lifters are being installed, push the valve lifters all the way in. If any of the lifters jam in the crankcase, have an automotive machine shop clearance the bores.

4   If not done already, fit the flanged number 1 bearing on the flywheel end of the crankshaft. Make sure the offset dowel hole goes toward the flywheel end. The bearing surfaces of the journal should be well lubricated with clean oil or assembly lube but keep the outside surfaces of the bearing clean and dry.

5   Place one half of the number 2 main bearing in the crankcase, engaging the dowel in the hole **(see illustration)**. On 1966 and later models, install new camshaft bearings **(see illustration)**. Lubricate the bearings with clean oil or assembly lube.

6   Place the crankshaft assembly into position in the left hand crankcase half. The three dowel holes in the circular crankshaft bearings must be lined up so that they will align with the dowels in the crankcase and number 3 and 4 connecting rods must pass through the openings **(see illustration)**. Do not force anything into place. Once the crankshaft is in place, rotate the circular bearings a little until you can feel the dowels engage. There will be a click and the crankshaft will drop slightly. Be sure the oil

32.7a   Position the connecting rods as shown here

32.7b   The marks on the teeth must mesh like this

32.7c   Check the endplay of the camshaft with a dial indicator

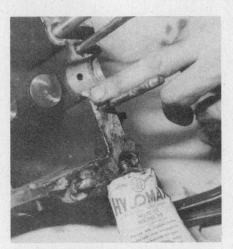

32.10   Apply sealant to the mating surfaces of the crankcase

32.11   Install the circular camshaft plug

slinger disc fits in the oil slinger recess in the casting. Once all the bearings are aligned, the crankshaft should drop into place.

7   Position the number one and two connecting rods up **(see illustration)**. Turn the crankshaft carefully until the two marked teeth are visible at the edge of the crankcase. Coat the lobes and journals of the camshaft with assembly lube. Install the camshaft into the crankcase bearings; mesh the single tooth on the camshaft gear between the two marks on the drive gear **(see illustration)**. Engage the teeth and roll the camshaft around, in mesh still, into its bearing location. Then turn the gears again to check that the timing marks are still correctly aligned. Check the camshaft endplay **(see illustration)** and gear backlash and compare the results to this Chapter's Specifications. **Note:** *Camshaft gears are available in various pitch radii; they are marked "-1, +1, +2, etc. to denote the size.*

8   Now apply assembly lube to the remaining four valve lifters and place them into the right-hand half of the crankcase. If they are the original lifters, install them in the same positions they were originally in.

9   Fit the other half of number 2 bearing into the right half of the crankcase locating it over its dowel correctly.

10   Apply a thin coat of sealant (VW Hylomar, or equivalent) to the mating surfaces of the crankcase halves **(see illustration)**. Make sure the two surfaces are coated completely, but thinly and evenly. Take care to cover around the base of the studs. Do not let any sealant get into oil passages or other places where it may cause problems.

11   Coat the circular camshaft sealing plug with sealant and place it in po-

sition in its groove in the left-hand half at the flywheel end of the camshaft **(see illustration)**. **Note:** *On manual transaxle models, the open end faces in, on Automatic Stick Shift models, reverse the plug.*

12   Install new sealing rings on 1967 and later models (beginning with engine number HO398526) over the six larger crankcase studs (M12 x 1.5).

13   Place the right-hand half of the crankcase over the studs of the left and carefully slide it down until it just touches the crankshaft bearings.

14   Push the two halves together, tapping lightly with a soft face mallet if necessary. Use no force – none should be necessary.

15   Now stop and check:

a)   Are all the connecting rods protruding from their proper holes? Cap bolts/nuts tight?

b)   Are all four bearings, two gears and oil slinger disc installed on the crankshaft?

c)   Are all eight valve lifters in position?

d)   Are the timing marks meshed properly?

e)   Is the camshaft sealing plug installed properly?

16   Install the oil pump housing in the crankcase with a new gasket. Start all the nuts on the crankcase studs finger tight. On 1967 and earlier models (from engine number HO230323 to HO398525), the center studs are sealed with special sealing nuts; the nuts are installed with the plastic ring inward, with no washers. Turn the crankshaft just to make sure that everything moves freely. It is important to tighten down the stud nuts evenly and in the correct order. Tighten the small nut near the lower large stud near

32.16 Tighten this nut (arrow) first

32.17   Tighten the crankcase nuts/bolts with a torque wrench

33.4   Insert each ring into the cylinder and measure the end gap with a feeler gauge

33.5   If the end gap is too small, clamp a file in a vise and file the ring ends (from the outside in only) to enlarge the gap slightly

33.9   Installing the spacer/expander in the oil control ring groove

number 1 main bearing **(see illustration)** to 14 ft-lbs in two steps.

17   Tighten the six large nuts (M12) to the torque listed in this Chapter's Specifications **(see illustration)**. **Note:** *Tighten sealing nuts, if equipped, to 18 ft-lbs.*

18   Tighten the remaining smaller nuts/bolts (M8) to the torque listed in this Chapter's Specifications.

19   Now rotate the crankshaft – it should revolve smoothly without any binding. If there is stiffness, loosen all the crankcase nuts. If it then turns freely, separate the crankcase again. Then check that all the bearings have been properly located on their dowel pegs and that the split bearings of the camshaft are seated properly. Any pressure spots on bearings will be visible. The cause is normally due to dirt or burrs behind them, particularly on the corners of the bearing bores and mating face edges. These can be chamfered lightly if necessary. Do not continue until you have found the reason for any binding. Start again from the beginning if necessary.

33   Pistons and rings – reassembly

Refer to illustrations 33.4, 33.5, 33.9, 33.11 and 33.16

1   Before installing the new piston rings, the ring end gaps must be checked. It's assumed that the piston ring side clearance has been checked and verified correct (see Section 22). **Note:** *The piston/cylinder diameter grades must be matched with the piston rings. Consult your dealer parts department or auto parts store for specific sizing information.*

2   Lay out the piston/connecting rod assemblies and the new ring sets so the ring sets will be matched with the same piston and cylinder during the end gap measurement and engine assembly.

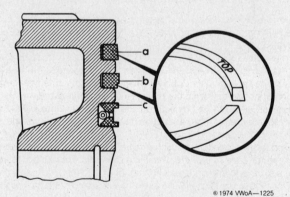

33.11   Piston ring side view

a)   *Upper compression ring*   c)   *Oil scraper ring*
b)   *Lower compression ring*

3   Insert the top (number one) ring into the first cylinder and square it up with the cylinder walls by pushing it in with the top of the piston. The ring should be near the bottom of the cylinder, at the lower limit of ring travel.

4   To measure the end gap, slip feeler gauges between the ends of the ring until a gauge equal to the gap width is found **(see illustration)**. The feeler gauge should slide between the ring ends with a slight amount of drag. Compare the measurement to this Chapter's Specifications. If the gap is larger or smaller than specified, double-check to make sure you have the correct rings before proceeding.

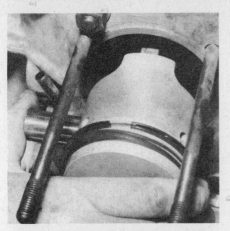

33.16 The wrist pin should go in with thumb pressure

34.2 Put a new gasket on the base of the cylinder

34.4 Tighten the ring compressor around the rings

34.6 Slip the cylinder over the piston

5   If the gap is too small, it must be enlarged or the ring ends may come in contact with each other during engine operation, which can cause serious damage to the engine. The end gap can be increased by filing the ring ends very carefully with a fine file. Mount the file in a vise equipped with soft jaws, slip the ring over the file with the ends contacting the file face and slowly move the ring to remove material from the ends. When performing this operation, file only from the outside in **(see illustration)**.

6   Excess end gap isn't critical unless it's greater than 0.040-inch. Again, double-check to make sure you have the correct rings for your engine.

7   Repeat the procedure for each ring that will be installed in the first cylinder and for each ring in the remaining cylinders. Remember to keep rings, pistons and cylinders matched up.

8   Once the ring end gaps have been checked/corrected, the rings can be installed on the pistons.

9   The oil control ring (lowest one on the piston) is usually installed first. It's usually composed of two or three separate components. Slip the expander into the groove **(see illustration)**. Then install the oil scraper ring(s).

10   After the oil ring components have been installed, check to make sure they can be turned smoothly in the ring groove.

11   The number two (lower compression) ring is installed next. Most rings will be marked "oben" or "top" which denotes which way they go. The lower of the two is installed first **(see illustration)**. **Note:** *Always follow the instructions printed on the ring package or box – different manufacturers may require different approaches.* Do not mix up the top and middle rings, as they have different cross-sections (profiles).

12   Use a piston ring installation tool and make sure the identification mark is facing the top of the piston, then slip the ring into the middle groove on the piston. Don't expand the ring any more than necessary to slide it over the piston.

13   Install the number one (top) ring in the same manner. Make sure the mark is facing up. Be careful not to confuse the number one and number two rings.

14   Repeat the procedure for the remaining pistons and rings.

15   Remove one circlip from each piston – if not already done – and push out the wrist pin to permit the end of the connecting rod to be positioned. If the pins are too tight to push out, do not force them. Warm up the pistons with an electric hair dryer.

16   If new pistons are being installed, they can go on any connecting rod. The side of the piston marked on the crown with an arrow goes towards the flywheel end of the engine. Lubricate the pin with oil and then push the it back into place **(see illustration)** and replace the circlip. Make sure that you use only the circlips supplied with the pistons. Do not use the old circlips. **Caution:** *When the crankshaft is rotated, the skirt of the piston can hit the crankcase at bottom dead center (BDC) unless it is guided into the cylinder opening.*

34   Cylinders – installation

Refer to illustrations 34.2, 34.4, 34.6, 34.7 and 34.11

1   The cylinders should go back in their original locations, unless new pistons and/or cylinders are being installed or they have been rebored.

2   Before installing the cylinders, you may wish to lightly grind them into the seats in the cylinder head. This can be done using fine valve lapping paste. Make sure that all traces of paste are flushed away afterwards. Light grinding in this way helps to ensure a gas-tight seal. Make sure that the mating faces at top and bottom of the cylinders are perfectly clean and free of old gasket material. Select the new thin, cylinder base gaskets from the set and put them in position on the cylinder base, held by sealant **(see illustration)**.

3   Stagger the piston ring gaps around the upper 180-degrees of each piston with the gap in the oil control ring facing the top of the engine.

4   The rings must be compressed into the piston grooves in order to get the cylinder over them. Use a special take-apart type ring compressor, because once the cylinder is on it will not be possible to lift it off over the top of the piston. Coat the piston with oil and fit the ring compressor clamp around the rings. Tighten it so that all three rings are compressed **(see illustration)**. Take care to see that no ring slips out from under the clamp; this can easily happen, particularly when first tightening up the compressor.

5   Tighten the compressor until the rings are flush with the piston but do not tighten it so much that the clamp grips the piston tightly. Otherwise, it will be difficult to slide the clamp down the piston.

6   With the lower cylinder gasket in place, slip the cylinder over the piston crown **(see illustration)**, narrow end first with the fin flats facing the adjacent cylinder position and with the four studs aligned in the passages in the fins.

34.7 Carefully tap the cylinder into place

34.11 Install the air deflector plates between the cylinders on the underside (engine mounted on stand and turned upside-down for ease of installation)

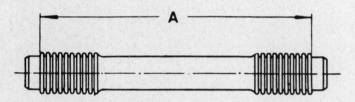

35.1 Measure dimension "A" to determine pushrod tube length

7   Press the base of the cylinder against the piston ring compressor and tap it down with a wooden block or soft face hammer (see illustration). If the compressor does not move, loosen it slightly and try again. If a ring does escape, it will be necessary to start again. If you break a ring you will probably have to buy a set of three for that piston.
8   Once all rings are inside the cylinder, remove the compressor.
9   Move the barrel down and locate it into the crankcase. It will not be a tight fit. Make sure that the gasket is not dislodged.
10 Rotate the crankshaft as each cylinder is installed. When this is done,

the cylinders must be tied down with wire to keep them from moving.
11 Install the air deflector plates (see illustration). It is a spring fit to the two center studs. Make sure it is tight – the flanges may be bent out a little to increase the tension, if necessary. Note that these deflectors are on the lower side near the pushrod tubes. They follow the contour of the cooling fins when installed, so make sure they are positioned properly. They cannot be installed after putting the cylinder heads and tubes in position.

35 Cylinders heads – installation

Refer to illustrations 35.1, 35.2, 35.3, 35.4, 35.7a and 35.7b

1   First check the pushrod tubes for damage and rust. They have compressible ends; stretch these out a little by pulling them so that the distance between the outer ends of the pleated sections is no less than dimension "A" (see illustration) – 7 7/64 inches on 1965 and earlier engines and 7 1/2 inches on 1966 and later engines. When stretching the tubes, pull straight to avoid any possibility of cracking them.
2   Install a new seal over each end so they will not leak (see illustration). Note: *On some early 1200 cc models, copper/asbestos sealing rings were used between the head and cylinder. If the engine was originally equipped with them, install new ones.*
3   Install the head onto the head studs just far enough to be secure. Then place the four pushrod tubes into position (see illustration) and hold them loosely in position by putting the pushrods back through them.
4   Move the head further into position so that the tube ends locate in their

35.2 Install new seals on the ends of the pushrod tubes

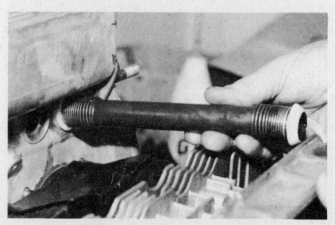

35.3 Position the pushrod tubes between the head and crankcase

35.4   Push the head on until the pushrod tubes are seated

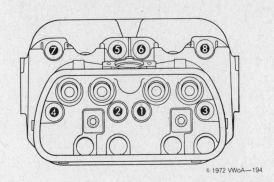

35.7a   Following this sequence, tighten the cylinder head nuts to the initial torque listed in this Chapter's Specifications

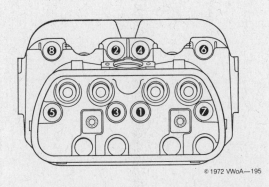

35.7b   Final cylinder head tightening sequence

36.2   Three shims are used to set crankshaft endplay

36.5   Mount a dial indicator to the crankcase to measure crankshaft endplay

6   Replace the stud washers and nuts and tighten them lightly and evenly by hand.

7   Tighten the nuts in two stages, in the correct sequence (see illustrations), to the torque listed in this Chapter's Specifications.

8   Repeat the operation for the other head.

9   Install the rocker arms and pushrods (see Section 3) and adjust the valves as described in Chapter 1.

36   Crankshaft endplay – check and adjustment

Refer to illustrations 36.2 and 36.5

1   Crankshaft endplay is governed by shims installed between the flywheel/driveplate flange and the crankshaft thrust bearing.

2   Three shims (see illustration) are always used to make up the required total thickness; they are available in five thicknesses: 0.0095 in (0.24 mm), 0.0118 in (0.30 mm), 0.0126 in (0.32 mm), 0.0134 in (0.34 mm) and 0.0142 in (0.36 mm). Install two shims to start with, then calculate the thickness of the third. Measure used shims with a micrometer – new ones have their size etched in them.

3   Replace the O-ring seal in the flywheel flange recess (if equipped) and then place the flywheel in position on the crankshaft.

4   Tighten the gland nut to at least 75 ft-lbs in order to accurately read crankshaft endplay.

5   Mount a dial indicator to the crankcase (see illustration).

respective seats at both ends (see illustration). Make sure that the pushrod seals seat securely. The seams in the tubes should face the cylinders.

5   The cylinder head studs should not be touching any of the cylinder barrel fins, so if necessary, turn the barrels a little to achieve this. A piece of postcard placed behind each stud will make a gap.

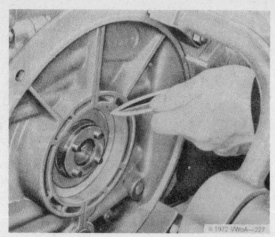

37.2   Lightly chamfer the outer edge of the opening to avoid damaging the seal – be sure to remove any chips

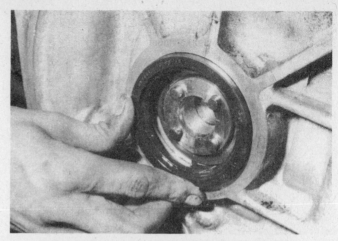

37.4a   Position the seal squarely in the seal bore . . .

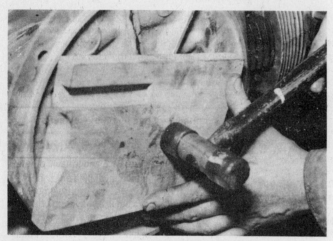

37.4b   . . . and press it into place with a hammer and a block of wood . . .

37.4c   . . . or a special seal driver

6   Move the crankshaft in, zero the dial indicator and move the flywheel out. Read the dial indicator to determine endplay. Calculate the thickness of the third shim by subtracting 0.10 mm (0.004 inch) from the measured endplay. Any three shims will do, provided they add up in total thickness to the sum of the two in position and the calculated third.

7   Once the correct shims have been selected, remove the flywheel, lightly oil the shims and install them.

8   Recheck the crankshaft endplay and compare the results to that listed in this Chapter's Specifications. **Caution:** *Endplay is critical on these engines – incorrect endplay can cause severe damage.*

9   Temporarily remove the flywheel and install the oil seal as described in Section 37.

37   Crankshaft oil seal – replacement

Refer to illustrations 37.2, 37.4a, 37.4b and 37.4c

1   The crankshaft oil seal must be replaced before the flywheel is installed. Do not install the flywheel or seal until the crankshaft endplay has been checked (see Section 36).

2   Lightly chamfer the outer edge of the seal opening **(see illustration)** to avoid damaging the seal – be sure to remove any chips.

3   Be sure the endplay shims are positioned over the crankshaft flange (see Section 36) and make sure they are perfectly clean and lightly oiled.

4   Coat the outer edge of the new oil seal with sealant and place it squarely in position into the crankcase with the spring side of the seal facing inwards. Press it into place using a block of wood and a hammer or a special tool **(see illustrations)**.

38   Flywheel/driveplate – installation

Refer to illustrations 38.2 and 38.3

1   Before flywheel/driveplate installation, check and adjust the crankshaft endplay and lightly oil the lips of the seal (see the two preceding Sections).

2   The four dowels should all be in the crankshaft flange **(see illustration)**. Be sure the paper or metal gasket or O-ring is in place between the crankshaft and flywheel (see Section 15). **Note:** *Beginning with engine number FO741385 (1967 models), a rubber O-ring is used instead of the gasket.*

3   Guide the flywheel/driveplate over the dowels **(see illustration)** with the balance marks (see Section 15) aligned. Once the flywheel is positioned on the dowels, install the gland nut and washer by hand.

4   Hold the flywheel/driveplate from turning as described in Section 15. Then very carefully tighten the bolt to draw the flywheel on. Tighten the gland nut to the torque listed in this Chapter's Specifications.

38.2   Insert the dowels, if they were removed

38.3   Guide the flywheel/driveplate onto the dowels

5   On manual transaxle models, apply about one gram of high temperature grease to the pilot bearing located in the gland nut. Then refer to
Chapter 8 and install the clutch assembly.

39   External engine components – reassembly

All external components must be installed on the rebuilt or replace-
ment engine, in the opposite order of removal. These include:
Crankshaft pulley
Exhaust manifolds/heat exchangers and muffler
Emissions control components (if equipped)
Fuel injection components or carburetor
Intake manifold
Fuel pump (carbureted models only)
Oil cooler
Cooling shrouds
Distributor and drive, spark plug wires and spark plugs
Generator/alternator and fan housing
Thermostat (1963 and later)
Clutch and flywheel or driveplate
Air cleaner assembly
Refer to the appropriate Sections and Chapters for detailed installation
instructions.

40   Engine – installation

1   On manual transaxle models, make sure the clutch friction disc has
been centered with an alignment tool. Apply a light coating of moly-base
grease to the splines of the transaxle input shaft and the face of the clutch
release bearing.
2   On Automatic Stick Shift models, detach the temporary torque converter retainer.
3   Clean the bellhousing-to-engine flanges.
4   Block the front wheels to prevent the vehicle from rolling. Raise the
rear of the vehicle and support it securely on jackstands. Position the jackstands under the torsion arms, just forward of the rear wheels.
5   Position the engine underneath the vehicle and raise it into place in
the reverse order of removal (see Section 12). **Caution:** *Do not force the
engine into position with the floor jack; the clutch or transaxle may be damaged. If something hangs up, check and correct the problem before proceeding.*
6   Ensure that the accelerator cable and wiring harness are positioned
where they will not get trapped or kinked.

7   Push the engine forward so that the lower mounting studs engage in
the holes and the crankcase moves right up to the transaxle. Reach between the engine and firewall and feed the accelerator cable though the
guide tube in the fan housing **(see illustration)**. It may be necessary to
wiggle the engine a little, or turn the crankshaft slightly, to seat it. Once the
engine is slid up against the transaxle, install the mounting nuts/bolts and
tighten them each a little at a time until they are all tightened securely. **Caution:** *Any attempt to draw the engine into position with the mounting bolts/
nuts when there is a considerable gap may crack the crankcase or
transaxle.*
8   When the engine is installed, reconnect all of the components that
were disconnected during engine removal, in the reverse order (see Section 12).
9   Adjust the accelerator cable (see adjustment details in Chapter 4). On
manual transaxle models, adjust the clutch pedal free play and on Automatic Stick Shift models, install the torque converter bolts and tighten
them to the torque listed in this Chapter's Specifications.
10   Install the rear cover assembly. The edge of the plate should fit neatly
in the rubber beading around the edge of the engine compartment.
11   Reconnect the battery.
12   Fill the engine with the recommended grade and quantity of oil, and
transaxle lubricant, on Automatic Stick Shift models (see Chapter 1).
13   Set ignition timing (see Chapter 1).

41   Initial start-up and break-in after overhaul

Warning: *Have a fire extinguisher handy when starting the engine for the
first time.*

1   Once the engine has been installed in the vehicle, double-check the
engine oil level.
2   With the spark plugs out of the engine and the ignition system dis-
abled (see Section 8), crank the engine until the oil pressure light goes out.
3   Install the spark plugs, connect the plug wires and restore the ignition
system functions (see Section 8).
4   Start the engine. It may take a few moments for the fuel system to
build up pressure, but the engine should start without a great deal of effort.
Note: *If backfiring occurs through the carburetor or throttle valve housing,
recheck the valve clearance, point gap and ignition timing.*
5   After the engine starts, it should be allowed to warm up to normal operating temperature. While the engine is warming up, make a thorough
check for fuel and oil leaks.
6   Shut the engine off and recheck the engine oil level. On Automatic
Stick Shift models, check the fluid level.
7   Drive the vehicle to an area with minimum traffic, accelerate at full
throttle from 30 to 50 mph, then allow the vehicle to slow to 30 mph with the

throttle closed. Repeat the procedure 10 or 12 times. This will load the piston rings and cause them to seat properly against the cylinder walls. Check again for oil and fuel leaks.

8   Drive the vehicle gently for the first 500 miles (no sustained high speeds) and keep a constant check on the oil level. It is not unusual for an engine to use oil during the break-in period.

9   At approximately 500 to 600 miles, change the oil (see Chapter 1).

10 For the next few hundred miles, drive the vehicle normally. Do not pamper it or abuse it.

11 After 2000 miles, change the oil and filter again and consider the engine broken in.

Chapter 3   Cooling and heating systems

Contents

Specifications

Torque specifications

Engine cooling fan-to-shaft nut .... 40 ft-lbs
Oil cooler mounting nuts .... 60 in-lbs

1   General information

The engine cooling system consists of a cooling fan, a thermostat and an oil cooler. The oil cooler is a multi-tube heat exchanger mounted on the crankcase, inside the fan housing. Air from the cooling fan is ducted past it.

The cooling fan is mounted on the front of the generator/alternator shaft, inside the fan housing. On 1964 and earlier models, an air control ring restricts air flow over the engine during warmup.

On 1965 and later models, engine cooling is regulated by a bellows type thermostat which is mounted under the right-hand pair of cylinders. The thermostat operates two linked control flaps in the fan housing. When the engine is cold the thermostat restricts the circulation of air over the engine. When the minimum operating temperature is reached, the thermostat begins to open, allowing air to flow freely over the engine cooling fins.

The heating system works by directing air over the engine cooling fins on 1962 and earlier models, or over fins on the heat exchangers on 1963 and later models. The heated air is routed into the interior of the vehicle by a system of ducts. Temperature is controlled by cable operated flaps at the heat exchanger outlets. Super Beetles also have an electric motor driven blower for ventilation.

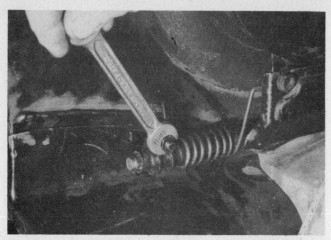

2.3a   Loosen the locknut to adjust the air control ring gap – it's located between the fan housing and the firewall

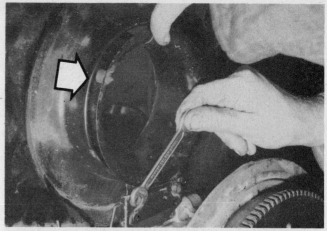

2.3b   The rubber pad (arrow) should just touch the fan shroud when the engine is cold – be sure the mounting bolts are tight (engine removed for clarity)

2   Air control ring – check and adjustment (1964 and earlier models)

Refer to illustrations 2.3a and 2.3b

1   Drive the vehicle for about ten minutes to allow the engine to warm up.
2   Shut the engine off and open the rear hood.
3   Check the gap between the air control ring and the fan housing while the engine is still warm. The gap at the top should be at least 3/4 inch (20 mm). If not, loosen the locknut **(see illustration)** and move the air control ring until the correct gap is set. Tighten the locknut and recheck the gap measurement. **Note:** *When the engine is cold the air control ring should be all the way in against the fan shroud* **(see illustration)**.

3   Thermostat – check and replacement (1965 and later models)

Refer to illustrations 3.3, 3.4, 3.5 and 3.7

1   Raise the rear of the vehicle and support it securely on jackstands.
2   Working under the engine, remove the sheet metal cover between the right (passenger's) side heat exchanger and the engine case.
3   With the engine cold, the thermostat bellows should be fully contracted. When the engine is warm, the bellows should be expanded **(see illustration)**.

4   Unbolt the thermostat from the mounting bracket and remove the bracket mounting nut from the engine case **(see illustration)**.
5   Unscrew the thermostat from the control rod **(see illustration)**. Grasp the rod and move it up and down. The linkage and control flaps

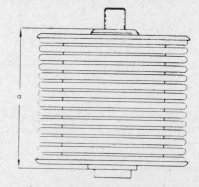

3.3   The thermostat can be checked with a thermometer and a ruler or vernier caliper

a = 1 13/16 inches minimum at 149 to 158-degrees F

3.4   Remove the thermostat bolt and the mounting bracket nut (arrows)

3.5   Unscrew the thermostat from the control rod – it may be necessary to hold the rod with locking pliers

3.7 Slip the mounting bracket into position

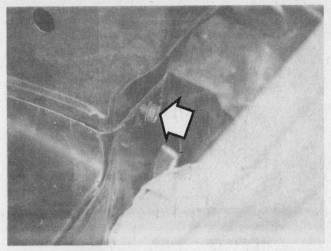

4.10 Remove the mounting screws from the sides and rear of the fan housing

should operate freely without binding and return to the closed position because of the return spring located on the firewall side of the fan housing.
6   Screw the thermostat onto the linkage rod and tighten it securely.
7   Slip the mounting bracket over the thermostat and guide the bracket over the stud on the engine case. **(see illustration)** Install the mounting nut loosely.
8   Move the thermostat bracket until the thermostat touches the top of the mounting bracket. Tighten the bracket nut securely.
9   Install the thermostat-to-bracket bolt and tighten it securely.
10   Reinstall the cover and bolts. Remove the jackstands and lower the vehicle.

---

4   Engine cooling fan and housing – removal and installation

Refer to illustrations 4.10, 4.13, 4.14, 4.15 and 4.16

Removal

1   Disconnect the negative cable from the battery.
2   Remove the drivebelt (see Chapter 1).
3   Remove the rear hood (see Chapter 11).
4   Remove the carburetor or air intake sensor (see Chapter 4).
5   Remove the heater hoses and various emissions/breather hoses (if equipped) that connect to the fan housing.
6   Label and then disconnect the wiring from the oil pressure sending unit, the ignition coil, back-up lights (1967 and later) and the voltage regulator (6 volt models) or the generator/alternator (12 volt models).
7   Reach around to the firewall side of the engine and pull the accelerator cable out through the tube in the fan housing.
8   Label the spark plug wires and remove them with the distributor cap (see Chapter 1).
9   Unbolt the generator/alternator retaining strap.
10   Remove the mounting screws on the sides **(see illustration)** and rear of the fan housing. On 1971 and later models, detach the small shroud at the front (firewall side) of the oil cooler.
11   On 1964 and earlier models, release the air control ring spring, then unbolt the ring and lift it out of the engine compartment (see Section 2, if necessary).
12   On 1965 and later models, remove the thermostat (see Section 3).
13   Carefully lift the fan housing straight up. If the oil cooler interferes with removal, temporarily support the fan housing with wood blocks, then unbolt and remove the oil cooler (see Section 5). **Caution:** *Take care to avoid bending the thermostat linkage rod* **(see illustration)**.

4.13 Carefully guide the thermostat linkage rod through the opening in the cooling fins (1965-on)

14   If you intend to remove the fan from the generator/alternator shaft, reinstall the pulley and mounting nut. To keep the shaft from turning while you loosen the fan nut **(see illustration)**, wrap an old drivebelt around the pulley and clamp it in a vise. Using a 36 mm (1 7/16 in) socket and breaker bar, remove the fan mounting nut. Note the position of the shims and washers for reassembly. **Note:** *If you are unable to get the nut loose, take the fan housing assembly to a repair shop or dealer for removal with an air impact tool.*
15   Check the air control flaps (1965 and later models) for binding and damage **(see illustration)**.

Installation

16   Installation is the reverse of removal. Tighten the fan-to-generator/alternator shaft nut to the torque listed in this Chapter's Specifications. Using a feeler gauge, measure the distance between the fan and fan cover **(see illustration)**. The recommended clearance is 0.08 inch (2.0 mm). If the clearance is incorrect, adjust it by varying the number of shims under the thrust washer. Store unused shims between the thrust washer and nut. Turn the fan by hand to check for binding.
17   Install the fan housing. Be sure to adjust the air control ring or thermostat as described in Section 2 or 3 and the drivebelt (see Chapter 1).

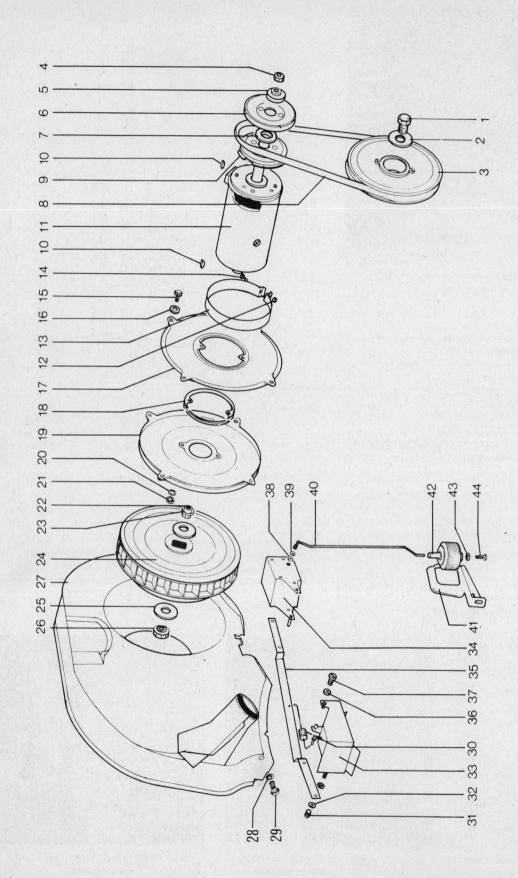

4.14   Typical fan housing components – exploded view.

1	Pulley securing bolt	17	Outer fan cover	33	Cooling air regulator. left
2	Dished washer	18	Reinforcement flange	34	Cooling air regulator. right
3	Crankshaft pulley	19	Inner fan cover	35	Regulator connectng rod
4	Pulley nut	20	Lockwasher	36	Washer
5	Washer	21	Nut	37	Screw
6	Pulley – rear half	22	Fan hub	38	Lockwasher
7	Spacer washer	23	Shim	39	Washer
8	V-belt	24	Fan	40	Connecting rod
9	Pulley – front half	25	Lockwasher	41	Thermostat bracket
10	Woodruff key	26	Special nut	42	Thermostat
11	Generator	27	Fan housing	43	Lockwasher
12	Nut	28	Washer	44	Bolt
13	Generator strap	29	Screw		
14	Bolt	30	Return spring		
15	Bolt	31	Spring		
16	Lockwasher	32	Washer		

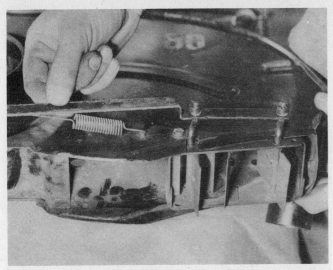

4.15 Move the linkage back and forth to check for binding – lubricate all moving parts

5 Oil cooler – removal and installation

Refer to illustrations 5.3, 5.5, 5.6, 5.9a and 5.9b

Removal

1 Disconnect the negative cable from the battery.
2 Unbolt the fan housing and lift it as high as possible (see Section 4). Place wood blocks under the ends to hold it in this position.

1970 and earlier models

3 Remove the three nuts holding the oil cooler to the engine **(see illustration)**.
4 Slip the cooler off the mounting studs and lift it out of the fan housing. Note the type of seals used and replace them with new ones of the same type.

1971 and later models

5 Remove the nuts holding the oil cooler adapter to the engine case **(see illustration)**.
6 Remove the air shroud bracket **(see illustration)**.

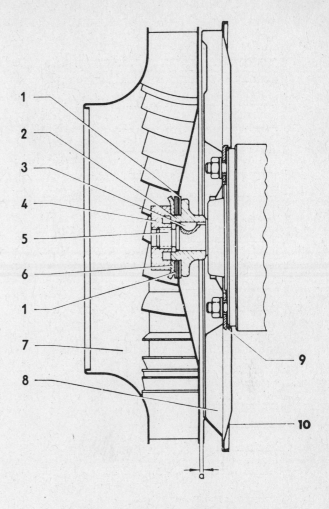

4.16 **Fan assembly – cross section**

1	Spacer washers	7	Fan
2	Fan hub	8	Fan cover, inner
3	Woodruff key	9	Reinforcement flange
4	Retaining nut	10	Fan cover, outer
5	Generator shaft		a=2 mm (.080 in)
6	Lockwasher (dished)		

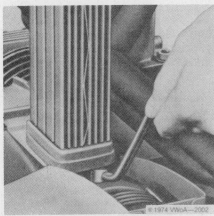

5.3 On 1970 and earlier models, use a curved wrench to remove the mounting nuts

5.5 Remove the adapter from the engine (1971 and later models)

5.6 Remove the bracket (1971 and later models)

3

5.9a   Some engines have flat seals . . .

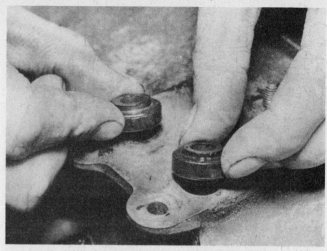

5.9b   . . . and others have stepped seals

6.3   Remove the upper luggage compartment liner

Installation (all models)

7   If the cooler appears to be leaking, it should be pressure tested by a Volkswagen dealer or radiator shop. If the cooler is leaking, the oil pressure relief valve should also be checked because excessive pressure may have caused the cooler failure (see Chapter 2).

8   If the fins of the cooler are clogged, soak it in solvent and then blow through the passages with compressed air at about 30 psi. **Warning:** *Wear eye protection.* If the passages are clogged with sludge or contain metal chips, replace the cooler.

9   Install new seals **(see illustrations)** between the oil cooler and engine (1970 and earlier models) or between the engine case and adapter and oil cooler and adapter (1971 and later models).

10   Install the mounting nuts and tighten them to the torque listed in this Chapter's Specifications. Be sure to tighten them evenly so the cooler seats properly.

11   Install the fan housing, run the engine and check for oil leaks.

---

6   Blower unit – removal and installation

Note: *All 1971 and later Super Beetles and Convertibles and all models 1973 and later are equipped with a two-speed fresh air ventilation fan powered by an electric motor.*

1971 and 1972 Super Beetles and Convertibles
Refer to illustrations 6.3, 6.11, 6.12a and 6.12b

1   Disconnect the negative cable from the battery.

2   Remove the control knobs. If necessary, loop a strong cord around the knob and use it as a pull handle.

3   Working under the front hood, remove the upper portion of the luggage compartment liner **(see illustration)**.

4   Detach the air ducts from the fresh air box.

5   Detach the bottom support of the fresh air box from the vehicle body and disconnect the drain hose from the underside.

6   Remove the three mounting screws from the front upper edge of the fresh air box.

7   Lift the fresh air control box away from the dash enough to reach behind it, then disconnect the wires from the back of the fan switch.

8   Detach the two mounting screws from the control bracket to the instrument panel. Remove the fresh air control box and control bracket and cables from the vehicle as an assembly. Mark the cables for correct reassembly.

9   Slip the fresh air hoses and ducts down and out of the instrument panel.

10   Push the fresh air vents up out of the dash.

11   Disassemble the fresh air box **(see illustration)** and lift out the fan assembly.

12   Separate the fan duct by removing the clips. Remove the four nuts and lift the motor/fan assembly out of the duct **(see illustrations)**.

13   Installation is the reverse of removal.

1973 and later models

14   Disconnect the negative cable from the battery.

15   Remove the instrument panel (see Chapter 12).

16   Label and disconnect the wiring on the blower unit.

17   Carefully remove the clips that hold the blower housing together. Remove the blower motor from the blower housing.

18   Installation is the reverse of removal.

---

7   Heater control cables – removal and installation

Refer to illustrations 7.4, 7.5, 7.7, 7.8a, 7.8b and 7.10

Removal

1   The heater control cables are connected together near the control knob or lever. If any part of the cable is broken, the whole assembly must be replaced.

2   Block the front wheels to prevent the vehicle from rolling. Raise the rear of the vehicle and support it securely on jackstands.

3   Locate the heater control cables where they come out of the floor pan on both sides of the transaxle. Follow the cables back to the heat exchanger (1963 and later models) or heat control flap (1962 and earlier models).

4   Hold the clamping sleeve with locking pliers and loosen the clamp bolt **(see illustration)**. Slip the cable out and remove the clamping sleeve from the control lever.

5   Remove the cable seals from the guide tubes **(see illustration)**.

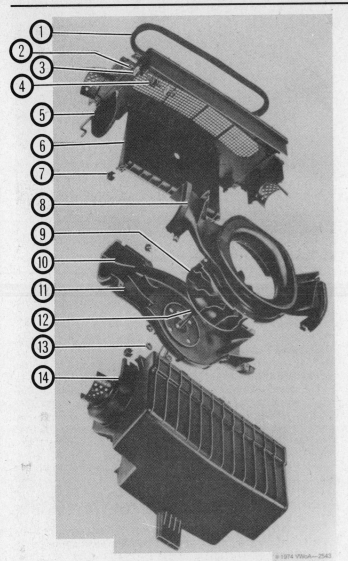

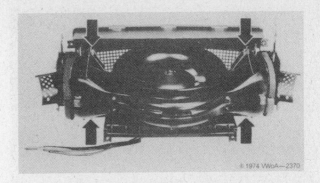

6.12a   Remove the clips (arrows) and separate the housing

6.11   Fresh air box – exploded view

1	Weatherstrip	8	Front of fan duct
2	Nut (8)	9	Fresh air fan with motor
3	Washer (8)	10	Rear of fan duct
4	Rubber mounting (4)	11	Sealing flap
5	Fresh air flap (2)	12	Wiring harness grommet
6	Upper fresh air box	13	Nut with washer (4)
7	Clip (10)	14	Lower fresh air box

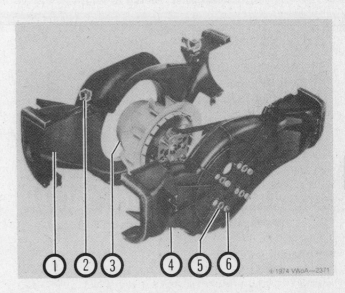

6.12b   Blower unit – exploded view

1 Front of fan duct
2 Clip
3 Fan with motor
4 Rear of fan duct
5 Washer
6 Nut

7.4   Loosen the bolt from the clamping sleeve (arrow)

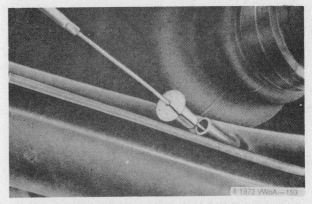

7.5   Pull the cable seals out of the guide tubes

7.7   Unscrew the threaded collar and pull the knob and cable up

7.8a   On 1963 and later models, remove the rubber handbrake boot

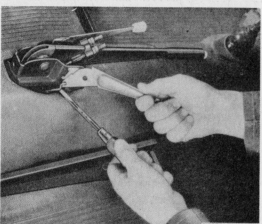

7.8b   Remove the nut from the right lever, then detach the cable

7.10   Guide the cables into the tube – on 1962 and earlier models, the longer cable goes into the right tube

6   Remove the right (passenger's) side front seat (see Chapter 11).
7   On 1962 and earlier models, unscrew the threaded collar below the heater control knob and pull the knob and cable out of the tube **(see illustration)**.
8   On 1963 and later models, remove the handbrake rubber boot **(see illustration)**. Remove the nut from the right (passenger's) side heater control lever and lift off the lever and friction discs. Detach the control cable from the lever **(see illustration)** and pull it out of the tube.
9   On all models, inspect all components for wear and damage and replace as needed.

Installation

10   Apply a light coat of grease to the new cable and insert it into the tube from the control knob/lever end **(see illustration)**.
11   On 1962 and earlier models, connect the cable to the heater control knob. Turn the knob left (counterclockwise) until it stops. Now turn it three turns to the right (clockwise). Install the heater control assembly.
12   On 1963 and later models, connect the cable to the control lever, then

install the lever, friction discs and mounting nut. Tighten the nut until sufficient friction is felt when the lever is moved. Reinstall the rubber boot over the handbrake assembly.
13   Working under the vehicle, insert the sealing plugs on the cables.
14   Reinstall the clamping sleeves and slip the cables into them. Take up all the slack in the cable and tighten the clamp bolt.
15   Have an assistant operate the heater control while you check for full movement of the lever.

8   Heat exchangers – removal and installation

The heat exchangers (also known as heater boxes) used on 1963 and later models direct heated air to the interior of the vehicle and connect the exhaust system to the cylinder heads. On earlier models, cooling air is ducted over the engine and then into the interior of the vehicle. See Chapter 2, Exhaust manifold/heat exchanger – removal and installation, for service procedures.

Chapter 4 Fuel and exhaust systems

Contents

4

Specifications

Fuel pressure
Carbureted models . . . .   2.8 psi at 3.400 rpm
Fuel injected models
   Regulator vacuum hose connected . . . .   26 to 30 psi
   Regulator vacuum hose disconnected . . . .   33 to 37 psi

Torque specifications
Carburetor mounting nuts . . . .   14 ft-lbs
Fuel injector retainer bolt . . . .   52 in-lbs

1 General information

All Volkswagen Beetles were equipped with carburetors through the 1974 model year. Beginning in 1975, they were fitted with Bosch electronic fuel injection as standard equipment.

Carbureted engines have a mechanical fuel pump mounted next to the distributor. All fuel injected models are equipped with an electric fuel pump mounted in the front of the vehicle below the fuel tank.

1961 and earlier models have no fuel gauge. Instead, a reserve valve is mounted under the dash. When the engine stalls for lack of fuel, the driver flips the lever to "reserve", allowing the vehicle to be driven to a filling station. In 1962, a mechanical cable-driven fuel gauge was added. 1968 and later models have an electric sending unit with a gauge mounted in the speedometer cluster.

The exhaust system consists of a muffler connected to the heat exchangers/exhaust manifolds. On carbureted models. two tail pipe tips extend rearward from the muffler. On 1975 and later models. the exhausts from both sides of the engine are routed together into a single header pipe and muffler. Most of these vehicles are also equipped with a catalytic converter. Each of these components is replaceable. For further information regarding the catalytic converter, refer to Chapter 6.

2 Fuel pressure relief procedure (fuel injected models only)

Warning: *Gasoline is extremely flammable. so take extra precautions when you work on any part of the fuel system. Don't smoke or allow open flames or bare light bulbs near the work area, and don't work in a garage where a natural gas-type appliance (such as a water heater or clothes dryer) with a pilot light is present. If you spill any fuel on your skin, rinse it off immediately with soap and water. When you perform any kind of work on the fuel tank, wear safety glasses and have a Class B type fire extinguisher on hand.*

1   Fuel injection systems operate with relatively high fuel pressures. This pressure remains in the system after the engine is shut down. Whenever repairs are performed on the fuel system, the pressure should be released first. If a line or fitting is opened without relieving this pressure, fuel may spray out, causing injury and/or fire.

3.9 Connect the fuel pressure tester as shown – be sure to use a gauge rated for at least 50 psi

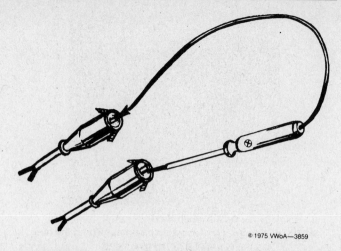

© 1975 VWoA—3859

3.12 Disconnect the wires from the fuel pump and connect a test light across them

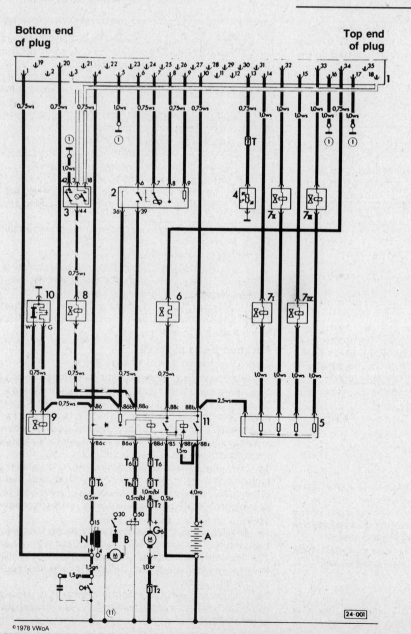

3.13 Fuel injection wiring diagram

1	Electronic control unit plug
2	Intake air sensor
3	Throttle valve switch/microswitch (except 1978 California models)
4	Temperature sensor II
5	Series resistance block
6	Auxiliary air regulator
7	Injectors
8	EGR valve (except 1977 and later California models)
9	Cold-start valve
10	Thermo-time switch
11	Double relay
N.	Ignition coil
G6	Fuel pump
A.	Battery
B.	Starter
T.	Electrical connector
Tlb	Electrical connector
T2.	Electrical connector, double
T6.	Electrical connector, 6-point
1.	Ground connector near alternator
11.	Ground connector, headlights

Color codes
ws = white
sw = black
br = Brown
ro = red
gn = green
ro/bl = red/blue

3.14 The double relay (arrow) is mounted behind the rear seat under a protective cover

2   If the engine runs, allow the engine to idle, then remove the fuel pump fuse. The injectors will use up the fuel under pressure and the engine will stall. The system may then be opened for servicing.

3   If the engine is inoperative, wait until the engine cools off completely, then disconnect a fuel line very slowly to release pressure. Wrap a rag around the fuel line to prevent the fuel from spraying and to soak up any spills. **Warning:** *Wear eye protection!*

3   Fuel pump/fuel pressure – check

Warning: *Gasoline is extremely flammable, so take extra precautions when you work on any part of the fuel system. Don't smoke or allow open flames or bare light bulbs near the work area, and don't work in a garage where a natural gas-type appliance (such as a water heater or clothes dryer) with a pilot light is present. If you spill any fuel on your skin, rinse it off immediately with soap and water. When you perform any kind of work on the fuel tank, wear safety glasses and have a Class B type fire extinguisher on hand.*

Carbureted models

1   With the engine OFF, connect a "tee" fitting in the fuel hose between the fuel pump and the carburetor.

2   Connect a fuel pump pressure tester to the "tee" fitting. Be sure the hose is routed away from the drivebelt.

3   Set the parking brake and block the wheels. Start the engine in neutral, allow it to warm up, then run it briefly at 3,400 rpm (this is approximately highway cruising speed). Use a portable tachometer to check engine speed if desired – follow the manufacturer's instructions. **Warning:** *Stay clear of the drivebelt, pulleys and exhaust system components!*

4   Note the pressure reading and compare it to that listed in this Chapter's Specifications.

5   Remove the test equipment and reconnect the fuel line. Start the engine and check for fuel leaks.

Fuel injected models

Fuel pump operational check

6   Set the parking brake and have an assistant turn the ignition switch to the On position while you listen at the fuel pump (located below the fuel tank near the right front wheel). You should hear a whirring sound, lasting for a couple of seconds. Start the engine. The whirring sound should now be continuous (although harder to hear with the engine running).

7   If there is no whirring sound, either the fuel pump or the fuel pump circuit is defective. Check the relay circuit first (proceed to Step 14).

Fuel pressure check

Refer to illustration 3.9, 3.12 and 3.13

8 - If you suspect low fuel pressure, first check for a leaking, clogged or otherwise damaged fuel line, or a clogged fuel filter (see Chapter 1).

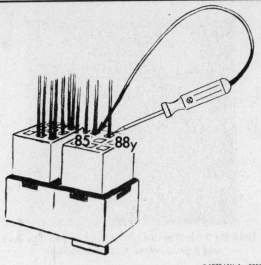

3.18   Check for power at terminal 88y

9   Start the engine and allow it to warm up. Shut the engine off, then disconnect the fuel line from the cold start valve. Connect a fuel pressure tester to the end of the fuel line **(see illustration)**.

10   Start the engine (or crank it if it won't start) and note the pressure reading on the gauge. Compare the reading to that listed in this Chapter's Specifications.

11   If the pump supplies pressure during the test but the pressure is way too low or too high, check the following:
   1) If the pressure is higher than specified:
     a) check for a faulty pressure regulator (see Section 13) or a pinched or clogged fuel return hose or pipe.
   2) If the pressure is lower than specified:
     a) Inspect the fuel filter – make sure it's not clogged.
     b) Look for a pinched or clogged fuel hose between the fuel tank and the fuel pump.
     c) Check the pressure regulator for a malfunction (see Section 13).
     d) Look for leaks in the fuel line.

12   If the pump is getting fuel but fails to supply pressure or doesn't run at all, check for voltage to the pump **(see illustration)**. Operate the starter – if the test lamp lights, replace the fuel pump.

13   If the test lamp doesn't light, check the wiring **(see illustration)** and check the fuel pump switch in the air intake sensor and the fuel pump relay (see below).

Fuel pump circuit check

Refer to illustrations 3.14, 3.18 and 3.23

14   Electrical power to the fuel pump is controlled by the double relay and the intake air sensor. The double relay **(see illustration)** controls electrical power to the fuel injection components. When the starter is activated, power from terminal 50 on the starter is routed to terminal 86a at the double relay. This energizes the fuel pump relay portion of the double relay and directs current from terminal 30 at the starter to the fuel pump through terminals 88d and 88y.

15   The fuel pump relay portion of the double relay controls power to the fuel pump, cold-start valve and the auxiliary air regulator. The other portion of the double relay (known as the power relay), which is activated whenever the ignition is ON, controls power to the remaining components in the system.

16   After the engine starts, power is routed to the fuel pump from the intake air sensor via terminal 86b and the resistor in the double relay.

17   When the ignition is shut off, terminal 86c of the double relay is no longer powered. The relay opens and power is disconnected from the fuel injection components.

18   Connect one end of a test light to terminal 85 (ground) of the double relay. Touch the test probe to terminal 88y **(see illustration)**, then probe terminal 88z. Both of these terminals should have power.

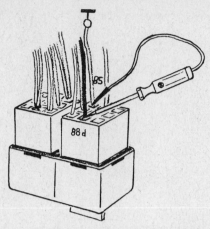

© 1975 VWoA—3853

3.23   Check for power at terminal 88d

19   Turn the ignition ON. Probe terminal 86c with the test light; it should have battery voltage when the ignition is ON.
20   Repeat the test of terminal 86c while an assistant operates the starter. Battery voltage should be present during cranking.
21   Test terminal 86a while an assistant operates the starter. Battery voltage should be present during cranking. **Note:** *If voltage is present at terminal 86a when the starter is not in use, the wires for terminals 50 and 30 on the starter may be reversed.*
22   If positive battery voltage is present in the above tests, perform the following steps. If voltage is not present, trace and repair the wiring.
23   Probe terminal 88d **(see illustration)** and operate the starter. If no voltage is present, replace the double relay. **Caution:** *Disconnect the battery ground cable before relay replacement.*
24   With the ignition On, probe terminal 88b. If no voltage is detected, replace the double relay.

---

4   Fuel pump – removal and installation

Warning: *Gasoline is extremely flammable, so take extra precautions when you work on any part of the fuel system. Don't smoke or allow open flames or bare light bulbs near the work area. and don't work in a garage where a natural gas-type appliance (such as a water heater or clothes dryer) with a pilot light is present. If you spill any fuel on your skin, rinse it off immediately with soap and water. When you perform any kind of work on* the fuel tank, wear safety glasses and have a Class B type fire extinguisher on hand.

Carbureted models

Refer to illustrations 4.4, 4.7, 4.9, 4.13 and 4.14

Removal

1   Disconnect the cable from the negative terminal of the battery.
2   The fuel pump is located between the distributor and the generator/alternator.
3   Detach the fuel lines/hoses from the fuel pump. On 1965 and earlier models, unscrew the inlet line with a line wrench. All others are a slip fit, simply loosen the clamps and pull the hoses off.
4   Remove the two mounting nuts **(see illustration)** and lift the pump off the engine.
5   Lift the pushrod out, then remove the intermediate flange and gaskets. Be careful not to damage the intermediate flange – it's made of plastic.

Installation

6   Position a gasket, the intermediate flange and another gasket over the mounting studs.
7   Inspect the pushrod for wear and damage. Roll it on a flat surface to check for bending. Install the pushrod with the tapered end down **(see illustration)**.
8   Using a wrench on the crankshaft pulley bolt, turn the crankshaft clockwise until the pushrod is at the highest point in its travel.
9   Measure the height of the pushrod above the flange and gaskets **(see illustration)**. It should be about 1/2 inch (13 mm).
10   Turn the crankshaft until the pushrod is at its lowest point. It should measure about 5/16 inch (8 mm). Subtract the smaller measurement from the larger one. This dimension is the stroke. It should be about 5/32 inch (4 mm).
11   If the height measurements are incorrect, add or subtract gaskets as needed. If the stroke is incorrect, replace the distributor drive gear.
12   Fill the bottom of the fuel pump mounting flange with grease.
13   Position the pump and gasket on the intermediate flange **(see illustration)**. Tighten the nuts securely.
14   Reconnect the fuel lines **(see illustration)** and battery cable.
15   Start the engine and check for fuel leaks.

Fuel injected models

16   Detach the cable from the negative battery terminal.
17   Relieve the fuel pressure (see Section 2).
18   Set the parking brake and block the rear tires. Loosen the lug nuts on the right front wheel. Raise the front of the vehicle and support it securely on jackstands.
19   Remove the right front wheel (see Chapter 1).
20   Using a pair of small clamps, pinch off the fuel lines.
21   Label and detach the fuel lines and wires from the fuel pump.

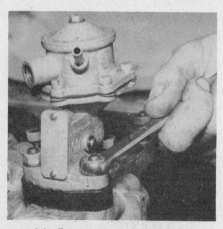

4.4   Remove the mounting nuts

4.7   Install the pushrod with the tapered end down

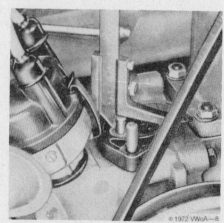

© 1972 VWoA—8

4.9   Measure the highest and lowest points of pushrod travel

4.13   Install the pump with the pushrod (arrow) in the down position

4.14   1971 and 1972 models are equipped with a fuel cutoff valve – be sure to reconnect it properly

1	Hose from fuel tank	3	Pressure line from pump
2	Suction line to pump	4	Hose to carburetor

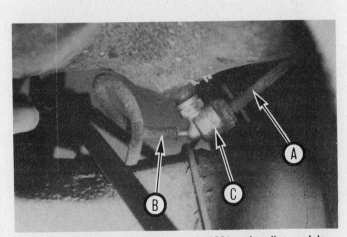

5.5   Fuel control valve components, 1961 and earlier models

A Control rod (to interior)   C   Control valve
B Fuel outlet hose

22   Unbolt the pump from its mounting bracket and remove it.
23   Installation is the reverse of removal.
24   After you have installed the new pump, temporarily disconnect the primary wire from the distributor to the coil and have an assistant activate the starter for about 20 seconds while you watch for any leaks where the fuel lines are attached to the pump. **Warning:** Be sure the transaxle is in neutral and the parking brake is applied.

5   Fuel tank – removal and installation

Refer to illustrations 5.5, 5.7a, 5.7b, 5.8, 5.9 and 5.10
Warning: Gasoline is extremely flammable, so take extra precautions when you work on any part of the fuel system. Don't smoke or allow open flames or bare light bulbs near the work area, and don't work in a garage where a natural gas-type appliance (such as a water heater or clothes dryer) with a pilot light is present. If you spill any fuel on your skin, rinse it off immediately with soap and water. When you perform any kind of work on the fuel tank, wear safety glasses and have a Class B type fire extinguisher on hand.

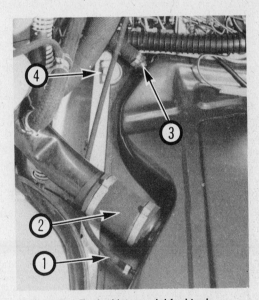

5.7a   Typical late model fuel tank

1	Vapor recovery hose	3	Vent return hose
2	Filler neck hose		

Note: The following procedure is much easier to perform if the fuel tank is empty. Try to schedule fuel tank removal when the tank is nearly empty.
1   Detach the cable from the negative terminal of the battery.
2   On 1970 and later models, remove the fuel tank filler cap to relieve fuel tank pressure.
3   If the vehicle is fuel-injected, relieve the fuel system pressure (see Section 2).
4   Raise the vehicle and place it securely on jackstands.
5   If the tank still has fuel in it, detach the fuel outlet line from the bottom of the tank and connect a drain hose to the outlet fitting on the bottom of the tank **(see illustration)**. Drain the fuel into an approved gasoline container.
6   Open the front hood and remove the luggage compartment liner.
7   Label, then disconnect the fuel line(s), the vapor recovery hoses and the vent hose, if equipped **(see illustrations)**.

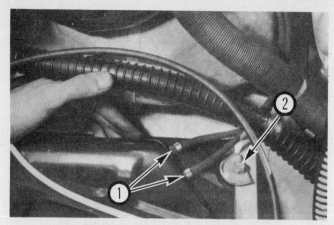

5.7b   Typical late model fuel tank

1   Vapor recovery line   2   Mounting bolt

5.8   Lift the cover off, then pull the outer cable out of the slotted holder and lift the cable straight up to disengage it from the float lever

5.9   Unplug the electrical connectors (arrows)

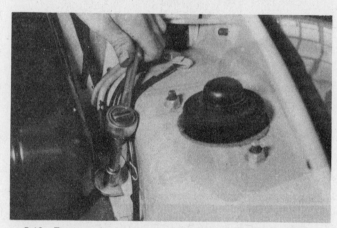

5.10   Remove the four mounting bolts and lift the fuel tank from the vehicle

dangerous work. Even after cleaning and flushing of the fuel system, explosive fumes can remain and ignite during repair of the tank.

2   If the fuel tank is removed from the vehicle, it should not be placed in an area where sparks or open flames could ignite the fumes coming out of the tank. Be especially careful inside garages where a natural gas-type appliance is located, because the pilot light could cause an explosion.

7   Air cleaner – removal and installation

Refer to illustrations 7.3, 7.4a, 7.4b, 7.5a, 7.5b, 7.6, 7.7a and 7.7b

Removal

1   Oil bath air cleaners were used on vehicles through the 1972 model year. 1973 and later models are equipped with dry paper air filter elements.

2   Detach the air preheater hose(s).

3   Disconnect the crankcase ventilation hose adjacent to the oil filler cap **(see illustration)**.

4   On 1968 through 1972 models, detach the preheater control cable **(see illustrations)**.

5   On later models with several vacuum hoses, label and disconnect the hoses **(see illustrations)**.

6   Loosen the clamp on the carburetor throat **(see illustration)** and any bracket bolts. On Karmann Ghias, remove the hose from the air cleaner to the carburetor and release the hold-down clamps.

7.3   Disconnect the crankcase ventilation hose

8   On 1962 through 1967 models, lift the cover and detach the gas gauge indicator cable **(see illustration)**.

9   On 1968 and later models, disconnect the fuel gauge sending unit wires **(see illustration)** and the fuel filler hose from the tank.

10   Remove the four fuel tank mounting bolts **(see illustration)**.

11   Remove the tank from the vehicle.

12   Installation is the reverse of removal. Inspect the anti-squeak seal and replace it if necessary.

6   Fuel tank cleaning and repair – general information

1   All repairs and cleaning of the fuel tank or filler neck should be carried out by a professional who has experience in this critical and potentially

7.4a Typical 1968 through 1972 Beetle engine air cleaner

1 Preheater cable
2 Preheater control lever
3 Clamp

A Preheater hose
B Clamp

7.4b Typical later model Karmann Ghia air cleaner

A Clamp
B Crankcase breather hose
C Hot air hose

D Preheater control cable
E Cable retainer
F Clamp

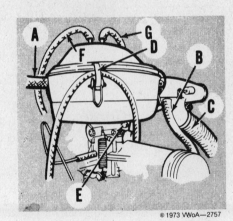

7.5a Typical late model Beetle air cleaner

A Hose from charcoal filter
B Crankcase ventilation hose
C Preheated intake air hose
D Release clip supporting
   green vacuum hose

E Air cleaner clamp screw
F Vacuum hose
   from carburetor
G Vacuum hose to intake
   air valve

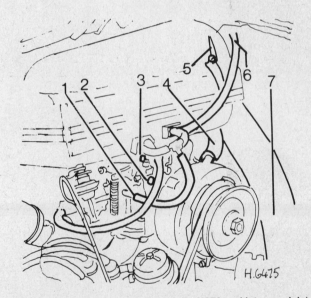

7.5b Paper element air cleaner details (1973 and later models)

1 Hose to carburetor
2 Screws in support plate
3 Carburetor clamp screw
4 Crankcase ventilation hose

5 Retaining clips, top-to-base
6 Vacuum hose
7 Warm air hose
   from preheater

7   Lift the air cleaner assembly out of the engine compartment **(see illustrations)**.
8   Do not tip oil bath filters over because the oil will pour out. On all models, remove the cover and service the air filter as described in Chapter 1.

Installation

9   Installation is the reverse of removal.
10   To adjust the preheater cable (where equipped), the engine must be cold. Push the cable housing onto the air cleaner as far as possible. Push the other end into the retainer on the fan housing and fasten it. Push the inner wire into the clamp on the preheater lever and fasten it. Push the wire into the clamp on the cooling air regulator. The flap should be closed and the spring slightly compressed.

8   Accelerator cable – replacement

Refer to illustrations 8.2a, 8.2b, 8.3, 8.7 and 8.12

Removal

1   The accelerator (or throttle) cable connects the carburetor or throttle valve with the accelerator pedal. The cable is routed through a tube in the fan housing, then into a flexible guide near the transaxle and through the floor pan to the accelerator pedal.

7.6   Loosen the clamp on the carburetor throat and remove the bolt from the bracket

1   Clamp   2   Bracket bolt

2   Detach the cable from the carburetor (**see illustrations**) or the intake air sensor.
3   Remove the spring and sleeve (**see illustration**).
4   Detach the cable end from the accelerator pedal.
5   Block the front wheels. Raise the rear of the vehicle and support it securely on jackstands.

6   Working under the vehicle, guide the cable through the fan housing.
7   Slip the flexible guide tube off the cable and remove the rubber boot (**see illustration**).
8   Pull the cable out of the tube near the accelerator pedal. Wipe it off with a cloth to prevent grease from getting on the floor covering.

Installation

9   Start the new cable into the guide tube in the floor pan near the accelerator pedal. Lubricate the cable with grease as you push it into the tube.
10   When the cable exits the tube near the transaxle, slip the rubber boot and flexible guide tube in place and push the cable into the metal tube in the fan housing.
11   Working in the engine compartment, pull the cable through the tube and install the spring and keeper. Reconnect the cable to the throttle lever.
12   Have an assistant fully depress the accelerator pedal while you adjust the cable. On carbureted models, there should be a slight gap between the throttle lever and stop (**see illustration**).

---

9   Carburetor – removal and installation

Refer to illustrations 9.3, 9.4, 9.6 and 9.9
Warning: *Gasoline is extremely flammable, so take extra precautions when you work on any part of the fuel system. Don't smoke or allow open flames or bare light bulbs near the work area, and don't work in a garage*

7.7a   Lift the air cleaner assembly straight up

7.7b   1973 and later models have a dry paper element filter – disconnect the hoses and lift it off

8.2a   Loosen the screw on the throttle lever near the base of the carburetor . . .

8.2b   . . . then remove the retaining clip (be careful not to lose the clamp screw assembly on the throttle lever)

8.3   Remove the spring and sleeve

8.7   Cable routing details (body removed for clarity)

1   Rubber boot   3   Clutch cable
2   Flexible guide tube

8.12   Clearance at "a" should be about 0.40 in (1 mm)

9.3   The throttle positioner (1) mounting bracket fits between the carburetor and intake manifold

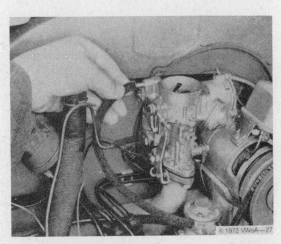

9.4   Disconnect the fuel line from the carburetor

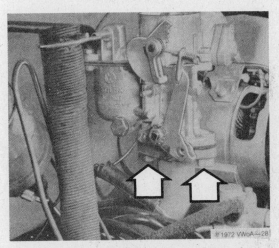

9.6   Remove the mounting nuts (arrows)

4

where a natural gas-type appliance (such as a water heater or clothes dryer) with a pilot light is present. If you spill any fuel on your skin, rinse it off immediately with soap and water. When you perform any kind of work on the fuel tank, wear safety glasses and have a Class B type fire extinguisher on hand.

Removal

1   Disconnect the negative cable from the battery.
2   Remove the air cleaner (see Section 7), or on Karmann Ghias, remove the air cleaner-to-carburetor duct.
3   Label and disconnect the vacuum hose(s) and any wires from the carburetor and throttle positioner, if equipped **(see illustration)**.
4   Disconnect the fuel line from the carburetor **(see illustration)**.
5   Detach the accelerator cable (see Section 8) and, on 1960 and earlier models, disconnect the manual choke cable. On models with a throttle positioner, detach the pull rod from the fast idle lever by prying off the retaining pin.
6   Remove the carburetor mounting nuts and lift the carburetor from the engine **(see illustration)**.
7   Temporarily stuff a rag in the intake manifold to prevent dirt from falling in.
8   Remove all traces of old gasket material from the intake manifold flange and the carburetor base (and the throttle positioner, if equipped).

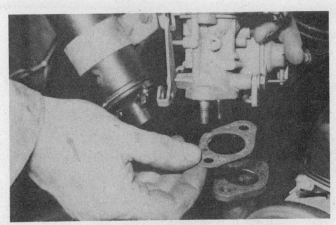

9.9   Place a new gasket between the carburetor and intake manifold

Installation

9   Installation is the reverse of removal. Be sure to use a new gasket **(see illustration)** and tighten the nuts to the torque listed in this Chapter's

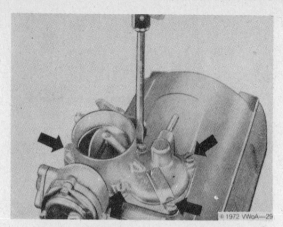

10.9a   Remove the cover screws (arrows)

Specifications. If the engine is equipped with a throttle positioner, install a gasket on both sides of the throttle positioner.
10   Run the engine and check for fuel leaks.

10   Carburetor – diagnosis and overhaul

Warning: *Gasoline is extremely flammable, so take extra precautions when you work on any part of the fuel system. Don't smoke or allow open flames or bare light bulbs near the work area, and don't work in a garage where a natural gas-type appliance (such as a water heater or clothes dryer) with a pilot light is present. If you spill any fuel on your skin, rinse it off immediately with soap and water. When you perform any kind of work on the fuel tank, wear safety glasses and have a Class B type fire extinguisher on hand.*

Diagnosis

1   A thorough road test and check of carburetor adjustments should be done before any major carburetor service work. Specifications for some adjustments are listed on the Vehicle Emissions Control Information (VECI) label found in the engine compartment on late model vehicles.
2   Carburetor problems usually show up as flooding, hard starting, stalling, severe backfiring and poor acceleration. A carburetor that's leaking fuel and/or covered with wet looking deposits definitely needs attention.
3   Some performance complaints directed at the carburetor are actually a result of loose, out-of-adjustment or malfunctioning engine or electrical components. Others develop when vacuum hoses leak, are disconnected or are incorrectly routed. The proper approach to analyzing carburetor problems should include the following items:

   a)   Inspect all vacuum hoses and actuators for leaks and correct installation (see Chapters 1 and 6).
   b)   Tighten the intake manifold and carburetor mounting nuts/bolts evenly and securely.
   c)   Perform a compression test (see Chapter 2).
   d)   Clean or replace the spark plugs as necessary (see Chapter 1).
   e)   Check the spark plug wires (see Chapter 1).
   f)   Inspect the ignition coil primary wires.
   g)   Check the ignition timing (see Chapter 1 or follow the instructions printed on the Emissions Control Information label).
   h)   Check the fuel pump pressure/volume (see Section 3).
   i)   Check/replace the air filter element (see Chapter 1).
   j)   Check the PCV system (see Chapter 6).
   k)   Check/replace the fuel filter (see Chapter 1). Also, the strainer in the fuel tank could be restricted.
   l)   Check for a plugged exhaust system.
   m)   Check EGR valve operation, if equipped (see Chapter 6).
   n)   Check the choke; it should be completely open at normal engine operating temperature (see Chapter 1).
   o)   Check for fuel leaks and kinked or dented fuel lines (see Chapters 1 and 4)

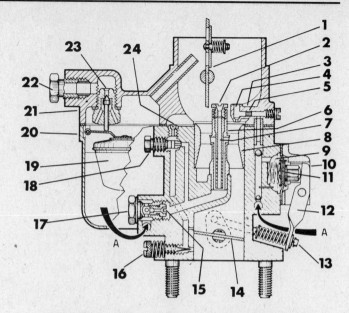

10.9b   Solex 28 PCI carburetor – cross-sectional view

1	Choke plate	14	Throttle valve
2	Correction jet	15	Main jet
3	Accelerator pump injector	16	Slow running mixture
4	Air bleed		adjusting screw
5	Pump jet	17	Main jet carrier plug
6	Main jet bridge	18	Pilot jet
7	Emulsion tube	19	Float
8	Choke tube	20	Carburetor body
9	Pump diaphragm spring	21	Top cover
10	Accelerator pump	22	Fuel inlet fitting
11	Pump diaphragm	23	Needle valve assembly
12	Pump lever	24	Pilot jet air bleed
13	Pump operating rod	A	Fuel inlet points

   p)   Check accelerator pump operation with the engine off (remove the air cleaner cover and operate the throttle as you look into the carburetor throat – you should see a stream of gasoline enter the carburetor).
   q)   Check for incorrect fuel or bad gasoline.
   r)   Check the valve clearances (see Chapter 1)
   s)   Have a dealer service department or repair shop check the engine on an electronic analyzer.
4   Diagnosing carburetor problems may require the engine be started and run with the air cleaner off. While running the engine without the air cleaner, backfires are possible. This situation is likely to occur if the carburetor is malfunctioning, but just the removal of the air cleaner can lean the fuel/air mixture enough to produce an engine backfire. **Warning:** *Do not position any part of your body, especially your face, directly over the carburetor during inspection and servicing procedures. Wear eye protection!*

Overhaul

Refer to illustrations 10.9a, 10.9b, 10.9c, 10.9d, 10.09e, 10.9f, 10.9g, 10.10a, 10.10b, 10.11, 10.15, 10.27, 10.28a, 10.28b and 10.29

5   Once you determine that the carburetor needs an overhaul, several options are available. If you're going to attempt to overhaul the carburetor yourself, first obtain a good quality carburetor rebuild kit (which will include all necessary gaskets, internal parts, instructions and a parts list). You'll also need some special solvent and a means of blowing out the internal passages of the carburetor with air.
6   An alternative is to obtain a new or rebuilt carburetor. They are readily available from dealers and auto parts stores. Make absolutely sure the exchange carburetor is identical to the original. A number is stamped on the

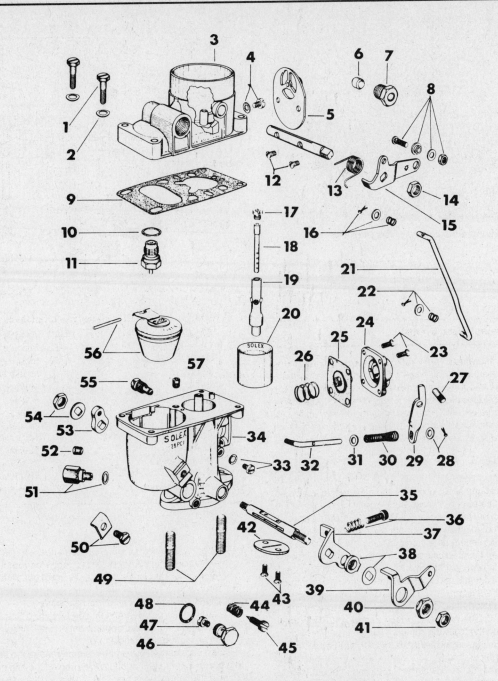

10.9c Solex 28 PCI Carburetor – exploded view

1	Cover screw	15	Choke lever	29	Pump lever	42
2	Washer	16	Connecting rod washer and	30	Return spring	43
3	Cover		retaining pin	31	Washer	44
4	Securing screw	17	Air correction jet	32	Operating rod	45
	and washer	18	Emulsion tube	33	Securing screw	46
5	Choke plate	19	Emulsion tube support		and washer	47
6	Fuel line ferrule	20	Choke tube	34	Main body	48
7	Fuel line union	21	Connecting rod	35	Throttle shaft	49
8	Choke cable connection	22	Connecting	36	Throttle stop screw	50
9	Gasket	23	Cover screws		and spring	51
10	Needle valve washer	24	Accelerator pump cover	37	Throttle lever	52
11	Needle valve	25	Accelerator pump diaphragm	38	Shaft washer	53
12	Choke plate screws	26	Spring	39	Intermediate lever	54
13	Choke shaft return spring	27	Pump lever pivot pin	40	Shaft nut	55
14	Shaft nut	28	Washer and cotter pin	41	Lock nut	56
						57

42 Throttle plate
43 Throttle plate screws
44 Spring
45 Volume control screw
46 Main jet holder
47 Main jet
48 Washer
49 Mounting studs
50 Cable clamp and screw
51 Vacuum pipe/distributor union
52 Vacuum pipe union ferrule
53 Intermediate lever
54 Shaft washer and nut
55 Pilot jet
56 Float and pivot
57 Pilot air bleed

4

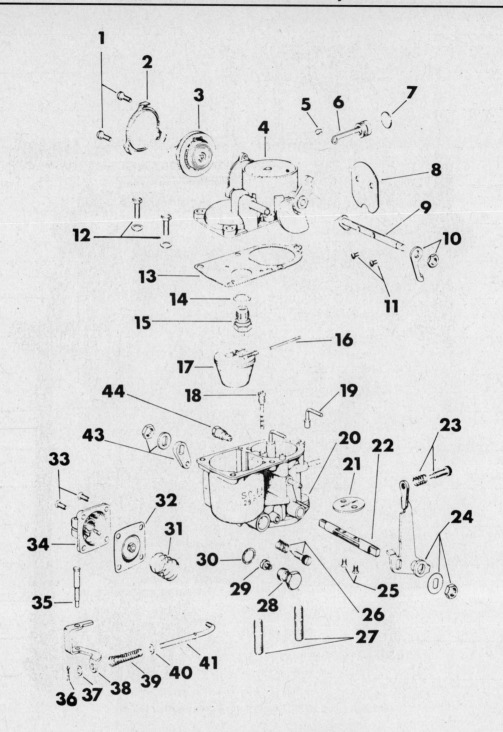

10.9d   Solex 28 PICT carburetor – exploded view

1	Retaining screws	12	Cover screws	23	Throttle stop screw	34	Pump cover
2	Cover retaining ring	13	Gasket	24	Throttle lever washer and nut	35	Pivot pin
3	Automatic choke element	14	Washer	25	Throttle plate screws	36	Cotter pin
4	Upper body	15	Needle valve	26	Volume control screw	37	Washer
5	Clip	16	Float pivot	27	Mounting studs	38	Pump lever
6	Vacuum piston link	17	Float	28	Main jet carrier	39	Spring
7	Plug	18	Emulsion tube	29	Main jet	40	Washer
8	Choke plate	19	Accelerator pump discharge	30	Washer	41	Pump rod
9	Choke shaft	20	Lower body	31	Pump spring	42	Not Used
10	Lever and nut	21	Throttle plate	32	Pump diaphragm	43	Intermediate lever, washer and nut
11	Choke plate screws	22	Throttle shaft	33	Pump cover screws	44	Pilot jet

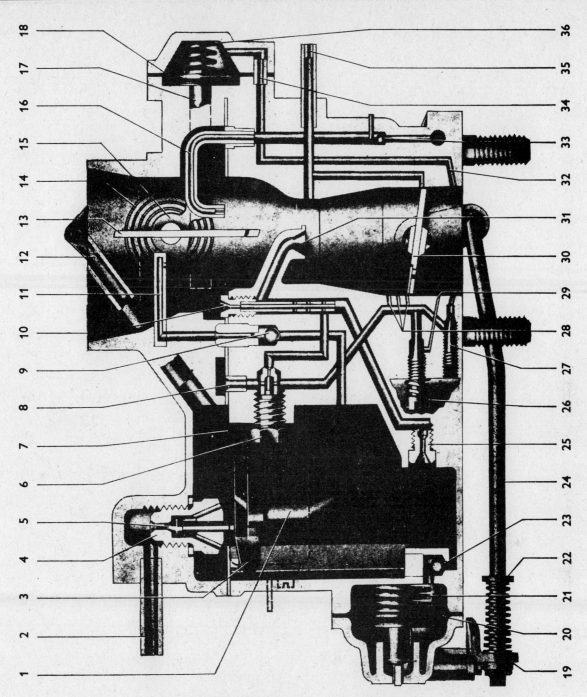

10.9e Solex 30 PICT carburetor – cross-sectional view

1 Float
2 Fuel line
3 Float lever
4 Needle valve
5 Needle
6 Pilot jet (electro-magnetic cut-off shown in dotted line)
7 Gasket
8 Pilot air orifice
9 Non-return ball
10 Air correction jet and emulsion tube
11 Power fuel tube
12 Vent tube
13 Choke plate
14 Bi-metal choke spring
15 Choke lever
16 Accelerator pump discharge tube
17 Vacuum diaphragm rod
18 Vacuum diaphragm
19 Pump lever
20 Pump diaphragm
21 Pump spring
22 Spring
23 Non-return ball, pump outlet
24 Pull rod for pump diaphragm
25 Main jet
26 Volume control screw
27 Idle bleed screw
28 By-pass ports
29 Idle port
30 Throttle plate
31 Main discharge beak
32 Vacuum drilling
33 Non-return ball, pump outlet
34 Jet orifice
35 Vacuum connection
36 Vacuum diaphragm spring

4

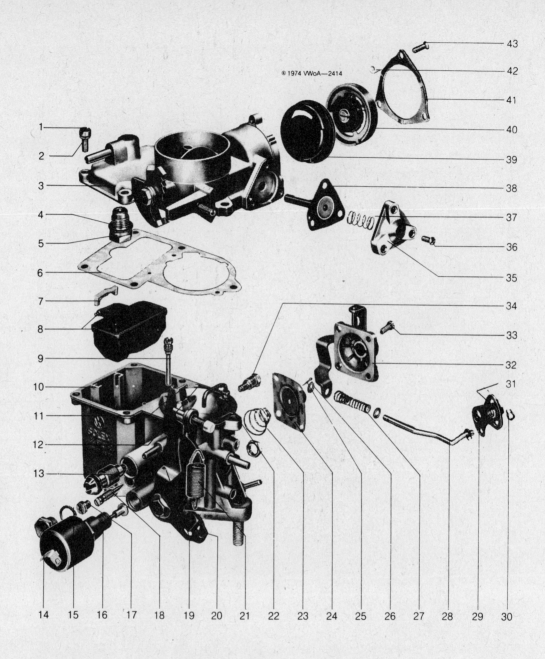

© 1974 VWoA—2414

10.9f   Solex 34 PICT-3 carburetor – exploded view

1	Fillister head screw	15	Main jet cover plug seal	30	Circlip
2	Spring washer	16	Electromagnetic cutoff valve	31	Adjusting segment
3	Carburetor upper part	17	Main jet	32	Pump cover
4	Float valve washer	18	Volume control screw	33	Screw
5	Needle valve	19	Fast idle lever	34	Pilot jet
6	Gasket	20	Throttle valve lever	35	Vacuum diaphragm cover
7	Float pin retainer	21	Throttle return spring	36	Oval head screw
8	Float with pivot pin	22	Accelerator pump injector	37	Vacuum diaphragm spring
9	Air correction jet with	23	Pump diaphragm spring	38	Vacuum diaphragm
	emulsion tube	24	Pump diaphragm	39	Plastic cap
10	Carburetor body	25	Cotter pin	40	Choke heating element
11	Pilot air drilling	26	1 mm (0.040 in.) thick washer	41	Cover retaining ring
12	Auxiliary air drilling	27	Connecting rod spring	42	Retaining ring spacer
13	Bypass screw	28	Connecting link	43	Small fillister head screw
14	Main jet cover plug	29	Adjustable bellcrank		

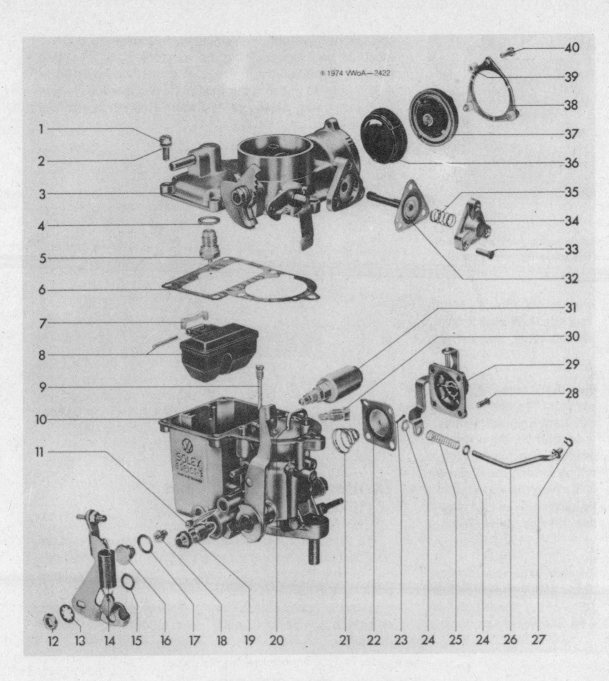

10.9g   Solex 30 PICT-3 carburetor – exploded view

1	Fillister head screw	14	Throttle return spring
2	Spring washer	15	Spring washer
3	Carburetor upper part	16	Main jet cover plug
4	Float valve washer	17	Main jet cover plug seal
5	Float valve	18	Main jet
6	Gasket	19	Bypass screw
7	Float pin retainer	20	Accelerator pump injector
8	Float with pivot pin	21	Pump diaphragm spring
9	Air correction jet with emulsion tube	22	Pump diaphragm
		23	Cotter pin
10	Carburetor body	24	1-mm (0.040 in.) thick washer
11	Volume control screw	25	Connecting rod spring
12	Nut	26	Connecting link
13	Lockwasher		

27	Clip
28	Screw
29	Pump cover
30	Pilot jet
31	Electromagnetic cutoff valve
32	Vacuum diaphragm
33	Oval head screw
34	Vacuum diaphragm cover
35	Vacuum diaphragm spring
36	Plastic cap
37	Choke heating element
38	Cover retaining ring
39	Retaining ring spacer
40	Small fillister head screw

10.10a   Remove the gasket . . .

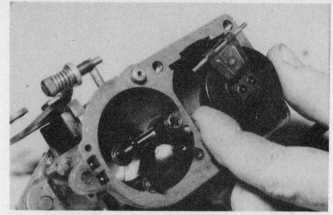

10.10b   . . . and lift the float out

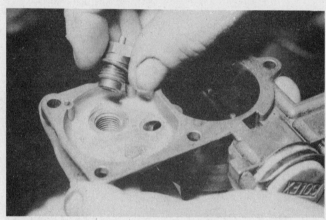

10.11   Loosen the float needle valve with a wrench and then unscrew it – save the washer for comparison with the replacement

10.15   Remove the pilot jet cutoff valve

float bowl. It will help determine the exact type of carburetor you have. When obtaining a rebuilt carburetor or a rebuild kit, make sure the kit or carburetor matches your application exactly. Seemingly insignificant differences can make a large difference in engine performance. Carburetors may be identified by the numbers on the float bowl:

28 PICT carburetors – 1963 and earlier models
28 PICT-1 carburetors – 1964 and 1965 models
30 PICT-1 carburetors – 1966 and 1967 models
30 PICT-2 carburetors – 1968 and 1969 models
30 PICT-3 carburetors – 1970 models
34 PICT-3 and 34 PICT-4 carburetors – 1971 through 1974 models

7   If you choose to overhaul your own carburetor, allow enough time to disassemble it carefully, soak the necessary parts in the cleaning solvent (usually for at least one-half day or according to the instructions listed on the carburetor cleaner) and reassemble it, which will usually take much longer than disassembly. When disassembling the carburetor, match each part with the illustration in the carburetor kit and lay the parts out in order on a clean work surface. Overhauls by inexperienced mechanics can result in an engine which runs poorly or not at all. To avoid this, use care and patience when disassembling the carburetor so you can reassemble it correctly.

8   Because carburetor designs were constantly modified by the manufacturer in order to meet increasingly more stringent emissions regulations, it isn't feasible to include a step-by-step overhaul of each type. You should receive a detailed, well-illustrated set of instructions with any carburetor overhaul kit; they will apply in a more specific manner to the carburetor on your vehicle. However, if instructions are not available, refer to the following Steps, and adapt them to the model you are working on.

9   Remove any external items such as springs and dashpots. Remove the five screws from the carburetor top **(see illustrations)** and carefully lift it off.

10   Detach the gasket and lift the float out **(see illustrations)**.
11   Unscrew the float needle valve **(see illustration)**.
12   Remove the three screws from the automatic choke cover (1961 and later models) and remove the heating element and plastic cap.
13   On 1964 and later models, remove the three vacuum diaphragm-to-cover screws.
14   Remove the air correction jet and emulsion tube.
15   On 1970 and earlier models, remove the pilot jet cutoff valve **(see illustration)**.
16   On 1971 and later models, remove the bypass mixture cutoff valve.
17   Remove the main jet plug, seal and jet.
18   Remove the idle mixture (volume) screw and spring (early models) or the air bypass screw (later models). **Caution:** *On 1971 and later carburetors, do not remove the small volume control screw located near the air bypass screw.*
19   Remove the cotter pin from the accelerator pump connector rod (if equipped).
20   Remove the four screws from the accelerator pump cover and detach the cover, diaphragm and spring.
21   Soak all the metal parts in a carburetor cleaning tank for several hours. **Caution:** *Do not place electrical, rubber or plastic parts in the cleaner.*
22   Remove the parts from the cleaning tank and rinse them with water. Blow out all the passages with compressed air. **Warning:** *Wear eye protection!* **Caution:** *Do not use wire to clean out the passages, the holes may be enlarged.*
23   Inspect all parts for wear and damage. Shake the float to see if it has absorbed fuel. Replace it if necessary.
24   Replace all gaskets and small components with the parts supplied in the rebuilding kit. Compare the old and new parts to ensure interchangeability.

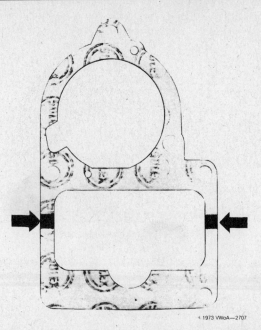

10.27   The color of the stripes (arrows) indicates which carburetor it belongs with

10.29   On 34 PICT-3 carburetors, the accelerator pump is adjusted by moving the screw (arrow) – on models with generators, the linkage is located where the dotted outline is shown

10.28a   Install the bimetallic spring so the hook engages the lever (arrows)

10.28b   Align the marks as described in the text

25   Check the choke and throttle shafts for looseness or binding.

26   Reassemble the carburetor in the reverse order of disassembly. Be sure to use the correct thickness washer under the fuel inlet needle valve, as this determines the float level. Refer to the adjustment instructions in the carburetor kit.

27   Be sure to use the correct carburetor body-to-cover gasket. On 30 PICT-3 carburetors, the gasket is marked with yellow stripes, 34 PICT-3 gaskets have black stripes **(see illustration)**.

28   When assembling the automatic choke (1961 and later models), be sure the hook on the bimetallic spring contacts the choke shaft lever **(see illustration)**. Install the cover and retainer and lightly tighten the screws. Turn the cover until the marks are aligned properly **(see illustration)**. On some 1970 models, the mark on the heating element must align with the upper mark on the housing. On other models, align the element with the middle mark on the housing. Refer to the instructions in the rebuilding kit for specific information. **Note:** *On 1972 through 1974 models, the heating elements are marked with a number 60 to identify them. These elements are not interchangeable with earlier models.*

29   When tightening the screws on the accelerator pump cover, move the lever away from the float bowl to ensure the diaphragm is in the correct position. The amount of fuel delivered by the accelerator pump is adjustable. Too little fuel will result in engine stumbling and hesitation, while excess fuel will reduce fuel economy and increase exhaust emissions. Several types of accelerator pump linkages are used. Adjustment is made by installing the rod or cotter pin in a different hole on early models. On later models with 34 PICT-3 carburetors, adjustment is made by moving a spring loaded screw **(see illustration)**. Refer to the adjustment instructions in the carburetor kit.

30   When the carburetor is completely assembled, install it (see Section 9) and adjust the idle speed (see Chapter 1).

11   Fuel injection system – general information

Refer to illustration 11.2

Warning: *Gasoline is extremely flammable, so take extra precautions when you work on any part of the fuel system. Don't smoke or allow open flames or bare light bulbs near the work area, and don't work in a garage where a natural gas-type appliance (such as a water heater or clothes dryer) with a pilot light is present. If you spill any fuel on your skin, rinse it off immediately with soap and water. When you perform any kind of work on the fuel tank, wear safety glasses and have a Class B type fire extinguisher on hand.*

Note: *Always check the ignition system and engine compression (see Chapter 2 and 5) before condemning the fuel injection for rough engine operation.*

Starting with the 1975 model year, VW Beetles are equipped with electronic fuel injection instead of carburetors.

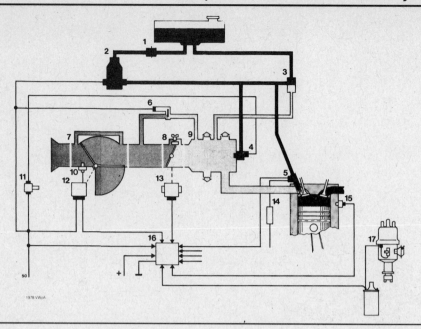

The fuel injection system **(see illustration)** is composed of three subsystems; fuel delivery, air control and electronic controls. We will discuss each one separately:

Fuel delivery

Fuel is pressurized by an electric fuel pump located below the fuel tank and pumped through a filter and lines from the front to the rear of the vehicle. In the engine compartment, a circle of fuel lines (known as the ring main) route fuel to the injectors and cold-start valve. A fuel pressure regulator maintains pressure at a preset level in the ring main and returns any excess fuel to the tank via a return line. The fuel injectors spray fuel under pressure into the air intake passages just upstream of the intake valves. The cold-start valve sprays fuel into the engine's air intake during cold starts, taking the place of a choke on carbureted models.

Air control

Air passes through the air filter and then into the intake air sensor. The stator flap moves according to the rate of air flow into the engine. A potentiometer connected to the flap varies resistance and signals the computer about air volume going into the engine. Air then flows through the rubber boot into the throttle valve housing. The accelerator cable is connected to the throttle valve; when the driver presses the accelerator pedal, the throttle valve opens, admitting more air through the intake air distributor into the engine.

Whenever the engine is cold, the auxiliary air regulator opens, allowing extra air into the engine for a fast idle. The regulator has an electrically heated bi-metallic spring which closes the valve gradually as the engine warms up.

Electronic control

An Electronic Control Unit (also known as a computer or ECU) monitors sensor output and adjusts fuel delivery accordingly by varying the time the fuel injectors are open. Air flow volume (measured by the intake air sensor) and engine speed (obtained from the ignition distributor) are the main parameters used by the ECU to meter fuel flow to the engine.

All models have a temperature sensor (known as Temperature Sensor 2) mounted in the cylinder head. The information provided by this sensor allows the ECU to adjust the fuel mixture for cold starts and warm-up as well as normal operation. On 1976 and later models, a temperature sensor (known as Temperature Sensor 1) is located inside the intake air sensor. It measures the temperature of air going through the sensor and allows the ECU to adjust fuel mixture for air density changes caused by temperature variation.

The thermo-time switch activates the cold-start valve when the engine is cold and allows it to spray fuel for a short time. After a pre-set time, the power to the cold-start valve is shut off to prevent flooding.

Additionally, a throttle valve switch is used on 1975 through 1977 models (microswitch on 1977 California models) to signal the ECU to supply full load mixture enrichment whenever the throttle is wide open. On 1978 and 1979 models, the system was deleted.

The throttle valve switch also controls opening of the EGR valve (except on 1977 and later California models). EGR is shut off at idle and full throttle.

12   Intake air sensor – check and replacement

Refer to illustrations 12.3a and 12.3b

Check

Note: *Sometimes the air flap inside the sensor will jam with dirt or break off from a backfire. If the engine won't run properly or won't start at all, inspect the throat of the sensor and clean or replace if necessary. Be sure to remove any broken parts.*

1   The intake air sensor has a moveable internal flap that is connected to a potentiometer (variable resistor) that signals the computer about throttle opening. Additionally, the intake air sensor controls the fuel pump through the double relay when the engine is running.

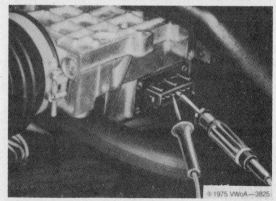

12.3a   Remove the plug and connect an ohmmeter to terminals 6 and 9

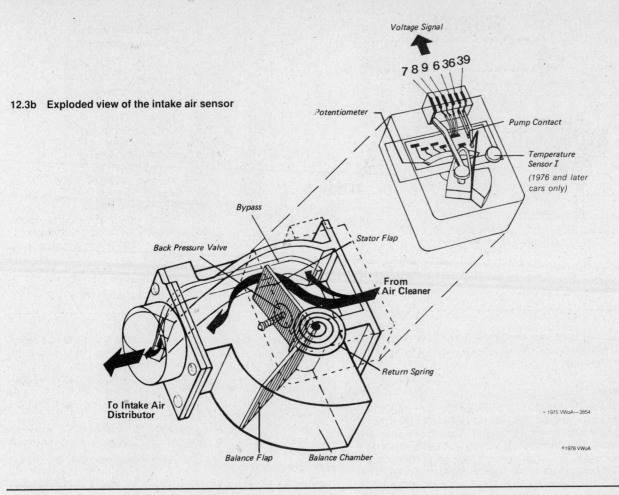

12.3b   Exploded view of the intake air sensor

Voltage Signal

7 8 9 6 36 39

Potentiometer

Pump Contact

Temperature Sensor I

(1976 and later cars only)

Bypass

Stator Flap

Back Pressure Valve

From Air Cleaner

Return Spring

To Intake Air Distributor

Balance Flap   *Balance Chamber*

1975 VWoA—3854

©1978 VWoA

4

Potentiometer test

2   Remove the air intake boot from the intake air sensor.

3   Carefully unplug the electrical connector from the intake air sensor and connect an ohmmeter to terminals 6 and 9 **(see illustration)**. Reach inside the throat and hand operate the balance flap **(see illustration)**. The ohmmeter reading should range from:

    1976 models – 100 to 300 ohms
    1975, 1978 and 1979 models – 200 to 400 ohms

Note: *The 200 to 400 ohm unit is usually installed on 1976 models as a service replacement unit.*

4   Connect the ohmmeter to terminals 7 and 8. The reading should range from:

    1975 models – 120 to 200 ohms
    1976 models – 80 to 200 ohms
    1977 and later models – 100 to 500 ohms

5   If the resistance is not as specified in either check, replace the intake air sensor.

Fuel pump switch test

6   Remove the air intake boot from the intake air sensor.

7   Carefully unplug the electrical connector from the intake air sensor and connect an ohmmeter to terminals 36 and 39. Reach inside the throat and hand operate the air flap. When the flap is closed there should be no continuity. As soon as the flap opens slightly there should be continuity. If not, replace the intake air sensor.

Replacement

8   Disconnect the negative cable from the battery.

9   Remove the air cleaner assembly (see Section 7).

10   Slide back the boot on the electrical connector, then carefully unplug the wiring harness from the intake air sensor.

11   Detach the rubber air intake duct from the intake air sensor.

12   Remove the mounting nuts and lift the intake air sensor from the vehicle.

13   Installation is the reverse of removal. Whenever a new intake air sensor is installed, adjust the idle speed (see Chapter 1) and have the fuel/air mixture adjusted using an exhaust gas analyzer.

---

13   Fuel pressure regulator – check and replacement

Warning: *Gasoline is extremely flammable, so take extra precautions when you work on any part of the fuel system. Don't smoke or allow open flames or bare light bulbs near the work area, and don't work in a garage where a natural gas-type appliance (such as a water heater or clothes dryer) with a pilot light is present. If you spill any fuel on your skin, rinse it off immediately with soap and water. When you perform any kind of work on the fuel tank, wear safety glasses and have a Class B type fire extinguisher on hand.*

Check

1   The fuel pressure regulator is mounted on the front cover plate of the engine, on the right (passenger's) side between the fan housing and firewall. It has a vacuum hose attached to it which connects with the intake air distributor.

2   If the engine is cold, start it and allow it to warm up. Shut the engine off and connect a fuel pressure gauge as shown in Section 3.

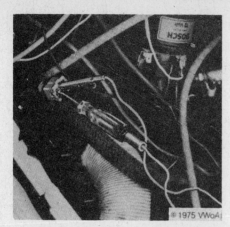

14.5   Check for voltage at each injector plug while an assistant operates the starter

14.9   Probe the series resistance block for voltage coming from terminal 88b of the double relay

3   Detach the vacuum hose from the pressure regulator and plug it.

4   Start the engine and note the fuel pressure. The pressure should be as listed in this Chapter's Specifications.

5   If the fuel pressure in the previous Step is correct, reconnect the vacuum hose and repeat the test. Pressure should now be as listed in this Chapter's Specifications. The fuel pressure regulator is non-adjustable. If the pressure is incorrect in either test, replace the fuel pressure regulator.

Replacement

6   Relieve the fuel pressure (see Section 2).

7   Disconnect the ground strap from the negative battery terminal.

8   Detach the vacuum hose from the fuel pressure regulator.

9   Disconnect the fuel lines from the pressure regulator and plug them.

10   Block the front tires. Raise the rear of the vehicle and support it securely on jackstands.

11   Working under the vehicle, remove the fuel pressure regulator mounting nut. It is threaded on the fuel outlet tube.

12   Lift the regulator from the engine compartment.

13   Install the new fuel pressure regulator with the pressure hose from the fuel pump connected to the side pipe of the regulator. The fuel lines and vacuum hose must be attached securely.

14   Connect the battery and repeat the pressure tests.

15   Check for fuel leaks after all fuel lines are reconnected.

---

14   Fuel injector – check and replacement

Warning: *Gasoline is extremely flammable, so take extra precautions when you work on any part of the fuel system. Don't smoke or allow open flames or bare light bulbs near the work area, and don't work in a garage where a natural gas-type appliance (such as a water heater or clothes dryer) with a pilot light is present. If you spill any fuel on your skin, rinse it off immediately with soap and water. When you perform any kind of work on the fuel tank, wear safety glasses and have a Class B type fire extinguisher on hand.*

Check

Refer to illustrations 14.5 and 14.9

1   The fuel injectors receive 12 volts positive from terminal 88b on the double relay whenever the ignition is ON. This current goes through four separate resistors in the series resistance block, which stabilizes the voltage going to the injectors.

2   The Electronic Control Unit (ECU) provides a negative (ground) return path for all injectors once per crankshaft revolution. When the solenoids in the injectors are energized in this fashion, the needle valves open. This permits fuel to spray out of the nozzle.

3   Two types of electrical malfunctions may occur; either the injector doesn't get power, or it gets grounded when it shouldn't.

4   If the engine is getting too much fuel (flooding), especially in wet weather, inspect the connections at the injectors for internal grounding. Unplug the connector from each fuel injector. Using an ohmmeter, touch one probe to the injector case and the other probe to one terminal on the injector and then the other. If there is continuity between the case and either terminal, replace the injector.

5   With the electrical connectors unplugged from the injectors, probe the connector terminals for voltage **(see illustration)** while an assistant operates the starter. If the system is working properly, the light should flicker on and off as the engine is cranked.

6   Test the wiring harness for shorts to ground. With the ignition OFF, unplug all of the injectors. Connect one ohmmeter probe to a clean engine ground and then probe each connector for continuity to ground. If any of the wires are grounded, replace the harness.

7   If the fuel pump works (see Section 3) but the engine won't start, determine if the fuel injectors are spraying fuel. Remove the injectors (see below) but leave the wiring and fuel hoses connected. Temporarily disable the ignition by disconnecting the primary wire between the distributor and the coil. Have an assistant operate the starter briefly while you observe the injector tips. **Warning:** *Perform this test only when the engine has cooled off completely. Wear eye protection and stay clear of the drivebelt and pulleys!* Fuel should spray out of all of the injectors in simultaneous squirts, once per crankshaft revolution. If it doesn't, there is a problem in the fuel injection system – continue the check procedure.

8   If any injectors don't spray fuel, unplug the electrical connectors. With an ohmmeter, check for continuity between the terminals of each injector that didn't spray. If there is no continuity, replace the injector.

9   If the injectors test OK, connect a test light **(see illustration)** and check for positive voltage at the series resistance block with the ignition On (do not operate the starter).

10   If voltage is getting to the series resistance block, check each resistor, the double relay and the wiring between the relay terminal 88b and the series resistance block (see Section 3).

11   Injectors should also be checked for leakage. First, check the fuel pressure (see Section 3). With the injectors out as described in the previous Step, wipe off the tips of the injectors. Have an assistant turn the ignition ON (do not activate the starter) while you observe the tips of the injectors. No more than two or three drops of fuel may leak from the nozzle. If the leakage is greater, replace the injector(s).

Replacement

12   Relieve fuel pressure (see Section 2).

13   Remove the heater air ducts that run between the heat exchangers and fan housing.

14   Unplug the electrical connectors from the fuel injectors.

15   Remove the retaining bolts from the injector retainers using a 10 mm socket wrench.

16   Gently pull the injectors out of the intake manifold, along with the retainers and seals. **Note:** *If the seals stick, remove them with a wire hook.*

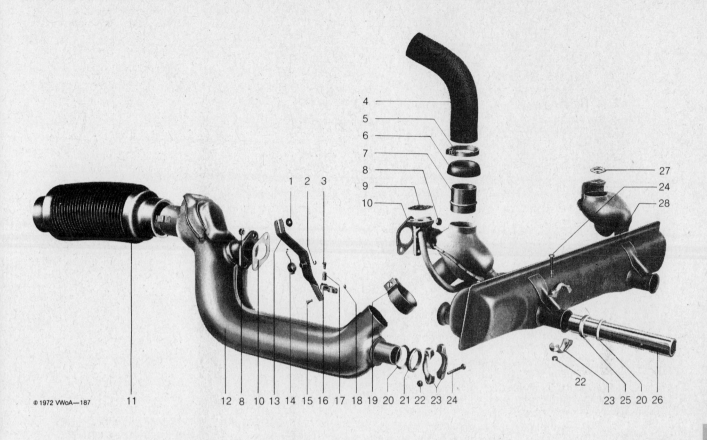

© 1972 VWoA—187

15.1   Exhaust system details (typical carbureted model)

1	Clamp washer	8	Nut	15	Pin	22	Nut
2	E-clip	9	Gasket	16	Cable connecting link	23	Clamp
3	Bolt	10	Gasket	17	Cable retaining pin	24	Bolt
4	Hot air tube	11	Heater air duct	18	E-clip	25	Sealing ring
5	Hose clamp	12	Heat exchanger	19	Clamp	26	Tailpipe
6	Air hose grommet	13	Heater flap lever	20	Retaining ring	27	Gasket
7	Connecting pipe	14	Lever return spring	21	Sealing ring	28	Muffler

17   Loosen the hose clamps and pull the injectors off the main fuel ring.

18   Replace the large seal around the injector body and the small seal at the tip of the injector. Installation is the reverse of removal. Tighten the retainers to the torque listed in this Chapter's Specifications.

15   Exhaust system servicing – general information

Refer to illustrations 15.1 and 15.4

Warning: *Inspection and repair of exhaust system components should be done only after enough time has elapsed after driving the vehicle to allow the system components to cool completely. Also, when working under the vehicle, make sure it is securely supported on jackstands.*

1   The exhaust system consists of the heat exchangers/exhaust manifolds, the catalytic converter (1975 and later models only), the muffler, the tailpipe(s) and all connecting parts, brackets, hangers and clamps **(see illustration)**. If any of the parts are improperly installed, excessive noise and vibration will be produced.

2   Conduct regular inspections of the exhaust system to keep it safe and quiet. Look for any damaged or bent parts, open seams, holes, loose connections, excessive corrosion or other defects which could allow exhaust fumes to enter the vehicle. Also check the catalytic converter (if equipped) when you inspect the exhaust system (see below). Deteriorated exhaust system components should not be repaired; they should be replaced with new parts.

3   If the exhaust system components are extremely corroded or rusted together, welding equipment will probably be required to remove them. The convenient way to accomplish this is to have a muffler repair shop remove the corroded sections with a cutting torch.

4   Here are some simple guidelines to follow when repairing the exhaust system:

   a) Apply penetrating oil to the exhaust system component fasteners to make them easier to remove.

   b) Use new gaskets and clamps when installing exhaust systems components.

   c) Apply anti-seize compound to the threads of all exhaust system fasteners during reassembly.

15.4   **The catalytic converter is located to
the left of the muffler**

d) Be sure to allow sufficient clearance between newly installed parts and all points on the underbody. Pay particularly close attention to the catalytic converter mounting **(see illustration)**.

Chapter 5   Engine electrical systems

Contents

1   General information

The engine electrical systems include all ignition, charging and starting components. Because of their engine-related functions, these components are discussed separately from chassis electrical devices such as the lights, the instruments, etc. (which are included in Chapter 12).

Volkswagen Beetles through model year 1966 were built with six-volt electrical systems; 1967 and later models have 12-volt systems. Beginning in June 1971, they were equipped with a special wiring harness that connects to the VW Computer Analysis system used by Volkswagen dealers. This harness terminates in the engine compartment with a special plug. **Caution:** *Never connect anything else to this plug or the components connected to it may be damaged.*

Always observe the following precautions when working on the electrical systems:

a) Be extremely careful when servicing engine electrical components. They are easily damaged if checked, connected or handled improperly.

b) Never leave the ignition switch ON for long periods of time with the engine off.

c) Don't disconnect the battery cables while the engine is running.

d) Maintain correct polarity when connecting a battery cable from another vehicle during jump starting.

e) Always disconnect the negative cable first and hook it up last or the battery may be shorted by the tool being used to loosen the cable clamps.

f) Never jump start a vehicle with a six-volt electrical system from a 12-volt vehicle or vice versa.

It's also a good idea to review the safety-related information regarding the engine electrical systems located in the *Safety first* Section near the front of this manual before beginning any operation included in this Chapter.

2   Battery – emergency jump starting

Refer to the *Booster battery (jump) starting* procedure at the front of this manual. **Warning:** *Never jump start a vehicle with a six-volt electrical system from a vehicle with a 12-volt electrical system or vice versa.*

3   Battery cables – check and replacement

1   Periodically inspect the entire length of each battery cable for damage, cracked or burned insulation and corrosion. Poor battery cable connections can cause starting problems and decreased engine performance.

2   Check the cable-to-terminal connections at the ends of the cables for cracks, loose wire strands and corrosion. The presence of white, fluffy deposits under the insulation at the cable terminal connection is a sign that the cable is corroded and should be replaced. Check the terminals for distortion, missing mounting bolts and corrosion.

3   When removing the cables, always disconnect the negative cable first and connect it last or the battery may be shorted by the tool used to loosen the cable clamps. Even if only the positive cable is being replaced, be sure to disconnect the negative cable from the battery first (see Chapter 1 for further information regarding battery cable removal).

4   Disconnect the old cables from the battery, then trace each of them to their opposite ends and detach them from the starter solenoid and ground terminals. Note the routing of each cable to ensure correct installation.

5   If you are replacing either or both of the old cables, take them with you when buying new cables. It is vitally important that you replace the cables with identical parts. Cables have characteristics that make them easy to identify: positive cables are usually covered with black or red insulation and have a larger diameter battery post clamp; ground cables are usually

4.7a   Six-volt batteries have three caps

4.7b   12-volt batteries have six caps

uninsulated and have a slightly smaller diameter clamp for the negative post.

6   Clean the threads of the solenoid or ground connection with a wire brush to remove rust and corrosion. Apply a light coat of battery terminal corrosion inhibitor, or petroleum jelly, to the threads to prevent future corrosion.

7   Attach the cable to the solenoid or ground connection and tighten the mounting nut/bolt securely.

8   Before connecting a new cable to the battery, make sure that it reaches the battery post without having to be stretched.

9   Connect the positive cable first, followed by the negative cable.

4   Battery – removal and installation

Refer to illustrations 4.7a and 4.7b
Caution: *Always disconnect the negative cable first and connect it last or the battery may be shorted by the tool being used to loosen the cable clamps.*

1   Remove the lower cushion from the rear seat (see Chapter 11, if necessary).

2   Release the hold-down clamp and remove the battery cover, if equipped.

3   Disconnect both cables from the battery terminals.

4   Remove the hold-down bracket located on the side of the battery near the bottom.

5   Lift out the battery. Be careful – it's heavy.

6   While the battery is out, inspect the tray and floorpan for corrosion and correct as necessary.

7   If you are replacing the battery, make sure that you get one that's identical, with the same voltage **(see illustrations)**, dimensions, amperage rating, cold cranking rating, etc.

8   Installation is the reverse of removal. **Caution:** *Be sure the battery is protected with an insulating cover to avoid short circuiting through the seat springs!*

5   Ignition system – general information

Refer to illustration 5.1

The purpose of the ignition system is to provide sparks to ignite the fuel in the combustion chambers. Ignition system components include the battery, ignition switch, coil, the primary (low voltage) and secondary (high voltage) wiring, the distributor and the spark plugs **(see illustration)**. The distributor contains the ignition breaker points (or "points"), the condenser, cap and rotor and an advance mechanism. The ignition coil is switched on and off by contact breaker points in the distributor. When the points close, electricity flows from the battery, through the ignition switch and wiring into the primary windings of the coil. As the points open, the magnetic field in the coil breaks down, inducing high voltage in the secondary windings. This voltage travels from the center post in the coil to the center post of the distributor cap, then through the rotor to the spark plug wire. When the voltage reaches the spark plug, it jumps the gap, creating a spark that fires the fuel/air mixture.

5.1   Ignition system
       schematic diagram

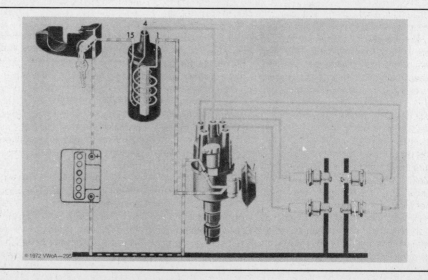

© 1972 VWoA—295

7.1   The ignition coil (arrow) is mounted on the fan housing

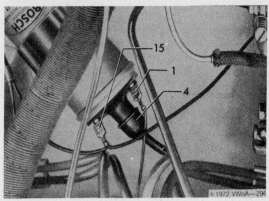

7.3   Ignition coil wiring

1	To distributor (points)	15	To ignition switch
4	To center post of distributor cap (high voltage)		

The optimum moment for the spark to ignite the fuel mixture varies with engine speed and load, as well as engine temperature and fuel octane. The advance mechanism in the distributor adjusts the firing point (known as spark timing or advance) to allow the engine to operate over a wide range of speeds and loads. All 1967 and earlier models use a vacuum chamber mounted externally on the distributor to provide spark advance. All 1968 and later automatic stick shift models and all 1971 and later models use a combination of vacuum and centrifugal advance mechanisms to more accurately monitor the engine and time the sparks. On later emission-controlled models, the vacuum chambers have an advance and a retard portion.

The ignition breaker points, condenser, distributor cap and rotor, spark plug wires and spark plugs are all routine maintenance items. Check and replacement procedures and ignition timing instructions are provided in Chapter 1.

6   Ignition system – check

Warning: *Because of the very high secondary (spark plug) voltage generated by the ignition system, extreme care should be taken when this check is done.*

Calibrated ignition tester method

1   If the engine turns over but won't start, disconnect the spark plug lead from any spark plug and attach it to a calibrated ignition tester (available inexpensively from most auto parts stores). Make sure the tester is designed for point-type ignition systems.

2   Connect the clip on the tester to a bolt or metal bracket on the engine, crank the engine and watch the end of the tester to see if bright blue, well-defined sparks occur.

3   If sparks occur, sufficient voltage is reaching the plug to fire it (repeat the check at the remaining plug wires to verify that the distributor cap and rotor are OK). However, the plugs themselves may be fouled, so remove and check them as described in Chapter 1 or install new ones.

4   If no sparks or intermittent sparks occur, remove the distributor cap and check the cap and rotor as described in Chapter 1. If moisture is present, dry out the cap and rotor, then reinstall the cap and repeat the spark test.

5   If there's still no spark, detach the secondary coil wire from the distributor cap and hook it up to the tester (reattach the plug wire to the spark plug), then repeat the spark check.

6   If no sparks occur, check the primary (small) wire connections at the coil to make sure they're clean and tight. Refer to Section 7 and check the ignition coil. Make any necessary repairs, then repeat the check again.

7   If sparks now occur, the distributor cap, rotor, plug wire(s) or spark plug(s) (or all of them) may be defective.

8   If there's still no spark, the coil-to-cap wire may be bad (check the resistance with an ohmmeter and compare it to the Specifications). If a known good wire doesn't make any difference in the test results, the ignition coil, points or other internal components may be defective.

Alternative method

Note: *If you're unable to obtain a calibrated ignition tester, the following method will allow you to determine if the ignition system has spark, but it won't tell you if there's enough voltage produced to actually initiate combustion in the cylinders.*

9   Remove the wire from one of the spark plugs. Using an insulated tool, hold the wire about 1/4-inch from a good ground and have an assistant crank the engine.

10   If bright blue, well-defined sparks occur, sufficient voltage is reaching the plug to fire it. However, the plug(s) may be fouled, so remove and check them as described in Chapter 1 or install new ones.

11   If there's no spark, check the remaining wires in the same manner. A few sparks followed by no spark is the same condition as no spark at all.

12   If no sparks occur, remove the distributor cap and check the cap and rotor as described in Chapter 1. If moisture is present, dry out the cap and rotor, then reinstall the cap and repeat the spark test.

13   If there's still no spark, disconnect the secondary coil wire from the distributor cap, hold it about 1/4-inch from a good engine ground and crank the engine again.

14   If no sparks occur, check the primary (small) wire connections at the coil to make sure they're clean and tight.

15   If sparks now occur, the distributor cap, rotor, plug wire(s) or spark plug(s) (or all of them) may be defective.

16   If there's still no spark, the coil-to-cap wire may be bad (check the resistance with an ohmmeter and compare it to the Specifications). If a known good wire doesn't make any difference in the test results, the ignition coil, points or other internal components may be defective. Refer further testing to a VW dealer or qualified electrical specialist.

7   Ignition coil – check and replacement

Refer to illustrations 7.1 and 7.3

Check

1   The ignition coil steps up battery voltage high enough to jump the gap on the spark plugs. The coil is mounted on the fan housing adjacent to and above the distributor **(see illustration)**.

2   Inspect the coil wires and insulating tower for damage, splits, cracks and carbon tracks.

3   Check the routing of the wires to the coil **(see illustration)**. If the wires to terminals 1 and 15 are reversed, the engine may run, but will misfire under certain conditions.

4   Using a voltmeter, turn the ignition ON, engine OFF (do not operate the starter) check for positive voltage at terminal 15. On six-volt models, at least 4.8 volts should be reaching terminal 15; on 12-volt models, a minimum of 9.6 volts must be available. If not, trace and repair the wiring.

8.4   Disconnect the vacuum hose(s) from the distributor – if there are two hoses, label them

8.5   Remove the distributor hold-down nut

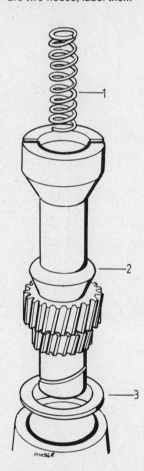

8.6   Distributor driveshaft components – exploded view (36 hp and fuel-injected models are slightly different)

| 1 | Spacer spring | 3 | Thrust washer |
| 2 | Distributor shaft | | (2 required) |

5   If sufficient voltage is reaching terminal 15 on the coil, disconnect the high-voltage wire (terminal 4) at the distributor cap end and check for a spark as described in Section 6.

6   If there is a strong spark, the coil is OK. If there is no spark, check the ignition points and condenser (see Chapter 1) and replace as necessary.

7   If the points and condenser are OK and sufficient voltage is present at terminal 15, replace the ignition coil. **Caution:** *Use the correct coil for the*

application. Coils used on 12-volt models have an internal resistor to re-duce power going to the windings. Models with six-volt systems do not have a built-in resistor. Use of a six-volt coil on a 12-volt system will result in burned points; a 12-volt coil on a six-volt model will not produce enough voltage.

Replacement

8   Label and then detach the wires from the coil.

9   Remove the two mounting bolts and lift the coil from the engine compartment.

10   Loosen the coil bracket clamp screw and slip the coil from the bracket.

11   Installation is the reverse of removal.

---

8   Distributor – removal and installation

Refer to illustration 8.4, 8.5, 8.6, 8.7, 8.8, 8.9a, 8.9b, 8.10, 8.11a and 8.11b

Removal

1   Disconnect the negative cable from the battery terminal.

2   Remove the distributor cap (see Chapter 1) and turn the crankshaft until the rotor is pointing toward the notch in the distributor body (below the terminal for the number one spark plug in the distributor cap) – see the TDC locating procedure in Chapter 2.

3   Detach the primary ignition wire that connects the ignition points and condenser in the distributor to the number 1 terminal on the ignition coil.

4   Disconnect the vacuum hose(s) from the distributor **(see illustration)**.

5   Remove the distributor hold-down nut **(see illustration)**.

6   Pull the distributor straight up to remove it. There is a spacer spring in the distributor driveshaft that may stick to the bottom of the distributor **(see illustration)**. Do not drop the spring into the crankcase. **Caution:** *DO NOT turn the crankshaft while the distributor is out of the engine.* If you intend to remove the distributor driveshaft, remove the fuel pump, pushrod and intermediate flange as described in Chapter 4 (not necessary on fuel-injected models).

7   Note the position of the slot in the distributor driveshaft and then re-move it by lifting and turning it slightly in a counterclockwise direction **(see illustration)**. Special tools are available from Volkswagen dealers or Schley Products (part no. 79150).

8   Remove the two thrust washers with a magnet or stiff wire **(see illustration)**. **Caution:** *Do not drop the washers into the crankcase.*

9   Inspect the distributor driveshaft for worn teeth and wear on the fuel pump eccentric (carbureted models only). If the teeth are damaged, check the teeth on the crankshaft gear. Measure the thrust washers with a mi-crometer. They should be 0.24 inch (0.60 mm). Replace any worn parts. Inspect the distributor components **(see illustrations)** and repair or re-place as necessary.

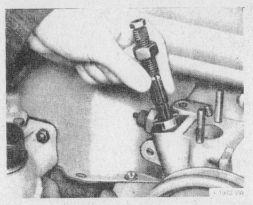

8.7 Pull the distributor driveshaft out with a special tool

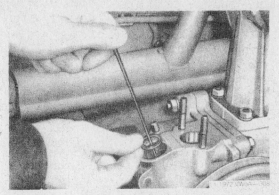

8.8 Remove the two thrust washers with a magnet or a stiff wire

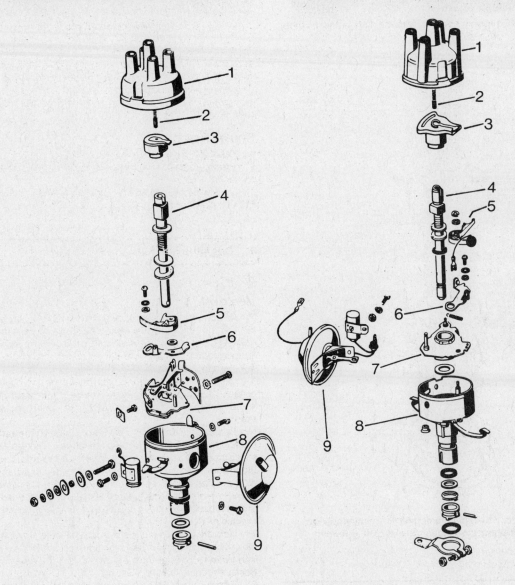

V.W.

BOSCH.

8.9a Early type distributor components

1	Cap	3	Rotor	6	Fixed contact	8	Distributor body
2	Carbon brush and spring	4	Shaft and cam	7	Contact base plate	9	Vacuum advance unit
		5	Moving contact				

5

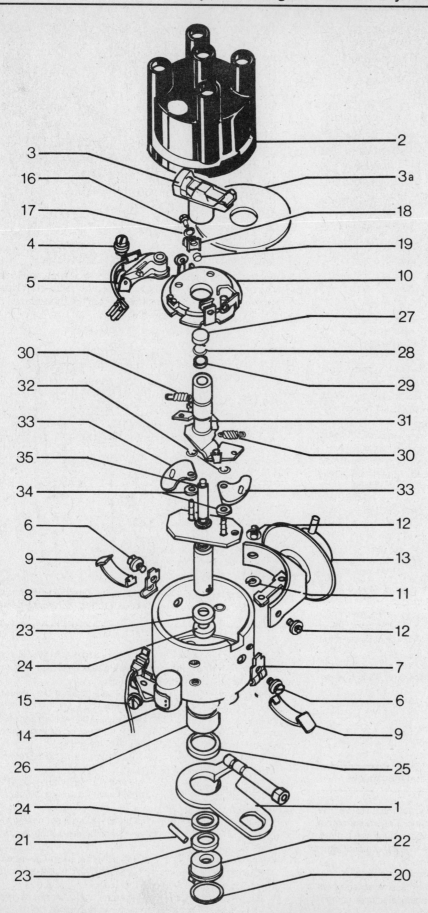

8.9b   Later type distributor with centrifugal advance mechanism

1   Mounting clamp bracket
2   Cap
3   Rotor
3a   Plastic cap
4   Contacts securing screw
5   Contact points
6   Clip screw
7   Clip retainer
8   Clip retainer
9   Cap clip
10   Contact points mounting plate
11   E-clip for pull rod
12   Screw
13   Vacuum unit
14   Condenser
15   Screw
16   Screw
17   Spring washer
18   Retaining spring
19   Ball
20   Circlip
21   Pin
22   Driving dog
23   Shim
24   Fiber washer
25   O-ring
26   Distributor body
27   Felt washer
28   Circlip
29   Thrust ring
30   Return spring
31   Cam
32   Circlip
33   Weights
34   Washer
35   Driveshaft

8.10 Slide the shims down the rod

8.11a Apply engine oil to the distributor driveshaft and install it with the slot approximately perpendicular to the crankcase centerline seam and the smaller segment toward the crankshaft pulley

Installation

Note: *If the crankshaft has been moved while the distributor is out, the number one piston must be repositioned at TDC. This can be done by feeling for compression pressure at the number one plug hole as the crankshaft is turned. Once compression is felt, align the ignition timing zero mark on the crankshaft pulley with the seam in the crankcase.*

10   Insert a rod or stiff wire straight into the spring hole. Apply grease to the two shims and slide them down the rod **(see illustration)**. Be sure the shims are properly seated before removing the rod.

11   Apply engine oil to the distributor driveshaft and install it with the slot perpendicular to the crankcase centerline seam and the smaller segment near the crankshaft pulley **(see illustrations). Note:** *On some late models with emission controls, the slot should be positioned one tooth left (counterclockwise) to allow for vacuum advance diaphragm clearance.*

12   Turn the crankshaft back and forth slightly with a wrench to determine if the distributor driveshaft is seated. If the driveshaft moves, it is seated. Realign the crankshaft pulley to TDC and check the slot in the driveshaft, also.

13   Insert a stiff wire into the center of the driveshaft and slide the spring down it and into place.

14   Install the fuel pump (carbureted models only).

15   Position the distributor to go into the engine. The hold-down bracket should be over the stud on the crankcase and the smaller segment of the drive tang on the bottom should face the crankshaft pulley. Slip the distributor into place. To mesh the slot in the distributor drive and the distributor, it may be necessary to turn the rotor slightly. The rotor should align with the mark on the edge of the distributor base.

16   Place the hold-down clamp in position and tighten the nut securely.

17   Install the distributor cap and reattach the spark plug wires to the plugs (if removed).

18   Connect the coil-to-distributor wires and the cable to the negative terminal of the battery.

19   Check the ignition timing (refer to Chapter 1).

9   Charging system – general information and precautions

The charging system supplies electrical power for the entire vehicle when the engine is running. The charging system includes a generator or an alternator, a voltage regulator, a charge indicator light, the battery, fuses and the wiring between all the components. The generator or alternator is driven by a drivebelt at the rear of the engine.

The purpose of the voltage regulator is to limit the generator's or alternator's voltage to a preset value. This prevents excessive voltage from overheating the generator/alternator and damaging electrical components when the engine is operated at high speeds.

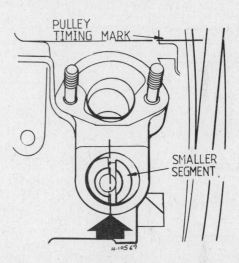

8.11b   With the engine at TDC, when the distributor driveshaft is seated, it should be perpendicular to the crankcase seam

Periodic maintenance of the charging system is not normally required. However, the drivebelt, battery and wires and connections should be inspected at the intervals outlined in Chapter 1.

The dashboard warning light should come on when the ignition key is turned to Start, then go off immediately after the engine starts. If it remains on, there is a malfunction in the charging system (see Section 10).

Be very careful when making electrical circuit connections to a vehicle equipped with an alternator and note the following:

a)   When reconnecting wires to the alternator from the battery, be sure to note the polarity.

b)   Before using arc welding equipment to repair any part of the vehicle, disconnect the wires from the alternator and the battery terminals.

c)   Never start the engine with a battery charger connected.

d)   Always disconnect both battery leads before using a battery charger.

e)   The generator/alternator is turned by an engine drivebelt which could cause serious injury if your hands, hair or clothes become entangled in it with the engine running.

f)   Wrap a plastic bag over the generator/alternator and secure it with rubberbands before steam cleaning the engine.

10.2   Checking battery voltage – the type of voltmeter shown here also incorporates lengths of resistance wire, allowing it to double as a battery load tester, which can check the battery's performance under a current draw that simulates the starter motor load; load testers, commonly available from auto parts stores, are a bit expensive, but make starting/charging system diagnosis easier

10   Charging system – check

Refer to illustration 10.2

1   If a malfunction occurs in the charging circuit, don't automatically assume the generator/alternator is causing the problem. First check the following items:

   a) Check the drivebelt tension and condition (see Chapter 1). Replace it if it's worn or deteriorated.
   b) Make sure the generator/alternator mounting bolts are tight.
   c) Inspect the generator/alternator wiring harness and the connectors at the alternator and voltage regulator. They must be in good condition and tight.
   d) Use a hydrometer (available at auto parts stores) to check the specific gravity of the battery electrolyte in each cell (doesn't apply to maintenance-free batteries). If it's low, charge the battery. Also, make sure each cell's reading is close to the readings of the other cells. One bad cell can cause the generator/alternator to overcharge the battery.
   e) Disconnect the battery cables (negative first, then positive). Inspect the battery posts and the cable clamps for corrosion. Clean them thoroughly if necessary (see Chapter 1). Reconnect the cable to the positive terminal.
   f) With the key off, connect a test light between the negative battery post and the disconnected negative cable clamp.
      1) If the test light does not come on, reattach the clamp and proceed to the next Step.
      2) If the test light comes on, there is a short (drain) in the electrical system of the vehicle. The short must be repaired before the charging system can be checked.
      3) Disconnect the generator/alternator wiring harness.
         (a) If the light goes out, the alternator is bad.
         (b) If the light stays on, pull each fuse until the light goes out (this will tell you which component is drawing power).

2   Using a voltmeter, check the battery voltage **(see illustration)** with the engine off. It should be approximately 6.3 volts on 1966 and earlier models and 12.6 volts on 1967 and later models.

3   Start the engine and run it at a fast idle (about 2,000 rpm). Check the

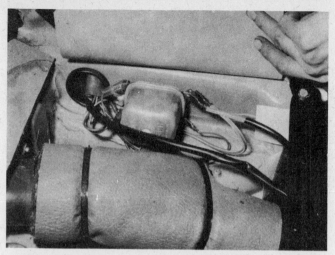

11.2a   On 1967 through late 1974 model Beetles, the voltage regulator is mounted under the rear seat on the driver's side

battery voltage again. It should now be approximately 7.4 to 8.1 volts on a 1966 or earlier models and 13.5 to 14.5 volts on 1967 and later models.

4   Turn on the headlights. The voltage should drop, and then come back up, if the charging system is working properly.

5   If the voltage reading is more than the specified charging voltage, replace the voltage regulator (refer to Section 11). If the voltage is less, the generator or alternator may be faulty or the voltage regulator may be malfunctioning. Replace the voltage regulator and if that doesn't correct the problem, replace the generator/alternator (the voltage regulator should be replaced whenever the generator/alternator is replaced anyway).

11   Voltage regulator – replacement

Refer to illustrations 11.2a, 11.2b, 11.4, 11.5, 11.8a, 11.8b and 11.9

1   Several types of voltage regulators are used on the models covered by this manual, and the one in the vehicle you are working on may not be the correct one. Whenever replacement is necessary, provide the parts counterperson with the vehicle chassis number, the engine serial number, the numbers on the generator/alternator and the numbers on the voltage regulator.

2   On 1966 and earlier models, the voltage regulator is mounted on the generator. On 1967 through late 1974 model Beetles, the voltage regulator is mounted under the back seat on the driver's side **(see illustration)**; vehicles produced after late 1974 have voltage regulators built into the alternators. On 1967 and later Karmann Ghias, the voltage regulator is mounted in the engine compartment next to the battery **(see illustration)**.

3   Disconnect the negative cable from the battery.

External voltage regulators

4   Label and then disconnect the wires from the voltage regulator **(see illustration)**.

5   Remove the mounting screws and lift the regulator. On six-volt models, turn the regulator over and disconnect the two wires underneath **(see illustration)**.

6   When reinstalling a six-volt regulator, be sure to connect the thick wire from the positive generator brush to the D+ terminal under the regulator. Connect the thin wire from the field to the DF or F terminal under the regulator.

7   On all models, mount the regulator and tighten the screws securely.

8   Reconnect the wires **(see illustrations)**.

Internal voltage regulators

9   Remove the cover plate from the top of the alternator **(see illustration)**.

11.2b On 1967 and later Karmann Ghias, the voltage regulator is located next to the battery

11.4 Label and then disconnect the wires (six-volt model shown)

11.5 On six-volt models, lift the regulator, then label and disconnect the wires underneath

11.8a On six-volt models, terminal 61 goes to the generator warning light and B+ (51) connects to the battery via the starter

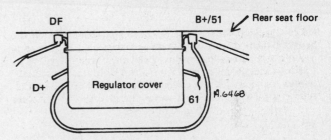

11.8b On 12-volt models with generators, the wires are connected as follows:

D+ – to battery
DF – to generator DF
B+/51 – to battery +ve and terminal 30
61 – to ignition warning light

10 Remove the two screws from the voltage regulator/brush holder assembly and lift it out.

11 Installation is the reverse of removal. Guide the brushes into place and seat the voltage regulator assembly in the alternator. Install the screws.

12 Generator – removal and installation (1972 and earlier models)

Refer to illustrations 12.2a, 12.2b, 12.3, 12.4, 12.5, 12.6, 12.7a, 12.7b, 12.8a, 12.8b, 12.9a, 12.9b, 12.9c and 12.14

Removal

1 Disconnect the negative cable from the battery.

2 Label and then disconnect the wiring from the generator on 12-volt models **(see illustrations)** or voltage regulator on six-volt models (see Section 11).

3 Make index marks on the outer fan cover and fan housing **(see illustration)** to ensure proper alignment during reassembly.

4 Remove the generator strap **(see illustration)**.

5 Detach the fan housing (see Chapter 3) and lift it up high enough to remove the screws from the outer fan cover **(see illustration)**.

6 Lift the generator from the fan housing **(see illustration)**.

7 Remove the engine cooling fan (see Chapter 3) and then the shims, washer and hub **(see illustrations)**.

8 Remove the inner fan cover, reinforcement flange and outer fan cover **(see illustrations)**.

11.9 Remove the cover plate and then the voltage regulator/brush holder assembly

1 *Cover plate*
2 *Voltage regulator/brush holder assembly*

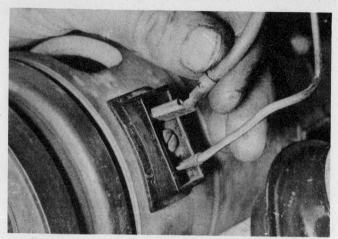

12.2a   These connectors pull off – be sure to pull the connector, not the wire (12-volt model shown)

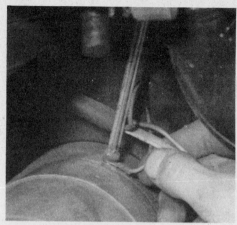

12.2b   Unscrew the small ground wire at the fan housing end of the generator (12-volt model)

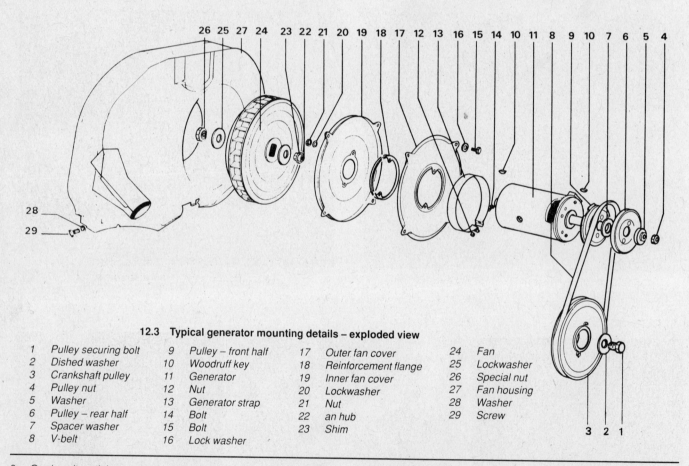

12.3   Typical generator mounting details – exploded view

1	Pulley securing bolt	9	Pulley – front half	17 Outer fan cover	24 Fan
2	Dished washer	10	Woodruff key	18 Reinforcement flange	25 Lockwasher
3	Crankshaft pulley	11	Generator	19 Inner fan cover	26 Special nut
4	Pulley nut	12	Nut	20 Lockwasher	27 Fan housing
5	Washer	13	Generator strap	21 Nut	28 Washer
6	Pulley – rear half	14	Bolt	22 an hub	29 Screw
7	Spacer washer	15	Bolt	23 Shim	
8	V-belt	16	Lock washer		

9   On six-volt models, remove the voltage regulator from the generator. Inspect the generator and repair or replace as necessary **(see illustrations)**.

Installation

10   Reinstall the components in the reverse order of removal. On six-volt models, install a new voltage regulator whenever the generator is replaced or rebuilt.

11   Make sure the hub is seated on the Woodruff key. Refer to Chapter 3 for engine cooling fan installation and clearance check and adjustment.

12   After installation, turn the generator pulley by hand to check for binding before installing the drivebelt.

13   Install the drivebelt and adjust as described in Chapter 1.

14   If a new, rebuilt or used generator was installed, it must be polarized **(see illustration). Warning:** *Connect the polarizing wires to the battery first, then momentarily touch them to the generator terminals. If you connect them to the generator first and touch them to the battery. you will create a spark near the battery that could ignite the hydrogen gas created in the battery and cause an explosion!*

15   Check the charging voltage to verify proper operation of the generator (see Section 10).

12.4   Remove the generator strap (six-volt shown, 12-volt similar)

12.5   Remove the four mounting screws (arrows)

12.6   Lift the generator from the fan housing

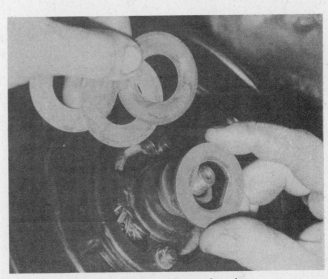

12.7a   Remove the shims and washer . . .

12.7b   . . . and slide the hub off

12.8a   Remove the inner fan cover . . .

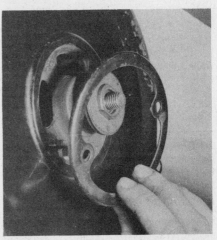

12.8b   . . . the reinforcement flange and outer fan cover

5

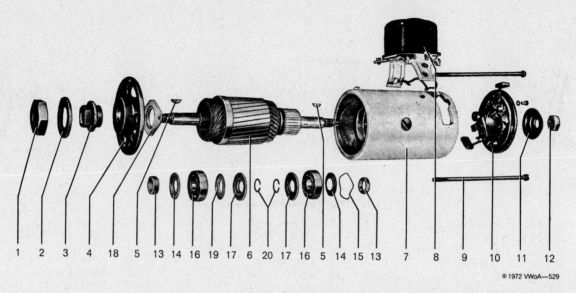

12.9a   Bosch six-volt generator (111903021H) – exploded view

1	Fan nut	6	Armature	11	Spacer washer	16	Ball bearing
2	Carrier plate	7	Housing and field assembly	12	Pulley nut	17	Oil slinger
3	Fan hub	8	Regulator	13	Spacer ring	18	Flange
4	End plate	9	Through bolt	14	Oil slinger	19	Cover washer
5	Woodruff key	10	Brush holder end plate	15	Spring ring	20	Circlips

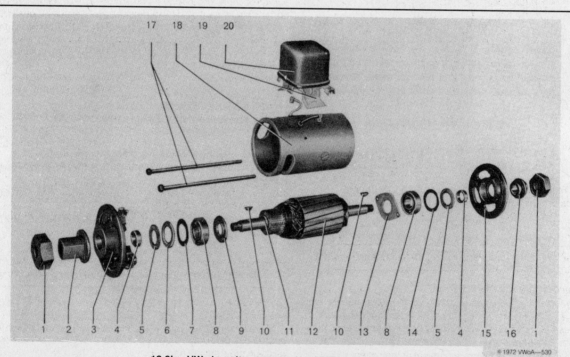

12.9b   VW six-volt generator (111903021J) – exploded view

1	Nut	6	Retainer	11	Spacer	16	Fan hub
2	Pulley hub	7	Thrust ring	12	Armature	17	Through bolts
3	Brush holder end plate	8	Ball bearing	13	Bearing retainer	18	Housing and field assembly
4	Spacer ring	9	Washer	14	Thrust ring	19	Slotted screw hole
5	Felt washer	10	Key	15	End plate	20	Voltage regulator

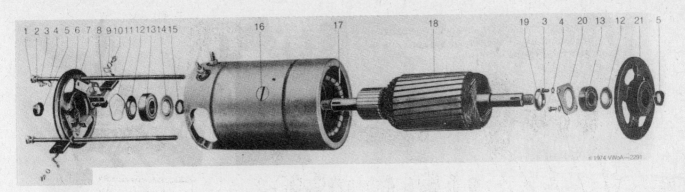

12.9c 12-volt generator – exploded view

1	Housing through bolt (2)	8	Carbon brush (2)	15	Thrust washer
2	B six lock washer (2)	9	B 4 lock washer (2)	16	Pole shoe screw (2)
3	AM 4 x 8 fillister head screw (3)	10	AM 4 x 6 fillister head screw	17	Field coil (2)
4	B 4 lock washer (3)	11	Lock washer	18	Armature
5	Spacer ring (2)	12	Dished washer (2)	19	Splash shield
6	Brush spring (2)	13	Ball bearing (2)	20	Retaining plate
7	End plate, commutator end	14	Splash shield	21	End plate, fan end

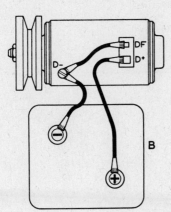

© 1974 VWoA—1202

12.14 To polarize the generator, connect a battery of the proper voltage momentarily as shown

13 Alternator – removal and installation (1973 and later models)

Refer to illustrations 13.8 and 13.9

Note: *Starting with chassis number 1132414931, 1973 models are equipped with alternators instead of generators. Alternator removal and installation is essentially the same as for the generator; refer to the illustrations in Section 12 as necessary.*

1   Detach the cable from the negative terminal of the battery.

2   Label and then detach the electrical connectors from the alternator.

3   Make index marks on the outer fan cover and fan housing to ensure proper alignment during reassembly.

4   Remove the alternator hold-down strap.

5   Detach the fan housing (see Chapter 3) and lift it up high enough to remove the mounting screws from the outer fan cover.

6   Lift the alternator from the fan housing.

7   Remove the engine cooling fan (see Chapter 3) and then the shims, washer and hub.

8   Remove the inner fan cover, stiffener and outer fan cover **(see illustration)**.

9   If you are replacing the alternator **(see illustration)**, take the old one with you when purchasing a replacement unit. Make sure the new/rebuilt unit looks identical to the old alternator. Look at the terminals – they should be the same in number, size and location as the terminals on the old alternator. Finally, look at the identification numbers – they will be stamped into the housing or printed on a tag attached to the housing. Make sure the numbers are the same on both alternators, or that the new numbers supersede the old ones.

10   Many new/rebuilt alternators DO NOT have a pulley installed, so you may have to switch the pulley from the old unit to the new/rebuilt one.

11   Installation is the reverse of removal.

12   Make sure the hub is seated on the Woodruff key. Refer to Chapter 3 for engine cooling fan installation and clearance check and adjustment.

13   After installation, turn the alternator pulley by hand to check for binding before installing the drivebelt.

14   After the alternator is installed, adjust the drivebelt tension (see Chapter 1).

15   Check the charging voltage to verify proper operation of the alternator (see Section 10).

Caution: *Alternators never need polarizing; do not attempt to polarize the alternator.*

14 Starting system – general information and precautions

The sole function of the starting system is to turn over the engine quickly enough to allow it to start.

The starting system consists of the battery, the starter motor, the starter solenoid and the wires connecting them. The solenoid is mounted directly on the starter motor.

The solenoid/starter motor assembly is installed on the lower part of the engine, next to the transmission bellhousing.

When the ignition key is turned to the Start position, the starter solenoid is actuated through the starter control circuit.

The starter solenoid then connects the battery to the starter. The battery supplies the electrical energy to the starter motor, which does the actual work of cranking the engine.

5

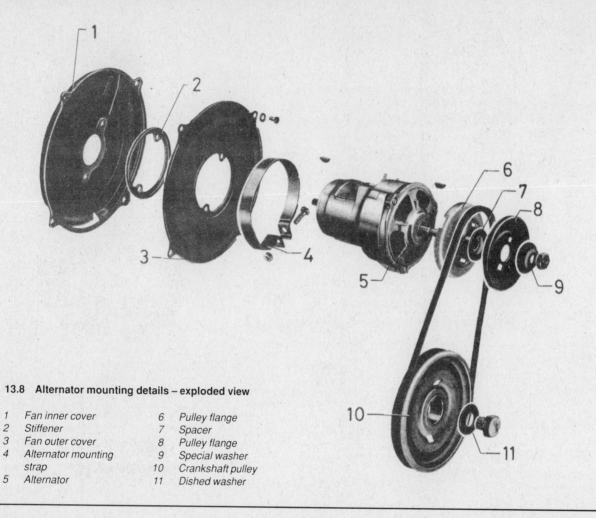

13.8   Alternator mounting details – exploded view

1	Fan inner cover	6	Pulley flange
2	Stiffener	7	Spacer
3	Fan outer cover	8	Pulley flange
4	Alternator mounting	9	Special washer
	strap	10	Crankshaft pulley
5	Alternator	11	Dished washer

The starter on a vehicle equipped with an automatic stick shift can only be operated when the transmission selector lever is in Neutral.

Always observe the following precautions when working on the starting system:

a) Excessive cranking of the starter motor can overheat it and cause serious damage. Never operate the starter motor for more than 15 seconds at a time without pausing to allow it to cool for at least two minutes.

b) The starter is connected directly to the battery and could arc or cause a fire if mishandled, overloaded or shorted out.

c) Always detach the cable from the negative terminal of the battery before working on the starting system.

15   Starter motor – testing in vehicle

1   If the starter motor does not turn at all on automatic stick shift models when the switch is operated, make sure that the shift lever is in Neutral.

2   Make sure that the battery is charged and that all cables, both at the battery and starter solenoid terminals, are clean and secure.

3   If the starter motor spins but the engine is not cranking, the overrunning clutch in the starter motor is slipping and the starter drive must be replaced.

4   If, when the switch is actuated, the starter motor does not operate at all but the solenoid clicks, then the problem lies with either a discharged battery, faulty solenoid contacts or the starter motor itself (or the engine is seized).

5   If nothing can be heard when the switch is actuated, the battery is dead or switch is bad, the circuit is open or the solenoid itself is defective.

6   To check the solenoid, connect a jumper lead between the battery positive terminal and the starter switch terminal (the small terminal) on the solenoid. If the starter motor now operates, the solenoid is OK and the problem is in the ignition switch, neutral start switch (automatic stick shift) or the wiring.

7   If the starter motor still does not operate, remove the starter/solenoid assembly for disassembly, testing and repair.

8   If the starter motor cranks the engine at an abnormally slow speed, first make sure that the battery is charged and that all terminal connections are tight. If the engine is partially seized, or has the wrong viscosity oil in it (in cold weather), it will crank slowly.

9   Run the engine until normal operating temperature is reached, then disconnect the coil wire from the distributor cap and ground it on the engine.

10   Connect a voltmeter positive lead to the positive battery post and connect the negative lead to the negative post.

11   Crank the engine and take the voltmeter readings as soon as a steady figure is indicated. Do not allow the starter motor to turn for more than 15 seconds at a time. A reading of 4.5 volts or more (on a 1966 or earlier model), or 9 volts or more (on a 1967 or later model), with the starter motor turning at normal cranking speed, is acceptable. If the reading is 4.5 volts or more (1966 or earlier models) or 9 volts or more (1967 and later models) but the cranking speed is slow, the solenoid contacts are burned, the starter is faulty or there is a bad connection. If the reading is less than 4.5/9 volts and the cranking speed is slow, the starter motor is bad, the battery is partly discharged or the engine is tight (it could be partially seized or, in cold weather, the oil viscosity could be too high).

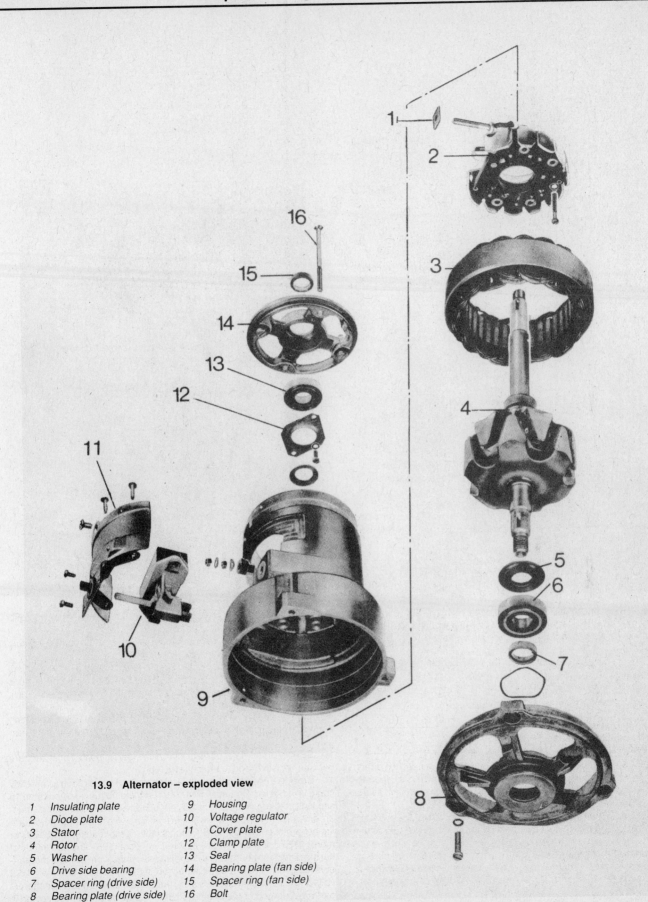

13.9 Alternator – exploded view

1	Insulating plate	9	Housing
2	Diode plate	10	Voltage regulator
3	Stator	11	Cover plate
4	Rotor	12	Clamp plate
5	Washer	13	Seal
6	Drive side bearing	14	Bearing plate (fan side)
7	Spacer ring (drive side)	15	Spacer ring (fan side)
8	Bearing plate (drive side)	16	Bolt

5

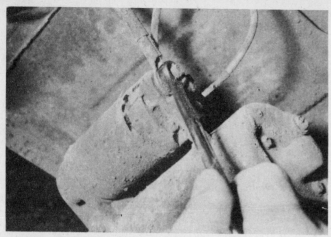

16.3   Unplug the small wires and remove the nut from the solenoid, then detach the battery cable

16.4   Remove the starter fasteners

17.3   Remove the nut and the electrical strap

17.4a   Detach the solenoid from the starter (early model shown)

17.4b   Later model Bosch solenoids are attached with screws

16   Starter motor – removal and installation

Refer to illustrations 16.3 and 16.4

1   Detach the cable from the negative terminal of the battery.
2   Block the front wheels to prevent the vehicle from rolling. Loosen the lug bolts on the right rear wheel. Raise the rear of the vehicle and support it securely on jackstands. Remove the right rear wheel.
3   Disconnect the wires from the terminals on the starter solenoid **(see illustration)**.
4   Have an assistant hold the nut in the engine compartment while you remove the inner starter bolt. Then remove the mounting nut and detach the starter **(see illustration)**.
5   Inspect the bushing where the tip of the starter fits into the transaxle and replace if necessary (Bosch starters only).
6   Lubricate the bushing with grease. Apply a bead of sealant to the transaxle where the starter contacts it and install the starter. Tighten the fasteners securely.
7   The remainder of the installation is the reverse of removal.

17   Starter solenoid – removal and installation

Removal

Refer to illustrations 17.3, 17.4a, 17.4b and 17.5

1   Disconnect the cable from the negative terminal of the battery.
2   Remove the starter motor (see Section 16).
3   Remove the nut **(see illustration)** and disconnect the electrical strap from the solenoid to the starter motor terminal.
4   Remove the nuts or screws which secure the solenoid to the starter motor **(see illustrations)**.
5   On Bosch starters (except Automatic Stick Shift), lift the solenoid slightly to disengage the pull rod from the starter **(see illustration)** and remove the solenoid. **Note:** *Starters may be manufactured by Bosch or Volkswagen; identification is imprinted in the case.*
6   On VW-built starters, remove the solenoid housing, the solenoid core remains with the starter.

Installation

Refer to illustrations 17.7, 17.8a, 17.8b, 17.8c, 17.8d, 17.8e and 17.8f

7   If you are replacing the solenoid on a Bosch starter, adjust the length of the pull rod **(see illustration)**. No pull rod adjustment is necessary on VW-built starters.
8   Apply sealant to the mating surfaces between the solenoid and the drive end plate **(see illustrations)**. Position the rubber seal (if equipped) on the drive end plate.
9   Pull the drive pinion out as far as possible and install the solenoid. On Bosch starters, be sure the opening in the pull rod fits over the engaging lever. On VW-built starters, slip the core into the solenoid.
10   Install the solenoid mounting nuts/screws and tighten them securely.
11   Install the starter as described in Section 16.

17.5   Lift the solenoid free of the starter (Bosch shown)

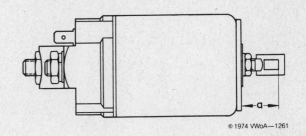

© 1974 VWoA—1261

17.7   To adjust the pull rod on Bosch starters, loosen the locknut, turn the rod until the distance "a" is 0.744 to 0.752 inch (18.90 to 19.10 mm), then tighten the locknut and remeasure "a"

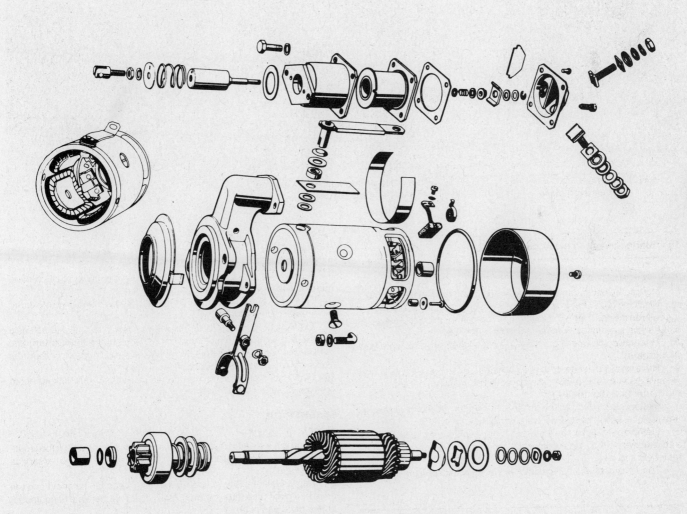

17.8a   Early six-volt Bosch starter motor – exploded view

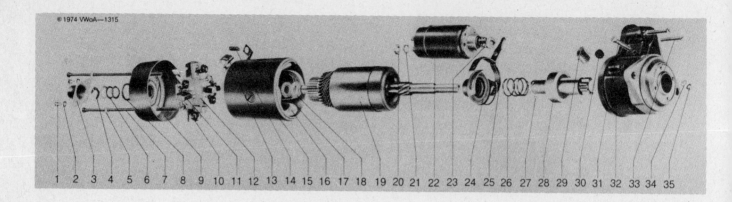

© 1974 VWoA—1315

17.8b   Bosch starter 003911023A – exploded view (Automatic Stick Shift)

1	Screw (2)	12	Brush holder	23	Solenoid return spring
2	Washer (2)	13	Positive brush (2)	24	Operating sleeve
3	End cap	14	Rubber grommet	25	Engaging lever
4	C-washer	15	Pole housing	26	Engaging spring
5	Washer (2)	16	Field winding	27	Detent balls (10)
6	Shim	17	Insulator washer	28	Drive pinion
7	Through bolt (2)	18	Thrust washer	29	Molded rubber seal
8	Sealing ring	19	Armature	30	Disk
9	End plate	20	Nut	31	Pin
10	Retaining spring (4)	21	Lock washer	32	Drive end plate
11	Negative brush (2)	22	Solenoid	33	Screw (2)
				34	Lock washer
				35	Nut

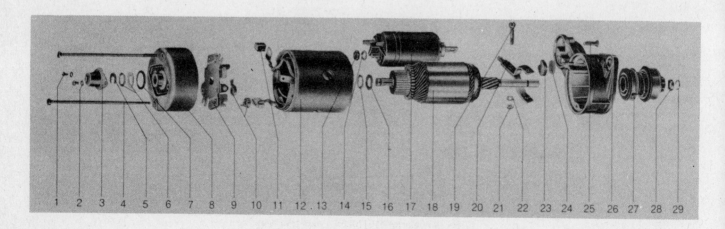

17.8c   Bosch starter 311911023B – exploded view

1	Screw (2)	9	Brush holder	17	Solenoid	25	Screw (2)
2	Washer (2)	10	Spring (2)	18	Armature	26	Drive end plate
3	End cap	11	Rubber grommet	19	Pin	27	Drive pinion
4	Through bolt (2)	12	Pole housing	20	Engaging lever	28	Stop ring
5	C-washer	13	Nut	21	Nut	29	Circlip
6	Shim	14	Lock washer	22	Lock washer		
7	Sealing ring	15	Insulating washer	23	Molded rubber seal		
8	End plate	16	Thrust washer	24	Disk		

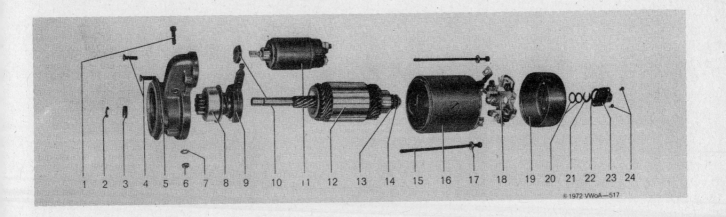

17.8d   Bosch starter 113911021B – exploded view

1	Lever bearing pin	7	Spring washer	13	Steel washer
2	Circlip	8	Pinion	14	Synthetic washer
3	Stop ring	9	Operating lever	15	Through bolts
4	Securing screw	10	Rubber seal	16	Housing
5	Mounting bracket	11	Solenoid	17	Washer
6	Nut	12	Armature	18	Brush holder

19   End plate
20   Shims
21   Lock washer
22   Sealing ring
23   End cap
24   Screws

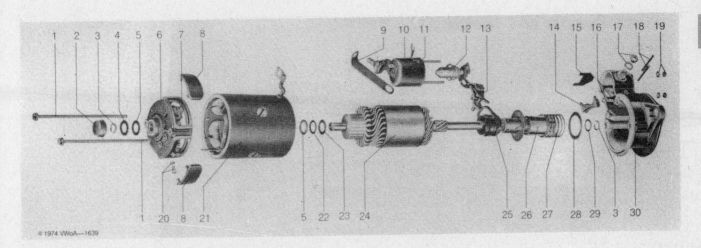

17.8e   VW starter 11911023A – exploded view

1   Through bolt (2)
2   Cap
3   Circlip (2)
4   Steel washer
5   Bronze washer (2)
6   Commutator end plate
7   Brush holder and
   brushes (2)

8   Brush inspection cover (2)
9   Connecting strap
10   Solenoid housing
   and winding
11   Insulating disk
12   Solenoid core
13   Linkage
14   Molded rubber seal

15   Insulating plate
16   Spring clip (2)
17   Nut and lock washer (2)
18   Pins (2)
19   Small nut and lock
   washer (2)
20   Screw and lock washer
21   Pole housing

22   Dished washer
23   Steel washer
24   Armature
25   Connecting bushing
26   Drive pinion
27   Spring
28   Intermediate washer
29   Dished washer
30   Drive end plate

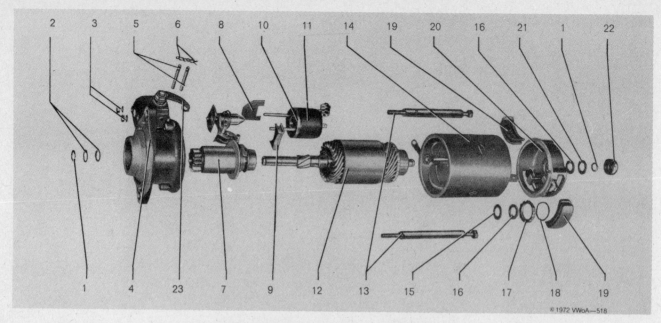

17.8f   VW starter 113911021A – exploded view

1	Circlip	7	Drive pinion with linkage	12	Armature
2	Cup washer		and solenoid core	13	Through bolts

1 Circlip
2 Cup washer
3 Nuts and lockwashers
4 Intermediate bracket
5 Pivot pins
6 Spring clips

7 Drive pinion with linkage
   and solenoid core
8 Insulating plate
9 Molded rubber seal
10 Insulating disc
11 Solenoid housing

12 Armature
13 Through bolts
14 Housing and field assembly
15 Steel washer
16 Bronze washer
17 Friction washer

18 Thrust ring
19 Brush inspection cover
20 Commutator end plate
21 Steel washer
22 Cap
23 Connecting strip

Chapter 6 Emissions control systems

Contents

6

---

1   General information

A number of emissions control systems are incorporated in later model VW Beetles to prevent pollution of the atmosphere from incompletely burned and evaporating gases, and to maintain good driveability and fuel economy. The principal systems are:

Automatic choke system
Carburetor mounted emission control devices
Catalytic converter (CAT)
Electronic fuel injection (EFI)
Exhaust Gas Recirculation (EGR) system
Fuel evaporative emission control system (EVAP)
Inlet air temperature control system
Positive Crankcase Ventilation (PCV) system

The Sections in this Chapter include general descriptions, checking procedures within the scope of the home mechanic and component replacement procedures (when possible) for each of the systems listed above.

Before assuming an emissions control system is malfunctioning, check the fuel and ignition systems carefully. The diagnosis of some emission control devices requires specialized tools, equipment and training. If checking and servicing become too difficult or if a procedure is beyond your ability, consult a dealer service department. Remember, the most fre-quent cause of emissions problems are simply a loose or broken vacuum hose or wire or a clogged passage, so always check these items first.

Emission control systems are not particularly difficult to maintain and repair. You can quickly and easily perform many checks and do most of the regular maintenance at home with common tune-up and hand tools.

Pay close attention to any special precautions outlined in this Chapter. It should be noted that the illustrations of the various systems may not exactly match the system installed on a particular vehicle because of changes made by the manufacturer during production or from year-to-year.

On later models, a Vehicle Emissions Control Information (VECI) label is located on the fan housing. This label contains important emissions specifications and adjustment information. When servicing the engine or emissions systems, the VECI label in the vehicle should always be checked for up-to-date information.

2   Positive Crankcase Ventilation (PCV) system

Refer to illustration 2.2
1   The Positive Crankcase Ventilation (PCV) system reduces hydrocarbon emissions by scavenging crankcase vapors. It does this by routing blow-by gases from the crankcase through the air cleaner and into the intake manifold for reburning.

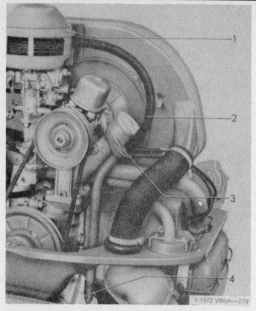

2.2   The PCV hose runs from the oil filler housing to the air cleaner

1	Air cleaner	3	Oil filler housing
2	PCV hose	4	Rubber drain valve

3.7a   On Beetles, the canister is located inside the right rear fender

1   Metal vent line from fuel tank
2   Plastic hose connects to metal tank line
3   Outlet hose to air cleaner

3.7b   On Karmann Ghias, the canister is located in the engine compartment

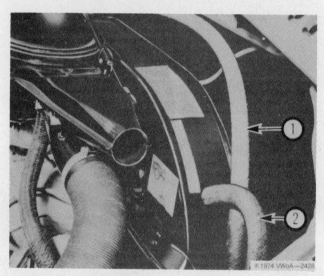

3.8   Hose routing on engine

1	Carries vapors from the canister to the air intake	2 Routes air from the fan housing to the canister

2   On 1971 and earlier models, the PCV hose runs from the oil filler housing to the air cleaner **(see illustration)**. On 1972 and later models, a hose runs from each valve cover to the air cleaner.

3   Check the hose(s) for cracks, splits and collapsing (see Chapter 1) and replace as necessary.

---

3   Evaporative emissions control (EVAP) system

Refer to illustrations 3.7a, 3.7b and 3.8

General description

1   This system is installed on 1970 and later models. It is designed to trap and store gasoline vapors that evaporate from the fuel system and would normally enter the atmosphere in the form of hydrocarbon (HC) emissions.

2   The system consists of an activated charcoal-filled canister, an expansion tank (on Super Beetles), connecting lines and fuel tank ventilating hoses.

3   When the engine is off and pressure begins to build up in the fuel tank (caused by fuel evaporation), the charcoal in the canister absorbs the fuel vapor. After the engine starts, the stored fuel vapors are routed to the intake manifold and combustion chambers where they are burned during normal engine operation.

Checking

4   The canister is located inside the right rear fender on Beetles and in the engine compartment on Karmann Ghias.

5   Check the canister, hoses and lines for cracks and other damage.

6   Check the gasket on the fuel filler cap for deformation, cracking or other damage that would allow vapors to leak into the atmosphere.

Charcoal canister replacement

7   To replace the canister, label and then disconnect the vacuum hoses, remove the mounting screws and separate the canister from the bracket **(see illustrations)**.

8   Installation is the reverse of removal. Check the routing of all the hoses **(see illustration)**.

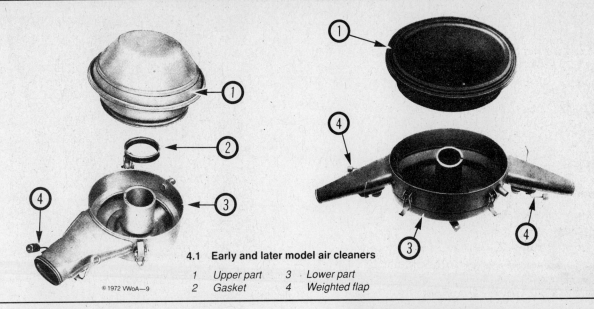

4.1   Early and later model air cleaners

1	Upper part	3	Lower part
2	Gasket	4	Weighted flap

© 1972 VWoA—9

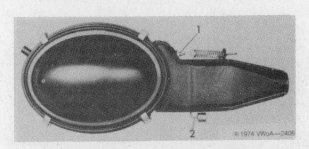

4.8a   1971 Beetle air cleaner (top view)

1	Thermostat	2	Weighted flap

© 1974 VWoA—2406

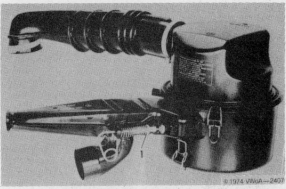

4.8b   1971 Karmann Ghia air cleaner

1   Thermostat

© 1974 VWoA—2407

4   Inlet air temperature control system

Refer to illustrations 4.1, 4.8a, 4.8b and 4.9

General description

1   All models have weighted flaps on the air cleaner **(see illustration)** to route heated air into the engine during low engine speed operation. This deters carburetor icing and reduces stumbling and hesitation. Check the arm for free movement while the air cleaner is installed.

2   Later emission controlled models also have a thermostatically controlled air cleaner system which provides heated intake air during warmup, then maintains the inlet air temperature at approximately 90-degrees F by mixing warm and cool air. This allows leaner fuel/air mixtures, which reduces emissions and improves driveability, especially during warmup.

3   Two sources of air – one warm and one cold – are used. The balance between the two is controlled by a thermostat. On 1968 through 1970 models, the engine cooling thermostat is connected to the air cleaner flap with a cable. On 1971 models, the flap is operated by a separate thermostat located in the air cleaner. On 1972 and later models, the flap is controlled by a thermostatically regulated vacuum unit. The bi-metallic thermostat expands and contracts according to the temperature of the incoming air. In turn, the flap will open and close with a cold or warm engine temperature.

4   When the underhood air temperature is cold, warm air radiating off the heat exchangers is routed up through hot air inlet tube(s) and into the air cleaner. This provides warm intake air to the engine. As the temperature of the air routed over the thermostat rises, the heat duct valve is gradually closed and the air cleaner draws air through a cool air duct instead. The result is a consistent intake air temperature.

Checking

Note: *Refer to Chapter 1 for the initial system check. If the system doesn't operate as described in Chapter 1, proceed as described below.*

5   Remove the air intake duct from the air cleaner. Check and make sure the air flap is not loose or damaged.

6   The flap should seal the cold air opening when the temperature is low. If the flap is sealing the warm air opening when the engine is cold, replace the thermostat. **Note:** *On 1968 through 1970 models, try to adjust the engine thermostat and cable first (see Chapters 3 and 4).*

Component replacement

7   On 1968 through 1970 models, see Chapter 3 for thermostat adjustment and replacement.

8   To remove the thermostat on the air cleaner (1971 models), temporarily remove the air cleaner housing from the engine (see Chapter 4). Carefully remove the thermostat and replace it with a new unit **(see illustrations)**.

9   To remove the thermostatic valve or vacuum unit **(see illustration)** on 1972 and later models, refer to Chapter 4 and remove the air cleaner. Carefully remove the thermostatic valve or vacuum unit and replace it with a new part. **Note:** *Thermostatic valves installed after December 1972 are different than earlier ones. They may be identified by the brass hose fitting for the vacuum unit. Also, later models use paper air filter elements instead of oil bath.*

6

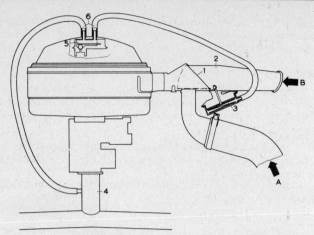

© 1974 VWoA—2401

4.9   1972 through 1974 air cleaner details

A	Heated air	3	Vacuum unit
B	Unheated air	4	Intake manifold
1	Control flap	5	Thermostatic valve
2	Air intake	6	Vacuum hose connections

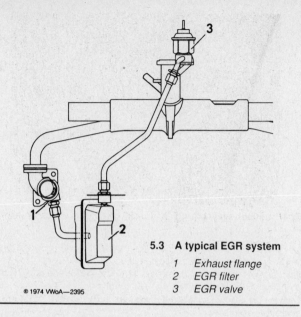

© 1974 VWoA—2395

5.3   A typical EGR system

1   Exhaust flange
2   EGR filter
3   EGR valve

5.7   Unplug the connector (arrow) and check for idle roughness, then probe the terminals with a test light

5   Exhaust Gas Recirculation (EGR) system

General description

Refer to illustration 5.3

1   Exhaust Gas Recirculation (EGR) systems are installed on 1972 and later California models with Automatic Stick Shift, all 1973 models with Automatic Stick Shift and all 1974 and later models.
2   The EGR system reduces nitrogen oxide (NOx) emissions by recirculating exhaust gases into the intake manifold. The exhaust gases lack oxygen which results in lower combustion chamber temperatures and a reduction in harmful emissions.
3   The EGR system consists of an EGR valve, an EGR filter and connecting tubing **(see illustration)**.
4   The EGR valve should not open during idle or full throttle conditions. The most common driveability problem associated with a malfunctioning EGR system is an engine that runs extremely rough at idle speed and smoothes out when speed is increased. This problem can be caused by an EGR valve stuck in the open position, an improperly adjusted linkage

(1977 and later California models) or a misrouted vacuum hose (allowing vacuum to the EGR valve at idle).
5   Another common problem is pinging (or spark knock) under acceleration. If the EGR valve is stuck closed or clogged with carbon, the hose is disconnected or misrouted or the linkage is improperly adjusted (1977 and later California models), the engine will be more prone to pinging.

Checking

Carbureted models

6   On all except 1974 California models, detach the vacuum hose from the EGR valve. Then, with the engine idling, temporarily connect a hose directly from the intake manifold to the EGR valve (such as the hose from the intake air preheating thermostat). If the engine stalls or runs rough when the hose is connected directly to the valve, the valve is functional. **Warning:** *Stay clear of the drivebelt and pulleys!* On 1974 California models with two-stage valves, check the EGR valve by watching for movement of the pin when the engine is revved up. To test the throttle valve switch on 1974 California models, operate the switch manually with the engine at idle. If the engine stalls or runs rough, the system is functional.

Fuel-injected models (except 1977 and later California models)

Refer to illustration 5.7

7   On these models, the EGR valve is vacuum operated and electrically controlled. To check these, detach the connector on the vacuum unit **(see illustration)** while the engine is idling. If the engine stalls or runs rough, the EGR valve is functional.
8   If no change occurs when the connector is unplugged, shut off the engine. Switch the ignition ON without starting the engine. Probe the terminals with a test light as shown in illustration 5.7 while an assistant moves the accelerator pedal slowly from idle to full throttle. If the test light doesn't come on at full throttle and at idle, check the throttle valve switch or microswitch. If that's OK, test the double relay (see Fuel pump/fuel pressure – testing in Chapter 4).
9   If the test light goes on at idle and full throttle and goes off in between, replace the EGR valve.

1977 and later California models

Refer to illustration 5.11

10   These models have a mechanically actuated EGR valve connected to the throttle valve. Check the valve by removing the E-clip and operating the rod while the engine is idling. **Warning:** *Stay clear of the drivebelt and pulleys!* The engine should run rough or stall when the valve is opened. If it doesn't, the passages are probably clogged with carbon; correct as necessary.

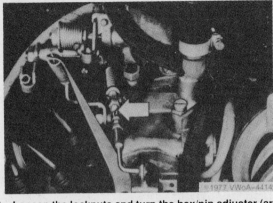

5.11 Loosen the locknuts and turn the hex/pin adjuster (arrow)

11   To adjust the mechanical EGR valve, warm the engine up and be sure the idle speed is within the range specified in Chapter 1. With the engine idling, loosen the locknuts on the adjusting rod **(see illustration)**. Turn the hex/pin to shorten the rod until the idle roughens.

12   Now turn the hex/pin the other way one and one half (1 1/2) turns and tighten the locknuts.

6   Throttle valve positioner

Refer to illustrations 6.2, 6.6, 6.8, 6.10, 6.11 and 6.12

General description

1   Most 1968 and 1969 models, all 1970 and 1971 models with manual transaxles and 1972 California models with manual transaxles are equipped with throttle valve positioners.

2   The throttle valve positioner slows the closing of the throttle when the driver lifts the accelerator pedal. This allows additional air to enter the intake manifold, which reduces the amount of pollutants in the exhaust. On 1968 and 1969 models, the altitude corrector is built into the throttle valve positioner **(see illustration)**. On some models beginning in 1971, a dashpot is mounted on the carburetor to assist this function.

Adjustment

3   To adjust the throttle valve positioner, first connect a tachometer to the ignition coil (see Chapter 1, Section 29). **Note:** *The engine should be in a good state of tune with the ignition points and timing correctly adjusted.*

1968 and 1969 models

4   Position an open end wrench in back of the pull rod stop washer and pull the rod until the stop washer contacts the throttle valve positioner housing.

5   Start the engine. Engine speed should be 1700 to 1800 rpm. Go to Step 8.

1970 and later models

6   Start the engine and pull the fast idle lever back against the adjusting screw **(see illustration)**. **Warning:** *Stay clear of the drivebelt and pulleys!*

7   Fast idle speed should be 1450 to 1650 rpm. Turn the adjusting screw as necessary. After engine warmup, fast idle speed should be 1700 rpm or less.

All models

8   Pull the throttle valve lever away from the fast idle lever until the engine runs at 3000 rpm. Release the lever and note how long it takes to return to idle; it should be about 3 seconds. If not, adjust it by turning the adjustment screw **(see illustration)**. **Note:** *See illustration 6.2 for the location of the adjustment screw on 1968 and 1969 models. Turning the screw clockwise causes the valve to operate slower.*

9   After engine warmup, the throttle valve shouldn't take more than six seconds to close. If adjustment fails to correct the problem, check the throttle positioner diaphragm and check the connecting hoses.

10   Whenever a diaphragm unit in the throttle valve positioner is replaced, the length of the pull rod must be adjusted. After the unit is installed, temporarily loosen the locknuts and turn the rod to shorten or extend it **(see illustration)**. The lever is adjusted properly if the fast idle lever doesn't touch the throttle valve lever or the carburetor body when the throttle valve is closed.

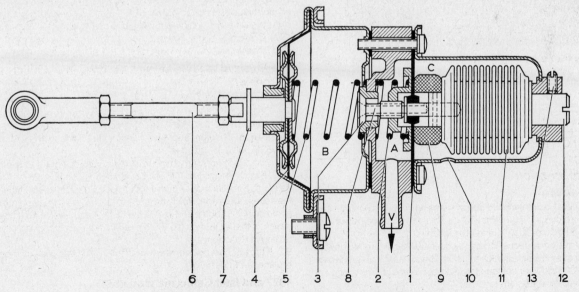

6.2   Throttle valve positioner (1968 and 1969 models)

1	Diaphragm	5	Spring	8	Hole	11	Altitude corrector
2	Spring	6	Pull rod	9	Filter	12	Adjusting screw
3	Valve	7	Washer	10	Air hole	13	Lock screw
4	Diaphragm						

6.6   Pull the fast idle lever against the screw

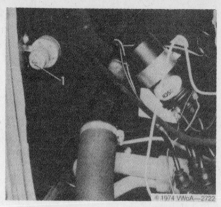

6.8   Turn the screw in the altitude corrector (1970 and later models)

1   *Adjuster screw*

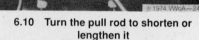

6.10   Turn the pull rod to shorten or lengthen it

6.11   Adjust the dashpot plunger tip clearance "a" by moving the locknuts

6.12   Detach the pull rod and remove the mounting screws (1968 and 1969 models)

1   *Pull rod*   2   *Mounting screws*

11   Some later models with manual transaxles have a dashpot mounted on the carburetor to slow throttle closing. To adjust it, warm the engine up and then shut the engine off. With the choke off of fast idle, compress the plunger and measure the clearance at "a" **(see illustration)**. It should be 0.40 inch (1 mm); if not, move the locknuts to increase or decrease clearance as necessary.

Removal and installation

12   To remove the throttle valve positioner, label and detach the vacuum hoses. Then disconnect the linkage at the throttle valve lever **(see illustration)** and remove the carburetor (see Chapter 4). The throttle valve positioner bracket mounts between the carburetor and intake manifold flange. Be sure to use new gaskets on both sides of the bracket under the carburetor during installation.

7   Catalytic converter

Warning: *The catalytic converter can become very hot! Allow it to cool completely before touching it or working nearby.*

General description

1   The catalytic converter is an emissions control device added to the exhaust system to reduce the levels of hydrocarbon (HC) and carbon monoxide (CO) pollutants in the exhaust gas stream. It consists of a honeycomb-like core coated with a thin layer of precious metals which assist in the chemical reaction between the exhaust gases and atmospheric oxygen.

Checking

2   Catalytic converters can fail in several ways: They can be physically damaged from the outside, the interior core can crumble and break up, the core can melt and become clogged, excessive oil consumption can coat the honeycomb and the metals in the converter can eventually be used up.

3   Whenever the vehicle is raised for servicing of underbody components, check the converter for leaks, corrosion, dents and other damage. Check the welds/flange bolts that attach the ends of the converter to the exhaust system. Tap the housing with the side of your fist to check for internal rattles, which may indicate a loose core. If damage is discovered, the converter should be replaced.

4   An exhaust gas analyzer is necessary to functionally test a catalytic converter. This is done by removing the test plug located upstream of the converter and sampling the exhaust gases before and after the catalyst. If the contents of the gases are the same before and after, the catalyst is non-functional. If you suspect the converter is not working, take the vehicle to a dealer service department or authorized emissions inspection facility for diagnosis and repair.

5   If the engine idles fairly well but won't accelerate normally, check for a partially clogged converter. The easiest way to test for a restricted converter is to use a vacuum gauge to measure the effect of a blocked exhaust on intake vacuum.

  a) Open the throttle until the engine speed is about 2000 rpm.
  b) Release the throttle quickly.
  c) If there's no restriction, the gauge will quickly drop to not more than 2 in-Hg or more above its normal reading.
  d) If the gauge doesn't show 5 in-Hg or more above its normal reading, or seems to momentarily hover around its highest reading for a moment before it returns, the exhaust system, or the converter, is plugged (or an exhaust pipe is bent or dented, or the core inside the muffler has shifted).

Removal and installation

6   Refer to the exhaust system servicing procedures in Chapter 4 for information on removal and installation. Remove the converter and visually inspect the core to confirm the diagnosis. Replace if necessary.

Chapter 7 Part A   Manual transaxle

Contents

Specifications

Overhaul

Gap between synchro rings and gear teeth
   Normal .... 0.043 inch (1.1 mm)
   Minimum .... 0.024 inch (0.6 mm)
Selector fork
   Maximum clearance in groove .... 0.012 inch (0.3 mm)
   Force required to overcome spring resistance .... 33 to 44 lbs (15-20 kgs)
   Spring free length .... 1 inch (25 mm)

Torque specifications

	Ft-lbs
Transaxle front mount nuts	14
Transaxle rear mount bolts	166

Split-case transaxle

Transaxle case nuts and bolts
   Initial torque .... 7 to 10
   Final torque 14
Oil drain plugs .... 22 to 29
Oil filler plugs 14
Gear shift cover-to-carrier nuts 11
Gear carrier-to-case nuts 14
Pinion shaft nut
   Early .... 80 to 87
   Later (new lock washer) .... 58 to 65
Input shaft nut .... 30 to 36
Reverse selector fork bolt 14
Selector fork clamp bolts 18
Pinion shaft slotted nut (non-synchro) 36

Torque specifications (continued)

Single-piece case

	Ft-lbs
Input and pinion shaft nuts	
Initial torque	87
Final torque	43
Selector fork clamp bolts	18
Pinion bearing flange bolts	36
Carrier-to-case nuts	14
Gear change housing nuts	11
Side cover nuts	22

1   General information

The vehicles covered by this manual are equipped with either a four-speed manual transaxle or an Automatic Stick Shift. Information on the manual transaxle is included in this Part of Chapter 7. Service procedures for the Automatic Stick Shift are contained in Chapter 7, Part B.

The manual transaxle is a compact, lightweight aluminum alloy split-case (two-piece) housing (early models) or a single-piece housing (later models) containing both the gearbox and differential assemblies. Early split-case units have four speeds, with a non-synchromesh first gear; later single-piece units are all full synchro four-speed designs.

Because of the complexity, unavailability of replacement parts and special tools required, internal repair of the manual transaxle by the home mechanic is not recommended. However, illustrated transaxle overhaul Sections are provided for readers who wish to tackle a transaxle rebuild.

Depending on the expense involved in having a faulty transaxle overhauled, it may be a good idea to replace it with either a new or rebuilt unit. Your local dealer or transmission shop should be able to supply you with information concerning cost, availability and exchange policy. Regardless of how you decide to remedy a transaxle problem, you can still save a lot of money by removing and installing the unit yourself.

2   Transaxle mounts – check and replacement

Check

Refer to illustration 2.3

1   Raise the rear of the vehicle and place it securely on jackstands.

2   Inspect the front and rear mounts for cracks and deterioration. If they look dried, cracked or otherwise damaged, replace them.
3   Wedge a large screwdriver or prybar between the front transaxle mount and the transaxle housing **(see illustration)** and try to lever the transaxle up and down and side to side. If the mount separates when you move the transaxle, replace it.
4   To check the rear mounts, slide a floor jack under the transaxle, place a block of wood between the jack and the transaxle and raise the floor jack until it's supporting the weight of the transaxle. If either of the rubber insulator pads between the carrier and the transaxle separates when the jack pushes up on the transaxle, replace them.

Replacement

Front mount

Refer to illustration 2.5

5   Remove the front mount nuts from the transaxle and the torsion housing **(see illustration)**.
6   Loosen the transaxle carrier bolts **(see illustration 2.11)** and pry the transaxle to the rear enough to remove the front mount.
7   Slide the new mount into position and install the mounting bolts loosely.
8   Tighten the transaxle carrier bolts to the torque listed in this Chapter's Specifications, then tighten the front mount nuts to the torque listed in this Chapter's Specifications.

Rear mounts

Refer to illustration 2.11

9   Remove the engine (see Chapter 2).
10   Place a floor jack under the transaxle, place a block of wood between the jack and the transaxle and raise the jack until it's supporting the transaxle.

2.3   Wedge a large screwdriver or prybar between the front mount and the transaxle and try to pry the transaxle up and down – if it moves easily, or the mount insulator separates, replace the mount

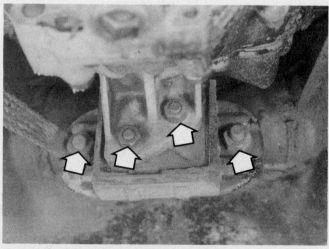

2.5   To remove the front mount, remove the four nuts (arrows) – two from the transaxle and two from the bracket on the torsion housing

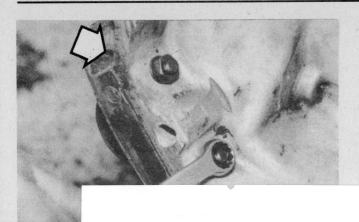

2.11 Remo[...] that retain[...] nut(s) fro[...]

11 Remove the two nuts for each mount from the carrier and the nut(s) from inside the bellhousing **(see illustration)**.
12 Raise the transaxle with the floor jack until it clears the insulator studs and remove the mount.
13 Installation is the reverse of removal.

---

3 Shift lever and shift rod – removal and installation

Shift lever

Refer to illustrations 3.1, 3.2, 3.4, 3.8, 3.9

If you're replacing the shift lever, make sure you obtain the correct replacement part. On vehicles produced before August 1967, the lever is straight; on later models, it's curved **(see illustration)**. Don't try to swap levers from one model to another unless they're identical. The lever on 1973 and later models is about 1-1/2 inches shorter than those on earlier models.

Pull back the floor mat, put the shift lever in Neutral and mark the posi-

3.1 Exploded view of a typical shift lever/shift rod assembly

1	Knob (curved lever)
1a	Knob (straight lever)
2	Shift lever (curved)
2a	Shift lever (straight)
3	Rubber dust boot
4	Bolt
5	Spring washer
6	Ball housing
7	Spring
8	Stop plate
9	Shift rod
10	Sleeve
11	Ring
12	Self-tapping screw
13	Locking cap
14	Insert
15	Housing
16	Bolt
17	Washer
18	Spring pin

7A

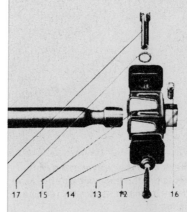

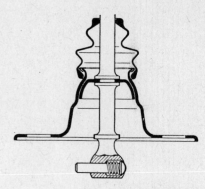

© 1972 VWoA—733

3.2   Before you loosen the bolts on the ball housing flange, mark the position of the stop plate in relation to the flange (arrow) – the plate must be properly adjusted at installation, or you'll have shifting problems

3.4   Remove the shift lever, ball housing, rubber boot and spring as a unit

3.8   Make sure the shift lever locating pin is secure and check the spring inside the steel ball for tension – replace it if it's worn

tion of the stop plate in relation to the ball housing flange **(see illustration)** to ensure proper alignment during installation. **Caution:** *Incorrect adjustment of the stop plate in the shift lever assembly can cause shifting problems.*

3   Remove the mounting bolts from the ball housing flange.

4   Remove the shift lever, ball housing, rubber boot and spring as a single unit **(see illustration)**.

5   Before removing the stop plate, note the orientation of the raised tab(s) on the stop plate. Some stop plates have a single tab on the right side of the hole which faces up; other plates have two tabs facing up, with the long, low, narrow tab near the driver and the shorter, higher tab on the right. Regardless of the design, the important thing to remember is that the stop plate must be reinstalled with the tab(s) oriented exactly the same way they were before removal.

6   Clean all parts thoroughly.

7   Inspect the shift lever collar, stop plate and shift lever ball socket in the shift rod for wear. Replace any worn parts.

8   Make sure the shift lever locating pin is secure **(see illustration)**. Check the spring in the steel ball for tension. Replace it if it's worn.

9   Install the stop plate. Make sure it's oriented with the tab(s) facing the same way as before removal **(see illustration)**.

10   Lubricate all moving parts with multi-purpose grease.

11   Inspect the condition of the rubber boot. Replace it if it's damaged.

12   Install the shift lever assembly (lever, ball housing and spring). Make sure the shift lever locating pin engages the slot in the ball socket and the stop plate seats in the hollow central part of the ball housing. If the lever is installed and seated properly, it will be vertical when its in Neutral.

13   Install the ball housing flange bolts loosely. Match up the alignment marks on the flange, stop plate and tunnel and tighten the bolts securely.

14   Recheck the position of the shift lever by engaging the gears. Readjust as necessary.

Shift rod

Refer to illustrations 3.17, 3.18a, 3.18b, 3.20, 3.21 and 3.24

Note: *If you're replacing a shift rod, make sure the replacement is the same length as the original – the rod on later models is shortened to fit the relocated mounting bracket for the guide bushing in the frame tunnel.*

15   Remove the shift lever assembly (see Steps 1 through 5).

16   Remove the rear seat.

17   Remove the inspection cover on the frame tunnel **(see illustration)**.

18   Remove the fasteners from the shift rod coupling **(see illustrations)**.

19   Remove the front bumper (see Chapter 11).

20   Remove the access cover in the frame head **(see illustration)** and in the front body apron.

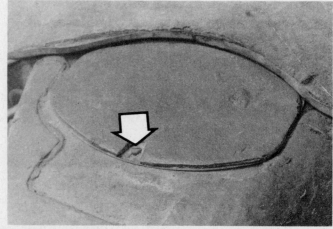

3.9   Make sure the stop plate is installed with the tab(s) facing the same way they were before removal

3.17   Remove the inspection cover from the frame tunnel

3.18a   To disconnect the earlier type shift rod coupling, remove this bolt

3.18b   To disconnect the later type shift rod coupling, remove this bolt and the self-tapping screw on the side, then knock out the spring pin with a hammer and punch

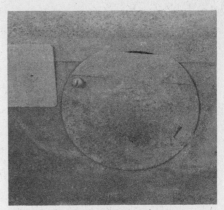

3.20   Remove the access cover from the frame head

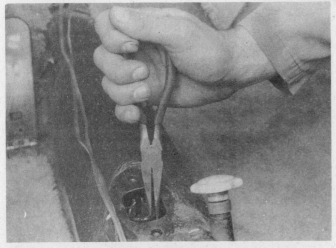

3.21   Using a pair of pliers through the hole in the tunnel for the shift lever, work the shift rod out of the coupling and through the shift rod guide bushing – keep working it forward until it's free of the bushing

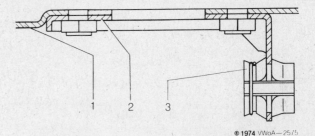

© 1974 VWoA–2575

3.24   Typical shift rod guide and bushing assembly

1   Frame tunnel
2   Reinforcement bracket
3   Guide bushing and wire ring

4   Input shaft oil seal – replacement

Refer to illustrations 4.4 and 4.6

1   Remove the engine (see Chapter 2).
2   Remove the clutch release bearing (see Chapter 8).
3   Clean the area around the seal.
4   Carefully pry out the oil seal **(see illustration)**.

21   Working through the hole in the frame tunnel, use a pair of pliers to separate the shift rod from the coupling and slide it through the shift rod guide bushing **(see illustration)**. If the grease on the shift rod – or the bushing itself – is dry, you may encounter some resistance.
22   Working through the hole in the frame head, pull the shift rod forward, through the tunnel and out the hole.
23   Inspect the shift rod for distortion. Replace it if it's warped or damaged (a bent shift rod can cause hard shifting and/or the loss of first and third gear).
24   Inspect the shift rod guide bushing for dryness, cracking or other damage. Replace it if necessary. To remove the old bushing, pull it – and the wire ring – out of the shift rod guide with a pair of pliers. To install a new bushing, slide a new wire ring onto the end of the bushing and install the bushing, slotted end first, into the shift rod guide **(see illustration)**.
25   Coat the entire shift rod with multi-purpose grease.
26   Insert the shift rod through the hole in the frame head, through the shift rod guide in the tunnel and push it all the way to the rear until it's fully engaged into the shift rod coupling. Install the frame head cover, the access cover in the front apron and the bumper.
27   Install the shift rod coupling fasteners and tighten them securely. Install the inspection cover on the frame tunnel. Install the rear seat.
28   Install the shift lever assembly (see Steps 6 through 12).
29   Adjust the shift lever (see Step 13).

4.4   Using a screwdriver or seal puller, carefully extract the old seal from its bore

7A

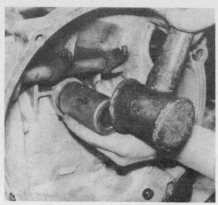

4.6 Use a large socket with an outside diameter slightly smaller than the outside diameter of the seal to drive the seal into place

5.18 Place a floor jack under the transaxle, place a board between the jack and the transaxle and raise the jack until it's supporting the transaxle

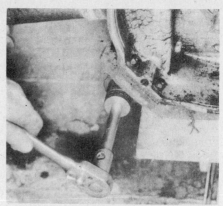

5.19 Remove the transaxle carrier bolts

5 Apply a thin coat of sealing compound to the outside of the new seal and lubricate the input shaft and seal lip with multi-purpose grease or transaxle lubricant.

6 Slide the new seal onto the input shaft and, using a large socket with an outside diameter slightly smaller than the outside diameter of the seal, drive the seal onto the shaft until it's fully seated **(see illustration)**.

7 Install the clutch release bearing (see Chapter 8).

8 Install the engine (see Chapter 2).

5   Transaxle – removal and installation

Removal

Refer to illustrations 5.18 and 5.19

1 Place the shift lever in first or third gear.

2 Remove the rear seat and disconnect the negative cable from the battery.

3 Remove the inspection cover for the shift rod coupling and remove the bolt behind the coupling (see Section 3).

4 To disconnect the shift rod from the coupling, move the shift lever to second or fourth.

5 Raise the vehicle and support it securely on jackstands. Remove the rear wheels (swing axle models only).

6 Drain the transaxle fluid (see Chapter 1).

7 Remove the engine (see Chapter 2).

8 On models with swing axles, disconnect and plug the rear brake lines and detach the parking brake cable (see Chapter 9).

9 On models with swing axles, remove the lower shock absorber mounting bolts (see Chapter 10).

10 On models with swing axles, loosen the clamps on the axle boots (see Chapter 8).

11 On models with swing axles, use a chisel to make alignment marks on the spring plate and the axleshaft bearing housing to ensure proper re-alignment during reassembly (see Chapter 10).

12 On models with swing axles, remove the bolts from the housing of the rear axleshaft bearing (see Chapter 10).

13 On models with driveaxles, detach the inner ends of both driveaxles from the transaxle if you're not going to move the vehicle. If you plan to move the vehicle, remove the driveaxles entirely (see Chapter 8). Cover the CV joints with plastic bags to keep out dirt and moisture and hang the driveaxles out of the way.

14 Disconnect the clutch cable from the clutch operating shaft lever, slide off the boot and remove the cable and sleeve from the bracket (see Chapter 8).

15 Disconnect the starter wires (see Chapter 5).

16 On later models, peel back the rubber caps and detach the back-up light electrical connectors from the transaxle (see Chapter 12).

17 Remove the nuts from the transaxle front mount (see Section 2).

18 Place a floor jack, with a piece of wood on the jack head, under the transaxle and raise the jack until it supports the transaxle **(see illustration)**.

19 Remove the transaxle carrier bolts **(see illustration)**.

20 Make a final check that all wires and hoses have been disconnected from the transaxle, then carefully pull the transaxle and jack to the rear and lower the jack.

21 On models with swing axles, disconnect the swing axles from the transaxle (see Chapter 8).

22 Remove and inspect the rear mounts (see Section 2). If they're dried, cracked or damaged, replace them.

Installation

23 Install the transaxle carrier and mounts, if removed (see Section 2). **Note:** *Don't tighten the three nuts for each rear mount until after the transaxle has been installed and you've tightened the front mount nuts.*

24 Install the swing axles, if removed (see Chapter 8).

25 Place the transaxle on the floor jack and, raise it into place. On models with swing axles, slide the swing axles into position in the spring plates. Grease and install the transaxle carrier bolts and tighten them to the torque listed in this Chapter's Specifications.

26 Install the front mount nuts and tighten them to the torque listed in this Chapter's Specifications. Now tighten the rear mount nuts securely.

27 On models with swing axles, align the marks on the axleshaft bearing housings with the match marks you made on the spring plates before disassembly, install the spring plate mounting bolts and tighten them to the torque listed in the Chapter 8 Specifications. Install the lower shock absorber mounting bolts and tighten them securely. Install the axle boots (see Chapter 8). Reattach the brake lines and bleed the brakes (see Chapter 9). Reattach and adjust the parking brake cable (see Chapter 9). Install the wheels.

28 On models with driveaxles, install the driveaxles or – if you only detached the inner ends – reattach the driveaxles to the transaxle (see Chapter 8).

29 Inspect all clutch components before proceeding. In most cases, new clutch components should be routinely installed any time the engine is removed (see Chapter 8).

30 Install the engine (see Chapter 2).

31 Reattach the clutch cable and adjust it (see Chapter 8).

32 Reattach all of the electrical connectors that were disconnected.

33 Make a final check that all wires, hoses and linkages have been connected.

34 Fill the transaxle with lubricant to the proper level (see Chapter 1).

35 Install the wheels, if removed.

36 Remove any jack(s) supporting the transaxle and/or engine and lower the vehicle.

37 Move the shift lever into neutral and reconnect the shift rod coupling (see Section 3).

38 Connect the negative battery cable.

39 Road test the vehicle for proper operation and check for leaks.

6   Transaxle overhaul – general information

Overhauling a manual transaxle is a difficult job for the do-it-yourselfer. Many small parts must be removed, inspected and installed correctly. Numerous clearances must be precisely measured and, if necessary, altered. Therefore, if transaxle problems arise, you can remove and install the transaxle yourself, but we recommend that you check with local dealer parts departments and auto parts stores regarding the availability of a rebuilt transaxle. Or, you can have it overhauled by a transmission repair shop, though the labor and parts charges for an overhaul will likely exceed the cost of purchasing a rebuilt unit.

Nevertheless, if you have the determination, time, skills and special tools, it's not impossible to rebuild a transaxle. You'll need various sizes of internal and external snap-ring pliers, a bearing puller, a slide hammer, a set of pin punches, a dial indicator and a hydraulic press. You'll also need a large, sturdy workbench, a bench vise and a transaxle stand.

During disassembly of the transaxle, make careful notes of how each piece comes off, where it fits in relation to other pieces and what holds it in place. Exploded views are included to show where the parts go – but actually noting how they are installed when you remove the parts will make it much easier to get the transaxle back together. Most importantly, work carefully and slowly in a deliberate step-by-step manner.

Before disassembling the transaxle, try to determine what area of the transaxle is malfunctioning. Certain problems can be traced to specific areas in the transaxle, which can make component examination and replacement easier. Refer to the Troubleshooting section at the front of this manual for information regarding possible sources of trouble.

7   Transaxle overhaul (split-case type)

Disassembly

Refer to illustrations 7.7, 7.8 and 7.18

1   Drain the transaxle lubricant (see Chapter 1).
2   Remove the transaxle from the vehicle (see Section 5).
3   Remove the front mount, the transaxle carrier and the rear mounts (see Section 2).
4   Remove the outer bearings and axle tubes (see Chapter 8). **Note:** *You can't remove the axleshafts until after the gear cases have been split.*
5   Remove the clutch release bearing (see Chapter 8).
6   Remove the nuts holding the gear selector rod housing at the front of the case and remove the housing.
7   Unlock the two tab washers from the large nuts on the ends of the input and pinion shafts **(see illustration)**. To loosen these two nuts (do it

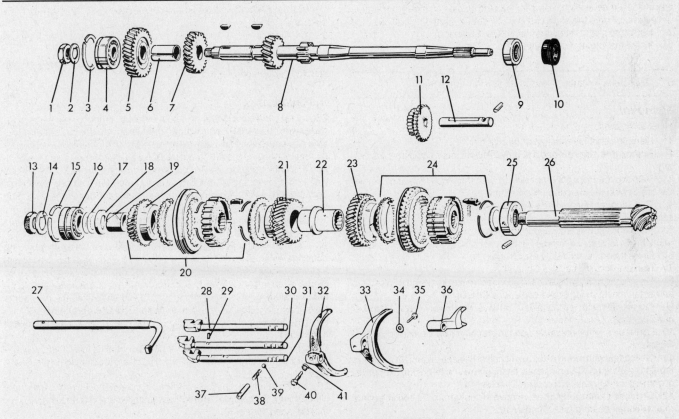

7.7   Exploded view of the internal components in the split-case transaxle

1	Shaft nut	12	Reverse gear shaft	22	Splined bushing
2	Lock washer	13	Shaft nut	23	Second gear
3	Circlip for bearing	14	Lock washer	24	Second gear synchronizer/
4	Bearing	15	Circlip for bearing		first gear hub
5	Fourth gear	16	Bearing	25	Roller bearing
6	Spacer sleeve	17	Shims	26	Pinion
7	Third gear	18	Thrust washer	27	Selector arm
8	Input shaft	19	Bushing	28	Reverse selector rail
9	Roller bearing	20	Third/fourth gear	29	Interlock plunger
10	Seal		synchronizer assembly	30	First/second selector rail
11	Reverse idler gear	21	Third gear	31	Third/fourth selector rail

32	Third/fourth selector fork
33	Second/third selector fork
34	Washer
35	Screw
36	Reverse selector fork
37	Sleeve
38	Detent spring
39	Detent ball
40	Screw
41	Washer

7A

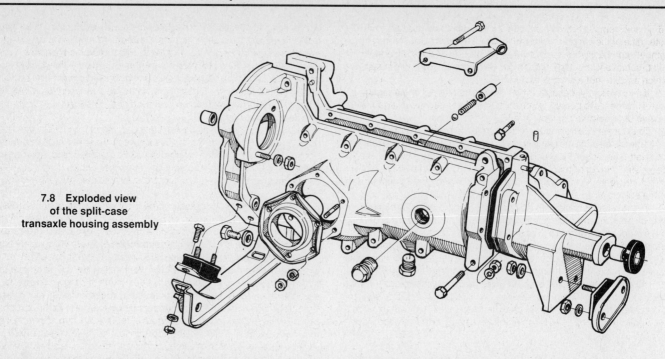

7.8   Exploded view of the split-case transaxle housing assembly

now while it's easy), engage two gears simultaneously by pulling out the outer two selector fork rails. This locks the two shafts. Loosen the nuts.

8   Remove all through bolts and nuts that clamp the two halves of the case together **(see illustration)**. Don't forget the bolts inside the bellhousing or the long thin through bolt that goes right through the center of the case.

9   Once all the bolts are removed, the only thing preventing the two halves from falling apart is the tight fit of the two side bearings. A few gentle taps with a mallet or block of wood will separate the two halves. **Caution:** *Do not, under any circumstances, use force or leverage between the two mating faces or serious damage could result: The fit around the bearings could become too loose, resulting in oil leaks.*

10   Pull one case half over the axleshaft and the two gearbox shafts can simply be lifted out of the other half.

11   Detach the axleshafts and differential assembly from the other case half.

12   Usually, the differential side bearings are left in place in each case

half, but the spacer rings and shims fitted on the differential housing can be removed. Just make sure you don't switch them! As you remove each case half, clearly label the set of shims for each side and put them away (tape them into position on the differential, if you wish). The transaxle is now disassembled into the main sub-assemblies.

13   To disassemble the pinion shaft, remove the nut and washer. Remove the ball bearing – with the retaining ring fitted in its outer groove – by holding the bearing so that the shaft hangs down and then striking the end of the shaft with a soft faced hammer. If you have no one to support the shaft, hold it just above the bench surface over a small pile of rags.

14   Remove the shims, the thrust washer, the bushing, the fourth gear synchro ring and the third/fourth synchro hub. If the third/fourth synchro assembly is difficult to break loose from the splines, tap it carefully with a small soft mallet but don't let it fall apart when it slides free.

15   Remove the third gear synchro ring, third gear, the bushing, second gear and the second/first synchro assembly. Don't lose the three springs which will pop out of the center sleeve when the shaft comes out.

7.18   Remove fourth and third gears from the input shaft with a small puller – don't lose the keyways or the spacer sleeve between the gears

7.24   Inspect the ring and pinion gear – if either of them looks like this badly damaged pinion gear, replace both as a matched set

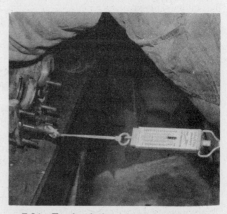

7.31   To check the pressure of the spring-loaded ball in the groove for each selector rail, attach a spring balance to the end of each selector fork – if the amount of pull required is significantly outside the specified pull, replace the spring(s)

16 Finally remove any shims – note their number and position – and the outer race of the pinion roller bearing. Don't try to remove the inner race without expert assistance. It's a very tight press fit on the shaft and is difficult to remove without the proper tool and a press. You can damage the pinion if you're not extremely careful.

17 If third or fourth gear on the input shaft is badly worn or damaged, or if one of the other two gears – which are part of the shaft – is damaged, you'll have to disassemble the input shaft.

18 To disassemble the input shaft, remove the nut and the washer. Remove the ball bearing the same way you removed the bearing from the pinion shaft (see Step 13). Using a puller, remove fourth gear, the spacer sleeve and third gear **(see illustration)**. Don't lose the keyways for third and fourth gears. Remove the seal and roller bearing from the other end with a puller too.

19 The reverse gear pinion runs on a shaft which is locked in place in the case by a pin, the protruding end of which also locates the rear ball bearing of the input shaft. Remove the pin and the shaft can be pulled out. Note that the gear spins on a bushing – if it's worn, replace it. Any radial play between the gear and shaft can may allow the gear to rock, which can cause it to jump out of engagement in reverse, under a load.

20 To remove the selector forks, remove the two threaded plugs from the case and loosen the clamping screws. Don't remove the rails or selector forks unless they need to be replaced (see Inspection). The selector forks need not be removed unless inspection indicates that they are too slack a fit in the sleeve grooves.

Inspection

Refer to illustrations 7.24 and 7.31

Note: *The following inspection procedure applies to both split-case and single-piece case transaxles, unless noted otherwise.*

21 The amount of wear determines the economics of repair vs. replacement. If, after inspecting the components, you calculate that a rebuild will cost almost as much as a rebuilt transaxle, you may wish to consider whether to proceed with an overhaul or simply purchase a rebuilt unit.

22 It's not usually necessary to immerse the gearbox components in solvent for inspection purposes. Just wipe them off with a clean cloth. However, you should wash the case with solvent. Just be sure to remove the roller bearings.

23 Examine the case for signs of cracks or damage, particularly near the bearing housings and on the mating surfaces where the gear carrier and side bearing plates join.

24 Inspect the ring and pinion **(see illustration)**. If they're badly worn – chipped teeth, excessive backlash, etc. – replace them as a sub-assembly. The special tools needed to reassemble and readjust a rebuilt differential and ring and pinion assembly are difficult to obtain and expensive.

25 Some gears run on separate bushings on the shaft, so make sure there's no play between the gear, bushing and shaft. If there is, a new bushing will usually solve the problem. Don't forget to check the reverse gear bushing.

26 Inspect all gear teeth for signs of pitted mating surfaces, chips or scoring. If one gear is damaged, then its counterpart on the other shaft will probably be damaged too.

27 Two types of bearings – ball and needle roller – are used. Generally, needle rollers wear very little because they're not subject to axial thrust. But note carefully how they spin. If any bearing exhibits the slightest roughness, drag or play, replace it. Inspect the two tapered roller bearings for the differential too. If they need to be replaced, have a VW transaxle specialist do it. Also have him inspect and, if necessary, reset the ring and pinion as well.

28 Using a hydraulic press, remove all synchro rings for examination. The grooved taper face of the ring provides the braking action on the mating face of the gear wheel cone. If the ridges are worn, the braking or synchro action will be less effective. The only way to effectively determine the condition of the rings is by comparing them with new parts. New rings are relatively inexpensive, so it's a good idea to simply replace all of them. When fitting a synchro ring over its cone on the gear wheel, the gap between the synchro ring and the gear teeth should be between the normal and minimum dimensions listed in this Chapter's Specifications. If the gap is near the lower limit, get new rings. **Caution:** *When buying new rings, make sure you obtain the correct parts. Production modifications have been made, so although the new rings will fit – and work – they're not necessarily identical to the ones you're replacing. The rings in a set are similar, but they're not identical – for example, some have wider cut-outs. Mixing them up is asking for trouble. So mark each ring to insure that you install it with its respective gear.*

29 The synchro hubs must be assembled for inspection. There must be no axial or radial play at the splines between the inner hub and outer sleeve. When replacing the synchro rings, it's a good idea to replace the sliding keys and their locating springs. The keys – which fit into the cutouts in the synchro rings – are subject to wear, and the springs eventually weaken.

30 The selector forks are some of the most critical components in the transaxle. The two forks run in grooves in the outer sleeves of the synchro hubs. If the clearance of the forks in the grooves is excessive, the gears they control may jump out. The clearance of the fork in the groove should not exceed the maximum clearance listed in this Chapter's Specifications. Excessive clearance can be caused by wear on the fork, or the groove or both. Take the forks to the dealer parts department or a transaxle specialist and ask them to compare the thickness of the used forks with new ones. If the difference in thickness isn't enough to compensate for the excess gap between the fork and the hub groove, replace the hub assembly as well. It's an expensive part, but the gap is critical, so there's no alternative.

31 The selector rails on which the forks are mounted need not be removed from the case. Some force is needed to overcome the pressure of the spring-loaded ball in the groove. To check it, measure it with a spring balance hooked on to the end of each selector fork **(see illustration)**. If the required pull is significantly outside the range listed in this Chapter's Specifications, check the detent springs and balls. Push the selector rods out of the case to release the ball and spring plugs from their respective bores (on earlier, split-type case transaxles, the detent balls and springs are released inside the case when the rails are pulled out – keep a hand over the hole to prevent them flying out). **Note:** *You'll need to obtain new plugs for reassembly.*

32 Check the spring free length and compare your measurements to the dimension listed in this Chapter's Specifications. If the springs are too short, replace them. Inspect the balls for pitting and grooves and make sure the selector rods themselves are a tight fit in their bores. Look at the detent grooves in the rails – they shouldn't be worn. While the rails are removed, don't lose the interlock plungers which fit between the selector rod grooves.

Reassembly

Refer to illustrations 7.38a, 7.38b, 7.40a, 7.40b, 7.40c, 7.40d, 7.40e, 7.40f, 7.40g, 7.41, 7.42a, 7.42b, 7.43, 7.44, 7.45, 7.46, 7.47, 7.48, 7.49a, 7.49b, 7.54, 7.55, 7.56, 7.57a, 7.57b, 7.68a, 7.68b, 7.70, 7.71a, 7.71b and 7.73

33 Prepare a clean space of adequate size on your work bench. Don't start until you've collected all the necessary parts and gaskets and have made sure that all of them fit. **Note:** *It's a good idea to keep the old gaskets you remove until the job is done – gasket sets often contain items for a variety of models, so you need to pick the right gaskets.*

34 Reassembly of the split-case type transaxle is generally simpler than reassembly of the later single-piece unit, as long as the ring and pinion don't have to be reset. Side bearing adjustment involves reassembly of the complete transaxle, then – if the side bearing shims must be changed – disassembly again.

35 The mating surfaces of both case halves must be perfectly clean and unmarked by dents or burrs. Use solvent to remove any traces of old sealing compound.

36 Obtain good quality sealing compound suitable for prepping the mating surfaces.

37 Make sure that new gaskets are available. This is particularly important when refitting the gear change end cover because the thickness of the gaskets determines the pressure on the shaft bearings which eliminates axial movement.

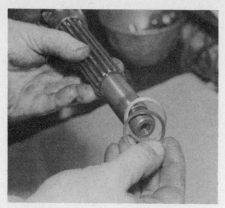

7.38a   Install the same number of shims, in the same order, that you removed from the pinion shaft

7.38b   Install the bearing on the pinion shaft

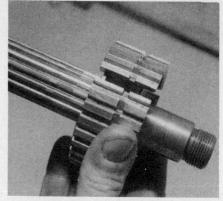

7.40a   To install the second gear synchronizer/first gear hub on the pinion shaft, fit the single, square section key retaining ring into the groove in the center section of the hub, slide the hub onto the shaft with the retaining ring nearest the pinion gear, . . .

7.40b   . . . place the three key springs into the holes, . . .

7.40c   . . . hook the flat, stepped end of each sliding key under the retaining ring so the raised dimple faces outward, . . .

7.40d   . . . look for marks inside the outer sleeve – make sure the depressions in three of the splines line up with the centers of the three sliding keys, . . .

7.40e   . . . slide the outer sleeve over the hub so the keys are held in place . . .

7.40f   . . . install the second gear synchro ring . . .

7.40g   . . . and install second gear

---

38   Install the shims and bearing on the pinion shaft (**see illustrations**). **Note:** *There shouldn't be any problems with shim settings – as long as you carefully noted their number and position during removal.*

39   If you're replacing the ring and pinion, assembly of the pinion shaft is a little more involved. You'll need to have access to an assortment of shims and be able to get the inner race of the pinion bearing heated and pressed off and onto the shaft. Be advised, however, that adjusting the ring gear, and side bearing pre-load, is more complex and requires a special gauge. It's best to leave this job to a specialist with the skills and tools.

40   To install the second gear synchronizer/first gear hub assembly, fit the single, square section key retaining ring into the groove in the center section of the hub, slide the hub onto the shaft with the retaining ring nearest

7.41   Install the splined, shouldered bushing on the pinion shaft

7.42a   Install third gear . . .

7.42b   . . . and the third gear synchro ring on the pinion shaft

7.43   Install the third/fourth synchro assembly on the pinion shaft

7.44   Install the fourth gear bushing on the pinion shaft

7.45   Install the fourth gear synchro ring on the pinion shaft

7.46   Install fourth gear on the pinion shaft

7.47   Install the thrust washer on the pinion shaft – note that the grooves in the thrust washer face the gear

7.48   Install the shims on the pinion shaft

7A

the pinion gear, place the three key springs into the holes and hook the flat, stepped end of each sliding key under the retaining ring so that the raised dimple faces outwards (see illustrations). Now slide the outer sleeve over the hub so that the keys are trapped and held in position. If marks exist or have been made on the inner and outer hubs, lining up the splines is no problem. If there aren't any marks, look inside the outer sleeve and make sure that the three depressions in three of the splines line up with the centers of the three sliding keys (see illustrations). Now install the second gear synchro ring and second gear (see illustrations).

41   Install the splined, shouldered bushing (see illustration).

42   Install third gear and the third gear synchro ring on the pinion shaft (see illustrations).

43   Install the third/fourth synchronizer assembly (see illustration). To verify that your reassembly is correct, when the third/fourth synchronizer hub has been fitted to the shaft the inner sleeve should line up with the end face of the splined part of the shaft. This alignment should not vary by more than 0.002 inch (0.05 mm). If it does, the assembly is wrong or the shim thickness next to the roller bearing is incorrect.

44   Install the fourth gear bushing (see illustration).

45   Install the fourth gear synchro ring (see illustration).

46   Install fourth gear (see illustration).

47   Install the thrust washer (see illustration). Note that the grooves in the washer face the gear.

48   Install the shims (see illustration).

7.49a Install the ball bearing on the end of the pinion shaft ...

7.49b ... and drive it on until it's fully seated against the shims

7.54 Install the bushing into reverse gear

7.55 Insert the reverse gear shaft through the case, plain end first, and align the cut-out with the hole in the bearing housing

7.56 Install the lock pin for the reverse gear shaft

7.57a To check the setting of the selector forks, temporarily place the assembled pinion shaft in position in the left case half (note the locating dowel (arrow) for the bearing), ...

49 Install the ball bearing (see illustration). Drive it on until it's fully seated against the shims (see illustration). The lockwasher and shaft nut should be installed but not tightened fully at this stage.

50 Lining up the keyways to tight fitting gears can be tricky. Heat the gears to about 194-degrees F (90-degrees C) in an oil bath, then slide them onto the shaft and position them over the Woodruff keys. Make sure the keys are a snug fit and fully engaged in their slots or they might shift – and jam – before the gear is positioned. Install third (the smaller) gear first – it should butt right up to the second gear on the shaft. Then install the spacer and, finally, fourth gear which should butt up tight to the spacer.

51 You can tap the two bearings onto the shaft with a pipe of sufficient diameter or use the hot oil bath to heat them up and slide them into place. Don't heat the the bearings any other way or you could damage them.

52 The bearing with the retaining circlip goes on the threaded end of the shaft with the circlip nearest to the threaded end. Inspect the transaxle case where the bearing fits. The circlip fits into a recess or groove in the front face. The bearing should not protrude more than a fraction of a millimeter in front of the case.

53 Replace, but do not fully tighten, the lockwasher and nut.

54 Fit the reverse gear to the case before installing the input shaft. Fit the sleeve into the gear (see illustration), then hold the gear in position in the case with the smaller of the two rows of gear teeth towards the front.

55 Insert the reverse gear shaft through the case, plain end first, and align the cut-out with the hole in the bearing housing (see illustration).

56 Install the lock pin (see illustration).

57 Have an assistant handy for the next Steps. Place the assembled pinion shaft in position in the left half of the case (see illustrations) and check the setting of the selector forks. If new forks or rails have been fitted, put the rails in the neutral position and – with the forks engaged correctly with their respective hub grooves – verify that both synchro hub outer sleeves

are in the neutral (central) position on their hubs. Then engage each gear to ensure that the sleeves mesh correctly. At this stage, no further adjustment is possible. If there's trouble later, you can make further adjustments after the transaxle is installed. The reverse gear selector fork, however, can't be adjusted later, so install the input shaft temporarily and verify that the gears line up correctly when reverse gear is engaged. If necessary, move the selector fork along the rail until the small gear of the sliding pinion meshes fully with the gear teeth of the first/second hub on the pinion shaft. The larger gear of the sliding pinion should be in mesh with the gear teeth on the input shaft at the same time. Then select neutral and first gear, in turn, to ensure that the sliding reverse gear pinion is well clear of engagement with anything else.

58 Determine the direction of rotation of the differential ring gear so that the axleshaft assembly turns in the right direction. The left case half carries the differential ring gear and the selector mechanism. So the axle/differential assembly must go in first.

59 Make sure the correct shims are in position on the ring gear side of the differential case.

60 Position the left half of the case in a suitable position. Bear in mind that the two axleshafts must be positioned – and supported – so that their weight doesn't upset the balance of the case.

61 Ensure that all parts are scrupulously clean and that the shims and spacers are correct for each side of the differential casing. Remember that the shims serve two functions – they pre-load the side bearings and they position the differential ring gear correctly in relation to the pinion.

62 You might argue that the shim combinations should be recalculated if new bearings are fitted. In practice, however, it's unnecessary as long as you're installing the same differential ring gear and pinion and have never altered the shim combinations.

63 When fitting new bearings, support the side cover evenly and secure-

7.57b . . . verify that both synchro hub outer sleeves are in the central (neutral) position on their hubs and engage each gear to ensure that the sleeves mesh correctly

7.68a Install the input shaft assembly – make sure the hole in the rear bearing engages with the protruding end of the reverse shaft lock pin (arrows) – and, if everything is installed correctly, . . .

7.68b . . . this is how it should look

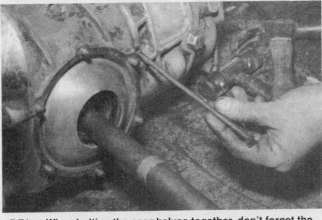

7.70 Before tightening the case fasteners, apply RTV sealant to the outside of the input shaft seal and install it onto the rear end of the input shaft – make sure the seal lip faces into the case

7.71a When bolting the case halves together, don't forget the long center bolt

ly and arrange the bearings so that the closed side of the ball race faces the outside of the case. The bore in the side cover must be scrupulously clean and free of any snags or burrs.

64   Tap the new bearing into place with a heavy mallet and a large socket or a piece of pipe with an outside diameter slightly smaller than the diameter of the outer race of the bearing. Make sure it doesn't cock in the bore when you start to drive it in. If it does, work it out and start again.

65   Make sure both mating surfaces are perfectly clean. Apply a thin even film of RTV sealant to the mating face of the case. Using a new O-ring, install the right side bearing and cover. Tighten the nuts evenly to the torque listed in this Chapter's Specifications.

66   Insert the axleshaft through the bearing and guide the differential into the case, ring gear side first (with the teeth visible). If necessary, tap the case so the bearing fully seats on the shoulder of the differential.

67   Install the pinion shaft assembly. The selector forks should be in the neutral position and they must engage in the grooves of the hub sleeves. At the same time the rear bearing outer race should be turned so that the peg in the case engages the case.

68   Install the input shaft. Make sure the hole in the rear bearing engages with the protruding end of the reverse shaft lock pin **(see illustrations)**.

69   Verify that the differential side bearing shims are in position on the differential. Install the right case over the shaft and against the differential so that the bearing locates on the shoulder. Simultaneously supporting the weight of the axles, holding the cases and aligning the bearings with the dowel pegs can be challenging. An assistant is helpful at this point. Or arrange the left shaft into a near vertical position by hanging it over the edge of the bench. Place two wooden boxes on end, side by side, on the floor, with the shaft hanging down between them. Tap the case half into position

onto the shoulder of the differential. If you have difficulty getting the two halves to butt together, one of the bearing dowel pegs isn't properly located. Don't force anything. Take it off, have a look and try again.

70   Before reattaching the case halves, apply RTV sealant to the outside of the input shaft oil seal and install it onto the rear end of the input shaft **(see illustration)**. Make sure the seal lip faces into the case.

71   Install all new nuts, bolts and washers. Note that one or two are longer than the others. Don't forget the long center bolt **(see illustration)**. Tighten the case bolts evenly and gradually in the pattern shown **(see illustration)** to the initial torque listed in this Chapter's Specifications. Make sure

7A

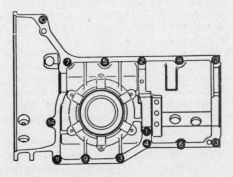

7.71b   Bolt tightening sequence for split-case type housing

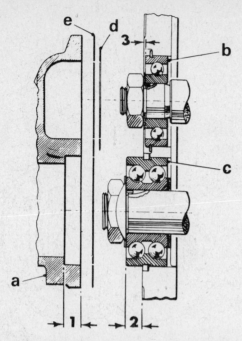

8.4a   If third gear jumps out, remove the front plug from the transaxle . . .

7.73   Layout of gaskets to load front bearings

a Gearshift lever housing	d Circular gasket
b Input shaft bearing	e Main cover gasket
c Pinion shaft bearing	

8.4b   . . . loosen the selector fork set screw, slide the fork to the rear on its rail, tighten the set screw, install the plug and road test the vehicle to check your work – you may have to repeat this process several times until the gear mesh feels right

both shafts revolve freely and each of the gears engage. If they don't, split the cases and have a look. If they do, tighten the case bolts in the sequence shown to the final torque listed in this Chapter's Specifications.

72   To tighten the input and pinion shaft nuts, engage two gears by pulling out the two outer selector rods. Tighten the larger, pinion shaft nut to the torque listed in this Chapter's Specifications. Bend up the block tabs against a flat on the nuts.

73   Fitting the gear change rod housing on the end of the case is critical because gasket thickness determines the pressure applied to the outer races of both ball bearings to prevent any movement when end thrust is applied **(see illustration)**. Use new gaskets and tighten the housing bolts securely.

74   When placing the gear shift cover in position, the selector rails should be in neutral and the change rod should fit into the cut-out slots in the ends of the rails. Replace the nuts and tighten them evenly to the torque listed in this Chapter's Specifications.

75   Install the mounting bracket and flexible mounting blocks, the clutch release thrust ring and the unit is ready for replacement in the car.

8   Selector forks – adjustment

Refer to illustrations 8.4a and 8.4b

1   You can make adjustments to the forward speed selector forks (not reverse) with the transaxle installed in the vehicle. Such adjustments, which prevent a gear from jumping out of mesh under power, are usually necessary just after the transaxle has been overhauled. Under any other circumstances, adjustment simply compensates for wear. The down side, however, is that adjusting a fork to prevent one gear from jumping out of mesh may very well cause another gear to jump instead. For example, if you adjust a fork to cure a third gear jump, you might well find that fourth gear then jumps out instead! The same applies to first and second, so before you start adjusting selector forks, decide which gear is going to bother you least if it jumps out!

2   On the lower forward end of the left side of the transaxle case, two large plugs cover holes through which you can access the clamp screws of the selector forks. The front one is for the third and fourth selector fork and the other for first/second.

3   To make an adjustment, select Neutral and remove the plug for the fork you wish to adjust.

4   If third gear jumps out, remove the front plug **(see illustration)**, loosen the fork set screw **(see illustration)**, slide the front selector fork backwards a fraction on its rail, retighten the set screw, install the plug and road test. If fourth gear jumps out, move the front selector fork forwards.

5   If first gear is jumping out, leave it alone – the fault is unlikely to be the selector fork setting. If second gear jumps out, slide the rear selector fork forward.

6   You may have to repeat this process several times for each fork until the mesh feels just right.

7   Sometimes, when the transaxle is badly worn, any adjustment results in all gears jumping out. You'll have to decide which ones cause the least inconvenience and take up the slack in the appropriate direction. Needless to say, jumping out of gear – particularly with the power on – can be dangerous, so don't be too casual about correcting this problem. If you get

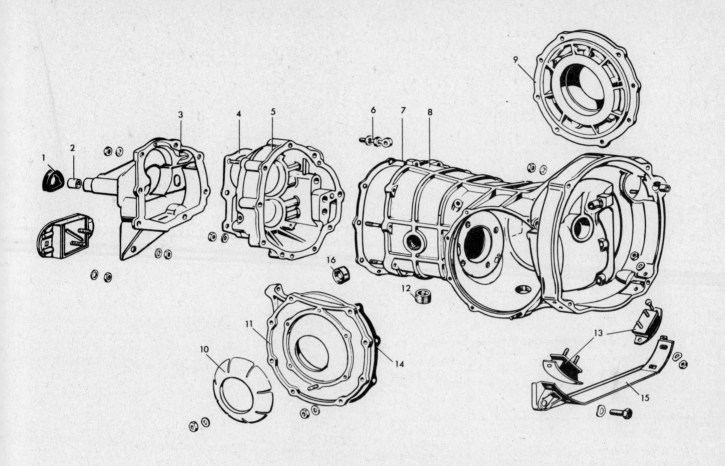

9.4 Exploded view of a typical early single-piece transaxle housing

1	Grommet	7	Gasket	12	Drain plug
2	Bushing	8	Case	13	Rear flexible mountings
3	Gearshift housing	9	Right side bearing cover	14	Gasket
4	Gasket	10	Plastic insert	15	Rear mounting bracket
5	Gear carrier	11	Left side bearing cover	16	Oil level plug
6	Reverse lever pivot post				

into the habit of holding a gear in mesh, you can expect accelerated wear of everything connected with the synchromesh mechanism.

8   There may also be wear in the shift lever mechanism (see Section 3). A certain amount of adjustment is possible at the shift lever. Loosen the two retaining bolts. The mounting bolt holes are elongated, so the shift lever assembly can be moved forward or backward a little. If you move the assembly forward, second and fourth gears will engage more positively; if you move it to the rear, first and third will be more positive. But remember: This adjustment is normally used only to seek the exact central position. Too much adjustment at the shift lever could have exactly the same results as too much adjustment at the selector forks.

9   Transaxle overhaul (single-piece case)

Disassembly

Refer to illustration 9.4, 9.5, 9.8, 9.13, 9.16a, 9.16b, 9.20 and 9.26
Note: *Gasket sets often contain items covering a variety of models. Save the old gaskets you remove during disassembly. You can use them to determine which gaskets in the new set are for your transaxle.*

1   Remove the transaxle from the vehicle (see Section 5).
2   Drain the oil, remove the front mount, transaxle carrier and rear mounts (see Section 2) and clean the transaxle exterior thoroughly.
3   On swing axle models, remove the axleshafts and axle tubes (see Chapter 8).
4   Remove the nuts holding the gear selector lever housing and remove the housing together with the lever **(see illustration)**.
5   Bend back the tabs of the lockwashers and remove the large nuts on the ends of the input and pinion shafts **(see illustration on next page)**. To prevent the shafts from rotating, pull or push the two outer selector fork rails which protrude from the end of the case. This will lock the two shafts by engaging two gears at once. **Note:** *On later models, circlips are used instead of these nuts. Remove the circlip on the input shaft end before attempting to withdraw the two shafts from the bearings in the gear carrier.* **Caution:** *Cover the end of the shaft with a shop rag when releasing this circlip. It's under tension from a dished thrust washer underneath, so it may fly off when released from its groove.*
6   Remove the nuts from the studs which secure the gear carrier (end case) to the main case. Also remove the ground strap.
7   Turn the whole unit on its side so that the left side bearing cover is facing up (remember, the narrow end of the case is the front).

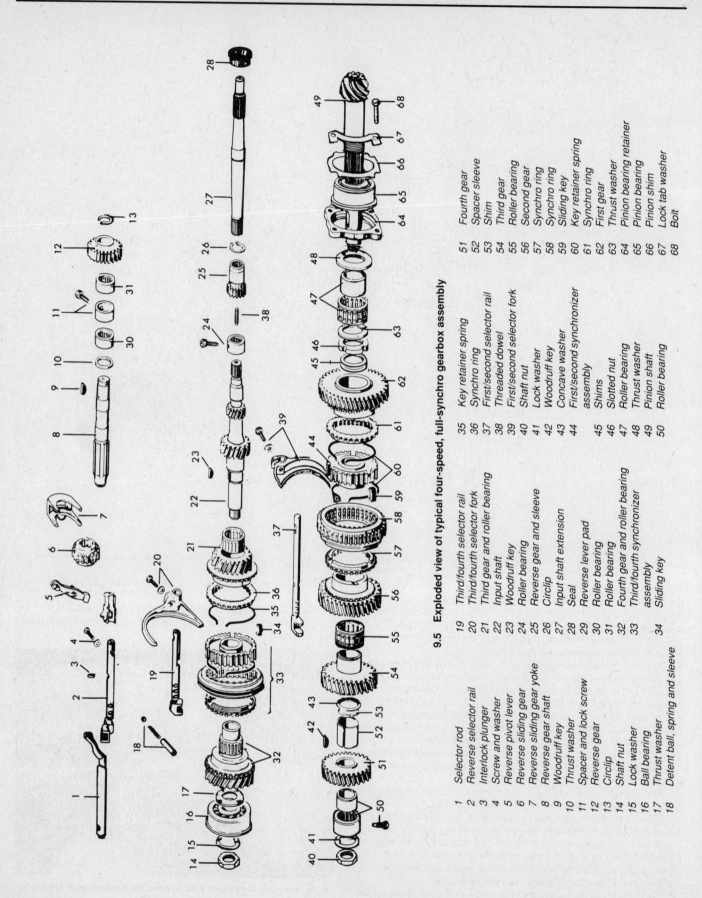

9.5　Exploded view of typical four-speed, full-synchro gearbox assembly

1　Selector rod
2　Reverse selector rail
3　Interlock plunger
4　Screw and washer
5　Reverse pivot lever
6　Reverse sliding gear
7　Reverse sliding gear yoke
8　Reverse gear shaft
9　Woodruff key
10　Thrust washer
11　Spacer and lock screw
12　Reverse gear
13　Circlip
14　Shaft nut
15　Lock washer
16　Ball bearing
17　Thrust washer
18　Detent ball, spring and sleeve

19　Third/fourth selector rail
20　Third/fourth selector fork
21　Third gear and roller bearing
22　Input shaft
23　Woodruff key
24　Roller bearing
25　Reverse gear and sleeve
26　Circlip
27　Input shaft extension
28　Seal
29　Reverse lever pad
30　Roller bearing
31　Roller bearing
32　Fourth gear and roller bearing
33　Third/fourth synchronizer
　　assembly
34　Sliding key

35　Key retainer spring
36　Synchro ring
37　First/second selector rail
38　Threaded dowel
39　First/second selector fork
40　Shaft nut
41　Lock washer
42　Woodruff key
43　Concave washer
44　First/second synchronizer
　　assembly
45　Shims
46　Slotted nut
47　Roller bearing
48　Thrust washer
49　Pinion shaft
50　Roller bearing

51　Fourth gear
52　Spacer sleeve
53　Shim
54　Third gear
55　Roller bearing
56　Second gear
57　Synchro ring
58　Synchro ring
59　Sliding key
60　Key retainer spring
61　Synchro ring
62　First gear
63　Thrust washer
64　Pinion bearing retainer
65　Pinion bearing
66　Pinion shim
67　Lock tab washer
68　Bolt

9.8   Exploded view of a typical differential assembly

1	Differential and ring gear	5	O-ring	10	Drive flange
2	Left side bearing cover	6	Circlip	11	Spacer
3	Bearing outer race	8	Nut	12	Circlip
4	Oil seal	9	Washer	13	Sealing plug

8   On driveaxle models, remove the sealing plugs from the centers of the drive flanges (**see illustration**) by punching the blade of a screwdriver through them and levering them out. Then remove the circlips from the grooves in the ends of the splined shafts and lever off the flanges. There's a spacer ring behind the flange. If you can dig it out now, remove it. If not, you can remove it after you pull off the side cover.

9   Remove the left side bearing cover retaining nuts and remove the cover. Give it a few taps with a soft face mallet if necessary – don't use force. When the cover comes off, the outer race of the tapered roller side bearing usually comes off with it. If the bearing comes off with the side cover, don't lose the shim(s) between the bearing inner race and the differential. These shims, which control the side bearing pre-load and ring and pinion backlash, are critical. Label them, tape them to the bearing to prevent mix-ups with the shims for the other side cover and set them aside. If the bearing stays on, leave it there for now. Note the paper gasket between the cover and case.

10   Turn the transaxle on its side with the opening for the left side cover facing up and carefully lift out the differential assembly.

11   If you can't lift it out, turn the transaxle over again, and, using a drift punch placed against the inner race of the right bearing, gently tap it out. Support the differential to prevent it from dropping under its own weight. If it's easier for you to tap out the differential with the bearing still in the side cover, by all means do it that way. Collect the shims for the other side bearing, label them, tape them together and set them aside.

12   Turn the transaxle over with the right side bearing cover facing up. On driveaxle models, remove the drive flange (see Step 8). Remove the right side bearing cover nuts and remove the cover. Again, note the paper gasket.

13   Remove the circlip which locks the reverse gear sleeve to the input shaft (**see illustration**). Slide it back along the shaft and slide the sleeve along behind it.

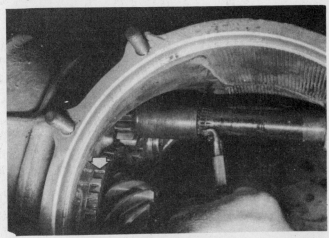

9.13   Remove the circlip which locks the reverse gear sleeve to the input shaft

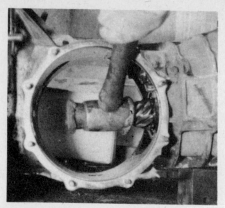

9.16a   To remove the gearbox assembly from the case, strike the end of the pinion with a heavy soft-faced mallet ...

9.16b   ... or place a small scissor-type jack inside the differential housing and push the gearbox assembly loose

9.20   To remove a differential side bearing from the differential, tap it off with a drift and hammer

14   Unscrew the rear end of the input shaft from the front half. Take off the gear/sleeve and remove the circlip from the shaft. Withdraw the shaft from the rear through the oil seal. Remove the input shaft seal and discard it. **Note:** *This seal can be replaced with the transaxle installed (see Section 4).*

15   On earlier units, four bolts secure the pinion shaft bearing retainer plate. Carefully pry up the lock tabs on each bolt. Don't let the tool slip and strike the pinion gear. Carefully remove the bolts. Later units use a locking castellated ring threaded onto the pinion bearing instead of a four-bolt flange. On these models, simply unscrew the lock ring. Again, make sure you don't damage the pinion teeth.

16   To remove the gearbox assembly from the case, use a heavy copper faced mallet and strike the end of the pinion **(see illustration)**. Or insert a jack small enough to fit between the pinion and the opposite side of the case **(see illustration)**. Cushion the head of the jack touching the pinion and press it out. Be sure to support the gear carrier when the gear shafts come free. As soon as they're clear, collect the shims(s) from the pinion flange and attach them to the flange or put them in a plastic bag to prevent loss.

17   To remove first gear and its shaft, remove the circlip. The gear is a slide fit on a key. Pull it off. Pry it a little with a screwdriver if necessary. Remove the key from the shaft and remove the shaft from the front.

18   To remove the needle roller bearings from the reverse shaft, unscrew the locating screw (secures the spacer sleeve between the two bearings) from the case. Use a drift of suitable diameter to drive the two needle rollers and spacer out towards the rear of the case.

19   The other needle bearing outer race is also secured by a screw in the case. Remove it too. Then tap out the needle roller bearing race. (This is the bearing that supports the rear end of the forward half of the input shaft.)

20   The large side bearings located in either the covers or on the differential can remain in place unless inspection indicates that they're worn. Knock them off the differential or out of the covers **(see illustration)**. If you're removing them from the covers, make sure the covers are firmly and evenly supported. Don't attempt to do it the other way round – support the bearings and knock the covers out – or you may damage the cover.

21   Separate the two shafts with their clusters of gears from the gear carrier.

22   Remove the small sliding gear and the reverse fork from the pivot on the reverse lever.

23   Loosen the clamping bolts which hold the two other selector forks to their respective rails. Slide back the rail for the first/second gear fork far enough to remove the fork. The other fork is trickier to remove because the gear carrier is in the way. Drive the rail back far enough to free it from the fork. **Caution:** *DO NOT drive the rails out of the gear carrier. If you do, the detent balls and springs will pop out and you will be looking at a lot of extra work.*

24   Remove the two gear shafts from the carrier. It's a good idea to tape both shafts together. Then, when you release the ends of the shafts, they won't fall apart. You'll need an assistant for this Step. Hold the carrier – with the shafts hanging down – while another person strikes the end of the

input shaft with a soft faced mallet and supports the weight of the gear shafts as they are driven out. Do NOT let them drop down.

25   Remove the two bearings in the carrier. The needle roller bearing is located by a screw similar to that used on the needle roller bearings you just removed. Drive out the input shaft front bearing from inside the carrier. The outer race of this bearing is flanged. The bearing will only come out one way.

26   To dismantle the input shaft, remove the spacer ring, then fourth gear and the needle bearing cage on which it runs. Remove the synchro rings. Using a hydraulic press and V-blocks, press off the inner race from the shaft **(see illustration)**. Position the 'V' blocks so they provide support behind the third gear wheel to prevent damage to the shaft or gears and prevent the synchro hub assembly from coming apart. Make sure all parts are supported and held while under pressure.

27   Remove third gear and its needle roller bearing. It's not necessary to remove the third gear bearing inner race or the key which locates the synchro hub. Keep the synchro rings with their respective gears for future reference – fix them with adhesive tape to prevent mix-ups.

28   Disassemble the pinion shaft only far enough to remove the gears, synchro hub and synchro rings. The double-taper pinion roller bearing held by the notched locking nut can be left on the shaft. Its removal requires the use of special tools which most home mechanics probably don't have.

29   Using a hydraulic press, remove fourth gear, the inner race of the needle bearing spacer, the shim, the concave washer, third gear, the needle roller bearing, second gear and the first/second gear synchro hub. Don't use a hammer instead of a press! Repeatedly striking the threaded end of the shaft – even with a soft headed mallet – can distort the threads and ruin the shaft. Remove the synchro rings.

30   On later models with circlips instead of retaining nuts on the ends of the two shafts, remove the circlips. Then press off fourth gear, the inner race, the spring spacer, the second circlip and third gear.

31   Unless the transaxle has been abused or has very high mileage, the synchro hub assemblies shouldn't require service. Handle the synchro hub assemblies with care to prevent them from coming apart. If the center hub and outer sleeve are accidentally separated, they must be properly reassembled. If you wish to disassemble the hubs, remove the spring retaining clip on each side and slide the sleeve out of the hub. Don't drop or lose the three sliding keys. Put the parts for each hub assembly in a plastic bag and set it aside for inspection.

32   Don't remove the selector fork rails from the carrier unless inspection indicates that there's something wrong with the detent balls and springs.

Inspection

Refer to illustration 9.40

33   As we mentioned in Section 1, the degree of component wear determines whether you should repair or replace the transaxle. If the differential ring gear and pinion are badly worn – causing significant backlash and noise – they can be repaired for about half the cost of a new unit. Such work is beyond the scope of the average owner so this manual doesn't

9.26 Using a hydraulic press and V-blocks, press the inner race from the input shaft – support third gear with the V-blocks to prevent damage to the shaft or gears, and to prevent the synchro hub from coming apart

9.40 Measure the clearance between the selector fork and the groove of the synchro hub sleeve – if this clearance is excessive, the gears can jump out of mesh

9.43a Install three new sliding keys, or blocker bars . . .

cover differential rebuilds. On the other hand, using no special tools aside from a hydraulic press, we fitted the transaxle in the accompanying illustrations with new ball bearings, synchro rings, synchro hub keys and retaining clips.

34   Normally, it shouldn't be necessary to immerse all the components in solvent. Wipe components with a clean cloth for examination. In this way the likelihood of dry spots during the first moments of use after reassembly are minimized. The case itself should be thoroughly washed out with solvent. Do not leave the needle roller bearings in position when doing this.

35   Thoroughly inspect all parts of the case for signs of cracks or damage, particularly near the bearing housings and on the mating surfaces where the gear carrier and side bearing plates join.

36   Using a small two or three-jaw puller, remove all synchro rings – if you haven't already done so – for inspection. The grooved taper face of each ring provides the braking action on the mating face of the gear wheel cone. If the ridges are worn, the braking or synchro action will be less effective. The only way to accurately assess the condition of this face is to compare it with a new part. As a rule of thumb, when a synchro ring is fitted over its cone on the gear wheel, there should be a minimum gap of 0.024 inch (0.6 mm) between the synchro ring and the gear teeth. The normal gap is 0.043 inch (1.1 mm), so it's obvious that, if the gap is near the lowest limit, new rings should be fitted. When buying new synchro rings, make sure the parts store identifies and marks each one to go with its respective gear. Modifications have taken place over the years, so although the new ones will still fit and may even work, they aren't necessarily identical to the ones you took off. If you mix them up, you could have problems. They're also not all the same in a set – for example, some have wider cut-outs. So carefully mark the new ones. **Note:** *These parts are cheap, so it makes good sense to simply replace them while the transaxle is disassembled.*

37   Two types of bearings are uses – ball and needle roller. As a rule, needle roller bearings wear very little because they're not subjected to end thrust of any sort. The two large side bearings are ball bearings which carry the forward end of the input shaft. Inspect all bearings for noise and roughness. If they sound even slightly rough or if they drag when they turn, replace them. Check the double-taper roller bearing for roughness and excessive endplay. If it allows any endplay, carefully inspect the condition of the pinion gear and differential ring gear. If they need to be replaced, the setting of the whole box is altered and clearances and shims have to be re-calculated and changed. This is a job for a specialist.

38   Inspect the teeth of all gears for signs of pitted mating surfaces, chips and scoring. If one gear is damaged, its counterpart on the other shaft will usually be just as badly worn.

39   Assemble the synchro hubs (see Step 43). With the keys removed, the inner and outer sections of the hub should slide easily, but there must be no axial play or backlash between the splines of the inner and outer parts. The actual amount of acceptable wear is difficult to describe. No play at all is ideal, but hardly likely. Ask someone with experience how

much slop is acceptable.

40   Some of the most critical parts of the transaxle are the selector forks. The two forks run in grooves in the outer sleeves of the synchro hubs. If the clearance of the forks in the grooves is excessive, the gears will probably jump out. Measure the clearance between the fork and the groove **(see illustration)**. It shouldn't exceed 0.3 mm (0.012 inch). Excessive clearance could be caused by wear on the fork, or the groove, or both. So take the forks to the parts department and ask them if you can compare the thickness of new parts with your old ones. If the difference in thickness isn't enough to compensate for the excessive clearance between the fork and the hub groove, then replace the hub assembly as well. This is an expensive item, but this gap is critical, so there's no alternative.

41   The selector rails on which the forks are mounted need not be removed from the case. A certain force is required for them to overcome the pressure of the spring loaded ball in the groove. Measure this force with a spring balance hooked on the end of each selector fork. If the required pull is significantly outside the range of 33 to 44 lbs (15 to 20 kgs), it's advisable to check the detent springs and balls. Push the selector rod out of the case to release the ball and spring. To remove the springs, pry out the plastic plugs. Be sure to get some new plugs for reassembly.

42   Check the spring free length. It should be one inch. If it's less, replace the spring(s). The balls should be free from pitting and grooves and the selector rods themselves shouldn't be a sloppy fit in the bores. The detent grooves in the rails shouldn't be worn. If they are, replace the rail(s). If you have to remove the rails, don't lose the interlock plungers which fit between the s
elector rod grooves.

Reassembly

Refer to illustrations 9.43a, 9.43b, 9.44a, 9.44b, 9.45a, 9.45b, 9.45c, 9.46a, 9.46b, 9.46c, 9.47a, 9.47b, 9.48, 9.49, 9.50a, 9.50b, 9.51, 9.52, 9.53, 9.54, 9.55, 9.56, 9.57a, 9.57b, 9.57c, 9.59, 9.60, 9.62a, 9.62b, 9.62c, 9.63, 9.64a, 9.64b, 9.64c, 9.64d, 9.64e, 9.65a, 9.65b, 9.65c, 9.66a, 9.66b, 9.67, 9.68a, 9.68b, 9.68c, 9.69, 9.70a, 9.70b, 9.70c, 9.71, 9.74a, 9.74b, 9.76a, 9.76b, 9.77, 9.78a, 9.78b, 9.79, 9.81, 9.82a, 9.82b, 9.83, 9.84, 9.85, 9.86, 9.87a, 9.87b, 9.87c, 9.87d, 9.88, 9.90a, 9.90b, 9.93, 9.94a, 9.94b, 9.95, 9.97, 9.98a, 9.98b, 9.98c, 9.100a, 9.100b, 9.100c, 9.100d and 9.100e

43   If you're rebuilding the synchro hubs, service them as a complete assembly. It isn't a good idea to fit an inner hub to an old outer sleeve, or vice versa. Keep in mind the following points when reassembling a synchro hub:

  a) When the synchro rings are replaced, it's a good idea to replace the three sliding keys and their locating spring rings as well. The keys fit into the cut-outs in the synchro rings and are subject to wear, and the springs weaken over time.

  b) Always use new blocker bars (sliding keys) **(see illustration)** and

7A

9.43b . . . and new retainer spring clips when rebuilding the synchro hubs

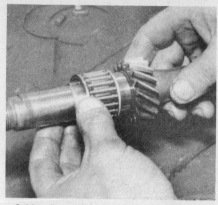

9.44a   Install the needle roller cage for third gear on the input shaft . . .

9.44b   . . . then install third gear with its matching synchro ring onto the roller bearings with the cone toward the front of the input shaft

9.45a   Install the third/fourth gear synchro hub assembly on the input shaft . . .

9.45b   . . . making sure it's lined up with the keyway . . .

9.45c   . . . then drive on the hub with a suitable piece of pipe and a heavy hammer

9.46a   Drive the inner race for the fourth gear needle bearing onto the input shaft . . .

9.46b   Install the needle roller cage . . .

9.46c   . . . and install the synchro ring and fourth gear

retaining spring clips **(see illustration)** in the hubs to take full advantage of the new, unworn cutouts in the rings.

c) The splines of the inner hub and outer sleeve are matched – either by selection on assembly or by wear patterns during use. Those matched on assembly have marks etched on the inner hub and outer sleeve to facilitate alignment. If a hub has no marks, make some of your own with a small dab of paint to ensure reassembly in the same position. If a hub falls apart accidentally, you'll have to live with the fact that it may wear out more quickly.

d) Fit the retaining spring clips so the ends fit behind, but not into, the keys, and so that the the clips overlap on each side, i.e. don't have more than two clip ends over one key.

44   Install the needle roller cage for third gear on the input shaft **(see illustration)**. Then install third gear with its matching synchro ring onto the roller bearings with the cone towards the front end of the shaft **(see illustration)**.

45   Install the third/fourth gear synchro hub assembly **(see illustration)**. It must line up with the key in the shaft **(see illustration)**. Once the keyway in the center part of the hub is lined up with the key in the shaft, drive on the hub with a suitable piece of pipe and a heavy hammer **(see illustration)**.

9.47a Install the thrust washer on the end of the input shaft with the V-cuts facing the front of the shaft

9.47b Loosely install the lockwasher and locknut and set the assembled input shaft aside

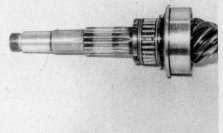

9.48 This is as far as you should disassemble the pinion shaft, unless you want to reshim the gearbox and final drive – a job that will take an expert with special tools

9.49 Install the thrust shim(s) on the pinion shaft that control first gear endplay

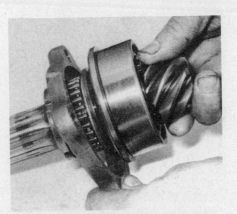

9.50a Install the bearing retainer over the shaft and up to the pinion bearing . . .

9.50b . . . with its smooth, machined side facing toward the pinion gear

Some later models have a groove in the outer sleeve 1 mm deep. Make sure the hub with this groove faces toward the front of the shaft. If there's no groove, you can install the hub facing either way. Drive the center part of the hub, or it could come apart. Line up the slots in the synchro ring with the keys in the hub. Have someone hold the synchro ring in position with the keys in place while you drive the hub into place.

46 Drive the inner race for the fourth gear needle bearing onto the shaft the same way you installed the hub in the previous Step (**see illustration**). Drive it right down to the hub. Then install the needle roller cage (**see illustration**) and the synchro ring and fourth gear (**see illustration**). The synchro ring also has three cut-outs which engage with the sliding keys in the hub.

47 Install the thrust washer on the end of the shaft with the V cuts (if any) facing the front end of the shaft (**see illustration**). Loosely install the locknut and lockwasher (**see illustration**), or install the circlip, and lay the input shaft assembly aside.

48 As it was pointed out earlier, we disassembled the pinion shaft only as far as the pinion bearing (**see illustration**). If you have replaced this bearing, the gearbox and final drive must be reshimmed. This is a skilled job requiring special equipment and a selection of special shims.

49 Install the shim(s) that control first gear endplay (**see illustration**). To measure the endplay after the first gear and hub are installed, measure the gap between the thrust washer (already locked in position behind the first gear needle bearing) and the face of the gear. If the gap is outside the limits of 0.004-0.010 inch (0.10-0.25 mm), you'll need different shims to correct it. In effect, the shims determine the position of the inner sleeve of the first/second gear synchro hub in relation to the captive thrust washer. First gear endplay is controlled between the thrust washer and center hub face.

50 Install the bearing retainer over the shaft and up to the pinion bearing with the smooth, machined face towards the pinion gear at the end of the shaft (**see illustrations**).

51 Install first gear (the largest one with helically cut teeth) in position on the needle roller bearings with the cone face of the synchro pointing away from the pinion gear (**see illustration**).

7A

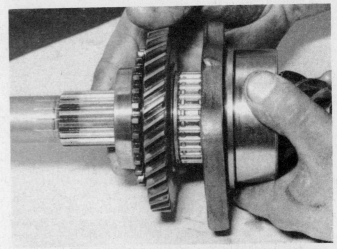

9.51 Install first gear (the big gear with the helically cut teeth) over the needle roller bearings with the cone side of the synchro facing away from the pinion gear

9.52   Install the first gear synchro ring over first gear, then the first and second gear hub over the splines of the shaft with the selector fork groove of the outer sleeve facing toward the front end of the shaft

9.53   Check first gear endplay again the same way you checked it in Step 49

9.54   Place the second gear synchro ring in position in the hub so that the slots engage with the sliding keys

9.55   Install second gear with the cone facing toward the hub

9.56   Install third gear – and the needle roller bearing which fits together with it – inside second gear

9.57a   Install the dished washer on the shaft with its raised inner circumference facing toward the end of the shaft . . .

9.57b   . . . install the shim, . . .

9.57c   . . . and install the spacer sleeve on top of the washer

9.59   After heating fourth gear to over 194-degrees F in hot oil, slide it onto the pinion shaft with the wider, raised hub facing toward the spacer collar

52   Install the first gear synchro ring over first gear (see illustration) and install the first and second gear hub over the splines of the shaft with the selector fork groove of the outer sleeve facing toward the front end of the shaft. Make sure that the three cut-outs in the synchro ring engage with the sliding keys in the hub before pushing the hub into place. Remember – the synchro rings for first and second gears are slightly different – first gear has narrower cut-outs than those in the second gear ring.

53   Check the first gear endplay as described in Step 49 (see illustration).

54   Place the second gear synchro ring in position in the hub so that the slots engage with the sliding keys (see illustration).

55   Install second gear with the cone facing toward the hub (see illustration).

56   Install third gear – and the needle roller bearing which fits together with it – inside second gear (see illustration). Note the large bearing boss integral with third gear.

57   Install the dished washer onto the shaft with the raised inner circumference facing toward the end of the shaft (see illustration). Install the

9.60 Tap the inner race for the needle roller bearing onto the pinion shaft

9.62a The needle roller bearings for the reverse drive shaft consists of two roller cages and a spacer between them

9.62b Drive one cage into the case with a socket on an extension so that it's flush with the one end of the bore – the metal face of the end of the needle should face in . . .

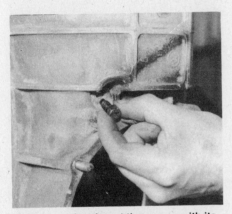

9.62c . . . then insert the spacer with its slot aligned so it engages with the lock bolt screwed into the side of the case

9.63 The other needle roller bearing supports the rear end of the front half of the input shaft – tap it into the larger bore (arrow) so that the circular recess in the outer race lines up with the lock screw hole in the case

9.64a Slide the spacer ring over the shaft so that it butts against the splined section of the reverse gear shaft . . .

shim (see illustration). If the only changes made to the pinion shaft have been new synchro rings, the existing washer and shim can be reused. If, however, the synchro hub or any gears have been replaced, then the shim thickness will likely need to be altered. The dished washer is designed to exert a pressure of about 220 pounds on third gear and the hub to eliminate sloppiness along the shaft. The critical dimension is the distance between the face of third gear and the shoulder on the shaft against which fourth gear will be installed. This length of shaft has a spacer collar which bears on the concave washer (and shim) when fourth gear is finally installed. Obviously a thicker shim will increase the pressure, and vice versa. If you have to recalculate the shim requirement, you'll need an accurate measuring device. The dished washer has a designed spring travel of 0.17 mm in order to exert its pressure and has a thickness of 1.04 mm. Thus the length of the distance collar plus the total concave washer dimensions (1.21 mm) should equal the shaft distance from the third gear face to the fourth gear shoulder. Select the appropriate shim sizes to make up the difference. Install the spacer sleeve on top of the washer and shim (see illustration).

58 On later gearboxes, install a selective circlip in place of the concave washer. Measure the endplay of third gear between the gear and the circlip. It should be between 0.004 and 0.010 inch (0.10 and 0.25 mm). Later models also use a spring spacer after the circlip.

59 Heat fourth gear to at least 194-degrees F (90-degrees C) in a bath of hot oil. This will expand it so you can slide it onto the shaft and over the key. Grasp the hot gear firmly with a pair of pliers and install it with the wider, protruding face of its hub toward the spacer collar (see illustration). Make sure it seats firmly against the shoulder on the shaft. Caution: Don't try to

press fourth gear on. Although it was pressed off, it's virtually impossible to press it on and align it with the keyway. Also, once you start it on, it can't be re-aligned.

60 Press, or drive, the inner race for the needle roller bearing onto the shaft (see illustration).

61 On later models, press or drive on the gear against the spring spacer and install a circlip. Force the circlip down against the concave washer in order to seat it into its groove. If you don't have a press and jig, select a piece of tubing which will fit round the shaft, wrap the whole assembly with shop rags, have an assistant grip it firmly and drive on the circlip against spring pressure. Then press on the inner race for the needle bearing. Put the pinion shaft aside.

62 Two sets of needle roller bearings are installed at the rear end of the main case. The set for the reverse drive shaft (see illustration) consists of two roller cages and a spacer between them. Drive one cage into the case with a socket on an extension, or a suitable drift, so that it's flush with one end of the bore (see illustration). The metal face of the end of the needle cage should face inward. Then insert the spacer with its slot aligned so it engages with the lock bolt screwed into the side of the case (see illustration). Then drive the other needle roller bearing into the other end of the bore.

63 The other bearing supports the rear end of the front half of the input shaft. Tap the single needle roller cage into the larger bore so that the circular recess in the outer race lines up with the lock screw hole in the case (see illustration). Install the lock screw and tighten it securely.

64 To install the reverse gear shaft, slide the spacer ring over the shaft so that it butts against the splined section (see illustration), insert the shaft

7A

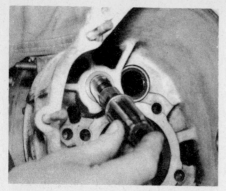

9.64b ... insert the shaft through the needle bearing from the front of the case ...

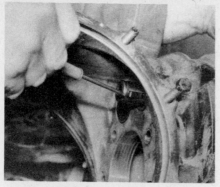

9.64c ... fit the key into the keyway ...

9.64d ... support the front end of the shaft, push the gear onto the shaft – make sure it engages the key and the projecting side of the gear hub faces out

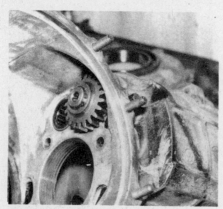

9.64e Install the circlip – make sure it seats into the groove

9.65a Position the needle roller bearing for the front end of the pinion shaft so that the hole for the locking screw is lined up with the recess in the bearing ..

9.65b ... tap it into position ...

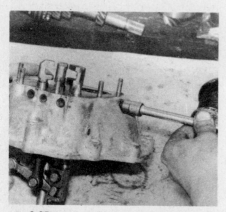

9.65c ... and install the lock bolt

9.66a Place the special ball bearing with the flanged outer race into position in the carrier with the flange facing up ...

9.66b ... and tap it into place in the carrier

through the needle bearings from the front of the case **(see illustration)**, install the key into the keyway **(see illustration)**, support the front end of the shaft and push the gear onto the shaft **(see illustration)**. Make sure it engages the key and the projecting side of the gear hub faces out. Install the circlip **(see illustration)**. Make sure it's fully seated into the groove.

65   Line up the needle roller bearing for the forward end of the pinion shaft so that the hole for the locking screw corresponds with the recess in the bearing **(see illustration)**. Tap it into position **(see illustration)** and install the lock bolt **(see illustration)**.

66   Drive the special ball bearing (with the flange outer race) into position

in the carrier case **(see illustrations)**.

67   Before installing the input and pinion shafts in the gear carrier, place them side-by-side, bind them together with strong tape and place the third/fourth selector fork in position **(see illustration)**.

68   You'll need an assistant for the next few Steps. Position the taped shafts in the carrier **(see illustration)**. Move the third/fourth selector fork into position in the synchro hub – and keep it there – as you push the shafts into position. Pull back the fork rail so it can be mated with the fork as it's carried in **(see illustrations)**.

69   Once the selector fork for third/fourth gear is in position in its groove –

9.67 Before you install the input and pinion shafts in the gear carrier, place them side-by-side, bind them together with strong tape and place the third/fourth selector fork in position

9.68a Position the taped shafts in the carrier, move the third/fourth selector fork into position in the synchro hub – and keep it there – as you push the shafts into position, . . .

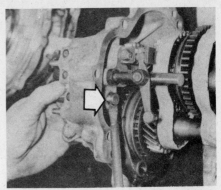

9.68b . . . then pull back the fork rail so it can be fitted on the fork as it's carried into place

9.68c This is how the third/fourth selector fork looks when it's properly positioned

9.69 Once the selector fork for third/fourth gear is in position in its groove – with the clamp lug facing out from the case – tap the two shafts into their respective bearings

9.70a Once both shafts are fully seated in the carrier bearings, install new lock washers – make sure the lock washer tangs engage the groove in each shaft . . .

9.70b . . . and install new shaft nuts

9.70c To hold the assembly while you tighten the nuts, stand the case on end and carefully lower the gear carrier assembly onto the studs

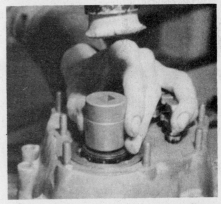

9.71 Use a socket to drive the circlip against the concave washer and pop it into the groove in the end of the input shaft on later units that don't use a nut

7A

with the clamp lug facing out from the case – tap the two shafts into their respective bearings (**see illustration**). Alternate taps between the two shafts and drive them into place as a single assembly. The ball bearing may come out of the carrier as you tap in the input shaft, so support it from behind to prevent it from falling out. As you tap the two shafts into the case, line up the selector fork with its appropriate rail. Make sure the fork doesn't jam. Once the fork's on the rail, move the rail back in line with the others.

70 Once both shafts are fully seated in the carrier bearings, install new lock washers and shaft nuts (**see illustrations**). Make sure the lock wash-

er tangs engage the groove in each shaft. To hold the assembly while tightening the nuts, stand the main case on end and carefully place the gear carrier assembly onto the studs (**see illustration**). Tighten both nuts to the initial torque listed in this Chapter's Specifications. Back them off and tighten them to the final torque listed in this Chapter's Specifications. Don't bend up the lock washers on to the nuts yet – if anything is amiss, you may have to remove them.

71 On later models with circlips instead of nuts, install a dished washer and circlip on each shaft (**see illustration**). The washer must be com-

9.74a   Install the selector pad and relay lever for reverse gear onto the rail . . .

9.74b   . . . then install the selector fork for first/second gear into its groove, mount it on the selector rail and tighten the clamp bolt to prevent slipping

9.76a   Install the small reverse sliding gear and yoke on the reverse gear shaft – the gear should be midway between the straight cut teeth on the synchro hub sleeve and the helical teeth of the second gear on the input shaft

9.76b   If it's necessary to reposition reverse gear, loosen and adjust the block clamped to the selector rail

9.77   Install a pair of three-inch long studs in the pinion bearing flange to help you line up the bolt holes (you can't move the flange when it's in position)

9.78a   Install the pinion setting shims on the flange (early units with four bolt pinion flange)

pressed to fit the circlip into its groove, so you'll need a press or a socket or pipe to do the job.

72   Once the shaft nuts have been tightened, remove the gear carrier from the case in preparation for setting the selector forks.

73   Setting the selector forks is critical. If the wear between the fork and groove is outside the limit, the likelihood of a gear not being fully engaged – and jumping out – is increased. Ideally, you should try to have the unit set up by a transaxle specialist for the next few Steps. If that isn't possible, lay the assembly on the bench and do it yourself, but work very carefully.

74   Install the selector pad and relay lever for reverse gear onto the rail **(see illustration)**, then install the selector fork for first/second gears into its groove and mount it on the selector rail **(see illustration)**. Set all three selector rails in the neutral position (cut-outs in their ends all line up) and set the synchro hub outer sleeves in neutral with the forks in position. Then tighten the fork clamp bolts sufficiently to prevent them slipping. Push each selector so that each gear is fully engaged. The outer sleeve of the appropriate synchro hub must move fully over the dogs of the synchro ring and gear. The fork must not bind in the groove in any gear.

75   If you have trouble engaging a gear, loosen the fork clamp nut, slide the synchro hub sleeve on the shaft until it's fully meshed and retighten the fork clamp. Then move the selector back to neutral and into the opposite gear position. In all three positions there must be no pressure in either direction between the fork and the sides of the groove in which it runs. Don't forget that the synchro hub and second and third gears on the pinion shaft are preloaded because of the dished washers and will rotate stiffly. This

can make it difficult to line up the dogs when engaging second gear. Once both forks have been correctly set, tighten the clamp bolts to the torque listed in this Chapter's Specifications.

76   Install the small reverse sliding gear and yoke on the reverse gear shaft **(see illustration)**. To position them correctly, engage second gear. The reverse sliding gear should be midway between the straight cut teeth on the synchro hub sleeve and the helical teeth of second gear on the input shaft. Then move out of second gear and shift into reverse and verify that the reverse gears mesh completely. If necessary, adjust the block clamped to the selector rail **(see illustration)**.

77   To help you line up the bolt holes in the pinion bearing flange on earlier units (impossible to move when fully in position), install two three-inch-long studs in the flange **(see illustration)**. These studs are pilots for the holes in the case and will automatically line up the flange. Later units don't use this flange. Instead, they use a castellated lock ring that screws onto threads at the base of the pinion bearing.

78   Install the pinion setting shims in position on the face of the flange **(see illustrations)**. Your two guide studs will help position them. If the flange has small bumps cast into the edge, line up the shim so that its shape matches the bumps. Put a dab of grease on the shim to prevent it falling off.

79   Place a new gasket over the studs on the case **(see illustration)**. Make sure no traces of old gasket remain on the mating surfaces, which must be perfectly clean and smooth.

80   Make sure the reverse sliding gear is still in place. To prevent it from

9.78b Install the pinion setting shims on a later pinion shaft with castellated locking nut instead of flange

9.79 Place a new gasket over the studs on the case – make sure the gasket mating surface is immaculate

9.81 As you install the gear carrier on the case, just remember these three things – make sure the pinion flange lines up correctly, don't let the pinion shim fall out of place and make sure the splined reverse gear shaft lines up with the sliding reverse gear!

9.82a Using new lock plates, install the four pinion flange bolts and tighten them in a criss-cross pattern, evenly and gradually, to the specified torque

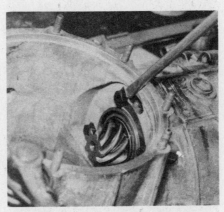

9.82b Bend up the lock plate tabs

9.83 Install the carrier nuts and tighten them in a criss-cross pattern, evenly and gradually, to the specified torque

sliding out of place, engage reverse gear.

81   Install the gear carrier to the case with the case standing upright (see illustration). Watch three things as you install the carrier. First, as you guide the temporary studs into the bolt holes in the case, make sure the flange lines up properly. Second, don't let the pinion shim fall out of place. Third, make sure the splined reverse gear shaft lines up with – and goes into – the sliding reverse gear. If you take care of these three things, the whole unit will drop into place easily. Tap the carrier a few times with a soft mallet to butt the mating faces together. If for any reason something binds during this procedure, stop and have a look. Don't force anything. Check the three areas mentioned above and try again.

82   Once the gear carrier is installed, turn the case on its side and remove the guide studs from the pinion bearing flange. Using new lock plates (included in the gasket set) install the four pinion flange bolts and tighten them in a criss-cross fashion, evenly and gradually, to the torque listed in this Chapter's Specifications (see illustration). Take care to avoid slipping and damaging the pinion while tightening these bolts. Turn the bolt head between reverse gear and the pinion shaft so that a flat on the head faces the pinion to prevent the reverse gear sleeve from fouling the bolt head. Don't exceed the specified torque to do this – back off the bolt if necessary and retighten to a slightly lower torque. Bend up the lock plate tabs (see illustration).

83   Install the carrier nuts. Tighten them in a criss-cross fashion, evenly and gradually, to the torque listed in this Chapter's Specifications. Don't

forget that one nut secures the ground strap (see illustration).

84   If all shafts rotate freely, bend up the lock tabs against flats on the nuts for the input and pinion shaft nuts (see illustration).

9.84 If all the shafts rotate freely, bend up the lock tabs against the flats on the nuts for the input and pinion shaft nuts

7A

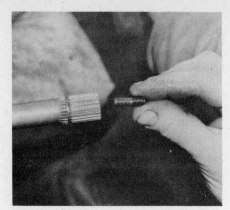

9.85   Install the small link stud into the end of the front shaft

9.86   Install a new circlip over the splines and beyond the groove on the smooth part of the shaft

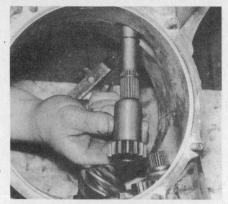

9.87a   Install the reverse gear/splined sleeve onto the shaft, plain end first . . .

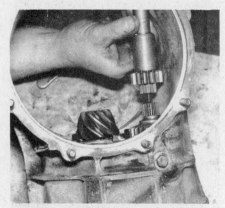

9.87b   . . . screw the shaft stud into the end of the protruding input shaft . . .

9.87c   . . . and move the sleeve forward so that the gears engage

9.87d   On later units, install the sleeve over the input shaft extension

9.88   Clean the mating surfaces on the end of the gear carrier and shift housing and position a new gasket onto the gear carrier

9.90a   When you install the shift housing, make sure the end of the gear change lever (arrow) seats in the cut-outs in the ends of the three selector rails

9.90b   A close-up view of the relationship between the gear change lever and the cut-outs

85   Before installing the front section of the input shaft, lubricate the land in the center which will run in the oil seal and screw the small link stud into the end of the front shaft **(see illustration)**. Then carefully insert the shaft through the oil seal from the rear of the main case.

86   Install a new circlip **(see illustration)** over the splines and beyond the groove on the smooth part of the shaft.

87   Install the reverse gear/splined sleeve onto the shaft, plain end first **(see illustration)**. Screw the shaft stud into the end of the protruding input

shaft **(see illustration)**. Screw it in as far as it will go, then back it off one turn to allow the splined collar to engage both halves of the shaft. DO NOT engage the sleeve with the ends of the shafts butted tightly together. Move the sleeve forward so that the gears engage **(see illustration)**, then move the circlip back along the shaft so that it engages fully into the groove. On later units, install the sleeve over the input shaft extension **(see illustration)**.

88   Clean the mating surfaces on the end of the gear carrier and shift

9.93   To install new side bearings, support the side cover evenly and securely, then tap the new bearing into place with a wide, flat metal bar or a block of wood – the closed side of the ball race must face toward the outside of the case

9.94a   Install a new O-ring on the side cover . . .

9.94b   . . . make sure the gasket mating surfaces are perfectly clean, install a new gasket over the case studs (no sealing compound is necessary), place the bearing side cover in position and install it

9.95   Install the differential shims and hold them in position with a dab of grease

9.97   Carefully install the differential ring gear assembly

9.98a   Make sure the shims are properly located on the differential ring gear, place a new gasket in position and install the left bearing side cover

housing and position a new gasket over the gear carrier studs (see illustration).

89   Verify that the transaxle is in neutral by checking the cut-outs in the ends of the three selector rods, which should be lined up. Install the gear change lever into the housing. It should easily slide into the housing, but there shouldn't be any sideplay. If the lever fits too loosely, it could cause jamming or other problems of changing gear.

90   Install the housing (see illustration). Make sure the end of the gear change lever seats in the cut-outs in the ends of the three selector rails (see illustration). Install the housing nuts and tighten them to the torque listed in this Chapter's Specifications.

91   Make sure all differential and side bearing parts are clean, and the shims and spacers are correct for each side of the differential casing. Remember that the shims have two functions, to put a pre-load on the side bearings, and to position the differential ring gear correctly in relation to the pinion gear.

92   In theory, you might think that if new bearings are installed, the shim requirements should be recalculated. In practice, this isn't necessary, provided that the same ring gear and pinion are installed and no shims have been previously altered in an attempt to improve some earlier malfunction.

93   To install new bearings, support the side cover evenly and securely and arrange the bearing so that the closed side of the ball race faces the outside of the case when the side cover is installed. The bore in the side cover must be scrupulously clean and free of any snags or burrs. Tap the new bearing into place with a heavy mallet and a wide, flat metal strap or

wood block to evenly distribute the force (see illustration). Make sure the bearing doesn't cock in the bore as you start to drive it in. If it does, remove it and start again.

94   Make sure the gasket mating surfaces are perfectly clean, install a new gasket over the case studs (no sealant is necessary), install a new O-ring (see illustration), place the side cover and bearing assembly in position (it will only fit one way) and install it (see illustration). Tighten the nuts in a criss-cross fashion, gradually and evenly, to the torque listed in this Chapter's Specifications.

95   Install the differential shims (see illustration). Hold them in position with a dab of grease. Make sure everything is perfectly clean. Note: If the shims are mixed up, you won't be able to set the pinion/ring gear backlash correctly. DON'T guess! Take the whole assembly to a transaxle specialist and have him reset it.

96   If you know which shims came off each side, make sure they're arranged with the thicker spacer ring fitted first – with its chamfered side facing in – and the shims after that (so they'll be between the spacer ring and the bearing).

97   With the spacer and shims in place, install the differential assembly (see illustration). Place the differential in the case very carefully and tap it into position. The shoulder must be fully seated against the inner race of the bearing in the cover.

98   Make sure the other set of shims is properly located on the ring gear end of the differential, place a new gasket in position and install the left bearing side cover (see illustration). The cover has to fit down onto the

7A

9.98b   Carefully tap the left bearing side cover down onto the differential – don't use the retaining nuts to draw it down or you may crack the cover

9.98c   Install the cover nuts only after you have driven it into place

9.100a   On later units with driveaxles, install the spacer ring into each side bearing cover, . . .

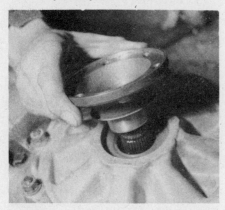

9.100b   . . . push the drive flange onto the shaft, . . .

9.100c   . . . install the circlip onto the shaft, . . .

9.100d   . . . tap it on the shaft with a socket until it pops into its groove . . .

differential, so tap it into position **(see illustration)** until the nuts can be installed onto the studs **(see illustration)**. DO NOT use the cover retaining nuts to pull the cover and bearing down. This could easily crack or break it. Tighten the nuts to the same torque as the other side cover.
99   On swing axle models, install the axleshafts and tubes (see Chapter 8).
100 On driveaxle models, install the spacer ring over the shaft, push the drive flange onto the shaft, fit the circlip over the end of the shaft, tap it into the groove using a socket of suitable diameter and fit a new sealing plug **(see illustrations)**. Repeat this procedure for the other side bearing cover.
101 Install the transaxle (see Section 5).

9.100e   . . . and install a new sealing plug

Chapter 7 Part B   Automatic Stick Shift

Contents

7B

Specifications

Shift lever contact gap . . . . .010 to .016 in (0.25 to 0.40 mm)

Torque specifications	Ft-lbs
Transaxle rear mounting bolts	166
Transaxle front mounting nuts	25
Clutch operating lever pinch bolt	22
Clutch pressure plate bolts	14
Bellhousing nuts	14

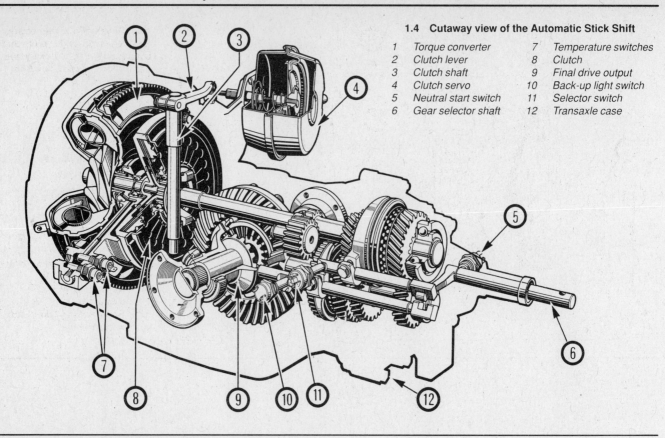

1.4   Cutaway view of the Automatic Stick Shift

1	*Torque converter*	*7*	*Temperature switches*
2	*Clutch lever*	*8*	*Clutch*
3	*Clutch shaft*	*9*	*Final drive output*
4	*Clutch servo*	*10*	*Back-up light switch*
5	*Neutral start switch*	*11*	*Selector switch*
6	*Gear selector shaft*	*12*	*Transaxle case*

1.6   Exploded view of torque converter and clutch assembly

1	*Torque converter*	*3*	*Clutch plate*
2	*Carrier plate*	*4*	*Pressure plate and diaphragm spring*

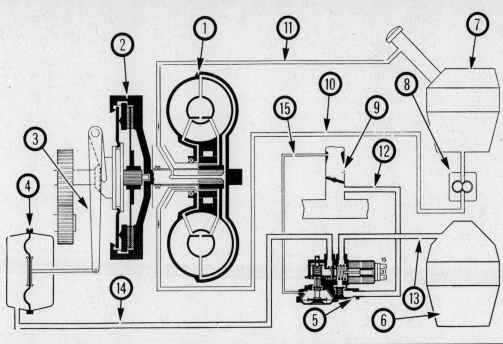

1.7 Schematic of the torque converter hydraulic system and vacuum operated clutch system for the Automatic Stick Shift

1   Torque converter
2   Clutch
3   Clutch lever
4   Servo
5   Control valve
6   Vacuum reservoir
7   Oil tank
8   Oil pump
9   Carburetor/throttle body
10 Pressure line
11 Return line
12 Intake manifold-to-control valve vacuum line
13 Vacuum reservoir-to-control valve vacuum line
14 Servo-to-control valve vacuum line
15 Reduction valve-to-venturi vacuum line

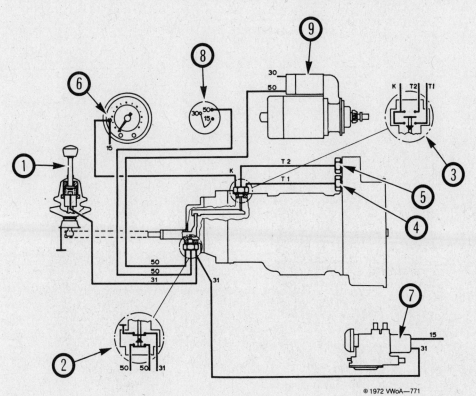

1.8a Schematic of pre-1972 electrical circuit for the Automatic Stick Shift

1   Shift lever and contact
2   Neutral start switch
3   Selector switch
4   Temperature switch for Drive 2 range
5   Temperature switch for Drive 1 range
6   Warning light
7   Control valve solenoid
8   Ignition switch
9   Starter motor solenoid

© 1972 VWoA—771

7B

1   General information and principles of operation

General information

All vehicles covered in this manual come equipped with either a four-speed manual transaxle or an Automatic Stick Shift transaxle. All information on the Automatic Stick Shift is included in this Part of Chapter 7. Information for the manual transaxle can be found in Part A of this Chapter.

Due to the complexity of the Automatic Stick Shift and the need for specialized equipment to perform most service operations, this Chapter contains only general diagnosis, routine maintenance, adjustment and removal and installation procedures.

If the Automatic Stick Shift requires major repair work, it should be left to a dealer service department or an automotive or transmission repair shop. You can, however, remove and install it and save the expense, even if the repair work is done by a transmission shop.

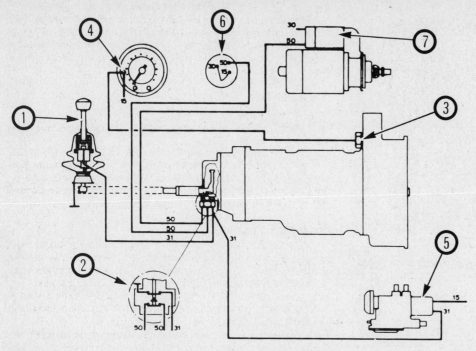

1.8b Schematic of the electrical circuit for the Automatic Stick Shift on 1972 and later models

1   Shift lever and contact
2   Neutral start switch
3   Temperature switch
4   Warning light
5   Control valve solenoid
6   Ignition switch
7   Starter motor solenoid

Principles of operation

Refer to illustrations 1.4, 1.6, 1.7, 1.8a and 1.8b

The Automatic Stick Shift **(see illustration)** was available as an option on 1968 through 1975 models. Like an automatic transmission, it has a torque converter, and like a manual, it has a three-speed gearbox. But the other components – and its operation – are unique. In effect, it's a semi-automatic transmission; gear changes are made manually, but without a clutch pedal.

Think of the torque converter as a hydraulic clutch or fluid coupling that provides a smooth transfer of power over a wide range of operation between the engine and the clutch. It also multiplies engine torque, which is greatest (2:1) when the vehicle starts moving from a dead stop (about 2000 to 2250 rpm). This is the point of maximum slippage between the impeller and the turbine inside the torque converter. As the speed difference between the turbine and impeller decreases, torque multiplication and slippage decrease. By the time slippage decreases to the point at which turbine speed is 84-percent of impeller speed, there's no longer any torque multiplication – coupling is almost one-to-one (The turbine's maximum coupling efficiency is about 96-percent of the impeller speed).

The torque converter doesn't share oil with the rear axle and transmission. An oil pump driven by the engine oil pump delivers automatic transmission fluid from a reservoir (located under the right fender) to the torque converter, and back through a return line to the reservoir. The torque converter drives a conventional three-speed transmission (the function of the manual's low gear is handled by the torque converter) through a single-plate, diaphragm-spring type clutch **(see illustration)**.

When you move the shift lever to select a drive range, an electrical contact at the bottom of the lever energizes a control valve solenoid which supplies engine vacuum from the intake manifold to a clutch servo unit that disengages the clutch, permitting you to complete your shift. The control valve opens or closes in accordance with the difference between atmospheric pressure and intake vacuum. A vacuum line **(see illustration)** between the carburetor, or throttle body, and the control valve transmits intake vacuum – which varies with engine load – from the carburetor/throttle body to the control valve. The interval between completion of the gear shift and engagement of the clutch is determined by the rate at which the spring pressure inside the control valve overcomes the intake vacuum-controlled diaphragm. When the spring overcomes the diaphragm,

the servo's vacuum supply is cut off and the clutch re-engages. The control valve engages the clutch quickly during acceleration (spring pressure quickly overcomes low intake vacuum), more slowly and smoothly during deceleration and downshifting (spring pressure takes longer to overcome high intake vacuum). A vacuum reservoir (located under the left rear fender), connected to the control valve, stores enough vacuum to permit five or six gear changes regardless of available engine vacuum.

On early models, two temperature switches **(see illustration)** monitor torque converter fluid temperature. A temperature selector switch connects the temperature switch for Drive 2 to a warning light on the instrument cluster when Drive 2 is selected, and it connects the switch for Drive 1 to the light when Drive 1 is selected. The Drive 2 switch turns on the light at 257-degrees F; the Drive 1 switch turns it on at 284-degrees F. When the light comes on, the driver must select the next lower range until the light goes out. On 1971 through 1975 models **(see illustration)**, the electrical circuit is simpler: A single temperature sender turns on the warning light when temperature exceeds 284-degrees F, and keeps it on until the fluid cools, regardless of the drive range.

A neutral start switch prevents the engine starter from operating unless the shift lever is in the Neutral (N) position. Any other gear position opens the switch (located between the ignition switch and the starter solenoid). This switch also grounds the clutch control valve solenoid, preventing the shift lever from affecting the clutch when in Neutral.

2   Diagnosis

1   Automatic Stick Shift malfunctions may be caused by four general conditions: poor engine performance, improper adjustments, hydraulic malfunctions or mechanical malfunctions. Diagnosis of these problems should always begin with a check of the eight items that must be routinely inspected or maintained at the prescribed mileage (maintenance intervals listed in Chapter 1):

Checking the selector lever contacts (see Section 3)
Cleaning the air filter on the control valve (see Chapter 1)
Checking and correcting the ATF level (see Chapter 1)
Checking the axle boots (see Chapter 1)

2.12   Connect a pressure gauge to the torque converter circuit to check the ATF pressure

Checking the constant velocity (CV) joint bolts (see Chapter 1)
Checking and correcting the transmission oil level (see Chapter 1)
Checking the clutch freeplay (see Section 4)
Lubricating the rear wheel bearings (see Chapter 10)

2   Before attempting to diagnose transmission troubles, try to determine whether the problem can be corrected with the transmission still installed or will require removal of the transmission. If the gears grind when you try to change Drive ranges, the gearbox isn't the probable cause – the clutch probably isn't disengaging. If there's no drive in *any* range, the clutch probably isn't engaging. You can distinguish converter or hydraulic system problems from clutch problems by performing stall speed and pressure tests. If the clutch *is* slipping, adjusting the freeplay (see Section 4) usually solves the problem. **Note:** *Always begin diagnosis with* Troubleshooting *at the front of this book. If you know the symptom, it will direct you to the appropriate Chapter or Section to help you correct the problem.*

Road test

3   If you suspect a malfunction in the Automatic Stick Shift, perform a road test to determine if the problem has been corrected or if more diagnosis is necessary. It's helpful to compare its performance with a Beetle equipped with an automatic known to be in good operating condition.
4   During the road test, check the operation of all Drive ranges. Pay particular attention to the speed of clutch engagement when you shift down and accelerate.
5   If the engine revs up excessively – especially in L, 1 and R ranges – the cause is probably a slipping clutch, faulty torque converter or poor supply of ATF to the torque converter.

Stall speed test

6   A stall speed test will help you decide whether the torque converter is operating the way it should. Perform this test only if the vehicle is incapable of reaching its specified maximum speed or if acceleration is poor. During this test, the ATF in the converter heats up rapidly, so stop the test as soon as you have the necessary reading.
7   Hook up an electric tachometer in accordance with the manufacturer's instructions.
8   Set the parking brake, start the engine and depress the brake pedal firmly to hold the vehicle in place.
9   Shift the selector lever to position 2 and, while still holding the brake pedal down, briefly press the accelerator pedal to the floor. Instead of revving up, the engine should drop in rpm (stall speed). Note the tachometer reading – stall speed should be about 2000 to 2250 rpm.
10   If the stall speed is below this range, but the engine is properly tuned,

the converter is faulty. Replace it (see Section 6).
11   If the stall speed is above this range, adjust the clutch servo (see Section 4). If it's still high, the converter may not be getting enough ATF pressure. Perform a pressure test (see next Step) or, if you don't have the correct pressure gauge, have the test done by a dealer service department or other repair shop.

Pressure test

Refer to illustration 2.12

12   Connect a pressure gauge to the torque converter circuit **(see illustration)**.
13   If the indicated pressure at 2000 rpm is below 52.6 psi, the ATF level is low (see Chapter 1), the pump outlet is low, the hoses to and from the converter are restricted or there's a leak somewhere. If it's above 52.6 psi, either the pressure relief valve or the pump is faulty, or they are clogged (they may also be clogged if they're bulging, or if seals are leaking).

Fluid leak diagnosis

14   Most fluid leaks are easy to locate visually, not always so easy to trace back to their source. Repair usually consists of tightening a loose fastener on the ATF hoses for the torque converter, or replacing a converter or pump hub seal. Sometimes the converter itself has sprung a leak.
15   If a leak is difficult to find, the following procedure may help. Identify the fluid. Make sure it's transmission fluid and not engine oil or brake fluid (automatic transmission fluid is a deep red color).
16   Try to pinpoint the source of the leak. Drive the vehicle several miles, then park it over a large sheet of cardboard. After a minute or two, you should be able to locate the leak by determining the source of the fluid dripping onto the cardboard.
17   Make a careful visual inspection of the suspected component and the area immediately around it. Pay particular attention to gasket mating surfaces. A mirror is often helpful for finding leaks in areas that are hard to see.
18   If you still can't find the leak, clean the suspected area thoroughly with a degreaser or solvent, then dry it.
19   Drive the vehicle for several miles at normal operating temperature and varying speeds. After driving the vehicle, visually inspect the suspected component again.
20   Once you've located the leak, determine the cause before making any further repairs.
21   Before attempting to repair a leak, check to make sure that the following conditions are corrected or they may cause another leak. **Note:** *Some of the following conditions cannot be fixed without highly specialized tools and expertise. Such problems must be referred to a transmission repair shop or a dealer service department.*

Seal leaks
22   If a converter seal or pump hub seal is leaking, the fluid level or pressure may be too high, the vent may be plugged, the seal bore may be damaged, the seal itself may be damaged or improperly installed, the surface of the shaft protruding through the seal may be damaged or a loose bearing may be causing excessive shaft movement.
23   Make sure the dipstick cap seal is in good condition.

Case leaks
24   If the case itself appears to be leaking, the casting is either porous or cracked and will have to be repaired or replaced.

Fluid comes out vent pipe or fill tube
25   If this condition occurs, the transmission is overfilled, the dipstick is incorrect, the vent is plugged or the drain back holes are plugged.

---

3   Shift lever and rod – removal, installation and adjustment

---

Refer to illustrations 3.1, 3.2, 3.4, 3.6, 3.10 and 3.13

1   Unscrew the shift lever knob and remove the shift lever dust boot **(see illustration)**. Loosen and unscrew the shift lever sleeve and remove the shift lever, sleeve, locknut and spring (don't lose the spring).

7B

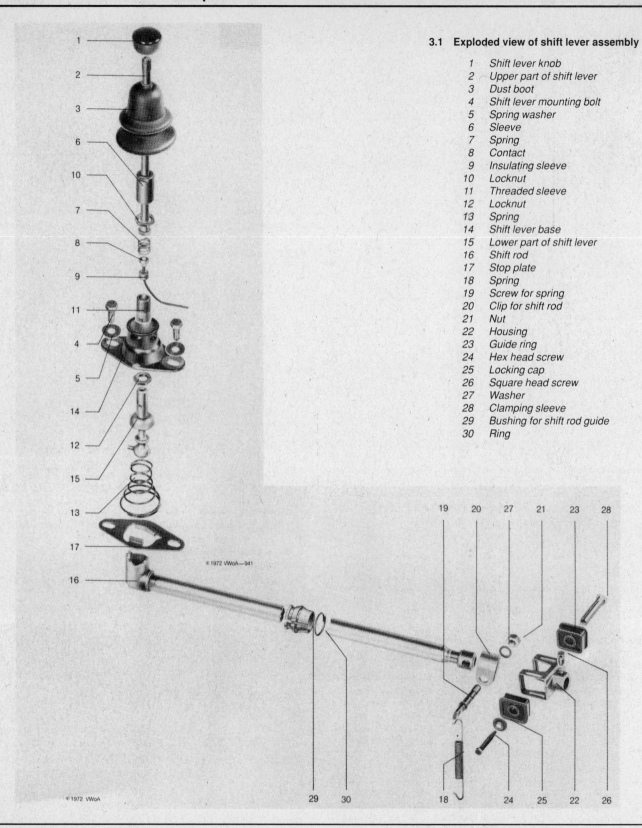

3.1   Exploded view of shift lever assembly

1   Shift lever knob
2   Upper part of shift lever
3   Dust boot
4   Shift lever mounting bolt
5   Spring washer
6   Sleeve
7   Spring
8   Contact
9   Insulating sleeve
10 Locknut
11 Threaded sleeve
12 Locknut
13 Spring
14 Shift lever base
15 Lower part of shift lever
16 Shift rod
17 Stop plate
18 Spring
19 Screw for spring
20 Clip for shift rod
21 Nut
22 Housing
23 Guide ring
24 Hex head screw
25 Locking cap
26 Square head screw
27 Washer
28 Clamping sleeve
29 Bushing for shift rod guide
30 Ring

© 1972 VWoA—941

© 1972 VWoA

2   Remove the rear seat cushion, locate the ground wire for the shift lever contact and unplug the connector **(see illustration)**.
3   Peel up the shift lever boot, remove the shift lever mounting bolts and
remove the shift lever assembly **(see illustration 3.1)**.
4   Remove the frame fork inspection cover, remove the shift rod coupling pin, remove the clamp and disconnect the spring **(see illustration)**.

5   Remove the two cover plates from the front body panels and the cover
plate on the frame head and pull the shift rod out through the front of the
vehicle with a pair of pliers.
6   Inspect the bushing in the shift rod mounting **(see illustration)**. If it's
cracked or deteriorated, replace it. To install a new bushing, slip the wire
ring **(see illustration 3.1)** around the bushing first, then, starting at the

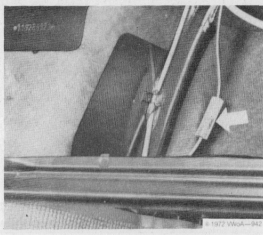

3.2 Look for the connector under the rear seat which connects the ground wire for the shift lever contact with the ground wire to the frame

3.4 Details of shift rod coupling (U-shaped part is the housing – square head screw is immediately above it)

1 Hex head screw   2 Spring   3 Nut

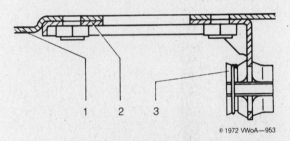

3.6 Frame tunnel (1), shift rod guide (2) and bushing for the shift rod mounting (3)

3.13 Attach the ground wire for the shift lever contact (upper arrow) to the base plate (lower arrow)

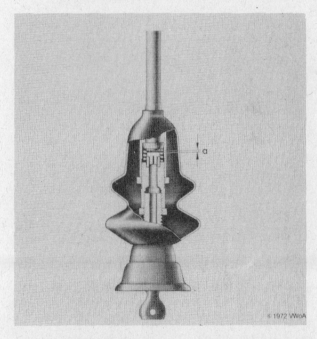

3.10 To adjust the gap between the shift lever contacts, screw the sleeve down until the contacts touch, then unscrew it half a turn and measure the gap – it should be within the range listed in this Chapter's Specifications

7B

slot, press on the bushing.

7   Apply a thin coat of grease to the selector rod, install it through the tunnel at the front of the vehicle, insert it into the bushing and carefully push it through.

8   Install the clamp, insert the pin in the shift rod coupling, tighten the screw and connect the spring.

9   Clean the shift lever contact surfaces with a point file or emery board. If they're damaged or worn, replace them.

10   Re-install the shift lever spring, locknut, sleeve, shift lever and mounting bolts. Screw the sleeve down until the contacts just touch, then back the sleeve off half a turn. Measure the contact gap **(see illustration)** and compare your measurement to the gap listed in this Chapter's Specifications

11   If necessary, screw the sleeve in or out until the gap is correct. When the gap is correct, hold the sleeve to prevent it from turning, tighten the locknut and re-check. Sometimes, the gap changes as you tighten the locknut, so it may be necessary to adjust the gap again until you get it right.

12   To adjust the shift lever, move it into drive range L, then carefully align the lever in the L position. The lever shouldn't tilt to either side but should be inclined backward about 10-degrees from vertical. Loosen the base plate mounting bolts a little, then, holding the lever to keep it from moving, press the stop plate under the base plate to the left until it contacts the shoulder on the lever. With the lever in this position, retighten the mounting bolts. Shift through all the drive ranges. You should be able to engage any range easily and without sticking.

13   Attach the ground wire for the shift lever contact at the base plate **(see illustration)**, route the wire under the rear seat and plug in the connector. Re-install the shift lever boot.

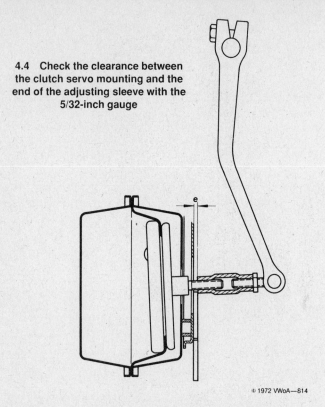

4.4   Check the clearance between the clutch servo mounting and the end of the adjusting sleeve with the 5/32-inch gauge

© 1972 VWoA—614

4.5   Check the clearance between the locknut and the adjusting sleeve with the 1/4-inch gauge

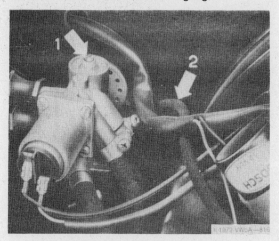

5.3   Details of the control valve assembly
1   Adjusting screw   2   Vacuum hose

4   Clutch servo – freeplay adjustment

Refer to illustrations 4.4 and 4.5

1   As the clutch lining wears, clutch freeplay is reduced. If the gap between the upper edge of the clutch servo mounting bracket and the lower edge of the adjusting sleeve on the servo rod isn't adjusted periodically, the clutch will eventually slip.

2   To perform the following procedure, you'll need a pair of pretty thick feeler gauges. Thick feeler gauges are unavailable from most tool suppliers, but you can easily fabricate your own. Take a strip of 1/16-inch (1 mm) sheet steel and trim one end to exactly 5/32-inch (4 mm) and the other end to 1/4-inch (6.5 mm). If you have trouble finishing the ends of your gauge to the specified dimensions, have a machine shop do it for you. You can also stack a bunch of feeler gauges together to attain the specified thicknesses, but since the following procedure is something you need to do regularly, it's worth the time to make a permanent tool.

3   Loosen the clamp and detach the vacuum hose from the servo, then pull the servo rod out of the servo as far as you can.

4   Using the 5/32-inch measuring strip, check the clearance between the servo mount and the end of the adjusting sleeve as indicated **(see illustration)**.

5   If the clearance is greater than 5/32-inch, loosen the adjusting sleeve locknut just enough to release the adjusting sleeve, then turn the sleeve five to five-and-a-half turns away from the locknut. The 1/4-inch measuring strip should fit between the locknut and the sleeve **(see illustration)**.

6   Screw the locknut up against the adjusting sleeve and tighten it enough to hold the adjusting sleeve in its new position. **Note:** *If this adjustment has been made so many times that the clutch operating lever is touching the bellhousing, further adjustment is impossible. The clutch plate is worn out and must be replaced (see Section 8).*

7   Screw the locknut up against the adjusting nut in its new position and tighten it.

8   Attach the vacuum hose to the servo and tighten the clamp.

9   Road test the vehicle to check your work. If you can accelerate without clutch slippage, the freeplay is correct. Try to put the shift lever in reverse. If it's difficult to engage reverse, freeplay may be excessive. Check and, if necessary, readjust.

5   Control valve – adjustment, removal, overhaul and installation

Adjustment

Refer to illustration 5.3

1   The control valve, located above and to the left of the engine, determines clutch engagement speed. If the clutch engages too slowly, slippage increases – and so does clutch lining wear. On the other hand, as service life increases, the contact pattern on the clutch plate improves, and the clutch may start to grab. Perform the following road test to determine whether the control valve requires adjustment. **Note:** *You can also use the road test to adjust the clutch engagement speed to your own driving habits.*

2   Driving at about 30 mph, move the shift lever from 2 to 1, but don't accelerate. About one second after taking your hand off the shift lever, the clutch should fully engage.

3   If the clutch engages too quickly, remove the protective cap from the top of the control valve **(see illustration)**. Turn the adjusting screw clockwise one-quarter to one-half turn, then replace the protective cap. Take the vehicle for a road test and re-check clutch engagement speed as described in Step 2. If it's still too quick, remove the cap and turn the screw clockwise a little more. Repeat this procedure until the engagement is acceptable.

4   If the clutch engages too slowly, remove the protective cap and turn the screw counterclockwise one-quarter to one-half turn, replace the cap and road test the vehicle. Readjust as necessary.

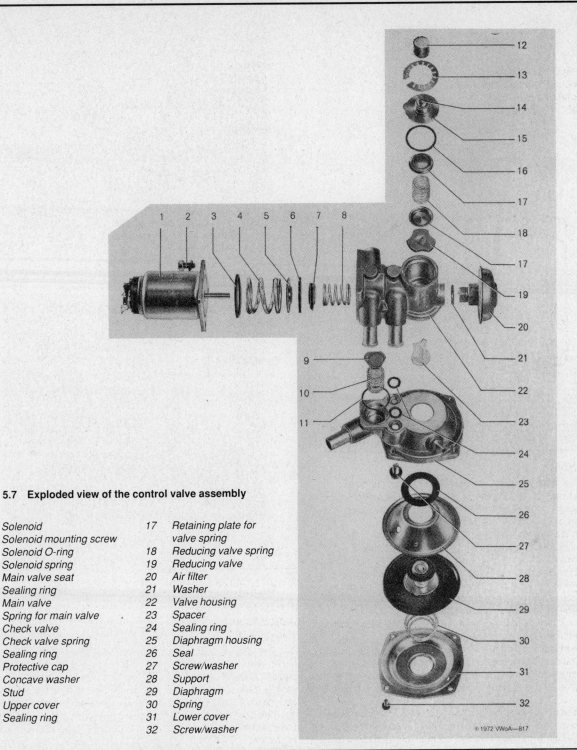

5.7 Exploded view of the control valve assembly

1	Solenoid	17	Retaining plate for
2	Solenoid mounting screw		valve spring
3	Solenoid O-ring	18	Reducing valve spring
4	Solenoid spring	19	Reducing valve
5	Main valve seat	20	Air filter
6	Sealing ring	21	Washer
7	Main valve	22	Valve housing
8	Spring for main valve	23	Spacer
9	Check valve	24	Sealing ring
10	Check valve spring	25	Diaphragm housing
11	Sealing ring	26	Seal
12	Protective cap	27	Screw/washer
13	Concave washer	28	Support
14	Stud	29	Diaphragm
15	Upper cover	30	Spring
16	Sealing ring	31	Lower cover
		32	Screw/washer

Removal

5   To remove the control valve, unplug the two electrical connectors, loosen the hose clamps and detach the three vacuum hoses. Remove the three mounting screws and take off the valve (see illustration 5.3).

Overhaul

Refer to illustrations 5.7 and 5.18

6   Remove the bracket.
7   Remove the special concave washer from the upper cover, and take off the upper cover and the seal **(see illustration)**.

8   Remove the upper retaining plate, the spring, the lower retaining plate and the reducing valve.
9   Remove the lower cover screws and the lower cover.
10   Remove the spring, the diaphragm, the support washer, the rubber washer and the spacer.
11   Remove the two screws from the diaphragm housing cover and re-move the housing.
12   Remove the check valve, spring and sealing ring from the diaphragm housing.
13   Unscrew the solenoid and remove the sealing ring, spacer spring, valve seat, seal, main valve and spring from the valve housing.

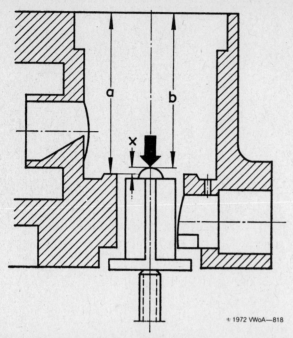

© 1972 VWoA—818

5.18   Working through the hole in the diaphragm housing cover, loosen the locknut and turn the adjusting screw in the center of the diaphragm until dimension b (from dome on spacer to top of valve housing) is .012 to .016-inch (0.30 to 0.40 mm) less than dimension a – the difference is dimension x (arrow)

14   Unscrew and remove the air filter.
15   Inspect the solenoid, valve seats, valve springs, diaphragms, seals and sealing rings. Replace as necessary – you can purchase individual parts or get a complete rebuild kit.
16   Install the check valve and sealing rings in the diaphragm housing, then reattach the diaphragm housing to the valve housing.
17   Insert the spacer into the valve housing. Install the diaphragm and related parts into the diaphragm housing. Install the diaphragm housing cover.
18   Working through the hole in the diaphragm housing cover, loosen the locknut and turn the adjusting screw in the center of the diaphragm to obtain the correct dimensions **(see illustration)**.

19   Tighten the diaphragm adjusting screw locknut.
20   Make sure the compensating port and valve seat for the reducing valve are clean. Install the reducing valve, lower retaining plate, valve, upper retaining plate, sealing ring and cover. Secure the cover with the concave washer.
21   Install the main valve along with its springs and related parts. Install the O-ring and the solenoid.

Installation

22   Installation of the control valve is the reverse of removal (see Step 5).
23   After you've installed the control valve, check the clutch engagement speed with a road test (see Steps 1 through 4).

---

6   Torque converter – removal, inspection, seal replacement and installation

---

Removal

1   Remove the engine (see Chapter 2).
2   Place a wide drain pan underneath the converter to catch any spilled ATF. Pull the torque converter straight off the one-way clutch support and remove it. Cover the opening in the converter hub to prevent contamination.

Inspection

3   Place the converter on a clean, well-lit workbench and inspect it to determine whether it's suitable for reinstallation. The converter is a welded assembly, so leaks are rarely caused by cracks in the housing. If the outside of the converter and the inside of the bellhousing are coated with ATF, a leaking converter is a possibility, though a leaking converter seal is more likely. There's still a considerable amount of ATF inside the converter. You can use it to help you find a leak in the converter housing. Wipe off the converter with a shop rag until it's completely dry. Then slowly rotate the converter and watch the welded seams and the points where the cooling vanes and starter ring gear brackets are welded to the housing. If ATF is leaking at any of these points, replace the converter.
4   Make sure none of the welds holding the starter ring gear are broken. Inspect the converter hub for evidence of scoring by the seal. If deep scoring is evident, replace the converter. Inspect the bushing inside the converter too. If worn or damaged, it's replaceable, but special tools are required, so have it done by a dealer service department or other repair shop.
5   The one-way clutch inside the converter hub should permit the stator to turn in only one direction. If acceleration has been poor, or if a stall speed

6.7   Using a small pry bar or seal remover, pry the old seal out of the one-way clutch

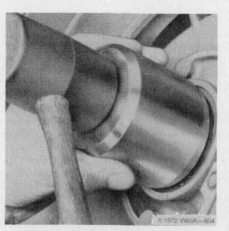

6.8   Using a socket with an outside diameter slightly smaller than the outside diameter of the seal, drive it into place

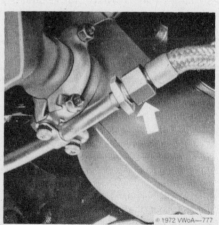

7.6   Disconnect the threaded coupling (arrow) for the ATF suction line below the rear of the right side heat exchanger

7.8   Drill a hole in a metal strap and attach it to one of the bellhousing studs with a nut to keep the torque converter from falling out during transaxle removal and installation

7.9   Disconnect both ATF hoses from the transaxle (upper arrow) and detach the electrical connectors from the temperature switches (lower arrow)

7.10a   Unplug the temperature switch electrical connector from the transaxle housing

test was outside specifications, check its operation. It's probably bad. If so, replace the converter. Remove all burrs and sharp edges from the converter hub with crocus cloth. Don't use emery cloth or sandpaper – it will produce a rough finish that can damage the seal.

Seal replacement

Refer to illustrations 6.7 and 6.8

6   **Note:** *Besides the converter seal discussed here, there's also a turbine shaft seal pressed into the other side of the bellhousing. But you can't replace it without removing the bellhousing and the entire clutch assembly, including the carrier plate. The procedure for removing the bellhousing and the clutch assembly (except the carrier plate) is outlined in Section 8. Because of the special tools required for further disassembly, you'll have to take the bellhousing/carrier plate assembly to a dealer service department or other repair shop to have the seal replaced.*

7   Using a small pry bar or seal remover, pry the old seal out of the one-way clutch **(see illustration)**.

8   Apply a coat of automatic transmission fluid to the sealing lip of the new seal and slip it onto the one-way clutch support. Using a large socket with an outside diameter slightly smaller than the outside diameter of the seal, drive the seal into place **(see illustration)**.

Installation

9   To install the converter, slowly turn it clockwise and counterclockwise until the turbine splines engage the splined shaft on the clutch carrier plate. Press the torque converter straight on without allowing it to tilt or rock. This could damage the seal or the converter bushing.

10   Install the engine (see Chapter 2).

---

7   Transaxle – removal and installation

Removal

Refer to illustrations 7.6, 7.8, 7.9, 7.10a, 7.10b, 7.15 and 7.16

1   Disconnect the strap from the negative battery terminal.

2   Place the shift lever in position 1.

3   Working through the opening in the frame tunnel, remove the square head set screw from the shift rod coupling (see Section 3). Move the shift lever to position 2 and detach the coupling from the transaxle's gear selector shaft.

4   Raise the rear of the vehicle and place it securely on jackstands.

7.10b   Unplug the electrical connector from the neutral start switch (upper arrow) – the two nuts (lower arrows) attach the front of the transaxle to the front mount on earlier models (note the ground strap attached to the left stud)

5   Detach the ATF pressure line from the engine. Raise the detached end and secure it to the chassis so the fluid doesn't drain out.

6   Detach the ATF suction line **(see illustration)**. Plug the end of the line to prevent leakage.

7   Remove the bolts that hold the torque converter to the engine driveplate and remove the engine (see Chapter 2).

8   Drill a hole in a metal strap and install the strap on the bellhousing **(see illustration)** to prevent the torque converter from falling out while the transaxle is being removed.

9   Disconnect both ATF hoses from the transaxle **(see illustration)**.

10   Clearly label the electrical connectors for the temperature switches and the neutral start switch, then disconnect them **(see accompanying illustrations and illustration 7.9)**.

11   Remove the driveaxles (see Chapter 8).

12   Detach the vacuum hose from the servo (see Section 4).

13   Clearly label the wires to the starter solenoid, then disconnect them (see Chapter 5).

14   Place a transmission jack, or a floor jack, under the transaxle. If you use a floor jack, put a block of wood between the jack and the transaxle to protect the transaxle from damage. Raise the jack until it's supporting the transaxle.

7B

7.15   The later style front transaxle mount is attached by two nuts (arrows) to the underside of the frame crossmember

7.16   Typical transaxle rear mounting bolt (arrow)

8.7   To get at the two bellhousing stud nuts (arrows) inside the final drive housing, you'll have to remove the transmission cover

15   Remove the front transaxle mounting nuts **(see illustration)** and, on earlier models, the ground strap connected to one of the bolts **(see illustration 7.10b)**.
16   Remove the transaxle rear mounting bolts **(see illustration)**.
17   On 1972 and earlier models, move the transaxle slightly to the rear and lower it. On 1973 and later models, lower the transaxle slightly, then move it toward the rear before lowering it from the vehicle.

Installation

18   Raise the transaxle into position with the floor jack or transmission jack and install the nuts at the front transaxle mount (don't forget to reattach the ground strap) and loosely install the bolts at the rear transaxle mount.
19   Attach the hose for the clutch servo and tighten the hose clamp.
20   Using new sealing washers, reconnect the ATF hoses and tighten the banjo bolts securely.
21   Plug in the connectors for the neutral start switch and oil temperature switches and reconnect the wires to the terminals on the starter solenoid.
22   Install the driveaxles (see Chapter 8).
23   Tighten the transaxle mounting bolts and nuts to the torque listed in this Chapter's Specifications.
24   Install the engine, followed by the torque converter-to-driveplate bolts, then tighten the bolts to the torque listed in the Chapter 2 Specifications.
25   Reconnect the ATF suction and pressure line banjo bolts and reattach the two electrical connectors to the transaxle.
26   Install the shift rod coupling (see Section 3).
27   Reconnect the negative battery cable.
28   Fill the transaxle and ATF tank with proper fluid (see the Specifications in Chapter 1).
29   Start the engine and make sure that ATF is flowing through the circuit, then check for leaks.
30   Perform a road test, pressure test and stall speed test (see Section 2).

---

8   Clutch – removal, inspection, overhaul, installation and adjustment

Removal

Refer to illustrations 8.7 and 8.9

1   Remove the engine (see Chapter 2).
2   Remove the torque converter (see Section 6). Cover the hole to prevent contamination.
3   Remove the transaxle (see Section 7) and place it on a clean work bench.
4   Remove the servo and its mounting bracket.
5   Loosen the pinch bolt that secures the clutch operating lever to the release shaft and remove the lever.

6   Turn the transaxle upside down and remove the eight nuts that attach the transmission cover to the bottom of the final drive housing.
7   Remove all eight nuts securing the bellhousing to the final drive housing. Two of them **(see illustration)** are located inside the final drive housing. The other six are evenly spaced around the bellhousing.
8   Separate the bellhousing and clutch assembly from the transaxle as a single unit.
9   Loosen all six bolts that hold the pressure plate to the clutch carrier plate **(see illustration)**. Loosen them a little at a time so the spring tension is relieved evenly and gradually.
10   Once spring tension has been relieved, remove the six bolts completely and lift the pressure plate assembly off the clutch disc and clutch carrier plate.
11   Lift the clutch disc out of the clutch carrier plate.

Inspection

Warning: *Dust produced by clutch wear and deposited on clutch components may contain asbestos, which is hazardous to your health. DO NOT blow it out with compressed air and DO NOT inhale it. DO NOT use gasoline or petroleum-based solvents to remove the dust. Brake system cleaner should be used to flush the dust into a drain pan.*

12   Before cleaning the clutch components, look at the clutch. If it's covered with transmission oil, the main driveshaft seal in the transaxle case must e replaced (see Step 24). If it's covered with ATF, the seal in the clutch carrier plate must be replaced. Take the bellhousing and carrier plate to the dealer for this service. And ask him to inspect, and if necessary, replace the carrier plate needle bearing and the ball bearing for the one-way clutch support in the center bore of the bellhousing.
13   Clean the clutch carrier plate, clutch disc, pressure plate and release bearing with brake system cleaner.
14   Inspect the friction surface of the clutch carrier plate for cracks and grooves. If it's worn, replace it (see Step 12).
15   Inspect the clutch disc lining for wear, cracks, oil and burns. Measure the thickness of the disc – it must be at least 23/64-inch thick. Look for loose rivets. Slide the disc onto the transaxle mainshaft spline and make sure it slides freely without excessive radial play. Replace the disc if necessary.
16   Inspect the pressure plate for cracked or broken spring fingers, cracked or scored friction surface and evidence of heat (bluish tint). Replace it if necessary.
17   Inspect the release bearing for noise and wear. **Note:** *In view of its modest cost, we recommend replacing this part regardless of its condition.*

Overhaul

Clutch release shaft

Refer to illustration 8.18

18   Remove the hexagonal bearing sleeve bolt and its spring washer **(see illustration)**.

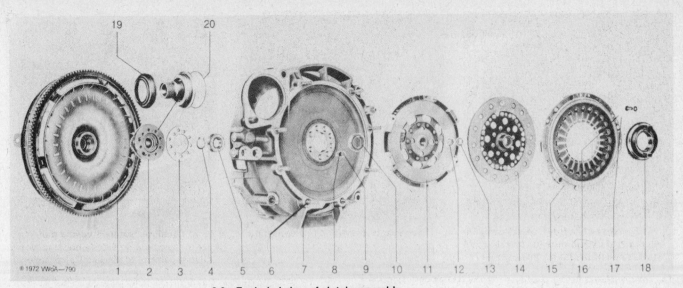

8.9 Exploded view of clutch assembly

1	Torque converter	6	O-ring for stud	11	Clutch carrier plate
2	One-way clutch support	7	Bellhousing	12	Needle bearing
3	Gasket	8	Spring washer	13	Carrier plate seal
4	Circlip for carrier plate	9	Bolt	14	Clutch disc
5	Ball bearing	10	Seal	15	Pressure plate

16	Spring washer
17	Bolt
18	Release bearing
19	Converter seal
20	One-way clutch O-ring

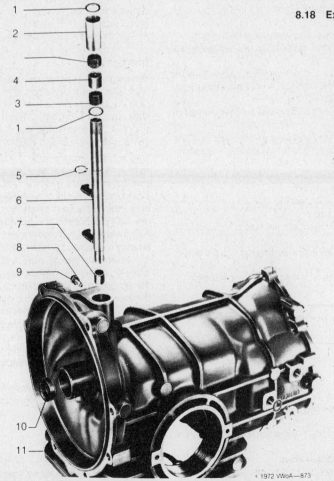

8.18 Exploded view of clutch release shaft assembly

1 Thrust washer
2 Bearing sleeve
3 Rubber seal
4 Spacer bushing
5 Circlip
6 Clutch release shaft
7 Slotted bushing
8 Spring washer
9 Bolt
10 Main driveshaft seal
11 Transaxle case

7B

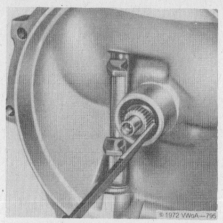

8.24 Using a small hook-type seal puller, dig the main driveshaft seal out of the guide sleeve for the clutch release bearing

8.27 Lightly coat the lugs of the clutch release bearing at the points indicated by the arrows

8.29 Center the clutch disc with a clutch alignment tool or a pilot cut from an old mainshaft, then tighten the clutch bolts evenly and gradually to the torque listed in this Chapter's Specifications

8.30 Insert the two lower engine mounting bolts from the torque converter side of the bellhousing and install new O-rings around them (and the other six mounting studs, not shown)

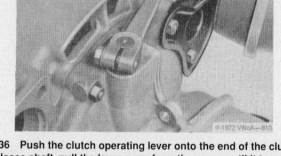

8.36 Push the clutch operating lever onto the end of the clutch release shaft, pull the lever away from the servo until it touches the bellhousing and snug – but don't tighten – the pinch bolt

19 Push the shaft upward to force the bearing sleeve, rubber seals and spacer bushing out of the top of the transaxle.

20 Remove the bearing sleeve and the other parts from the shaft, then pull the shaft down and out through the clutch housing.

21 Pry open the slotted bushing with a screwdriver and remove it.

22 Press a new slotted bushing into the case.

23 Installation is the reverse of removal. Referring to illustration 8.18, make sure you install the parts in their correct order.

Main driveshaft seal

Refer to illustration 8.24

24 Using a seal remover or pry bar, carefully hook the old seal and pull it out **(see illustration)**.

25 Some converters have a slight chamfer on the hub to facilitate installation of a new seal and to make insertion of the converter hub easier. Look for burrs on this chamfer. If it's gouged or scratched, carefully smooth it out with crocus cloth, then polish and round it to protect the oil seal from damage when the converter is installed.

26 Lubricate the lip of the new seal with hypoid gear oil and, using a socket with an outside diameter slightly smaller than the outside diameter of the seal, drive it into place.

Installation

Refer to illustrations 8.27, 8.29 and 8.30

27 Lightly coat the guide sleeve for the clutch release bearing and the

lugs of the clutch release bearing **(see illustration)** with moly-base grease.

28 Lubricate the needle bearing and seal in the carrier plate hub with a small amount of lithium grease.

29 Install the clutch disc, pressure plate and release bearing into the clutch housing. Center the clutch disc with a clutch alignment tool or a pilot cut from an old mainshaft **(see illustration)**. Make sure the release bearing is properly centered in the diaphragm spring. Tighten the pressure plate bolts evenly by hand, then tighten them to the torque listed in this Chapter's Specifications.

30 Insert the two lower engine mounting bolts from the torque converter side of the bellhousing **(see illustration)**. Install new O-rings around them and the other six bellhousing mounting studs.

31 Install the bellhousing/clutch assembly onto the transaxle. Make sure the clutch release shaft engages behind the release bearing lugs. Tighten all nuts evenly and gradually to the torque listed in this Chapter's Specifications.

32 Reattach the clutch servo mounting bracket and servo.

33 Adjust the clutch to its basic setting (see Step 36).

34 Install the torque converter (see Section 6).

35 Install the engine (see Chapter 2).

Clutch adjustment

Refer to illustrations 8.36, 8.37, 8.38 and 8.39

Note: *The purpose of the following procedure is to give you a basic setting for a new clutch plate.*

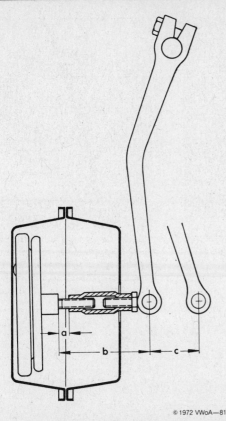

© 1972 VWoA—81

8.37 Using the adjustment sleeve on the servo rod, adjust the linkage to dimensions "a" (the distance from the end of the sleeve to the hub of the servo diaphragm) and "b" (the distance from the hub to the eye of the sleeve), then push the servo rod all the way into the servo unit, loosen the pinch bolt and rotate the clutch operating lever toward the clutch servo until the distance between the eye of the lever and the eye of the threaded sleeve on the servo rod is dimension "c"

Dimension "a" – 0.335-inch (8.5 mm)
Dimension "b" – 3.03-inches (77 mm)
Dimension "c" – 1.574-inches (40 mm)

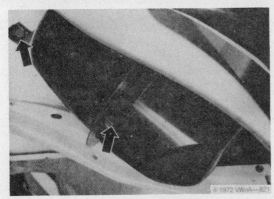

9.3 Typical vacuum tank assembly (Beetle shown) – to remove the tank, remove the strap bolt (lower arrow) and bracket bolt (upper arrow)

36 Slide the clutch operating lever onto the clutch release shaft. Pull the lever away from the servo until it touches the bellhousing **(see illustration)**, then snug the pinch bolt, but don't tighten it completely yet.
37 Using the adjustment sleeve on the servo rod, adjust the linkage to dimensions "a" and "b" as indicated **(see illustration)**.

8.38 The special VW measuring jig used for setting dimension "c" – you can use a vernier caliper or a steel ruler to measure the distance between the bore centerlines of the servo rod and operating lever

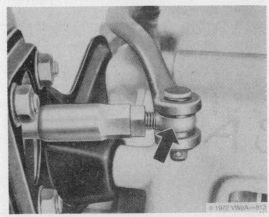

8.39 Using a new plastic bushing, connect the operating lever to the servo rod, insert the clevis pin from the top and secure it with a washer and a new cotter pin

38 Push the servo rod all the way into the servo unit until it bottoms against the end of the vacuum chamber. Loosen the pinch bolt and rotate the clutch operating lever toward the clutch servo until the distance between the eye of the lever and the eye of the threaded sleeve on the servo rod is 1.574-inches (40mm) (measurement "c" in illustration 8.37). **Note:** *Volkswagen has a special measuring jig* **(see illustration)** *for this critical dimension, but you can use a steel ruler to measure between eye centers on the servo rod and operating lever.* Tighten the pinch bolt to the torque listed in this Chapter's Specifications.
39 Using a new plastic bushing, connect the clutch operating lever to the servo rod **(see illustration)**. Insert the clevis pin from the top and secure it at the bottom with a washer and a new cotter pin.
40 After about 300 miles of operation, check the clutch freeplay (see Section 4).

9   Vacuum tank – removal and installation

Refer to illustration 9.3
1   On Beetles, you'll find the vacuum tank inside the left rear fender; on Karmann-Ghias, it's either inside the right rear wheel housing (earlier models), or on the left side of the engine compartment (later models).
2   Loosen the hose clamps on the vacuum hoses and detach the hoses from the tank.
3   Remove the retaining strap bolt and the mounting bracket bolt **(see illustration)** and remove the tank.
4   Installation is the reverse of removal.

7B

10.2   Disconnect the ATF return line fitting from the filler neck (upper arrow) – the two lower arrows point to the nuts that attach the trim plate to the quarter panel

10   ATF tank – removal and installation

Refer to illustrations 10.2 and 10.4

1   On Beetles and Super Beetles, you'll find the ATF tank inside the right rear fender; on Karmann-Ghias, it's on the right side of the engine compartment.
2   Place a drain pan under the return line fitting and disconnect it from the ATF tank **(see illustration)**.
3   Remove the trim plate retaining nuts and the filler neck rubber seal at the quarter panel.
4   Place a drain pan under the ATF return line fitting **(see illustration)** and disconnect the fitting from the ATF tank.
5   Remove the retaining strap bolt and remove the tank.
6   Installation is the reverse of removal. Refill the tank with the proper amount and type of fluid (see Chapter 1).

11   Neutral start switch – check and replacement

Check

1   The neutral start switch (see illustrations 1.4, 1.8a and 1.8b) prevents the engine starter from operating unless the shift lever is in the Neutral (N) position. Any other gear position opens the switch (located between the ignition switch and the starter solenoid). This switch also grounds the clutch control valve solenoid, preventing the shift lever from affecting the clutch when in Neutral.

10.4   Typical ATF tank assembly (Beetle shown) – to remove it, disconnect the ATF suction line fitting (lower arrow), take off the nuts attaching the trim plate to the quarter panel (see illustration 10.2) and remove the strap bolt

2   Here's a quick check for the neutral start switch: Place your foot firmly on the brake and turn the ignition key to Start while you move the shift lever through all its positions. If the starter operates in any position other than Neutral – or fails to operate when in Neutral – either the switch itself is faulty or there's a problem somewhere in the circuit.
3   Raise the rear of the vehicle and place it securely on jackstands.
4   Unplug the electrical connector from the switch and connect a jumper wire between the terminal for the wire from the ignition switch and the terminal for the wire that leads to the starter solenoid. If the starter now works, replace the switch. If it doesn't, proceed to the next Step.
5   Have an assistant move the shift lever to each gear position. Using a self-powered continuity checker or an ohmmeter, verify that the neutral start switch has no continuity in any gear position except Neutral.
6   If the switch doesn't show continuity in Neutral, replace it switch. If it does show continuity, verify that the circuit is powered, or verify continuity in the circuit itself, and repair as necessary. See Wiring Diagrams at the end of Chapter 12.

Replacement

7   Unplug the electrical connector, unscrew the switch, screw in a new switch, tighten it securely and plug in the connector.

Chapter 8 Clutch and driveline

Contents

Specifications

Clutch disc
Minimum lining thickness . . . . 1/16-inch (2.00 mm)
Runout . . . . 0.020 inch (0.50 mm)

Clutch cable guide sag . . . . 1 to 1 13/16-in (25 to 45 mm)

Swing axle
Rounded portion of axleshaft-to-side gear . . . . 0.001 to 0.004 in (0.03 to 0.1 mm)
Flat portion of axleshaft-to-fulcrum plates . . . . 0.001 to 0.010 in (0.035 to 0.244 mm)
Axleshaft runout . . . . 0.002 in (0.05 mm)
Axleshaft and side gear replacement sets
  Yellow
    Side gear inner diameter . . . . 2.3595 to 2.3610 in (59.93 to 59.97 mm)
    Axleshaft outer diameter . . . . 2.3570 to 2.3582 in (59.87 to 59.90 mm)
  Blue
    Side gear inner diameter . . . . 2.3614 to 2.3622 in (59.98 to 60.00 mm)
    Axleshaft outer diameter . . . . 2.3586 to 2.3598 in (59.91 to 59.94 mm)
  Pink
    Side gear inner diameter . . . . 2.3602 to 2.3638 in (60.01 to 60.04 mm)
    Axleshaft outer diameter . . . . 2.3602 to 2.3610 in (59.95 to 59.97 mm)

Torque specifications
	Ft-lbs
Clutch pressure plate-to-flywheel bolts	18
Axle tube retainer nuts	14
CV joint bolts	25
Rear axle bearing cover	40

1 General information

The information in this Chapter deals with the components from the front of the engine to the the drive wheels, except for the transaxle, which is covered in the previous Chapter. For the purposes of this Chapter, these components are grouped into two categories: clutch and driveline. Separate Sections within this Chapter offer general descriptions and checking procedures for components in each of the two groups.

Since nearly all the procedures covered in this Chapter involve working under the vehicle, make sure it's securely supported on sturdy jackstands or on a hoist where the vehicle can be easily raised and lowered.

8

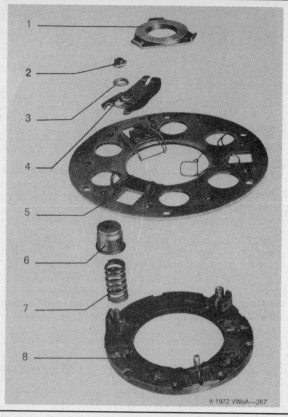

2.1a   Exploded view of a typical coil spring type clutch assembly

1   *Release ring*
2   *Adjusting nut*
3   *Washer*
4   *Release lever*
5   *Clutch cover*
6   *Spring cap*
7   *Spring*
8   *Pressure plate*

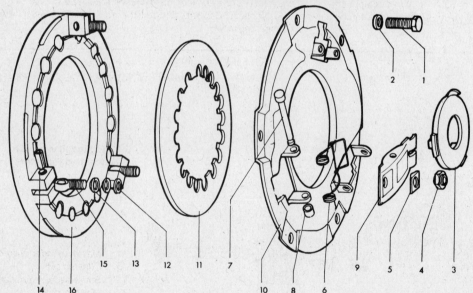

2.1b   Exploded view of a typical diaphragm spring type clutch assembly

1   *Bolt*
2   *Lock washer*
3   *Release ring*
4   *Adjusting nut*
5   *Thrust piece*
6   *Spring*
7   *Clutch cover pin*
8   *Bushing*
9   *Release lever*
10   *Clutch cover*
11   *Diaphragm spring*
12   *Pivot pin washer*
13   *Concave washer*
14   *Spring pin*
15   *Pivot pin*
16   *Pressure plate*

2   Clutch – description and check

Refer to illustrations 2.1a, 2.1b and 2.1c

1   All vehicles with a manual transaxle use a single dry-plate, coil spring clutch (1972 and earlier models) or diaphragm spring clutch (1973 and later models). The clutch disc has a splined hub which allows it to slide along the splines of the transaxle input shaft. The clutch and pressure plate are held in contact by spring pressure exerted by the coil springs or the diaphragm spring in the pressure plate **(see illustrations)**.

2   The clutch release system is cable operated. The release system includes the clutch pedal, the clutch cable, the clutch release lever, the clutch release shaft and the clutch release bearing.

3   When the clutch pedal is depressed, its movement is transmitted by the cable to the clutch release lever. As the lever pivots, the forks on the release shaft push against the release bearing, which slides along the input shaft toward the flywheel. On earlier clutches, the release bearing pushes against the release ring, which pushes on the inner ends of the three release levers, which releases the pressure plate from the clutch disc, allowing the clutch disc to disengage from the flywheel. On later clutches, the release bearing pushes against the fingers of the diaphragm spring of the pressure plate assembly, lifting the pressure plate off the clutch disc and allowing it to disengage from the flywheel.

4   Terminology can be a problem when discussing the clutch components because common names are in some cases different from those

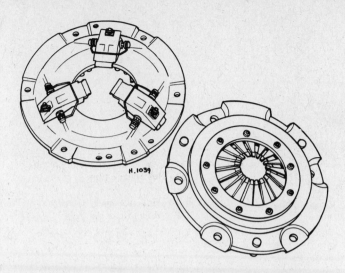

H.1039

a) Check clutch "spin down time." Run the engine at normal idle speed with the transaxle in Neutral and the clutch pedal up. Disengage the clutch (depress the clutch pedal), wait several seconds and shift the transaxle into Reverse. You shouldn't hear any gears grinding. A grinding noise indicates a problem in the pressure plate or the clutch disc (see Section 5).

b) Verify that the clutch releases completely. Run the engine (with the parking brake applied to prevent the vehicle from moving) and hold the clutch pedal about 1/2-inch from the floor. Shift the transaxle between 1st gear and Reverse several times. If the shift is hard or the transaxle grinds, something in the clutch release mechanism is broken (see Section 6).

c) Inspect the pivot bushing between the clutch pedal and the pedal shaft for binding or excessive play (see Section 3).

d) If the clutch pedal is difficult to operate, the most likely cause is a faulty clutch cable. Remove the cable (see Section 4) and check it for kinks, frayed wires, rust and other signs of corrosion. If it's in bad shape, replace it; if it looks like it's in good condition, lubricate it with penetrating oil and try it again.

2.1c   Typical early (left) and later (right) diaphragm spring clutch pressure plates: Early version uses release levers like older coil spring types – on later version, levers are eliminated and diaphragm spring is attached to plate (you can swap the earlier version for the later one at overhaul time)

used by the manufacturer. For example, the driven plate is also called the clutch plate or disc, the clutch release bearing is sometimes called a throwout bearing, etc.

5   Unless you're planning to replace obviously damaged components, always perform the following preliminary checks to pinpoint the source of clutch problems.

3   Pedal cluster – removal and installation

Refer to illustrations 3.1, 3.3, 3.4a, 3.4b, 3.5, 3.6, 3.7, 3.8, 3.10, 3.11 and 3.12

1   On models equipped with a manual transaxle, the accelerator, brake and clutch pedals are mounted on a common shaft which is bolted to the left side of the center tunnel. On models with equipped with an Automatic Stick Shift, there's no clutch pedal – the brake pedal is wider and has two arms attached to a common bushing **(see illustration)**.

2   Disconnect the clutch cable from the clutch release lever at the transaxle (see Section 4).

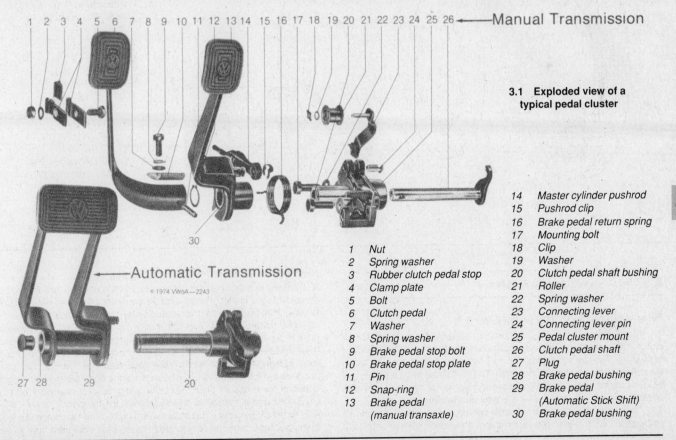

Manual Transmission

3.1   Exploded view of a typical pedal cluster

Automatic Transmission

© 1974 VWoA – 2243

#	Part
1	Nut
2	Spring washer
3	Rubber clutch pedal stop
4	Clamp plate
5	Bolt
6	Clutch pedal
7	Washer
8	Spring washer
9	Brake pedal stop bolt
10	Brake pedal stop plate
11	Pin
12	Snap-ring
13	Brake pedal (manual transaxle)
14	Master cylinder pushrod
15	Pushrod clip
16	Brake pedal return spring
17	Mounting bolt
18	Clip
19	Washer
20	Clutch pedal shaft bushing
21	Roller
22	Spring washer
23	Connecting lever
24	Connecting lever pin
25	Pedal cluster mount
26	Clutch pedal shaft
27	Plug
28	Brake pedal bushing
29	Brake pedal (Automatic Stick Shift)
30	Brake pedal bushing

8

3.3   To remove the accelerator pedal, pry the pedal return spring out of the way and pull out the pedal pivot pin

3.4a   To disconnect the brake master cylinder pushrod, pry the master cylinder pushrod clip out of the way . . .

3.4b   . . . and remove the pivot pin

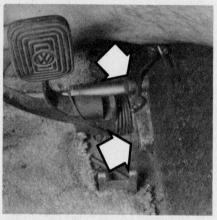

3.5   Remove the pedal cluster mounting bolts (arrows)

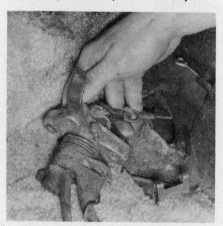

3.6   Pull out the pedal cluster and disconnect the clutch cable from the clutch pedal shaft

3.7   Mark the end of the clutch pedal and the pedal shaft to ensure proper reassembly

3.8   Drive out the pin which secures the clutch pedal to the shaft

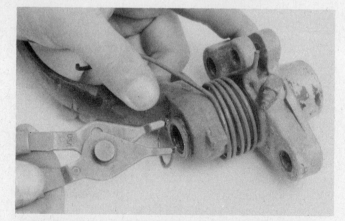

3.10   Remove the snap-ring that holds the brake pedal to the pedal cluster mount

3   Pry the accelerator pedal return spring aside, pull out the accelerator pedal pivot pin **(see illustration)** and remove the accelerator pedal.

4   Pry the master cylinder pushrod clip out of the way and remove the pivot pin **(see illustrations)**.

5   Remove the pedal cluster mounting bolts **(see illustration)**.

6   Pull out the pedal cluster and the (still connected) clutch cable **(see illustration)**. Disconnect the clutch cable.

7   The clutch pedal is pressed onto the end of the clutch pedal shaft and secured with a small pin driven through the pedal and the shaft. Mark the

end of the shaft and the pedal **(see illustration)** to ensure that the hole in the pedal and the hole in the shaft are realigned during reassembly.

8   Using a hammer and a narrow punch, drive out the pin which secures the clutch pedal to the shaft **(see illustration)**.

9   Pull off the clutch pedal. If it won't budge, tap it off with a soft faced hammer.

10   Remove the snap-ring that holds the brake pedal on the pedal cluster **(see illustration)**.

11   Pull the brake pedal off the pedal cluster **(see illustration)**.

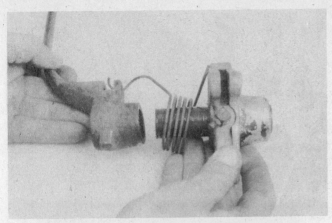

3.11   Pull the brake pedal off the pedal cluster mount

3.12   Remove the clutch pedal shaft from the pedal cluster mount

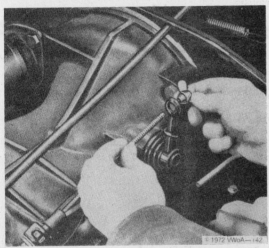

4.2   After you've raised the rear of the vehicle and placed it on jackstands, you'll find the clutch release lever on the upper left side of the transaxle – to disconnect the clutch cable, simply remove the wing nut

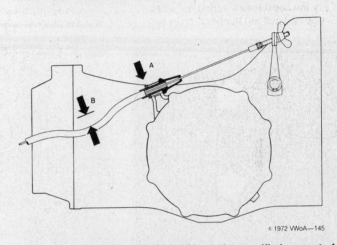

4.8   The clutch cable tube should have the specified amount of sag at point B (where the cable guide leaves the frame tunnel) – to alter the sag, install washers at point A between the end of the guide and the bracket on the transaxle

12   Remove the clutch pedal shaft **(see illustration)**. Wipe the shaft off and inspect it for burrs and nicks. Clean it up with emery or crocus cloth if it's damaged.

13   Installation is the reverse of removal. It's a good idea to adjust the brake master cylinder pushrod clearance (see Chapter 9) and the clutch cable (see Section 4).

4   Clutch cable – removal and installation

Removal

Refer to illustration 4.2

1   Loosen the lug bolts of the left rear wheel, raise the rear of the vehicle and support it securely on jackstands. Remove the wheel.

2   Locate the clutch release lever on the upper left side of the transaxle and disconnect the cable from the lever **(see illustration)**.

3   Remove the pedal cluster and disconnect the clutch cable from the clutch shaft (see Section 3).

4   Pull the clutch cable forward, through the center tunnel, and out the hole for the pedal cluster.

Installation

Refer to illustration 4.8

5   Coat the new cable with multi-purpose grease.

6   Reach into the hole for the brake and clutch pedal cluster and locate the front end of the cable guide tube. Grasp the tube with your fingers and

insert the new cable into the tube.

7   Once you've started the cable into the tube, push it to the rear, through the tube. If necessary, lubricate the cable with multi-purpose grease as you push it into the tube.

8   The "sag," or bend, in the clutch cable guide tube is critical – the friction it imposes on the cable minimizes clutch chatter. Measure the sag at point B **(see illustration)** and compare your measurement to the sag listed in this Chapter's Specifications. To alter the sag, install or remove washers between the holding bracket and the end of the cable tube (point A).

9   Adjust the clutch pedal freeplay (see Chapter 1).

5   Clutch components – removal, inspection and installation

Warning: *Dust produced by clutch wear and deposited on clutch components may contain asbestos, which is hazardous to your health. DO NOT blow it out with compressed air and DO NOT inhale it. DO NOT use gasoline or petroleum-based solvents to remove the dust. Brake system cleaner should be used to flush the dust into a drain pan. After the clutch components are wiped clean with a rag, dispose of the contaminated rags and cleaner in a covered, marked container.*

Removal

Note: *Any time the engine is removed for major overhaul, check the clutch for wear and replace worn components as necessary. The relatively low*

8

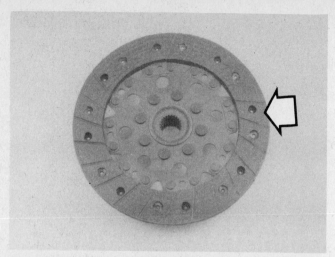

5.7a　Inspect the clutch lining material (arrow) – there should be at least 1/16-inch of lining above the rivet heads – also look for loose rivets, distortion, cracks, broken springs and other damage

5.7b　Check the clutch disc for runout as shown and compare your measurement to the amount listed in this Chapter's Specifications – replace the clutch if runout is excessive

5.9a　Inspect the friction surface of the pressure plate for wear, cracks and grooves – alternating bright and dull areas indicate a warped plate

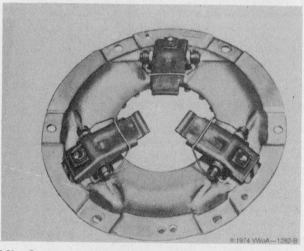

5.9b　On pressure plates with coil springs, inspect the friction surfaces of the release ring (removed for clarity) and the release levers (arrows) for excessive wear

cost of the clutch components compared to the time and trouble spent gaining access to them warrants their replacement – unless they are new or in near perfect condition – anytime the engine is removed.

1　Remove the engine (see Chapter 2).

2　If the old pressure plate is to be reused, scribe or paint alignment marks on the pressure plate and the flywheel to ensure proper realignment of the pressure plate during reassembly.

3　Loosen the pressure plate-to-flywheel bolts by turning each bolt only a little at a time. Work in a criss-cross pattern until all spring pressure is relieved. Hold the pressure plate securely and completely remove the bolts, followed by the pressure plate and clutch disc. **Caution:** *The pressure plate is under a great deal of spring pressure. If you work your way around the cover, removing each bolt one at a time, it will warp.*

Inspection

Refer to illustrations 5.7a, 5.7b, 5.9a, 5.9b and 5.9c

4　Ordinarily, clutch problems are caused by a worn out clutch driven plate (clutch disc). But it's a good idea to inspect the other components too, just in case any of them are worn or damaged.

5　Inspect the flywheel for cracks, heat checking, grooves and other obvious defects. If the imperfections are slight, a machine shop can machine the surface flat and smooth (highly recommended, regardless of the sur-

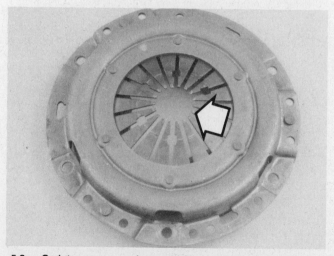

5.9c　On later pressure plates with diaphragm springs, inspect the spring fingers (arrow) for excessive wear and make sure they're not distorted – shake the pressure plate and make sure the diaphragm spring doesn't rattle

5.13 Center the clutch disc with an alignment tool, then tighten the pressure plate bolts

6.3 Note how the clips on the release bearing engage the release forks (you'll need to remember this for reassembly), then pry the clips loose from the release forks with a screwdriver

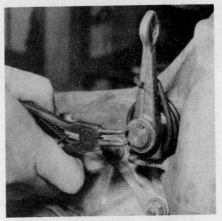

6.4a On 1965 and later models, the release lever is secured to the release shaft with a snap-ring (on earlier models, it's held on with a pinch bolt)

face appearance). If necessary, replace the flywheel (see Chapter 2).

6   Clean the needle bearings inside the flywheel gland nut (the large nut in the center of the flywheel). Using a small flashlight, inspect the needle bearings. If they're flattened from excessive wear or otherwise damaged, replace the gland nut (see Chapter 2). If you decide to re-use the old gland nut, be sure to repack the bearings with multi-purpose grease (just enough to coat all needles lightly). Then squirt a little oil onto the felt ring just in front of the needle bearings. **Note:** *In view of the low replacement cost for a new gland nut, it's a good idea to replace it anytime the clutch is removed, even if the needle bearings look okay.*

7   Inspect the lining on the clutch disc **(see illustration)**. There should be at least 1/16-inch of lining above the rivet heads. Check for loose rivets, distortion, cracks, broken springs and other obvious damage. As mentioned above, ordinarily the clutch disc is routinely replaced, so if in doubt about the condition, replace it with a new one. If you're planning to re-use the old clutch disc, it's also a good idea to check it for runout **(see illustration)**. The indicated runout shouldn't exceed the amount listed in this Chapter's Specifications.

8   Carefully inspect the splines inside the hub of the clutch disc and the splines on the input shaft. They must not be broken or distorted. Lubricate the splines in the disc hub and the splines on the input shaft with graphite, then verify that the clutch disc slides freely on the drive shaft splines without excessive radial play. You're probably replacing the clutch disc anyway, but if the splines on the input shaft are damaged, you'll have to replace the input shaft as well (see Chapter 7 Part A).

9   Inspect the friction surface of the pressure plate for wear, cracks and grooves **(see illustration)**. Alternating bright and dull areas indicate a warped plate. Light glazing can be removed with medium grit emery cloth. On earlier (coil spring type) plates, inspect the friction surfaces of the release ring and the release levers for excessive wear **(see illustrations)**. On later (diaphragm spring type) plates, inspect the diaphragm spring fingers for excessive wear and make sure they're not distorted. Shake the pressure plate assembly and verify that the diaphragm spring doesn't rattle. If the pressure plate is damaged or worn in any way, replace it with a new or rebuilt unit.

10   Inspect the release bearing. Replace it if it's noisy or rough (see Section 6). Also inspect the bushings for the clutch release shaft and replace if necessary. **Note:** *Like the gland nut, the release bearing should normally be replaced anytime the clutch is replaced (see Section 6).*

Installation

Refer to illustrations 5.13

11   Install the flywheel, if removed (see Chapter 2).

12   Clean the flywheel and pressure plate friction surfaces with lacquer thinner or acetone. **Caution:** *DO NOT use oil or grease on these surfaces or on the clutch disc lining. And clean your hands before handling the parts.*

13   Position the clutch disc and pressure plate against the flywheel with the clutch held in place with an alignment tool – the best alignment tool is an old input shaft **(see illustration)**. Make sure the clutch disc is installed properly (most replacement clutch plates will be marked "flywheel side" or something similar – if not marked, install the clutch disc with the damper springs toward the transaxle). Also make sure the marks you made on the pressure plate and the flywheel are matched up (if you're using the old pressure plate. Working around the pressure plate, tighten the pressure plate-to-flywheel bolts finger tight.

14   Center the clutch disc by ensuring the alignment tool extends through the splined hub and into the needle bearing in the gland nut. Wiggle the tool up, down or side-to-side as needed to bottom the tool into the gland nut. Tighten the pressure plate-to-flywheel bolts a little at a time, working in a criss-cross pattern to prevent distorting the cover. After all of the bolts are snug, tighten them to the torque listed in this Chapter's Specifications. Remove the alignment tool.

15   Install the release bearing, if removed (see Section 6). Be sure to lubricate the bore of the release bearing and (on 1971 and later models) the outer surface of the central guide sleeve with high-temperature grease, and apply multi-purpose grease to the contact areas of the forks on the release shaft.

16   Install the engine (see Chapter 2).

17   Adjust the clutch pedal freeplay (see Chapter 1).

---

6   Clutch release assembly – removal, inspection and installation

Warning: *Dust produced by clutch wear and deposited on clutch components may contain asbestos, which is hazardous to your health. DO NOT blow it out with compressed air and DO NOT inhale it. DO NOT use gasoline or petroleum-based solvents to remove the dust. Brake system cleaner should be used to flush the dust into a drain pan. After the clutch components are wiped clean with a rag, dispose of the contaminated rags and cleaner in a covered, marked container.*

Removal

Refer to illustrations 6.3, 6.4a 6.4b, 6.5, 6.6 and 6.7

1   Remove the engine (see Chapter 2).

2   Remove the clutch assembly and inspect it for wear (see Section 5).

3   Note how the release forks engage the retaining clips on the release bearing. Unhook the retaining clips **(see illustration)** and slide the bearing off the input shaft.

4   On 1964 and earlier models, loosen the pinch bolt on the clutch release lever. On 1965 and later models, remove the snap-ring from the end of the shaft **(see illustration)**. Remove the lever, return spring and seat **(see illustration)**.

8

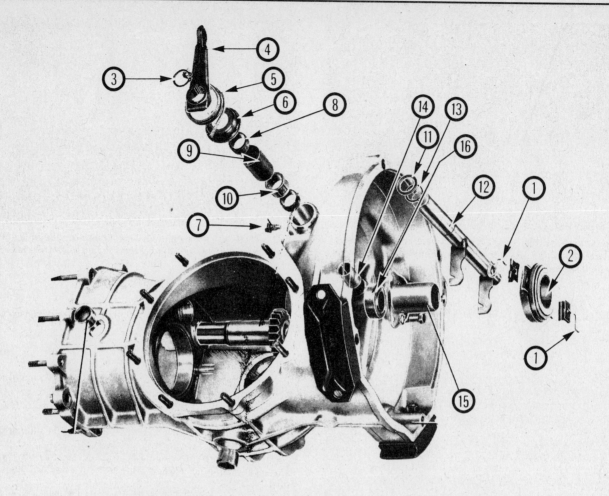

6.4b   Exploded view of a typical (1965 and later) clutch release assembly

1	Release bearing clips	7	Lock bolt	12	Release shaft
2	Release bearing	8	Outer rubber grommet	13	snap-ring
3	snap-ring	9	Left release shaft bushing	14	Right release shaft bushing
4	Release lever	10	Inner rubber grommet	15	Guide sleeve
5	Return spring	11	O-ring	16	Input shaft bearing
6	Spring seat				

6.5   Remove this lock bolt to unlock the release shaft bushing

6.6   From inside the bellhousing, push the release shaft out the left side far enough to remove the outer rubber grommet, bushing, inner rubber grommet and O-ring (if the O-ring doesn't come out, you can remove if from the shaft after pulling the shaft out)

6.7   To remove the release shaft, slide it back to the right and down at the same time (don't remove that snap-ring you see on the shaft – it serves as a stop to prevent the shaft from backing out of its right bushing)

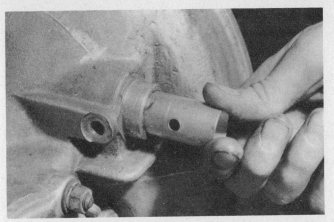

6.12   When you install the bushing, make sure the hole in the bushing is aligned with the hole in the transaxle case for the lock bolt

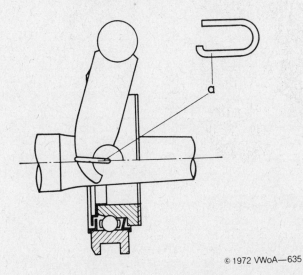

© 1972 VWoA—635

6.16   This is how the clips on the release bearing retain the release forks when they're properly engaged – the bent end of the clip is indicated at "a"

5   Remove the lock bolt for the release shaft bushing **(see illustration)**
6   Slide the release shaft to the left (driver's side) until the outer rubber grommet and the shaft bushing appear, then pull off the outer grommet, bushing, inner grommet and O-ring **(see illustration)**.
7   To remove the release shaft, slide it back to the right, and down **(see illustration)**.

Inspection

8   Wipe the release bearing with a clean rag. It's a sealed bearing, so don't immerse it in solvent. If the lubricant inside is diluted by solvent, the bearing is ruined. Inspect the bearing for obvious damage, wear and cracks. Hold the center of the bearing and rotate the outer portion while applying pressure. If the bearing is rough or noisy, replace it with a new one.
9   Clean the release lever, shaft and bushing in solvent. Inspect them for wear or other damage. Inspect the right (passenger's side) bushing too. Replace any worn parts. Never re-use the rubber grommets and O-ring for the left bushing. Their fit can't be duplicated once they've been compressed, so replace them.

10   Inspect the oil seal for the input shaft. If it's leaking, replace it (see Chapter 7, Part A).

Installation

Refer to illustrations 6.12 and 6.16

11   Lubricate the release shaft with lithium base grease and slide the inner rubber sleeve and O-ring onto the shaft and, from inside the bellhousing, carefully slide the shaft into the hole in the bellhousing. Make sure you don't damage the rubber grommet or O-ring.
12   Lubricate the left bushing and slide it into place **(see illustration)**. Make sure the hole for the lock bolt in the bushing is aligned with the hole for the bolt in the transaxle case. Screw in the bolt. Make sure the cylindrical part of the bolt fits into the hole in the bushing. Install the outer rubber sleeve.
13   Install the spring seat, the return spring and the release lever. Install the lever snap-ring or pinch bolt.
14   If you're using a genuine VW release bearing, there may be a plastic coating on the thrust face (the ring around the side of the bearing that pushes against the release ring on the pressure plate). Remove this coating with medium sandpaper or emery cloth and apply a thin coat of moly-base grease.
15   Lightly lubricate the contact points between the fork and the bearing with grease. Slide the bearing onto the input shaft.
16   Install the retaining clips **(see illustration)**. The small bend in each clip must tightly grip the fork.
17   Install the clutch components, if removed (see Section 5).
18   Install the engine (see Chapter 2).

7   Rear axles – general information

All 1968 and earlier VW Beetles and Karmann Ghias (except the 1968 Automatic Stick Shift model) are equipped with swing axles, which pivot only at their inner ends. When a rear wheel hits a bump or a dip, the axle swings up or down in an arc with the transaxle at its center.
The swing axle assembly consists of a pair of axle tubes, the outer ends of which are attached to spring plates (kind of like trailing arms that are able to flex). The axleshafts inside these axle tubes are attached to the differential side gears via spade-type universal joints. Their outer ends ride in bearings, which are lubricated by oil from the transaxle which sloshes into the axle tubes. The rubber boot at the inner end of axle tube prevents lubricant from leaking out.
The 1968 Automatic Stick Shift model and all 1969 and later models are equipped with double-jointed driveaxles which – because of the constant velocity (CV) joints attached to each end – can pivot at either end. The rear wheels have a slight negative camber, which increases with a load or during cornering.

8

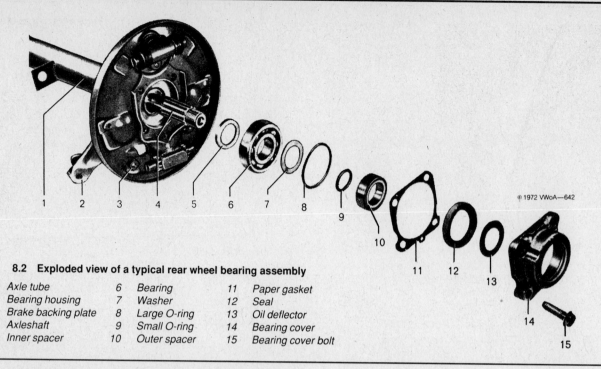

8.2   Exploded view of a typical rear wheel bearing assembly

1	Axle tube	6	Bearing	11	Paper gasket
2	Bearing housing	7	Washer	12	Seal
3	Brake backing plate	8	Large O-ring	13	Oil deflector
4	Axleshaft	9	Small O-ring	14	Bearing cover
5	Inner spacer	10	Outer spacer	15	Bearing cover bolt

The driveaxle assembly consists of a pair of axleshafts with CV joints at each end. The inner CV joints are attached to the flanges of the differential side gears and the outer CV joints are bolted to the flanges on the inner ends of the stub axles for the wheels. Both inner and outer CV joints are removable and rebuildable.

8   Oil seal and wheel bearing – replacement

Swing axle models

Refer to illustrations 8.2, 8.5, 8.6, 8.7, 8.8a, 8.8b, 8.8c, 8.9, 8.10 and 8.12

1   Remove the brake drum and the brake shoes (see Chapter 9).

2   Remove the bearing cover bolts. Remove the cover, the paper gasket, the oil deflector and the seal **(see illustration)**.

3   Remove the spacer, the two sealing rings and the large washer.

4   Detach the brake line (see Chapter 9) and remove the brake backing plate.

5   VW recommends that the rear wheel bearings be removed with a hydraulic press, but you can fabricate an inexpensive puller in less than an hour. Obtain a pair of 3/8-inch diameter bolts at least six inches long. Cut the heads off with a hacksaw and carve out notches near the unthreaded end of each bolt with a round file **(see illustration)**. Then, get a 3/16-inch thick steel plate, about six inches long by two inches wide. Insert the hooked ends of the bolts into position between the inner and outer races as shown, lay the plate across their opposite (threaded) ends and mark where they hit the plate. Drill out two holes for the bolts, add washers and nuts and your puller is ready! Hook it up as shown and remove the bearing. Remove the inner spacer and set it aside.

6   Install the inner spacer **(see illustration)**.

7   Install the new bearing with the sealed side facing the transaxle and the open side (numbers on the outer race) facing out **(see illustration)**. Use a brass drift to drive the new bearing into place. Start it onto the axleshaft by tapping all the way around the inner race. When the bearing reaches the axle housing, start tapping on the outer race as well. Alternate your taps between the inner and outer races until the bearing is fully seated.

8   Install the large O-ring, washer and small O-ring **(see illustrations)**, then smear the O-rings with a film of oil. **Note:** *Make sure all the parts are absolutely clean. Always use new O-rings. You can re-use the large washer if it's clean and rust free. Inspect the spacer carefully. It must not be scored, cracked or rusty.*

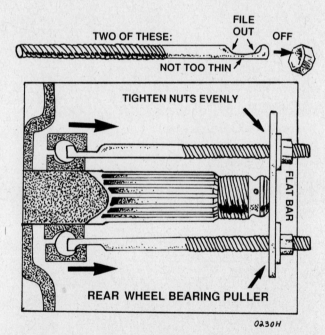

8.5   Take two 3/8-inch diameter bolts about six inches long, cut off the heads and notch the unthreaded ends as shown, then drill two holes in a six-inch by two-inch by 3/16-inch plate – insert the notched ends of the bolts between the races with the notches facing the outer race, install the plate, washers and nuts and pull off the rear wheel bearing

9   Install the brake backing plate **(see illustration)**, making sure the large O-ring doesn't slip off the bearing. Attach the brake line (see Chapter 9).

10   Place a new seal in position, square with the bore in the bearing cover **(see illustration)**, and drive it into place with a seal driver or a hammer and a flat piece of wood.

11   Slip the outer spacer onto the axleshaft. Push or tap it into place

8.6 Install the inner spacer

8.7 Install the rear wheel bearing

8.8a Install the large O-ring onto the bearing

8.8b Install the washer

8.8c Install the small O-ring

8.9 Install the brake backing plate

8.10 Place the bearing cover on a block of wood, position the new seal – numbers facing up, open side facing down – square with the recessed bore in the cover and carefully tap the seal into place

8.12 Be careful when you install the bearing cover, or you could easily damage the seal lip on the axleshaft splines

against the new bearing. Lubricate the outside of the spacer with a little oil to protect the sealing lip of the new bearing cover seal. Also lubricate the lip of the seal.

12 Place a new paper gasket in position and install the bearing cover **(see illustration)**. Make sure the oil drain hole in the cover faces down. Tighten the bearing cover bolts to the torque listed in this Chapter's Specifications. **Caution:** *When you slip the bearing cover over the end of the axleshaft, make sure you don't damage the seal lip on the shaft splines.*

13 Install the brake shoes and the brake drum (see Chapter 9).

14 Check the transaxle lubricant and refill if necessary (see Chapter 1).

15 Adjust and bleed the brakes (see Chapter 9).

Driveaxle models

16 Remove the diagonal arm (see Chapter 10) and take it to a dealer service department or other repair shop. A press and a number of special adapters are necessary to replace the bearings, bushings and spacers inside the diagonal arm.

8

9.4   Apply a thin coat of sealing compound to the mating surfaces of the boot

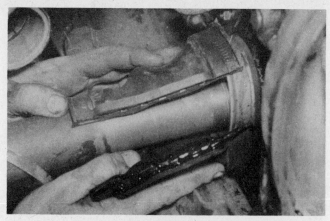

9.5   Don't get any oil on the sealing compound when you install the new boot

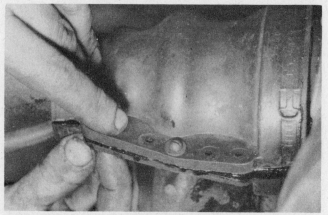

9.6a   Pinch the mating surfaces along the seam together, then install the screws, washers and nuts – don't overtighten them or the boot will leak

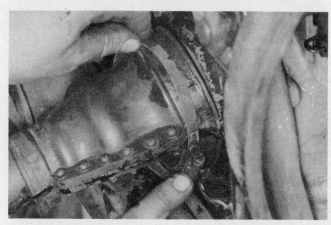

9.6b   Seat the hose clamps and tighten them securely

4   Apply a thin layer of sealing compound to the mating surfaces of the new boot (**see illustration**).
5   Carefully slip the new boot into place (**see illustration**). Don't get oil on the mating surfaces of the seam.
6   Make sure the axle tube is level and the boot isn't distorted, then squeeze the mating surfaces together at the seam and install the screws, washers and nuts (**see illustration**). The seam of the boot should point to the front or rear of the vehicle – not straight up. Install the hose clamps at each end (**see illustration**). **Caution:** *Overtightening the fasteners will distort the boot and cause leaks, so use discretion.*
7   Remove the jackstands and lower the vehicle.

---

10   Swing axle – removal, inspection and installation

Removal

Refer to illustrations 10.6a, 10.6b and 10.8
Note: *You can remove and install the axle tubes and axleshafts with the transaxle installed in the vehicle, but VW doesn't recommend it. In order to determine the clearance at the inner end of the axle tube, you need to be able to swing the axle tube around freely. That's difficult to do with the transaxle installed on the vehicle. It's also a struggle to install new gaskets or shims from under the vehicle without damaging them. Finally, it's almost impossible to prevent dirt from getting into the differential.*

1   Remove the engine (see Chapter 2).
2   Remove the brake drums and brake shoes (see Chapter 9).
3   Remove the bearing cover, brake backing plate and wheel bearing (see Section 8).
4   Drain the transaxle lubricant (see Chapter 1).

10.6a   Remove the six nuts on the axle tube retainer

17   Install the diagonal arm (see Chapter 10) after the bearings are installed.

---

9   Rear axle boots (swing axle models) – replacement

Refer to illustrations 9.4, 9.5, 9.6a and 9.6b
1   Raise the rear of the vehicle and place it securely on jackstands.
2   Remove the hose clamps from both ends of the old boot and cut it off (don't bother to remove the screws that attach the seam).
3   Wipe off the axle tube and axle tube retainer.

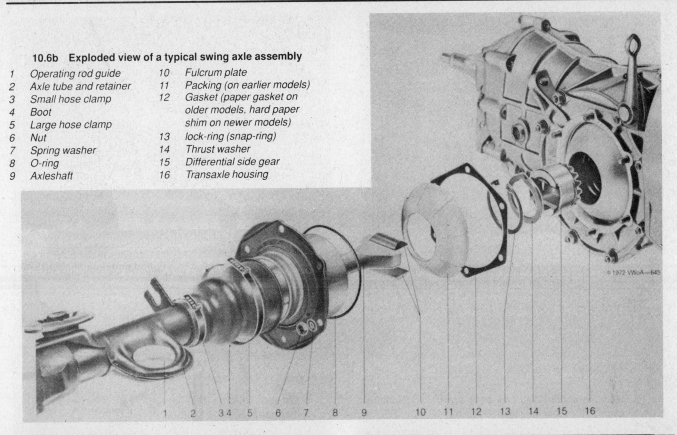

10.6b Exploded view of a typical swing axle assembly

1	Operating rod guide	10	Fulcrum plate
2	Axle tube and retainer	11	Packing (on earlier models)
3	Small hose clamp	12	Gasket (paper gasket on older models, hard paper shim on newer models)
4	Boot		
5	Large hose clamp		
6	Nut	13	lock-ring (snap-ring)
7	Spring washer	14	Thrust washer
8	O-ring	15	Differential side gear
9	Axleshaft	16	Transaxle housing

10.8   Reach through the final drive cover with a pair of snap-ring pliers and remove the lock-ring (snap-ring) that secures the axleshaft and side gear in the differential

10.17   Using a feeler gauge of the correct thickness, measure the thickness between the rounded ends of the flat-bladed tip of the axleshaft and the inner diameter of the differential side gear

5   Remove the transaxle (see Chapter 7, Part A).

6   Remove the nuts on the axle tube retainer (**see illustration**) and slip the axle tube, boot and retainer off the axleshaft (**see illustration**).

7   On 1961 through 1967 models, remove the plastic packing and the paper gasket. On later models, remove the hard paper shims and O-ring. Count the number of shims and write it down.

8   Using a pair of snap-ring pliers, remove the large lock-ring (snap-ring) that locks the axleshaft and side gear into the differential (**see illustration**).

9   Remove the differential side gear thrust washer and pull the axleshaft out.

10   Remove the differential side gear and the fulcrum plates from the differential housing.

11   Drive the lock pin out of the housing for the axleshaft bearing at the other end of the shaft.

12   Loosen the axle boot clamps.

13   Take the axle tube to an automotive machine shop and have the bearing housing pressed off, if necessary.

Inspection

Refer to illustrations 10.17, 10.18a, 10.18b, 10.20a and 10.20b

14   Clean all axleshaft parts and the axle tube retainer seat on the final drive cover with solvent.

15   Inspect the axle boot for damage and replace it if necessary.

16   Inspect the axleshaft, differential side gear, thrust washer and lock-ring for damage or wear. Replace any damaged parts.

17   If the clearance between the flat-bladed inner end of each axleshaft and the differential side gear is inadequate, axle noise or seizure can result. Measure the clearance between the rounded portions of the inner end of the axleshaft and the differential side gear (**see illustration**). Compare

8

10.18a   Install the old fulcrum plates between the flat sides of the axleshaft tip and the differential side gear, . . .

10.18b   . . . and, using a feeler gauge of the correct thickness, measure the clearance between the axleshaft and the fulcrum plates

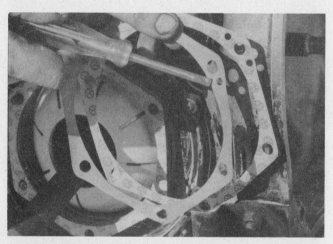

10.20a   The paper gaskets are identified by means of holes punched into them: one hole indicates a 0.004-inch thickness; two holes indicate an 0.008-inch thickness

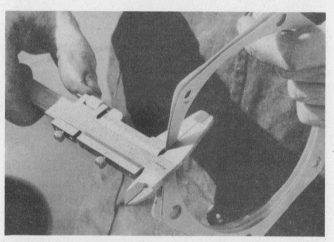

10.20b   Use a vernier caliper (or a micrometer) to measure the thickness of the original combination of paper gaskets or hard paper shims that you removed, then try to duplicate that same thickness with an assortment of new gaskets/shims

your measurements with the clearance listed in the Specifications at the beginning of this Chapter. If the clearance is outside the specified clearance, you'll have to replace the axleshaft and differential side gear as a matched set. There are three sets available and they're color coded yellow, blue or pink. The gear set color code is painted in a recess on the gear; the axleshaft has a painted ring six inches from the end. Make sure the axleshaft and gear colors match.

18   Measure the clearance between the flat portions of the shaft and the fulcrum plates **(see illustrations)**. Compare your measurements with the clearance listed in the Specifications at the beginning of this Chapter. If the clearance is excessive, replace the fulcrum plates. New standard size and oversize fulcrum plates are available.

19   Have the axleshafts checked for runout by an automotive machine shop. If it's excessive, replace them.

20   The concave inner end of the axle tube pivots up or down on the convex surface of the final drive cover. On earlier models, a plastic packing between the two acts as an extra bearing surface; on later models, the packing is eliminated. Either way, the clearance between the axle tube and the final drive cover must be within a range of zero to 0.008 inch (0.2 mm) clearance. The number and thickness of paper gaskets or hard paper shims between the axle boot retainer and the final drive cover determine how much clearance is available. If the clearance is too small, the swing axle can't move up or down smoothly; if there's too much clearance, the axleshaft will have too much endplay. The trick is to determine how many

paper gaskets or hard shims to use with the retainer. There's really no accurate way to measure axleshaft endplay at home. The best practice is to use the exact same number and size of paper gaskets and hard shims as you removed, then move the swing axle through every possible angle of motion and verify that it feels firm but doesn't stick or jam. If the swing axle feels hard to move, substitute a thicker gasket or add another; if it moves too freely, remove a gasket or substitute a thinner one. The thickness of a gasket is indicated by the number of holes punched in it: One hole indicates a 0.004 inch (0.1 mm) thickness; two holes indicate an 0.008 inch (0.2 mm) thickness **(see illustration)**. Use a vernier caliper or micrometer to measure the thickness of various assortments of gaskets or shims **(see illustration)**.

Installation

Refer to illustrations 10.22a, 10.22b, 10.22c, 10.23, 10.24, 10.25a and 10.25b

21   Make sure all seating surfaces are clean and lubricated with clean oil, then have the bearing housing pressed onto the axle tube at an automotive machine shop.

22   Install the differential side gear, axleshaft and thrust washer into the the differential housing and secure them with the lock-ring **(see illustrations)**.

23   Install the plastic packing, if equipped **(see illustration)**.

10.22a   Insert the differential side gear and axleshaft through the final drive cover and into the differential – push them in until the side gear meshes with the spider gears in the differential . . .

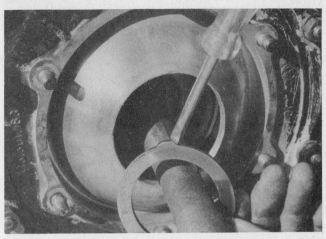

10.22b   . . . slide the thrust washer into place against the outer face of the side gear . . .

10.22c   . . . and install the lock-ring (snap-ring) – make sure it seats properly into its groove in the axle bore of the differential

10.23   Install the plastic packing (older models)

10.24   Install the paper gaskets or hard paper shims

10.25a   Slide the axle tube, boot and retainer onto the axleshaft

10.25b   Make sure the axle tube is installed with the notch in the bearing housing facing up and the boss for the shock absorber facing down

8

24   Install the paper gaskets or hard paper shims **(see illustration)**.
25   Slide the axle tube, boot and retainer onto the axleshaft **(see illustration)**. Install the retainer nuts and washers and tighten the nuts to the torque listed in this Chapter's Specifications. Install the hose clamp for the outer end of the boot but don't tighten it until the transaxle/swing axle as-

sembly is installed. **Note:** *The axle tubes aren't interchangeable. If you removed both axle tubes, make sure the notch in each bearing housing faces up and the shock absorber mounting boss faces forward and down* **(see illustration)**.
26   Install the transaxle and swing axle assembly (see Chapter 7, Part A).

11.3   To remove a driveaxle, simply unbolt the inner and outer CV joints from the final drive flange and the stub axle, respectively (outer CV joint shown)

12.4   Use a hammer and punch to dislodge the boot collar from the CV joint

12.5   Mark the CV joint component relationship before disassembly

12.6   Use snap-ring pliers to expand the snap-ring and lift it out of the groove

12.7   Hold the CV joint securely and push the axleshaft out with your thumbs

12.8a   Remove the concave washer by working it up the shaft with pliers

27   Install the wheel bearing, brake backing plate and bearing cover (see Section 8).
28   Fill the transaxle with clean lubricant (see Chapter 1).
29   Install the brake drums and brake shoes (see Chapter 9).
30   Bleed and adjust the brake system (see Chapter 9).
31   Install the engine (see Chapter 2). **Note:** *Before installing the engine, be sure to inspect the needle bearing in the flywheel gland nut (see Chapter 2), the clutch components (see Section 5) and the release bearing (see Section 6).*

11   Driveaxles – removal and installation

Refer to illustration 11.3

1   Raise the rear of the vehicle and support it securely on jackstands.
2   Remove the rear wheel(s). (This isn't actually necessary, but it does make access to the outer CV joint bolts easier.)
3   Remove the CV joint bolts from the inner and outer CV joints. Detach

12.8b Slide the boot off

12.9 Tilt the inner race out of the outer race and separate them

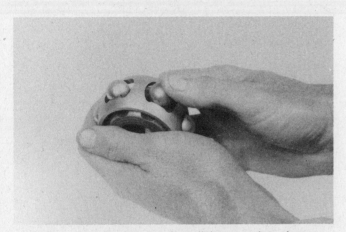

12.14 Press the bearings in until they snap into place

12.17 Use a hammer and deep socket to tap on the concave washer until it's at the base of the splines

the inner CV joint from the final drive flange and the outer CV joint from the stub axle flange **(see illustration)**. Grasp the driveaxle securely, supporting the CV joints, and lower the assembly from the vehicle. Be sure to note which CV joint bolts to the final drive flange and which one bolts to the stub axle flange. **Caution:** *Earlier models use Allen bolts; later models use spline-drive bolts. Don't try to loosen Allen bolts with spline-drive bits, or vice versa. You'll strip out the recessed centers of the bolts, making removal much more difficult.*

4   Inspect the CV joint dust boots for cracks and tears. If the boots are in good condition, the CV joints are probably clean and adequately lubricated. But if either boot is cracked, torn or leaking, remove it, clean, inspect and repack the CV joint and install a new boot. If a CV joint requires replacement, replace it (see Section 12).

5   Installation is the reverse of removal. Tighten the CV joint-to-flange bolts to the torque listed in this Chapter's Specifications. **Note:** *The threaded portions of all CV joint-to-flange bolts are the same, so Allen bolts are interchangeable with spline-drive bolts (just make sure you use the right bits!).*

6   Install the wheel(s) and lower the vehicle.

---

12   Constant Velocity (CV) joints – overhaul and boot replacement

Refer to illustrations 12.4, 12.5, 12.6, 12.7, 12.8a, 12.8b, 12.9, 12.14, 12.17, 12.18 and 12.19
Note: *The following procedure applies to either CV joint on either*

driveaxle.

1   Raise the rear of the vehicle and support it securely on jackstands.
2   Remove the driveaxle(s) (see Section 11).
3   Place the driveaxle on a clean working surface.
4   Use a punch and hammer to work around the outer circumference and dislodge the collar from the joint housing **(see illustration)**.
5   Paint or scribe across the components so they can be reinstalled in the same relationship **(see illustration)**.
6   Remove the snap-ring from the end of the axle **(see illustration)**.
7   Push the axleshaft out of the joint with your thumbs **(see illustration)**.
8   To remove the boot, note the direction in which it is installed, remove the concave washer from the axleshaft with pliers and then slide the boot off the end of the axleshaft **(see illustrations)**.
9   Align the ball bearings with the grooves in the outer race and separate the outer race from the inner **(see illustration)**.
10   Remove the balls from the race.
11   Wash the components in solvent and dry them thoroughly.
12   Inspect the balls, splines and races for damage, corrosion, wear and cracks.
13   If any of the components are not serviceable, the entire CV joint must be replaced with a new one.
14   Press the balls into the race until they snap into place **(see illustration)**.
15   Reassemble the inner and outer bearing races.
16   Install the boot on the shaft, carefully guiding it over the splines.
17   Slide the concave washer onto the shaft splines and press it into position with a suitable deep socket **(see illustration)**.

8

12.18　Press the grease into the boot with your fingers

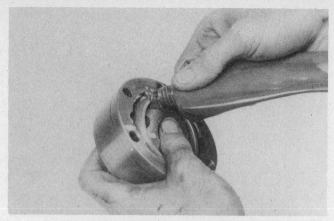

12.19　Force the grease into the rollers and races

18　Place a small amount of CV joint grease into the boot **(see illustration)**.

19　Pack the bearing assembly with CV joint grease **(see illustration)**.

20　Lubricate the splines with a small amount of grease and slide the CV joint into place, making sure the marks made during removal are aligned.

21　Secure the joint with the snap-ring and tap the boot collar onto the joint groove. Install the hose clamps and tighten them securely.

22　Install the driveaxle(s) (see Section 11).

23　Lower the vehicle.

Chapter 9 Brakes

Contents

Specifications

Brake fluid type .... See Chapter 1

Drum brakes
Minimum brake shoe lining thickness .... See Chapter 1

Disc brakes
Minimum disc thickness* .... 0.315 in (8.00 mm)
Disc runout (maximum) .... 0.007 in (0.2 mm)

Refer to marks cast or stamped into the disc (they supersede information printed here)

Torque specifications   Ft-lbs
Drum brakes
Brake backing plate-to-steering knuckle bolts 36
Wheel cylinder-to-backing plate 18
Rear axle nut
   Swing axle models 217
   Driveaxle models 253

Disc brakes
Allen bolts for caliper halves .... 14 to 18
Caliper mounting bolts 30

9

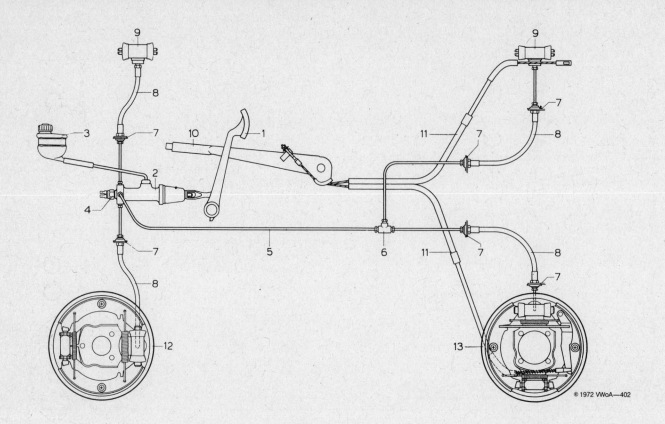

© 1972 VWoA—402

1.2a   Schematic of a typical single-circuit brake system (1966 and earlier models)

1	Brake pedal	6	Three-way connection	10	Parking brake lever
2	Master cylinder	7	Brake hose bracket	11	Cable and guide tube
3	Fluid reservoir	8	Brake hose	12	Front wheel brake
4	Brake light switch	9	Wheel cylinder	13	Rear wheel brake
5	Brake line				

1   General information

The vehicles covered by this manual are equipped with hydraulically operated front and rear brake systems. All models except later model Karmann Ghias have drum brakes at the front and rear. Later model Ghias have disc brakes at the front, drums at the rear.

Hydraulic system

Refer to illustrations 1.2a and 1.2b

The hydraulic system on 1966 and earlier models is a single-circuit design – one circuit operates both front and rear brakes **(see illustration)**. All 1967 and later models are equipped with dual-circuit systems **(see illustration)**. In the dual-circuit system, one circuit operates the front brakes and the other operates the rear brakes. The master cylinder has separate reservoirs for the two circuits, so in the event of a leak or failure in one hydraulic circuit, the other circuit will remain operative.

When you press the brake pedal down, it pushes on the piston(s) in the master cylinder, which increases brake fluid "pressure" by decreasing the interior volume of the brake system. Brake fluid isn't compressible, so it can't be squeezed into a smaller space. Instead, it "transmits" the force of your foot pressure against the brake pedal to a pair of moving pistons inside a wheel cylinder (on drum brakes) or two pistons inside a caliper (on disc brakes). When the pistons in the wheel cylinder move outward, they push the brake shoes against the inside of the brake drum. When the pistons in a brake caliper moves out of the caliper, they push the pads against the brake disc.

Brake lights and warning lights

A brake light switch on the front end of single-circuit master cylinders activates the brake lights when brake fluid pressure in the master cylinder increases. Dual-circuit master cylinders have two switches to ensure that the lights still work even if one circuit fails. Circuit failure is indicated on the instrument cluster by a red warning light. On early dual-circuit master cylinders, the light is activated by a switch controlled by two small pistons in an auxiliary chamber in the master cylinder. On 1972 and later models, the auxiliary chamber and extra switch are eliminated and the warning light is controlled by the brake light switches.

Parking brake

The parking brake system consists of a lever between the front seats, an actuating lever on each rear brake shoe and the two cables connecting the parking brake lever to the levers on the rear shoes. When the lever is pulled up, it pulls on the two cables, which in turn pull the levers on the rear brake shoes. When the lower ends of these levers are pulled forward, they move connecting links that push the front shoes against the drum.

The parking brake should be adjusted whenever the rear brake shoes have worn enough to allow you to raise the lever five clicks without noticeable braking action. Although the compensating lever on top of the parking

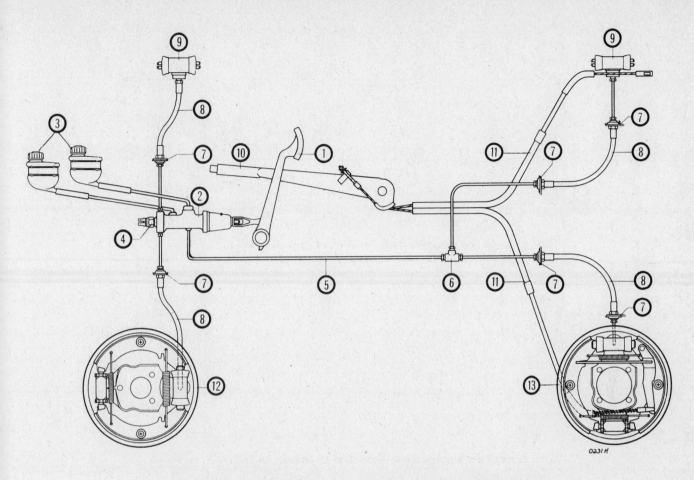

1.2b Schematic of a typical dual-circuit brake system (1967 and later models)

1	Brake pedal	6	Three-way connection	10	Parking brake lever
2	Master cylinder	7	Brake hose bracket	11	Cable and guide tube
3	Fluid reservoirs	8	Brake hose	12	Front wheel brake
4	Brake light switch	9	Wheel cylinder	13	Rear wheel brake
5	Brake line				

brake lever makes up for some of the difference in adjustment between the left and right cables, it's critical that the cables be adjusted so that the lever is horizontal when the parking brake lever is applied. If the rear brake shoes are adjusted properly but the compensating lever isn't horizontal after adjustment of the parking brake cables, one cable may be stretching and – if left in service – will eventually break.

After completing any operation involving disassembly of any part of the brake system, always test drive the vehicle to check for proper braking performance before resuming normal driving. When testing the brakes, perform the tests on a clean, dry, flat surface. Conditions other than these can lead to inaccurate test results. Test the brakes at various speeds with both light and heavy pedal pressure. The vehicle should stop evenly without pulling to one side or the other. Avoid locking the brakes because this slides the tires and diminishes braking efficiency and control of the vehicle.

Tires, vehicle load and front-end alignment – all these factors affect braking performance.

2 Drum brake shoes – replacement and adjustment

Warning: *The dust created by the brake system may contain asbestos, which is harmful to your health. Never blow it out with compressed air and*

don't inhale any of it. Wear an OSHA-approved filtering mask when working on the brakes. Do not, under any circumstances, use petroleum-based solvents to clean brake parts. Use brake cleaner or denatured alcohol only. Always replace drum brake shoes in pairs (front or rear) – never replace the shoes on only one wheel. Work on one brake assembly at a time to avoid mixing up parts.

Caution: *Whenever the brake shoes are replaced, the retractor and hold-down springs should also be replaced. Due to the continuous heating/cooling cycle that the springs are subjected to, they lose their tension over a period of time and may allow the shoes to drag on the drum and wear at a faster rate than normal. When replacing the brake shoes, use only high quality, nationally recognized brand-name parts.*

Replacement

Refer to illustrations 2.2a, 2.2b and 2.3a through 2.3u

1   Loosen the wheel lug bolts, raise the front or rear of the vehicle and place it securely on jackstands. Block the wheels on the ground. If you're removing the front wheels, apply the parking brake to keep the vehicle from rolling. Remove the wheels.

2   On the left front wheel, remove the clip which secures the speedom-

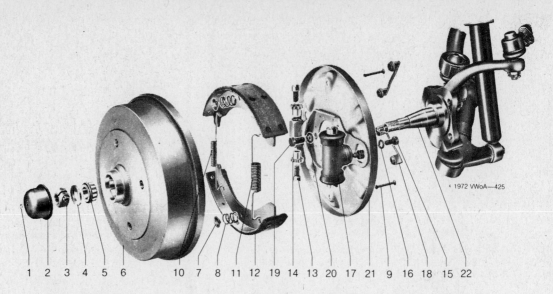

2.2a   Exploded view of a typical front drum brake assembly on a torsion bar model

1	C-clip for speedometer cable (left side only)	9	Retaining pin	16	Lock washer
2	Dust cap	10	Return spring	17	Wheel cylinder
3	Clamp nut	11	Return spring	18	Sealing plugs
4	Thrust washer	12	Brake shoe	19	Bolt
5	Wheel bearing	13	Adjusting screw	20	Lock washer
6	Brake drum	14	Adjusting nut (star wheel)	21	Backing plate
7	Spring cup	15	Wheel cylinder mounting bolt	22	Spindle/steering knuckle assembly
8	Shoe retaining (or hold-down) spring				

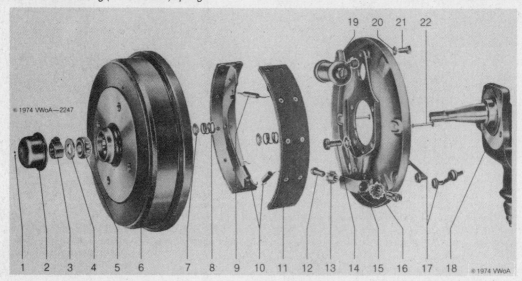

2.2b   Exploded view of a typical front drum brake assembly on a Super Beetle model

1	E-clip for speedometer cable (left side only)	8	Shoe retaining spring	16	Backing plate
2	Dust cap	9	Shoe retaining spring	17	Rubber plugs
3	Clamp nut	10	Brake shoe	18	Spindle/steering knuckle assembly
4	Thrust washer	11	Brake shoe	19	Wheel cylinder
5	Outer wheel bearing	12	Adjuster screw	20	Lock washer
6	Brake drum	13	Adjuster nut (star wheel)	21	Wheel cylinder mounting bolt
7	Spring cup	14	Backing plate bolt	22	Shoe retaining pin
		15	Lock washer		

eter cable to the left dust cap **(see illustrations)**. On all wheels, pry off the dust cap that protects the wheel bearing.

3   Follow the accompanying photos (illustrations 2.3a through 2.3j for the front brakes, 2.3k through 2.3u for the rears) for the brake shoe replacement procedure. Follow the photos in sequence and read each caption.

2.3a   If the front brake drum is binding on the brake shoes, insert a screwdriver through the adjustment hole in the drum, turn the adjuster until the shoes are no longer binding . . .

2.3b   . . . and pull off the drum

2.3c   A typical front brake shoe assembly on a torsion bar model

2.3d   A typical front brake shoe assembly on a Super Beetle model

2.3e   Remove the smaller rear return spring with a pair of pliers (wear a pair of safety goggles, just in case a spring gets away from you)

2.3f   Remove the hold-down cups and springs – a special tool (available at most auto parts stores) can be used to push down on the cups and turn them to align the slot in the cup with the blade on the pin, but a pair of pliers can be used also

2.3g   Pull the rear end of the lower shoe out of the slot in the adjuster . . .

2.3h   . . . then pull the front end out of the slot in the wheel cylinder, remove the front return spring and the upper shoe

2.3i   Even if the wheel cylinder doesn't appear to be leaking, it's a good idea to pull the pistons and seals out and inspect them while the brake is disassembled – if they're rusted, pitted or scored, replace or rebuild the wheel cylinder (see Section 3)

9

2.3j   If the adjuster screws are rusted or pitted, replace them – to install the new brake shoes, reverse the previous Steps

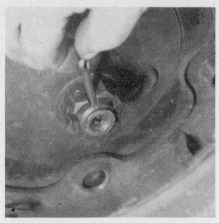

2.3k   To begin the rear brake shoe replacement procedure, remove the cotter pin from the castle nut on the rear axle

2.3l   Break the rear axle nut loose with a breaker bar

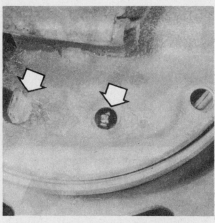

2.3m   If the drum is difficult to remove, retract the brake shoes by turning the adjuster star wheels (arrows – the one on the left is still covered by the rubber plug) – on this model, the adjuster hole is in the backing plate; on some models, it's in the drum itself

2.3n   Remove the drum and inspect the braking surface

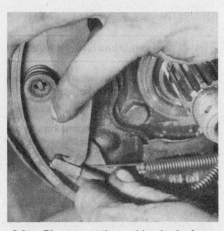

2.3o   Disconnect the parking brake from the lever

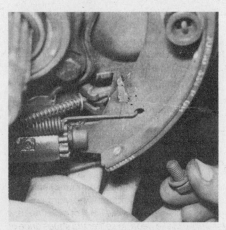

2.3p   Disconnect the bolt that attaches the parking brake cable guide to the backing plate (the bolt's on the rear of the backing plate)

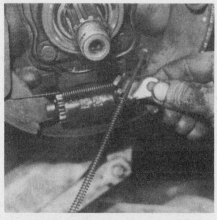

2.3q   Pull the parking brake cable guide and cable through the backing plate and detach the cable from the guide

2.3r   Disconnect the lower return spring with a pair of pliers (wear a pair of safety goggles to protect your eyes just in case the spring gets away from you)

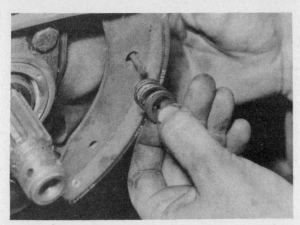

2.3s   Remove the brake shoe hold-down cups and springs – a special tool (available at most auto parts stores) can be used to push down on the cups and turn them to align the slot in the cup with the blade on the pin, but a pair of pliers can be used also

2.3t   Remove the brake shoes, connecting link and upper return spring

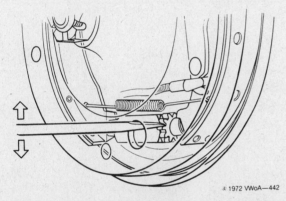

2.9   Rotate the wheel and turn the adjuster nut (star wheel) until the brake shoe drags on the drum slightly, then turn the star wheel in the opposite direction three or four clicks

4   Before reinstalling the drum, inspect it for cracks, score marks, deep scratches and hard spots, which will appear as small discolored areas. Remove hard spots with fine emery cloth. If that doesn't do it, or if any of the other conditions described above are evident, have the drum turned by an automotive machine shop. **Note:** *Professionals recommend resurfacing the drums every time you do a brake job. Resurfacing eliminates the possibility of out-of-round drums. If the drums are worn so much that they can't be resurfaced without exceeding the maximum allowable diameter (stamped or cast into the drum), replace them. If you decide to skip resurfacing, remove the glazing from the surface with emery cloth or sandpaper, using a swirling motion.*

5   Install the brake drum. On front wheels, install the bearing, the thrust washer and the axle nut and adjust the bearing (see Chapter 1, Section 32).

6   Mount the wheel, hand tighten the lug bolts and lower the vehicle. Tighten the wheel lug bolts to the torque listed in the Chapter 1 Specifications. On rear wheels, tighten the axle nut to the torque listed in this Chapter's Specifications.

Adjustment

Refer to illustration 2.9

7   Raise the vehicle and support it securely on jackstands. If you're adjusting the rear brakes, release the parking brake.

8   Depress the brake pedal several times, using firm pressure, to center the brake shoes in the drum. On 1969 and earlier models, rotate the wheel until the hole in the brake drum is aligned with one of the star wheel adjust-

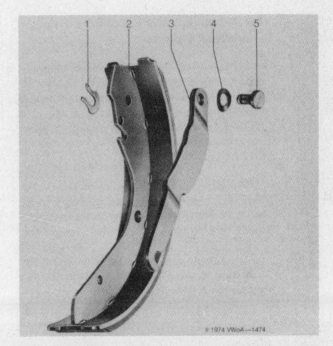

2.3u   Pry apart the ends of the retaining clip and transfer the parking brake lever to the new rear brake shoe – to install the new shoes, reverse Steps 2.3k through 2.3t

1	Retaining clip	4	Spring washer
2	Brake shoe	5	Pin
3	Parking brake lever		

ers. On 1970 and later models, remove the rubber plugs from the brake backing plate.

9   Using a brake adjusting tool or a screwdriver, turn the star wheel of the adjuster, while rotating the wheel, until the brake shoe slightly drags on the drum **(see illustration)**. **Note:** *If the brakes are way out of adjustment, it may be necessary to press on the brake pedal to center the shoes once or twice during the adjustment procedure.* Now, turn the star wheel in the opposite direction three or four clicks so the wheel can turn freely.

10   Repeat Step 9 on the star wheel of the other brake shoe, then perform the adjustment procedure to the remaining wheels.

11   Check brake operation before driving the vehicle in traffic.

9

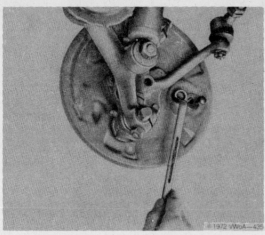

3.5a   To remove a front wheel cylinder, disconnect the brake line
fitting and remove the single mounting bolt

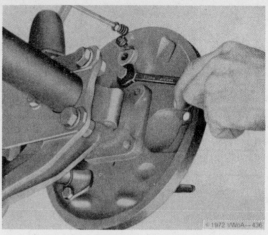

3.5b   To remove a rear wheel cylinder, disconnect the brake line
and remove the two mounting bolts

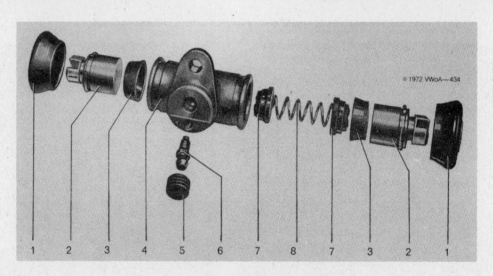

3.7   Exploded view of a typical wheel cylinder

1	Boot	3	Cup	5	Dust cap
2	Piston	4	Cylinder	6	Bleeder valve

7	Cup expander
8	Spring

---

3   Wheel cylinder – removal, overhaul and installation

Note: *If an overhaul is indicated (usually because of fluid leakage or sticky
operation) explore all options before beginning the job. New wheel cylinders are available, which makes this job quite easy. If it's decided to rebuild
the wheel cylinder, make sure that a rebuild kit is available before proceeding. Never overhaul or replace only one wheel cylinder – always rebuild or
replace them in pairs (front or rear).*

Removal

Refer to illustrations 3.5a and 3.5b

1   Loosen the wheel lugs nuts. Raise the front, or rear, of the vehicle and
support it securely on jackstands. Block the wheels still on the ground to
keep the vehicle from rolling. Remove the wheel(s).

2   Remove the brake drum and the brake shoes (see Section 2).

3   Remove all dirt and foreign material from around the wheel cylinder.

4   Unscrew the brake line fitting. Don't pull the brake line away from the
wheel cylinder.

5   Remove the wheel cylinder mounting bolt(s) **(see illustrations)**.

6   Detach the wheel cylinder from the brake backing plate and place it on
a clean workbench. Immediately plug the brake line to prevent fluid loss
and contamination. **Note:** *If the brake shoe linings are contaminated with
brake fluid, install new brake shoes.*

Overhaul

Refer to illustration 3.7

7   Remove the bleeder valve, cups, pistons, boots and spring assembly
from the wheel cylinder body **(see illustration)**.

8   Clean the wheel cylinder with brake fluid, denatured alcohol or brake
system cleaner. **Warning:** *Do not, under any circumstances, use petroleum-based solvents to clean brake parts!*

9   Use compressed air to remove excess fluid from the wheel cylinder
and to blow out the passages.

10   Check the cylinder bore for corrosion and score marks. Crocus cloth
can be used to remove light corrosion and stains, but the cylinder must be
replaced with a new one if the defects can't be removed easily, or if the
bore is scored.

11   Lubricate the new cups with brake fluid.

12   Assemble the wheel cylinder components. Make sure the cup lips
face in.

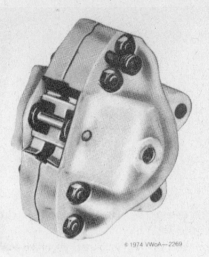

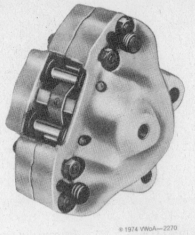

1971 and earlier models (ATE)   *1972 and 1973 models (ATE)*   *1973 and later models (Girling)*

4.4   The three different calipers used on Karmann Ghias

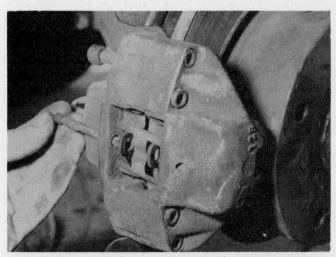

4.5   Knock the pad retaining pin(s) out with a hammer and drift, then pull them out of the caliper housing – be careful not to let the pad spreader spring fly out

4.6   Before you remove the pad spreader spring, make sure you note how it's installed

Installation

13   Place the wheel cylinder in position and install the bolt(s) loosely.
14   Connect the brake line, but don't tighten it yet. Tighten the wheel cylinder bolt(s) securely, then tighten the brake line fitting. Install the brake shoes and the brake drum (see Section 2).
15   Bleed the brakes (see Section 9).
16   Check brake operation before driving the vehicle in traffic.

---

4   Disc brake pads – replacement

Refer to illustration 4.4
Warning: *Disc brake pads must be replaced on both front wheels at the same time – never replace the pads on only one wheel. Also, the dust created by the brake system may contain asbestos, which is harmful to your health. Never blow it out with compressed air and don't inhale any of it. An approved filtering mask should be worn when working on the brakes. Do not, under any circumstances, use petroleum-based solvents to clean brake parts. Use brake cleaner or denatured alcohol only!*
Note: *When servicing the disc brakes, use only high quality, nationally recognized name brand pads.*

1   Remove the cover from the brake fluid reservoir. When you push the caliper pistons back into their bores, the fluid in the lines will back up into the reservoir and overflow, so remove some fluid with a syringe.
2   Loosen the wheel lug bolts, raise the front of the vehicle and support it securely on jackstands. Remove the front wheels.
3   Inspect the brake disc carefully as outlined in Section 6. If machining is necessary, follow the information in that Section to remove the disc, at which time the pads can be removed from the calipers as well.
4   Work on one brake assembly at a time, using the assembled brake for reference if necessary. Refer to the accompanying illustration to determine which kind of caliper the vehicle you are working on has **(see illustration)**.

ATE calipers
Refer to illustrations 4.5, 4.6, 4.8, 4.13 and 4.15
Note: *1971 and earlier ATE calipers have only one retaining pin; 1972 and 1973 units, which were redesigned to offer greater brake pad area, use two pins. The two versions are otherwise virtually identical.*
5   Knock the pad retaining pin(s) out of the caliper housing with a hammer and drift punch **(see illustration)**. Discard them and buy new pins.
6   Note the orientation of the pad spreader spring in the caliper housing, then remove it **(see illustration)**. Discard the spring and buy a new one (see Note in Step 15).

9

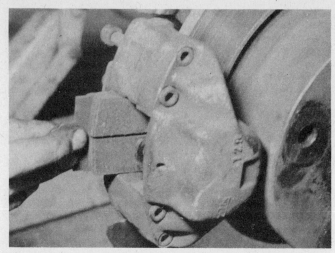

4.8   Note how the brake pads are oriented in the caliper, then as you remove each of them, depress its respective piston back into the caliper to make room for the new pad

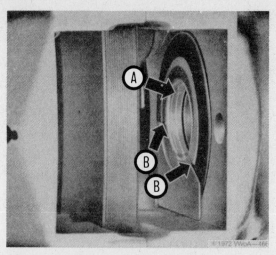

4.13   After the brake pad cavity in the caliper housing is cleaned, install the retaining plate by pushing the circular part (a) into the piston crown – make sure the plate is situated below the relieved portion of the crown (b)

7   Using a pair of adjustable pliers, grip the upper edge of each brake pad backing plate and the caliper housing and squeeze the pistons back into their bores. If you don't do this now, there won't be enough room between the pistons and the brake disc to install new pads. If you can't push the piston back into its bore with both pads in place, go to the next Step. **Caution:** *If you intend to re-use the same pads – for instance, if you're simply removing the pads so you can remove the caliper – be sure to mark the pads now. If you reverse them during installation, uneven braking will result.*

8   If you had trouble depressing either or both pistons in the last Step, pull one brake pad out of the brake caliper **(see illustration)** and try to depress the piston for that pad with adjustable pliers, a large screwdriver or a pry bar. Don't pull out both pads at once. One pad must remain installed while you depress the piston on the opposite side, or else one piston will protrude from its bore when you depress the other piston. After you've depressed one piston all the way into the caliper, install a new pad on that side, pull out the other old pad and repeat the above process.

9   Inspect the brake pads for cracks, chunking, oily film deposits and separation from their backing plates. If any of these conditions are evident, replace them. Measure the pads for wear (see Chapter 1). Replace them if they're at or below the minimum allowable thickness.

10   Inspect the brake disc for wear. If it's worn or damaged, have it machined or replace it (see Section 6).

11   Remove the piston retaining plates from the pistons (see exploded view in Section 5). Inspect the cavity for hard accumulations of dirt and rust. Clean the seating and sliding surfaces of the brake pads in the caliper with brake system cleaner (the seating surface is the end of the piston which pushes against the brake pad backing plate; the sliding surfaces are the upper and lower ends of the brake pad cavity against which the edges of the pads slide during operation).

12   Inspect the rubber piston seals. If either of them is cracked, hard or swollen, remove the caliper and replace it (see Section 5).

13   Note how the crown of each piston is relieved (cut out). Make sure this relieved portion is aligned correctly to receive the retaining plate. If it isn't, rotate the piston a little with a pair of pliers. To install the retaining plate, press the circular part (a) firmly into the piston crown **(see illustration)**. When installed properly, the retaining plate lies below the relieved portion of the piston crown (b) as shown.

14   Install the pads. If you're re-using the old pads, make sure you install them in their original locations to prevent uneven braking.

15   On single-pin calipers, install the pad retainer spring, depress the spring with your thumb and insert a new pad retaining pin. On later two-pin units, insert the new lower retaining pin, install a new pad retainer spring, depress the top of the spreader spring with your thumb and insert the new upper pin. Push the new pin(s) into place by hand as far as possible, then

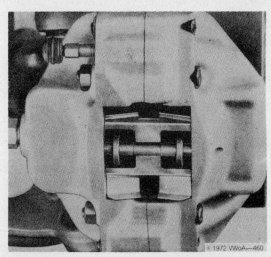

4.15   The pad spreader spring on 1971 and later ATE calipers is wider at the bottom to reduce rattling caused by play between the pads and the caliper housing – you can also retrofit this spreader spring onto older calipers – just make sure you install it with the wide part at the bottom as shown

use a small hammer to tap the pin(s) the rest of the way. DON'T use a punch – it could shear off the shoulder(s) of the pin(s). **Warning:** *DO NOT grease the retaining pins. Heat produced by braking can melt the lubricant and cause it to flow onto the pads or disc.* **Note:** *Later single-pin calipers have better spreader springs than earlier units. The bottom half of the spring is wider to provide more support, which reduces rattling noises caused by the play between the brake pads and caliper housing. You can use this spring on older calipers. Just be sure you install it with the wider part at the bottom* **(see illustration)**.

16   The remainder of installation is otherwise the reverse of removal. Pump the brake pedal several times to bring the pads into contact with the disc. Check the operation of the brakes before driving the vehicle in traffic.

Girling calipers

Refer to illustrations 4.17a, 4.17b, 4.21 and 4.24

17   Remove the locking clip **(see illustration)** from the upper leg of the U-shaped retaining pin, then pull out the pin **(see illustration)**. Make sure the spreader spring doesn't fly out.

18   Remove the pad spreader spring.

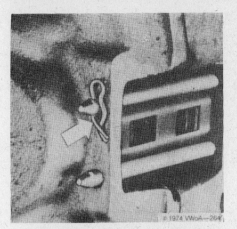

4.17a   Remove this locking clip from the U-shaped retaining pin . . .

4.17b   . . . and pull the retaining pin out of the caliper housing

4.21   Rotate the pads 90-degrees in the caliper and remove them

19   Remove the caliper (see Section 5) and hang it from the steering tie-rod with a piece of wire.

20   Depress the pistons into their bores (see Steps 7 and 8 above).

21   Rotate the brake pads 90-degrees in the caliper and remove them **(see illustration)**. **Warning:** *If you plan to reuse the same pads, be sure to mark them to ensure that they're installed on the same sides again. Changing their location will cause uneven braking.*

22   Remove the anti-squeal shims (thin plates that go between the pads and the pistons).

23   Inspect the brake pads, brake disc, disc pad cavity in the caliper and piston seals (see Steps 9 through 12 above).

24   Install the anti-squeal shims in the caliper with their arrows pointing in the same direction as forward wheel rotation **(see illustration)**.

25   Install the brake pads with the grooved surface facing the disc. If you're re-using the old pads, make sure you install them on the same sides as before.

26   Install the caliper (see Section 5).

27   Install a new pad spreader spring, the U-shaped retaining pin and a new locking clip. Bend the straight side of the locking clip so that it looks like the clip in illustration 4.17a.

28   Installation is otherwise the reverse of removal. Pump the brake pedal several times to bring the pads into contact with the disc. Check the operation of the brakes before driving the vehicle in traffic.

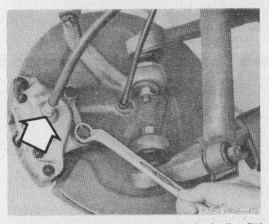

4.24   Install the anti-squeal shims in the caliper with their arrows pointing in the same direction as forward wheel rotation

---

5   Disc brake caliper – removal, overhaul and installation

Warning: *Dust created by the brake system may contain asbestos, which is harmful to your health. Never blow it out with compressed air and don't inhale any of it. An approved filtering mask should be worn when working on the brakes. Do not, under any circumstances, use petroleum-based solvents to clean brake parts. Use brake cleaner or denatured alcohol only!* **Note:** *If an overhaul is indicated (usually because of fluid leakage) explore all options before beginning the job. New and factory rebuilt calipers are available on an exchange basis, which makes this job quite easy. If it's decided to rebuild the calipers, make sure a rebuild kit is available before proceeding. Always rebuild the calipers in pairs – never rebuild just one of them.*

Removal

Refer to illustration 5.5

1   Remove the cover from the brake fluid reservoir, siphon off two-thirds of the fluid into a container and discard it.

2   Loosen the wheel lug bolts, raise the front of the vehicle and support it securely on jackstands. Remove the front wheels.

3   Inspect the caliper housing halves. If there are leaks along the seam, the O-rings surrounding the fluid pathways are leaking. If the caliper is an ATE unit **(see illustration 4.4)**, you can separate it into two halves and replace the O-rings after you take it off the vehicle. If the caliper is a Girling

5.5   To remove the caliper, disconnect the brake line fitting (arrow) and the mounting bolts (if you're only removing the caliper to get at the brake disc or some other component, it's not necessary to disconnect the brake line – just remove the caliper and hang it with a piece of wire)

unit, no O-rings are available, so you'll have to exchange the damaged caliper for a rebuilt unit or buy a new caliper.

4   If the caliper is an ATE unit, remove the brake pads (see Section 4).

5   Disconnect the brake hose fitting from the caliper **(see illustration)**. Have a rag handy to catch spilled fluid and wrap a plastic bag tightly

9

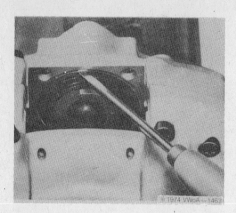

5.9a   Pry out each boot retaining ring with a small screwdriver

5.9b   Carefully pry out each piston boot with a pick or small screwdriver – be careful not to scratch the piston or the bore

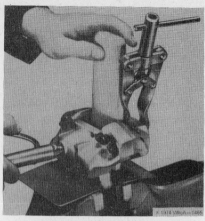

5.10   Lock one piston into place with a pair of adjustable or locking pliers, position a strip of wood (or several rags) between the two pistons, then apply compressed air to the inlet fitting

around the end of the hose to prevent fluid loss and contamination. **Note:** *Don't detach the brake hose from the caliper if you are only removing the caliper for access to other components. Remove the caliper and hang it from the underbody by a piece of wire. Don't let the caliper hang by the brake hose!*

6   Remove the two mounting bolts and detach the caliper from the vehicle.

7   If the caliper is a Girling unit, remove the brake pads (see Section 4).

Overhaul

Refer to illustrations 5.9a, 5.9b, 5.10, 5.11, 5.18 and 5.23

Note: *The illustrations for the following overhaul procedure depict an ATE caliper. Basically, overhaul of a Girling caliper is similar, with one important difference: You can separate an ATE unit into two halves to replace leaking O-rings, but DO NOT separate a Girling caliper. O-rings for the fluid pathways between the housing halves aren't available as spare parts. If fluid is leaking out the seams (see Step 3), replace the caliper with a new or rebuilt unit.*

8   Clean the exterior of the caliper with brake cleaner or denatured alcohol. Never use gasoline, kerosene or petroleum-based cleaning solvents. Place the mounting flange of the caliper in a bench vise. Use soft-jaws or clamp the flange between two pieces of wood to protect it from damage and prevent misalignment of the installed caliper.

9   Pry out the dust boot retaining rings and the dust boots with a small screwdriver **(see illustrations)**.

10   Lock one piston into place with a pair of adjustable or locking pliers, position a 1/4 to 3/8-inch thick wood block or several rags in the caliper as a cushion, then use compressed air to remove the piston from the caliper **(see illustration)**. Use only enough air pressure to ease the piston out of the bore. If the piston is blown out, even with the cushion in place, it may be damaged. **Warning:** *Never place your fingers in front of the piston in an attempt to catch or protect it when applying compressed air, as serious injury could occur.* **Note:** *Once a piston is removed, no air pressure can build up to remove the other piston, so service one piston, seal and bore at a time.*

11   Using a wood or plastic tool, remove the piston seal from the groove in the caliper bore **(see illustration)**. Metal tools may cause bore damage.

12   Clean the piston and the bore with brake system cleaner or denatured alcohol. Inspect the piston and bore for nicks, rust, loss of plating or other damage. If the piston is damaged, replace it. If the bore is slightly corroded or stained, lightly polish it with crocus cloth. If that doesn't clean it up, replace the caliper – the bore can't be honed.

13   Coat the piston bore and the new seal with clean brake fluid.

14   Install the new seal.

15   Lubricate the piston with clean brake fluid. Place the piston in position so it's square with the bore and try to push it into the bore with your thumbs. If it's difficult to depress, you can use a pair of adjustable pliers or a large

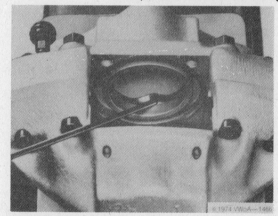

5.11   Using a non-metallic tool, carefully pry the piston seal from its groove in the caliper bore – make sure you don't scratch the surface of the bore

screwdriver to depress it. Just be SURE you don't cock the piston in its bore. Push it all the way in until it stops.

16   Repeat Steps 10 through 15 for the other piston, seal and bore.

17   If the caliper is an ATE unit and was leaking along its seam when you inspected it, the following sequence describes how to separate the two caliper halves and replace the O-rings. If the caliper is a Girling unit, skip this part and proceed to Step 25.

18   Remove the four Allen bolts which hold the two halves of the housing together and pull the two halves apart **(see illustration)**.

19   Remove the old O-rings.

20   Clean the caliper halves in brake system cleaner or denatured alcohol.

21   Install the new O-rings.

22   Using NEW Allen bolts and nuts, reattach the two caliper halves together. There are two long bolts and two short ones – the short ones go in the outer holes.

23   Check the alignment of the two halves, then tighten the four bolts, in the sequence shown **(see illustration)**, to the torque listed in this Chapter's Specifications.

24   Check the alignment of the two caliper halves again. If it's off, loosen the bolts, realign the two halves and retighten the bolts in the specified sequence.

25   Install a new dust boot and retaining ring on each piston.

Installation

26   If the caliper is a Girling unit, install the brake pads (see Section 4).

27   Install the caliper, a new lock plate and new caliper mounting bolts.

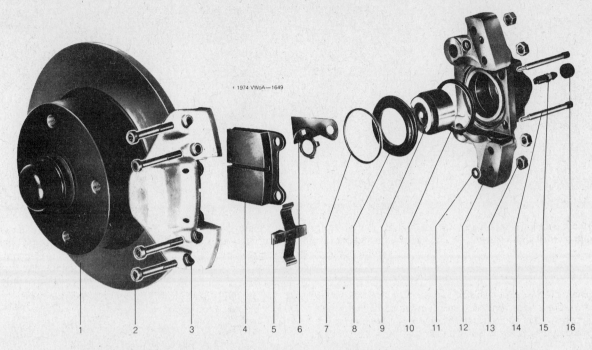

5.18   **Exploded view of a typical caliper assembly (later style ATE caliper shown, others similar)**

1   Brake disc
2   Allen bolt
3   Caliper outer housing
4   Brake pad
5   Pad spreader spring
6   Piston retaining plate

7   Dust boot retaining ring
8   Piston dust boot
9   Piston
10   Rubber seal
11   O-ring

12   Caliper inner housing
13   Nut
14   Brake pad retaining pin
15   Bleeder valve
16   Bleeder valve dust cap

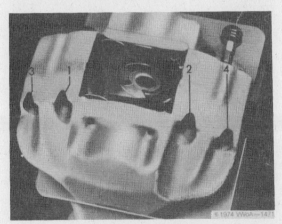

5.23   **When you tighten the four Allen bolts for the ATE caliper halves, tighten them evenly and gradually in this order, then check the alignment of the halves**

6.2   **After detaching the caliper, hang it from the tie-rod with a piece of wire – don't ever hang the caliper by the brake hose!**

Tighten the bolts to the torque listed in this Chapter's Specifications. Bend the tabs on the lock plate up to prevent the bolts from backing out.
28   If the caliper is an ATE unit, install the brake pads (see Section 4).
29   Reattach the brake line threaded fitting and tighten it securely.
30   Install the wheels and lower the vehicle. Tighten the lug bolts to the torque listed in the Chapter 1 Specifications.
31   Add brake fluid to the reservoir and bleed the brake system (see Section 9).
32   After the job has been completed, firmly depress the brake pedal a few times to bring the pads into contact with the disc.
33   Check the operation of the brakes before driving the vehicle in traffic.

6   Brake disc – inspection, removal and installation

Inspection
Refer to illustrations 6.2, 6.3, 6.4a, 6.4b and 6.5
1   Loosen the wheel lug bolts, raise the vehicle and support it securely on jackstands. Remove the wheel.
2   Remove the brake caliper (see Section 5). It's not necessary to disconnect the brake hose. After removing the caliper bolts, suspend the caliper out of the way with a piece of wire **(see illustration)**. Don't let the caliper hang by the hose and don't stretch or twist the hose.

6.3   The brake pads on this vehicle were obviously neglected, as they wore deep grooves into the disc – wear this severe will require replacement of the disc

6.4a   Use a dial indicator to check disc runout (this is the factory setup from ATE – an indicator with a magnetic base will work just as well)

6.4b   If you decide to skip machining, be sure to break the glaze on the disc surface with emery cloth or sandpaper

6.5   Check the thickness of the disc with a micrometer at several points

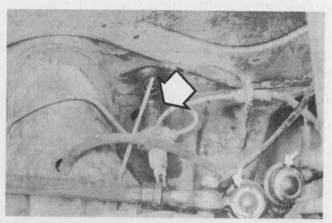

7.3   The master cylinder is located on the left side of the pan, bolted to the firewall

3   Inspect the disc surface for score marks and other damage (see illustration). Light scratches and shallow grooves indicate normal wear and aren't necessarily detrimental to brake operation. But if the disc has deep score marks – over 0.015-inch (0.38 mm) – remove the disc and have it refinished by an automotive machine shop. Be sure to check both sides of the disc. If you've noticed pulsating when applying the brakes, suspect disc runout. Be sure to check the wheel bearings to make sure they're properly adjusted (see Chapter 1).

4   To check disc runout, place a dial indicator at a point about 1/2-inch from the outer edge of the disc (see illustration). Set the indicator to zero and turn the disc. The indicator reading should not exceed the runout limit listed in this Chapter's Specifications. If it does, the disc needs refinishing (can be done by an automotive machine shop) or the wheel bearing is damaged or out of adjustment. Note: Professionals recommend resurfacing of brake discs regardless of the dial indicator reading (to produce a smooth, flat surface that will eliminate brake pedal pulsations and other undesirable symptoms related to questionable discs). At the very least, if you elect not to have the discs resurfaced, deglaze them with sandpaper or emery cloth (use a swirling motion to ensure a nondirectional finish) (see illustration).

5   The disc must not be machined to a thickness less than the minimum thickness listed in this Chapter's Specifications. The minimum thickness is also cast or stamped into the disc. The disc thickness can be checked with a micrometer (see illustration).

Removal

6   See Chapter 1, Section 32, for the hub/disc removal procedure.

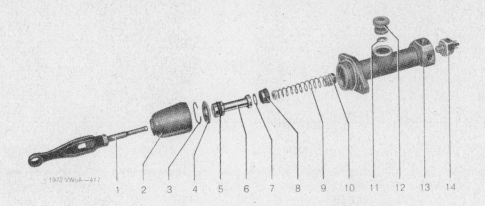

7.13   Exploded view of a typical single-circuit master cylinder

1	Pushrod	6	Piston	11	Washer for plug
2	Boot	7	Piston washer	12	Sealing plug
3	Lock ring	8	Primary cup	13	Cylinder housing
4	Stop washer	9	Return spring	14	Brake light switch
5	Secondary cup	10	Check valve		

Installation

7   Install the disc/hub assembly and adjust the wheel bearing (see Chapter 1).

8   Install the caliper (see Section 5) and brake pad assembly (see Section 4).

9   Install the wheel, then lower the vehicle to the ground. Tighten the lug bolts to the torque listed in the Chapter 1 Specifications. Depress the brake pedal a few times to bring the brake pads into contact with the disc. Bleeding the system isn't necessary unless the brake hose was disconnected from the caliper. Check the operation of the brakes carefully before driving.

7   Master cylinder – removal, overhaul and installation

Note: *Several different master cylinders have been used on the vehicles covered by this manual. Earlier versions are single-circuit designs; later units are dual-circuit types. If you're buying a rebuild kit, or a rebuilt master cylinder, make sure you get the right components. It's a good idea to take your master cylinder with you to the auto parts store to prevent confusion. Also, if you're rebuilding the master cylinder, don't discard the internal parts right away. Instead, lay them out in the exact order in which you remove them. Even though you're going to replace them with the parts in the rebuild kit, this will help you install everything in the correct sequence. And if – after comparing the old parts with the parts in the rebuild kit – anything from the rebuild kit is missing, you'll know you have the wrong kit. Finally, be aware that more than one vendor manufactures master cylinders for these vehicles. It's okay to swap entire master cylinders, but don't try to swap the internals of one brand for another – they won't fit.*

Removal

Refer to illustration 7.3

1   Remove the fluid from the master cylinder reservoir with a syringe.

2   Loosen the left front wheel lug bolts, raise the vehicle and place it securely on jackstands. Remove the left front wheel.

3   You'll find the master cylinder on the pan, immediately in front of the firewall between the passenger compartment and the luggage compartment **(see illustration)**.

4   Clearly label the wires from the brake light and fluid warning switches, then disconnect them.

5   Have some rags handy. Pull out the rubber plug(s) and elbow(s) for the lines between the reservoir and the master cylinder (in the top of the master cylinder) and place rags under them to soak up the brake fluid in the lines.

6   Using a flare nut wrench, disconnect the threaded fittings for the brake lines. Plug the ends of the lines to prevent contamination from dirt or water.

7   Inside the passenger compartment, locate the master cylinder pushrod pin that connects the master cylinder pushrod to the brake pedal. Bend the clip up and remove this pin (see Chapter 8, Section 3).

8   Remove the brake pedal stop plate (see Chapter 8, Section 3).

9   Remove the pushrod **(see illustration 7.13). Warning:** *Don't loosen the locknut on the pushrod. The factory has set the overall length of the pushrod and it must not be changed.*

10   Remove the master cylinder mounting bolts.

11   Remove the master cylinder.

Overhaul

Single-circuit master cylinder

Refer to illustration 7.13

12   Clean the master cylinder with denatured alcohol.

13   Remove the rubber boot, the lock ring and the stop washer **(see illustration).**

14   Remove the piston. If it's stuck, plug all holes and force the piston out with compressed air (point the end of the master cylinder into a pile of rags, just in case it comes out with force). It doesn't take much pressure – even a hand pump will do the trick. Wear safety goggles to protect your eyes just in case any residual brake fluid inside the master cylinder squirts out.

Note: *If the piston is stuck, pay particular attention to the bore of the master cylinder upon disassembly – it may be pitted or rusty (see Step 23).*

15   Remove the piston washer, primary cup, return spring and check valve.

16   Remove the brake light switch.

Dual-circuit master cylinder

Refer to illustration 7.18

17   Clean the master cylinder with denatured alcohol.

9

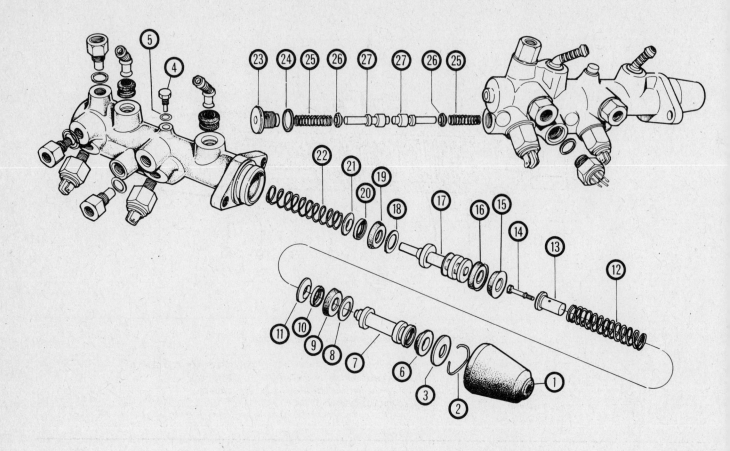

7.18   Exploded view of a typical dual-circuit master cylinder

1	Boot	10	Spring seat	19	Cup
2	Lock ring	11	Spring support ring	20	Spring seat
3	Stop washer	12	Spring	21	Spring support ring
4	Stop screw	13	Stop sleeve	22	Spring
5	Stop screw seal	14	Stroke limiting screw	23	Plug
6	Secondary piston cup	15	Cup	24	Seal
7	Secondary piston	16	Cup	25	Spring
8	Washer	17	Primary piston	26	Cup seal
9	Cup	18	Washer	27	Piston

18   Remove the rubber boot, the lock ring and the stop washer **(see illustration)**.

19   Remove the stop screw and the stop screw seal.

20   Remove the secondary (rear) piston cup, the piston, the washer, the cup, the spring seat, the spring support ring, the rear piston spring, the stop sleeve, the stroke limiting screw and the other cup. If the piston is stuck, see Step 14 above.

21   Remove the primary (front) piston cup, the piston, the washer, the other cup, the spring seat, the spring support ring and the spring. If the piston is stuck, see Step 15 above.

22   On some master cylinders (late 1967 through 1971), there's an auxiliary chamber with two small pistons which operate a switch controlling a warning light on the instrument cluster. To disassemble this part of the master cylinder, unscrew the plug and remove the seal, spring, cup seal, the two pistons, the other cup seal and the other spring.

All master cylinders

Refer to illustrations 7.24a and 7.24b

23   Clean the master cylinder with denatured alcohol or brake system cleaner. Don't use gasoline, kerosene or any petroleum-based solvent. Inspect the cylinder bore for corrosion, pitting and scoring. Remove light scratches and corrosion with crocus cloth. If that doesn't clean up the bore, replace the master cylinder.

24   Insert a small copper – not steel – wire through the compensating ports and intake ports **(see illustrations)**. Steel wire might damage the walls of the ports. Make sure there are no burrs at the bottom of these ports which might damage the cup(s).

25   Lubricate the master cylinder walls with brake fluid. Do NOT use mineral oil or grease. They'll attack rubber brake parts.

26   Reassembly is the reverse of disassembly. Make sure you reassemble the master cylinder in the exact reverse order in which it was disassembled.

Installation

Refer to illustrations 7.28a and 7.28b

27   Installation is the reverse of removal. Use a new clip to secure the pushrod-to-brake pedal clevis pin.

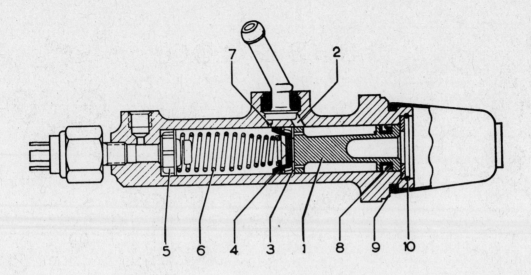

7.24a   Cutaway of a typical single-port master cylinder

1	Piston	5	Check valve	8	Secondary cup seal
2	Intake port (fluid	6	Check valve spring	9	Stop plate
	from reservoir)	7	Compensating port (excess	10	Lock ring
3	Piston washer		fluid back to reservoir)		
4	Primary cup seal				

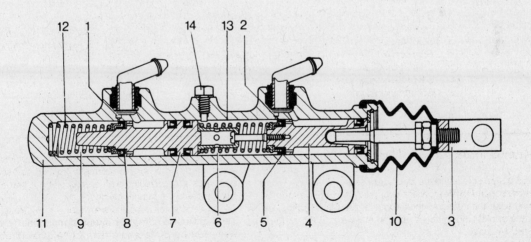

7.24b   Cutaway of a typical dual-port master cylinder

1	Secondary compensating port	7	Secondary piston (front	11	Cylinder body
2	Primary compensating port		brake system)	12	Secondary piston
3	Pushrod	8	Cup seal		return spring
4	Primary piston	9	Secondary pressure chamber	13	Primary piston return spring
5	Cup seal	10	Rubber boot	14	Stop screw
6	Primary pressure chamber				

9

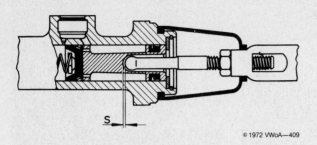

© 1972 VWoA—409

7.28a   The clearance between the pushrod and the piston recess (dimension "s") is set at the factory by the overall length of the pushrod

28   Volkswagen has set the length of the pushrod so there's 0.04 inch (1 mm) clearance between the tip of the rod and the recess in the rear of the piston **(see illustration)**. This clearance is adequate to keep the compensating port open between brake applications, to bleed off hot (expanding) brake fluid which could otherwise cause the brakes to drag. As long as you're not pushing on the brake pedal, the piston won't move forward and close the port. Obviously, the pushrod-to-piston recess clearance is critical. Anytime you remove the master cylinder, you should check and, if necessary, adjust it. But don't adjust it by loosening the locknut on the pushrod. Reposition the brake pedal stop plate so that the brake pedal has 3/16 to 9/32-inch (5 to 7 mm) freeplay **(see illustration)**. This will produce the specified clearance between the pushrod and the piston recess.

8   Brake hoses and lines – inspection and replacement

Inspection
Refer to illustration 8.1
1   About every six months, or whenever there's brake trouble or you're servicing the brakes, raise the vehicle, place it on jackstands and inspect the rubber hoses which connect the steel brake lines with the front and rear brake assemblies. These are important and vulnerable parts of the brake system, so conduct a thorough inspection (a light and mirror are helpful). Look for cracks, chafing of the outer cover, leaks, blisters and other damage **(see illustration)**. If a hose exhibits any of the above conditions, replace it.

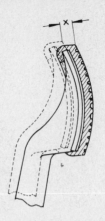

© 1972 VWoA—410

7.28b   To set dimension "s" in Fig. 7.28a, move the brake pedal stop plate backward or forward to produce a freeplay of 3/16 to 9/32-inch (5 to 7 mm) at the top of the brake pedal (dimension "x")

Replacement
Brake hoses
Refer to illustrations 8.3a and 8.3b
2   Loosen the wheel lug bolts. Raise the end of the vehicle you're working on and place it securely on jackstands. Remove the wheel.
3   Using a flare nut wrench, disconnect the metal brake line from the hose fitting **(see illustrations)**. Don't bend the frame bracket or the metal brake line. If the fitting is very tight and the bracket starts to bend, place an open end wrench on the hose fitting.
4   Pry the U-clip from the female fitting at the bracket, then detach the hose from the bracket.
5   Unscrew the brake hose from the wheel cylinder or (on some Karmann Ghias) the disc brake caliper.
6   To install the hose, screw the threaded fitting into the wheel cylinder or caliper and tighten it securely.
7   Without twisting the hose, install the female fitting in the hose bracket. It will fit the bracket in only one position.
8   Install the U-clip retaining the female fitting to the frame bracket.
9   Using a flare nut wrench, attach the metal brake line to the hose fitting.
10   When the brake hose installation is complete, there should be no

8.1   If you find a brake hose that looks like this – dried and cracked – replace it immediately!

8.3a   To disconnect the front brake hose from the metal line, loosen the fitting with a flare nut wrench, pry off the U-clip that secures the female hose fitting to the bracket and slide the connection out of the bracket

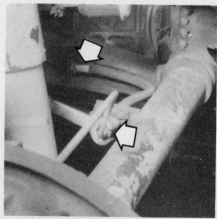

8.3b   Disconnect the rear brake hose and metal brake line the same way as the front

9.7   When bleeding the brakes, a hose is connected to the bleeder valve at the wheel cylinder (or caliper) and then submerged in brake fluid – air will be seen as bubbles in the hose and container when the pedal is depressed and the bleeder valve is opened

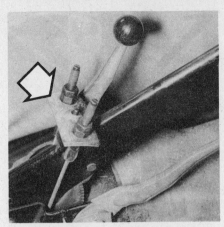

11.3   Remove the locknuts and adjusting nuts from the parking brake cables and remove the compensating lever (arrow)

11.5   Remove the snap-ring from the parking brake lever pivot pin and remove the pin

kinks in the hose. Make sure the hose doesn't contact any part of the suspension. Check this by turning the wheels to the extreme left and right positions. If the hose makes contact, remove it and correct the installation as necessary.

11   Fill the master cylinder reservoir and bleed the system (see Section 9).

Metal brake lines

12   When replacing brake lines be sure to use the correct parts. Don't use copper tubing for any brake system components. Purchase steel brake lines from a dealer or auto parts store.

13   Prefabricated brake line, with the tube ends already flared and fittings installed, is available at auto parts stores and dealers. These lines are also bent to the proper shapes.

14   When installing the new line make sure it's securely supported in the brackets and has plenty of clearance between moving or hot components.

15   After installation, check the fluid level in the master cylinder and add fluid as necessary. Bleed the brake system as outlined in the next Section and test the brakes carefully before driving the vehicle in traffic.

9   Brake system bleeding

Refer to illustration 9.7

Warning: *Wear eye protection when bleeding the brake system. If the fluid comes in contact with your eyes, immediately rinse them with water and seek medical attention.*

Note: *Bleeding the hydraulic system is necessary to remove any air that manages to find its way into the system when it's been opened during removal and installation of a hose, line, caliper or master cylinder.*

1   It will probably be necessary to bleed the system at all four brakes if air has entered the system due to low fluid level, or if the brake lines have been disconnected at the master cylinder.

2   If a brake line was disconnected at only one wheel, then only that caliper or wheel cylinder must be bled.

3   If a brake line is disconnected at a fitting located between the master cylinder and any of the brakes, that part of the system served by the disconnected line must be bled.

4   Remove the master cylinder reservoir cover and fill the reservoir with the recommended brake fluid (see Chapter 1). Reinstall the cover. **Note:** *Check the fluid level often during the bleeding operation and add fluid as necessary to prevent the fluid level from falling low enough to allow air bubbles into the master cylinder.*

5   Have an assistant on hand, as well as a supply of new brake fluid, a clear container partially filled with clean brake fluid, a length of 3/16-inch

plastic, rubber or vinyl tubing to fit over the bleeder valve and a wrench to open and close the bleeder valve.

6   Beginning at the right rear wheel, loosen the bleeder valve slightly, then tighten it to a point where it's snug but can be loosened quickly and easily.

7   Place one end of the tubing over the bleeder valve and submerge the other end in brake fluid in the container **(see illustration)**.

8   Have the assistant pump the brakes slowly a few times to get pressure in the system, then depress the pedal firmly and hold it down.

9   While the pedal is depressed, open the bleeder valve just enough to allow a flow of fluid to leave the valve. Watch for air bubbles to exit the submerged end of the tube. When the fluid flow slows after a couple of seconds, close the valve and have your assistant release the pedal.

10   Repeat Steps 8 and 9 until no more air bubbles appear in the tube, then tighten the bleeder valve and proceed to the left rear wheel, the right front wheel and the left front wheel, in that order, and perform the same procedure. Be sure to check the fluid in the master cylinder reservoir frequently.

11   Never use old brake fluid. It contains moisture which will deteriorate the brake system components.

12   Refill the master cylinder with fluid at the end of the operation.

13   Check the operation of the brakes. The pedal should feel solid when depressed, with no sponginess. If necessary, repeat the entire process.

Warning: *Do not operate the vehicle if you are in doubt about the effectiveness of the brake system.*

10   Brake pedal – removal and installation

See Chapter 8, Section 3, for the brake pedal removal and installation procedure.

11   Parking brake lever – removal and installation

Refer to illustrations 11.3, 11.5, 11.6 and 11.9

Removal

1   On 1967 and earlier models, remove the front seats (see Chapter 11) and the rear floor covering.

2   Remove the rubber dust boot from the parking brake lever.

3   Remove the locknut and adjusting nut from each cable **(see illustration)**.

4   Remove the compensating lever.

5   Remove the snap-ring from the lever pivot pin and take out the pin **(see illustration)**.

11.6 Without depressing the release button, lift out the parking brake lever (if you depress the button before you get the lever out, the ratchet segment will fall into the tunnel!) – after you've got the lever out far enough, put your hand under the ratchet segment, push the release button and the ratchet segment will fall out of the lever

6 Push the lever to the rear and lift it out (see illustration). Caution: *Don't press the release button as you're lifting the lever out, or the ratchet segment inside the bottom of the lever assembly will fall into the tunnel.*
7 Place one hand under the ratchet segment, press the release button and remove the ratchet segment.
8 Disassemble the lever and clean the pawl rod, release button, pawl spring and ratchet segment. Grease all parts and reassemble.

Installation

9 Insert the ratchet segment so that the recess fits over the tube in the

lever (see illustration, point A) and the teeth engage in the pawl. Make sure the rounded end of the pawl is positioned correctly (point B in illustration).
10 Reposition the lever and insert the threaded ends of the cables through the cable guides. As you insert the lever, make sure the slot in the front of the ratchet segment engages the frame edge (point C in illustration 11.9).
11 Grease the lever pin, install it and secure it with the snap-ring.
12 Install the compensating lever.
13 Install the cable adjusting nuts and locknuts loosely.
14 Adjust the cables (see Section 12).
15 Install the lever dust boot.
16 On 1967 and earlier models, install the rear floor covering and the front seats.
17 Check the operation of the parking brake.

---

12   Parking brake cable – replacement and adjustment

Note: *The parking brake should be adjusted whenever the rear brake shoes have worn enough to allow you to raise the lever five clicks without noticeable braking action. Although the compensating lever on top of the parking brake lever makes up for some of the difference in adjustment between the left and right cables, it's essential that the cables be adjusted so that the compensating lever is horizontal when the parking brake lever is applied. If the rear brake shoes are adjusted properly but the compensating lever isn't horizontal after adjustment of the parking brake cables, one cable may be stretching and – if left in service – will eventually break. If only one of the cables is broken or damaged, you don't have to replace the other one, but one cable will be more stretched than the other. It's easier to adjust two cables of the same age, so we recommend replacing both cables when one breaks.*

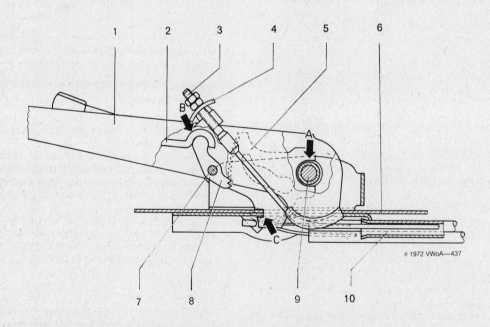

11.9 Installation details of a typical parking brake lever

1	Parking brake lever	5	Ratchet segment	8	Pawl
2	Pawl rod	6	Frame	9	Lever pin
3	Brake cable	7	Pawl pin	10	Cable guide tube
4	Compensating lever				

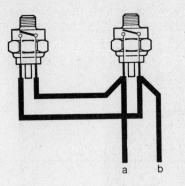

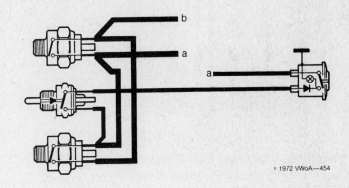

c 1972 VWoA—453

c 1972 VWoA—454

13.2 Electrical schematic for early dual-circuit type brake light switches – wire "a" goes to terminal 15, wire "b" goes to the brake lights; switch at left is for front wheels, switch at right is for rear wheels

13.7 Electrical schematic for early dual-circuit type brake light switches and warning light switch – wire "a" goes to terminal 15, wire "b" to brake lights

Replacement

1   Detach the cable(s) from the parking brake lever (see Section 11).
2   Loosen the rear wheel lug bolts, raise the vehicle, place it securely on jackstands and remove the rear wheel(s).
3   Remove the brake drum(s) and shoes (see Section 2).
4   Detach the cable clip from the backing plate. **Note:** *If you're replacing both cables, do one cable at a time so you'll have the other cable as a reassembly guide.*
5   Pull the rear end of the cable and guide hose out of the backing plate and pull the front end of the cable out of the guide tube.
6   Clean the cable and guide tube.
7   On models manufactured since August 1, 1966, the rear wheel track is wider. These models have longer parking brake cables. Compare the lengths of the new cable and the old cable to make sure you have the right replacement cable.
8   Lubricate the cable with multi-purpose grease.
9   Thread the front end of the cable through the guide tube and the rear end of the cable through the brake backing plate.
10   Install the brake shoes and attach the parking brake cable to the lever on the rear shoe (see Section 2).
11   Loosely install the cable adjusting nut and locknut at the parking brake lever.
12   If you're replacing both cables, repeat Steps 4 through 11 for the other cable.
13   Adjust the parking brake cable (see below).

Adjustment

14   Adjust the rear brakes (see Section 2).
15   Fold back the slots in the rubber dust boot on the parking brake lever to get at the cable locknuts and adjusting nuts.
16   Insert a screwdriver in the slotted end of the cable and loosen the cable locknuts (see Section 11).
17   On 1972 and earlier models, tighten the adjusting nuts on both cables until the rear brake shoes stop the rear wheels from turning, then back off the adjusting nuts half a turn, or until the wheels turn freely. Raise the parking brake lever two clicks and verify that braking effort is the same on both rear wheels. Pull the lever up two or three more clicks – you should no longer be able to turn the wheels by hand.
18   On 1973 and later models, raise the parking brake lever three clicks,

hold the cable end with a screwdriver and tighten the adjusting nuts until you can just turn each rear wheel by hand. Braking effort must be equal on both sides.
19   The compensating lever should be horizontal. If it isn't, replace the cables (see above).
20   Tighten the locknuts securely.
21   Push the cover flaps for the adjusting slots forward and install the rubber boot.

13   Brake light/warning light switch – check and replacement

Single-circuit and early dual-circuit systems
Brake light switch
Refer to illustration 13.2

1   Raise the front of the vehicle and place it securely on jackstands. Remove the left front wheel.
2   Locate the master cylinder (see Section 7) and disconnect the brake light switch wires from the front switch (single-circuit system) or for the front brake circuit (dual-circuit system) **(see illustration)**.
3   Turn the ignition switch to On and operate the brake pedal. The brake lights should come on.
4   Reconnect the wires. Disconnect the wires from the rear switch and repeat the test in Step 3. The brake lights should come on again.
5   If either switch fails to turn on the brake lights, replace it.
6   Bleed the brake system (see Section 9).

Warning light
Refer to illustration 13.7

7   Turn the ignition switch to On and test the warning light by pressing the pushbutton on the warning light lens **(see illustration)**. The warning light should come on. If it doesn't, replace the bulb and retest.
8   Remove the warning light switch from the master cylinder (see Section 7). **Caution:** *Make sure you don't remove one of the brake light switches by mistake.*
9   Depress the plunger on the warning light switch and note whether the light comes on. If it doesn't, replace the switch. It isn't necessary to bleed the brakes after replacing the warning light switch.

9

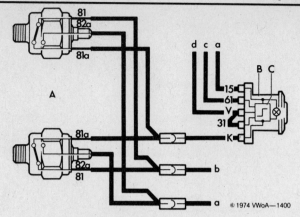

Later model dual-circuit systems

Refer to illustration 13.11

10   On 1972 and later models, the warning light switch is eliminated and its function is integrated into the circuit for the brake light switches. On these models, it isn't necessary to functionally check the warning light by pushing the pushbutton on the lens. The warning light comes on when the ignition is turned to On and, just like the alternator and oil pressure warning lights, goes out once the engine has started.

11   The test for the circuit **(see illustration)** is essentially the same as for the earlier type (see Steps 1 through 5 above).

13.11   Electrical schematic for later dual-circuit type combination brake light/warning light switches

A	Brake light switches	b	To brake lights
B	Dual-circuit brake warning light	c	From regulator switch (terminal 61)
C	Electronic switch	d	To ground
a	To terminal 15		

Chapter 10
Suspension and steering systems

Contents

Specifications

10

General

Offset between upper and lower torsion arms	5 to 9 mm
Balljoint play	
Upper balljoint	0.08 in (2.0 mm)
Lower balljoint	0.04 in (1.0 mm)
Spring plate setting angles	
Swing axle models	
Without equalizer spring	17-degrees. 30-minutes + 50-minutes
With equalizer spring	20-degrees + 50-minutes
Driveaxle models	20-degrees. 30-minutes + 50-minutes

Torque specifications

	Ft-lbs
Front suspension	
Balljoint nuts/bolts	
Torsion bar models	
10 mm nuts	29 to 36
12 mm nuts	36 to 51
MacPherson strut models	
Strut-to-balljoint bolts	29
Self-locking nut on balljoint stud (pre-1974)	29
Clamp bolt for balljoint stud (1974 on)	25
Strut-to-steering knuckle bolts (1974 on)	61
Strut-to-body nuts	14
Strut piston rod nut	
1973 and earlier	50 to 61
1974 on	43
Front axle beam mounting bolts	
Axle-to-frame head bolts	36
Body-to-axle bolts	14
Control arm	
Castellated nut for stabilizer bar	22
Self-locking nut on eccentric bolt	29
Rear suspension	
Spring plate bolts	80 to 87
Diagonal arm pivot bolt	87
Steering	
Worm-and-roller steering gear	
Steering worm adjustment screw locknut	36 to 43
Roller shaft adjustment screw locknut	16 to 18
Steering gear clamp bolts (torsion bar models)	18 to 22
Steering gear mounting bolts (MacPherson strut models)	29
Universal joint self-locking nut	18
Rack-and-pinion steering gear	
Side member bracket bolts	32
Steering gear-to-bracket bolts	18
Tie-rod-to-steering rack bolts	40
Steering wheel nut	36
Castellated tie-rod nuts (all models)	22
Pitman arm nut	72
Idler arm self-locking nut	29

1   General information

Front suspension

Refer to illustrations 1.2 and 1.5

All pre-1968 and many 1968 and later Beetles and Karmann Ghias are equipped with torsion bar front ends. A MacPherson strut front end was introduced in 1968 on the Super Beetle with Automatic Stick Shift, but 1968 Super Beetles with manual transaxles and some 1969 and 1970 Super Beetles have the torsion bar front end. All 1971 and later Super Beetles and convertibles have MacPherson struts.

On torsion bar models, the front axle is a rigid beam with pivoting members **(see illustrations)**. The beam is constructed from two steel tubes, one above the other, welded into a rectangular assembly with four stamped steel crossmembers. The outer crossmembers between the tubes, known as side plates (or shock towers), also serve as the upper mounting points for the shock absorbers. Inside each axle tube is a torsion bar, consisting of 10 spring steel leaves.

A torsion arm is attached to each end of the axle tube. The inner ends of the torsion arms have square holes cut into them to fit onto the outer ends of the torsion bars. Set screws secure the arms to the bars. On pre-1966 models, the outer ends of the torsion arms are attached to the steering knuckle with a pair of linkpins; on 1966 and later models, they're attached with balljoints. The lower torsion arms are linked by a stabilizer bar. The shock absorbers are mounted between the lower torsion arms and the upper shock mounts, or sideplates.

If the axle, body or frame are bent or damaged in an accident, you can unbolt the entire front end from the frame head and remove it as a single unit for replacement, or for repairs to the front of the vehicle (see Section 9).

On MacPherson strut models, the torsion bar front end, and the frame head to which it's attached, are replaced by a new frame head which provides the inner mounting points for a pair of control arms **(see illustration)**. The outer ends of these control arms are attached to the lower ends of the steering knuckles with balljoints. The steering knuckles are bolted to the lower ends of the MacPherson struts. The upper ends of the struts are bolted to the vehicle body. The control arms are linked by a stabilizer bar.

Rear suspension

Refer to illustration 1.8

All pre-1969 models, except the 1968 Super Beetle with Automatic Stick Shift, are equipped with swing axles at the rear. The 1968 Super Beetle with Automatic Stick Shift and all 1969 and later models are equipped with driveaxles with constant velocity (CV) joints.

Regardless of axle type, the rear wheels are independently sprung on all models. A splined tube welded to the rear crossmember of the frame

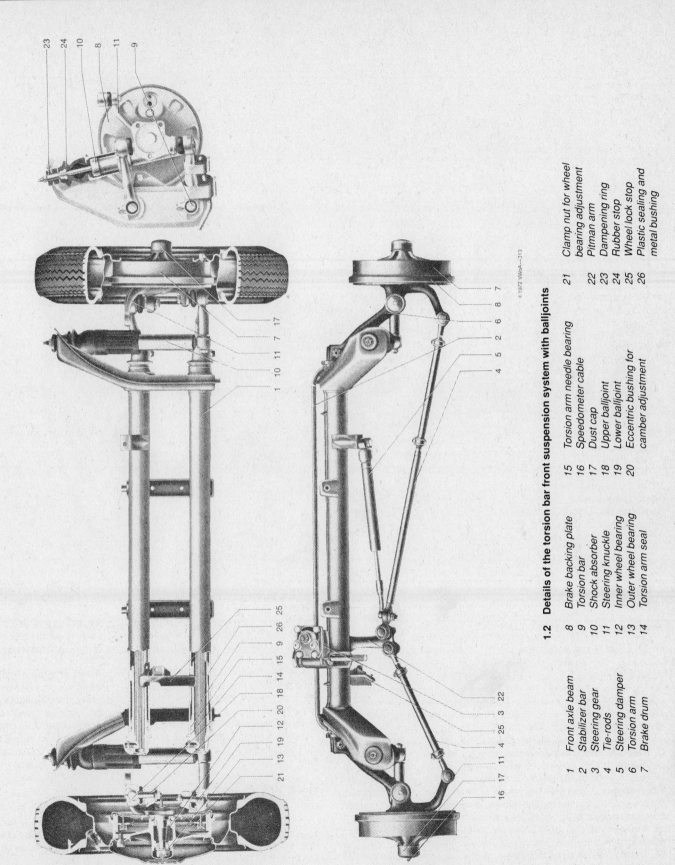

1.2   Details of the torsion bar front suspension system with balljoints

1	Front axle beam	8	Brake backing plate	15	Torsion arm needle bearing
2	Stabilizer bar	9	Torsion bar	16	Speedometer cable
3	Steering gear	10	Shock absorber	17	Dust cap
4	Tie-rods	11	Steering knuckle	18	Upper balljoint
5	Steering damper	12	Inner wheel bearing	19	Lower balljoint
6	Torsion arm	13	Outer wheel bearing	20	Eccentric bushing for
7	Brake drum	14	Torsion arm seal		camber adjustment

21	Clamp nut for wheel bearing adjustment
22	Pitman arm
23	Dampening ring
24	Rubber stop
25	Wheel lock stop
26	Plastic sealing and metal bushing

© 1972 VWoA—313

10

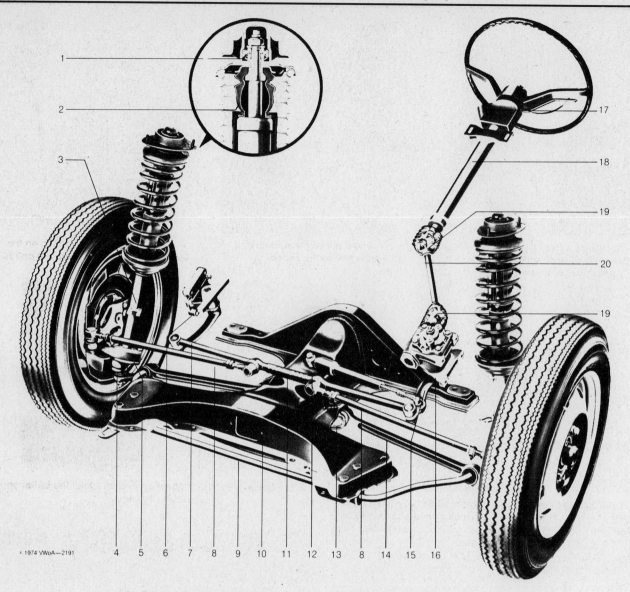

1.5   Details of the earlier strut-type front suspension with worm-and-roller steering

1	Ball thrust bearing	6	Idler arm bracket	11	Center tie-rod	16	Steering gear
2	Rubber bump stop	7	Idler arm	12	Steering damper	17	Steering column switch
3	Strut assembly	8	Tie-rod	13	Camber adjustment		housing
4	Balljoint	9	Stabilizer bar		eccentric bolt	18	Steering column tube
5	Steering knuckle	10	Frame head	14	Control arm	19	Universal joint
				15	Pitman arm	20	Intermediate shaft

anchors transverse torsion bars at their inner ends. The splined outer ends of the torsion bars carry hubbed spring plates, to which the axle tube (swing axle models) or diagonal arm (driveaxle models) is attached. The splined hubs at the front ends of the spring plates also allow suspension adjustment. Shock absorbers control damping.

On 1967 and 1968 swing axle models, an equalizer spring **(see illustration)** provides additional progressive spring action to assist the torsion bars when the vehicle is loaded down. Because its operating levers slant in opposite directions, the action of the equalizer spring doesn't affect body roll, so the front end of the vehicle is able to absorb more roll to provide improved cornering.

On later models with driveaxles and CV joints, a pair of large trailing arms, known as diagonal arms, absorb lateral forces generated by the outer ends of the driveaxles and transfer them to the frame. The rear suspensions on early and later models are otherwise fairly similar.

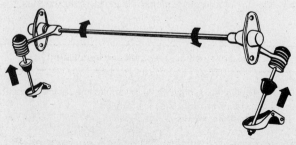

1.8   On 1967 and 1968 swing axle models, an equalizer spring assists the rear torsion bars when the vehicle is under load

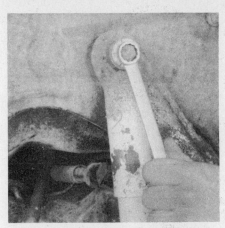

2.3a To replace a front shock absorber on a linkpin type front end, remove the upper mounting bolt . . .

2.3b . . . and the lower mounting bolt, and remove the shock

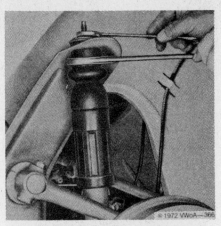

2.4a Place a backup wrench on the buffer stud and remove the nut on top

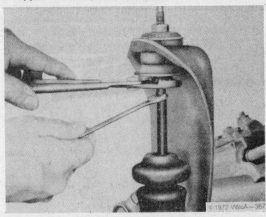

2.4b If you can't get the nut on top loose, slide the plastic cover and buffer down the damper rod, put a pair of pliers on the buffer stud and a wrench on the damper rod and unscrew the rod from the stud

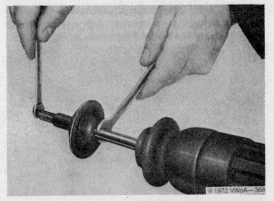

2.7a You'll need to use a backup wrench to get the buffer stud off the old shock

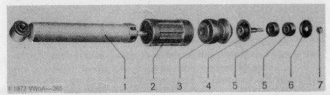

2.7b Exploded view of a typical shock absorber for balljoint models

1	Shock absorber	5	Bushings or damping rings for pin
2	Outer tube		
3	Buffer	6	Plate for bushings
4	Buffer stud or pin	7	Upper mounting nut

Steering

All 1954 through 1974 Beetles and Super Beetles are equipped with a worm-and-roller steering gear. The Pitman arm moves the steering knuckles through adjustable tie-rods. A steering damper reduces road shock to the steering wheel.

1971 through 1975 Super Beetle models also use a worm-and-roller steering gear, but the linkage is different from the Beetle unit. The Pitman arm moves a center tie-rod, supported at the other end by an idler arm. The center tie-rod moves the steering knuckles through adjustable outer tie-rods. A steering damper reduces road shock to the steering wheel.

All 1975 and later Super Beetles have rack-and-pinion steering. Outer tie-rods relay the movement of the rack to the steering knuckles.

2 Front shock absorbers – removal and installation

1 Loosen the wheel lug bolts, raise the front of the vehicle, place it securely on jackstands and block the rear wheels.
2 Remove the front wheels.

1965 and earlier models (kingpin type front end)

Refer to illustrations 2.3a and 2.3b

3 Remove the upper and lower shock mounting bolts (see illustrations) and remove the shock. Installation is the reverse of removal.

1966 and later models (balljoint type front end)

Refer to illustrations 2.4a, 2.4b, 2.7a, 2.7b and 2.12

4 Place a floor jack under the torsion arm and raise the arm just enough to release tension from the torsion bar. Remove the nut that attaches the shock absorber to the shock tower. If you're not using an air tool to break the nut loose, you'll probably need to use a back-up wrench (42 mm) on the buffer stud screwed into the end of the damper rod (see illustration). If you can't loosen the upper nut, slide the plastic cover and rubber buffer down the shaft, grasp the lower end of the buffer stud with a pair of pliers and, using an open end wrench, screw the damper rod out of the buffer stud (see illustration).
5 Remove the nut from the mounting pin on the lower torsion arm.
6 Remove the shock absorber.
7 If you're installing a new shock, remove the buffer and buffer stud from the old shock (see illustration) and install them on the new shock (see illustration). If either part is worn, replace it.

10

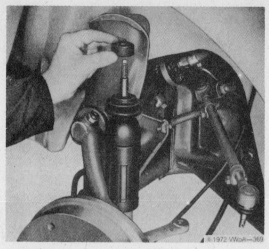

2.12 Install the damping ring on the shock absorber before you slip the damper rod through the upper mounting hole in the shock tower

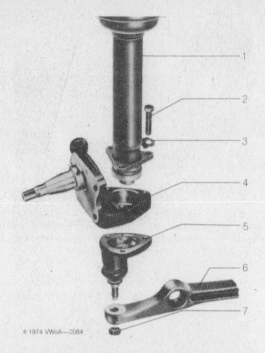

3.4 Exploded view of 1968 through 1973 MacPherson strut and steering knuckle assembly

1	Strut	5	Balljoint
2	Strut-to-knuckle bolt	6	Control arm
3	Lockplate	7	Self-locking nut
4	Steering knuckle		

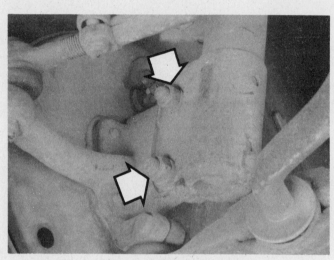

3.5 Remove the strut-to-steering knuckle bolts (arrows)

8　If you're going to reuse the old shock, inspect the upper and lower mounting bushings and, if necessary, replace them.
9　Inspect the mounting pin on the lower torsion arm. Replace it if damaged.
10　Apply a light coat of multi-purpose grease to the mounting pin on the lower torsion arm.
11　Slide the lower end of the shock absorber onto the mounting pin and install the nut, but don't tighten it completely yet.
12　Install the damping ring (bushing) on the buffer stud with the shoulder facing up **(see illustration)**.
13　Extend the piston damper rod up and push it through the hole in the shock tower. Install the second damping ring plate and the upper mounting nut.
14　Raise the floor jack until the shock bump stop is firmly pressing against the underside of the shock tower. Tighten the upper and lower mounting nuts securely.

All models

15　Lower the floor jack and remove it. Install the wheel and tighten the wheel lug bolts snugly. Remove the jackstands and lower the vehicle. Tighten the wheel lug bolts to the torque listed in the Chapter 1 Specifications.

---

3   Struts – removal and installation

Refer to illustrations 3.4, 3.5, 3.6 and 3.7

Removal

1　Loosen the wheel lug bolts, raise the front of the vehicle, place it securely on jackstands and remove the wheels.
2　Pry off the speedometer cable clip from the left brake drum and pull out the speedometer cable through the back of the steering knuckle.
3　Pry off the U-clip from the threaded fitting between the brake hose and the metal brake line and pull the fitting out of its bracket on the strut. Don't disconnect the fitting or you'll have to bleed the brakes!
4　On 1968 through 1973 models, bend down the lockplates and remove the three bolts that hold the balljoint and steering knuckle on the strut **(see illustration)**.
5　On 1974 and later models, remove the two bolts and nuts that attach the strut to the steering knuckle **(see illustration)**.
6　Pull the strut off the steering knuckle. On 1968 through 1973 models, install one bolt to support the knuckle while the strut's out **(see illustration)**.
7　Working from inside the luggage compartment, remove the three upper mounting nuts **(see illustration)**. When you get to the third nut, reach under the fender and hold the strut to prevent it from falling.

Installation

8　Installation is the reverse of removal. Use new lock plates for the three lower mounting bolts on 1968 through 1973 models. Tighten the three upper mounting nuts and the three, or two, lower mounting bolts to the torque listed in this Chapter's Specifications.
9　Repeat Steps 2 through 8 for the other side.
10　Have the wheel alignment checked and, if necessary, adjusted after installing the struts.

3.6 On 1968 through 1973 models, put one of the strut-to-knuckle bolts back through the knuckle mounting flange and screw it into the balljoint flange to support the knuckle while the strut's removed

3.7 Working from inside the luggage compartment, remove these three upper mounting nuts – when you get to the third nut, reach under the fender and hold the strut so it doesn't fall when you remove the nut

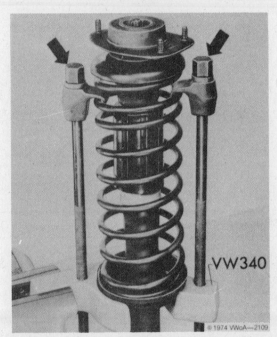

4.4 Install the spring compressor according to the tool manufacturer's instructions and compress the spring until all pressure is relieved from the upper seat

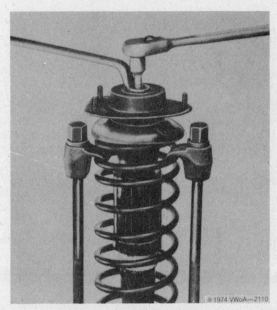

4.6 Using an offset box wrench and an Allen wrench as shown, remove the nut from the piston rod

3   Place the strut in a bench vise. Be sure to line the jaws of the vise with wood, and don't tighten the vise excessively, or the strut tube could be damaged. Pry off the dust cap from the top of the strut.
4   Install a spring compressor in accordance with the manufacturer's instructions (**see illustration**).
5   If you're using the type of spring compressor with two separate threaded rods, tighten them a few turns at a time, alternating back and forth. Continue to tighten the compressor until there is no more spring tension on the spring seat (you'll be able to wiggle the spring).
6   Using an offset box end wrench and an Allen wrench as shown, remove the self-locking nut from the strut piston rod (**see illustration**).
7   Remove the components from the strut (**see illustration**). If the coil spring is to be replaced, gradually loosen the compressor, alternating back and forth, until all tension is removed from the spring. Remove the spring compressor.
8   Inspect the rubber bump stop for cracks or deterioration. If it's worn, replace it.
9   Inspect the strut. Try extending and compressing it. It should operate smoothly, with uniform resistance throughout the range of its stroke.

4   Struts – replacement

Refer to illustrations 4.4, 4.6, 4.7, 4.13 and 4.16
1   Remove the strut (see Section 3).
2   Check the strut assembly for leaking fluid, dents, cracks or other obvious damage. Check the coil spring for chips or cracks which could cause premature failure, and inspect the rubber components for hardness or general deterioration. Complete strut assemblies are available on an exchange basis. This eliminates much time and work. So, before disassembling the strut to replace individual components, check on the availability of parts and the price of a complete rebuilt unit. **Warning:** *Disassembling a strut assembly is a potentially dangerous undertaking. Utmost attention must be directed to the job, or serious injury may result. Use only a high quality spring compressor and carefully follow the manufacturer's instructions furnished with the tool. After removing the coil spring from the strut, set it aside in a safe, isolated area (a steel cabinet is preferred).*

10

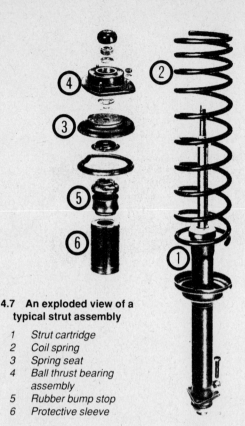

4.7   An exploded view of a typical strut assembly

1   *Strut cartridge*
2   *Coil spring*
3   *Spring seat*
4   *Ball thrust bearing assembly*
5   *Rubber bump stop*
6   *Protective sleeve*

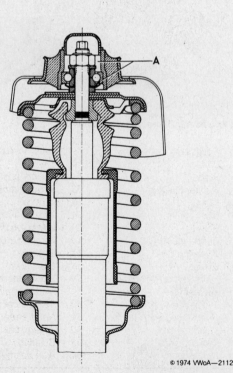

4.16   To ensure adequate lubrication for the ball thrust bearing assembly, fill the cavity around the top of the strut (area A) with lithium grease

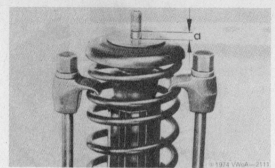

4.13   Gradually compress the spring until the unthreaded portion of the piston rod projects about 5/16 to 3/8-inches above the spring seat (dimension "a")

10   If the strut doesn't work properly, replace it.
11   Install the rubber bump stop and protective sleeve on the piston rod.
12   Install the spring.
13   Gradually compress the spring until the unthreaded portion of the piston rod projects about 5/16 to 3/8-inches above the spring seat **(see illustration)**.
14   Install the ball thrust bearing assembly.
15   Install a new self-locking nut on the piston rod and tighten it to the torque listed in this Chapter's Specifications.
16   Fill the indicated spaces of the ball thrust bearing with lithium grease **(see illustration)**.
17   Install the strut on the vehicle (see Section 3).

---

5   Steering knuckles – removal, overhaul and installation

Removal

1   Loosen the front wheel lug bolts, raise the front of the vehicle, place it securely on jackstands and remove the wheel.
2   Disconnect the speedometer cable from the left dust cap and pull the cable out of the steering knuckle.
3   Disconnect the brake hose-to-metal line fitting at the bracket (see Chapter 9). Plug both the hose and the line to prevent contamination.
4   Disconnect the tie-rod end from the steering knuckle (see Section 17).
5   Remove the brake drum, the brake shoes – or the brake caliper and disc – and the backing plate (see Chapter 9).

1965 and earlier models
Refer to illustrations 5.6 and 5.7
6   Remove the clamp bolts and nuts for the linkpin bolts **(see illustration)**.

5.6   Before you can remove the linkpins from the steering knuckle, you'll have to remove these clamp bolts and nuts

5.7   Exploded view of a 1965 and earlier steering knuckle and torsion arm assembly

1	Body mounting bolt	17	Bearing	33	Dowel pin	49	Lock washer
2	Washer	18	Seal	34	Clip	50	Sleeve
3	Plate	19	Spacer	35	Plate	51	Rubber bushing
4	Rubber packing	20	Steering knuckle	36	Rubber bushing	52	Shock absorber
5	Rubber packing	21	Linkpin	37	Clamp	53	Locknut
6	Axle assembly	22	Bushing	38	Clip	54	Torsion arm set screw
	mounting nut	23	Shim	39	Plate	55	Upper torsion arm
7	Spring washer	24	Seal	40	Rubber bushing	56	Lower torsion arm
8	Bearing dust cover	25	Seat retainer	41	Stabilizer bar	57	Seals
9	Tab washer	26	Kingpin	42	Clamp	58	Dowel pin
10	Adjustment nut	27	Bushing	43	Linkpin pinch bolt nut	59	Shock absorber
11	Thrust washer	28	Grease fitting	44	Washer		mounting pin
12	Bearing	29	Kingpin carrier (link)	45	Linkpin pinch bolt	60	Bump stop
13	Brake drum	30	Cover for thrust washer	46	Shock absorber	61	Needle bearing
14	Backing plate bolt	31	Plastic thrust washer		mounting bolt	62	Torsion bar
15	Washer	32	Steel thrust washer	47	Lock washer	63	Bushing
16	Backing plate			48	Nut	64	Axle beam (tube)

10

7   Remove the linkpin bolts that secure the steering knuckle to the torsion arms. Count the number of camber shims and note their location on each linkpin **(see illustration)** – just in case you mix up some of the shims while the linkpins are out. On pre-1960 models, each linkpin has ten shims; on 1960 and later models, each has eight (the number of shims on the vehicle you are working on may be different, however, depending on prior service). **Caution:** *Don't lose any shims or install them in the wrong location. If you install the linkpins with shims missing or out of place, the camber will be altered and will have to be adjusted by an alignment shop.* Tap the knuckle off the torsion arms with a rubber hammer.

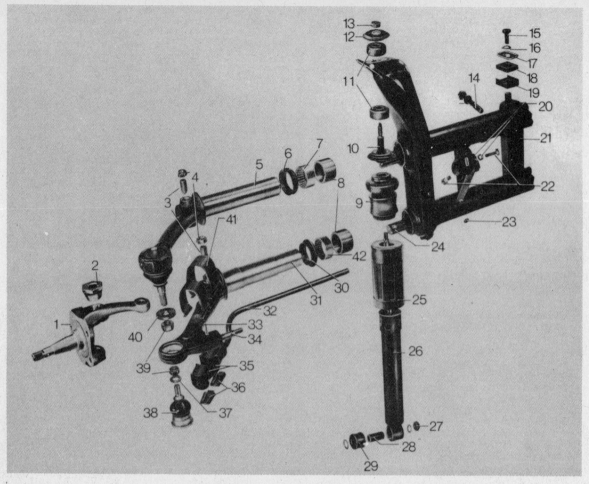

5.8 Exploded view of a 1966 and later torsion bar front end assembly

1	Steering knuckle	12	Plate	23	Grease fitting	33	Pin
2	Camber adjuster	13	Nut	24	Torsion bar	34	Damper lower mounting stud
3	Retaining screw	14	Bolt	25	Outer tube	35	Rubber block
4	Retaining screw locknut	15	Bolt	26	Damper	36	Clip
5	Upper torsion arm	16	Spring washer	27	Nut	37	Washer
6	Seal	17	Plate	28	Sleeve	38	Balljoint
7	Bearing	18	Rubber packing	29	Bushing	39	Self-locking nut
8	Bushing	19	Rubber packing	30	Seal	40	Washer
9	Buffer	20	Locknut	31	Lower torsion arm	41	Clamp
10	Pin	21	Axle beam	32	Stabilizer bar	42	Needle bearing
11	Damper ring	22	Steering stop screw				

1966 and later torsion bar models

Refer to illustrations 5.8 and 5.10

8   Remove the lower balljoint nut **(see illustration)**. Install a balljoint separation tool. With the balljoint tool exerting pressure on the stud, tap the side of the steering knuckle boss with a hammer and the joint will pop loose.

9   Remove the upper balljoint nut and loosen the eccentric bushing for camber adjustment. Press out the upper balljoint stud the same way you did the lower one in Step 8.

10   Raise the upper torsion arm and remove the steering knuckle. **Note:** *A special tool is available for lifting the upper torsion arm* **(see illustration)**. *If this tool isn't available, support the lower torsion arm with a jack, unbolt the lower end of the shock absorber and allow the torsion arm to extend down as far as possible. Position a prybar between the top of the steering knuckle and the upper torsion arm and pry the torsion arm up until the camber adjuster is free of the knuckle.*

MacPherson strut models

11   Remove the stabilizer bar (see Section 6).

12   On 1968 through 1973 models, remove the three bolts connecting the strut, steering knuckle and balljoint (see Section 3). Push the control arm down and remove the steering knuckle (It's not necessary to disconnect the balljoint from the control arm).

13   On 1974 and later models, loosen the balljoint stud pinch bolt and disconnect the balljoint from the steering knuckle. Remove the two bolts securing the steering knuckle to the strut (see Section 3). Remove the knuckle.

Inspection

14   Inspect the steering knuckle for bends, cracks or other damage. If it's bent or cracked, replace it. Don't try to straighten a bent steering knuckle or repair a cracked unit. If you're in any doubt as to the condition of the

5.10 You'll need to raise the upper torsion arm to remove the steering knuckle – the tool in this photo is a special VW tool

5.15 Drive the old linkpin bushings out of the carrier

5.16 Drive the old kingpin out of the carrier and knuckle with a hammer and punch (if you can't drive them out, they'll have to be removed with a hydraulic press)

5.18 Drive in the new kingpin bushing with the same bushing tool, socket or pipe you used to remove it – make sure the notches in the bushing are aligned with the notches in the upper part of the carrier (if the bushing doesn't have any notches, you'll have to make some with a file)

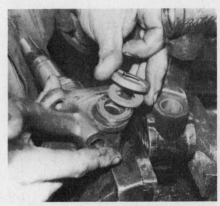

5.19a When you install the new steel thrust washer, plastic thrust washer and thrust washer cover . . .

knuckle, take it to a dealer service department or other repair shop and have it checked. Inspect the bearing surfaces – if they're rusted, pitted, scored or otherwise damaged, replace the knuckle.

Overhaul (1965 and earlier models only)

Refer to illustrations 5.15, 5.16, 5.18, 5.19a, 5.19b, 5.20a, 5.20b, 5.21a, 5.21b and 5.21c

15 Support the knuckle in a vise. Using a socket or a section of pipe with an outside diameter slightly smaller than the outside diameter of the linkpin bushings, drive the old bushings out of the linkpin carrier **(see illustration)**.

16 Drive the old kingpin out of the linkpin carrier and the steering knuckle with a hammer and a large drift punch **(see illustration)**. Discard the thrust washer cover, plastic thrust washer and steel thrust washer. **Note:** *If you can't drive out the kingpin, the bushing and the pin have fused together and are stuck. You'll need a hydraulic press to remove them. If you don't have a press, take the knuckle and carrier assembly to a dealer service department, automotive machine shop or other repair shop, and have the kingpin and bushing pressed out. Also, be sure to take your repair kits with you. As long as you're there, you might as well have them press in the new kingpin bushing, kingpin and linkpin bushings.*

17 If you did manage to get the old kingpin out, drive the kingpin bushing out of the carrier with a socket or a section of pipe with an outside diameter slightly smaller than the outside diameter of the bushing.

18 Drive in the new kingpin bushing with the same socket or pipe. Make sure the notches in the bushing are aligned with the notches in the upper part of the carrier **(see illustration)**. If the bushing has no notches, make some with a small file. **Note:** *At this point, the kingpin carrier must be taken to a machine shop to ream the kingpin bushing to size.*

19 Install a new steel thrust washer, plastic thrust washer and thrust washer cover **(see illustration)**. Make sure the washers and cover are aligned with the dowel in the knuckle **(see illustration)**.

20 Place the kingpin carrier (link) and steering knuckle in position and drive the new kingpin through the upper part of the carrier, through the knuckle and into the bottom part of the carrier **(see illustration)**. Make sure it's fully seated **(see illustration)**.

21 Place the new linkpin bushings in position. Make sure the lubrication holes in the bushings are facing toward the cavity for the grease fitting, so lubricant can reach the clearance between the linkpins and the bushings **(see illustration)**. Install the linkpin bushings with a socket (the same way you removed the old bushings) or use the vise to press them into place **(see illustration)**. If they're installed properly, the bushings will be flush with the ends of the carrier **(see illustration)**.

10

5.19b   . . . make sure the dimples in the cover and washers are aligned with the dowel in the knuckle

5.20a   Place the carrier and knuckle in position and drive in the new kingpin . . .

5.20b   . . . until it's fully seated

5.21a   Install the new linkpin bushings with the lubrication hole adjacent to the grease fitting to ensure that lubricant gets to the linkpin and bushing

5.21b   You can tap the new bushings into place with a bushing installer, socket or pipe, or you can press them into place with a vise, like this

5.21c   The linkpin bushings should be flush with the end of the carrier when installed

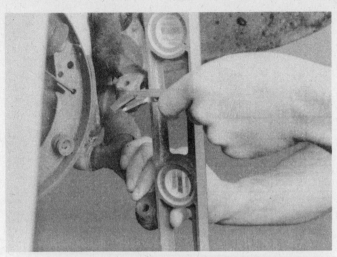

5.22   To measure the offset between the ends of the torsion arms, place a straightedge vertically between the two arms (a level works great), then measure the distance from the straightedge to the end of the upper arm with a vernier caliper

Installation

1965 and earlier models

Refer to illustrations 5.22 and 5.23

22   Measure the offset between the ends of the torsion arms **(see illustration)** and compare your measurement to the acceptable offset range listed in this Chapter's Specifications. If your measurement is within the acceptable range, record the exact figure and save it. You'll need it later. If it isn't, suspect bent torsion arms or defective axle tube needle bearings (see Section 7).

23   Compare the number of shims required for the offset measured in the previous Step to the number you removed in Step 6. If the numbers don't agree, use the numbers in the accompanying chart to produce the correct offset **(see illustration)**.

24   Install the shims and linkpins on the steering knuckle.

25   Install the steering knuckle on the torsion arms.

26   Insert the linkpin clamp bolts into their holes. A groove for the clamp bolt is machined into each linkpin. Turn the linkpins until the bolts slide all the way in.

27   Adjust each linkpin by tightening it (turning it against the clamp bolt), then loosen it about 1/8-turn. Retighten the pin to the point at which you can feel resistance. Tap the end of the pin lightly and tighten the clamp bolt. Repeat this procedure for each linkpin.

1966 and later torsion bar models

28   Lift the upper torsion arm as described in Step 10.

29   Install the steering knuckle and lower the torsion arm. Make sure the notch in the camber adjuster points forward.

30   Install the balljoint nuts and tighten them to the torque listed in this Chapter's Specifications.

MacPherson strut models

31   On 1968 through 1973 models, place the steering knuckle in position on the bottom of the strut, raise the control arm and balljoint into position and install the three bolts which attach the strut, knuckle and balljoint. Tighten the bolts to the torque listed in this Chapter's Specifications.

32   On 1974 and later models, place the steering knuckle in position on the strut, install the strut-to-knuckle bolts, raise the control arm into position, push the balljoint stud into the knuckle and install the pinch bolt. Tighten the bolts to the torque listed in this Chapter's Specifications.

All models

33   Connect the tie-rod to the steering knuckle (see Section 17).

34   Install the brake backing plate and brake shoes and connect the brake hose (see Chapter 9).

35   Install the brake drum (or disc and caliper) and adjust the front wheel bearings (see Chapter 1).

36   Bleed and adjust the brakes (see Chapter 9).

37   Connect the speedometer cable (driver's side only).

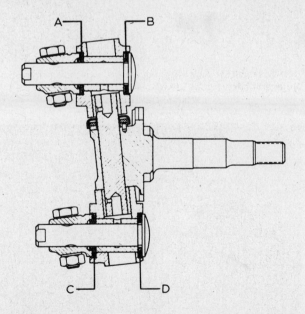

5.23   This chart shows how much offset between the torsion arms can be created with various shim combinations: The letters "A," "B," "C" and "D" above each column on the chart refer to the four points – two inner and two outer – at which the linkpins can be shimmed (if you haven't lost any shims, and you put them all back on at the same locations, the camber should be the same as it was before you removed the steering knuckle)

1959 and earlier models (10 shims)

	Washers installed on linkpins at:			
	A	B	C	D
Offset (mm)				
5	3	7	7	3
5.5	3	6	7	3
6	4	6	6	4
6.5	5	5	6	4
7	5	5	5	5
7.5	6	4	5	5
8	6	4	4	6
8.5	7	3	4	6
9	7	3	3	7

1960 and later models (8 shims)

	Washers installed on linkpins at:			
	A	B	C	D
Offset (mm)				
5.5	2	6	5	3
6	2	6	4	4
6.5	3	5	4	4
7	3	5	3	5
7.5	4	4	3	5
8	4	4	2	6
8.5	5	3	2	6

10

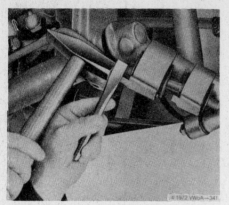

6.2   To remove the clips which hold the clamps together, bend up the lugs and slide the clips off

6.6   Install the new clamps with the slot tapering toward the steering knuckle

6.7   Compress the clamps with adjustable pliers and slide on the clips with the lugs facing toward axle beam

38   Install the wheel and lug bolts, lower the vehicle and tighten the lug bolts to the torque listed in the Chapter 1 Specifications.

---

6   Stabilizer bar – removal and installation

Torsion bar models

Refer to illustrations 6.2, 6.6 and 6.7

1   Loosen the front wheel lug bolts. Apply the parking brake. Raise the front of the vehicle and support it securely on jackstands. Remove the front wheels.

2   Bend up the lugs on the stabilizer bar clips **(see illustration)** and remove them from the clamps on both sides.

3   Open the clamps and remove the metal plates.

4   Remove the stabilizer bar. Discard the clips, plates and clamps.

5   Inspect the rubber bushings for cracks, hardness and other signs of deterioration. If the bushings are damaged, replace them.

6   Using new clips, plates and clamps, install the clamps with the slot tapering toward the steering knuckle **(see illustration)**.

7   Compress the clamps with adjustable pliers and slide on the clips.

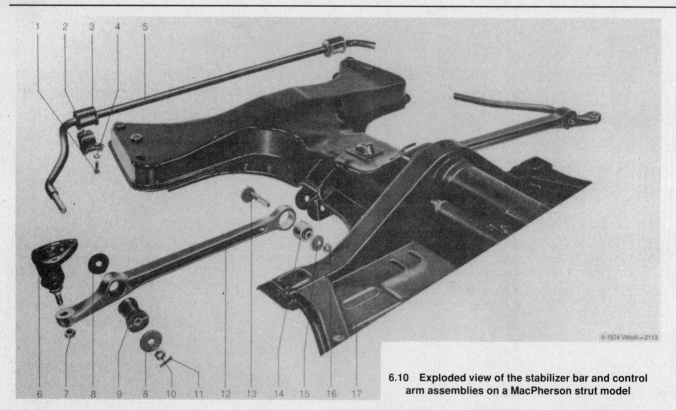

6.10   Exploded view of the stabilizer bar and control arm assemblies on a MacPherson strut model

1 Stabilizer bar mounting bolts	5 Stabilizer bar	9 Bonded rubber bushing for stabilizer bar
2 Mounting clamp	6 Balljoint (1968 through 1973 models)	10 Castellated nut
3 Rubber bushing	7 Self-locking nut	11 Cotter pin
4 Spring washer	8 Bushing washer	12 Control arm
		13 Eccentric camber adjusting bolt

14   Bonded rubber bushing for control arm
15   Eccentric camber adjusting washer
16   Self-locking nut
17   Frame head

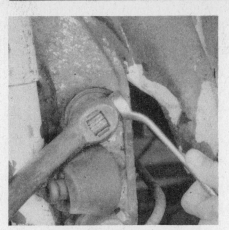

7.5a   To detach a torsion arm from the torsion bar, loosen the locknut on the set screw on the inner end of the arm , . . .

7.5b   . . . loosen the set screw with an Allen wrench and pull the arm off

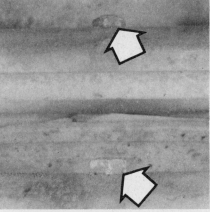

8.5   Remove the locknut which secures the torsion bar retaining bolt and remove the (8mm Allen) retaining bolt (if you're removing the upper bolt, you may find it necessary to grind down the short part of an L-shaped Allen wrench in order to get the wrench into the recessed head of the retaining bolt)

The lugs on the clips must face the axle beam **(see illustration)**.
8   Installation is otherwise the reverse of removal.

MacPherson strut models

Refer to illustration 6.10
Note: *The stabilizer bar on these models influences front wheel alignment. If it's bent, it must be replaced.*

9   Loosen the front wheel lug bolts. Apply the parking brake. Raise the front of the vehicle and support it securely on jackstands. Remove the front wheels.
10   Remove the cotter pins from the castellated nuts on the control arms, then remove the nuts **(see illustration)**.
11   Remove the bolts that attach the two stabilizer clamps to the underside of the frame head, remove the clamps and lower the center part of the stabilizer.
12   Pull the two ends of the stabilizer out of the rubber bushings in the control arms.
13   Inspect the stabilizer bar bushings for hardness and other signs of deterioration. If they're damaged, replace them.
14   Installation is the reverse of removal.

---

7   Torsion arms – removal and installation

Refer to illustrations 7.5a and 7.5b
1   Loosen the wheel lug bolts, raise the front of the vehicle, place it securely on jackstands and remove the front wheel.
2   Remove the brake drum, brake shoes and backing plate, or the caliper and disc (see Chapter 9).
3   Remove the steering knuckle (see Section 5).
4   If you're removing a lower torsion arm, remove the shock absorber (see Section 2) and the stabilizer bar (see Section 6).
5   Loosen the locknuts on the Allen head set screw for the torsion arm and back out the screw **(see illustrations)**.
6   Pull the torsion arm off the end of the axle tube.
7   Clean the torsion arm and linkpins, or balljoints, thoroughly. Inspect the bearing surfaces of the torsion arm for rust, pitting or scoring. If it's worn or damaged, replace it.
8   On early models with linkpins, inspect the linkpins carefully. If they're pitted, rusted or worn, examine the linkpin bushings in the kingpin carrier for the same kind of wear. If they're damaged, replace them (see Section 5).
9   On later models with balljoints, inspect the balljoints carefully. If the balljoints are worn or damaged, replace them (see Section 11).

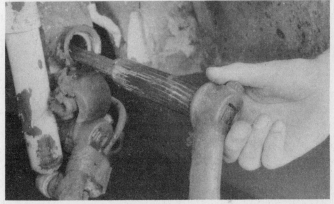

8.6   Use one of the torsion arms to pull the torsion bars out of the axle tube

10   Inspect the lower shock mounting pin. If it's pitted, rusted or worn, take the torsion arm to a dealer service department, automotive machine shop or other repair shop and have a new pin installed.
11   If you're planning to reinstall an old torsion arm, but you're in doubt about its condition, take it to a dealer service department or other repair shop and have it inspected. A number of special tools are needed to properly check a torsion arm.
12   Installation is the reverse of removal.

---

8   Front torsion bars – removal and installation

Refer to illustrations 8.5, 8.6 and 8.10
Removal
1   Loosen the wheel lug bolts, raise the front of the vehicle, place it securely on jackstands and remove the front wheels.
2   Remove the brake drums, brake shoes and backing plates, or the calipers and discs (see Chapter 9).
3   Remove the steering knuckles (see Section 5).
4   Remove a torsion arm on one end of the torsion bars you intend to remove (see Section 7).
5   Remove the torsion bar retaining bolt locknut and remove the retaining bolt **(see illustration)**.
6   Pull the torsion bar out with the torsion arm on the other end of the torsion bars **(see illustration)**.

10

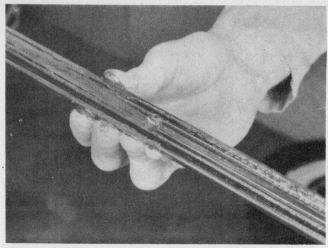

8.10   Before you insert the torsion bars through the axle tube, make sure they're aligned like this so that the recessed dimple is oriented toward the hole for the retaining bolt – when the bars are installed in the tube, the retaining bolt must seat into this dimple

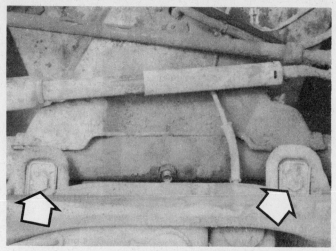

9.10   Remove the two bolts (arrows) that attach the body to the upper axle tube

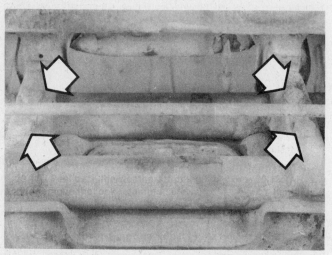

9.11   Remove the four bolts (arrows) that attach the axle assembly to the frame head

7   Clean the torsion bars with solvent. Inspect them for rust, cracks and fractures. If any damage is evident, replace the torsion bar(s).
8   Inspect the torsion arms (see Section 7). Inspect the needle bearings and bushings in the axle tubes. If they're rusted, pitted or worn, remove the front axle assembly (see Section 9) and have them replaced by a dealer service department or other repair shop.

Installation

9   Coat the bars liberally with multi-purpose grease. Make sure the grease gets in between the individual leaves.
10   Insert the torsion bars back into the axle tube. Align the countersunk recess **(see illustration)** with the torsion arm retaining bolt. Make sure you install the same number of leaves that you removed. If the torsion bars prove difficult to insert through the axle tube, wrap a piece of mechanic's wire around the leaves to keep them together. If that doesn't work, try installing them a layer at a time – two thin strips – side-by-side – on bottom, four thick strips – one on top of the next – and, finally, two more thin strips on top – side-by-side.
11   With the recess in the center of the bar aligned with the hole for the retaining bolt, install the retaining bolt and secure it with the locknut.
12   The remainder of installation is the reverse of removal.

9   Front axle beam assembly – removal and installation

Warning: *Gasoline is extremely flammable, so take extra precautions when you work on any part of the fuel system. Don't smoke or allow open flames or bare light bulbs near the work area. Also, don't work in a garage where a natural gas type appliance with a pilot light is present. Finally, when you perform any kind of work around the fuel tank, wear safety glasses and have a Class B type fire extinguisher on hand. If you spill any fuel on your skin, clean it off immediately with soap and water.*
Note: *Have an assistant handy to help you balance the axle assembly on the floor jack during removal.*

Removal

Refer to illustrations 9.10 and 9.11
1   Loosen the front wheel lug bolts, raise the front of the vehicle, place it securely on jackstands and remove the front wheels.
2   Disconnect the cable from the negative battery terminal.
3   Disconnect the fuel tank feed and vent lines and remove the fuel tank (see Chapter 4).
4   Disconnect the steering column from the flexible coupling flange (see Section 18).
5   Disconnect the horn wire near the flexible coupling (see Chapter 12).
6   Remove the retaining clip from the speedometer cable at the dust cap of the left front wheel and pull the cable out of the steering knuckle.
7   Disconnect the brake hoses from the metal lines at the brackets and plug the hoses and lines to prevent contamination (see Chapter 9).
8   Bend down the lockplate that secures the bolt for the steering damper at its mounting bracket on the axle. Detach the steering damper bolts from the axle bracket and from the long tie-rod and remove the damper (see Section 17).
9   Disconnect the long tie-rod from the steering knuckle and from the Pitman arm and remove it (see Section 17). (Remove the short tie-rod too, if you wish, but its removal isn't necessary for axle removal).
10   Remove the two bolts that attach the vehicle body to the top of the axle beam **(see illustration)**. Discard the rubber spacers, washers and spring washers.
11   Loosen the four bolts that attach the axle beam to the frame head **(see illustration)**.
12   Position a floor jack under the axle beam, remove the four axle beam retaining bolts and remove the axle beam assembly. The axle beam is heavy, so it's a good idea to have an assistant help balance the axle on the floor jack until it's safely lowered.
13   Remove the front axle bolts and lower it on the floor jack. Keep it balanced on the floor jack head. Remove the rubber spacers from the threaded bushings and discard them.

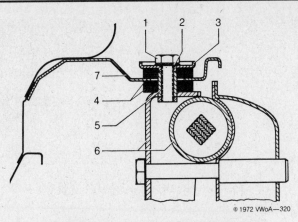

© 1972 VWoA—320

9.16   Cutaway view of axle attachment to body

1	Bolt	5	Threaded bushing
2	Lock washer	6	Axle
3	Washer for spacer	7	Vehicle body
4	Rubber spacer		

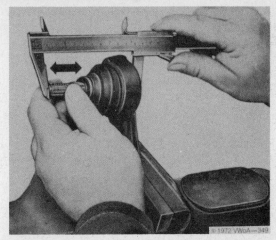

11.3   To check the play of a balljoint in a torsion arm, place the torsion arm in a bench vise, push the balljoint stud all the way in, measure it, pull it all the way out, measure it, calculate the difference and compare your measurement to the play listed in this Chapter's Specifications

Installation

Refer to illustration 9.16

Note: *You'll need an assistant to help you install the axle assembly.*

14   Install a new rubber spacer on each threaded bushing on the front axle.

15   Place the axle assembly on a floor jack, guide it under the front of the vehicle and, with your assistant helping you balance the axle on the floor jack, raise the axle into position and install the mounting bolts. Use new spring washers on the bolts. Tighten the bolts to the torque listed in this Chapter's Specifications.

16   Install new rubber spacers, washers and spring washers on the upper axle retaining bolts that attach the body to the axle **(see illustration)**. Tighten the bolts to the torque listed in this Chapter's Specifications.

17   Install the tie-rod(s) and the steering damper (see Section 17).

18   Reattach the steering column to the flexible coupling flange (see Section 18).

19   Reconnect the horn wire.

20   Reattach the fuel tank feed line and the return line and install the fuel tank (see Chapter 4).

21   Connect the brake hoses to the metal lines (see Chapter 9).

22   Install the wheels, loosely install the wheel lug bolts, lower the vehicle and tighten the wheel lug bolts to the torque listed in the Chapter 1 Specifications.

23   Have the wheel alignment checked and, if necessary, adjusted.

10   Control arms (strut-type front end only) – removal and installation

Removal

1   Loosen the wheel lug bolts, raise the front of the vehicle, place it securely on jackstands and remove the front wheel.

2   On 1973 and earlier models, remove the self-locking nut from the balljoint stud. On 1974 and later models, loosen the pinch bolt for the balljoint stud.

3   On 1973 and earlier models, pull the control arm off the balljoint stud (see Section 11). On 1974 and later models, pull the control arm down and out of the steering knuckle.

4   Disconnect the stabilizer bar from the control arm (see Section 6).

5   Remove the self-locking nut and the camber adjusting nut at the frame head **(see illustration 6.10)**.

6   Pull the control down and remove it.

7   Inspect the control arm. Make sure it's not cracked or bent. Inspect the bonded rubber bushings – at the inner end of the arm and for the stabi-

lizer bar – for cracks and deterioration. If they're damaged or worn, take the control arm to a dealer service department or other repair shop and have them replaced. **Note:** *When installed, the rubber lugs on the bushing for the stabilizer bar must be in a horizontal position* **(see illustration 6.10)**.

Installation

8   Insert the stabilizer bar through its bushing in the control arm and install the castellated nut finger tight.

9   Make sure the hole in the control arm for the balljoint stud and the stud itself are clean and dry (no lubricant). Push the outer end of the arm up onto the stud and install the castellated nut.

10   Push the inner end of the control arm up into its mounting bracket on the frame head and insert the camber adjusting bolt through the bracket and the control arm. Install the eccentric washer and a new self-locking nut.

11   Tighten the castellated nut on the balljoint stud to the torque listed in this Chapter's Specifications. If necessary, turn the nut a little further to expose a hole for the cotter pin. Install a new cotter pin.

12   Tighten the self-locking nut on the camber adjusting bolt to the torque listed in this Chapter's Specifications.

13   On 1973 and earlier models, install a new self-locking nut on the balljoint stud and tighten it to the torque listed in this Chapter's Specifications. You may need to hold the flat sides of the balljoint stud with a wrench to prevent the stud from turning as you tighten the nut. On 1974 and later models, tighten the clamp bolt to the torque listed in this Chapter's Specifications.

14   Install the wheel and lug bolts. Lower the vehicle and tighten the wheel lug bolts to the torque listed in the Chapter 1 Specifications.

15   Have the wheel alignment checked and, if necessary, adjusted.

11   Balljoints – check and replacement

Torsion bar models

Refer to illustration 11.3

Note: *A special tool is required to measure balljoint play with the torsion arm installed. However, you can check balljoint play with the torsion arm removed.*

1   Remove the torsion arm (see Section 7).

2   Carefully clean the torsion arm and balljoint.

3   Move the balljoint stud in and out and measure the difference between the limits of travel with a vernier caliper **(see illustration)**. Compare

10

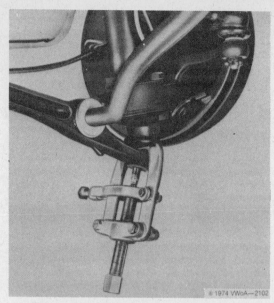

11.5   To detach the balljoint from the control arm, press it out with a balljoint separator or a two-jaw puller

your measurements to the wear limits listed in this Chapter's Specifications. If the indicated play exceeds the wear limits, take the torsion arm to a dealer service department or other repair shop and have a new balljoint installed.

MacPherson strut models
1970 through 1973 models
Refer to illustration 11.5

4   Remove the self-locking nut from the balljoint stud at the outer end of the control arm **(see illustration 3.4)**.
5   Using balljoint separator tool (or a two-jaw puller), push the balljoint stud out of the control arm **(see illustration)**.
6   Bend down the lockplates and remove the bolts that attach the balljoint, steering knuckle and strut together **(see illustration 3.4)**.
7   Hang the steering knuckle and brake assembly from the brake hose bracket or the strut with a piece of wire. Don't disconnect the brake hose.
8   Remove the balljoint.
9   Installation is the reverse of removal. Be sure to use new lock plates and a new self-locking nut on the balljoint stud. To immobilize the balljoint stud while tightening the self-locking nut, grip the flat sides of the lower end

of the stud with an open end wrench. Tighten the nut to the torque listed in this Chapter's Specifications.
10   Have the camber and toe checked and adjusted when you're done.

1974 and later models
11   Remove the control arm (see Section 10).
12   Take the control arm to a dealer service department or other repair shop and have the balljoint pressed out and a new balljoint pressed in.
13   Install the control arm (see Section 10).

---

12   Rear shock absorbers – removal and installation

Refer to illustrations 12.2a and 12.2b

1   Loosen the rear wheel lug bolts, raise the rear of the vehicle, place it securely on jackstands and remove the wheels.
2   Remove the upper and lower shock absorber mounting nuts and bolts **(see illustrations)**.
3   Remove the shock absorber.
4   Installation is the reverse of removal.

---

13   Spring plates and rear torsion bars – removal, installation and adjustment

Removal
Refer to illustrations 13.4, 13.5, 13.7, 13.8, 13.9a, 13.9b and 13.10

1   Loosen the rear wheel lug bolts, raise the rear of the vehicle, place it securely on jackstands and remove the wheels.
2   On driveaxle models, remove the driveaxle (see Chapter 8).
3   Disconnect the parking brake cables at the parking brake lever (see Chapter 9).
4   On swing axle models, mark the relationship of the spring plate to the axle bearing housing with a chisel **(see illustration)**.
5   On driveaxle models, mark the relationship of the spring plate to the diagonal arm with a chisel **(see illustration)**.
6   Disconnect the lower end of the shock absorber (see Section 12).
7   On swing axle models, remove the bolts securing the spring plate to the axle tube **(see illustration)**. Pull the axle tube to the rear, out of the spring plate. Suspend the axle tube with a piece of wire or support it on a jackstand.
8   On driveaxle models, remove the bolts securing the spring plate to the diagonal arm **(see illustration)**. Remove the diagonal arm pivot bolt and the diagonal arm (see Section 15).

12.2a   Upper shock mounting bolt and nut

12.2b   Lower shock mounting bolt and nut

13.4   On swing axle models, mark the spring plate position in relation to the housing for the rear axle bearing

13.5   On driveaxle models, mark the spring plate position in relation to the diagonal arm

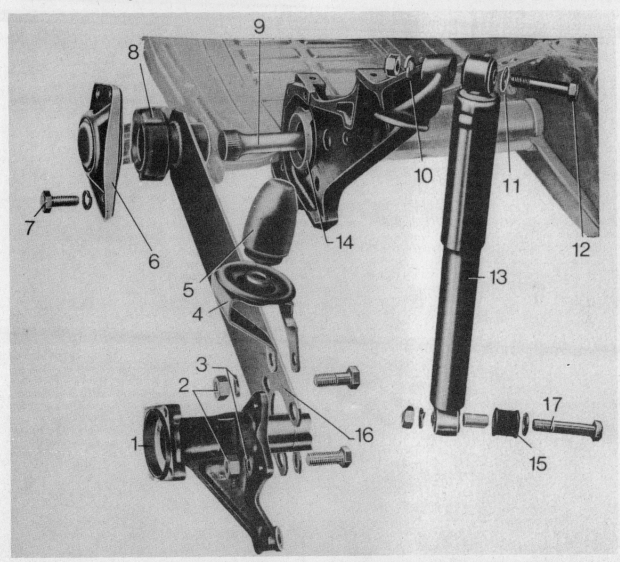

13.7   An exploded view of the rear suspension on a swing axle model

1	Bearing housing	6	Cover for hub	11	Washer	15	Rubber bushing
2	Nuts	7	Bolt	12	Shock absorber	16	Spring plate
3	Spring washers	8	Outer rubber bushing		mounting bolt	17	Shock absorber
4	Bump stop seat	9	Torsion bar	13	Shock absorber		mounting bolt
5	Bump stop	10	Nut and washer	14	Inner rubber bushing		

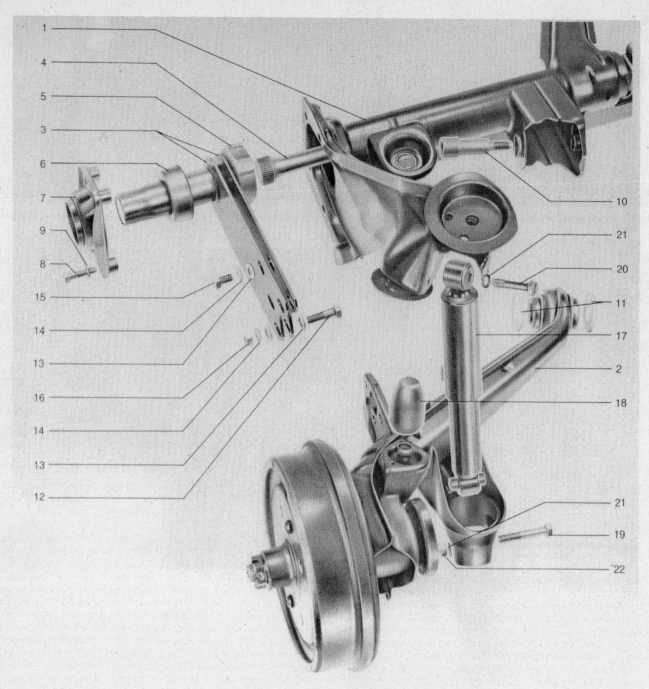

13.8   An exploded view of the rear suspension on a driveaxle model

1	Torsion housing	8	Hub cover bolt	15	Spring plate-to-diagonal arm bolt
2	Diagonal arm	9	Lock washer	16	Nut
3	Double spring plate	10	Diagonal arm pivot bolt	17	Shock absorber
4	Torsion bar	11	Spacer	18	Rubber bump stop
5	Inner rubber bushing	12	Spring plate-to-diagonal arm bolt	19	Shock absorber mounting bolt
6	Outer rubber bushing	13	Washer	20	Shock absorber mounting bolt
7	Cover for spring plate hub	14	Lock washer	21	Lock washer
				22	Nut

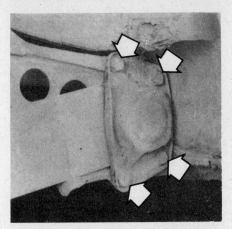

13.9a   Remove the cover for the spring plate hub

13.9b   Remove the rubber bushing from the hub

13.10   Carefully pry the spring plate off the stop

13.19   Place a protractor (angle finder) on the tunnel to measure the angle at which the vehicle is setting

13.20   Lift the spring plate slightly to remove any freeplay, place the protractor (angle finder) on top of the spring plate and record the indicated angle

9   Remove the bolts securing the spring plate hub cover **(see illustration)** and remove the cover. Also remove the rubber bushing **(see illustration)**. **Warning:** *The spring plate is under tremendous spring pressure. DO NOT place any part of your body under the spring plate while performing the next step, or anytime the spring plate hub cover is removed and the spring plate is resting on its stop.*

10   Place a floor jack under the end of the spring plate and raise it just until it comes off the stop. Lever the spring plate out away from the vehicle using a prybar **(see illustration)**, while simultaneously lowering the jack until the spring plate has reached the end of its travel and the torsion bar is relaxed. Pull the spring plate off the torsion bar.

11   Remove the fender (see Chapter 11).

12   Carefully slide the torsion bar out. Check it for nicks or cracks. Sometimes cracks may not be visible to the eye, so it's a good idea to have them checked by a dealer service department, automotive machine shop or other repair shop that is equipped to do the work.

Installation and adjustment

Refer to illustrations 13.19 and 13.20

13   Grease the splines on the torsion bar and carefully guide it into the torsion housing until you feel the splines engage. **Note:** *Torsion bars are marked L (left) and R (right). If you have removed both torsion bars, make sure you install them on the correct side.*

14   Coat the inner and outer rubber bushings with talcum powder to prevent the spring plate from turning them.

15   Install the inner bushing with the word "Oben" at the top. Note that the inner bushing is different from the outer bushing – don't mix them up.

16   Install the spring plate.

17   To ensure proper wheel alignment and sufficient spring travel under varying loads, the spring plate must be adjusted on the torsion bar. There are 40 splines on the inner end and 44 splines on the outer end of the torsion bar. If you rotate the inner end of the bar one spline, it alters the spring plate angle 9-degrees, 0-minutes; if you rotate the spring plate one spline on the bar, it alters the angle 8-degrees, 10-minutes. So, you can set the spring plate at any multiple of 50-minutes by rotating the splines in opposite directions. VW has a special tool for this job, but it's expensive and hard to find. Using the following procedure, you can adjust the spring plate with easily obtainable tools. **Note:** *Be sure to adjust both spring plates, even if only one has been removed, especially on a high mileage vehicle.*

18   Measure the spring plate angle in relation to the bottom of the door opening or the frame tunnel. Of course, it's unlikely that either the door opening or the frame tunnel are level, since the rear of the vehicle is elevated. First, you need to determine the angle at which the vehicle is inclined from the horizontal.

19   Place a protractor (angle finder) on the frame tunnel **(see illustration)**. Prop up the opposite end of the level until its bubble is centered. Note the angle of the tunnel and record this measurement.

20   Now place the protractor (angle finder) on top of the spring plate, lift the spring plate by hand slightly to remove any play, then measure the spring plate angle **(see illustration)**. Again, record your measurement.

21   Subtract the angle you measured in Step 19 from the angle you measured in Step 20. The difference should equal the spring plate angle listed in this Chapter's Specifications for model and year of the vehicle. If it doesn't, rotate the inner end of the torsion bar on its splines, or rotate the spring plate on the torsion bar, or both, until the correct angle is attained.

10

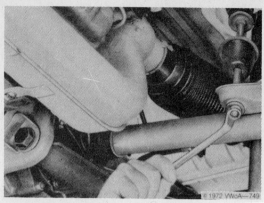

14.2   Remove the nuts from the lower ends of the operating rods

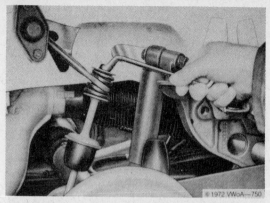

14.3   Remove the protective rubber caps and remove the nuts from the upper ends of the operating rods

14.14   Reassemble the inner and outer supports and rubber bushing like this (the support with flat flange should be positioned on the outside, and the support with the rolled flange should be on the inside)

22   Coat the outer rubber bushing with talcum powder and install it with the word "oben" at the top.
23   Install the spring plate hub cover and loosely install the bolts.
24   Using a floor jack, lift the spring plate until its lower edge clears the lower stop.
25   Tighten the spring plate hub cover bolts securely.
26   Clean the mating surfaces between the spring plate and the axle bearing housing or diagonal arm.
27   Install the spring plate-to-bearing housing or spring plate-to-diagonal arm bolts (and the diagonal arm pivot bolt), make sure the chisel marks on the spring plate and bearing housing or diagonal arm are aligned and tighten the bolts to the torque listed in this Chapter's Specifications.
28   On driveaxle models, install the driveaxle (see Chapter 8).
29   Reattach the parking brake cable and adjust it (see Chapter 9).
30   Install the fender.
31   Install the wheel(s), lower the vehicle and tighten the wheel lug bolts to the torque listed in the Chapter 1 Specifications.
32   If you installed a new spring plate, have the wheel alignment checked and, if necessary, adjusted.

14   Equalizer spring – removal, inspection and installation

Removal

Refer to illustrations 14.2 and 14.3
1   Loosen the rear wheel lug bolts, raise the rear of the vehicle, place it securely on jackstands and remove the rear wheels.
2   Remove the nuts from the operating rod guides **(see illustration)**.

3   Remove the protective rubber caps from the upper ends of the operating rods and remove the nuts **(see illustration)**.
4   Remove the operating rods and rubber damper rings.
5   Remove the nuts securing the outer and inner supports. Remove the supports and the bushings.
6   Loosen the locknut and remove the Allen screw securing the left spring lever. Remove the lever.
7   Remove the right spring lever and equalizer spring as a single assembly.

Inspection

8   Inspect the operating rod guide rings. Replace them if they're damaged or worn. To replace a ring, pry it out with a screwdriver.
9   Inspect the equalizer spring, bushings and rubber stops for wear and other deterioration. Replace as necessary.

Installation

Refer to illustration 14.14
10   Install the left spring lever on the equalizer spring. Tighten the Allen screw and locknut. **Note:** *The left spring lever is marked with an "L" and the right lever is unmarked. Make sure the left spring lever points down and toward the rear, with the clamping screw facing the front of the vehicle.*
11   Tighten the clamping screw and locknut securely.
12   Install the equalizer spring rod and left spring lever from the right side of the vehicle.
13   Install the right spring lever. Make sure the right spring lever points down and toward the front of the vehicle when installed.
14   Install the rubber washers, the supports and the rubber bushings **(see illustration)**.
15   Install the operating rods into the spring levers (the longer rod goes on the right side). Don't forget the damping rings above and below the spring levers. Tighten the nuts and install the rubber caps.
16   Insert the operating rods into the guides, install the washers and tighten the nuts.
17   Install the wheels and lug bolts. Lower the vehicle and tighten the wheel lug bolts to the torque listed in the Chapter 1 Specifications.

15   Diagonal arms – removal and installation

Removal

Refer to illustration 15.9
1   Loosen the rear wheel lug bolts, raise the rear of the vehicle, place it securely on jackstands and remove the rear wheel(s).
2   Remove the brake drum (see Chapter 9).
3   Remove the driveaxle (see Chapter 8).
4   Disconnect the brake hose and parking brake cable from the brake backing plate (see Chapter 9).

15.9   Remove the Allen pivot bolt from the front end of the diagonal arm

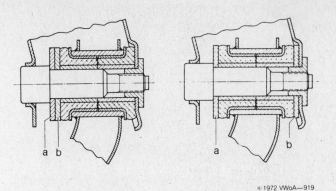

15.11a   Make sure both of the spacer washers are on the outside of the bushing as shown on the left, not on either side as shown on the right

15.11b   Peen the metal shoulder as shown to prevent the pivot bolt from backing out

5   Remove the bearing cover and backing plate (see Chapter 8).
6   Mark the position of the spring plate in relation to the diagonal arm with a chisel **(see illustration 13.5)**.
7   Disconnect the lower end of the shock absorber **(see illustration 13.8)**.
8   Remove the bolts securing the spring plate to the diagonal arm **(see illustration 13.8)**.
9   Remove the Allen pivot bolt which attaches the front end of the diagonal arm to its mounting bracket on the torsion bar tube **(see illustration)**. Remove the diagonal arm.
10   Inspect the rubber bushing at the front of the diagonal arm. If it's dried or cracked, it must be replaced. Inspect the bearings. If they're scored, pitted or worn, they must be replaced. Take the diagonal arm to a dealer service department or other repair shop.

Installation

Refer to illustrations 15.11a and 15.11b

11   Attach the diagonal arm to its mounting bracket on the torsion bar tube with the Allen pivot bolt. Make sure the spacer washers are both on the *outside* of the rubber bushing **(see illustration)**. Tighten the bolt to the torque listed in this Chapter's Specifications. To prevent tension in the bonded rubber bushing, pull the diagonal arm down to its fully extended position when you tighten the bolt. Lock the bolt by peening the bracket collar into a bolt head groove with a dull chisel **(see illustration)**.
12   Align the chisel marks, install the spring plate-to-diagonal arm bolts and tighten them to the torque listed in this Chapter's Specifications.
13   Attach the lower end of the shock absorber to the diagonal arm (see Section 12).

16.2   Exploded view of a typical late model steering wheel assembly

1	Padded horn ring	3	Trim
2	Steering wheel	4	Contact ring

14   Install the bearing cover (see Chapter 8).
15   Connect the brake hose and parking brake cable (see Chapter 9).
16   Install the driveaxle (see Chapter 8).
17   Install the brake drum (see Chapter 9).
18   Install the wheel and lug bolts, lower the vehicle and tighten the lug bolts to the torque listed in the Chapter 1 Specifications. Have the rear wheel alignment checked and, if necessary, adjusted.

---

16   Steering wheel – removal and installation

Removal

Refer to illustrations 16.2 and 16.3

1   Disconnect the cable from the negative terminal of the battery.
2   Pry the horn ring or horn pad **(see illustration)** from the steering wheel and disconnect the wire to the horn switch.

10

16.3   Remove the steering wheel nut and the spring washer

16.6   On older models, the steering wheel is equipped with a brass washer – make sure the cutaway portion of this washer faces to the right when the wheels are pointed straight ahead

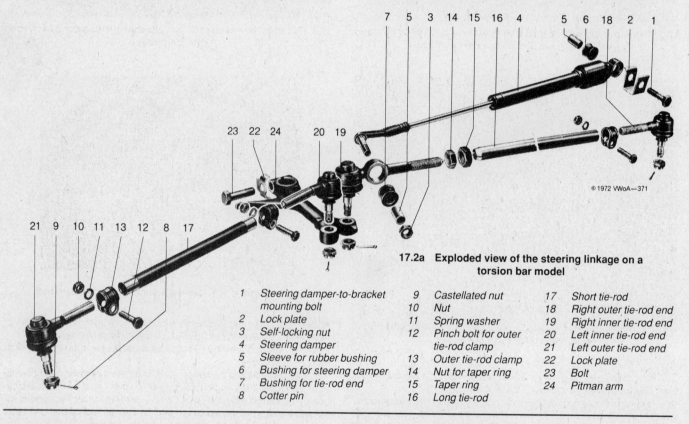

17.2a   Exploded view of the steering linkage on a torsion bar model

1	Steering damper-to-bracket mounting bolt	9	Castellated nut	17	Short tie-rod
2	Lock plate	10	Nut	18	Right outer tie-rod end
3	Self-locking nut	11	Spring washer	19	Right inner tie-rod end
4	Steering damper	12	Pinch bolt for outer tie-rod clamp	20	Left inner tie-rod end
5	Sleeve for rubber bushing	13	Outer tie-rod clamp	21	Left outer tie-rod end
6	Bushing for steering damper	14	Nut for taper ring	22	Lock plate
7	Bushing for tie-rod end	15	Taper ring	23	Bolt
8	Cotter pin	16	Long tie-rod	24	Pitman arm

3   Remove the steering wheel nut **(see illustration)** and the spring washer.

4   Mark the relationship of the steering shaft to the hub (if marks don't already exist or don't line up) to simplify installation and ensure steering wheel alignment.

5   Use a puller to detach the steering wheel from the shaft. Don't hammer on the shaft to dislodge the steering wheel.

Installation

Refer to illustration 16.6

6   On older models with a brass washer under the steering wheel nut, make sure the cutaway portion of the washer is facing to the right when the wheels are pointed straight ahead **(see illustration)**.

7   To install the wheel, align the mark on the steering wheel hub with the mark on the shaft and slip the wheel onto the shaft. **Note:** *If the wheel was previously installed incorrectly, the alignment marks won't ensure that it is installed with the spokes horizontal. If this is the case, make sure the wheels are pointed straight ahead and the steering gear is centered, then slip the wheel onto the steering column shaft with the spokes horizontal.*

The steering gear is centered when the split in the circlip is aligned with the raised boss on the gearbox.

8   Install the spring washer and nut. Tighten the nut to the torque listed in this Chapter's Specifications.

9   Connect the horn wire and install the horn ring or horn pad.

10   Connect the negative battery cable.

17   Steering gear linkage – removal and installation

1   For all of the following procedures, loosen the wheel lug bolts (where applicable), raise the front of the vehicle, support it securely, block the rear wheels and set the parking brake. Remove the front wheel(s) if necessary.

Torsion bar models
Steering damper

Refer to illustrations 17.2a, 17.2b and 17.3

2   Remove the bolt that attaches the steering damper to its mounting bracket on the upper axle tube **(see illustrations)**.

17.2b   Remove the bolt (arrow) that attaches the steering damper to its mounting bracket on the upper axle tube

17.3   Remove the nut (arrow) that attaches the damper piston rod to the long tie-rod

17.9   Press the tie-rod ends out of the steering knuckle and Pitman arm with a two-jaw puller

17.15   Remove the steering damper-to-Pitman arm bolt

3   Remove the nut that attaches the damper piston rod to the long tie-rod **(see illustration)** and remove the steering damper.

4   To check the steering damper, extend and compress the piston rod by hand. It should move slowly and uniformly. If there's a slack or stiff spot anywhere in the range of movement, replace the damper. Look for leaks too. If fluid is leaking past the seal, replace the damper. It's not rebuildable.

5   Inspect the rubber bushing and sleeve in the bracket end of the damper and on the tie-rod for wear and damage. If either needs to be replaced, take the damper and/or tie-rod to a dealer service department or other repair shop to have the old sleeve(s) and bushing(s) pressed out and new one(s) pressed in.

6   Installation is the reverse of removal. Tighten the nut at the tie-rod end and the bolt at the bracket end of the damper securely.

Tie-rods and tie-rod ends
Refer to illustration 17.9

7   If you're removing the right (long) tie-rod, detach the steering damper (see above).

8   Remove the cotter pins and castellated nuts from the tie-rod ends.

9   Press the tie-rod ends out of the Pitman arm and steering knuckle with a balljoint separator or a two-jaw puller **(see illustration)**.

10   Inspect the tie-rod(s) for damage and wear. If a tie-rod is bent, replace it – don't try to straighten it. If there's any play in the balljoints or if you can't move either balljoint stud by hand, replace the tie-rod end (see next Step).

Inspect the rubber boots for tears. If a tie-rod boot has been torn or punctured, replace the tie-rod end. Dirt has probably contaminated the balljoint. If you've removed the long tie-rod, inspect the bushing for the steering damper (see above).

11   If you're replacing the tie-rod itself, mark the inner and outer tie-rod ends with a paint stripe to ensure proper reassembly. If you're replacing one of the tie-rod ends, that won't work – instead, count the number of threads exposed on the old tie-rod end. Loosen the clamp bolt, slide the clamp out of the way and unscrew the old tie-rod end.

12   If you're installing the old tie-rod end, screw it into the tie-rod until the paint stripe is touching the tie-rod. If you're installing a new tie-rod end, screw it into the tie-rod until the same number of threads are exposed as on the old tie-rod. Place the clamp in position and tighten the clamp bolt securely.

13   Installation is the reverse of removal. Be sure to tighten the balljoint stud nuts to the torque listed in this Chapter's Specifications.

14   Take the vehicle to a dealer service department or alignment shop and have the front end alignment checked and, if necessary, adjusted.

MacPherson strut models with worm-and-roller steering
Steering damper
Refer to illustrations 17.15 and 17.17

15   Remove the Pitman arm-to-steering damper bolt **(see illustration)**.

16   To get at the bolt that attaches the steering damper to the frame head, remove the spare wheel from the front luggage compartment and pry the cover out of the access hole.

10

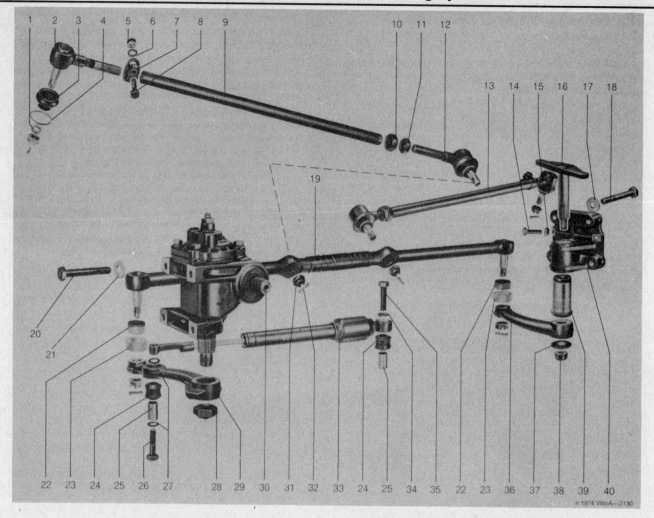

17.17   An exploded view of the steering linkage on 1970 through 1974 MacPherson strut models

1 Boot O-ring	11 Nut	21 Flat washer	31 Castellated nut
2 Tie-rod end	12 Tie-rod end	22 Spacer	32 Cotter pin
3 Boot	13 Right tie-rod assembly	23 Sealing ring	33 Steering damper
4 Boot retaining ring	14 Adjusting bolt	24 Rubber bushing	34 Lock washer
5 Nut	15 Locknut	25 Bushing sleeve	35 Bolt
6 Spring washer	16 Idler arm shaft	26 Bolt	36 Idler arm
7 Tie-rod clamp	17 Flat washer	27 Lock washer	37 Washer
8 Tie-rod clamp bolt	18 Bolt	28 Nut	38 Self-locking nut
9 Left tie-rod	19 Center tie-rod	29 Pitman arm	39 Idler arm bracket bushing
10 Tapered ring	20 Bolt	30 Steering gearbox	40 Idler arm bracket

17   Remove the steering damper-to-frame head bolt **(see illustration)** and remove the steering damper.

18   To check the steering damper, extend and compress the piston rod by hand. It should move through its stroke slowly and uniformly. If there's a slack or stiff spot anywhere in the range of movement, replace the damper. Look for leaks too. A small amount of fluid leaking past the seal is acceptable. But if the damper is empty, replace it. It's not rebuildable.

19   Installation is the reverse of removal. Tighten the damper-to-frame head bolt and the damper-to-Pitman arm bolt securely. Apply caulking compound around the access cover.

Tie-rods

Refer to illustration 17.22

20   Because models with worm-and-roller steering have a center tie-rod, it's easier to remove the center tie-rod and left and right tie-rods as a single unit, then separate them once the assembly is off the vehicle. But you can,

if you wish, remove either tie-rod by itself.

21   Remove the cotter pins and castellated nuts from the outer ends of both tie-rods **(see illustration 17.17)**.

22   Press the left and right tie-rod ends out of the steering knuckles with a balljoint separator or a two-jaw puller **(see illustration)**. Don't hammer on the tie-rod ends or you'll ruin the threads.

23   Press the center tie-rod ends out of the Pitman arm and idler arm **(see illustration 17.17)**.

24   Remove the tie-rod assembly as a single unit and clamp the center tie-rod in a vise. Remove the cotter pins and castellated nuts from the inner tie-rod ends. Press the inner ends of the tie-rods out of the center tie-rod.

25   Clean the tie-rods with a wire brush, then inspect them for cracks. Check for distortion by rolling the tie-rods over a flat surface. Inspect the tie-rod end boots for cracks. If a boot is damaged, it can be replaced, but be sure to inspect the tie-rod itself for contamination. Once dirt gets into a tie-rod end through a tear in the boot, replace the tie-rod end. If any of the

17.22 Press the tie-rod ends out of the steering knuckles with a two-jaw puller – don't hammer on the tie-rod end or you'll ruin the threads

17.32 After installing the nut that attaches the Pitman arm to the roller shaft, peen the lower part of the nut (arrows) until it engages the slots in the roller shaft

17.34 To remove the idler arm and bracket assembly, remove these three bolts from the body – support the idler arm as you remove the last bolt (arrow)

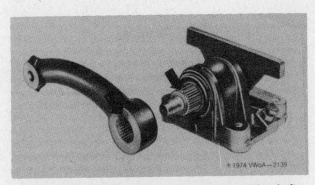

17.38 When installing the idler arm back onto the shaft, make sure the wide splines inside the shaft bore are aligned with the wide splines on the shaft

tie-rod ends are worn, replace them. Before removing a tie-rod end from a tie-rod, mark the threads with paint to ensure proper reinstallation.

26   Installation is the reverse of removal.

Pitman arm

Refer to illustration 17.32

27   Disconnect the steering damper's piston rod from the Pitman arm (see Steps 15 through 19).

28   Remove the cotter pin and castellated nut.

29   Press the center tie-rod end out of the Pitman arm. Don't hammer out the tie-rod end or you may damage the threads.

30   Remove the nut that attaches the Pitman arm to the roller shaft of the steering box and pull the Pitman arm off the shaft.

31   Inspect the rubber bushing and metal sleeve for the bolt that attaches the steering damper to the Pitman arm. If either is worn, press it out, lubricate the new bushing with silicone spray and press it in. If you don't have a hydraulic press, take the Pitman arm and new parts to a dealer service department or other repair shop to have this done.

32   Installation is the reverse of removal. Note that some of the splines on the roller shaft are wider than others to ensure proper realignment. If you're replacing the Pitman arm, make sure it's got the same size splines as the old arm. Tighten all fasteners to the torque listed in this Chapter's Specifications. After you've tightened the nut that attaches the Pitman arm to the roller shaft, peen the nut as shown (**see illustration**).

Idler arm

Refer to illustrations 17.34 and 17.38

33   Disconnect the tie-rod end from the idler arm.

34   Remove the three bolts that attach the idler arm to the body (**see illustration**).

35   Remove the idler arm and bracket as a single unit.

36   To remove the idler arm from the bracket, simply remove the self-locking nut and washer and pull the arm off the splined shaft.

37   Inspect the bonded rubber bushing inside the bracket. If it's worn, press it out along with the inner metal bushing, then press out the outer metal bushing. Press the new inner metal bushing, bonded rubber bushing and outer metal bushing into the bracket together. If you don't have a hydraulic press, take the bracket and new parts to a dealer service department or other repair shop to have this done.

38   Installation is the reverse of removal. Make sure the splines are aligned as shown (**see illustration**). Tighten the new self-locking nut and all other fasteners to the torque listed in this Chapter's Specifications.

MacPherson strut models with rack-and-pinion steering

Tie-rods and tie-rod ends

39   Remove the cotter pins and castellated nuts from the outer ends of both tie-rods.

40   Press the tie-rod end out of the steering knuckle with a two-jaw puller. Don't hammer on the tie-rod end or you'll ruin the threads.

41   To remove an outer tie-rod end, loosen the locknut, paint an alignment mark where the threads meet the tie-rod and unscrew the tie-rod end.

42   To remove a tie-rod, bend up the lockplate and remove the bolt that attaches the inner tie-rod end to the steering rack.

43   To remove an inner tie-rod end, loosen the locknut, paint an alignment mark where the threads meet the tie-rod and unscrew the tie-rod end.

44   Installation is the reverse of removal. Tighten the bolts at the inner tie-rod ends to the torque listed in this Chapter's Specifications.

---

18   Steering gear – removal and installation

Torsion bar models

Refer to illustrations 18.5, 18.9 and 18.10

1   Remove the fuel tank (see Chapter 4).

2   Loosen the front wheel lug bolts, raise the front of the vehicle, support it securely on jackstands, apply the parking brake and remove the front wheels.

3   Separate the tie-rod ends from the Pitman arm (see Section 17).

4   If you're planning to install a new steering gear, remove the Pitman arm (see Section 17).

10

18.5   Loosen the clamp (arrow) below the universal joint at the lower end of the steering column

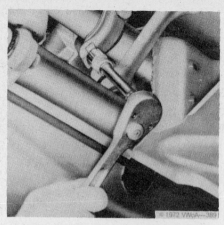

18.9   Remove the mounting clamp bolts, the clamp and the steering gear

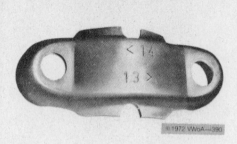

18.10   The steering gear mounting clamp has two cutouts – one for the Beetle and one for the Karmann Ghia – if you're installing the clamp on a Beetle axle tube, make sure the arrow at "13" points forward; on a Karmann Ghia, the "14" arrow must point forward

18.20   Push the protective boot up over the U-joint at the lower end of the steering column and loosen the clamp bolt (arrow) that attaches the steering column to the steering gear pinion

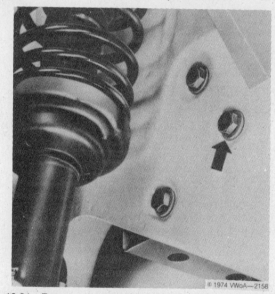

18.21   Remove the three bolts that attach the steering gear to the body

5   Loosen the clamp below the universal joint at the bottom of the steering column **(see illustration)**.
6   Disconnect the horn wire from the steering coupling contact.
7   Pull up on the steering column until the coupling flange clears the steering gear pinion.
8   Mark the position of the steering gear mounting clamp on the upper axle tube to ensure proper reinstallation.
9   Remove the mounting clamp bolts **(see illustration)**, the clamp and the steering gear.
10   Position the steering gear between the two welded-on stops on the upper axle tube. Use new lock plates under the mounting clamp bolts but don't fully tighten the bolts. Note the different cutouts on the edges of the clamp – make sure you orient the clamp correctly **(see illustration)**.
11   Set the steering to the center position and – with the spokes of the steering wheel horizontal – push the steering column coupling onto the steering gear pinion.
12   Reattach the tie-rods to the Pitman arm (see Section 17).
13   With the steering wheel centered and the brake drums (or discs) pointing straight ahead, tighten the steering column clamp bolt securely. Use a new lockplate for the bolt.
14   Tighten the steering gear clamp bolts to the torque listed in this Chapter's Specifications.
15   Install the wheels, lower the vehicle and tighten the wheel lug bolts to the torque listed in the Chapter 1 Specifications.

16   Test the steering. Make sure there's no binding anywhere in the range. If there is, you haven't aligned the steering gear correctly.

MacPherson strut models
Worm-and-roller steering gear
Refer to illustrations 18.20, 18.21, 18.23 and 18.24
17   Loosen the front wheel lug bolts, raise the front of the vehicle, support it securely on jackstands, apply the parking brake and remove the front wheels.
18   Disconnect the steering damper from the Pitman arm (see Section 17). Push the piston rod all the way into the damper to give yourself plenty of room, or swing the damper toward the front of the vehicle where it will be out of the way.
19   Disconnect the center tie-rod from the Pitman arm (see Section 17).
20   Push the lower boot up over the intermediate shaft U-joint to uncover the lower universal joint and remove the bolt that attaches the universal joint to the steering gear pinion shaft **(see illustration)**.
21   Remove the three bolts that attach the steering gear to the body **(see illustration)**.

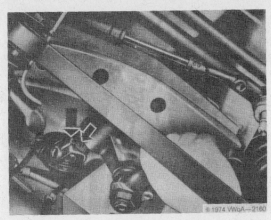

18.23   When you reattach the steering column to the steering gear, make sure the groove in the steering gear pinion (right arrow) is aligned with the hole in the lower U-joint (upper arrow)

18.24   If you're installing a new boot retaining ring, center the steering and align the lug with the mark (arrow)

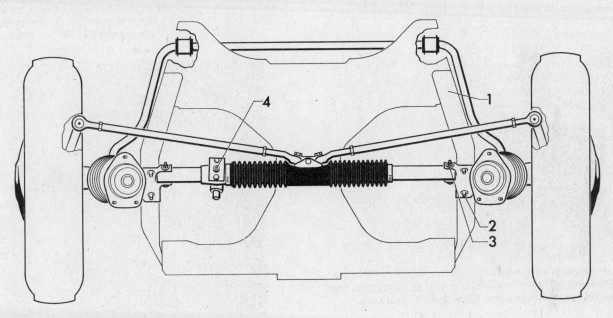

© 1976 VWoA

18.34   Installation details of the rack-and-pinion steering gear on late model MacPherson strut models

1	Body side member	3	Steering rack-to-mounting bracket bolt
2	Mounting bracket-to-side member bolt	4	Adjusting screw

22   Pull down on the steering gear, slide the pinion shaft out of the universal joint and remove the gear from the vehicle.

23   To install the steering gear, push the pinion shaft into the lower universal joint. Make sure the groove in the pinion is aligned with the bolt hole in the universal joint **(see illustration)**.

24   If you're installing a new boot retaining ring on the worm pinion, center the steering and align the lug with the mark as shown **(see illustration)**.

25   Install the three bolts that attach the steering gear to the body. Tighten the bolts to the torque listed in this Chapter's Specifications.

26   Install the bolt in the universal joint with a new self-locking nut and tighten it to the torque listed in this Chapter's Specifications.

27   Pull down the boot and engage it in the groove in the retaining ring.

28   Reattach the center tie-rod to the Pitman arm (see Section 17).

29   Install the wheels, lower the vehicle and tighten the wheel lug bolts to the torque listed in the Chapter 1 Specifications.

Rack-and-pinion steering gear

Refer to illustration 18.34

30   Push the lower boot up over the universal shaft to uncover the lower universal joint.

31   Remove the bolt that attaches the lower universal joint to the steering gear pinion.

32   Pry the universal joint off the steering gear pinion.

33   Bend up the lockplate, remove the bolts that attach the inner tie-rod ends to the steering rack and disconnect them from the rack (see Section 17).

34   Remove the nuts and bolts that attach the ends of the steering rack to the brackets on the body side members **(see illustration)**.

35   Remove the steering gear from the vehicle.

36   Installation is the reverse of removal. Tighten the two bolts that attach each bracket, the bolts that attach the rack to the brackets and the bolts that attach the tie-rods to the rack to the torque listed in this Chapter's Specifications.

37   Install the wheels, lower the vehicle and tighten the wheel lug bolts to the torque listed in the Chapter 1 Specifications.

38   Have the wheel alignment checked and, if necessary, adjusted.

10

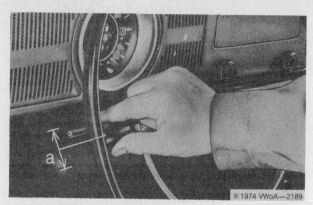

19.2 To check steering play, turn the steering wheel until the wheels are pointed straight ahead, then turn the wheel back and forth with your fingers as shown – the range in which you feel no resistance (distance "a") should be about one inch

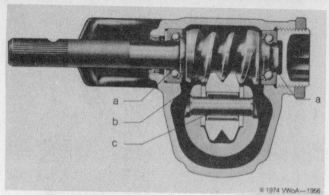

19.3 There are three areas where excessive play develops in the steering gear

a) *Axial play of the worm*
b) *Play between the roller and the worm*
c) *Axial play of the roller*

19 Steering gear – adjustment

Refer to illustrations 19.2 and 19.3

Note: *The following procedure applies to all worm-and-roller steering gears. whether on torsion bar or MacPherson strut models.*

1 With the vehicle on the ground. turn the front wheels to the straight-ahead position.

2 With the front wheels in the straight-ahead position. move the steering wheel lightly back and forth with your fingers as shown **(see illustration)**. The steering freeplay is that range of motion between the two points at which you feel resistance in each direction. Up to an inch of movement is acceptable.

3 If the steering play at the center position is excessive. verify that it's not caused by worn tie-rod ends (see Section 17) or a loose Pitman arm (see Section 18). Also. make sure the steering gear mounting bolts are tight. If these possible causes are eliminated. too much freeplay is caused by excessive axial play of the worm. play between the roller and the worm or axial play of the roller **(see illustration)**.

To adjust axial play of the worm

Refer to illustrations 19.4. 19.5 and 19.6

4 From underneath the front of the vehicle. turn the steering column U-joint coupling back and forth from left to right and watch the section of the pinion between the U-joint flange and the steering gear **(see illustration)**.

5 Loosen the locknut for the steering worm adjuster **(see illustration)**.

6 Turn the steering worm back and forth at the steering coupling while simultaneously tightening the adjuster **(see illustration)** until all play in the worm is removed.

7 Hold the adjuster and tighten the locknut to the torque listed in this Chapter's Specifications.

8 Turn the steering worm from lock to lock. It should rotate smoothly. with no "tight spots." If there are. the adjuster is too tight. Loosen it a little and check again. If you can't eliminate play by adjusting the worm. try adjusting the play between the roller and the worm.

To adjust play between the roller and the worm

Refer to illustration 19.11

9 Turn the steering wheel 90-degrees to the left or right of its centered position.

10 Raise the luggage compartment hood. remove the spare tire and re move the access panel for the steering gear.

11 Loosen the locknut for the roller shaft adjustment screw **(see illustration)**. Loosen the adjustment screw about one turn.

12 Tighten the adjustment screw until you feel the roller touching the steering worm.

13 Hold the adjustment screw and tighten the locknut securely

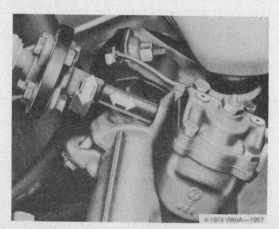

19.4 Turn the steering column U-joint flange back and forth, from left to right, and watch the section of the pinion between the U-joint and the steering gear – if it moves up and down (arrow), adjust the axial play of the worm

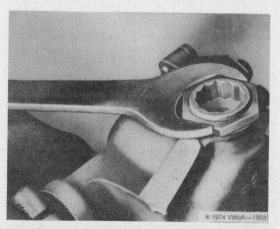

19.5 Loosen the locknut for the steering worm adjuster

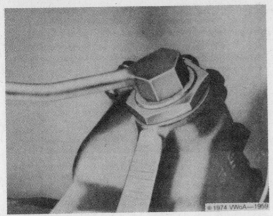

19.6   Tighten the adjuster while turning the steering worm back and forth at the steering coupling until all play is removed from the worm

19.11   Loosen the locknut for the roller shaft adjustment screw (arrow) and turn the screw out about one turn, then tighten the screw until you feel the roller touching the worm

METRIC TIRE SIZES

P 185 / 80 R 13

TIRE TYPE
P – PASSENGER
T – TEMPORARY
C – COMMERCIAL

ASPECT RATIO
(SECTION HEIGHT)
(SECTION WIDTH)
70
75
80

RIM DIAMETER
(INCHES)
13
14
15

SECTION WIDTH
(MILLIMETERS)
185
195
205
ETC

CONSTRUCTION TYPE
R – RADIAL
B – BIAS – BELTED
D – DIAGONAL (BIAS)

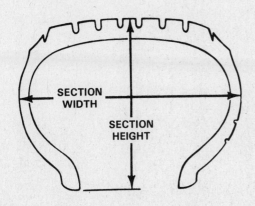

SECTION
WIDTH

SECTION
HEIGHT

20.1   Metric tire size code

14   With the vehicle on the ground, check the adjustment with the wheel turned 90-degrees to each side. Play must not exceed one inch at the circumference of the steering wheel. If there's more play on one side than the other, readjust the roller to worm play for that side.

15   Road test the vehicle. Carefully negotiate a corner at 10 to 12 mph. The steering should return to within 45-degrees of its centered position after you exit the corner. If it doesn't, the roller is still too tight. Repeat the adjustment procedure or the worm and roller will be damaged.

16   If you can't get the steering to perform as specified after several at-

tempts to readjust the play between the worm and roller, the axial play of the steering roller must be checked. This is a job for the dealer service department or other repair shop, because adjustment requires special tools and disassembly of the steering gear.

20   Wheels and tires – general information

Refer to illustration 20.1

Most vehicles covered by this manual are equipped with metric-sized fiberglass or steel belted radial tires **(see illustration)**. Use of other sizes or types of tires may affect the ride and handling of the vehicle. Don't mix different types of tires, such as radials and bias belted, on the same vehicle, or handling may be seriously affected. We recommend that tires be replaced in pairs on the same axle, but if only one tire is being replaced, make sure it's the same size, structure and tread design as the other.

Because tire pressure has a substantial effect on handling and wear, the pressure on all tires should be checked at least once a month or before any extended trips (see Chapter 1).

Wheels must be replaced if they are bent, dented, leak air, have elongated bolt holes, are heavily rusted, out of vertical symmetry or if the lug bolts won't stay tight. We don't recommend wheel repairs that use welding or peening.

Tire and wheel balance is important to the overall handling, braking and performance of the vehicle. Unbalanced wheels can adversely affect handling and ride characteristics as well as tire life. When a tire is installed on a wheel, the tire and wheel should be balanced by a shop with the proper equipment.

21   Wheel alignment – general information

Refer to illustration 21.1

Wheel alignment refers to the adjustments made to the wheels so they're in proper angular relationship to the suspension and the ground. Front wheels that are out of alignment not only affect steering control, but also increase tire wear. The front end adjustments normally required on most models are camber, caster and toe-in **(see illustration)**. The rear wheels can also be adjusted for camber and toe-in.

Aligning the wheels is an exacting process which requires complicated and expensive equipment. Have an alignment shop with the proper equipment perform this job. The following brief description of the mechanics of wheel alignment will provide you with enough information to deal intelligently with the shop that does the work.

10

Toe-in is the turning in of the wheels. The purpose of a toe specification is to ensure parallel rolling of the front wheels. In a vehicle with zero toe-in, the distance between the front edges of the wheels will be the same as the distance between the rear edges of the wheels. The actual amount of toe-in is normally only a fraction of an inch. Toe-in adjustment of the front wheels is controlled by the tie-rod end position on the tie-rod; toe-in of the rear wheels is adjusted by altering the relationship of the bearing housings – or, on later models, the diagonal arms – and the spring plates. Incorrect toe-in will cause the tires to wear improperly by making them scrub against the road surface.

Camber is the tilting of the wheels from the vertical when viewed from the end of the vehicle. When the wheels tilt out at the top, the camber is said to be positive (+). When the wheels tilt in at the top the camber is negative (-). The amount of tilt is measured in degrees from the vertical and this measurement is called the camber angle. This angle affects the amount of tire tread which contacts the road and compensates for changes in the suspension geometry when the vehicle is cornering or travelling over an undulating surface.

Caster is the tilting of the top of the steering axis from the vertical. A tilt toward the rear is positive caster and a tilt toward the front is negative caster.

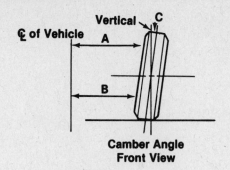

Camber Angle
Front View

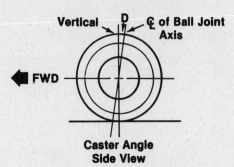

Caster Angle
Side View

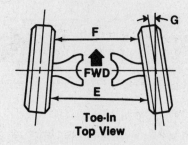

Toe-In
Top View

21.1   Front end alignment details

1   *A minus B = C (degrees camber)*
2   *E minus F = toe-in (measured in inches)*
3   *G = toe-in (expressed in degrees)*

Chapter 11   Body

Contents

1   General information

Refer to illustration 1.1

The body is made of many individual parts welded into a single structure, which is bolted onto a platform frame (floorpan), an assembly of welded sheet metal stampings consisting of a backbone (central) tunnel, a floor pan, cross bracing at the front and rear ends and a frame fork which supports the engine. The floor pan and central tunnel of the platform provide the majority of the load-carrying structure. Torsion bar axle beams – or, on Super Beetle models, a MacPherson strut front end – are bolted to a frame head at the front of the platform. At the rear, another torsion bar beam is welded to the frame fork **(see illustration)**. The platform itself is quite strong, but gains even further rigidity when the body is bolted onto it.

Some body parts – such as the bumpers, the front and rear hoods, the doors, the fenders and the running boards – can be removed for repair or replacement.

Only general body maintenance practices, body panel repair and simple component replacement procedures within the scope of the do-it-yourselfer are included in this Chapter.

2   Body – maintenance

1   The condition of your vehicle's body is very important, because the resale value depends a great deal on it. It's much more difficult to repair a neglected or damaged body than it is to repair mechanical components. The hidden areas of the body, such as the wheel wells, the frame and the engine compartment, are equally important, although they don't require as frequent attention as the rest of the body.

2   Once a year, or every 12,000 miles, it's a good idea to have the underside of the body steam cleaned. All traces of dirt and oil will be removed and the area can then be inspected carefully for rust, damaged brake lines, frayed electrical wires, damaged cables and other problems. The front suspension components should be greased after completion of this job.

3   At the same time, clean the engine and the engine compartment with a steam cleaner or water soluble degreaser.

4   The wheel wells should be given close attention, since undercoating can peel away and stones and dirt thrown up by the tires can cause the paint to chip and flake, allowing rust to set in. If rust is found, clean down to the bare metal and apply an anti-rust paint.

11

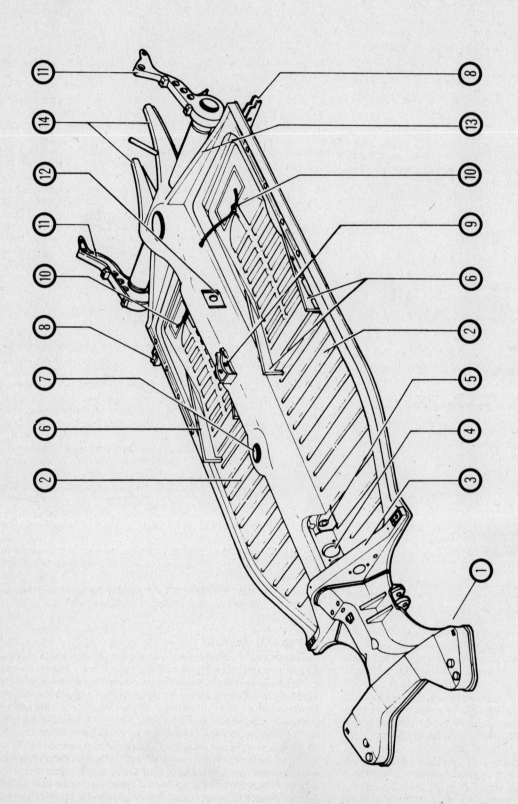

1.1   **Typical Super Beetle floorpan with frame head for MacPherson strut-type front suspension**

1	Frame head	5	Accelerator pedal	11 Spring plate brackets
2	Floorpan		mounting	12 Seat belt anchoring points
3	Front cross bracing	6	Seat runners	13 Rear cross bracing
4	Pedal cluster shaft aperture	7	Shift lever hole	14 Frame fork
		8	Jacking points	
		9	Parking brake	
			mounting bracket	
		10	Heater control cable tube	

5   The body should be washed about once a week. Wet the vehicle thoroughly to soften the dirt, then wash it down with a soft sponge and plenty of clean soapy water. If the surplus dirt is not washed off very carefully, it can wear down the paint.

6   Spots of tar or asphalt thrown up from the road should be removed with a cloth soaked in solvent.

7   Once every six months, wax the body and chrome trim. If a chrome cleaner is used to remove rust from any of the vehicle's plated parts, remember that the cleaner also removes part of the chrome, so use it sparingly.

3   Vinyl trim – maintenance

Don't clean vinyl trim with detergents, caustic soap or petroleum-based cleaners. Plain soap and water works just fine, with a soft brush to clean dirt that may be ingrained. Wash the vinyl as frequently as the rest of the vehicle.

After cleaning, application of a high quality rubber and vinyl protectant will help prevent oxidation and cracks. The protectant can also be applied to weatherstripping, vacuum lines and rubber hoses, which often fail as a result of chemical degradation, and to the tires.

4   Upholstery and carpets – maintenance

1 Every three months remove the carpets or mats and clean the interior of the vehicle (more frequently if necessary). Vacuum the upholstery and carpets to remove loose dirt and dust.

2   Leather upholstery requires special care. Stains should be removed with warm water and a very mild soap solution. Use a clean, damp cloth to remove the soap, then wipe again with a dry cloth. Never use alcohol, gasoline, nail polish remover or thinner to clean leather upholstery.

3   After cleaning, regularly treat leather upholstery with a leather wax. Never use car wax on leather upholstery.

4   In areas where the interior of the vehicle is subject to bright sunlight, cover leather seats with a sheet if the vehicle is to be left out for any length of time.

5   Body repair – minor damage

See photo sequence

Repair of minor scratches

1   If the scratch is superficial and does not penetrate to the metal of the body, repair is very simple. Lightly rub the scratched area with a fine rubbing compound to remove loose paint and built up wax. Rinse the area with clean water.

2   Apply touch-up paint to the scratch, using a small brush. Continue to apply thin layers of paint until the surface of the paint in the scratch is level with the surrounding paint. Allow the new paint at least two weeks to harden, then blend it into the surrounding paint by rubbing with a very fine rubbing compound. Finally, apply a coat of wax to the scratch area.

3   If the scratch has penetrated the paint and exposed the metal of the body, causing the metal to rust, a different repair technique is required. Remove all loose rust from the bottom of the scratch with a pocket knife, then apply rust inhibiting paint to prevent the formation of rust in the future. Using a rubber or nylon applicator, coat the scratched area with glaze-type filler. If required, the filler can be mixed with thinner to provide a very thin paste, which is ideal for filling narrow scratches. Before the glaze filler in the scratch hardens, wrap a piece of smooth cotton cloth around the tip of a finger. Dip the cloth in thinner and then quickly wipe it along the surface of the scratch. This will ensure that the surface of the filler is slightly hollow. The scratch can now be painted over as described earlier in this Section.

Repair of dents

4   When repairing dents, the first job is to pull the dent out until the affected area is as close as possible to its original shape. There is no point in trying to restore the original shape completely as the metal in the damaged area will have stretched on impact and cannot be restored to its original contours. It is better to bring the level of the dent up to a point which is about 1/8-inch below the level of the surrounding metal. In cases where the dent is very shallow, it is not worth trying to pull it out at all.

5   If the back side of the dent is accessible, it can be hammered out gently from behind using a soft-face hammer. While doing this, hold a block of wood firmly against the opposite side of the metal to absorb the hammer blows and prevent the metal from being stretched.

6   If the dent is in a section of the body which has double layers, or some other factor makes it inaccessible from behind, a different technique is required. Drill several small holes through the metal inside the damaged area, particularly in the deeper sections. Screw long, self tapping screws into the holes just enough for them to get a good grip in the metal. Now the dent can be pulled out by pulling on the protruding heads of the screws with locking pliers.

7   The next stage of repair is the removal of paint from the damaged area and from an inch or so of the surrounding metal. This is easily done with a wire brush or sanding disk in a drill motor, although it can be done just as effectively by hand with sandpaper. To complete the preparation for filling, score the surface of the bare metal with a screwdriver or the tang of a file or drill small holes in the affected area. This will provide a good grip for the filler material. To complete the repair, see the Section on filling and painting.

Repair of rust holes or gashes

8   Remove all paint from the affected area and from an inch or so of the surrounding metal using a sanding disk or wire brush mounted in a drill motor. If these are not available, a few sheets of sandpaper will do the job just as effectively.

9   With the paint removed, you will be able to determine the severity of the corrosion and decide whether to replace the whole panel, if possible, or repair the affected area. New body panels are not as expensive as most people think and it is often quicker to install a new panel than to repair large areas of rust.

10   Remove all trim pieces from the affected area except those which will act as a guide to the original shape of the damaged body, such as headlight shells, etc. Using metal snips or a hacksaw blade, remove all loose metal and any other metal that is badly affected by rust. Hammer the edges of the hole in to create a slight depression for the filler material.

11   Wire brush the affected area to remove the powdery rust from the surface of the metal. If the back of the rusted area is accessible, treat it with rust inhibiting paint.

12   Before filling is done, block the hole in some way. This can be done with sheet metal riveted or screwed into place, or by stuffing the hole with wire mesh.

13   Once the hole is blocked off, the affected area can be filled and painted. See the following subsection on filling and painting.

Filling and painting

14   Many types of body fillers are available, but generally speaking, body repair kits which contain filler paste and a tube of resin hardener are best for this type of repair work. A wide, flexible plastic or nylon applicator will be necessary for imparting a smooth and contoured finish to the surface of the filler material. Mix up a small amount of filler on a clean piece of wood or cardboard (use the hardener sparingly). Follow the manufacturer's instructions on the package, otherwise the filler will set incorrectly.

15   Using the applicator, apply the filler paste to the prepared area. Draw the applicator across the surface of the filler to achieve the desired contour and to level the filler surface. As soon as a contour that approximates the original one is achieved, stop working the paste. If you continue, the paste will begin to stick to the applicator. Continue to add thin layers of paste at 20-minute intervals until the level of the filler is just above the surrounding metal.

11

These photos illustrate a method of repairing simple dents. They are intended to supplement *Body repair - minor damage* in this Chapter and should not be used as the sole instructions for body repair on these vehicles.

1   If you can't access the backside of the body panel to hammer out the dent, pull it out with a slide-hammer-type dent puller. In the deepest portion of the dent or along the crease line, drill or punch hole(s) at least one inch apart . . .

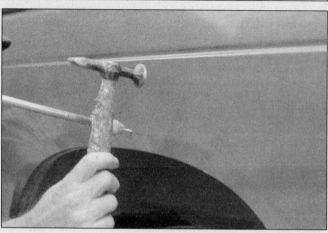

2   . . . then screw the slide-hammer into the hole and operate it. Tap with a hammer near the edge of the dent to help 'pop' the metal back to its original shape. When you're finished, the dent area should be close to its original contour and about 1/8-inch below the surface of the surrounding metal

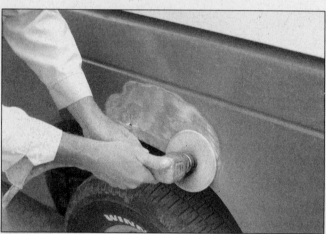

3   Using coarse-grit sandpaper, remove the paint down to the bare metal. Hand sanding works fine, but the disc sander shown here makes the job faster. Use finer (about 320-grit) sandpaper to feather-edge the paint at least one inch around the dent area

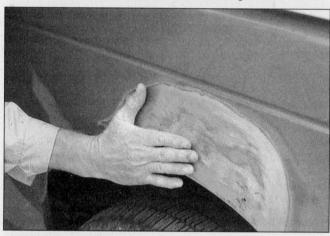

4   When the paint is removed, touch will probably be more helpful than sight for telling if the metal is straight. Hammer down the high spots or raise the low spots as necessary. Clean the repair area with wax/silicone remover

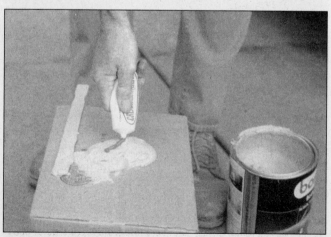

5   Following label instructions, mix up a batch of plastic filler and hardener. The ratio of filler to hardener is critical, and, if you mix it incorrectly, it will either not cure properly or cure too quickly (you won't have time to file and sand it into shape)

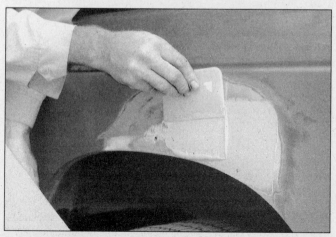

6   Working quickly so the filler doesn't harden, use a plastic applicator to press the body filler firmly into the metal, assuring it bonds completely. Work the filler until it matches the original contour and is slightly above the surrounding metal

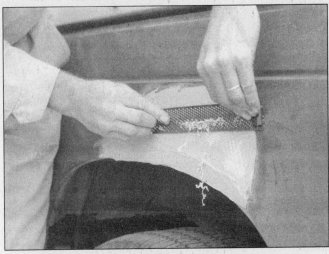

7 Let the filler harden until you can just dent it with your fingernail. Use a body file or Surform tool (shown here) to rough-shape the filler

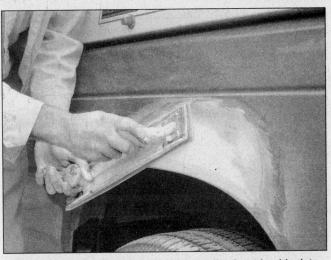

8 Use coarse-grit sandpaper and a sanding board or block to work the filler down until it's smooth and even. Work down to finer grits of sandpaper - always using a board or block - ending up with 360 or 400 grit

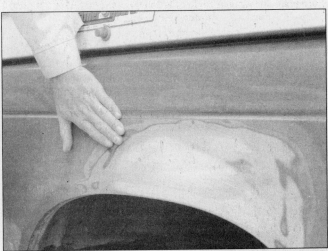

9 You shouldn't be able to feel any ridge at the transition from the filler to the bare metal or from the bare metal to the old paint. As soon as the repair is flat and uniform, remove the dust and mask off the adjacent panels or trim pieces

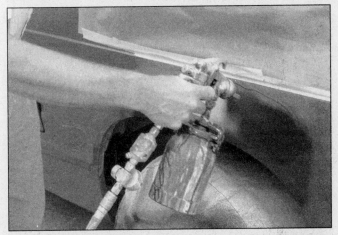

10 Apply several layers of primer to the area. Don't spray the primer on too heavy, so it sags or runs, and make sure each coat is dry before you spray on the next one. A professional-type spray gun is being used here, but aerosol spray primer is available inexpensively from auto parts stores

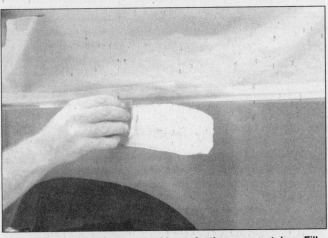

11 The primer will help reveal imperfections or scratches. Fill these with glazing compound. Follow the label instructions and sand it with 360 or 400-grit sandpaper until it's smooth. Repeat the glazing, sanding and respraying until the primer reveals a perfectly smooth surface

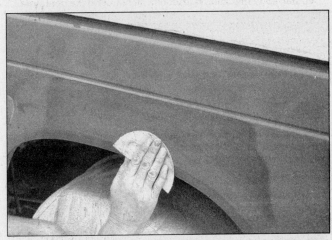

12 Finish sand the primer with very fine sandpaper (400 or 600-grit) to remove the primer overspray. Clean the area with water and allow it to dry. Use a tack rag to remove any dust, then apply the finish coat. Don't attempt to rub out or wax the repair area until the paint has dried completely (at least two weeks)

16   Once the filler has hardened, the excess can be removed with a body file. From then on, progressively finer grades of sandpaper should be used, starting with a 180-grit paper and finishing with 600-grit wet-or-dry paper. Always wrap the sandpaper around a flat rubber or wooden block, otherwise the surface of the filler will not be completely flat. During the sanding of the filler surface, the wet-or-dry paper should be periodically rinsed in water. This will ensure that a very smooth finish is produced in the final stage.

17   At this point, the repair area should be surrounded by a ring of bare metal, which in turn should be encircled by the finely feathered edge of good paint. Rinse the repair area with clean water until all of the dust produced by the sanding operation is gone.

18   Spray the entire area with a light coat of primer. This will reveal any imperfections in the surface of the filler. Repair the imperfections with fresh filler paste or glaze filler and once more smooth the surface with sandpaper. Repeat this spray-and-repair procedure until you are satisfied that the surface of the filler and the feathered edge of the paint are perfect. Rinse the area with clean water and allow it to dry completely.

19   The repair area is now ready for painting. Spray painting must be carried out in a warm, dry, windless and dust free atmosphere. These conditions can be created if you have access to a large indoor work area, but if you are forced to work in the open, you will have to pick the day very carefully. If you are working indoors, dousing the floor in the work area with water will help settle the dust which would otherwise be in the air. If the repair area is confined to one body panel, mask off the surrounding panels. This will help minimize the effects of a slight mismatch in paint color. Trim pieces such as chrome strips, door handles, etc., will also need to be masked off or removed. Use masking tape and several thicknesses of newspaper for the masking operations.

20   Before spraying, shake the paint can thoroughly, then spray a test area until the spray painting technique is mastered. Cover the repair area with a thick coat of primer. The thickness should be built up using several thin layers of primer rather than one thick one. Using 600-grit wet-or-dry sandpaper, rub down the surface of the primer until it is very smooth. While doing this, the work area should be thoroughly rinsed with water and the wet-or-dry sandpaper periodically rinsed as well. Allow the primer to dry before spraying additional coats.

21   Spray on the top coat, again building up the thickness by using several thin layers of paint. Begin spraying in the center of the repair area and then, using a circular motion, work out until the whole repair area and about two inches of the surrounding original paint is covered. Remove all masking material 10 to 15 minutes after spraying on the final coat of paint. Allow the new paint at least two weeks to harden, then use a very fine rubbing compound to blend the edges of the new paint into the existing paint. Finally, apply a coat of wax.

6   Body repair – major damage

1   Major damage must be repaired by an auto body shop specifically equipped to perform unibody repairs. These shops have the specialized equipment required to do the job properly.

2   If the damage is extensive, the body must be checked for proper alignment or the vehicle's handling characteristics may be adversely affected and other components may wear at an accelerated rate.

3   Due to the fact that all of the major body components (hood, fenders, etc.) are separate and replaceable units, any seriously damaged components should be replaced rather than repaired. Sometimes the components can be found in a wrecking yard that specializes in used vehicle components, often at considerable savings over the cost of new parts.

7   Hinges and locks – maintenance

Once every 3000 miles, or every three months, the hinges and latch assemblies on the doors, hood and trunk should be given a few drops of light oil or lock lubricant. The door latch strikers should also be lubricated

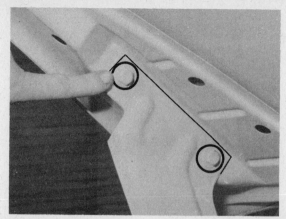

9.2   Draw or scribe a circle around each washer to ensure correct hood alignment with the hinges during reattachment – to adjust the hood, make alignment marks along the edge of each hinge so you can judge how much you're moving the hood relative to each hinge

with a thin coat of grease to reduce wear and ensure free movement. Lubricate the door and trunk locks with spray-on graphite lubricant.

8   Fixed glass – replacement

Replacement of the windshield and fixed glass requires the use of some specialized tools and techniques. These operations should be left to a dealer service department or a shop specializing in glass work.

9   Front hood – removal, installation and adjustment

Refer to illustration 9.2
Note: *The hood is heavy and somewhat awkward to remove and install – two people should perform this procedure.*

Removal and installation

1   Open the hood. Use blankets or pads to cover the cowl area of the body and the fenders. This will protect the body and paint as the hood is lifted off.

2   Scribe or draw alignment marks on the hood hinges around the washer for each bolt head **(see illustration)** to insure proper alignment during installation.

3   Disconnect any cables or wire harnesses which will interfere with removal.

4   Have an assistant support the weight of the hood. Remove the hinge-to-hood nuts or bolts.

5   Lift off the hood.

6   Installation is the reverse of removal.

Adjustment

7   Fore-and-aft and side-to-side adjustment of the hood is done by moving the hood in relation to the hinge plate after loosening the bolts.

8   Scribe a line around the entire hinge plate so you can judge the amount of movement **(see illustration 9.2).**

9   Loosen the bolts and move the hood into correct alignment. Move it only a little at a time. Tighten the hinge bolts and carefully lower the hood to check the alignment.

10   If necessary after installation, the hood lock assembly can be adjusted up-and-down so the hood closes securely and is flush with the fenders (see Section 10).

11   The hood hinges should be periodically lubricated with white lithium-base grease.

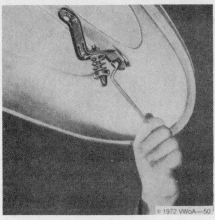

10.1 To remove the upper part of the old style lock, simply remove the mounting bolts

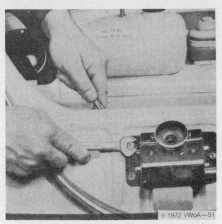

10.2 To remove the lower part of the old style lock, remove the mounting bolts . . .

10.3 . . . pull out the lock, loosen the clamping screw and detach the cable

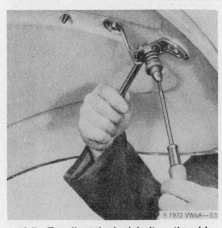

10.7 To adjust the lock bolt on the old style lock, loosen the locknut and turn the bolt in (to lower the hood) or out (to raise the hood)

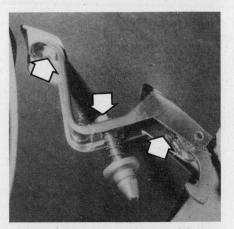

10.10 To remove the upper part of the new style lock, remove the bolts (outer arrows) – to adjust the lock bolt (center arrow), turn the bolt in (to lower the hood) or out (to raise the hood)

10.11 To remove the lower part of the new style lock, loosen the clamping screw to remove the cable

10   Front hood lock – removal, installation and adjustment

1967 and earlier models

Removal

Refer to illustrations 10.1, 10.2, 10.3 and 10.7

Note: *Older hood locks rely solely on a cable-actuated locking mechanism, so it's imperative that this cable be adjusted properly. If it isn't, you won't be able to open the front hood.*

1 Open the hood. Remove the bolts from the upper part of the lock **(see illustration)** and remove the handle and the upper part of the lock.

2 Remove the bolts securing the lower part of the lock **(see illustration)**.

3 Remove the cover plate from the lower part of the lock, loosen the cable clamping screw **(see illustration)**, detach the cable, pull it out of the cable guide and remove the lower part of the lock.

Installation

4 Thread the cable through the cable guide, push the lever with the cable clamping screw against spring tension until the lever is below the opening for the lock bolt. Insert the cable in the lever and tighten the clamping screw securely. **Note:** *Tensioning the lever insures that it will automatically spring back if the cable breaks, freeing the lock bolt so the hood can be opened.*

5 The remainder of installation is the reverse of removal.

Adjustment

6 Open and close the hood several times to verify that the lower part of the lock is correctly centered. If it isn't, loosen the bolts and center the lock.

7 Make sure the lock bolt in the upper part of the lock is long enough to catch the lever in the lower part of the lock. If it isn't, loosen the locknut above the bracket and screw the bolt in (to lower the hood) or back it out (to raise the hood) **(see illustration)**. Be sure to tighten the locknut when you're finished.

8 Make sure the cable locks and unlocks the hood properly. If necessary, remove the cover plate and readjust the cable. Bend back any excess cable.

9 Lubricate the lock with white lithium base grease.

1968 on

Removal

Refer to illustrations 10.10, 10.11 and 10.12

Note: *The upper part of the lock on later models is similar to older designs. It also uses an adjustable, cable-actuated lock bolt on the upper part of the hood lock, but there's also a pushbutton-actuated safety latch which you must release to open the hood.*

10 Open the hood. Remove the bolts from the upper part of the lock **(see illustration)**. Remove the handle, the plastic grommets and the upper part of the lock.

11 Loosen the cable clamping screw **(see illustration)**.

12 Using a chisel, cut off the pop rivets that secure the lower part of the

11

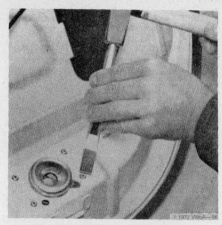

10.12   Cut the rivets with a chisel, or drill them out, and remove the lock from underneath the vehicle

11.4   Lift the hood off its hinge brackets so the spring can unhook from the bracket on the roof panel

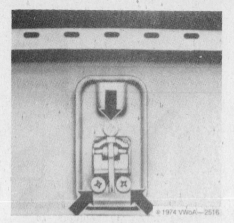

12.1a   Older (pre-1968) rear hood locks use three Phillips head screws

12.1b   Newer (1968 on) rear hood locks have a single Phillips head mounting screw

12.3   On 1967 and earlier models, move the striker plate to adjust the lock (the plate is welded in place on 1968 and later models, so you'll have to move the upper lock instead)

13.1a   Typical bumper assembly on a 1967 or earlier Beetle – to remove the bumper, simply unbolt it from the brackets (right bracket shown) – to remove the bracket itself, remove the spare tire and unbolt it from the body

lock to the body **(see illustration)**, or drill them out. Remove the lower part of the lock from underneath the vehicle.

Installation

13   If you're reinstalling the old lower part of the lock, lubricate it with white lithium-base grease.

14   Insert the lock cable through the guide on the lower part of the lock and temporarily attach it with the clamping screw.

15   Place the lower part of the lock in position and rivet it back in place. If you don't have a pop rivet gun, attach the lower part of the lock with four pairs of nuts and bolts of a suitable diameter and length.

16   Loosen the clamping screw slightly and pull all slack out of the cable. Retighten the clamping screw.

17   Install the plastic grommets, the hood handle, the upper part of the lock and the bolts. Tighten the bolts securely.

Adjustment

18   Open and close the hood several times to ensure that it's working properly. If necessary, adjust the length of the lock bolt by loosening the locknut and turning the bolt in or out **(see illustration 10.10)**.

---

11   Rear hood – removal and installation

Removal

Refer to illustration 11.4

1   Open the hood. Use blankets or pads to cover the firewall area of the body and the fenders. This will protect the body and paint as the hood is lifted off.

2   On some newer models, it may be necessary to remove the air cleaner (see Chapter 4). If you remove the air cleaner, be sure to cover the carburetor intake to protect the engine from contamination.

3   Disconnect the wire harness for the license plate light, detach the harness clip(s) from the hood and set the harness aside.

4   Remove the four bolts that attach the hood hinges to the curved hinge brackets on the body **(see illustration)**.

5   Pull the hood up against spring pressure and unhook the load spring from the bracket on the vehicle's body (the spring remains with the hood when the hood is removed).

6   If necessary, remove the curved hinge brackets from the vehicle body by removing the three bolts at each bracket.

Installation

7   Check the condition of the rubber weatherstrip. If it's coming loose, re-glue it; it's dried or cracked, replace it. Be sure to remove all of the old trim cement with solvent so the new weatherstrip adheres properly.

8   Loosely install one hood hinge on the curved bracket on the vehicle body.

9   Holding the hood at an angle so you can reach behind it, engage the spring in the bracket on the body.

10   Push the hood up and toward the vehicle. Loosely install the remaining hinge.

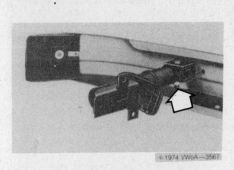

13.1b Typical bumper on a late model Beetle with energy absorbers – to remove it, simply remove each clevis bolt and nut (arrow)

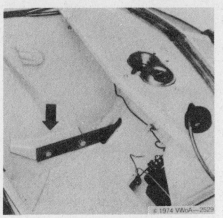

13.3a To get at the bumper bracket bolts on 1967 and earlier Beetles and pre-1972 Karmann-Ghias (shown), open the hood and remove the spare tire

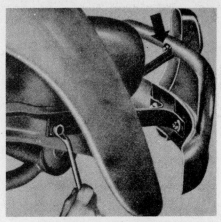

13.3b Typical 1967 or earlier rear bumper bracket installation

11   Move the hood in the elongated bolt holes until it contacts the weatherstrip evenly all around. Tighten the bolts securely.

12   Rear hood lock – removal, installation and adjustment

Refer to illustrations 12.1a, 12.1b and 12.3

1   Open the rear hood. Remove the Phillips head screws which attach the lock and handle to the rear hood **(see illustrations)**. Remove the lock, handle and plastic grommets.
2   Installation is the reverse of removal.
3   Open and close the hood several times to verify that the lock is positioned properly. If it isn't, move the striker plate on 1967 and earlier models **(see illustration)**, or adjust the position of the upper lock on 1968 and later models.

13   Bumpers and bumper brackets/energy absorbers – removal and installation

Refer to illustrations 13.1a, 13.1b, 13.3a, 13.3b and 13.5
Note: *Several bumper and bumper bracket designs have been employed on Beetles and Karmann-Ghias, but – aside from differences in the height of the bumper or the size of the bumper bracket – they're all basically similar, except for 1974 and later models, on which bumpers with energy absorbers were added to comply with Federal regulations.*

1   Remove the bolts attaching the bumper to the brackets or energy absorbers **(see illustrations)** and remove the bumper. **Note:** *On 1967 models, disconnect the leads to the back-up lights, which are attached to the rear bumper, and detach the lights from the bumper before removing it. On 1968 through 1973 models, a reinforcement strap connects the two bumper brackets. Although you can remove the bumper from the strap with the strap/bracket assembly still attached to the vehicle on these models, it's easier to remove the entire bumper assembly first, then detach the bumper from the strap (see Step 5).*
2   The bumpers on 1967 and earlier models are reinforced with single or double "bows" (the thin horizontal tubing that looks like a towel rack) and "overriders" (the stout vertical pieces which are bolted to the bow(s) and the bumper). To remove the bow(s) and overriders, simply remove all bolts and nuts attaching them to each other, and to the old bumper, and reattach them to the new bumper.
3   To replace a front bumper bracket on 1967 and earlier Beetle models, or pre-1972 Karmann-Ghia models, open the front hood and remove the spare tire **(see illustration)**. The bolts for the rear bumper brackets on these models are inside the rear wheel wells **(see illustration)**. On all other models, the bolts for the front brackets, or energy absorbers, and the

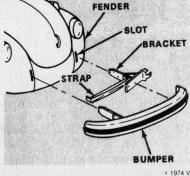

13.5 Exploded view of a typical bumper assembly on 1968 through 1973 Beetles (Karmann-Ghias similar) – the easiest way to replace parts on these models is to remove the entire bumper/strap/bracket assembly and disassemble it off the vehicle

rear brackets, are inside the wheel wells. **Note:** *On 1968 through 1973 models, the horn bracket is attached to the left front bumper bracket by two of the mounting bolts, so unplug the horn wires and carefully set the horn aside – don't hang it by the wires.* Remove the bumper assembly.
4   Once the bumper bracket or energy absorber is unbolted, simply pull it out through the slot in the fender.
5   Once the bumper assembly is removed on 1968 through 1973 models, remove the three nuts which attach each bracket to the strap, then remove the fasteners which attach the bumper to the strap and detach the bumper **(see illustration)**.
6   Be sure to inspect the rubber grommet in the fender. If it's cracked, dried or deteriorated, replace it.
7   Installation is the reverse of removal. The bumper bracket mounting holes are slotted, so make sure there's a uniform gap between both ends of the bumper and the body before tightening the bracket bolts.

14   Fenders – removal and installation

Removal
Refer to illustrations 14.5 and 14.6
Note: *The following procedure applies only to Beetle fenders. Karmann-Ghia fenders are welded to the body, so if they need to be replaced, take the car to a reputable body shop.*

1   Raise the vehicle and place it securely on jackstands.

11

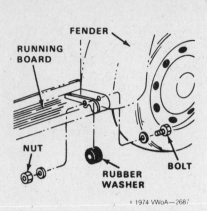

14.5   Remove the nut, washer, bolt and rubber spacer washer that attach the fender to the running boards

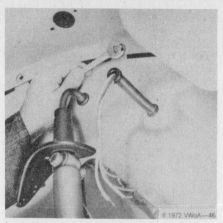

14.6   Remove the headlight and turn signal/sidemarker light, or taillight, pull out the wires, then remove the bolts that attach the fender to the body

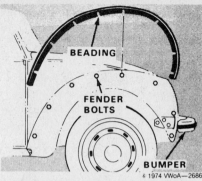

14.11   To install the beading on the fender, place the fender in position and install the bolts loosely, then slip the beading into place between the fender and the body – make sure the notches in the beading slip over the bolts, then tighten the bolts evenly and gradually

2   If you're removing the left front fender on a 1968 through 1973 model, unplug the horn wires and remove the horn. Don't hang the horn by the wires.
3   Remove the bumper and bumper bracket (or brackets, if you're replacing both fenders) (see Section 13).
4   If you're replacing a front fender, remove the headlight and turn signal/side marker light; if you're replacing a rear fender, remove the taillight assembly (see Chapter 12).
5   Remove the nut, washer and bolt that attach the fender to the running board (see illustration).
6   Remove the bolts/nuts attaching the fender to the body (see illustration).
7   Remove the fender, the beading and the rubber spacer washer between the fender and the running boards. Inspect the beading and rubber spacer washer. If they're cracked, dried or deteriorated, replace them.
8   Check the threaded holes in the body and clean them up with a tap if necessary. Lubricate the bolt threads.

Installation
Refer to illustration 14.11
9   Place the fender in position against the body without the beading and loosely install one bolt at the top to support the fender. Now start the rest of the bolts (and nut, if applicable). Tighten them just enough to hold the fender in position.
10   Install a new rubber spacer washer between the fender and the running board, then install the bolt, washer and nut that attaches the fender to the running board, but don't tighten it yet.
11   Push the beading into place with your hand. Make sure the slots in the beading slip over the bolts (see illustration). Be extremely careful about the fit of the beading as you gradually and evenly hand tighten the fender bolts a few turns.
12   Gradually and evenly tighten all the bolts.
13   The remainder of installation is the reverse of removal.

15   Running boards – removal and installation

1   Raise the vehicle and place it securely on jackstands.
2   Remove the nuts, washers, bolts and rubber spacer washers that attach the running board to the fenders (see illustration 14.5).
3   Remove the bolts and rubber washers that attach the running board to the body.
4   Clean up the threads of the running board bolts and lubricate the threads to protect them from corrosion.
5   Place the new running board in position and, using new rubber washers, install the running board-to-body bolts first and tighten them evenly and gradually.
6   Install the bolts, rubber spacer washers, washers and nuts that attach

the running board to the fenders.
7   Lower the vehicle.

16   Door latch striker plate – replacement and adjustment

1   If the door rattles or is hard to shut, the door latch striker plate is probably out of adjustment.

1966 and earlier models
Refer to illustrations 16.4, 16.5a, 16.5b and 16.6
2   To replace the striker plate, simply remove the screws and install a new one. Leave the screws loose enough so that you can still move the striker plate, if necessary, to adjust it.
3   Loosen the locknut on the wedge adjusting screw and turn the screw clockwise until the stop bushing bottoms against the striker plate.
4   To adjust the striker plate horizontally (see illustration), move it in or out until the door and rear quarter panel are flush with one another.
5   To adjust the striker plate vertically, hold the door almost shut and peel away the weatherstripping so you can see how the latch will fit into the striker plate (see illustration). Adjust the plate as shown (see illustration).
6   Open and close the door a few times to check the alignment of the latch housing with the striker plate. The bearing surfaces of the striker plate must make even contact with the latch housing (see illustration). If the latch isn't fitting evenly into the striker plate, tilt the plate slightly to align it with the latch.
7   Once the latch and striker are aligned with each other, tighten the striker plate retaining screws securely.
8   The plastic wedge is held in place in the striker place by an adjustable stop. To adjust the wedge, loosen the locknut of the adjusting screw while holding the adjusting screw with a screwdriver. Turn the adjusting screw counter-clockwise to move the stop toward the wedge. The position of the wedge is correct if you feel an increase in resistance as you open the door. If the resistance feels excessive, or if the door springs back when you try to close it, you've moved the stop too far. Turn the adjusting screw clockwise to reduce wedge pressure. Holding the adjusting screw with the screwdriver, tighten the locknut.
9   Apply a thin film of grease on the contact surfaces of the door latch and wedge. Wipe off the excess.

1967 on
Refer to illustrations 16.10, 16.11, 16.12, 16.13a, 16.13b, 16.17a, 16.17b, 16.20 and 16.21
10   Remove the striker plate (see illustration).
11   Engage the striker plate with the latch on the door (see illustration) and press the latch down into its fully locked position, then rotate the striker

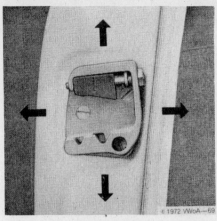

16.4   The striker plate can be adjusted horizontally and vertically to bring the door into proper alignment

16.5a   Peel back the weatherstripping around the latch and striker plate, almost close the door . . .

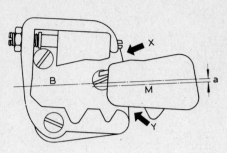

16.5b   . . . and note the height of dimensions of X and Y: X should be a little bigger than Y, to allow the latch to rise (a) about 0.08-inch (2 mm) as the latch enters the striker plate, and is lifted up by the lower bearing surface of the striker

16.6   Open and close the door a few times, then look at the bearing surfaces (arrows) of the striker plate: They must make even contact with the latch housing; if they don't, the latch isn't fitting evenly into the striker – tilt the plate slightly until the latch and striker are aligned

16.10   You may need an impact screwdriver to remove the four Phillips head screws that retain the striker plate

16.11   After you've removed the striker plate from the body, engage it with the latch on the door and press the latch down into its fully locked position, then rotate the top of the striker toward the outside of the door

16.12   Try to move the striker plate up and down – if you feel any play, the wedge must be shimmed (1967 through 1971 models) or replaced (1972 and later models)

plate toward the outside of the door (counterclockwise on driver's side, clockwise on passenger side).

12   Try to move the striker plate up and down **(see illustration)**. If you can feel any play, the wedge must be shimmed or replaced.

13   To shim a wedge (1967 through 1971 models), remove the two Phillips screws on the angled arm of the striker plate, insert the shim between the angled arm and the wedge and reinstall the screws **(see illustration)**. To replace a wedge (1972 on), simply pull the old wedge and rubbing block out, switch the rubbing block to the new wedge and insert the new wedge into the striker plate **(see illustration)**.

14   After the wedge is shimmed, or replaced, readjust the position of the door in the door opening as follows:

15   With the striker plate still removed, close the door and note whether the front edge of the door is flush with the front panel. If it isn't, loosen the hinges and move the door in, out, up or down as necessary (see Section 22).

16   Note the alignment of the trim strip on the door with the strip on the front quarter. If they're out of alignment, adjust the door as outlined in the previous Step.

11

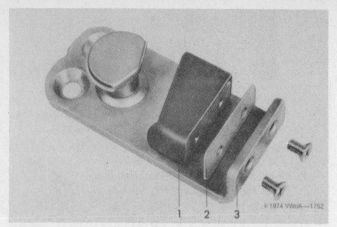

16.13a Striker plate assembly on 1967 through 1971 models

| 1 | Rubber wedge | 3 | Striker plate |
| 2 | Shim | | |

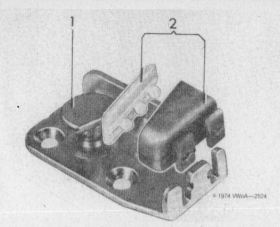

16.13b Striker plate assembly (1972 and later models)

| 1 | Striker plate | 2 | Rubbing block and wedge |

16.17a Use these notches (arrows) at the top and bottom of the striker plate as the reference points for adjusting the plate in the door frame recess

16.17b The striker plate mounting screws are threaded into this moveable plate (A) inside the rear quarter panel – the dimples (arrows) in the body are the adjustment points that match up with the notches in the striker plate (shown in the previous illustration)

17 Install the striker plate in its proper position **(see illustrations)** and tighten the screws snug enough to hold the plate in position but loose enough to allow you to move it.

18 Close the door. Note the alignment of the door and rear quarter panel. If they're not flush, move the striker plate in or out.

19 Note the alignment of the trim strip on the door with the strip on the rear quarter panel. If they're out of alignment, move the striker plate up or down.

20 If the door is difficult to close, and the pushbutton is hard to operate, the top of the striker plate is inclined inward too much, which forces the wedge against the latch too tightly. Loosen the screws, rotate the plate outward slightly **(see illustration)** and check again.

21 If the door springs back to the safety position instead of remaining closed when you slam it, the top of the striker plate is inclined outward too much, which prevents the wedge from applying sufficient pressure to hold the latch in place. Loosen the screws, rotate the plate inward slightly **(see illustration)** and check again.

22 If it's hard to open the door with the pushbutton and the door drops noticeably – instead of holding its horizontal position – when you open it, the striker plate is too high. Lower the striker plate.

23 If the door springs out of the closed position when you slam it and engages the safety notch, the striker plate is too low. Raise the plate.

24 Once the door is flush with the lock pillar, the trim strip on the door is aligned with the strip on the rear quarter panel, there's no play between the lock and the striker plate when the door is opened or closed with the handle, and the door opens from inside without excessive effort, the striker plate adjustment is correct.

17 Door trim panel – removal and installation

Refer to illustrations 17.2, 17.4, 17.5, 17.6a, 17.6b and 17.6c

1 Remove the window crank. On 1966 and earlier models, press the window crank escutcheon (the ring around the base of the crank) against the door trim panel and drive out the crank retaining pin with a punch.

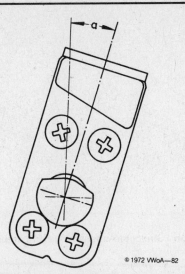

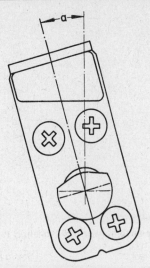

16.20 If the striker plate is tilted inward too much (plate for right door shown), it will make the door difficult to close and the pushbutton hard to push – to fix it, rotate the top of the plate outward the amount indicated by dimension "a" and try the door again

16.21 If the striker plate is tilted outward too much (plate for right door shown), it will cause the door to spring back to the safety position when you close it – to fix it, rotate the top of the plate inward the amount indicated by dimension "a" and try the door again

17.2 To remove the window regulator crank on 1967 and later models, pry the plastic cover off the crank and remove the Phillips screw

17.4 To remove the trim around the handle on 1967 and later models, pry out the recessed plastic cover and remove the Phillips screw

17.5 On 1973 and later models, remove the screws from the hollow recess under the door handle and remove the door handle

2   On 1967 and later models, pry the plastic cover off the window crank, remove the Phillips screw **(see illustration)** and pull off the crank assembly.

3   To remove the door handle on 1966 and earlier models, press the handle escutcheon against the door trim panel and drive out the crank retaining pin with a punch.

4   On 1967 and later models, pry out the recessed plastic cover with a screwdriver and remove it **(see illustration)**, then remove the Phillips screw and lift off the handle trim.

5   On 1972 and earlier models, it's unnecessary to remove the armrest – which is attached only to the door trim panel – unless you want to replace the armrest itself or switch it to a new door trim panel. On 1973 and later models, remove the screws from the hollow underside of the armrest and remove it **(see illustration)**.

6   Insert a wide-blade screwdriver, putty knife or similar tool under the edge of the door trim panel and pop loose the nearest fastener. Carefully work your way around the periphery of the panel until all the fasteners are detached. It's a good idea to tape the tip of the tool to prevent it from scratching the paint. Remove the panel and the spring at the window regulator crank **(see illustrations)**. **Note:** *On pre-1973 models, you'll need to*

17.6a Once all the fasteners are detached, remove the door trim panel . . .

11

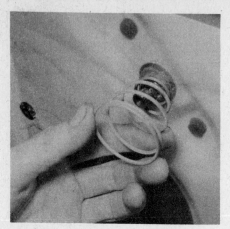

17.6b . . . and remove the spring for the window regulator crank

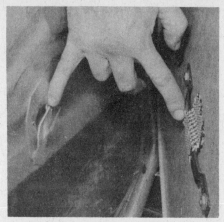

17.6c On 1972 and earlier models, you'll need to lift the door trim panel up a little so this armrest support strap on the backside of the panel clears the hook on the door – when you reinstall the panel, make sure that the strap engages the hook

18.4 Lower the window and remove the bolts that attach the window lifter channel to the window regulator mechanism

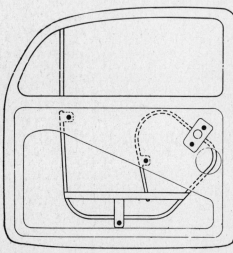

18.5 Push the door glass up and remove the five bolts that attach the regulator assembly to the door

raise the trim panel up a little to unhook the armrest support strap on the backside of the trim panel **(see illustration)**.

7   Installation is the reverse of removal. Be sure to reinstall any clips in the panel which may have been damaged or lost during removal and don't forget to reinstall the spring for the window regulator crank.

18   Door window and regulator – removal and installation

1   To open the door fully, remove the small circlip on the end of the pin for the door check strap and drive the pin out.
2   Remove the door trim panel (see Section 17).
3   Remove the waterproofing sheet from the door. If you tear the sheet during removal, discard it and get a new one – don't reuse torn waterproofing material. You can cut your own (use the old one as a template) out of heavy duty poly vinyl.

Earlier models

Refer to illustrations 18.4, 18.5, 18.6, 18.7 and 18.8
4   Lower the window and remove the bolts which attach the window lifter channel to the window regulator mechanism **(see illustration)**.

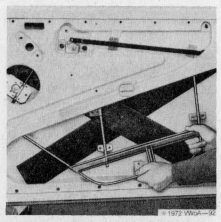

18.6   To remove the window regulator assembly from the door, raise the window and lifter as far as they'll go, push the regulator toward the outer skin of the door, then pull it down and toward you, through the opening in the door

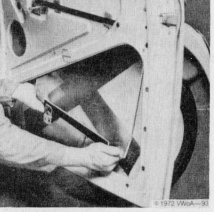

18.7   To remove the window, pull it down and toward you, through the opening in the door

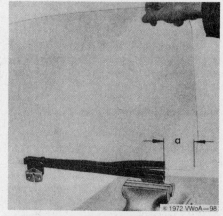

18.8 Make sure this dimension is about 3 5/32-inches (80 mm)

18.9   Lower the window and remove the bolts that attach the lifter channel to the regulator

18.10   Remove the bolts that attach the regulator to the door, ease the regulator forward and pull the window down and out

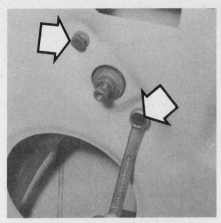

18.11   Remove the two bolts that attach the winder mechanism to the door

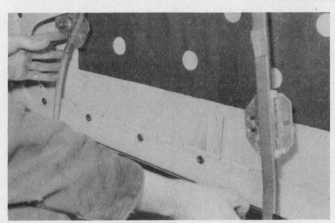

18.12   Pull the regulator assembly down and out through the opening in the door

5   Push the glass up and remove the five bolts which attach the window regulator to the door **(see illustration)**.
6   After the window has been pushed up as far as it will go, push the regulator assembly toward the outer panel of the door, then pull it down and toward you, through the opening in the door panel **(see illustration)**.
7   Pull the window and lifter channel down and toward you **(see illustration)**.
8   Installation is the reverse of removal. Make sure the channel is properly centered before you tighten any fasteners **(see illustration)**. Also, be sure to check the operation of the regulator before installing the door trim panel.

Later models
Refer to illustrations 18.9, 18.10, 18.11 and 18.12
9   Lower the window and remove the bolts attaching the window lifter channel to the regulator **(see illustration)**.
10   Remove the bolts which attach the regulator to the door, ease the regulator forward and pull the window down and out **(see illustration)**.
11   Remove the screws which attach the winder mechanism to the door **(see illustration)**.
12   Pull the regulator assembly down and out through the opening in the door **(see illustration)**.
13   To install the regulator, guide the regulator through the opening in the door, winder mechanism first, then shove the rest of the regulator assembly in and up into the door until the regulator mounting bracket holes are lined up with the holes in the door, but don't install the bolts yet.
14   Have an assistant hold the regulator assembly in place while you

carefully slip the window up through the opening in the door and into place on the lifter channel.
15   With the glass in position, install the bolts attaching the window lifter channel to the regulator. Attach the bottom end of the regulator to the door, then install the other three bolts which attach the regulator mounting brackets to the door. Tighten all fasteners hand tight, then check the operation of the regulator assembly. If necessary, loosen the bolts attaching the lifter channel to the regulator and readjust the window a little and recheck. Repeat this process until the regulator operates satisfactorily.
16   The remainder of installation is the reverse of removal.

19   Vent window – removal and installation

Earlier models
1   Remove the door trim panel (see Section 17).
2   Remove the window regulator and door glass (see Section 18).
3   Remove the Phillips head screw which attaches the top of the vent window frame to the door frame and lift out the vent window and frame assembly.
4   Installation is the reverse of removal.

Later models
Refer to illustration 19.5
5   Drill out the pivot pin at the top of the vent window **(see illustration)** and lift out the vent window glass and frame.

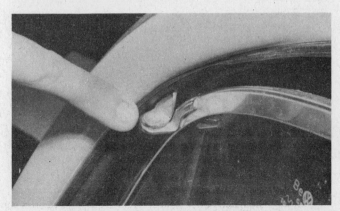

19.5   To remove the vent window on newer models, simply drill out this rivet from the upper pivot and remove the vent window glass and frame

11

20.9a   Remove the retaining bolts from the inside door handle, pull the handle away . . .

20.9b   . . . and remove the handle, remote control rod and foam packing as an assembly

20.10   Unclip the inside lock control rod from the lock mechanism

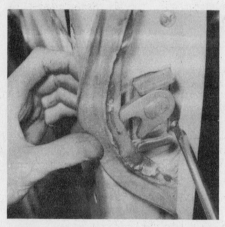

20.11   Peel back the weatherstripping and remove the lock retaining screws

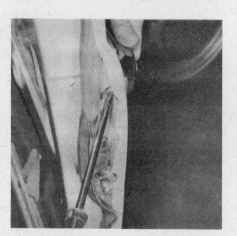

20.12a   Remove the outside door handle retaining screw . . .

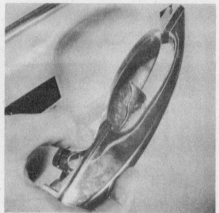

20.12b   . . . and remove the outside door handle and rubber seals

6   Place the new vent window glass and frame in position and install a rivet in the upper pivot. **Note:** *If you don't have a rivet gun, you can use a small nut and screw, but vehicle security will be compromised.*

20   Door outside handle, latch mechanism and inside handle – removal and installation

1   Remove the door window regulator handle, the inside door handle (older type) or the inside door handle escutcheon (newer type) and the door trim panel (see Section 17).

Early type

2   Remove the window regulator (see Section 18).
3   Peel back the weatherstripping, remove the two screws that secure the outside door handle and remove the handle and rubber seals.
4   Remove the four lock retaining screws from the door.
5   Remove the two screws adjacent to the door handle.
6   Remove the screw which secures the rear glass-run channel. Lift up the glass and remove the lock and remote control assembly.
7   Clean and grease all moving parts.
8   Installation is the reverse of removal.

Later type

Refer to illustrations 20.9a, 20.9b, 20.10, 20.11, 20.12a, 20.12b and 20.13

9   Remove the retaining bolts from the inside door handle **(see illustration)** and remove the handle, remote control rod and foam packing **(see**

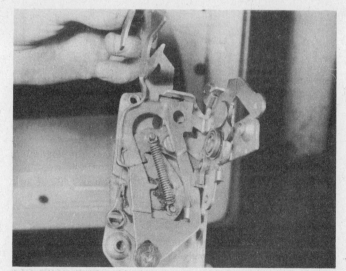

20.13   Typical lock mechanism – replace the lock if it's broken – don't bother trying to fix it

illustration) as an assembly.
10   Disconnect the inside lock mechanism **(see illustration)**.
11   Peel back the weatherstripping and remove the lock retaining screws **(see illustration)** and the lock.

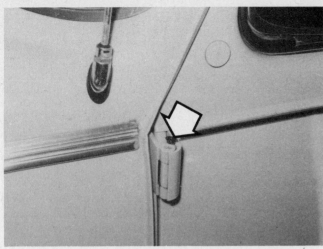

21.1   To install a mirror in the tapped hole in the door, pry out this removable plug (arrow)

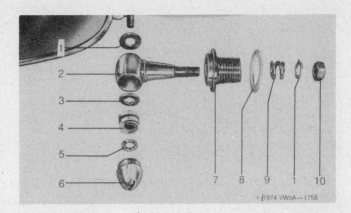

21.2   Exploded view of a typical mirror mounting assembly

1	Washer	6	Cap nut
2	Mirror arm	7	Mirror socket
3	Washer with hexagonal hole	8	Sealing washer
4	Coil spring	9	Spiral spring
5	Lock washer	10	Mirror arm nut

2   If you're switching the old mirror to a new door, be sure to disassemble the mirror mounting assembly **(see illustration)** and lubricate the parts. After the mirror mount is reassembled, be sure to stake the mirror arm nut before reinstalling the mirror in the door.

22   Door – removal and installation

Removal

1   Remove the clip from the pin for the door check strap and remove the pin.
2   Remove the cover plugs for the hinge screws.
3   Loosen the Phillips head hinge screws with an impact screwdriver, then remove them.
4   Grasping the door firmly, pull the hinges out of the pillar and remove the door.

Installation

Refer to illustration 22.6

5   Inspect the weatherstrip around the door opening and replace it if it's cracked, dried or deteriorated.
6   Basically, two types of doors have been used on Beetles. The only door currently available is the newer type (unless you find one in a wrecking yard). So, if you're installing a new door on an older car and you want to use the old door trim panel, you'll need to weld an armrest retainer bracket onto the inner panel **(see illustration)**.
7   Slide the hinges into position and install the hinge screws tight enough to support the door without moving.
8   Close the door carefully and note the fit between the top of the door and the roof and the fit between the rear edge of the door and the pillar and rear quarter panel. Adjust the hinges as necessary. You may also have to adjust the striker plate (see Section 16).
9   Tighten the hinge screws securely and replace the cover plugs. Lubricate the hinges with multi-purpose grease.

22.6   The door for 1973 and later models (the only door still available as a new part) has no retainer for the old-style armrest (which attaches only to the trim panel) – if you mix a new door with an old trim panel/armrest, you'll need to weld on an armrest retainer (four small protrusions mark the position for the armrest retainer)

12   Remove the outside door handle retaining screws **(see illustration)** and remove the outside door handle **(see illustration)**.
13   Remove the lock mechanism **(see illustration)**. The lock is quite complex – if it doesn't work right, replace it.
14   Installation is the reverse of removal.

21   Outside mirror – removal and installation

Refer to illustrations 21.1 and 21.2

1   The outside mirror is installed in a tapped hole **(see illustration)** in the door. It's not necessary to remove the door trim panel to install a mirror or replace the existing unit. If you're installing an accessory mirror, simply pry out the plug and screw in the new mirror. If you're replacing the existing mirror, remove the mirror mounting assembly from the door with a wrench.

23   Seats – removal and installation

1972 and earlier models

Refer to illustrations 23.2 and 23.4

1   If the vehicle is a 1972 model with a seat belt warning buzzer, unplug the electrical connector.

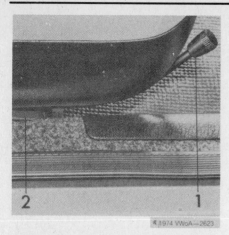

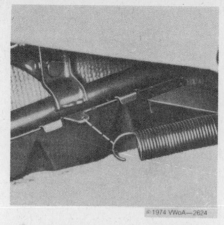

23.2   Raise the adjustment lever (1) and slide the seat forward until its runner contacts the leaf-spring stop (2)

23.4   Reach under the seat and detach the tension spring

23.10   Pry off the plastic cover from the rear end of each seat runner

2   Raise the adjustment lever and slide the seat forward until its runner contacts the leaf-spring stop **(see illustration)**.
3   Depress the leaf-spring stop with a screwdriver, raise the adjustment lever and slide the seat forward about 1 1/2-inches.
4   Reach under the seat and detach the tension spring **(see illustration)**.
5   Slide the seat forward, lift it off the tracks and and remove it.
6   To install the seat, grasping it with the backrest folded forward for better balance, place it in position over the tracks and slip the inner runner into its track. Pull the seat toward you slightly and insert the outer runner into its track.
7   Raise the adjusting lever, slide the seat back and reconnect the tension spring.
8   Plug in the electrical connector for the seat belt warning buzzer, if equipped.

1973 on

Refer to illustrations 23.10 and 23.12

9   Unplug the electrical connector for the seat belt warning buzzer.
10   Pry off the plastic cover from the rear end of each seat runner **(see illustration)**.
11   Pull back on the adjusting lever and slide the seat back to its next-to-last position.
12   Insert a screwdriver into the front of the seat bracket **(see illustration)** and, using it as a lever, push down the leaf-spring stop.
13   Release the seat adjusting lever and slide the seat to the rear and off its runners.
14   Inspect the four friction pads on the seat runners and make sure the two springs clips are pressed into the upper friction pads (if the clips are worn out, missing or not fully pressed into place, the seat will rattle).
15   Slide the seat into the rear ends of the runners.
16   Pull back the seat adjusting lever and slide the seat forward and into the central bracket.
17   Press the plastic covers back into the rear ends of the runners.
18   Plug in the electrical connector for the seat belt warning buzzer.

24   Seat belt check

1   Check the seat belts, buckles, latch plates and guide loops for obvious damage and signs of wear.
2   On 1972 and later models, a seat belt warning buzzer comes on, and a Fasten Seat Belts light comes on, if the key is turned to the Run or Start positions and a gear is selected before you – or a passenger – buckle up. Try starting the vehicle and putting it into gear to verify that the system is operating properly. **Note:** *On 1974 models, the engine can't be started while the buzzer is sounding.*
3   Passive restraint type seat belts on late-model vehicles are designed to lock up during a sudden stop or impact, yet allow free movement during normal driving. Verify that the retractors return the belt against your chest while driving and rewind the belt fully when the buckle is unlatched.
4   If any of the above checks reveal problems with the seat belt system, replace parts as necessary.

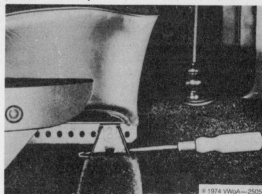

23.12   Insert a screwdriver into the front of the seat bracket and push down the leaf-spring stop

Chapter 12   Chassis electrical system

Contents

---

1   General information

The electrical system on these vehicles is either a 6-volt (pre-1967 models) or 12-volt, negative ground type. Power for the lights and all electrical accessories is supplied by a lead/acid-type battery which is charged by the alternator or generator.

This Chapter covers repair and service procedures for the various electrical components not associated with the engine. Information on the battery, alternator/generator, distributor and starter motor can be found in Chapter 5.

It should be noted that when portions of the electrical system are serviced, the negative battery cable should be disconnected from the battery to prevent electrical shorts and/or fires.

2   Electrical troubleshooting – general information

A typical electrical circuit consists of an electrical component, any switches, relays, motors, fuses, fusible links or circuit breakers related to that component and the wiring and connectors that link the component to both the battery and the chassis. To help you pinpoint an electrical circuit problem, wiring diagrams are included at the end of this book.

Before tackling any troublesome electrical circuit, first study the appropriate wiring diagrams to get a complete understanding of what makes up that individual circuit. Trouble spots, for instance, can often be narrowed down by noting if other components related to the circuit are operating properly. If several components or circuits fail at one time, chances are the problem is in a fuse or ground connection, because several circuits are of-

12

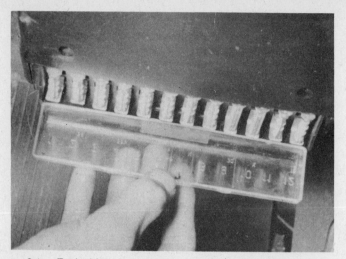

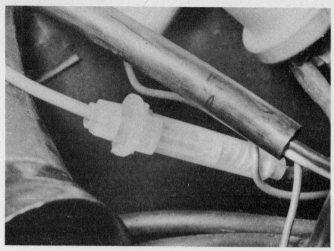

3.1a   Typical fuse box – to replace a fuse, remove the clear plastic cover (note the numbered fuse positions on the cover – compare these to the accompanying fuse box charts to quickly determine what each fuse is for)

3.1b   Typical in-line fuse

ten routed through the same fuse and ground connections.

Electrical problems usually stem from simple causes, such as loose or corroded connections, a blown fuse, a melted fusible link or a bad relay. Visually inspect the condition of all fuses, wires and connections in a problem circuit before troubleshooting it.

If testing instruments are going to be utilized, use the diagrams to plan ahead of time where you will make the necessary connections in order to accurately pinpoint the trouble spot.

The basic tools needed for electrical troubleshooting include a circuit tester or voltmeter (a 6 or 12-volt bulb with a set of test leads can also be used), a continuity tester, which includes a bulb, battery and set of test leads, and a jumper wire, preferably with a circuit breaker incorporated, which can be used to bypass electrical components. Before attempting to locate a problem with test instruments, use the wiring diagram(s) to decide where to make the connections.

Voltage checks

Voltage checks should be performed if a circuit is not functioning properly. Connect one lead of a circuit tester to either the negative battery terminal or a known good ground. Connect the other lead to a connector in the circuit being tested, preferably nearest to the battery or fuse. If the bulb of the tester lights, voltage is present, which means that the part of the circuit between the connector and the battery is problem free. Continue checking the rest of the circuit in the same fashion. When you reach a point at which no voltage is present, the problem lies between that point and the last test point with voltage. Most of the time the problem can be traced to a loose connection. **Note:** *Keep in mind that some circuits receive voltage only when the ignition key is in the Accessory or Run position.*

Finding a short

One method of finding shorts in a circuit is to remove the fuse and connect a test light or voltmeter in its place to the fuse terminals. There should be no voltage present in the circuit. Move the wiring harness from side to side while watching the test light. If the bulb goes on, there is a short to ground somewhere in that area, probably where the insulation has rubbed through. The same test can be performed on each component in the circuit, even a switch.

Ground check

Perform a ground test to check whether a component is properly grounded. Disconnect the battery and connect one lead of a self powered test light, known as a continuity tester, to a known good ground. Connect the other lead to the wire or ground connection being tested. If the bulb goes on, the ground is good. If the bulb does not go on, the ground is not good.

Continuity check

A continuity check is done to determine if there are any breaks in a circuit - if it is passing electricity properly. With the circuit off (no power in the circuit), a self powered continuity tester or an ohmmeter can be used to check the circuit. Connect the test leads to both ends of the circuit (or to the "power" end and a good ground), and if the test light comes on (or the ohmmeter needle indicates continuity) the circuit is passing current properly. If the light doesn't come on, there is a break somewhere in the circuit. The same procedure can be used to test a switch, by connecting the continuity tester to the switch terminals. With the switch turned On, the test light should come on.

Finding an open circuit

When diagnosing for possible open circuits, it is often difficult to locate them by sight because oxidation or terminal misalignment are hidden by the connectors. Merely wiggling a connector on a sensor or in the wiring harness may correct the open circuit condition. Remember this when an open circuit is indicated when troubleshooting a circuit. Intermittent problems may also be caused by oxidized or loose connections.

Electrical troubleshooting is simple if you keep in mind that all electrical circuits are basically electricity running from the battery, through the wires, switches, relays, fuses and fusible links to each electrical component (light bulb, motor, etc.) and to ground, from which it is passed back to the battery.

---

3   Fuses – general information

Refer to illustrations 3.1a, 3.1b, 3.2a, 3.2b, 3.2c, 3.2d, 3.2e and 3.3

The electrical circuits of the vehicle are protected by fuses. The fuse box is located under the dashboard to the left (Super Beetles) or right of the steering column. To replace a fuse, simply open the clear plastic cover on the box **(see illustration)**, pull the bad fuse out and install a new one of the same amperage. On air conditioned models, the fuse box is located ahead of the instrument cluster. To get at it, remove the protective cover on the firewall. In line fuses **(see illustration)** are also located throughout the vehicle, usually in the luggage or engine compartments.

Each fuse protects a specific circuit. The accompanying charts cover most fuse box versions **(see illustrations)**

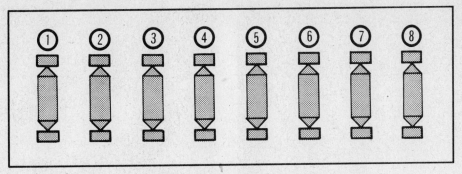

3.2a   Typical fuse box layout on pre-1967 (six-volt) models

1   Brake lights, turn signals, windshield wipers and horn (except 1961) (16-amp)
2   Left high beam and high beam warning light (8-amp)
3   Right high beam (8-amp)

4   Left low beam (8-amp)
5   Right low beam (8-amp)
6   Left tail light and left front parking brake (8-amp)

7   Right tail light, license plate light and right front parking light (except 1966) (8-amp)
8   Radio, interior light, horn (1961 only) and emergency flasher (1966 only) (8-amp, through 1965; 16 amp, 1966 only)

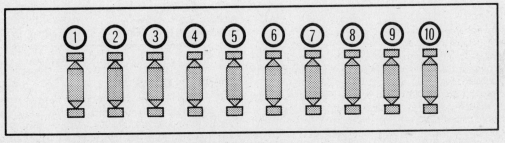

3.2b   Typical fuse box layout on 1967 through 1972 standard Beetles and 1970 convertibles

1   Horn (except 1968), turn signals, brake lights (except 1969 and 1970), fuel gauge (except 1967), Automatic Stick Shift warning lights (except 1967) and rear window defroster switch (1969 and 1970 only) (8-amp)
2   Windshield wipers, brake lights (1969 and 1970 only) and horn (1967 only) (8-amp)
3   Left high beam and high beam warning light (8-amp)

4   Right high beam (8-amp)
5   Left low beam (8-amp)
6   Right low beam (8-amp)
7   Right tail light (1967 and 1968 only), left tail light (1969 and 1970 only), license plate light (1967 only) and left front parking light (except 1967) (8-amp)
8   Left tail light (1967 only), right tail light (except 1967), right front parking light (except 1967) and license plate light (except 1967) (8-amp)

9   Radio (1967 only), dome light (except 1967), emergency flasher (except 1967) and ignition warning light (1969 and 1970) (8-amp, 1967; 16-amp, 1968 through 1971)
10   Dome light (1967 only), emergency flasher (1967 only) and radio (except 1967) (8-amp, 1968 through 1971; 16-amp, 1967 only)

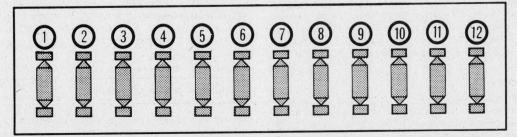

3.2c   Typical fuse box layout on 1971 and 1972 Super Beetle and convertible models

1   Turn signals, speedometer warning lights and fuel gauge (8-amp)
2   Windshield wipers, brake warning light, Automatic Stick Shift warning lights and rear window defroster switch (8-amp)
3   Brake lights and horn (8-amp)

4   Emergency flasher (8-amp)
5   Unassigned (8-amp)
6   Dome light and ignition warning buzzer (8-amp)
7   Left high beam and high beam warning light (8-amp)

8   Right high beam (8-amp)
9   Left low beam (16-amp)
10   Right low beam (8-amp)
11   Left tail light (16-amp)
12   Right tail light, side marker lights and license plate light (8-amp)

12

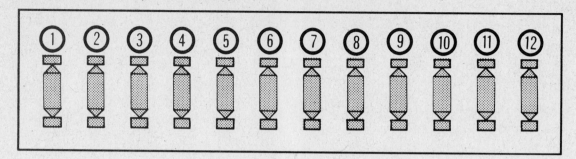

3.2d　Typical fuse box layout on 1973 and later Beetles

1 Front turn and parking light, front side marker lights, right tail light and license plate light (8-amp)
2 Left tail light (8-amp)
3 Left low beam (8-amp)
4 Right low beam (8-amp)

5 Left high beam and high beam indicator (8-amp)
6 Right high beam (8-amp)
7 Unassigned
8 Emergency flasher (8-amp)

9 Dome light and ignition warning buzzer (16-amp)
10 Windshield wipers (16-amp)
11 Horn and brake lights (8-amp)
12 Turn signals, fuel gauge and seat belt warning (8-amp)

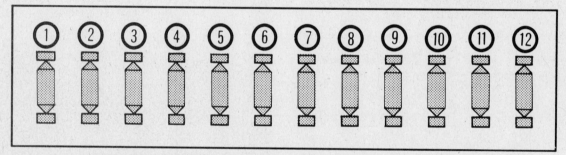

3.2e　Typical fuse box layout on 1973 and later Super Beetles and convertibles

1 Left tail light, left front turn and parking lights, left side marker light and license plate light (8-amp)
2 Right tail light, right side marker light and right front turn and parking light (8-amp)
3 Left low beam (8-amp)

4 Right low beam (8-amp)
5 Left high beam and high beam indicator (8-amp)
6 Right high beam (8-amp)
7 Unassigned
8 Emergency flasher (8-amp)

9 Dome light (16-amp)
10 Rear window fogger relay, fresh air fan and windshield wipers (16-amp)
11 Horn, brake lights and control valve (Automatic Stick Shift models only) (8-amp)
12 Seat belt interlock, instrument cluster lights, fuel gauge and turn signals (8-amp)

3.3　A blown fuse (on right) is easy to spot – the metal strip in the middle is burnt

If an electrical component fails, always check the fuse first. A blown fuse is easy to identify – there will be a gap in the metal strip in the middle of the fuse (see illustration).

Be sure the replacement fuse has the correct amperage rating. Fuses of different ratings are physically interchangeable, but replacing a fuse with one of a higher or lower value than specified isn't recommended. Each electrical circuit needs a specific amount of protection. The amperage rating of each fuse is determined by the color of the fuse body – red denotes 16 amp fuses and white denotes 8 amp fuses.

If the replacement fuse immediately fails, don't replace it again until the cause of the problem is isolated and corrected. In most cases, the cause will be a short circuit in the wiring caused by a broken or deteriorated wire.

4　Relays – general information

Refer to illustrations 4.2a, 4.2b and 4.2c

Relays are remote switches that allow a small current to control a larger one. On later models, electrical accessories such as the lights, horn, turn signal emergency flasher, intermittent wipers, fog lights and ignition

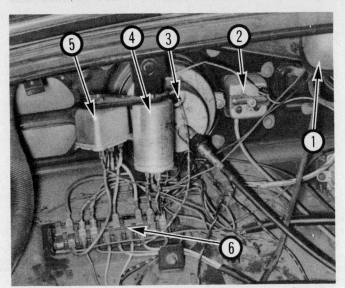

4.2a Some relays are located on the firewall under a protective cover (removed for clarity)

1 Windshield wiper motor	*5 Headlight dimmer flasher relay*
2 Fuel gauge	*6 Fused terminal block (fuses are*
3 Speedometer head	*on the other side. facing driver)*
4 Turn signal flasher relay	

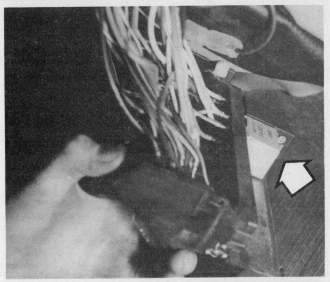

4.2b Some relays (arrow) are plugged into a special panel on the backside of the fuse box

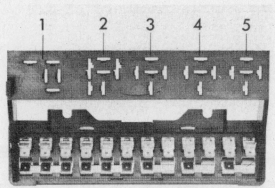

© 1974 VWoA—1341

4.2c Typical relay locations on the fuse box (Super Beetles and 1971 and later convertibles)

1 Low beam		*4 Open*	
2 Open		*5 Buzzer*	
3 Turn signal emergency			
flasher			

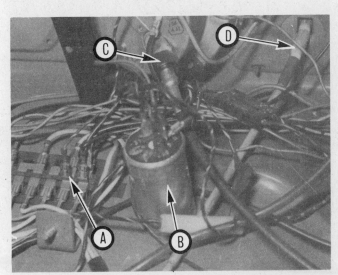

5.1 A typical turn signal flasher relay on an earlier model

A Fuse block	*C Speedometer cable*
B Flasher relay	*retaining collar*
	D Fuel gauge line

key and seat belt warning device all use relays to transmit the electrical signal to the components.

Relays are located on the firewall **(see illustration)**. on the steering column support behind the instrument panel. or on a special bracket behind the fuse box **(see illustrations)**. Replacing some relays is simply a matter of removing the instrument cluster cover from the firewall in the luggage compartment. pulling out the old relay and pushing a new one in: on others. you'll have to unscrew the fuse box from the dash and lower it far enough to unplug the relay(s).

If a relay is defective. the circuit it controls won't operate properly. If you suspect a faulty relay. remove it and have it tested by a dealer service department or a repair shop. or install a replacement unit and see if the circuit resumes proper operation.

---

5 Turn signal and hazard flashers – check and replacement

Turn signal flasher

Refer to illustration 5.1

1 The turn signal flasher **(see illustration)**. flashes the turn signals. On earlier models. the flasher relay is a small. metal canister located on the firewall. On later models. it's a small. plastic cube mounted on the steering column support behind the instrument panel. next to the headlight dimmer relay. On Super Beetles. it's plugged into the back of the fuse box (see Section 4).

2 Dirty. corroded or loose-fitting turn signal bulb contacts will cause the turn signal system to malfunction. Before assuming the problem is at the turn signal relay. always make sure all bulb contacts are clean and tight.

3 In operation. the flasher makes an audible clicking sound if it's working properly. If the turn signals fail on one side or the other and the flasher

12

6.18   Steering column components – exploded view

1   Slip-ring
2   Direction indicator switch
3   Snap-ring
4   Bearing
5   Retainer
6   Switch housing
7   Ignition/starter switch
8   Steering lock body
9   Lock cylinder
10   Steering wheel

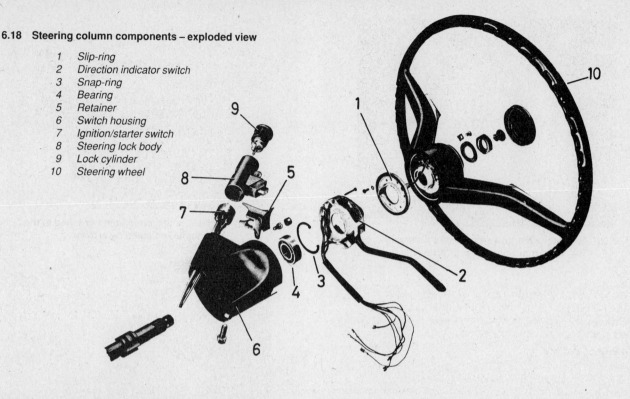

unit doesn't make its characteristic clicking sound, or clicks faster or slower than normal, a turn signal bulb is blown. **Note:** *Flasher frequency depends on the available voltage. The voltage varies with engine speed, so the flasher's frequency will be slower at idle than at high rpm. A good relay will operate at anywhere from 60 to 120 impulses a minute.*

4   If both turn signals fail to blink, the problem may be a blown fuse, a loose or open connection, a faulty flasher unit or a broken turn signal switch. If a quick check of the fuse box indicates that the turn signal fuse has blown, check the wiring for a short before installing a new fuse.

5   To replace the flasher on non-Super Beetle models, disconnect the cable from the negative battery terminal, open the front hood, remove the instrument panel protective cover, clearly label the three wires at the flasher, detach them, loosen the flasher mounting bracket and remove the flasher. Installation is the reverse of removal. Make sure the replacement unit is identical in specification to the old unit.

6   To replace the flasher on Super Beetle models, drop the fuse box down, unplug the flasher from the back of the fuse box and plug in a new unit. Make sure that the replacement unit is identical to the original.

7   If the problem is neither the fuse, the wiring nor the relay, check the turn signal switch (see Section 6).

Hazard flasher relay

8   All models manufactured since August 1966 are equipped with a hazard flasher system. When activated by a switch on the dash, it flashes all four turn signal lights simultaneously. Originally, the system consisted of a switch and a relay wired into the turn signal circuit. In January 1968, the flasher relay functions were integrated into the turn signal flasher relay. Early versions of this system located the integrated turn signal/emergency flasher relay on the firewall, under the protective cover for the instrument panel. On later models, the relay is on the back of the fuse box.

9   The turn signals and emergency flashers share the same relay on most models, so if the emergency flashers work – but the turn signals don't – the relay isn't at fault. Conversely, if the turn signals work – but the emergency flasher doesn't – the relay is still okay. The following check will help you avoid the unnecessary replacement of a relay.

10   With the ignition turned off, use a jumper wire to bridge terminal "+" or "49" (depending on manufacturer) of the relay to terminal "30" of the fuse block and operate the turn signal switch in both directions. If both signals work properly, the relay and switch are okay. If they don't, test the emergency flasher switch, then test the turn signal switch (see Section 6).

11   To replace the hazard flasher, follow the proceure outlined above for the turn signal flasher. Make sure the replacement is identical to the old unit.

---

6   Turn signal switch/emergency flasher switch – check and replacement

Check

Flasher switch

1   Make sure all contacts on the turn signal bulbs are connected properly and the bulb holders are corrosion free.

2   Remove the steering wheel (see Chapter 10).

3   Remove the flasher switch and turn it on.

4   Connect an ohmmeter across terminals "30" and "+ at the fuse block, and across terminals "49a," "R" and "L" on the switch, and check for continuity.

5   If any resistance is indicated, replace the emergency flasher switch.

Turn signal switch

6   Disconnect the black/green/white wire to the turn signal switch at the plug guide.

7   Using an ohmmeter, check for continuity between terminal 54BL (1970 models), or terminal 49a (1971 and later models), and terminals "R" and "L" of the turn signal switch.

8   If any resistance is indicated, replace the turn signal switch.

Replacement

Flasher switch

9   Disconnect the cable from the negative battery cable.

10   Raise the front hood and remove the instrument panel cover. On 1968 and later models, take out the fresh air box, too.

6.20   To remove the turn signal switch, remove these four mounting screws (arrows)

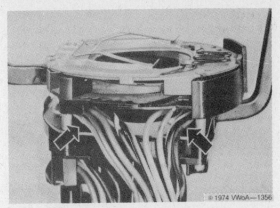

6.25   Make sure the wires aren't crushed at the points indicated by arrows

11   Clearly label. then disconnect. the wires at the switch.
12   Pull the switch knob out and unscrew the knob.
13   Remove the lock-ring and remove the switch.
14   Installation is the reverse of removal.

Turn signal switch

Refer to illustrations 6.18. 6.20 and 6.25

15   Detach the cable from the negative battery terminal.
16   Turn the ignition key to the On position. Place the turn signal lever in its central position.
17   Remove the steering wheel (see Chapter 10).
18   On 1971 and earlier models. remove the slip-ring **(see illustration)**. Also disconnect the wires to the turn signal switch from behind the dash and push the wires through the opening in the body toward the switch.
19   On 1972 and later models. remove the circlip from the groove below the steering wheel splines on the steering column.
20   Remove the four screws securing the switch **(see illustration)**.
21   Lift the switch out of the switch housing.
22   Disconnect the electrical connectors from the switch and remove the switch.
23   On 1972 and later models. bleed the air from the windshield washer reservoir and disconnect the windshield washer hose from the switch.
24   On 1972 and later models. the turn signal and windshield wiper switches must be removed together and separated after removal. These switches have channels that guide the wires from the switches. You can disconnect the guide channel by unplugging it from a connector in the bottom of the steering column switch housing.
25   Installation is the reverse of removal. Make sure the contact ring between the steering column bearing and the steering column is positioned properly and the turn signal switch lever is in its central position. or the the cancelling cam will be damaged by the tongue of the contact ring when the steering wheel is installed. On 1972 and later models. make sure the wires for the turn signals aren't crushed by contact with the windshield wiper switch at the points indicated **(see illustration)**.
26   After installing the switch. adjust the clearance between the steering column switch housing and the steering wheel hub. The distance between the hub and the column switch housing must be 1/16 to 1/8-inch (2 to 3 mm). To adjust this dimension. loosen the two screws that secure the switch to the vehicle body or steering column tube and move the switch housing in the slotted holes. **Caution:** *Move the turn signal switch only with the lever in its central position or the cancelling cam may be damaged.*

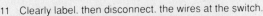

7   Ignition switch/lock cylinder – check and replacement

1967 and earlier models

1   Detach the cable from the negative battery terminal.

7.9   To remove the lock cylinder on 1958 through 1971 models, remove the retaining plate (A), insert the ignition key and turn it slightly, pull out the lock cylinder until the retaining spring is visible in the opening (B) and press on the retaining ring through the opening with a stiff piece of wire while pulling out the lock cylinder

2   Open the front hood and remove the protective cover for the instrument panel.
3   Clearly label. then disconnect. the wires to the ignition switch terminals.
4   Remove the screw which secures the switch bracket and remove the switch.
5   Installation is the reverse of removal.

1968 through 1971 models

Refer to illustration 7.9

6   Detach the cable from the negative battery terminal.
7   Remove the steering wheel (see Chapter 10).
8   Remove the circlip and plastic bushing from the steering column.
9   Loosen the turn signal switch and remove the two screws which secure the retaining plate **(see illustration)**.
10   Insert the ignition key and turn it slightly. Pull the lock cylinder out unil the retaining spring is visible in the opening.
11   Press on the retaining spring through the opening with a stiff piece of wire while pulling out the lock cylinder.
12   Installation is the reverse of removal.

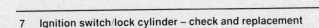

12

7.19 On 1976 and later models, if there's no hole in the cylinder for releasing the retaining spring, make one – carefully drill a small hole at the intersection of dimensions "a" and "b" (a and b are each 11 mm)

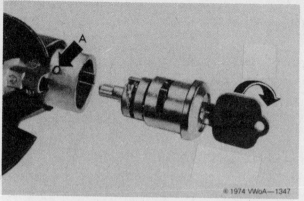

7.21 To remove the lock cylinder, insert a nail or piece of wire through the hole at A, depress the retaining spring, turn the key and pull the cylinder out of the housing

1972 and later models

Lock cylinder

Refer to illustrations 7.19, 7.21, 7.22 and 7.23

13 Detach the cable from the negative battery terminal.
14 Remove the steering wheel (see Chapter 10).
15 Remove the circlip and plastic bushing from the steering column.
16 Remove the turn signal switch and, if applicable, the wiper switch.
17 Remove the steering/ignition lock retainer plate.
18 On 1972 and later models, unplug the wire harness from the switch; on earlier models, push the wires through while you pull the lock cylinder out far enough to work on it.
19 On 1976 and later models, inspect the lock cylinder housing. If there's no hole at the point indicated **(see illustration)**, carefully drill one.
20 Insert a nail or a piece of steel wire through the hole and depress the retaining spring on the lock cylinder.
21 Remove the lock cylinder by turning the key and pulling the lock cylinder out of the housing as shown **(see illustration)**.
22 Before installing the cylinder, examine the guide pin **(see illustra-**

tion). When the pin is depressed slightly, you should be able to move the slide for the steering column lock to the right until the slide pin is flush with the housing.
23 If you're installing an earlier cylinder (no black plastic ring) **(see illustration)**, insert it with the key installed in the lock cylinder and turn the cylinder to the left stop position and remove the key. If the lock cylinder has a black plastic ring **(see illustration)**, install the cylinder by pushing it in without the key. Then turn the cylinder to the left stop position and remove the key.
24 If you're installing an earlier type lock cylinder with the helical groove for the pin, verify that the key pulls itself into the lock cylinder housing when you turn the lock cylinder (this check is unnecessary if you're installing the later type lock cylinder with the black plastic ring).
25 The remainder of installation is the reverse of removal.

Ignition switch

Refer to illustrations 7.28 and 7.30

26 Detach the cable from the negative battery terminal.
27 Remove the steering wheel (see Chapter 10).
28 Detach the steering column from the dash **(see illustration)** and remove the housing.
29 Unplug the harness from the ignition switch.
30 Remove the set screw from the lock cylinder housing **(see illustration)** and remove the ignition switch.
31 Installation is the reverse of removal.

7.22 Before you install the new cylinder, verify that the guide pin (left arrow) isn't bent or broken and the slide pin (right arrow) moves freely

7.23 Earlier cylinder on left has no black plastic ring and a helical groove for the pin – later cylinder on right has black plastic ring, no helical groove

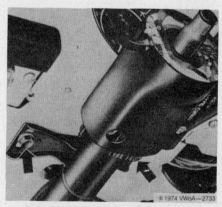

7.28 Remove the two bolts (arrows) that attach the steering column to the underside of the dash, lower the column, then remove the screws that attach the steering column housing

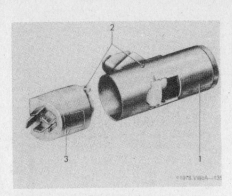

7.30   To remove the ignition switch (3) from the lock cylinder housing (1), remove the set screw (2)

8.2   To release the headlight assembly from the fender on 1966 and earlier models, remove the retaining screw from the bottom of the headlight trim ring

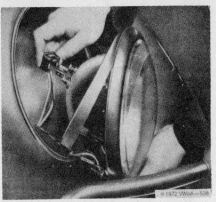

8.3   Unplug the electrical connector for the headlight unit and disconnect the wires for the parking light (at the bottom)

---

8   Headlights – removal and installation

1966 and earlier models

Refer to illustrations 8.2. 8.3 and 8.6

1   Disconnect the negative cable from the battery.
2   Remove the retaining screw from the headlight trim ring **(see illustration)** and pull out the entire headlight assembly.
3   Unplug the electrical connector from the headlight **(see illustration)**.
4   Disconnect the two wires from the parking light bulb socket.
5   Remove the parking light bulb.
6   Holding the headlight unit, pry one end of the retaining spring out with one thumb while you hold the other end of the spring with your other thumb **(see illustration)**. Be careful – the spring is under considerable tension.
7   Pull out the retaining ring and sealed beam unit.
8   Installation is the reverse of removal.
9   Adjust the headlights when you're done (see Section 9).

1967 and later models

Refer to illustration 8.11

10   Detach the cable from the negative battery terminal.
11   Remove the screw from the bottom of the trim ring and remove the

ring **(see illustration)**.
12   Remove the three screws which attach the retaining ring and remove the ring.
13   Pull out the headlight and unplug the wire harness.
14   Installation is the reverse of removal.
15   Adjust the headlights when you're done.

---

9   Headlights – adjustment

Refer to illustrations 9.1a and 9.1b

Note: *The headlights must be aimed correctly. If adjusted incorrectly they could blind the driver of an oncoming vehicle and cause a serious accident or seriously reduce your ability to see the road. The headlights should be checked for proper aim every 12 months and any time a new headlight is installed or front end body work is performed. It should be emphasized that the following procedure is only an interim step which will provide temporary adjustment until the headlights can be adjusted by a properly equipped shop.*

1   Headlights have two spring loaded adjusting screws. one on the top controlling up-and-down movement and one on the side controlling left-and-right movement **(see illustrations)**.

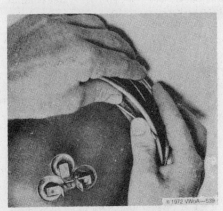

8.6   To remove the sealed beam unit, carefully pry one end of the retaining spring out with one thumb while holding the other end of the spring down with your other thumb – the spring is under tension, so watch what you're doing

8.11   An exploded view of the headlight assembly on 1967 and later models

a   *Trim ring retaining screw*
b   *Retaining ring screws for sealed beam unit*
c   *Headlight adjustment screws (upper screw is for vertical adjustment and lower screw is for horizontal adjustment)*

9.1a   Headlight adjustment screw locations on 1966 and earlier models – screw A controls vertical adjustment, screw B controls horizontal adjustment

12

9.1b   Typical headlight adjustment screw locations on a Karmann Ghia – screw a controls vertical adjustment, screw b controls horizontal adjustment (1967 and later Beetles are similar)

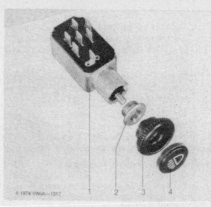

10.3   Exploded view of typical push-pull and rotary type headlight switch

1   Light switch
2   Lock-ring
3   Light switch knob
4   Light switch cap

10.10   Remove these cover strips from each end of the instrument panel switch cluster

2   There are several methods of adjusting the headlights. The simplest method requires a blank wall 25 feet in front of the vehicle and a level floor.

3   Position masking tape vertically on the wall in reference to the vehicle centerline and the centerlines of both headlights.

4   Position a horizontal tape line in reference to the centerline of all the headlights. **Note:** *It may be easier to position the tape on the wall with the vehicle parked only a few inches away.*

5   Adjustment should be made with the vehicle sitting level. the gas tank half-full and no unusually heavy load in the vehicle.

6   Starting with the low beam adjustment. position the high intensity zone so it is two inches below the horizontal line and two inches to the right of the headlight vertical line. Adjustment is made by turning the top adjusting screw clockwise to raise the beam and counterclockwise to lower the beam. The adjusting screw on the side should be used in the same manner to move the beam left or right.

7   With the high beams on. the high intensity zone should be vertically centered with the exact center just below the horizontal line. **Note:** *It may not be possible to position the headlight aim exactly for both high and low beams. If a compromise must be made. keep in mind that the low beams are the most used and have the greatest effect on driver safety.*

8   Have the headlights adjusted by a dealer service department or service station at the earliest opportunity.

10   Headlight switch – check and replacement

Check

1   If the headlight switch fails to activate the headlights. pull out the switch so you can get at the wire terminals on the back (see below) and. using a test light or voltmeter. check for voltage from the battery to the switch. If there's voltage to the switch. check for voltage across the terminals. If the circuit is open at the switch. replace the switch. If there's voltage across the terminals. check for voltage from the switch to the headlights. Repair the circuit as necessary.

Replacement

Push-pull and rotary types

Refer to illustration 10.3

Note: *A special tool is needed to remove the lock-ring that secures the switch to the dash. If you can't borrow this tool. try to buy one from your local VW dealer service department or an auto parts store.*

2   Remove the rear seat and disconnect the negative cable from the battery.

3   Unscrew the knob from the switch **(see illustration)**.

4   Remove the lock-ring with the special tool.

10.11   Remove this plug right above the steering column and remove the screw underneath it

10.12   Remove these sheet metal screws from each end of the instrument panel switch cluster

10.13a   Remove the instrument panel switch cluster from the dash

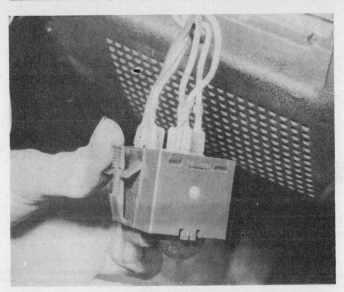

10.13b Squeeze the locking tabs (arrow) on the top and bottom of the rocker switch toward the switch and remove the switch, then clearly label the wires and disconnect them

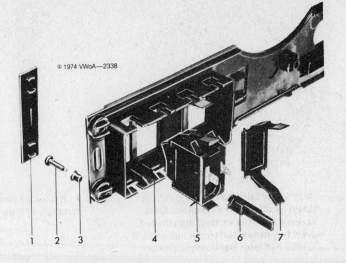

10.15 Exploded view of typical rocker-type headlight switch

1	Cover strip	5	Switch
2	Sheet metal screw	6	Warning light
3	Spacer sleeve	7	Cover plate
4	Instrument panel switch cluster		

5 Open the front hood, remove the two knurled nuts that attach the dashboard access panel to the firewall and remove the panel.
6 Pull the switch out of the dash.
7 Clearly label, then disconnect, the wires attached to the switch terminals.
8 Installation is the reverse of removal. Make sure the notches in the body of the switch engage the projections in the hole in the dashboard.

Rocker types
Refer to illustrations 10.10, 10.11, 10.12, 10.13a, 10.13b and 10.15

9 Detach the negative cable from the battery.
10 Carefully pry off the cover strips (**see illustration**) at each end of the instrument panel switch cluster.
11 Pry off the plug above the steering column (**see illustration**).
12 Remove the five sheet metal screws – two at each end (**see illustration**) and one in the center – that secure the instrument panel switch cluster to the dash. Don't lose the spacer sleeves for the screws.
13 Pull the cluster out of the dash (**see illustration**), pinch the tabs on the switch together and pull the switch out toward the back of the instru-

ment panel switch cluster (**see illustration**).
14 Clearly label, then disconnect, the wires attached to the switch terminals.
15 Installation is the reverse of removal (**see illustration**).

---

11 Bulb replacement

Refer to illustrations 11.1a, 11.1b, 11.1c, 11.1d, 11.1e, 11.1f, 11.1g, 11.1h, 11.1i, 11.1j, 11.2a, 11.2b, 11.4a, 11.4b, 11.4c, 11.4d and 11.4e

1 To replace most light bulbs, remove the lens screws, remove the lens and gasket, push in lightly on the bulb, turn it counterclockwise and remove it (**see illustrations**). To install the new bulb, insert it into the bayonet mount, push in lightly and turn it clockwise.

11.1a To replace a front turn signal bulb, simply remove the retaining screw from the top of the housing, ...

11.1b ... remove the housing ...

11.1c ... press the bulb down lightly, turn it counterclockwise and remove it

12

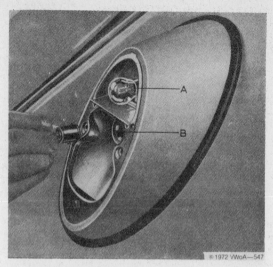

11.1d   To replace a rear turn signal bulb (at A) or brake/tail light bulb (at B), remove the lens retaining screws and the lens ...

11.1e   ... and remove the bulb that's burned out by pressing down lightly and turning it counterclockwise

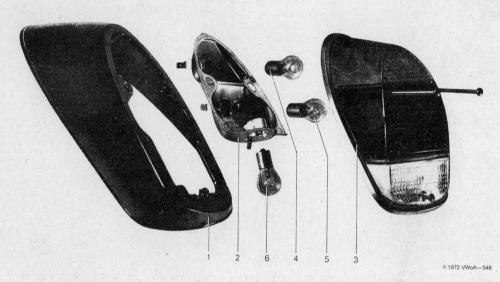

11.1f   An exploded view of a later tail light assembly with integral back-up bulb (earlier units don't have back-up bulb – it's mounted on bumper)

1   Housing
2   Bulb holder
3   Lens
4   Turn signal bulb
5   Brake/tail light bulb
6   Back-up bulb

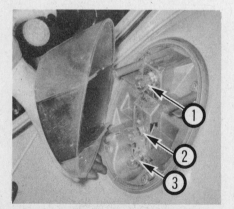

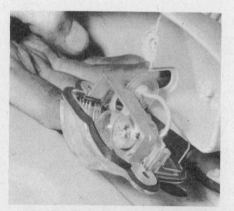

11.1g   Later model tail light assembly

1   Turn signal bulb
2   Brake/tail light bulb
3   Back-up bulb

11.1h   Typical early Karmann Ghia tail light assembly

1   Turn signal bulb
2   Brake light bulb
3   Tail light bulb

11.1i   To replace the license plate light on a Beetle, open the rear hood, remove the lens screw and lens, push the bulb into the socket, turn it counterclockwise and remove it

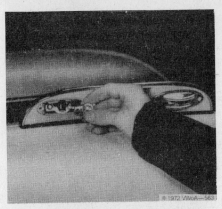

11.1j To replace a license plate light on a Karmann Ghia, open the rear hood, remove the lens screws and lens, push the bulb into the socket, turn it counterclockwise and remove it

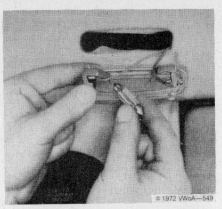

11.2a To replace a dome light in a Beetle, pop the lens off with a small screwdriver and pull the light straight down from its socket

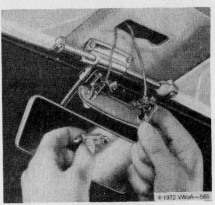

11.2b To replace a dome light in a Karmann Ghia, grip the edge of the lens with both hands and pull it down out of the headliner, then pull the bulb straight down from its socket

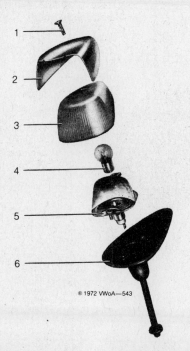

11.4a Details of a front turn signal light assembly

1 *Lens retaining screw*
2 *Cover*
3 *Lens*
4 *Bulb*
5 *Bulb holder*
6 *Packing*

2   Some bulbs, like the dome lights, can simply be pulled straight out of their sockets (**see illustrations**).

3   To replace lights in the instrument cluster lights, remove the instrument cluster (see Section 12).

4   If you need to replace an entire light assembly, it's usually simply a matter of unbolting it from inside the fender (**see illustration**).

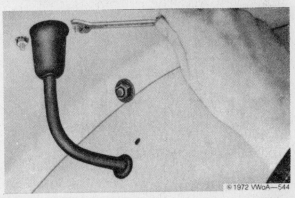

11.4b To detach the bulb holder from the fender, remove these two nuts from inside the wheel well

11.4c To remove the turn signal assembly from a Karmann Ghia, remove the lens screws, lens and chrome trim ring . . .

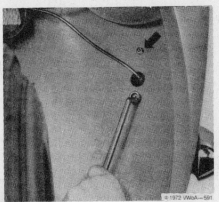

11.4d . . . from inside the wheel well, remove the two nuts from the front fender . . .

11.4e . . . pull the bulb holder out of the housing in the fender and disconnect the electrical connector

12

12.6   To remove a non-Super Beetle instrument cluster, simply unplug the wires – or pull out the bulbs – for the warning lights and instrument light, disconnect the speedometer cable and remove the two slotted screws

12.7   To remove a Super Beetle or convertible instrument cluster from the dash, disconnect the speeedometer cable, push the cluster out of its rubber grommet, label all wires and disconnect them

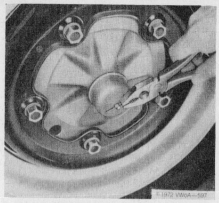

13.4   To detach the speedometer cable from the wheel bearing dust cap, remove the cotter pin (earlier models) or the circlip (later models), then pull the cable out of the steering knuckle from behind the wheel

12   Instrument cluster – removal and installation

Refer to illustrations 12.6 and 12.7

1   Detach the cable from the negative battery terminal.
2   On 1973 and later Super Beetles and convertibles, remove the instrument panel switch cluster (see Section 10).
3   Open the hood and remove the instrument panel cover from the firewall.
4   On pre-1973 models and 1973 and later non-Super Beetle models, pull out the warning bulbs and the instrument light from the back of the instrument cluster.
5   Disconnect the speedometer cable from the speedometer (see Section 13).
6   On pre-1973 models and 1973 and later non-Super Beetle models, remove the two slotted screws that attach the instrument cluster to the instrument panel **(see illustration)**. Pull the instrument cluster out of the dash.
7   On 1973 and later Super Beetles and convertibles, the instrument cluster is held in place by a ribbed rubber boot. Pull it out of the dash **(see illustration)**, clearly label all wires and disconnect them. Remove the cluster.
8   Installation is the reverse of removal.

13   Speedometer cable – replacement

Refer to illustrations 13.4 and 13.7

1   On pre-1973 models and 1973 and later non-Super Beetle models, open the front hood and remove the protective cover from the instrument panel.
2   On 1973 and later Super Beetle models and convertibles, remove the instrument panel switch cluster (see Section 10).
3   Working from the luggage compartment side on all pre-1973 models and 1973 and later non-Super Beetle models, or through the hole for the switch cluster on 1973 and later Super Beetle models and convertibles, unscrew the threaded fitting that attaches the speedometer cable to the speedometer assembly.
4   Remove the circlip or cotter pin which secures the end of the speedometer cable to the wheel bearing dust cap **(see illustration)**.
5   Working from the back side of the wheel, pull the cable out of the steering knuckle.
6   On pre-1973 models and 1973 and later non-Super Beetle models, pull the cable out of the guide channel, through the grommet in the vehicle

13.7   This cutaway shows the relationship between the speedometer cable and the rubber sleeve inside the steering knuckle which prevents water from entering and contaminating the wheel bearings

1	Cable	4	Rubber sleeve
2	Plastic sheathing of cable	5	Squared drive end
3	Metal sleeve	6	Cotter pin
		7	Dust cap with square hole

body and out through the luggage compartment. On 1973 and later Super Beetles and convertibles, pull the cable out through the hole in the dash.
7   It's a good idea to install a new rubber sleeve in the steering knuckle **(see illustration)**. If water gets into the knuckle, it can damage the bearings and allow the cable to freeze – and stick – in the winter.
8   Installation is the reverse of removal. Route the cable to eliminate sharp bends (no radius less than six inches). Make sure it isn't kinked or pulled too tight anywhere in the turning radius of the front wheel. And don't unseat the grommet when threading the new cable through. Finally, be sure to use a new cotter pin or circlip at the dust cap.

14   Instruments – replacement

Warning: *Gasoline is extremely flammable, so take extra precautions when you work on any part of the fuel system. Don't smoke or allow open flames or bare light bulbs near the work area, and don't work in a garage*

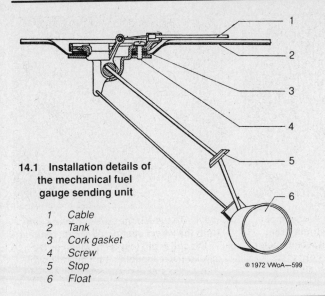

14.1   Installation details of the mechanical fuel gauge sending unit

1   Cable
2   Tank
3   Cork gasket
4   Screw
5   Stop
6   Float

© 1972 VWoA—599

where a natural gas-type appliance (such as a water heater or clothes dryer) with a pilot light is present. If you spill any fuel on your skin, rinse it off immediately with soap and water. When you perform any kind of work on the fuel system, wear safety glasses and have a Class B type fire extinguisher on hand.

Mechanical fuel gauge

Sending unit

Refer to illustrations 14.1 and 14.7

1   This gauge is mechanically operated by a cable from a sending unit mounted in the fuel tank **(see illustration)**. The sending unit transmits movement of the fuel tank float to the gauge in the instrument panel to indicate the amount of fuel in the tank. The sending unit must be removed to be checked.
2   Make sure the fuel level is low to avoid spilling fuel when the sending unit is removed.
3   Detach the cable from the negative battery terminal.
4   Remove the spare tire, jack and tools from the front luggage compartment. Remove the luggage compartment lining.
5   Remove the cover of the sending unit.
6   Disconnect the cable or wire to the gauge.
7   Remove the flange mounting screws **(see illustration)** and remove the sending unit and gasket.
8   Installation is the reverse of removal. Be sure to use new washers for the mounting screws and a new gasket for the flange. Adjust the gauge when you're done (see Steps 17 through 19).

Fuel gauge

Refer to illustrations 14.14 and 14.19

9   Remove the luggage compartment lining.
10   Remove the sending unit cover.
11   Disconnect the cable to the gauge.
12   Pull the cable out from under the felt pad on the floor of the luggage compartment.
13   Remove the light bulb from the gauge.
14   Remove the knurled nut and remove the gauge mounting bracket **(see illustration)**.
15   From inside the passenger compartment, remove the gauge from the dash.
16   Installation is the reverse of removal. Adjust the gauge when you're done.
17   To adjust the gauge, remove the cover from the sending unit to expose the lever to which the gauge cable is attached.
18   Press the lever to force the fuel tank float to its lowest position.
19   With the lever depressed, adjust the gauge by turning the knurled screw on the gauge in a clockwise direction until the gauge needle is on the stop at the low end of it scale **(see illustration)**. This adjustment insures that at least 1.3 gallons of fuel will be in the tank when the needle points to the Reserve mark.
20   Install the sending unit cover.

Electric fuel gauge

Refer to illustrations 14.28 and 14.32

21   This gauge is controlled by an electromechanical sending unit in the tank. If the gauge itself is inaccurte, replace it or send it to an instrument repair specialist.
22   If the gauge never moves from the 1/1 position, it has a grounded control circuit. Disconnect the control wire from the sending unit on top of the fuel tank. If the gauge falls from the 1/1 mark, the sending unit is faulty. If it doesn't, the control wire is grounded somewhere between the sending unit and the gauge.
23   If the gauge fails to register at all, disconnect the gauge wire from the sending unit and ground it against the a clean, unpainted part of the vehicle. If the gauge moves up to 1/1, the sending unit is faulty or isn't properly grounded. If the gauge still fails to move, the gauge or wire is faulty.
24   If an ohmmeter indicates infinite resistance when it's connected between the gauge terminal on the sending unit and ground, the sending unit is burned out. Replace it.

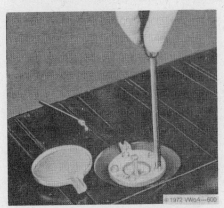

14.7   To remove the mechanical fuel gauge sending unit, remove the cover, disconnect the cable or wire to the gauge and remove the flange mounting screws

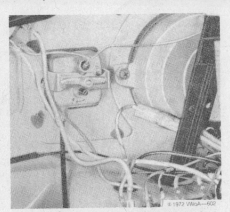

14.14   To remove the fuel gauge, disconnect the cable, pull it out from under the felt pad, remove the light bulb, remove the knurled nut and remove the gauge mounting bracket and pull the gauge out of the dash

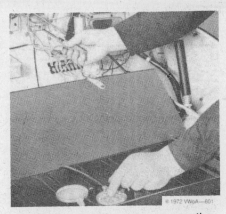

14.19   To adjust the gauge, remove the cover from the sending unit, press the lever to force the fuel tank float to its lowest position and turn the knurled screw on the gauge in a clockwise direction until the guage needle is on the stop at the low end of its scale

12

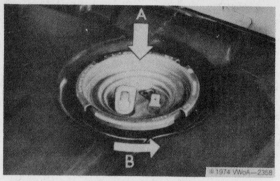

14.28   To remove the later type sending unit (shown), press down at (A) and turn the bayonet flange (B) counterclockwise to unlock it (to remove earlier unit, not shown, remove five flange mounting bolts)

25   Detach the cable from the negative battery terminal.
26   Remove the liner from the luggage compartment. On 1972 Super Beetles and convertibles, remove the fresh air box.
27   Disconnect the wire(s) from the sending unit (in 1972, a new sending unit with a second terminal for a separate ground wire was introduced).
28   Remove the five flange mounting bolts (early units), or unscrew the bayonet type locking flange (later units) **(see illustration)**.
29   Remove the sending unit.
30   To check the sending unit, connect a battery and voltmeter in series between the sending unit housing (or ground terminal) and the gauge wire terminal. Move the float by hand through its full range of motion. Note whether the voltmeter reading changes continuously as the sending unit float is moved. If the voltmeter needle doesn't move smoothly, the sending unit is defective. Replace it. **Warning:** *DO NOT perform these tests near the fuel tank. An electric spark could cause an explosion.*
31   Installation is the reverse of removal. Make sure the rubber gasket has a good ground connection clip on its edge (this clip isn't necessary on the later unit with its own separate ground wire). The clip must contact a clean and bare spot on the tank.
32   The fuel gauge can be checked in place. Earlier units have an external voltage stabilizer mounted next to the gauge **(see illustration)**. To check the stabilizer, switch on the ignition and connect a voltmeter as shown. If the stabilizer is good, the voltmeter will give a pulsating voltage reading. If it doesn't, replace the voltage stabilizer.
33   To check the gauge itself, switch on the ignition, detach the sending unit lead from the gauge and momentarily ground the gauge terminal. If the gauge gives no reading when grounded, it's defective. Replace the gauge. If the needle moves when the gauge is grounded, the problem is in the circuit between the sending unit or in the sending unit itself.
34   To replace the voltage stabilizer or the fuel gauge, remove the instrument cluster (see Section 12), then unsrew the defective unit from the cluster and install a new one.

Clock (Karmann Ghias)

Refer to illustrations 14.37
35   Raise the front hood and remove the instrument panel protective cover at the rear of the luggage compartment.
36   Pull out the two bulbs and disconnect the electric lead.
37   Remove the two attaching screws **(see illustration)**.
38   Remove the clock.
39   Installation is the reverse of removal.

---

15   Windshield wiper motor – check and replacement

Check

1   Early (six-volt) versions of the wiper motor are one-speed units; 1967 and later units (12-volts) have two speeds.
2   If the windshield wiper motor won't operate, and it is receiving power when the wiper switch is On and the grounds are good, replace the motor.

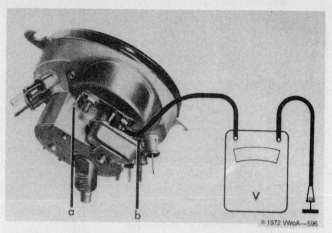

14.32   To test the stabilizer, turn on the ignition and hook up a voltmeter between terminal b and ground – if the stabilizer is good, the voltmeter needle will pulsate (if it's bad, the needle won't pulsate) – to check the fuel gauge, hook up the voltmeter to terminal a, detach the sending unit wire from the gauge and ground the gauge terminal – if the gauge gives no reading when grounded, it's bad

14.37   To replace the clock on a Karmann Ghia, pull out the two bulbs, detach the wire and remove the two attaching screws

Generally, if a motor has some internal problem, it's cheaper and quicker to simply exchange it for a rebuilt or new unit.

Replacement

1969 and earlier models

Refer to illustration 15.9
3   Detach the cable from the negative battery terminal.
4   Loosen the clamp screws on the wiper arm brackets and remove the wiper arms.
5   Remove both wiper bearing nuts with washers and outer bearing seals.
6   Remove the instrument panel protective cover in the front luggage compartment.
7   Disconnect the wires from the motor.
8   Remove the glove box.
9   Remove the bolt that secures the wiper frame. Remove the wiper frame with the motor and linkage **(see illustration)**.
10   Remove the lock washer and spring washer from the driveshaft and detach the driving link.
11   Loosen the wiper shaft nut, remove one motor retaining nut and separate the motor from the frame.
12   Installation is the reverse of removal.

15.9 To remove the windshield wiper motor on a pre-1970 model, remove the bolt that secures the wiper frame

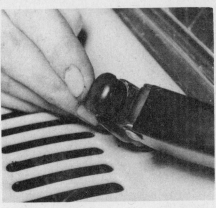

15.14a   Remove the wiper arm caps . . .

15.14b   . . . and nuts

15.15a   Remove the wiper shaft covers . . .

15.15b   . . . and nuts

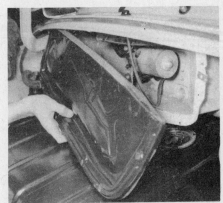

15.16   On 1973 and later Super Beetles and convertibles, remove the screws from the fresh air box and remove the cover

1970 and later models

Refer to illustrations 15.14a, 15.14b, 15.15a, 15.15b, 15.16, 15.18a, 15.18b, 15.20 and 15.21

13   Detach the cable from the negative battery terminal.
14   Remove the wiper arm caps and nuts **(see illustrations)**, then remove the arms.
15   Remove the wiper shaft covers and nuts **(see illustrations)**, washers and bearing seals.
16   On 1970 to 1973 models and 1973 and later non-Super Beetles, remove the instrument panel protective cover. On 1973 and later Super Beetles and convertibles, remove the screws from the cover for the fresh air box and remove the cover **(see illustration)**.
17   On 1970 to 1973 models and 1973 and later non-Super Beetles, remove the fresh air box (see Chapter 3), then remove the glove compartment and remove the right fresh air vent.
18   On 1970 to 1973 models and 1973 and later non-Super Beetles, disconnect the motor wire from the switch in the dash. On 1973 and later Super Beetles and convertibles, trace the motor harness through the firewall and unplug the electrical connector below the steering column **(see illustrations)**.

15.18a   On 1973 and later Super Beetles and convertibles, trace the motor wiring harness through the firewall . . .

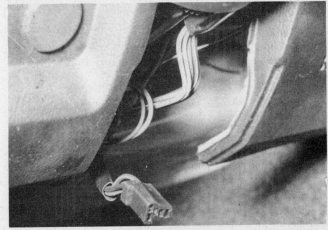

15.18b   . . . and unplug the electrical connector under the steering column

12

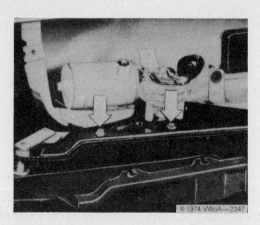

15.20   On 1973 and later Super Beetles and convertibles, remove the rain cover

15.21   Remove the motor (1973 or later type shown, others similar)

19   Remove the motor mounting bolt(s).
20   On 1973 and later Super Beetles and convertibles, remove the plastic rain cover **(see illustration)**.
rear window through a relay under the left side of the rear seat. The relay controls the temperature of the grid by shutting it off when the temperature (resistance) gets too hot. A green light in the speedometer indicates the circuit is operating.
21   Remove the motor **(see illustration)**.
22   Installation is the reverse of removal.

16   Windshield wiper switch – removal and installation

Early models

1   Detach the cable from the negative battery terminal.
2   Empty the windshield washer fluid lines.
3   Unscrew the switch knob and remove the push-button for the windshield washer.
4   Unscrew the switch escutcheon (retaining ring). You'll may need a special wrench for this job.
5   Remove the instrument panel protective cover from the luggage compartment.
6   Remove the two hoses running from the fresh air control box to the fresh air outlets (if equipped).
7   Pull the switch out of the dash, disconnect the wires and detach the water hoses.
8   To install the new type (push-pull) switch on an early (pre-1967) model with a single-speed, six-volt motor, connect terminal 53 to terminal 53b before installing the new switch (the push-pull switch used on early models is no longer available, but the rotary switch works with this modification). On 1967 and later models, skip this modification. Connect the terminals in accordance with the wiring diagrams at the end of this Chapter. And don't forget to connect the water hoses too.
9   The remainder of installation is the reverse of removal.

Later models

10   The later type windshield wiper switch is integrated into the turn signal switch. To replace it, see Section 6.

17   Horn – check and replacement

Check

1   On Beetles and Super Beetles, the horn is mounted under the left front fender. On Karmann Ghias, dual horns are mounted in the spare tire compartment. Current to the horns on Beetles and Super Beetle horns is controlled by the horn ring. On Karmann Ghias, it's controlled by a horn relay located at the left side of the spare tire compartment.
2   If the horn doesn't work, first remove the horn ring and look for dirty, worn or corroded contacts (Beetles and Super Beetles) or in the horn relay (Karmann Ghias). Loose or corroded contacts are a common cause of horn trouble. If necessary, clean them up with emery or crocus cloth.
3   If the contacts are in good condition, use a test light or a voltmeter to verify that there's battery voltage at the horn(s).
4   If there's no voltage at the horn(s), try activating it with a jumper wire from the battery. If the horn works, the circuit has an open or a short somewhere. If the horn doesn't work, replace it.
5   Look for an open or short in the (usually black and yellow) wire between the horn and the fuse (usually the first, third or eleventh fuse in the

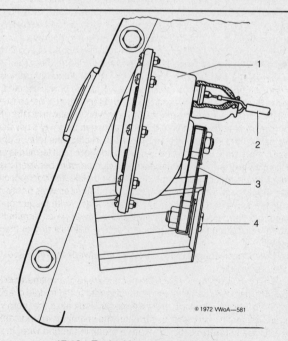

© 1972 VWoA—581

17.10   **Typical horn installation**

1	Horn	3	Mounting bracket
2	Wire	4	Mounting bolt

box, depending on model – see Section 3). If the fuse is good, check the ground for the horn ring.

6   On pre-1971 models, the contact ring on the steering wheel is grounded by a wire to the steering column U-joint coupling that runs through the hollow steering column. When you depress the horn ring, it grounds the steering column tube to the contact ring in the steering wheel. Also check the brown wire that runs from the horn to the steering column.

7   On 1971 and later models, the steering wheel is grounded by contact with the steering column. The column itself is grounded by a short wire that bypasses the steering coupling's flexible disk. When the horn control is depressed, it's grounded against the steering wheel contact ring. A wire from the horn control to the slip-ring grounds the horn circuit contact spring that's connected to the horn's brown ground wire.

8   If everything else in good condition on a Karmann Ghia, replace the relay. There's also a condenser in the relay. Since the relay won't work properly with a good condenser, and since you can't check the condenser at home without a special tool, we recommend that you replace the condenser too.

Replacement

Refer to illustration 17.10

9   Detach the cable from the negative battery terminal.
10   Disconnect the horn wire **(see illustration)**.
11   Remove the mounting bracket bolt.
12   Remove the horn.
13   Installation is the reverse of removal.

---

18   Heated rear window – check, switch replacement and grid repair

---

Check

Refer to illustration 18.6

1   1969 and later models have a heated rear window. A toggle switch under the dash, to the left of the ashtray, actuates the defogger grid on the
2   To check the switch, first verify that it's getting 12 volts. If it isn't, check the power wire to the switch. If it is, check voltage across the switch terminals with the power on. If there's no voltage, replace the switch. If there is voltage, check the circuit back to the grid, including the relay.
3   Refer to the wiring diagrams at the end of this Chapter and check for an open or short in the circuit between the switch and the relay.
4   Check the relay. Make sure it's not stuck closed, shorting out or burned out (open). The two thicker wires are for the power circuit; the two thinner wires are for the control circuit from the switch. Detach the cable from the negative battery terminal and remove the relay from the vehicle. Using an ohmmeter, check for continuity between the relay's power circuit terminals. There shouldn't be any. If there is, replace the relay. Connect a fused jumper wire between one of the two control circuit terminals and the positive battery terminal. Connect another jumper wire between the other control circuit terminal and ground. When you make the connections, the relay should click. If it doesn't, try swapping the jumper wires on the control circuit terminals (the polarity may be backwards). With the jumper wires connected, check for continuity between the power circuit terminals. Now there should be continuity. Replace the relay if it fails any of the above checks.
5   Check for an open or short in the circuit between the relay and the grid in the rear window.
6   Check the grid itself. Attach the negative lead of a voltmeter to a good ground. Attach the positive lead of the voltmeter to the middle of each grid wire. If a grid wire is broken, the voltmeter will indicate either zero volts or battery voltage. If a grid wire is unbroken, the voltmeter will indicate about six volts **(see illustration)**. To locate a break in the grid wire, move the positive lead of the voltmeter along the grid wire until the voltmeter needle suddenly jumps. Repair as necessary.

Switch replacement

7   Detach the cable from the negative battery terminal, remove the instrument panel protective cover in the luggage compartment, unscrew the

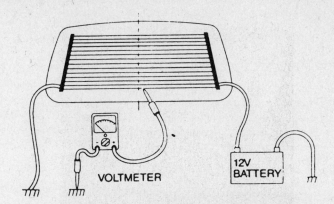

18.6   To check the grid, attach the negative lead of a voltmeter to ground and touch the positive lead of the voltmeter to the middle of each grid wire – if a grid wire is broken, the voltmeter will indicate either zero or 12 volts; if a grid wire is unbroken, the voltmeter will indicate about six volts; to locate a break in the grid wire, move the positive lead of the voltmeter along the wire until the needle jumps

---

escutcheon (lock-ring), remove the switch and disconnect the wire. Installation is the reverse of removal.

Grid repair

8   If any break in the rear window is longer than one inch, the rear window must be replaced.
9   Using a defroster grid repair kit (available at most auto parts stores), breaks less than one inch can be repaired. Follow the instructions included in the repair kit.

---

19   Wiring diagrams – general information

Refer to illustration 19.7

Since it isn't possible to include all wiring diagrams for every year covered by this manual, the following diagrams are those that are typical and most commonly needed.

Prior to troubleshooting any circuits, check the fuse and circuit breakers (if equipped) to make sure they're in good condition. Make sure the battery is properly charged and check the cable connections (see Chapter 1).

When checking a circuit, make sure that all connectors are clean, with no broken or loose terminals. When unplugging a connector, do not pull on the wires. Pull only on the connector housings themselves.

Note that two types of wiring diagrams are included. Those for earlier models show individual components as line drawings; those for later models are the current flow type and represent components schematically. In VW factory manuals, both types show the color of the wires. In our book, however, the wiring diagrams are in black and white, so you'll have to rely on the function of each wire, rather than its color (check where it's coming from and where it's going).

The small numbers in the wire lines indicate their gauge in square millimeters.

On wiring diagrams for vehicles built since 1971, the test connections for the VW Computer Analysis system are included. Always reattach these wires when servicing the electrical system. **Caution:** *If you connect any device other than the test plug of the VW Computer Analysis system to the test circuit socket in the engine compartment, it could damage the circuit or its components.*

The wiring diagrams for 1973 and later models use symbols for the

12

electrical components **(see illustration)**, instead of pictorial representations as in earlier diagrams. The thin black lines in the diagrams aren't actual wires, but ground connections via the vehicle chassis.

Along the bottom of each diagram is a row of numbers which will help you find electrical components. After each component listed in the accompanying legend are numbers labeled "current track." These numbers indicate the current track in the wiring diagram that contains the part you're looking for.

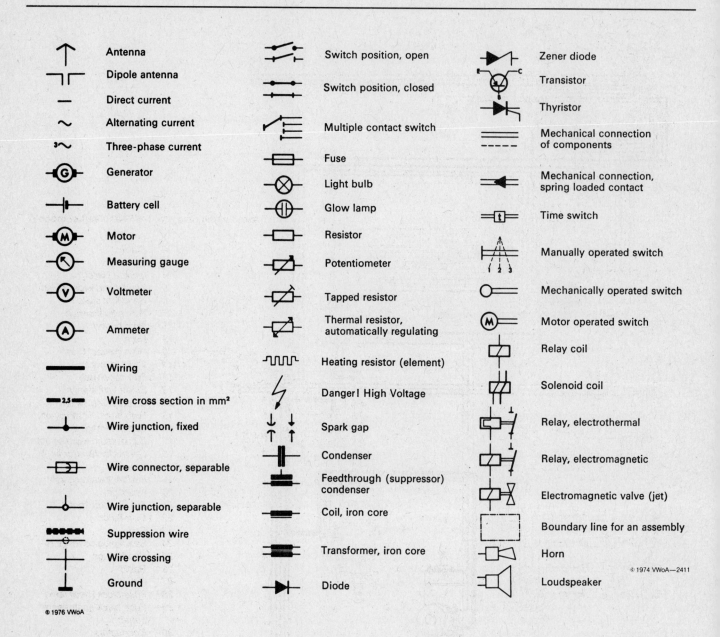

Antenna	Switch position, open	Zener diode
Dipole antenna	Switch position, closed	Transistor
Direct current		Thyristor
Alternating current	Multiple contact switch	Mechanical connection of components
Three-phase current	Fuse	
Generator	Light bulb	Mechanical connection, spring loaded contact
Battery cell	Glow lamp	Time switch
Motor	Resistor	Manually operated switch
Measuring gauge	Potentiometer	Mechanically operated switch
Voltmeter	Tapped resistor	Motor operated switch
Ammeter	Thermal resistor, automatically regulating	Relay coil
Wiring	Heating resistor (element)	Solenoid coil
Wire cross section in mm²	Danger! High Voltage	Relay, electrothermal
Wire junction, fixed	Spark gap	Relay, electromagnetic
Wire connector, separable	Condenser	Electromagnetic valve (jet)
Wire junction, separable	Feedthrough (suppressor) condenser	Boundary line for an assembly
Suppression wire	Coil, iron core	Horn
Wire crossing	Transformer, iron core	Loudspeaker
Ground	Diode	

© 1974 VWoA—2411

© 1976 VWoA

19.7   Legend for later model wiring diagrams

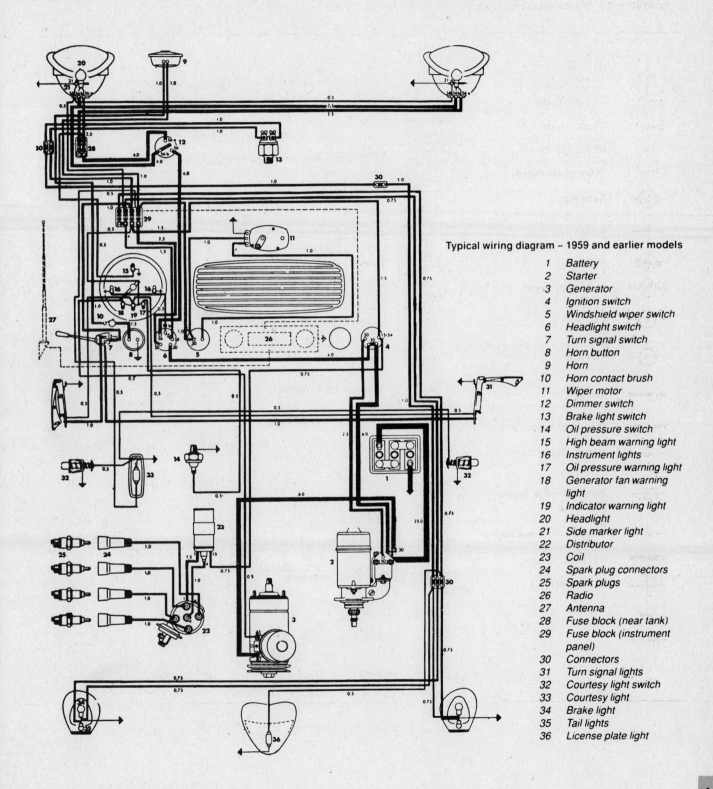

Typical wiring diagram – 1959 and earlier models

1   Battery
2   Starter
3   Generator
4   Ignition switch
5   Windshield wiper switch
6   Headlight switch
7   Turn signal switch
8   Horn button
9   Horn
10 Horn contact brush
11 Wiper motor
12 Dimmer switch
13 Brake light switch
14 Oil pressure switch
15 High beam warning light
16 Instrument lights
17 Oil pressure warning light
18 Generator fan warning
    light
19 Indicator warning light
20 Headlight
21 Side marker light
22 Distributor
23 Coil
24 Spark plug connectors
25 Spark plugs
26 Radio
27 Antenna
28 Fuse block (near tank)
29 Fuse block (instrument
    panel)
30 Connectors
31 Turn signal lights
32 Courtesy light switch
33 Courtesy light
34 Brake light
35 Tail lights
36 License plate light

12

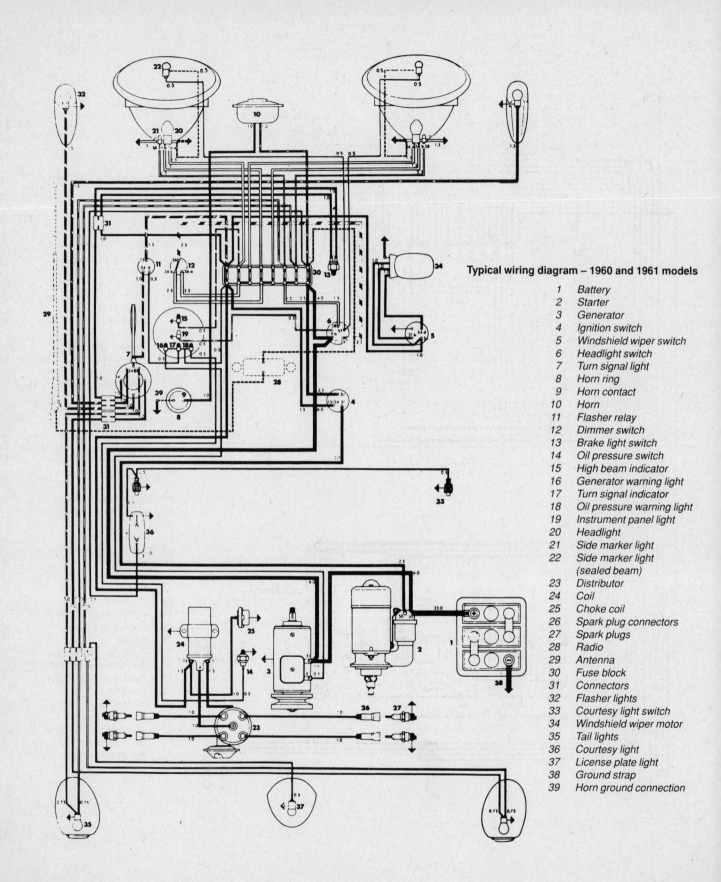

Typical wiring diagram – 1960 and 1961 models

1   Battery
2   Starter
3   Generator
4   Ignition switch
5   Windshield wiper switch
6   Headlight switch
7   Turn signal light
8   Horn ring
9   Horn contact
10 Horn
11 Flasher relay
12 Dimmer switch
13 Brake light switch
14 Oil pressure switch
15 High beam indicator
16 Generator warning light
17 Turn signal indicator
18 Oil pressure warning light
19 Instrument panel light
20 Headlight
21 Side marker light
22 Side marker light
    (sealed beam)
23 Distributor
24 Coil
25 Choke coil
26 Spark plug connectors
27 Spark plugs
28 Radio
29 Antenna
30 Fuse block
31 Connectors
32 Flasher lights
33 Courtesy light switch
34 Windshield wiper motor
35 Tail lights
36 Courtesy light
37 License plate light
38 Ground strap
39 Horn ground connection

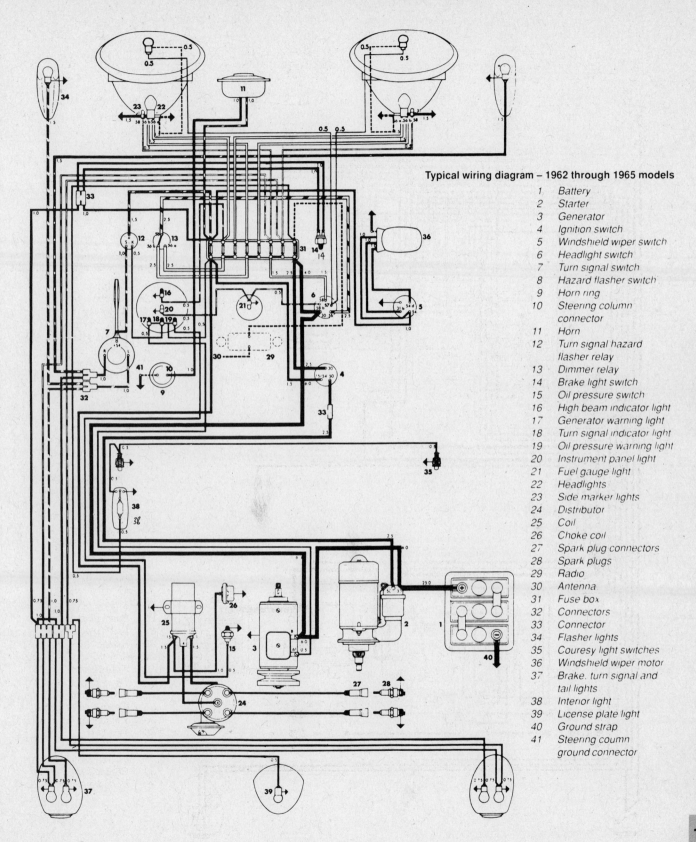

Typical wiring diagram – 1962 through 1965 models

1. Battery
2. Starter
3. Generator
4. Ignition switch
5. Windshield wiper switch
6. Headlight switch
7. Turn signal switch
8. Hazard flasher switch
9. Horn ring
10. Steering column connector
11. Horn
12. Turn signal hazard flasher relay
13. Dimmer relay
14. Brake light switch
15. Oil pressure switch
16. High beam indicator light
17. Generator warning light
18. Turn signal indicator light
19. Oil pressure warning light
20. Instrument panel light
21. Fuel gauge light
22. Headlights
23. Side marker lights
24. Distributor
25. Coil
26. Choke coil
27. Spark plug connectors
28. Spark plugs
29. Radio
30. Antenna
31. Fuse box
32. Connectors
33. Connector
34. Flasher lights
35. Couresy light switches
36. Windshield wiper motor
37. Brake, turn signal and tail lights
38. Interior light
39. License plate light
40. Ground strap
41. Steering column ground connector

12

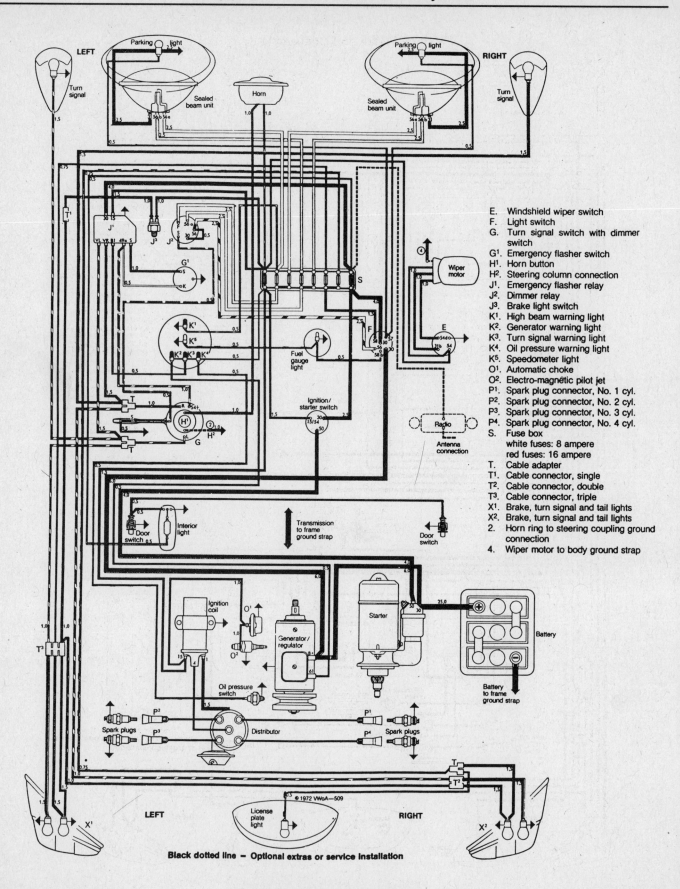

E.   Windshield wiper switch
F.   Light switch
G.   Turn signal switch with dimmer switch
G¹.   Emergency flasher switch
H¹.   Horn button
H².   Steering column connection
J¹.   Emergency flasher relay
J².   Dimmer relay
J³.   Brake light switch
K¹.   High beam warning light
K².   Generator warning light
K³.   Turn signal warning light
K⁴.   Oil pressure warning light
K⁵.   Speedometer light
O¹.   Automatic choke
O².   Electro-magnetic pilot jet
P¹.   Spark plug connector, No. 1 cyl.
P².   Spark plug connector, No. 2 cyl.
P³.   Spark plug connector, No. 3 cyl.
P⁴.   Spark plug connector, No. 4 cyl.
S.   Fuse box
     white fuses: 8 ampere
     red fuses: 16 ampere
T.   Cable adapter
T¹.   Cable connector, single
T².   Cable connector, double
T³.   Cable connector, triple
X¹.   Brake, turn signal and tail lights
X².   Brake, turn signal and tail lights
2.   Horn ring to steering coupling ground connection
4.   Wiper motor to body ground strap

Black dotted line – Optional extras or service installation

Typical wiring diagram for 1966 Beetles

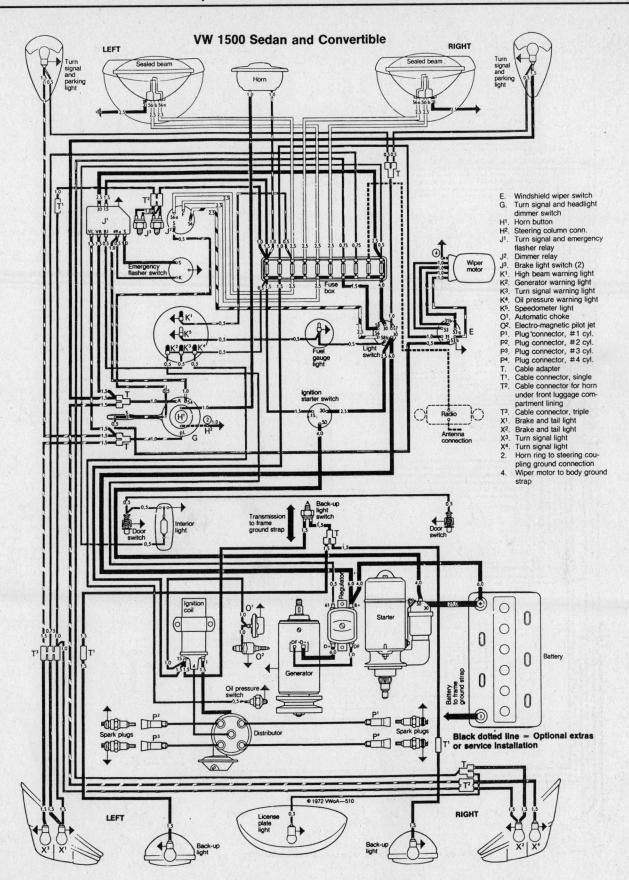

VW 1500 Sedan and Convertible

E. Windshield wiper switch
G. Turn signal and headlight dimmer switch
H1. Horn button
H2. Steering column conn.
J1. Turn signal and emergency flasher relay
J2. Dimmer relay
J3. Brake light switch (2)
K1. High beam warning light
K2. Generator warning light
K3. Turn signal warning light
K4. Oil pressure warning light
K5. Speedometer light
O1. Automatic choke
O2. Electro-magnetic pilot jet
P1. Plug connector, #1 cyl.
P2. Plug connector, #2 cyl.
P3. Plug connector, #3 cyl.
P4. Plug connector, #4 cyl.
T. Cable adapter
T1. Cable connector, single
T2. Cable connector for horn under front luggage compartment lining
T3. Cable connector, triple
X1. Brake and tail light
X2. Brake and tail light
X3. Turn signal light
X4. Turn signal light
2. Horn ring to steering coupling ground connection
4. Wiper motor to body ground strap

Black dotted line = Optional extras or service installation

© 1972 VWoA—510

Typical wiring diagram for 1967 Beetles

12

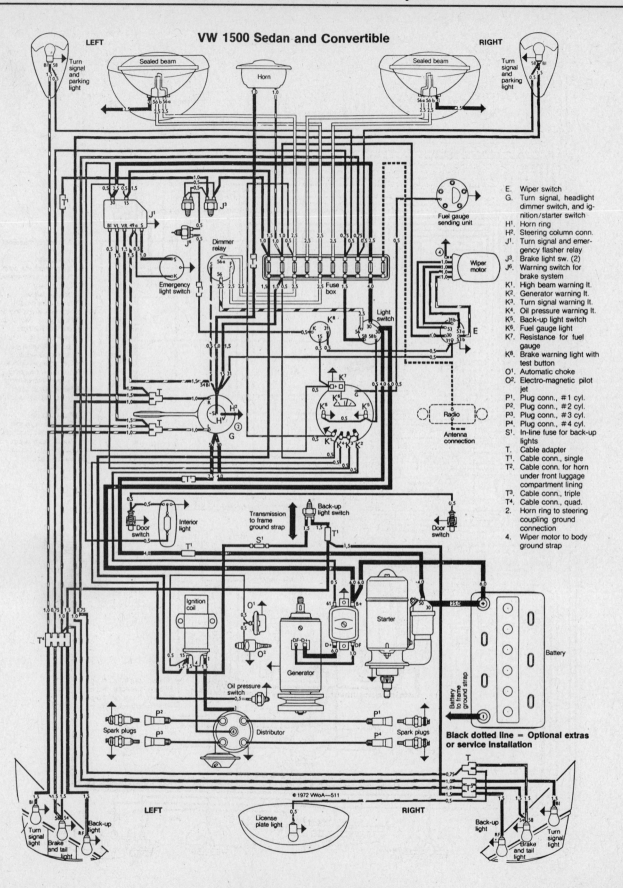

VW 1500 Sedan and Convertible

E.   Wiper switch
G.   Turn signal, headlight dimmer switch, and ignition/starter switch
H¹.   Horn ring
H².   Steering column conn.
J¹.   Turn signal and emergency flasher relay
J³.   Brake light sw. (2)
J⁶.   Warning switch for brake system
K¹.   High beam warning lt.
K².   Generator warning lt.
K³.   Turn signal warning lt.
K⁴.   Oil pressure warning lt.
K⁵.   Back-up light switch
K⁶.   Fuel gauge light
K⁷.   Resistance for fuel gauge
K⁸.   Brake warning light with test button
O¹.   Automatic choke
O².   Electro-magnetic pilot jet
P¹.   Plug conn., #1 cyl.
P².   Plug conn., #2 cyl.
P³.   Plug conn., #3 cyl.
P⁴.   Plug conn., #4 cyl.
S¹.   In-line fuse for back-up lights
T.   Cable adapter
T¹.   Cable conn., single
T².   Cable conn. for horn under front luggage compartment lining
T³.   Cable conn., triple
T⁴.   Cable conn., quad.
2.   Horn ring to steering coupling ground connection
4.   Wiper motor to body ground strap

Black dotted line = Optional extras or service installation

© 1972 VWoA—511

Typical wiring diagram for 1968 and 1969 Beetles

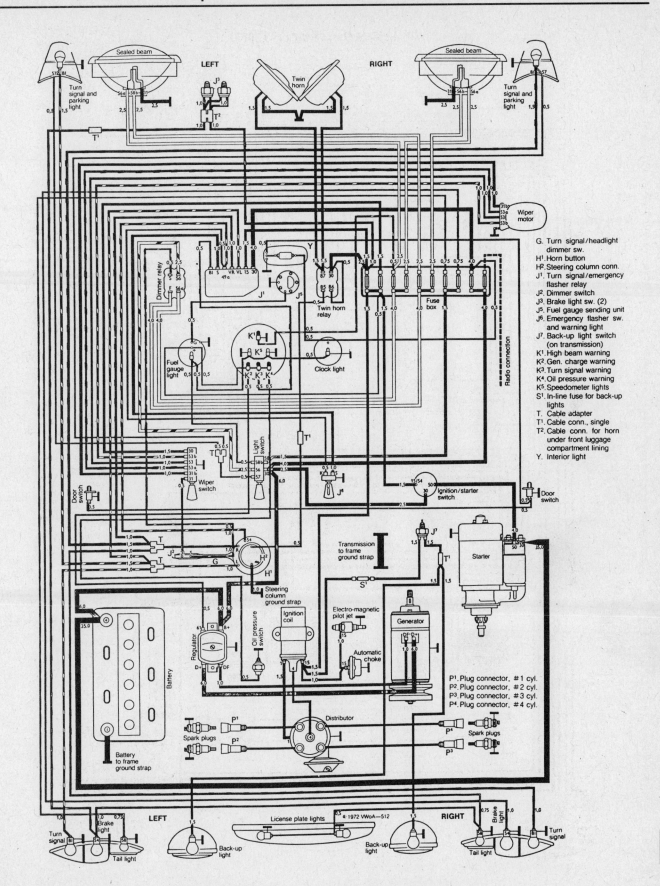

Typical wiring diagram for 1967 through 1969 karmann Ghias

G. Turn signal/headlight dimmer sw.
H[1]. Horn button
H[2]. Steering column conn.
J[1]. Turn signal/emergency flasher relay
J[2]. Dimmer switch
J[3]. Brake light sw. (2)
J[5]. Fuel gauge sending unit
J[6]. Emergency flasher sw. and warning light
J[7]. Back-up light switch (on transmission)
K[1]. High beam warning
K[2]. Gen. charge warning
K[3]. Turn signal warning
K[4]. Oil pressure warning
K[5]. Speedometer lights
S[1]. In-line fuse for back-up lights
T. Cable adapter
T[1]. Cable conn., single
T[2]. Cable conn. for horn under front luggage compartment lining
Y. Interior light

P[1]. Plug connector, #1 cyl.
P[2]. Plug connector, #2 cyl.
P[3]. Plug connector, #3 cyl.
P[4]. Plug connector, #4 cyl.

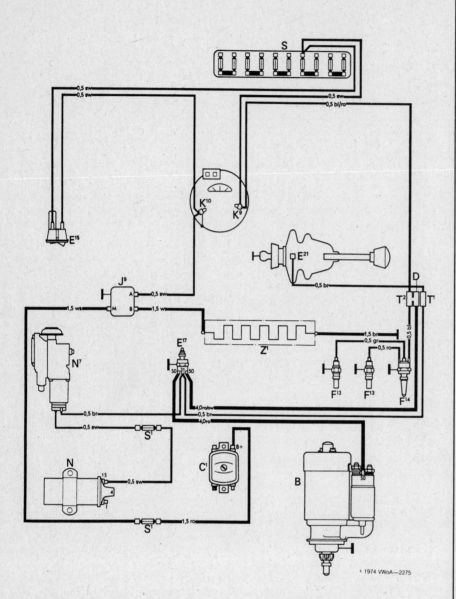

Note: *Legend is for diagram on facing page.*

A – Battery
B – Starter
C – Generator
C¹ – Regulator
D – Ignition/starter switch
E – Windshield wiper switch
E¹ – Light switch
E² – Turn signal and headlight dimmer switch
E³ – Emergency flasher switch
F – Brake light switch with warning switch
F¹ – Oil pressure switch
F² – Door contact switch, left, with contact for buzzer H 5
F³ – Door contact switch, right
F⁴ – Back-up light switch
G – Fuel gauge sending unit
G¹ – Fuel gauge
H – Horn button
H¹ – Horn
H⁵ – Ignition key warning buzzer
J – Dimmer relay
J² – Emergency flasher relay
J⁶ – Vibrator for fuel gauge
K¹ – High beam warning light
K² – Generator charging warning light
K³ – Oil pressure warning light
K⁵ – Turn signal warning light
K⁶ – Emergency flasher warning light
K⁷ – Dual circuit brake system warning light
L¹ – Sealed beam unit, left headlight
L² – Sealed beam unit, right headlight
L¹⁰ – Instrument panel light
M² – Tail and brake light, right
M⁴ – Tail and brake light, left
M⁵ – Turn signal and parking light, front, left
M⁶ – Turn signal, rear, left
M⁷ – Turn signal and parking light, front, right
M⁸ – Turn signal, rear, right
M¹¹ – Side marker light, front
N – Ignition coil
N¹ – Automatic choke
N³ – Electro-magnetic pilot jet
O – Ignition distributor
P¹ – Spark plug connector, No. 1 cylinder
P² – Spark plug connector, No. 2 cylinder
P³ – Spark plug connector, No. 3 cylinder
P⁴ – Spark plug connector, No. 4 cylinder
Q¹ – Spark plug, No. 1 cylinder
Q² – Spark plug, No. 2 cylinder
Q³ – Spark plug, No. 3 cylinder
Q⁴ – Spark plug, No. 4 cylinder
R – Radio connection
S – Fuse box
S¹ – Back-up light fuse
T – Cable adapter
T¹ – Cable connector, single
T² – Cable connector, double
T³ – Cable connector, triple
T⁴ – Cable connector (four connections)
V – Windshield wiper motor
W – Interior light
X – License plate light
X¹ – Back-up light, left
X² – Back-up light, right

① – Battery to frame ground strap
② – Transmission to frame ground strap

B – Starter
C¹ – Regulator
D – To ignition/starter switch, terminal 50
E¹⁵ – Switch for rear window defogger
E¹⁷ – Starter cut-out switch
E²¹ – Contact at selector lever
F¹³ – Temperature sensor
F¹⁴ – ATF temperature sensor selector
J⁹ – Rear window defogger relay
K⁹ – ATF temperature warning light
K¹⁰ – Rear window defogger warning light
N – Ignition coil
N⁷ – Automatic Stick Shift control valve

S – Fuse box
S¹ – Fuse for rear window defogger, Automatic Stick Shift control valve
T¹ – Cable connector, single
T² – Cable connector, double
Z¹ – Rear window defogger heating element

Color of cables:

sw = black
ro = red
br = brown
gr = grey
bl = blue

**Automatic Stick Shift and rear window defogger diagram
for 1970 and 1971 Beetles**

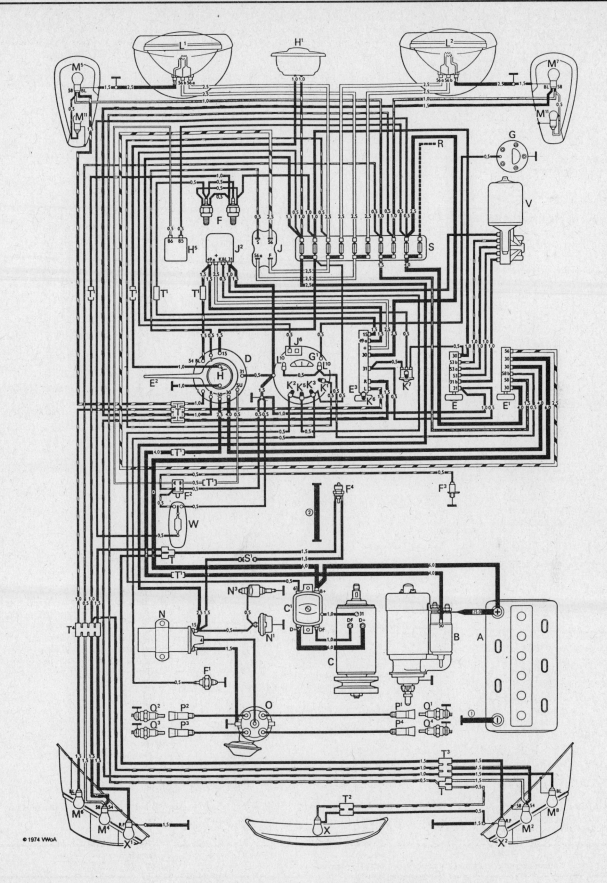

Typical wiring diagram for 1970 and 1971 Beetles

© 1974 VWoA

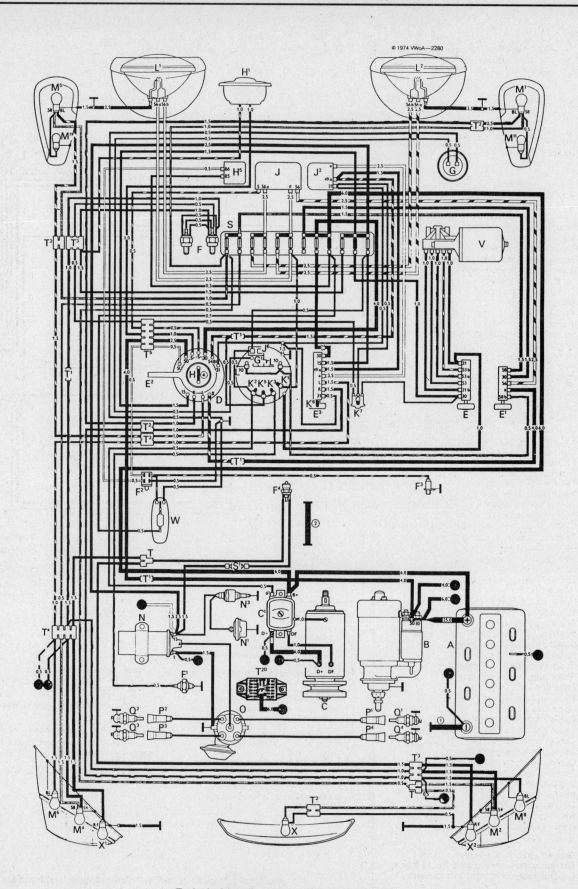

Typical wiring diagram for 1971 Super Beetle

Note: *Legend is for diagram on facing page.*

A – Battery
B – Starter
C – Generator
C^1 – Regulator
D – Ignition / starter switch
E – Windshield wiper switch
E^1 – Light switch
E^2 – Turn signal and headlight dimmer switch
E^3 – Emergency flasher switch
F – Brake light switch
F^1 – Oil pressure switch
F^2 – Door contact and buzzer alarm switch, left
F^3 – Door contact switch, right
F^4 – Back-up light switch
G – Fuel gauge sending unit
G^1 – Fuel gauge
H – Horn button
H^1 – Horn
H^5 – Ignition key warning buzzer
J – Dimmer relay
J^2 – Emergency flasher relay
J^6 – Fuel gauge vibrator
K^1 – High beam warning light
K^2 – Generator charging warning light
K^3 – Oil pressure warning light
K^5 – Turn signal warning light
K^6 – Emergency flasher warning light
K^7 – Dual circuit brake warning light
L^1 – Sealed-Beam unit, left headlight
L^2 – Sealed-Beam unit, right headlight
L^{10} – Instrument panel light
M^1 – Parking light, left
M^2 – Tail / brake light, right
M^4 – Tail / brake light, left
M^5 – Turn signal and parking light front left
M^6 – Turn signal, rear, left
M^7 – Turn signal and parking light front right
M^8 – Turn signal, rear, right
M^{11} – Side marker light, front
N – Ignition coil
N^1 – Automatic choke
N^3 – Electro-magnetic pilot jet
O – Distributor
P^1 – Spark plug connector, No. 1 cylinder
P^2 – Spark plug connector, No. 2 cylinder
P^3 – Spark plug connector, No. 3 cylinder
P^4 – Spark plug connector, No. 4 cylinder
Q^1 – Spark plug, No. 1 cylinder
Q^2 – Spark plug, No. 2 cylinder
Q^3 – Spark plug, No. 3 cylinder
Q^4 – Spark plug, No. 4 cylinder
S – Fuse box
S^1 – Back-up light in-line fuse
T – Cable adapter
T^1 – Cable connector, single
T^2 – Cable connector, double
T^3 – Cable connector, triple
T^4 – Cable connector (four connections)
T^5 – Cable connector (five connections)
T^{20} – Test network, central plug
V – Windshield wiper motor
W – Interior light
X – License plate light
X^1 – Back-up light, left
X^2 – Back-up light, right

① – Ground strap from battery to frame
② – Ground strap from transmission to frame
④ – Ground cable from front axle to frame

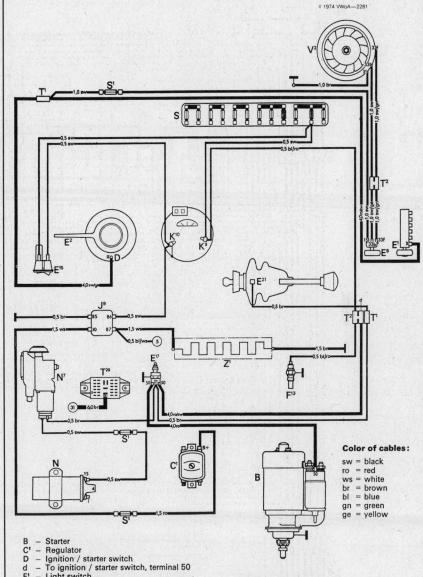

B – Starter
C^1 – Regulator
D – Ignition / starter switch
d – To ignition / starter switch, terminal 50
E^1 – Light switch
E^2 – Turn signal and headlight dimmer switch
E^9 – Fan motor switch
E^{15} – Rear window defogger switch
E^{17} – Starter cut-out switch
E^{21} – Contact at selector lever
F^{13} – ATF temperature control switch
J^9 – Rear window defogger relay
K^9 – ATF temperature warning light
K^{10} – Rear window defogger warning light
N – Ignition coil
N^7 – Automatic Stick Shift control valve
S – Fuse box
S^1 – Fuse for:
  rear window defogger,
  Automatic Stick Shift control valve,
  fan motor

T^1 – Cable connector, single
T^2 – Cable connector, double
T^{20} – Test network, central plug
V^2 – Fan motor
Z^1 – Rear window defogger heating element

Color of cables:

sw = black
ro = red
ws = white
br = brown
bl = blue
gn = green
ge = yellow

Test network (from June 1971 only)

The circles with the numbers 5 and 31 are connections in the test network which are wired to the central plug.
The numbers in the circles correspond to the terminals in the central plug.

Automatic Stick Shift, rear window defogger and fresh air fan diagram for 1971 Super Beetles

12

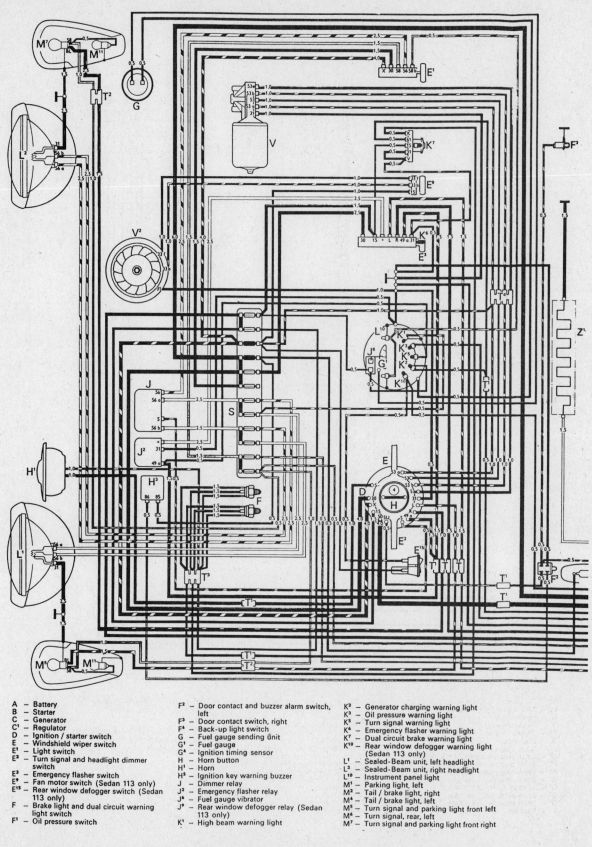

A – Battery
B – Starter
C – Generator
C¹ – Regulator
D – Ignition / starter switch
E – Windshield wiper switch
E¹ – Light switch
E² – Turn signal and headlight dimmer
      switch
E³ – Emergency flasher switch
E⁹ – Fan motor switch (Sedan 113 only)
E¹⁵ – Rear window defogger switch (Sedan
      113 only)
F – Brake light and dual circuit warning
      light switch
F¹ – Oil pressure switch

F² – Door contact and buzzer alarm switch,
      left
F³ – Door contact switch, right
F⁴ – Back-up light switch
G – Fuel gauge sending unit
G¹ – Fuel gauge
G⁴ – Ignition timing sensor
H – Horn button
H¹ – Horn
H³ – Ignition key warning buzzer
J – Dimmer relay
J² – Emergency flasher relay
J⁶ – Fuel gauge vibrator
J⁹ – Rear window defogger relay (Sedan
      113 only)
K¹ – High beam warning light

K² – Generator charging warning light
K³ – Oil pressure warning light
K⁵ – Turn signal warning light
K⁶ – Emergency flasher warning light
K⁷ – Dual circuit brake warning light
K¹⁰ – Rear window defogger warning light
      (Sedan 113 only)
L¹ – Sealed-Beam unit, left headlight
L² – Sealed-Beam unit, right neadlight
L¹⁰ – Instrument panel light
M¹ – Parking light, left
M² – Tail / brake light, right
M⁴ – Tail / brake light, left
M⁵ – Turn signal and parking light front left
M⁶ – Turn signal, rear, left
M⁷ – Turn signal and parking light front right

Typical wiring diagram for 1972 Beetles and Super Beetles

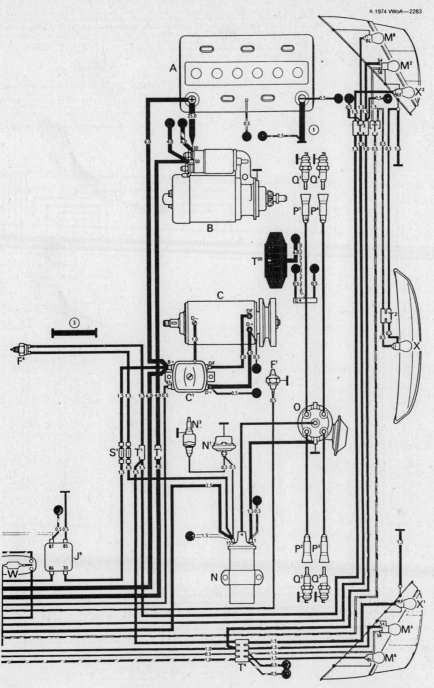

© 1974 VWoA—2283

M⁸ – Turn signal, rear, right	S¹ – Fuses for rear window defogger, back-up light (8 Amp.)	Z¹ – Rear window defogger heating element (Sedan 113 only)
M¹¹– Side marker light, front	T – Cable adapter	
N – Ignition coil	T¹ – Cable connector, single	① – Ground strap from battery to frame
N¹ – Automatic choke	T² – Cable connector, double	② – Ground strap from transmission to frame
N³ – Electro-magnetic pilot jet	T³ – Cable connector, triple	③ – Ground cable on steering coupling
O – Distributor	T⁴ – Cable connector (four connections)	
P¹ – Spark plug connector, No. 1 cylinder	T⁵ – Cable connector (five connections)	
P² – Spark plug connector, No. 2 cylinder	T²⁰ – Test network, central plug	
P³ – Spark plug connector, No. 3 cylinder	V – Windshield wiper motor	
P⁴ – Spark plug connector, No. 4 cylinder	V² – Fan motor (Sedan 113 only)	
Q¹ – Spark plug, No. 1 cylinder	W – Interior light	
Q² – Spark plug, No. 2 cylinder	X – License plate light	
Q³ – Spark plug, No. 3 cylinder	X¹ – Back-up light, left	
Q⁴ – Spark plug, No. 4 cylinder	X² – Back-up light, right	
S – Fuse box		

Typical wiring diagram for 1972 Beetles and Super Beetles (continued)

12

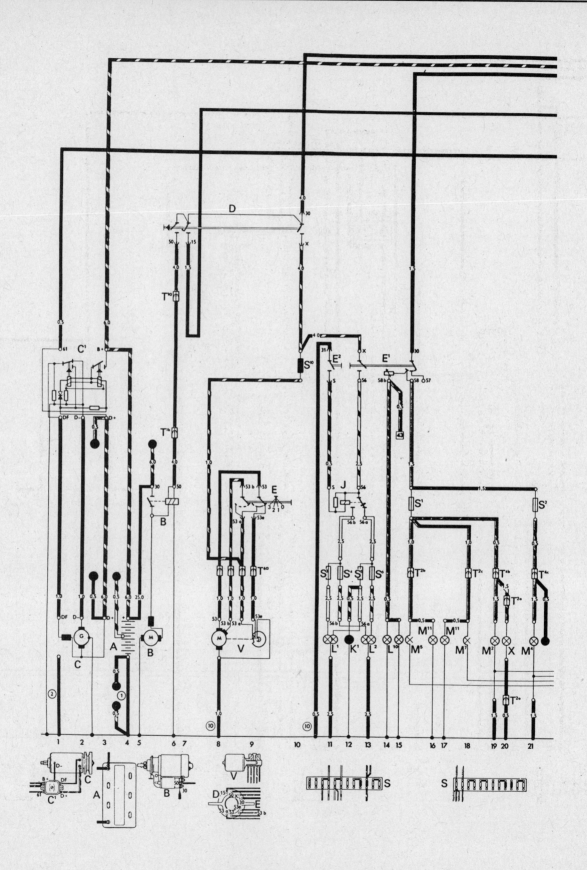

Typical wiring diagram for 1973 and later Beetles

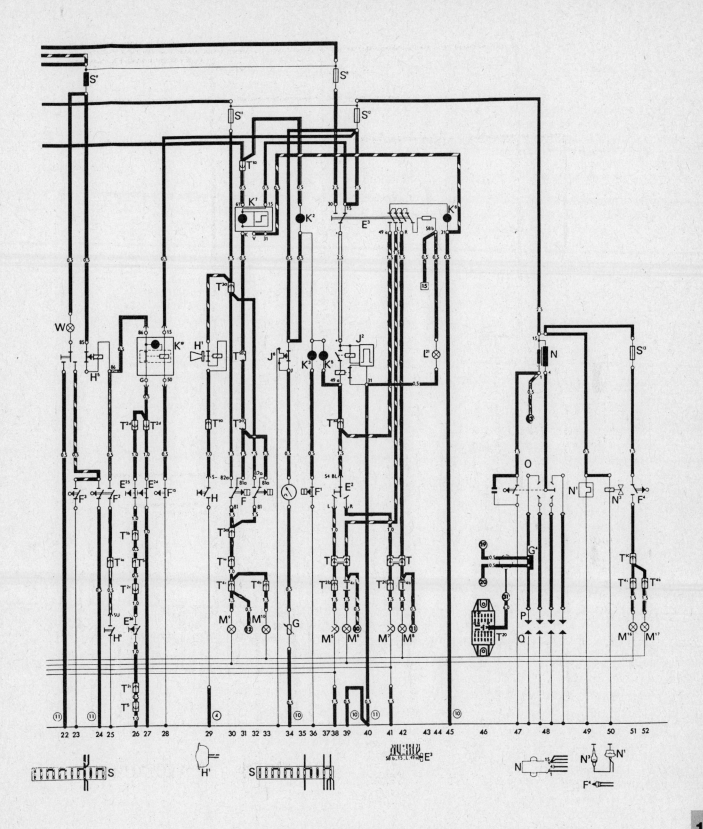

Typical wiring diagram for 1973 and later Beetles (continued)

Description	current track
A – Battery	4
B – Starter	5, 6
C – Generator	1, 2, 3
C¹ – Regulator	1, 2, 3
D – Ignition / starter switch	6, 7, 10, 25
E – Windshield wiper switch	9
E¹ – Light switch	12, 14, 15
E² – Turn signal and headlight dimmer switch	11, 38, 39
E³ – Emergency flasher switch	38, 39, 42, 44, 45
E²⁴ – Safety belt lock, left	27
E²⁵ – Safety belt lock, right	26
E²⁶ – Contact strip in passenger seat	26
F – Brake light switch	30, 31, 32, 33
F¹ – Oil pressure switch	36
F² – Door contact and buzzer alarm switch, left	24, 25
F³ – Door contact switch, right	23
F⁴ – Backup light switch	51
F¹⁵ – Transmission switch for safety belt warning system	28
G – Fuel gauge sending unit	34
G⁴ – Fuel gauge	34
G⁴ – Ignition timing sensor	47
H – Horn button	29
H.¹ – Horn	29
H⁵ – Ignition key warning buzzer	24, 25
H⁶ – Steering lock contact for ignition key warning system	25
J – Dimmer relay	11, 13
J² – Emergency flasher relay	39, 40
J⁶ – Fuel gauge vibrator	34
K¹ – High beam warning light	12
K² – Generator charging warning light	35
K³ – Oil pressure warning light	36
K⁵ – Turn signal warning light	37
K⁶ – Emergency flasher warning light	45
K⁷ – Dual circuit brake warning light	31, 33
K¹⁹ – Safety belt warning system light	27, 28
L¹ – Sealed beam unit, left headlight	11
L² – Sealed beam unit, right headlight	13
L¹⁰ – Instrument panel light	14, 15
L²¹ – Light for heater lever illumination	44
M² – Tail light, right	19
M⁴ – Tail light, left	21
M⁵ – Turn signal and parking light front left	15, 38
M⁶ – Turn signal, rear, left	39
M⁷ – Turn signal and parking light front right	18, 41
M⁸ – Turn signal, rear, right	42
M⁹ – Brake light, left	30
M¹⁰– Brake light, right	33
M¹¹– Side marker light, front	16, 17
M¹⁶– Backup light, left	51
M¹⁷– Backup light, right	52

Description	current track
N – Ignition coil	48
N¹ – Automatic choke	49
N³ – Electromagnetic pilot jet	50
O – Distributor	48
P – Spark plug connectors	48
Q – Spark plugs	48
S¹ to S¹² – Fuse box	10, 11, 13, 15, 21, 24, 30, 38, 40
S¹³ – Fuse for backup light (8 Amp.)	51
T – Wire connector (close to fuse box)	
T¹ – Wire connector, single	
a – close to fuse box	
b – below rear seat bench	
c – behind the engine compartment insulation, front	
T² – Wire connector, double	
a – in engine compartment lid	
b – in luggage compartment, front, left	
c – in passenger seat	
d – below rear seat bench	
T³ – Wire connector, triple	
a – in luggage compartment, front, left	
T⁴ – Wire connector, four connections	
a – close to fuse box	
b – behind engine compartment insulation, right	
c – behind engine compartment insulation, left	
T⁵ – Wire connector, double on passenger seat rail	
T²⁰ – Test network, test socket	46
V – Windshield wiper motor	8, 9
W – Interior light	23
X – License plate light	20

① – Ground strap from battery to frame		4
② – Ground strap from transmission to frame		1
④ – Ground wire on steering coupling		29
⑩ – Ground connector, dashboard		
⑪ – Ground connector, speedometer		

Ignition Switch/Safety Belt Interlock—see page N.

Legend for wiring diagram – 1973 and later Beetles

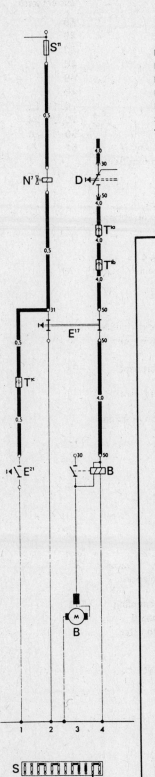

Description

B	–	Starter
D	–	Ignition / starter switch
E¹⁷	–	Starter cutout switch
E²¹	–	Selector lever contact
N⁷	–	Control valve
S¹¹	–	Fuse in fuse box
T¹	–	Wire connector, single
		a – below dashboard
		b – under rear seat bench
		c – on frame tunnel, right

Description	current track
M⁸ – Turn signal, rear, right	46
M⁹ – Brake light, left	34
M¹⁰– Brake light, right	36
M¹¹– Side marker light, front left + right	22, 25
M¹⁶– Backup light, left	55
M¹⁷– Backup light, right	56
N – Ignition coil	52
N¹ – Automatic choke	53
N³ – Electromagnetic pilot jet	54
O – Distributor	50, 52
P – Spark plug connectors	51, 52
Q – Spark plugs	51, 52
S¹	12, 15, 17,
to – Fuse box	20, 26, 27,
S¹²	34, 40, 41
S¹³ – Fuse for backup light (8 Amp.)	55
S¹⁴ – Fuse for rear window defogger, (8 Amp.)	8
T¹ – Wire connector, single	
a – below rear seat bench	
b – one connector of the eight terminals (strip) behind the dashboard	35
c – behind the engine compartment insulation	
T² – Wire connector, double, one of the eight terminals (strip)	33
a – in engine compartment lid	
b – in luggage compartment, front, left two of the eight terminals (strip)	21, 42 42, 45
c – in luggage compartment, front, right	
d – below rear seat bench	
e – two of the eight terminals (strip) behind the dashboard	29, 34
f – in passenger seat	
T³ – Wire connector, triple, in luggage compartment, front, left	
T⁴ – Wire connector, four connections, behind engine compartment insulation, left	
T⁵ – Wire connector, fire connections, behind engine compartment insulation, right	
T⁶ – Wire connector, six connections, above fuse box, left	
T⁷ – Wire connector, double, on passenger seat rail	
T²⁰ – Test network, test socket	49
V – Windshield wiper motor	9, 10, 11
V² – Fan motor	14
W – Interior light	27
X – License plate light	23
Z¹ – Rear window defogger heating element	8

		current track
① –	Ground strap from battery of frame	4
② –	Ground strap from transmission to frame	1
④ –	Ground cable on steering coupling	33
⑩ –	Ground connector, dashboard	
⑪ –	Ground connector, speedometer housing	

Description	current track
A – Battery	4
B – Starter	5, 6
C – Generator	1, 2, 3
C¹ – Regulator	1, 2, 3
D – Ignition / starter switch	6, 7, 12, 29
E – Windshield wiper switch	10, 11
E¹ – Light switch	16, 18, 20
E² – Turn signal and headlight dimmer switch	15, 43
E³ – Emergency flasher switch	41, 42, 43, 45, 47, 48
E⁹ – Fan motor switch	14
E¹⁵ – Rear window defogger switch	12
E²⁴ – Safety belt lock, left	31
E²⁵ – Safety belt lock, right	30
E²⁶ – Contact strip in passenger seat	30
F – Brake light and dual circuit warning light switch	34, 35, 36
F¹ – Oil pressure switch	38
F² – Door contact and buzzer alarm switch, left	29
F³ – Door contact switch, right	27
F⁴ – Backup light switch	55
F¹⁵ – Transmission switch for safety belt warning system (man. transm.)	32
G – Fuel gauge sending unit	40
G¹ – Fuel gauge	40
G⁴ – Ignition timing sensor	51
H – Horn button	33
H¹ – Horn	33
H⁵ – Ignition key warning buzzer	28
H⁶ – Steering lock contact for ignition key warning system	29
J – Dimmer relay	15, 16
J² – Emergency flasher relay	41
J⁶ – Fuel gauge vibrator	40
J⁹ – Rear window defogger relay	8, 12
K¹ – High beam warning light	16
K² – Generator charging warning light	37
K³ – Oil pressure warning light	38
K⁵ – Turn signal warning light	39
K⁶ – Emergency flasher warning light	48
K⁷ – Dual circuit brake warning light	35,36
K¹⁰– Rear window defogger warning light	13
K¹⁹– Safety belt warning system light	31, 32
L¹ – Sealed beam unit, left headlight	15
L² – Sealed beam unit, right headlight	17
L¹⁰– Instrument panel light	18, 19
L²¹ – Light for heater lever illumination	47
M² – Tail light, right	24
M⁴ – Tail light, left	20
M⁵ – Turn signal and parking light front, left	21, 42
M⁶ – Turn signal, rear, left	43
M⁷ – Turn signal and parking light front, right	26, 45

© 1974 VWoA

12

Legend for wiring diagram for 1973 Super Beetle – Also shown is Automatic Stick Shift circuit

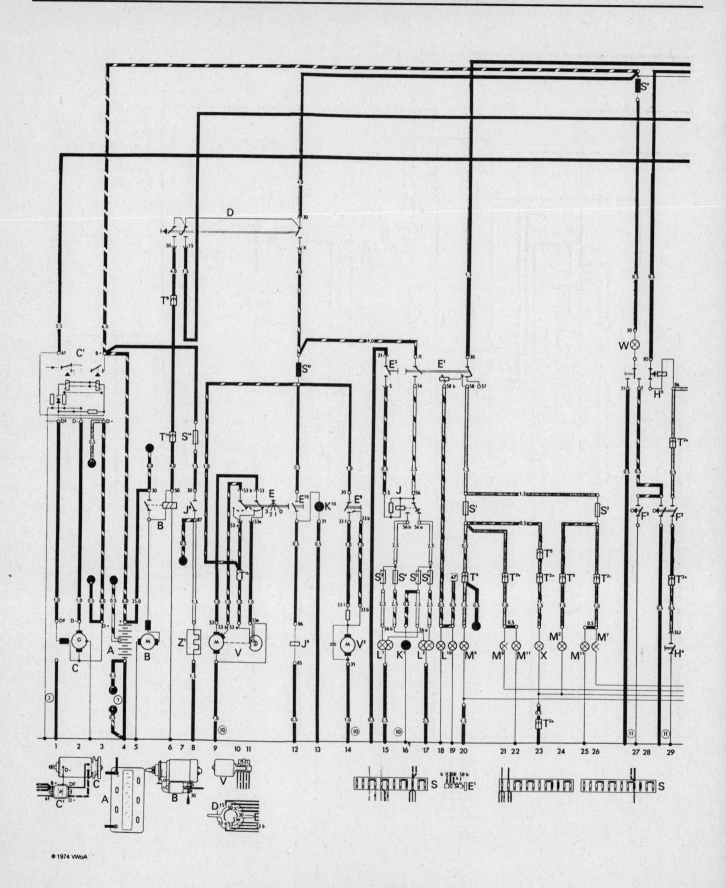

© 1974 VWoA

Typical wiring diagram for 1973 Super Beetle

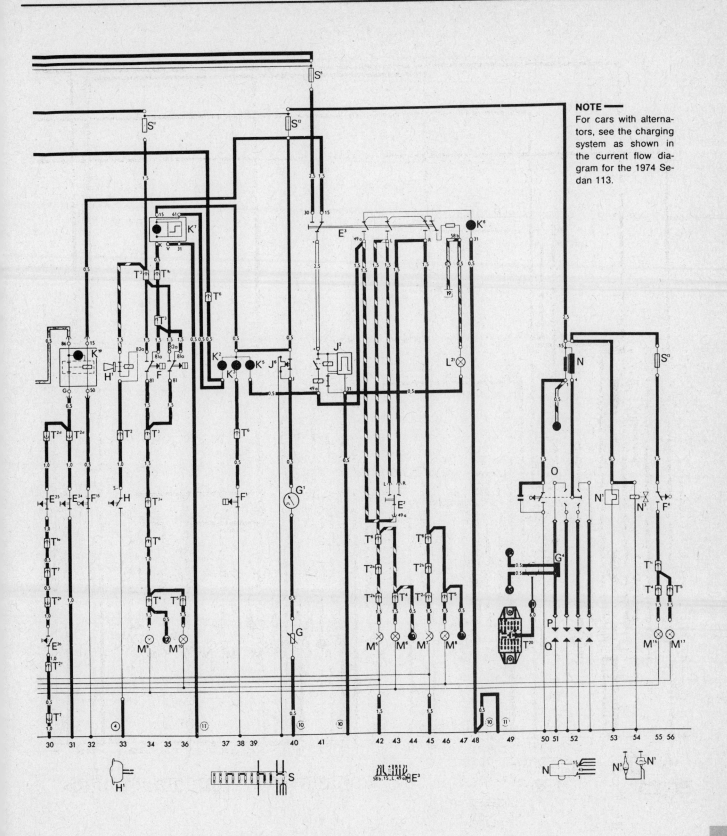

NOTE
For cars with alternators, see the charging system as shown in the current flow diagram for the 1974 Sedan 113.

Typical wiring diagram for 1973 Super Beetle (continued)

© 1974 VWoA

12

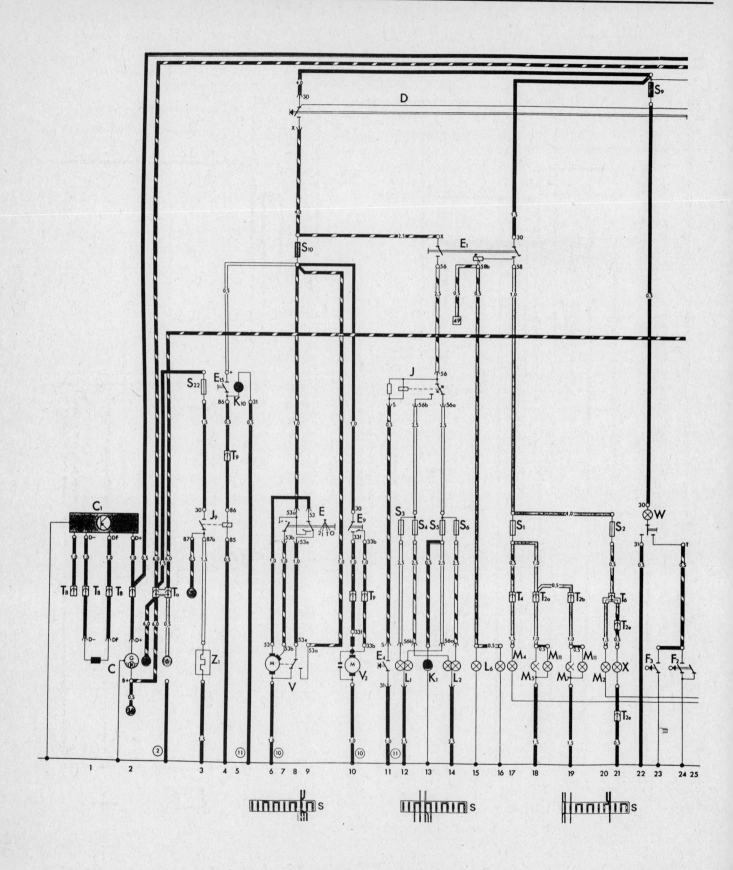

Typical wiring diagram for 1974 and later Super Beetles (1 of 3)

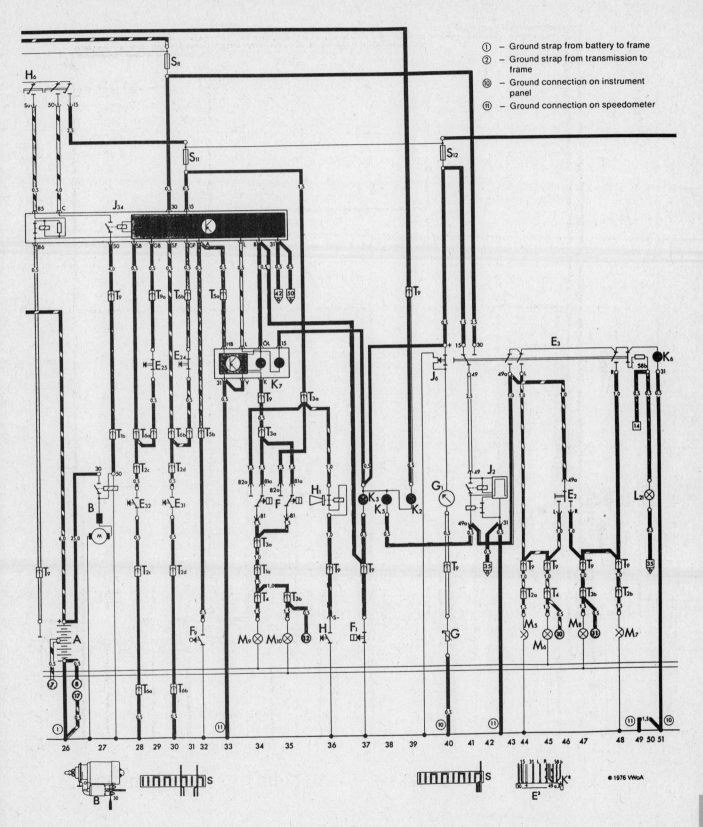

① – Ground strap from battery to frame
② – Ground strap from transmission to frame
⑩ – Ground connection on instrument panel
⑪ – Ground connection on speedometer

© 1976 VWoA

Typical wiring diagram for 1974 and later Super Beetles (2 of 3)

Description	current track	Description	current track
A – Battery	26	K¹ – High beam warning light	13
B – Starter	27	K² – Alternator charging warning light	39
C – Alternator	1, 2	K³ – Oil pressure warning light	37
C¹ – Regulator	1, 2	K⁵ – Turn signal warning light	38
D – Ignition/starter switch	8, 25, 26	K⁶ – Emergency flasher warning light	51
E – Windshield wiper switch	7, 9	K⁷ – Dual circuit brake warning and	
E¹ – Light switch	13, 15, 17	safety belt interlock warning system	33, 34, 35
E² – Turn signal switch	46	L¹ – Sealed beam unit, left headlight	12
E³ – Emergency flasher switch	41, 43, 44,	L² – Sealed beam unit, right headlight	14
	48, 50	L⁶ – Speedometer light	15, 16
E⁴ – Headlight dimmer switch	11	L²¹ – Light for heater lever illumination	50
E⁹ – Fresh air fan motor switch	10	M² – Tail light, right	20
E¹⁵ – Rear window defogger switch	4, 5	M⁴ – Tail light, left	17
E²⁴ – Safety belt lock, left	31	M⁵ – Parking light front, left	18
E²⁵ – Safety belt lock, right	29	M⁵ – Turn signal, front, left	44
E³¹ – Contact strip in driver seat	30	M⁶ – Turn signal, rear, left	45
E³² – Contact strip in passenger seat	28	M⁷ – Parking light front, right	19
F – Brake light switch	34, 35	M⁷ – Turn signal, front, right	48
F¹ – Oil pressure switch	37	M⁸ – Turn signal, rear, right	47
F² – Door contact and buzzer alarm	24, 25	M⁹ – Brake light, left	34
switch, left		M¹⁰ – Brake light, right	35
F³ – Door contact switch, right	23	M¹¹ – Sidemarker light front, left and right	18, 19
F⁴ – Backup light switch	52	M¹⁶ – Backup light, left	52
F⁹ – Parking brake control light switch	32	M¹⁷ – Backup light, right	53
G – Fuel gauge sending unit	40	N – Ignition coil	55
G¹ – Fuel gauge	40	N¹ – Automatic choke	59
G⁴ – Ignition timing sensor	56	N³ – Electro-magnetic cutoff valve	58
G⁷ – TDC marker unit	60	O – Ignition distributor	55, 57
H – Horn button	36	P – Spark plug connectors	55, 56, 57
H¹ – Horn	36	Q – Spark plugs	55, 56, 57
H⁶ – Contact in ignition / starter switch	25	S¹	8, 12, 14,
for buzzer		to – Fuses in fuse box	17, 20, 22,
J – Dimmer relay	11, 13, 14	S¹²	30, 31, 40
J² – Emergency flasher relay	41, 42	S²¹ – Fuse for backup lights (8 Amp.)	52
J⁶ – Voltage vibrator	40	S²² – Fuse for rear window defogger	3
J⁹ – Rear window defogger relay	3, 4	(8 Amp.)	
J³⁴ – Safety belt warning system relay	25, 26, 27	T – Cable adapter, behind insulation	
	28, 29, 30,	in engine compartment	
	31, 32, 33,	a – under rear seat bench	
	34, 35	T¹ – Wire connector, single	
		a – behind instrument panel	
		b – under rear seat bench	
		T² – Wire connector, double	
		a – in luggage compartment, left	
		b – in luggage compartment, right	
		c – under passenger seat	
		d – under driver's seat	
		e – in hood of engine compartmnet	
		T³ – Wire connector, 3 point	
		a – in luggage compartment, left	
		b – behind insulation in engine	
		compartment, right	
		T⁴ – Wire connector, 4 point	
		behind insulation in engine	
		compartment, left	
		T⁵ – Wire connector, single	
		a – behind instrument panel	
		b – on passenger seat rail	
		T⁶ – Wire connector, double	
		a – under passenger seat	
		b – under driver's seat	
		T⁷ – Wire connector, 3 point, in engine	
		compartment	
		T⁸ – Wire connector, 4 point, under rear	
		seat bench	
		T⁹ – Wire connector, 8 point, behind	
		instrument panel	
		T²⁰ – Test network, test socket	54
		V – Windshield wiper motor	6, 7, 8
		V² – Fresh air motor	10
		W – Interior light	22
		X – License plate light	21
		Z¹ – Rear window defogger heating	3
		element	

© 1976 VWoA

Typical wiring diagram and legend for 1974 and later Super Beetles (3 of 3)

© 1974 VWoA—2282

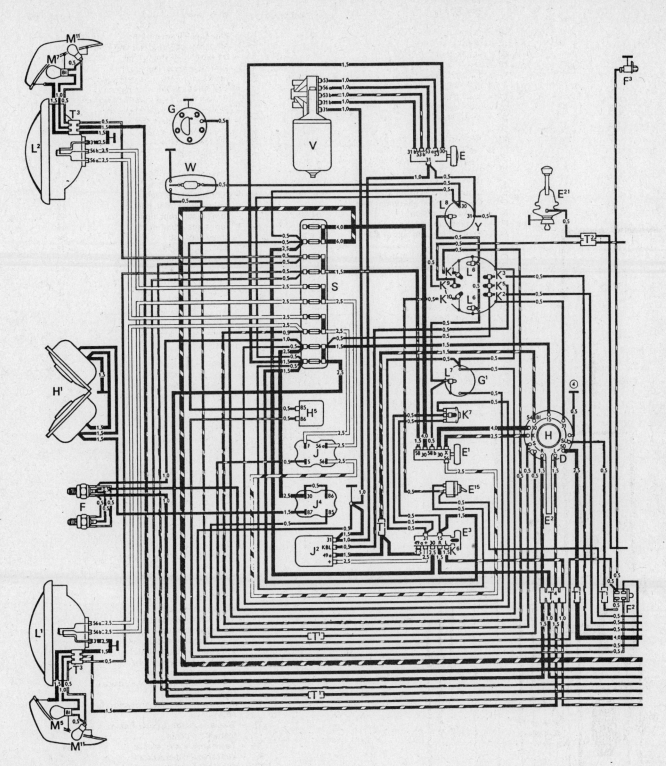

NOTE

On 1970 and early 1971 models (built before June 1971), the mainline from the battery's post to terminal B+ on the regulator is a solid red wire. A solid red wire also joins regulator terminal B+ with a terminal 30 on the light switch—this terminal 30 being in the location shown by terminal X in this diagram. On these earlier models, there is no terminal X on the steering column switch and no black and yellow wire joining it to a terminal X on the light switch.

Typical wiring diagram for 1970 and 1971 Karmann Ghias

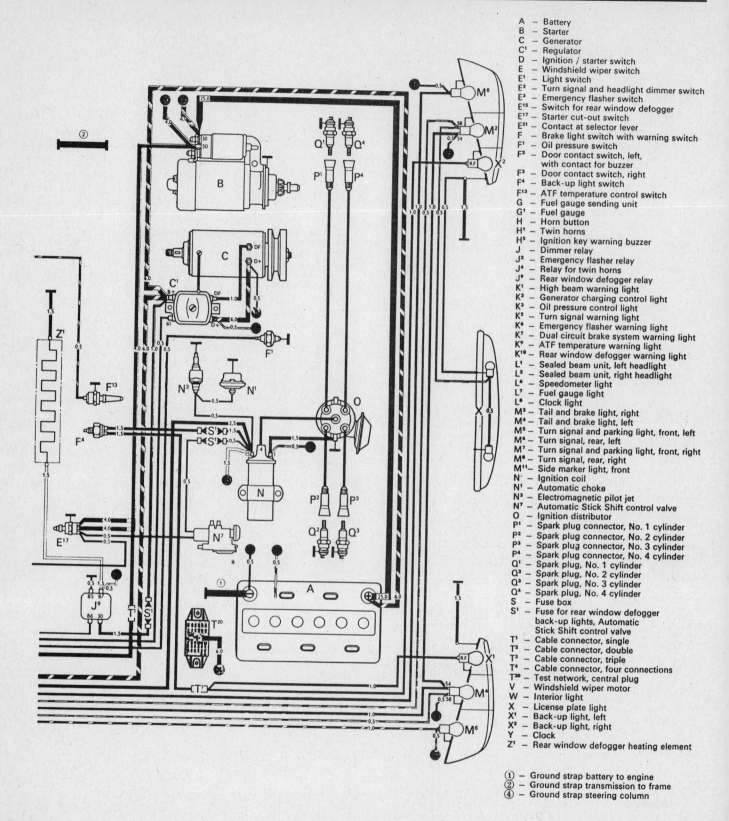

A – Battery
B – Starter
C – Generator
C^1 – Regulator
D – Ignition / starter switch
E – Windshield wiper switch
E^1 – Light switch
E^2 – Turn signal and headlight dimmer switch
E^3 – Emergency flasher switch
E^{15} – Switch for rear window defogger
E^{17} – Starter cut-out switch
E^{21} – Contact at selector lever
F – Brake light switch with warning switch
F^1 – Oil pressure switch
F^2 – Door contact switch, left,
         with contact for buzzer
F^3 – Door contact switch, right
F^4 – Back-up light switch
F^{13} – ATF temperature control switch
G – Fuel gauge sending unit
G^1 – Fuel gauge
H – Horn button
H^1 – Twin horns
H^5 – Ignition key warning buzzer
J – Dimmer relay
J^2 – Emergency flasher relay
J^4 – Relay for twin horns
J^9 – Rear window defogger relay
K^1 – High beam warning light
K^2 – Generator charging control light
K^3 – Oil pressure control light
K^5 – Turn signal warning light
K^6 – Emergency flasher warning light
K^7 – Dual circuit brake system warning light
K^9 – ATF temperature warning light
K^{10} – Rear window defogger warning light
L^1 – Sealed beam unit, left headlight
L^2 – Sealed beam unit, right headlight
L^6 – Speedometer light
L^7 – Fuel gauge light
L^8 – Clock light
M^2 – Tail and brake light, right
M^4 – Tail and brake light, left
M^5 – Turn signal and parking light, front, left
M^6 – Turn signal, rear, left
M^7 – Turn signal and parking light, front, right
M^8 – Turn signal, rear, right
M^{11} – Side marker light, front
N^{-} – Ignition coil
N^1 – Automatic choke
N^3 – Electromagnetic pilot jet
N^7 – Automatic Stick Shift control valve
O – Ignition distributor
P^1 – Spark plug connector, No. 1 cylinder
P^2 – Spark plug connector, No. 2 cylinder
P^3 – Spark plug connector, No. 3 cylinder
P^4 – Spark plug connector, No. 4 cylinder
Q^1 – Spark plug, No. 1 cylinder
Q^2 – Spark plug, No. 2 cylinder
Q^3 – Spark plug, No. 3 cylinder
Q^4 – Spark plug, No. 4 cylinder
S – Fuse box
S^1 – Fuse for rear window defogger
         back-up lights, Automatic
         Stick Shift control valve
T^1 – Cable connector, single
T^2 – Cable connector, double
T^3 – Cable connector, triple
T^4 – Cable connector, four connections
T^{20} – Test network, central plug
V – Windshield wiper motor
W – Interior light
X – License plate light
X^1 – Back-up light, left
X^2 – Back-up light, right
Y – Clock
Z^1 – Rear window defogger heating element

① – Ground strap battery to engine
② – Ground strap transmission to frame
④ – Ground strap steering column

Typical wiring diagram and legend for 1970 and 1971 Karmann Ghias

A – Battery
B – Starter
C – Generator
C¹ – Regulator
D – Ignition/starter switch
E – Windshield wiper switch
E¹ – Light switch
E² – Turn signal and headlight dimmer switch
E³ – Emergency flasher switch
E¹⁵ – Switch for rear window defogger
E¹⁷ – Starter cut-out switch
E²¹ – Contact at selector lever
F – Brake light switch with warning switch
F¹ – Oil pressure switch
F² – Door contact switch, left,
     with contact for buzzer
F³ – Door contact switch, right
F⁴ – Back-up light switch
F¹³ – ATF temperature control switch
G – Fuel gauge sending unit
G¹ – Fuel gauge
G⁴ – Ignition timing sensor
H – Horn button
H¹ – Twin horns
H⁵ – Ignition key warning buzzer
J – Dimmer relay
J² – Emergency flasher relay
J⁴ – Relay for twin horns
J⁹ – Rear window defogger relay
K¹ – High beam warning light
K² – Generator charging control light
K³ – Oil pressure control light
K⁵ – Turn signal warning light
K⁶ – Emergency flasher warning light
K⁷ – Dual circuit brake system warning light
K⁹ – ATF temperature warning light
L¹ – Sealed beam unit, left headlight
L² – Sealed beam unit, right headlight
L⁶ – Speedometer light
L¹⁰ – Instrument panel light
M² – Tail and brake light, right
M⁴ – Tail and brake light, left
M⁵ – Turn signal and parking light, front, left
M⁶ – Turn signal, rear, left

M⁷ – Turn signal and parking light, front, right
M⁸ – Turn signal, rear, right
M¹¹ – Side marker light, front
N – Ignition coil
N¹ – Automatic choke
N³ – Electromagnetic pilot jet
N⁷ – Automatic Stick Shift control valve
O – Ignition distributor
P¹ – Spark plug connector, No. 1 cylinder
P² – Spark plug connector, No. 2 cylinder
P³ – Spark plug connector, No. 3 cylinder
P⁴ – Spark plug connector, No. 4 cylinder
Q¹ – Spark plug, No. 1 cylinder
Q² – Spark plug, No. 2 cylinder
Q³ – Spark plug, No. 3 cylinder
Q⁴ – Spark plug, No. 4 cylinder
S – Fuse box
S¹ – Fuse for rear window defogger, (8 Amp)
     back-up lights, (8 Amp)
T – Cable adapter
T¹ – Cable connector, single
T² – Cable connector, double
T³ – Cable connector, triple
T⁴ – Cable connector, four connections
T²⁰ – Test network, central plug
V – Windshield wiper motor
W – Interior light
X – License plate light
X¹ – Back-up light, left
X² – Back-up light, right
Y – Clock
Z¹ – Rear window defogger heating element

① – Ground strap battery to engine
② – Ground strap transmission to frame
④ – Ground strap steering column

12

Legend for wiring diagram for 1972 Karmann Ghia

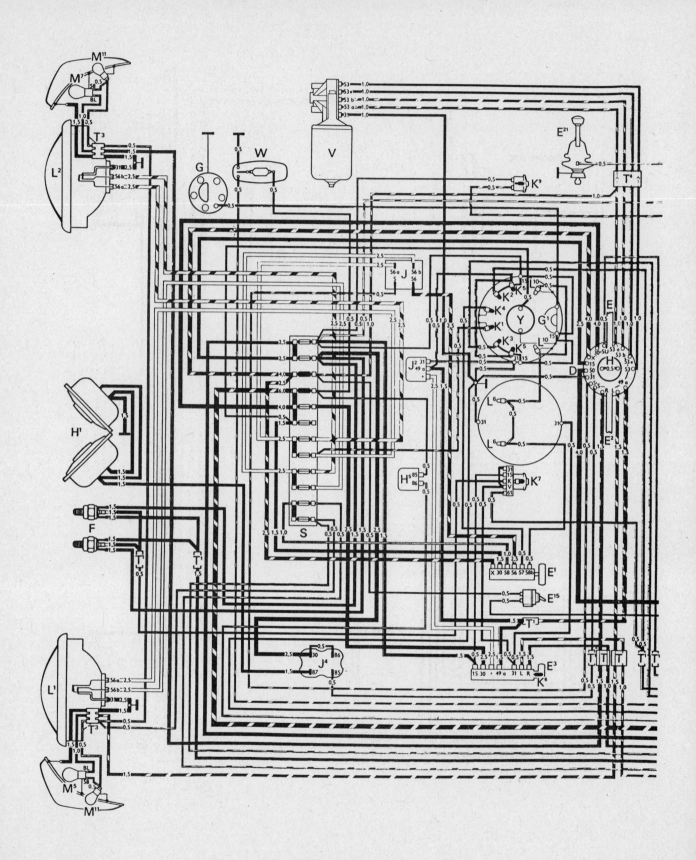

Typical wiring diagram for 1972 Karmann Ghia

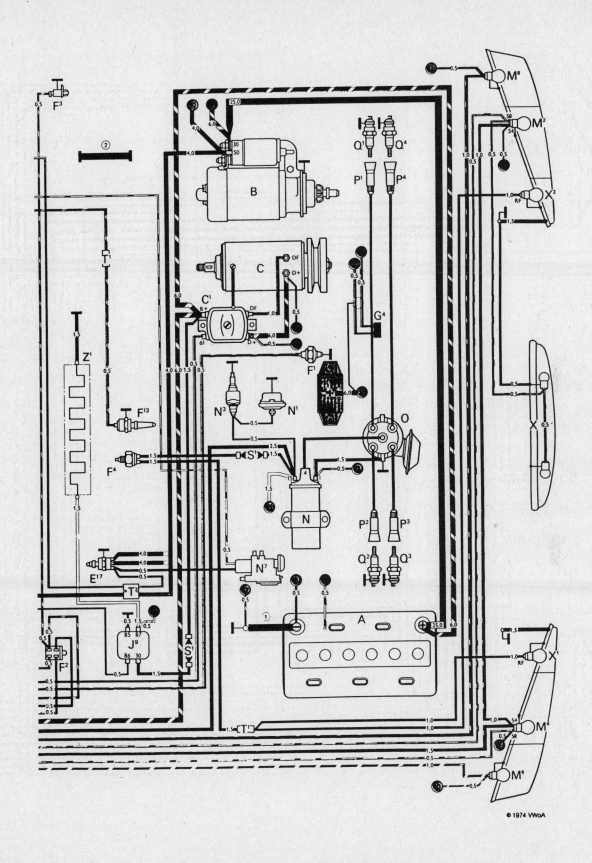

© 1974 VWoA

Typical wiring diagram for 1972 Karmann Ghia (continued)

Description	current track
A – Battery	5
B – Starter	6, 7
C – Generator	1, 2, 3
C¹ – Regulator	1, 2, 3
D – Ignition / starter switch	7, 11, 12
E – Windshield wiper switch	9, 10
E¹ – Light switch	16, 18, 22
E² – Turn signal and headlight dimmer switch	13, 50
E³ – Emergency flasher switch	50, 53, 54, 56, 58
E¹⁵ – Rear window defogger switch	11
E²⁴ – Safety belt lock, left	37
E²⁵ – Safety belt lock, right	36
E²⁶ – Contact strip in passenger seat	36
F – Brake light and dual circuit warning light switch	42, 43
F¹ – Oil pressure switch	46
F² – Door contact and buzzer alarm switch, left	34, 35
F³ – Door contact switch, right	33
F⁴ – Backup light switch	59
F¹⁵ – Transmission switch for safety belt warning system	38
G – Fuel gauge sending unit	48
G¹ – Fuel gauge	48
G⁴ – Ignition timing sensor	62
H – Horn button	39
H¹ – Twin horns	40, 41
H⁵ – Ignition key warning buzzer	33, 35
H⁶ – Steering lock contact for ignition key warning system	35
J – Dimmer relay	13, 16
J² – Emergency flasher relay	50, 52
J⁴ – Relay for twin horns	39
J⁹ – Rear window defogger relay	4, 11
K¹ – High beam warning light	15
K² – Generator charging warning light	45
K³ – Oil pressure warning light	46
K⁴ – Parking light warning light	22
K⁵ – Turn signal warning light	47, 49
K⁶ – Emergency flasher warning light	58
K⁷ – Dual circuit brake warning light	42, 43
K¹⁹ – Safety belt warning system light	37, 38
L¹ – Sealed beam unit, left headlight	14
L² – Sealed beam unit, right headlight	16
L⁸ – Speedometer light	18, 19
L¹⁰ – Instrument panel light	20, 21
L³¹ – Light for heater lever illumination	56
M² – Tail/brake light, right	28, 43
M⁴ – Tail/brake light, left	23, 42
M⁵ – Turn signal and parking light front, left	24, 50
M⁶ – Turn signal, rear, left	51
M⁷ – Turn signal and parking light front, right	27, 53
M⁸ – Turn signal, rear, right	54
M¹¹ – Side marker light, front left + right	25, 26
M¹⁶ – Backup light, left	59
M¹⁷ – Backup light, right	60
N – Ignition coil	62
N¹ – Automatic choke	64
N³ – Electromagnetic pilot jet	65
O – Distributor	62, 63
P – Spark plug connectors	62, 63
Q – Spark plugs	62, 63
S¹ to S¹² – Fuse box	11, 14, 16, 25, 28, 33, 40, 50, 51
S¹³ – Fuse for backup light (8 Amp.)	59
S¹⁴ – Fuse for rear window defogger, (8 Amp.)	4
T – Cable adapter, behind dashboard	
T¹ – Wire connector, single a – below rear seat bench b – behind the dashboard c – behind the engine compartment insulation	
T² – Wire connector, double a – below rear seat bench b – in the passenger seat	
T³ – Wire connector, triple a – in headlight housing, left b – in headlight housing, right	
T⁴ – Wire connector, four connections, behind the dashboard	
T⁷ – Wire connector, double on passenger seat rail	
T²⁰ – Test network, test socket	61
V – Windshield wiper motor	8, 9, 10
W – Interior light	32
X – License plate light	29, 30
Y – Clock	31
Z¹ – Rear window defogger heating element	4

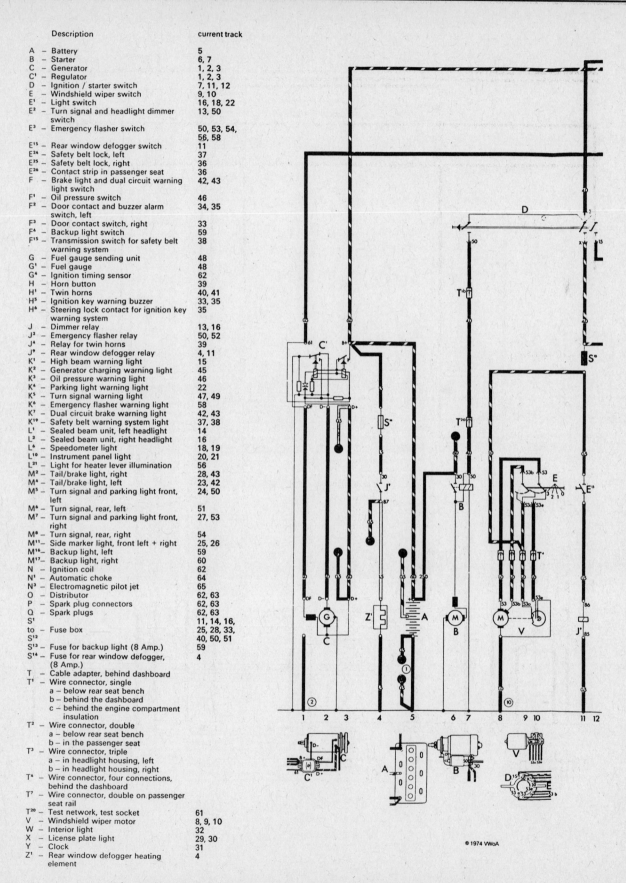

© 1974 VWoA

Legend and typical wiring diagram for 1973 and 1974 Karmann Ghias (1 of 3)

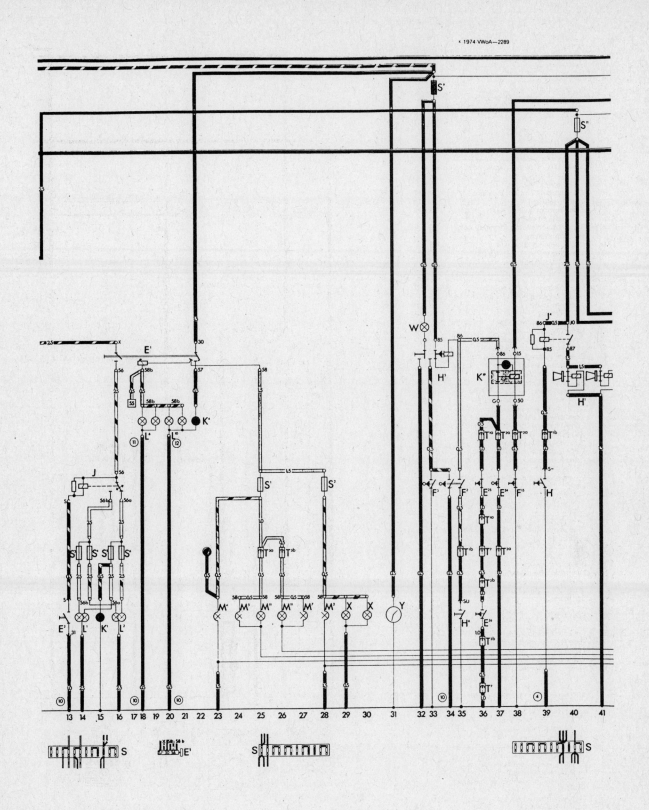

Typical wiring diagram for 1973 and 1974 Karmann Ghias (2 of 3)

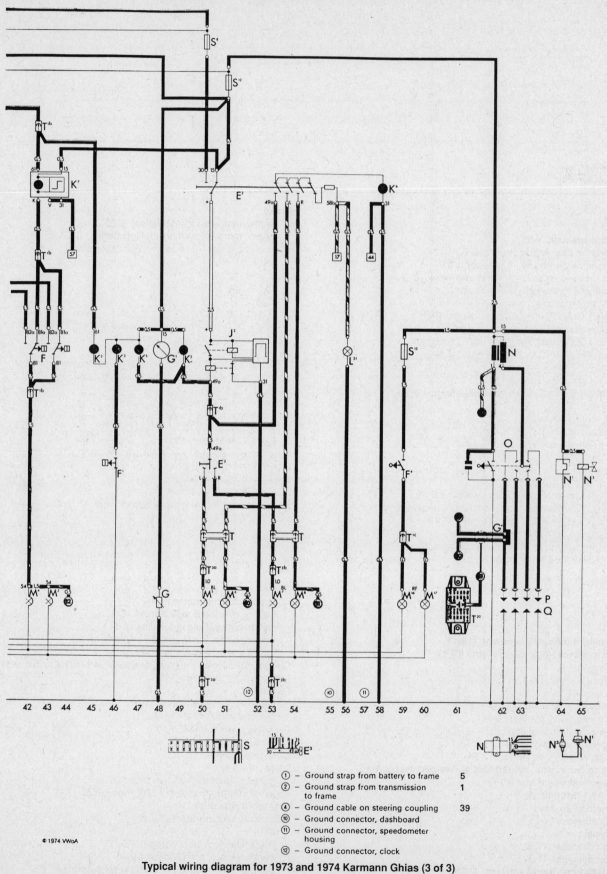

① – Ground strap from battery to frame   5
② – Ground strap from transmission   1
      to frame
④ – Ground cable on steering coupling   39
⑩ – Ground connector, dashboard
⑪ – Ground connector, speedometer
      housing
⑫ – Ground connector, clock

© 1974 VWoA

Typical wiring diagram for 1973 and 1974 Karmann Ghias (3 of 3)

Index

HAYNES AUTOMOTIVE MANUALS

ACURA
*1776 **Integra & Legend** all models '86 thru '90

AMC
Jeep CJ - see JEEP (412)
694 **Mid-size models,** Concord, Hornet, Gremlin & Spirit '70 thru '83
934 **(Renault) Alliance & Encore** all models '83 thru '87

AUDI
615 **4000** all models '80 thru '87
428 **5000** all models '77 thru '83
1117 **5000** all models '84 thru '88

AUSTIN
Healey Sprite - see MG Midget Roadster (265)

BMW
*2020 **3/5 Series** not including diesel or all-wheel drive models '82 thru '92
276 **320i** all 4 cyl models '75 thru '83
632 **528i & 530i** all models '75 thru '80
240 **1500 thru 2002** all models except Turbo '59 thru '77
348 **2500, 2800, 3.0 & Bavaria** all models '69 thru '76

BUICK
Century (front wheel drive) - see GENERAL MOTORS (829)
*1627 **Buick, Oldsmobile & Pontiac Full-size (Front wheel drive)** all models '85 thru '93
Buick Electra, LeSabre and Park Avenue; **Oldsmobile** Delta 88 Royale, Ninety Eight and Regency; **Pontiac** Bonneville
1551 **Buick Oldsmobile & Pontiac Full-size (Rear wheel drive)**
Buick Estate '70 thru '90, Electra'70 thru '84, LeSabre '70 thru '85, Limited '74 thru '79
Oldsmobile Custom Cruiser '70 thru '90, Delta 88 '70 thru '85,Ninety-eight '70 thru '84
Pontiac Bonneville '70 thru '81, Catalina '70 thru '81, Grandville '70 thru '75, Parisienne '83 thru '86
627 **Mid-size Regal & Century** all rear-drive models with V6, V8 and Turbo '74 thru '87
Regal - see GENERAL MOTORS (1671)
Skyhawk - see GENERAL MOTORS (766)
552 **Skylark** all X-car models '80 thru '85
Skylark '86 on - see GENERAL MOTORS (1420)
Somerset - see GENERAL MOTORS (1420)

CADILLAC
*751 **Cadillac Rear Wheel Drive** all gasoline models '70 thru '92
Cimarron - see GENERAL MOTORS (766)

CAPRI
296 **2000 MK I Coupe** all models '71 thru '75
Mercury Capri - see FORD Mustang (654)

CHEVROLET
*1477 **Astro & GMC Safari Mini-vans** '85 thru '93
554 **Camaro V8** all models '70 thru '81
866 **Camaro** all models '82 thru '92
Cavalier - see GENERAL MOTORS (766)
Celebrity - see GENERAL MOTORS (829)
625 **Chevelle, Malibu & El Camino** all V6 & V8 models '69 thru '87
449 **Chevette & Pontiac T1000** '76 thru '87
550 **Citation** all models '80 thru '85

*1628 **Corsica/Beretta** all models '87 thru '92
274 **Corvette** all V8 models '68 thru '82
*1336 **Corvette** all models '84 thru '91
1762 **Chevrolet Engine Overhaul Manual**
704 **Full-size Sedans** Caprice, Impala, Biscayne, Bel Air & Wagons '69 thru '90
Lumina - see GENERAL MOTORS (1671)
Lumina APV - see GENERAL MOTORS (2035)
319 **Luv Pick-up** all 2WD & 4WD '72 thru '82
626 **Monte Carlo** all models '70 thru '88
241 **Nova** all V8 models '69 thru '79
*1642 **Nova and Geo Prizm** all front wheel drive models, '85 thru '92
420 **Pick-ups '67 thru '87** - Chevrolet & GMC, all V8 & in-line 6 cyl, 2WD & 4WD '67 thru '87; Suburbans, Blazers & Jimmys '67 thru '91
*1664 **Pick-ups '88 thru '93** - Chevrolet & GMC, all full-size (C and K) models, '88 thru '93
*831 **S-10 & GMC S-15 Pick-ups** all models '82 thru '92
*1727 **Sprint & Geo Metro** '85 thru '91
*345 **Vans - Chevrolet & GMC,** V8 & in-line 6 cylinder models '68 thru '92

CHRYSLER
*2058 **Full-size Front-Wheel Drive** '88 thru '93
K-Cars - see DODGE Aries (723)
Laser - see DODGE Daytona (1140)
*1337 **Chrysler & Plymouth Mid-size** front wheel drive '82 thru '93

DATSUN
402 **200SX** all models '77 thru '79
647 **200SX** all models '80 thru '83
228 **B - 210** all models '73 thru '78
525 **210** all models '78 thru '82
206 **240Z, 260Z & 280Z** Coupe '70 thru '78
563 **280ZX** Coupe & 2+2 '79 thru '83
300ZX - see NISSAN (1137)
679 **310** all models '78 thru '82
123 **510 & PL521 Pick-up** '68 thru '73
430 **510** all models '78 thru '81
372 **610** all models '72 thru '76
277 **620 Series Pick-up** all models '73 thru '79
720 Series Pick-up - see NISSAN (771)
376 **810/Maxima** all gasoline models, '77 thru '84
368 **F10** all models '76 thru '79
Pulsar - see NISSAN (876)
Sentra - see NISSAN (982)
Stanza - see NISSAN (981)

DODGE
400 & 600 - see CHRYSLER Mid-size (1337)
*723 **Aries & Plymouth Reliant** '81 thru '89
*1231 **Caravan & Plymouth Voyager Mini-Vans** all models '84 thru '93
699 **Challenger & Plymouth Saporro** all models '78 thru '83
Challenger '67-'76 - see DODGE Dart (234)
236 **Colt** all models '71 thru '77
610 **Colt & Plymouth Champ** (front wheel drive) all models '78 thru '87
*1668 **Dakota Pick-ups** all models '87 thru '93
234 **Dart, Challenger/Plymouth Barracuda & Valiant** 6 cyl models '67 thru '76
*1140 **Daytona & Chrysler Laser** '84 thru '89
*545 **Omni & Plymouth Horizon** '78 thru '90
*912 **Pick-ups** all full-size models '74 thru '91
*556 **Ram 50/D50 Pick-ups & Raider and Plymouth Arrow Pick-ups** '79 thru '93
*1726 **Shadow & Plymouth Sundance** '87 thru '93
*1779 **Spirit & Plymouth Acclaim** '89 thru '92
*349 **Vans - Dodge & Plymouth** V8 & 6 cyl models '71 thru '91

EAGLE
Talon - see Mitsubishi Eclipse (2097)

FIAT
094 **124 Sport Coupe & Spider** '68 thru '78
273 **X1/9** all models '74 thru '80

FORD
*1476 **Aerostar Mini-vans** all models '86 thru '92
788 **Bronco and Pick-ups** '73 thru '79
*880 **Bronco and Pick-ups** '80 thru '91
268 **Courier Pick-up** all models '72 thru '82
1763 **Ford Engine Overhaul Manual**
789 **Escort/Mercury Lynx** all models '81 thru '90
*2046 **Escort/Mercury Tracer** '91 thru '93
*2021 **Explorer & Mazda Navajo** '91 thru '92
560 **Fairmont & Mercury Zephyr** '78 thru '83
334 **Fiesta** all models '77 thru '80
754 **Ford & Mercury Full-size,** Ford LTD & Mercury Marquis ('75 thru '82); Ford Custom 500,Country Squire, Crown Victoria & Mercury Colony Park ('75 thru '87); Ford LTD Crown Victoria & Mercury Gran Marquis ('83 thru '87);
359 **Granada & Mercury Monarch** all in-line, 6 cyl & V8 models '75 thru '80
773 **Ford & Mercury Mid-size,** Ford Thunderbird & Mercury Cougar ('75 thru '82); Ford LTD & Mercury Marquis ('83 thru '86); Ford Torino,Gran Torino, Elite, Ranchero pick-up, LTD II, Mercury Montego, Comet, XR-7 & Lincoln Versailles ('75 thru '86)
*654 **Mustang & Mercury Capri** all models including Turbo. Mustang, '79 thru '92; Capri, '79 thru '86
357 **Mustang V8** all models '64-1/2 thru '73
231 **Mustang II** 4 cyl, V6 & V8 models '74 thru '78
649 **Pinto & Mercury Bobcat** '75 thru '80
1670 **Probe** all models '89 thru '92
*1026 **Ranger/Bronco II** gasoline models '83 thru '93
*1421 **Taurus & Mercury Sable** '86 thru '92
*1418 **Tempo & Mercury Topaz** all gasoline models '84 thru '93
1338 **Thunderbird/Mercury Cougar** '83 thru '88
*1725 **Thunderbird/Mercury Cougar** '89 and '90
*344 **Vans** all V8 Econoline models '69 thru '91

GENERAL MOTORS
*829 **Buick Century, Chevrolet Celebrity, Oldsmobile Cutlass Ciera & Pontiac 6000** all models '82 thru '93
*766 **Buick Skyhawk, Cadillac Cimarron, Chevrolet Cavalier, Oldsmobile Firenza & Pontiac J-2000 & Sunbird** all models '82 thru '92
1420 **Buick Skylark & Somerset, Oldsmobile Calais & Pontiac Grand Am** all models '85 thru '91
*1671 **Buick Regal, Chevrolet Lumina, Oldsmobile Cutlass Supreme & Pontiac Grand Prix** all front wheel drive models '88 thru '90
*2035 **Chevrolet Lumina APV, Oldsmobile Silhouette & Pontiac Trans Sport** all models '90 thru '92

GEO
Metro - see CHEVROLET Sprint (1727)
Prizm - see CHEVROLET Nova (1642)
*2039 **Storm** all models '90 thru '93
Tracker - see SUZUKI Samurai (1626)

GMC
Safari - see CHEVROLET ASTRO (1477)
Vans & Pick-ups - see CHEVROLET (420, 831, 345, 1664)

(Continued on other side)

HAYNES AUTOMOTIVE MANUALS

NOTE: New manuals are added to this list on a periodic basis. If you do not see a listing for your vehicle, consult your local Haynes dealer for the latest product information.

HONDA
351	**Accord CVCC** all models '76 thru '83
1221	**Accord** all models '84 thru '89
2067	**Accord** all models '90 thru '93
160	**Civic 1200** all models '73 thru '79
633	**Civic 1300 & 1500 CVCC** '80 thru '83
297	**Civic 1500 CVCC** all models '75 thru '79
1227	**Civic** all models '84 thru '91
*601	**Prelude CVCC** all models '79 thru '89

HYUNDAI
*1552	**Excel** all models '86 thru '93

ISUZU
*1641	**Trooper & Pick-up,** all gasoline models Pick-up, '81 thru '93; Trooper, '84 thru '91

JAGUAR
*242	**XJ6** all 6 cyl models '68 thru '86
*478	**XJ12 & XJS** all 12 cyl models '72 thru '85

JEEP
*1553	**Cherokee, Comanche & Wagoneer Limited** all models '84 thru '93
412	**CJ** all models '49 thru '86
*1777	**Wrangler** all models '87 thru '92

LADA
*413	**1200, 1300. 1500 & 1600** all models including Riva '74 thru '91

MAZDA
648	**626 Sedan & Coupe (rear wheel drive)** all models '79 thru '82
*1082	**626 & MX-6 (front wheel drive)** all models '83 thru '91
267	**B Series Pick-ups** '72 thru '93
370	**GLC Hatchback (rear wheel drive)** all models '77 thru '83
757	**GLC (front wheel drive)** '81 thru '85
*2047	**MPV** all models '89 thru '93
460	**RX-7** all models '79 thru '85
*1419	**RX-7** all models '86 thru '91

MERCEDES-BENZ
*1643	**190 Series** all four-cylinder gasoline models, '84 thru '88
346	**230, 250 & 280** Sedan, Coupe & Roadster all 6 cyl sohc models '68 thru '72
983	**280 123 Series** gasoline models '77 thru '81
698	**350 & 450** Sedan, Coupe & Roadster all models '71 thru '80
697	**Diesel 123 Series** 200D, 220D, 240D, 240TD, 300D, 300CD, 300TD, 4- & 5-cyl incl. Turbo '76 thru '85

MERCURY
See FORD Listing

MG
111	**MGB** Roadster & GT Coupe all models '62 thru '80
265	**MG Midget & Austin Healey Sprite** Roadster '58 thru '80

MITSUBISHI
*1669	**Cordia, Tredia, Galant, Precis & Mirage** '83 thru '93
*2022	**Pick-up & Montero** '83 thru '93
*2097	**Eclipse, Eagle Talon & Plymouth Laser** '90 thru '94

MORRIS
074	**(Austin) Marina 1.8** all models '71 thru '78
024	**Minor 1000** sedan & wagon '56 thru '71

NISSAN
1137	**300ZX** all models including Turbo '84 thru '89
*1341	**Maxima** all models '85 thru '91
*771	**Pick-ups/Pathfinder** gas models '80 thru '93
876	**Pulsar** all models '83 thru '86
*982	**Sentra** all models '82 thru '90
*981	**Stanza** all models '82 thru '90

OLDSMOBILE
	Bravada - see CHEVROLET S-10 (831)
	Calais - see GENERAL MOTORS (1420)
	Custom Cruiser - see BUICK Full-size RWD (1551)
*658	**Cutlass** all standard gasoline V6 & V8 models '74 thru '88
	Cutlass Ciera - see GENERAL MOTORS (829)
	Cutlass Supreme - see GM (1671)
	Delta 88 - see BUICK Full-size RWD (1551)
	Delta 88 Brougham - see BUICK Full-size FWD (1551), RWD (1627)
	Delta 88 Royale - see BUICK Full-size RWD (1551)
	Firenza - see GENERAL MOTORS (766)
	Ninety-eight Regency - see BUICK Full-size RWD (1551), FWD (1627)
	Ninety-eight Regency Brougham - see BUICK Full-size RWD (1551)
	Omega - see PONTIAC Phoenix (551)
	Silhouette - see GENERAL MOTORS (2035)

PEUGEOT
663	**504** all diesel models '74 thru '83

PLYMOUTH
	Laser - see MITSUBISHI Eclipse (2097)
	For other PLYMOUTH titles, see DODGE listing.

PONTIAC
	T1000 - see CHEVROLET Chevette (449)
	J-2000 - see GENERAL MOTORS (766)
	6000 - see GENERAL MOTORS (829)
	Bonneville - see Buick Full-size FWD (1627), RWD (1551)
	Bonneville Brougham - see Buick Full-size (1551)
	Catalina - see Buick Full-size (1551)
1232	**Fiero** all models '84 thru '88
555	**Firebird** V8 models except Turbo '70 thru '81
867	**Firebird** all models '82 thru '92
	Full-size Rear Wheel Drive - see BUICK Oldsmobile, Pontiac Full-size RWD (1551)
	Full-size Front Wheel Drive - see BUICK Oldsmobile, Pontiac Full-size FWD (1627)
	Grand Am - see GENERAL MOTORS (1420)
	Grand Prix - see GENERAL MOTORS (1671)
	Grandville - see BUICK Full-size (1551)
	Parisienne - see BUICK Full-size (1551)
551	**Phoenix & Oldsmobile Omega** all X-car models '80 thru '84
	Sunbird - see GENERAL MOTORS (766)
	Trans Sport - see GENERAL MOTORS (2035)

PORSCHE
*264	**911** all Coupe & Targa models except Turbo & Carrera 4 '65 thru '89
239	**914** all 4 cyl models '69 thru '76
397	**924** all models including Turbo '76 thru '82
*1027	**944** all models including Turbo '83 thru '89

RENAULT
141	**5 Le Car** all models '76 thru '83
079	**8 & 10** 58.4 cu in engines '62 thru '72
097	**12 Saloon & Estate** 1289 cc engine '70 thru '80
768	**15 & 17** all models '73 thru '79
081	**16** 89.7 cu in & 95.5 cu in engines '65 thru '72
	Alliance & Encore - see AMC (934)

SAAB
247	**99** all models including Turbo '69 thru '80
*980	**900** all models including Turbo '79 thru '88

SUBARU
237	**1100, 1300, 1400 & 1600** '71 thru '79
*681	**1600 & 1800** 2WD & 4WD '80 thru '89

SUZUKI
*1626	**Samurai/Sidekick and Geo Tracker** all models '86 thru '93

TOYOTA
1023	**Camry** all models '83 thru '91
150	**Carina** Sedan all models '71 thru '74
935	**Celica Rear Wheel Drive** '71 thru '85
*2038	**Celica Front Wheel Drive** '86 thru '92
1139	**Celica Supra** all models '79 thru '92
361	**Corolla** all models '75 thru '79
961	**Corolla** all rear wheel drive models '80 thru '87
*1025	**Corolla** all front wheel drive models '84 thru '92
636	**Corolla Tercel** all models '80 thru '82
360	**Corona** all models '74 thru '82
532	**Cressida** all models '78 thru '82
313	**Land Cruiser** all models '68 thru '82
200	**MK II** all 6 cyl models '72 thru '76
*1339	**MR2** all models '85 thru '87
304	**Pick-up** all models '69 thru '78
*656	**Pick-up** all models '79 thru '92
*2048	**Previa** all models '91 thru '93

TRIUMPH
112	**GT6 & Vitesse** all models '62 thru '74
113	**Spitfire** all models '62 thru '81
322	**TR7** all models '75 thru '81

VW
159	**Beetle & Karmann Ghia** all models '54 thru '79
238	**Dasher** all gasoline models '74 thru '81
*884	**Rabbit, Jetta, Scirocco, & Pick-up** gas models '74 thru '91 & Convertible '80 thru '92
451	**Rabbit, Jetta & Pick-up** all diesel models '77 thru '84
082	**Transporter 1600** all models '68 thru '79
226	**Transporter 1700, 1800 & 2000** all models '72 thru '79
084	**Type 3 1500 & 1600** all models '63 thru '73
1029	**Vanagon** all air-cooled models '80 thru '83

VOLVO
203	**120, 130 Series & 1800 Sports** '61 thru '73
129	**140 Series** all models '66 thru '74
*270	**240 Series** all models '74 thru '90
400	**260 Series** all models '75 thru '82
*1550	**740 & 760 Series** all models '82 thru '88

SPECIAL MANUALS
1479	**Automotive Body Repair & Painting Manual**
1654	**Automotive Electrical Manual**
1667	**Automotive Emissions Control Manual**
1480	**Automotive Heating & Air Conditioning Manual**
1762	**Chevrolet Engine Overhaul Manual**
1736	**GM and Ford Diesel Engine Repair Manual**
1763	**Ford Engine Overhaul Manual**
482	**Fuel Injection Manual**
2069	**Holley Carburetor Manual**
1666	**Small Engine Repair Manual**
299	**SU Carburetors** thru '88
393	**Weber Carburetors** thru '79
300	**Zenith/Stromberg CD Carburetors** thru '76

Over 100 Haynes motorcycle manuals also available

5-94

* Listings shown with an asterisk (*) indicate model coverage as of this printing. These titles will be periodically updated to include later model years - consult your Haynes dealer for more information.

Haynes North America, Inc., 861 Lawrence Drive, Newbury Park, CA 91320 • (805) 498-6703